Jeep®

OWNER'S BIBLE™

By Moses Ludel

A Hands-on Guide to Getting the Most From Your Jeep

RB

ROBERT BENTLEY
AUTOMOTIVE PUBLISHERS

Jeep OWNER'S BIBLE™

Jeep's history, see Chapter 1

Operator's tips, see Chapter 3

Ignition tune-up, see Chapter 7

Clutch replacement tips, see Chapter 10

Table Of Contents

Disc brake service, see Chapter 13

Electrical system upgrades, see Chapter 15

Conversion engines, see Chapter 17

Off-road geartrain mods, see Chapter 18

Suspension lift kits, see Chapter 19

RB ROBERT BENTLEY, INC. | AUTOMOTIVE PUBLISHERS

Information that makes
the difference.®

1734 Massachusetts Avenue
Cambridge, MA 02138 USA
800-423-4595 / 617-547-4170
http://www.rb.com
e-mail: sales@rb.com

WARNING—Important Safety Notice

In this book we have attempted to describe repairs, modifications and accessories which may be used with Jeep vehicles using examples and instructions which we believe to be accurate. However, the examples, instructions, and other information are intended solely as illustrations and should be used in any particular application only by experienced personnel who are trained in the repair and modification of Jeeps and who have independently evaluated the repair, modification or accessory. Implementation of a modification or attachment of an accessory described in this book may render the vehicle, attachment or accessory unsafe for use in certain circumstances.

Do not perform work described in this book unless you are familiar with basic automotive repair procedures and safe workshop practices. This book illustrates procedures required for some service and modification work; it is not a substitute for full and up-to-date information from the vehicle manufacturer or aftermarket supplier, or for proper training as an automotive technician. Note that it is not possible for us to anticipate all of the ways or conditions under which vehicles may be serviced or modified or to provide cautions as to all of the possible hazards that may result.

The vehicle manufacturer and aftermarket suppliers will continue to issue service information updates and parts retrofits after the editorial closing of this book. Some of these updates and retrofits will apply to procedures and specifications in this book. We regret that we cannot supply updates to purchasers of this book.

We have endeavored to ensure the accuracy of the information in this book. Please note, however, that considering the vast quantity and the complexity of the information involved, we cannot warrant the accuracy or completeness of the information contained in this book.

FOR THESE REASONS, NEITHER THE PUBLISHER NOR THE AUTHOR MAKES ANY WARRANTIES, EXPRESS OR IMPLIED, THAT THE EXAMPLES, INSTRUCTIONS OR OTHER INFORMATION IN THIS BOOK ARE FREE OF ERRORS OR OMISSIONS, ARE CONSISTENT WITH INDUSTRY STANDARDS, OR THAT THEY WILL MEET THE REQUIREMENTS FOR A PARTICULAR APPLICATION, AND WE EXPRESSLY DISCLAIM THE IMPLIED WARRANTIES OF MERCHANTABILITY AND OF FITNESS FOR A PARTICULAR PURPOSE, EVEN IF THE PUBLISHER OR AUTHOR HAVE BEEN ADVISED OF A PARTICULAR PURPOSE, AND EVEN IF A PARTICULAR PURPOSE IS INDICATED IN THE BOOK. THE PUBLISHER AND AUTHOR ALSO DISCLAIM ALL LIABILITY FOR DIRECT, INDIRECT, INCIDENTAL OR CONSEQUENTIAL DAMAGES THAT RESULT FROM ANY USE OF THE EXAMPLES, INSTRUCTIONS OR OTHER INFORMATION IN THIS BOOK. IN NO EVENT SHALL OUR LIABILITY WHETHER IN TORT, CONTRACT OR OTHERWISE EXCEED THE COST OF THIS BOOK.

Your common sense and good judgment are crucial to safe and successful automotive work. Read procedures through before starting them. Think about how alert you are feeling, and whether the condition of your vehicle, your level of mechanical skill or your level of reading comprehension might result in or contribute in some way to an occurrence which might cause you injury, damage your vehicle, or result in an unsafe repair or modification. If you have doubts for these or other reasons about your ability to perform safe work on your vehicle, have the work done at an authorized Jeep dealer or other qualified shop.

This book is only intended for persons who have a great deal of experience in repairing automobiles and who are seeking specific information about Jeep vehicles. It is not for those who are looking for general information on automobile repair. REPAIR AND MODIFICATION OF AUTOMOBILES IS DANGEROUS UNLESS UNDERTAKEN WITH FULL KNOWLEDGE OF THE CONSEQUENCES.

Chrysler Corporation has not reviewed and does not warrant the accuracy or completeness of the technical specifications and procedures described in this book.

Before attempting any work on your Jeep, read the Warnings and Cautions on the inside front cover, and any warning or caution that accompanies a procedure or description in the book. Review the Warnings and Cautions each time you prepare to work on your Jeep.

Copies of this book may be purchased from authorized Jeep dealers, most automotive accessories and parts dealers specializing in Jeeps, from selected booksellers, or directly from the publisher by mail. The publisher encourages comments from the reader of this book. These communications have been and will be considered in the preparation of this and other manuals. Please write to Robert Bentley Inc., Publishers at the address listed on the top of this page.

Jeep Owner's Bible™: A Hands-on Guide to Getting the Most From Your Jeep, by Moses Ludel

Library of Congress Catalog Card No. 92-54440
ISBN 0-8376-0154-1
Bentley Stock No. GJEE
Chrysler/Jeep Part No. OOPM3361

03 02 01 00 99 98   13 12 11 10 9

Jeep® is a registered trademark of Chrysler Corporation

The paper used in this publication is acid free and meets the requirements of the National Standard for Information Sciences-Permanence of Paper for Printed Library Materials. ⊗

Manufactured in the United States of America

Front cover: Photo by Kirk Willis. **Back cover**: Clockwise from top: a) Chrysler/Jeep Corporation's 1988 Jeep Cup Rally Regional, Casa Grande, AZ, photo by Moses Ludel; b) 1999 Grand Cherokee, courtesy Chrysler Corporation; c) 1999 Wrangler, photo by Moses Ludel; d) Cherokee, courtesy Chrysler Corporation; e) late CJ-7 (Owner: Jim Powell), photo by Moses Ludel; f) pristine '48 CJ-2A Jeep (Owner: Randy Martin and family), photo by Moses Ludel. All other photography in this book, except for that supplied by vehicle manufacturers or aftermarket suppliers, is by Moses Ludel.

Preface

Author's note: In the fall of 1992, the first edition of my Jeep Owner's Bible reached the Jeep community. Support for the original book encouraged me to update material, include new Jeep vehicles and share aftermarket product developments. I wish to thank those readers who purchased and liked the first edition. Your enthusiasm inspired my line-by-line edit and revision of material, which you will discover in this new edition. First time and former readers, be assured that, while bringing forth current information and making the book a more accessible read, I have maintained all content that readers of the first edition found valuable. Whether your preference is a restored CJ-2A, a hybridized CJ-7, the latest Wrangler, a Grand Cherokee or any other Jeep 4WD truck, enjoy this book and your Jeep vehicle for all it's worth!

The oil heater grill glowed red, as flickering grey shadows danced across the hand planed plank floor of the C.O.D. Garage at Minden, Nevada. The dealership had served local ranchers and town residents for nearly half a century, taking orders and delivering new Buicks, Chevrolets and, for several years now, Jeep trucks.

Among the few vehicles purchased for stock, a bright green 1964 model CJ-5 Jeep stood patiently in the dusty storage barn. The topless utility truck, equipped with a heavy duty T-98A four-speed transmission, factory directional signals, and the split full front seat, would receive several "dealer installed" options.

As crisp autumn leaves skitted across the curbed streets of Minden, my father bought our first four-wheel drive Jeep. Add-ons, including a full cloth top, free-wheeling front hubs, a passenger side wiper motor, the factory heater package and a drawbar hitch, raised the selling price of $2400 to just over $2700.

At fifteen years of age, I hardly imagined the significance of that event. Nevada, boasting a scant population of 200,000 people and seemingly endless expanses of remote public land, would serve as my introduction to Jeep four-wheeling. The odyssey began with the first crisp start of that feisty F-head engine and the distinctive "gr-r-r" accompanying the shift to compound low gear.

In the spring of 1965, I passed my original driver's license test behind the large, flat steering wheel of the CJ-5, aware that a world of unbridled adventure lay ahead. A rugged Jeep truck, sure access to lone desert valleys, bands of wild horses and austere mountain ranges, became my companion and rite of passage.

The eager start-ups and reassuring drone of that F-head 134 engine are easy to recall. Those earliest travels tested the Sierra Nevada's rugged Rubicon Trail, pushed axle deep snow over Devil's Gate Summit, shared the Pine Nut Range with long-maned wild stallions and their harems, and wound along the 150-mile stretch of desolate gravel roads linking Tonopah with Austin, Nevada. Unfettered by extremes of weather, courageous on treacherous terrain, the CJ-5 never faltered, serving faithfully as my off-highway partner and mentor.

Years spent as a master truck mechanic, heavy equipment operator and four-wheel drive magazine writer, technical columnist and photojournalist have deepened my appreciation for Jeep products. Utility value and innovative engineering make these four-wheel drive vehicles a leader worldwide. Jeep 4WD trucks remain the undaunted workhorse, adventurous trail runner and consummate complement to contemporary suburban life....

In the rugged outback, every Jeep owner's concern is *dependability*. Safe four-wheeling requires predictable vehicle performance, precise driver skill and proper equipment. Preventive maintenance, periodic inspection, thorough tune-ups and the right accessories will provide reliability and maximum service from your Jeep 4x4 truck. Toward this end, I offer the *Jeep Owner's Bible*.

Whether or not you intend to work on your Jeep, this book also serves as a consumer guide, technical reference, data source and orientation to Jeep 4x4 trucks and their proper care. Equipped with this book and a genuine Jeep service manual for your model, you can perform quality repairs or even the complete mechanical restoration of a Jeep four-wheel drive truck.

My Jeep journey began with a shiny new 1964 CJ-5. Thirty-four years later, I share my experience as an inveterate Jeep enthusiast, 4WD truck mechanic, shop teacher, magazine and newspaper journalist, "low environmental impact" 4WD instructor and consultant to Jeep and other 4WD truck/SUV manufacturers.

Through my words and photos, discover why "Jeep 4WD" stands as a benchmark for rugged utility, the ultimate vehicle for outback fun. Whether accessing remote country or providing all-season security, the Jeep trademark and legend stand alone. May this book complement your Jeep adventures and lifestyle!

Chapter 1

Jeep: Building a Legend

War was inevitable in 1939, and American industry began to mobilize. Engineering draftsmen penned an arsenal of new weapons, planes, ships, tanks and trucks for the battlefields of Europe and the Far East. Among the needed war materiel were alternatives to the antiquated horse cavalry and reconnaissance motorcycles of World War I.

American manufacturers responded rapidly in their bid for contracts. Mechanical oddities, ranging from a motorized platform on wheels to half-tracks and heavily armored trucks, emerged for testing.

At American Bantam Car Company, the engineering staff headed by Karl Probst pioneered a no frills, four wheeled vehicle with limited sheet metal. The

Fig. 1-1. *The Willys-Overland prototype of a general purpose military truck demonstrated a practical, four-wheel drive design. Minor front end sheet metal changes distinguish this early MA model from the popular World War II Model MB Jeep. The versatility and utility of these 1/4-ton capacity trucks would revolutionize the concept of all-terrain vehicles.*

Fig. 1-2. *Rollout of the original Jeep, September 23, 1940. Karl Probst (leaning on the spare tire) and this small team at American Bantam built this prototype in 49 days, delivering it a mere 15 minutes before the Army contract deadline. Willys and Ford examined the Bantam and subsequently produced a similar design.*

prototype, essentially a scaled-down utility truck with an uncomplicated water-cooled engine, featured a useful four-wheel drive system with simple controls. Probst's design appeared well suited for the rigors of wartime field service.

Between September 1940 and mid-1941, American Bantam, Ford Motor Company and Willys-Overland tested vehicles of this type. In June of 1941, vehicles from each of these firms won U.S. Government approval, but in a pivotal decision, the Army concluded that the tiny American Bantam Car Company would be unable to produce the quantity of vehicles needed. As Willys-Overland and Ford forged ahead with production, American Bantam, innovator of the design, ceased manufacturing at a mere 2,675 units.

Willys-Overland's Winning Bid

The contract was crucial to Willys-Overland. Once a major car producer, Willys sales during the Depression Era had fallen well behind Ford, General Motors and Chrysler. Willys-Knight models vanished, along with the company's six- and eight-cylinder engines. By the mid-1930s, Willys cars and pickups were all four-cylinder powered, an effort to establish stable market share through the sale of lighter, more economical transportation.

Fig. 1-3. *Historical plaque marks the location of the American Bantam Car Co. in Butler, Pennsylvania, where the original Jeep was designed in 18 hours.*

Experience with a lightweight pickup, powered by a 134.2 cubic inch valve-in-block (L-head) four-cylinder engine, contributed to Willys' success with the U.S. Army contract. Two design attempts produced the prototype Model MA, followed by the mass built Model MB. Each was a four-wheel drive, 1/4-ton truck design incorporating several powertrain features from existing Willys civilian vehicles.

The widely used MB Jeep featured a Spicer 25 live front axle assembly. A full-floating design, the concept combined the stability of a conventional, solid (hypoid) driving axle with steerable knuckles at the outer ends of a rigid axle housing. The Spicer 25 front axle withstood all tests.

To meet military specifications, Willys built the Models MA and MB with a Spicer two-speed transfer case. This gear unit, mounted behind a three-speed Borg-Warner T-84 transmission, performed several tasks. As a power divider, the transfer case connected and disconnected power flow to the front and rear axles. An extra gearset, Low Range, gave the four-wheel drive mode an optional reduction gear ratio for climbing severe grades and pulling heavy loads.

A ladder frame and semi-elliptic leaf springs supported each axle. Wheel suspension included airplane shocks and anchor-and-shackle spring attachments. Sturdy and serviceable, Willy's first Jeep went to war.

Fighting to Victory

The MB Jeep played a major role in the European and Pacific theatres of the Second World War. Used by the Allies in Northern Europe, the Soviet Union, the Mediterranean, North Africa, the South Pacific Islands and throughout Asia, these utility 4x4s demonstrated indomitable traction and a remarkable ability to move personnel and materials.

Jeep MBs firmly established their role as lightweight utility trucks, amassing a long list of uses. For pulling, hauling, carrying or crawling, the low-range

Fig. 1-4. *Identification plate on this World War II Ford-built GPW shows familiar Ford script trademark. Differences between Willys-Overland and Ford trucks is subtle. Parts interchange without problem.*

The L-Head 134 Engine

Rated 60 horsepower with 6.48:1 compression ratio, the L-head 134 engine was right for the task. Ease of service, including a flat oil pan mating surface and adjustable valve lifters at the left side of the engine block, made the cast-iron, in-line four popular. For field service, the water pump, distributor and down draft one-barrel carburetor could each be replaced in minutes.

The very low compression ratio and willingness to start made hand cranking possible in an emergency. On flat ground, at just over one-ton dry weight, two people could easily push-start a Model MB Jeep. The three-main bearing engine design was light, strong and capable of operating on poor grades of gasoline. With a conventional six-volt breaker point ignition system, field tuning and troubleshooting proved simple.

gearset proved worthy. The weight distribution and tractability of the Jeep complemented the benefits of low gearing, which also offset the modest horsepower rating. On main roads, the low ratio 4.88:1 axle gearsets with 6.00"x16" tires caused the engine to whine well above 3000 rpm at 50 miles per hour.

By the War's end, military personnel from GIs to five-star generals praised the MB Jeep. Most ground troops had experienced the ride, noise and feel of a Jeep. At the battlefront, many witnessed the heroic role which these trucks played, as personnel carriers, light weapons carriers, mobile machine gun stations and Medevac vehicles. The Jeep's story plied deeply into frontline news.

On Home Soil

As troops came home to civilian life, the Jeep followed. The easily recognized MB model was soon available at surplus equipment sales, and Willys-Overland, recognizing a civilian market for the Jeep, had tooled for peacetime production. By 1946, the civilian model CJ-2A appeared, primarily intended as a work

Fig. 1-5. *The lightweight Model MB Jeep that served Allied forces featured Willys' 134 cubic inch L-head four, six-volt electrics, full-floating Spicer 25 front and similar 23-2 rear axles, a two-piece windshield and rear-mounted spare tire. Weak links were the chain camshaft drive, T-84/GPW transmission and Spicer 23-2 rear axle. These models were plentiful in the postwar surplus market.*

Fig. 1-6. *1950/51 Model MC/M38 military Jeep still had flat front fenders, however, a one-piece windshield, a tailgate and 24-volt electrical system differed from MB models. Rear axle was stronger Spicer 44, and the L-head 134 engine boasted timing gears. By the mid-'50s, following the Korean War, these trucks became available as surplus.*

truck for ranchers, farmers, utility companies, contractors and mine operators.

Tested thoroughly during the war years, the MB Jeep had revealed a few weaknesses. In civilian dress, the new CJ-2A soon abandoned the full-floating Spicer 23-2 rear axle (beginning with serial number 13453) in favor of a heftier Spicer 41-2 type. Gone too was the GPW/T-84 transmission with its weak countershaft bushings and light duty shift control unit. The replacement gearbox, a durable Borg Warner T-90 three speed, successfully served Jeep trucks for the next quarter century.

For utility, the postwar civilian Jeep featured a tailgate and side mounted spare tire. Surface-mounted headlights and the use of chrome trim items enhanced

Jeep Aftermarket Equipment Emerges

Arthur Warn pioneered free-wheeling front wheel hubs. His contribution increased the driving ease, reliability and economy of four-wheel drive Jeep trucks and greatly enhanced their popularity. Today, Warn Industries produces manual and automatic locking hubs, electric winches and a host of accessories for four-wheel drive vehicles.

Warn's first "free-wheeling" front end was extreme! This kit eliminated the transfer case and live front drive axle from a surplus model MB Jeep. Apparently, some

the civilian and military surplus Jeep. 1946 circa photo (below left) of CJ-2A shows Ramsey Model 101 PTO winch. Rated 4,000 lbs. capacity, the winch receives power from the Jeep's transfer case. A shift lever extends through the floor of cab.

Rare photo of pre-Wagoneer/J-truck era Jeep dealership shows (left to right) a Forward Control 4WD pickup, two four-cylinder CJs, a Jeep 4x4 Pickup, The CJ3-B and a 4x4 Utility Wagon. These new Kaiser/Willys trucks featured Ramsey mechanical winches.

A Farm Equipment invoice (below) of 1947 indicates the scope of Jeep utility. A Jeep could operate as a cultivating tractor, bulldozer, snow plow, post hole digger, buzz saw and portable cement mixer! At just over one-ton curb weight, with four-wheel drive traction, a two-speed transfer case and power take-off capability, the 60 horsepower MB and CJ-2A models worked hard.

owners needed a lightweight utility truck but not four-wheel drive. Surplus Jeep trucks were abundant and inexpensive.

Arthur Warn owned a Willys/Jeep dealership in Seattle, Washington. Above, a new CJ-2A sales invoice illustrates the wide variety of equipment available for early civilian Jeep models. Shipped from Toledo in raw form, a Jeep truck relied on dealer installed options.

The Warn Converter, which eliminated the transfer case, transformed a Jeep surplus engine and transmission into a stationary power source. Rugged, lightweight and capable of 60 horsepower, the Willys/Jeep L-head 134 engine became a motive force at fixed and portable worksites.

Likewise, the power take-off (PTO) access at the rear of the Spicer Model 18 transfer case provided a practical source of energy for a winch or posthole digger. Ramsey and Koenig developed PTO systems to harness engine power for winching and other chores. PTO winches and accessories increased the versatility of both

Fig. 1-7. *MC/M38 military models yielded to the MD/M38A1, which Willys-Overland introduced in 1951 and Kaiser continued to produce until 1968. M38A1 models employed the newer F-head 134 four-cylinder engine. The rounded front fender truck served as prototype for the CJ-5 civilian Jeep.*

Fig. 1-9. *As World War II ended, Willys-Overland introduced the first civilian model CJ-2A Jeep. Surface mounted headlights, a tailgate, side-mounted spare tire, Spicer 41-2 rear axle (after Serial No. 13453) and a stronger T-90 transmission quickly distinguished the CJ-2A from the Model MB military Jeep.*

the truck's appearance and distinguished this civilian 1/4-ton capacity vehicle from the military MB model. Six-volt electrics remained, along with the split windshield and sixteen-inch wheel rims. Intended for work, the CJ-2A maintained a spartan profile, including round, military-type gauges and instrumentation.

Building America

A robust postwar U.S. economy and industries afforded immediate opportunities for the Jeep. Capable of hauling workers and materials to remote minesites, up high-tension cable routes and through desert gullies and knee high streams, the CJ-2A and surplus MB Jeep further proved the Willys-Overland design. Ranchers and farmers welcomed the Jeep to American agriculture, discovering a multitude of uses for these all-wheel drive trucks.

Fig. 1-10. *Original owner of this Oregon based 1948 CJ-2A purchased the Jeep to pull three lawn mowers. Immaculately maintained, the truck is now collectible. Willys-Overland brought durability and rugged utility to the civilian truck market.*

The rugged design of the CJ-2A and later Willys CJ models was obvious. An industrial strength albeit low horsepower engine, the rear axle designed for much larger 1/2-ton trucks, and a transmission and transfer case that easily met the needs of larger Jeep Pickup and Station Wagon models contributed to the stamina of Willys and Kaiser era CJs. Subjected to constant work loads and severe off-pavement pounding, the Jeep CJ performed dutifully.

Off-Highway Recreational Jeep

Among those attracted to the Jeep 4x4s were a growing number of outdoor enthusiasts. Jeep trucks brought primitive back country, fishing, hunting, and exploring ghost towns within easy reach.

Fig. 1-8. *Early prototype of postwar civilian Jeep reveals several features common to the CJ-2A production models. Sidemount spare tire, surface mounted headlights and sixteen-inch diameter wheels distinguished the 1946 civilian models. Spicer Model 23-2 full-floating rear axle (shown here) and the experimental column shift mechanism appeared only in the very early CJ-2A trucks.*

Fig. 1-11. *The most obvious difference between the CJ-2A and CJ-3A was the one-piece windshield glass. Less evident, the CJ-3A boasted a stronger Spicer 44 rear axle and an improved front axle shaft design (beginning with chassis #37549). All CJ-3A and newer L-134s used a gear-driven camshaft. Six-volt electrics, a tailgate and side mount spare tire remained.*

Fig. 1-13. *In the postwar years, Jeep pioneered the all-steel station wagon. The 4x4-63 models featured a Borg-Warner T-90 transmission, Spicer Model 18 transfer case and Spicer drive axles. Although reliable, these trucks were grossly underpowered with the L-head 134 engine.*

Jeep 4x4s soon gave families access to remote desert and mountain camping. The zest of postwar American life, in direct contrast to the austere years of the Depression and horrors of World War II, created a greater interest in recreation. Inexpensive fuel and a relatively low cost of living introduced more people to outdoor activity. For those who enjoyed quietude and "getting away," Jeep 4x4s provided the means.

By 1948, when Willys-Overland introduced the flat fender CJ-3A with a one-piece windshield, the first Jeep 1/2-ton Pickup and Station Wagon had already earned attention. The earliest version of the Jeep Pickup was an L-head four-cylinder model. Grossly underpowered, these 4x4 trucks spent most of their four-wheel drive work time in low range. A two-wheel drive counterpart, weighing much less, served as a light duty pickup for suburban and farm use.

Fig. 1-14. *A more stylish, 104.5" wheelbase V-grilled 4x473 model introduced the F-head 134 four-cylinder engine in 1950. The F-134 four-cylinder engine produced nearly as much power as the Model 6-73 Station Wagon sixes.*

The Jeep Station Wagon entered the market in 1946, first in the Model 4-63 four-cylinder version. A meager 148.5 cubic inch in-line L-head six powered the 1948 Model 6-63. By 1950, a slightly larger 161 six replaced the 148.5 engine in the Model 6-73 Wagon, but at a mere 75 horsepower, the 161 was still underpowered.

134 F-head Four Cylinder Emerges

1953 was a significant change year for the CJ. The new, flat fendered CJ-3B featured a taller hood to clear the 134.2 cubic inch F-head four-cylinder engine. This engine design first appeared in the 1950 model 473HT chassis and the 1951 model M38A1 military Jeep, a prototype for the 1955–71 CJ-5 civilian Jeep.

In CJ-3B models, the F-head's low 6.9:1 compression ratio produced 70 horsepower @4000 rpm, while the four-cylinder Station Wagon and Pickup

Fig. 1-12. *Spartan looks of flat grill and fenders on postwar pickups matched the L-head 134 engine's sparse horsepower. Early L-head six-cylinder engines were also small displacement, low horsepower designs. As a consequence, pickup trucks spent a good deal of their off-highway working hours in 4WD Low Range.*

Fig. 1-15. *The CJ-3B, regarded by many as a marque, was actually a transitional model between the 80" wheelbase flat fender models and the 81" wheelbase CJ-5. Installation of the taller F-Head 134 four engine required raising the hood line. These models were popular from 1953–64, although the CJ-5 somewhat diminished CJ-3B sales after 1955.*

coaxed five extra horsepower from a higher 7.4:1 compression ratio. The 134 F-head's unique in-block exhaust valve with valve-in-head intake design served in U.S. models to 1973. Foreign licensee-built Jeep trucks continue to benefit from this frisky, high stamina engine.

F-134 Valvetrain Design

The unique F-head design maintains the same bore and stroke as the L-head 134. Intake valves, however, no longer set beside the exhaust valves in the engine block. A removable cylinder head casting supports large 2" diameter intake valves. This gives the F-head a combination of overhead and in-block valves, each featuring adjustable stem clearances.

Access to the exhaust valve tappets remains at the left side of the block. A rocker arm cover atop the removable cylinder head allows access to the rocker shaft assembly and adjustable intake valve rocker arms. The L- and F-134s share many components. (See service chapter for valve adjustment procedure.)

The Original Jeepster

The classic 2WD Jeepster VJ-2 and VJ-3 models of 1948–51 produced modest sales. Underpowered and offered only as a two-wheel drive phaeton, Willys-Overland's most stylish truck failed to find a market niche but may well have survived if the 226 six had been available. Four-wheel drive would also have increased early Jeepster VJ sales, as Kaiser's introduction of such a concept in a 1967 model proved highly successful. Among the rare, collectible VJ models that remain today, four-wheel drive conversions, using early Station Wagon/Pickup components, are common.

Jeep Models For A Broader Market

The most significant Willys Station Wagon and Pickup breakthrough was the 1954 introduction of the "Hurricane 6," a 226 cubic inch in-line powerplant. Rated 115 horsepower @3650 rpm with an impressive 190 lbs./ft. of torque @1800 rpm, the 226 served until the J-truck/Wagoneer era of the 1960s. A conventional valve-in-block, L-head design, this engine was essentially Kaiser's Continental Six powerplant.

As testimony to Jeep stamina, all Willys/Kaiser era CJ, 4WD Station Wagon and 4WD Pickup models shared Spicer's Model 18 transfer case. The T-90 Borg-Warner transmission was standard, with some pickups and Kaiser era CJ-5/CJ-6 models opting for the heavy duty T-98 Borg-Warner four-speed gearbox. These components held up well with four- and six-cylinder powerplants in trucks through 1/2-ton capacity.

Although various Spicer axles served the early Jeep trucks, the chassis layout remained similar. Kaiser's purchase of Willys-Overland in 1953, with corporate restructuring as Willys Motors, had limited impact on Jeep engineering until 1962. Even Kaiser's innovative cab forward control FC150 (F-head 134 four-cylinder) and FC170 (226 six powered) pickups

Fig. 1-16. *The 6-226 Kaiser powerplant provided 115 horsepower @3650 rpm and 190 lbs./ft. of torque @1800 rpm. Utility Pickup trucks and the Utility Wagon gave excellent service with these Hurricane Six L-head engines.*

Fig. 1-18. *In 1957, Kaiser's Willys Motors unveiled the cab-forward FC150 and FC170 models. Styling differences between the four-cylinder FC150 and six-cylinder FC170 models were subtle, although the larger FC170 featured a longer wheelbase. These innovative trucks aimed at the utility market. Sales figures, however, indicate only modest consumer interest in these rare, collectible models.*

Fig. 1-17. *By 1956, Kaiser influence at Willys Motors produced the 4x4 Utility Wagon, a considerably more stylish vehicle with the bigger 6-226 Kaiser/Continental engine. Modern styling and a V-shaped grill distinguished 1950–64 Utility 4x4 models. Many Hurricane Six-powered station wagons and pickups continue to deliver quality service.*

Fig. 1-19. *Introduced in 1962, the J-truck pickups and Wagoneer models, including this rare Model 1413 Jeep Panel Delivery truck, offered similar powertrain options. The original engine was Kaiser's Tornado 230 cubic inch OHC six, replaced in 1965 by AMC's 232 six and the 327 Vigilante V-8.*

of 1957 had powertrains and axle designs that reflected other Jeep models.

The Kaiser/Jeep Corporation Years

Kaiser, anticipating rapid growth in crossover four-wheel drive truck sales, planned changes for the 1960s. In 1962, a bold new Kaiser Jeep Corporation targeted the suburban and rural markets with the highly innovative Wagoneer. Considered the pioneer sport/utility four-wheel drive model or "SUV," the Wagoneer and its 1963 J-truck counterpart competed in the full-size American truck market. Jeep vehicles were no longer sparse, outmoded Willys trucks.

The new body size and wheelbase dimensions of the Wagoneer and "Gladiator" J-trucks came on time. While the 81" wheelbase 1/4-ton capacity CJ-5 held a unique edge in the lightweight utility market, the up-

scale Wagoneer and Gladiator pickup satisfied an emerging market of full sized four-wheel drive wagon and truck buyers.

Ford, General Motors and Dodge lagged years behind Jeep. The Big Three offered cumbersome, strictly work-oriented 4x4 pickup trucks and the staid Suburban while Kaiser's Jeep Corporation progressed in every area of vehicle design. Introducing luxury appointments, bold styling and power accessory options, the new Jeep Wagoneer and Gladiator models dominated the four-wheel drive market.

Wagoneer/J-Trucks: A Formidable Presence In the Marketplace

Soon, International Harvester's Travelall offered a modest challenge to the Wagoneer. Similarly, the 1961 I-H Scout, intended to meet the needs of agricultural customers, became the first true competitor for Jeep's CJ-5 and the longer, 101-inch wheelbase CJ-6.

Finally, in 1966, Ford responded with the Bronco six-cylinder utility models, initially aimed at the Jeep CJ and Scout buyer rather than the Wagoneer market. A less spartan 1969 Suburban 4x4 and new Chevrolet Blazer, followed by GMC's 1970 Jimmy, also made direct bids for the Wagoneer's market. Chrysler entered the competition in 1974 with the Dodge Ramcharger and Plymouth Trailduster.

North American consumers clearly stated their tastes, and sales have soared ever since the birth of the SUV market. The Wagoneer spearheaded this trend in

1962, rapidly filling the parking lots of gun clubs and suburban country clubs while amply meeting the toughest worksite challenges. Soon, the broad, roguish grins of Wagoneer grills glistened everywhere.

Beyond a facelift and attractive interior appointments, the Wagoneer and Gladiator 4x4s were real trucks. Carefully calibrated leaf spring suspension created a smooth ride, despite a thoroughly "truck" chassis. A stout ladder frame, hypoid driving axles and rugged powertrain options gave these models an edge.

Upscale suburban and rural buyers quickly recognized the Wagoneer's virtues. By the mid-'Sixties, a Super Wagoneer model boasted deluxe interior and

Fig. 1-20. *Popular CJ-5 Universal, built from 1955–83, originally offered F-134 engine. Kaiser added the Buick 225 Dauntless V-6 as an "official" option in 1966. By 1972, AMC 232 and 258 sixes and 304 V-8 replaced these earlier engines. Three extra inches of wheelbase accommodated AMC in-line sixes. Shown is a faithfully maintained '74 AMC/Jeep CJ-5 Renegade V-8 model.*

Fig. 1-21. *Original 81-inch wheelbase CJ-5 looked much like Model MD/M38A1 military Jeep. In civilian form, CJ-5s featured a tailgate, trim items and, generally, a one-piece windshield. Jeff Tunem's wholly original 1956 model, however, came with a military-type two-piece windshield. My original, early '55 CJ-5 restoration project featured an M38A1 style frame. Parts went into these rigs as available.*

Innovative Wagoneer and J-Truck Models

Wide popularity was Kaiser's reward for the versatile and stylish 110-inch wheelbase Wagoneer. The low profile chassis features heavy duty Spicer/Dana geartrain components, including the original through-drive Model 20 transfer case. Appealing power options, like an automatic transmission, helped drive sales.

Early J-trucks and Wagoneers feature Kaiser's advanced 230 cubic inch Tornado overhead camshaft six. Unfortunately, valve guide sealing problems and other bugs undermined this progressive engineering. By 1965, the American Motors overhead valve 232 six and 327 V-8 served as the standard and optional powerplants. These AMC engines allowed Jeep J-trucks and Wagoneers to compete with the Big Three trucks.

J-trucks and Wagoneers pioneered factory power steering as a 4x4 option. Wagoneer also experimented with an optional independent, live swinging front axle system fifteen years before Ford Motor Company introduced such a design. These Jeep trucks pioneered use of the all new Spicer/Dana 20 transfer case, a much improved through-drive design. In 1962, other truck manufacturers still packaged crude, less efficient side-drive transfer cases.

J-trucks and Wagoneers set a standard for the entire four-wheel drive industry. The Wagoneer proved that a four-wheel drive utility wagon could work hard yet drive easily. Seven years after Kaiser's Jeep Corporation initiative, General Motors introduced the Blazer/Jimmy models.

Fig. 1-22. *1965 was a change year for Wagoneer. A new low and wide grill enhanced styling. General Motors' rugged Turbo-Hydramatic 400 automatic transmission and power steering were Wagoneer options.*

exterior trim, bucket seats and a console mounted shifter. Tilt wheel power steering and a four-barrel carbureted AMC 327 V-8 placed Jeep several years ahead of other 4x4 truck builders.

By 1968, upgrade packages included either the 327 AMC V-8 or Buick's 350 Dauntless V-8 (as available) with the choice of GM's rugged THM400 three-speed automatic transmission or a proven Borg-Warner three- or four-speed manual transmission. ('Sixties J-trucks often have rugged Borg-Warner four-speed truck transmissions.) Air conditioning with heavy duty engine cooling and power assisted steering were also popular.

Evolution Of the CJ-5 and CJ-6 Models

In 1956, one year after the introduction of the CJ-5 model, Kaiser expanded the utility of the Jeep Universal models with an optional CJ-6 package on a 101" wheelbase. 20" longer than the popular CJ-5, the CJ-6 served a variety of work environments. Many CJ-6s featured accessories like a posthole digger or even a backhoe.

Additionally, the growing number of V-8 and six-cylinder engine conversions into the Jeep CJ, early truck and military surplus models attracted Kaiser's attention. By the mid-1960s, many Jeep owners had converted their earlier utility 4x4s into more versatile transportation or high performance machines. The trend toward sport/utility use was also clear.

In the autumn of 1965, as Ford introduced the sluggish 170 cubic inch displacement six-cylinder Bronco, Kaiser/Jeep brandished a Buick 225 "Dauntless" V-6 as an option in the '66 model CJs. The popular CJ V-6 package spearheaded an industry-wide horsepower race.

Bring On the Sport/Utility Trucks!

As other manufacturers targeted sport/utility vehicle sales, Jeep accepted the challenge. The Jeepster, on a 101" CJ-type wheelbase, appeared as a 1967 model. The timing was right.

1964 CJ 225 V-6 and a CJ-4?

I refer to the Jeep/Buick "Dauntless" 225 V-6 as a 1966 option. Parts listings support this statement, however, consumers and original owners have shared information about rare 1965 CJ-5 models equipped with this engine. A Canadian gentleman felt very sure his '64 CJ-3B had an original 225 V-6 engine.

As Kaiser/Jeep did a great deal of pre-production and testing work, it is highly likely that these cases are true—along with many other "one-off" model and equipment claims. Keep in mind that both Willys and Kaiser's Jeep Corporation were smaller production and engineering entities with plenty of interesting parts around.

I can vouch for one inquiry made around 1963 at Gardnerville, Nevada. The Postmaster, Hank Rosenbrock, received a visit from Jeep Corporation staff. His attractive CJ Jeep had a very nice GM 215 cubic inch aluminum V-8 conversion. Corporate curiosity might easily have led to Jeep's CJ and Jeepster being the first production 4WD trucks to use the Buick 215 V-8. Instead, an evolved version of that engine eventually found its place in the British Land Rover. Jeep focused, quite sensibly, on the torquey, odd-firing, all-iron 225 Buick V-6 powerplant.

For those who enjoy trivia, there were also many Jeep models that either never saw production or were built in small numbers. One isolated rarity was the CJ-4, a prototype developed coincidently with the military M38A1. Stylized front fenders and an oddball windshield frame distinguish this critter from both the M38A1 and the CJ-5 that emerged in 1955. The one and only CJ-4, a year older than the production M38A1, has a title with Serial Number '01.' An account of other Willys, Kaiser and AMC concept vehicles and "experiments" would easily fill another book.

Improved steering, better brakes and an overdue automatic transmission option created a ready market niche for the new Jeepster. V-6 equipped CJs and Jeepsters boasted single-lever transfer cases and the hefty T-86AA three speed manual transmission. (The all-synchromesh T-14 three-speed came on line in 1968 V-6 models.)

The impressive Buick 225 all-iron V-6 produced 160 horsepower, more than twice the 75 horsepower figure of the late F-head 134 engines. 1966 CJ models offered a power-to-weight ratio unavailable in any of the earlier utility 4x4s. At approximately 2500 pounds curb weight, the V-6 CJ-5 Jeep was an all-around performer.

The stability of a longer 101" wheelbase gave the V-6 Jeepster light towing capability. Unfortunately, the more rugged T-98A truck four speed was an option re-

Fig. 1-23. *The Buick Dauntless V-6 engine spearheaded a sport/utility four-wheel drive boom. 1966 CJ-5s and the new Jeepster offered this powerplant option.*

Fig. 1-24. *Kaiser's Jeepster Commando was available with either a full top or half-cab. On a 101-inch wheelbase, these sport/utility models competed with the Ford Bronco and I-H Scout. A more luxurious interior and an automatic transmission option gave the Jeepster a marketing edge.*

served for four-cylinder CJ models. For heavy loads or serious off-road crawling, the T98A transmission proved the better gearbox. Jeepster buyers settled for a Borg-Warner manual three-speed or an optional GM automatic transmission, a special edition TH400 built for Kaiser's Jeep Corporation.

Aware of trends, Jeep began packaging image, much like competitive manufacturers. As GM and Ford made their late-sixties bid for 4x4 sport/utility market share, Kaiser responded with the Super Wagoneer and CJ Renegade. (The rare, original Kaiser/Jeep CJ Renegades feature a superior boxed frame and heavy duty suspension package.) Upgrade trim packages and options would characterize truck marketing through the next decade.

By the 1970 model year, light truck marketing went well beyond powertrain options. The new four-wheel drive buyer was susceptible to image and concept appeal, much like automobile buyers in American society. Brand identification, distinctive styling packages and improved performance helped generate sales.

AMC Acquires Jeep Corporation

In 1970, Kaiser sold Jeep Corporation to American Motors (AMC). Acknowledging the value and impact of the Jeep trademark, American Motors immediately created a subsidiary, the Jeep Corporation. Despite ominous forecasts of stifling federal pollution controls and drastic fuel economy demands, AMC's acquisition of Jeep proved both timely and a major success.

The Jeep and AMC connection dated to 1965. Kaiser/Jeep Corporation's J-truck/Wagoneer use of the 327 AMC V-8 and 232 in-line six eased the transition to 304 and 360 AMC V-8s and the 232/258 sixes during 1971 and 1972. AMC dropped use of the Buick V-6 and 350 V-8 after 1971.

AMC inherited an impressive roster of quality geartrain components with the purchase of Kaiser Jeep Corporation. Rugged Spicer 44, 60 and 70 rear axles, Model 27 and 44 front axles and the Spicer Model 18 and 20 transfer cases were in the Kaiser parts inventory. T-18 and T98A Borg Warner four speeds, the all-synchromesh T-14 three-speed, a surviving version of the T-90 three speed and tough GM THM400 automatic transmissions meant rugged, proven service.

During the last years of Kaiser production even the superior GM Saginaw steering gears appeared in most of the Jeep models. Only a few Ross gear applications carried over. By 1971, Kaiser built ample trucks around the best powertrain and chassis pieces available in the United States.

1972: AMC's Influence Is Everywhere!

Through 1971, AMC/Jeep models remain largely unchanged from Kaiser designs. True AMC engineering first appears in 1972 models, as major shifts in engine technology and minor body alterations reflected AMC/Jeep's new marketing goals.

The CJ model lineup and Commando (Jeepster) models underwent significant powerplant changes with the introduction of the longer seven-main bearing 232/258 AMC in-line sixes and the broader, weightier 304 V-8. These powerplants required reshaping of the engine compartment, and a three-inch wheelbase length increase was necessary to accommodate the longer six-cylinder engines.

The CJ's new 304 V-8 was a proven AMC automotive engine with a noted capacity for torque. AMC made the 304 a standard powerplant for the new CJ-5 Renegade package. A carryover from the V-6 Renegade theme of the Kaiser/Jeep era, AMC's 1972 Renegade featured a roll bar, full gauges and identification trim. The Renegade epitomized AMC/Jeep's theme for 1972: "Jeep (4 Wheel Drive)—The toughest 4-letter word on wheels."

The CJ-6 and CJ-8 Utility Trucks

Kaiser introduced the CJ-6 work truck in 1956. A growing number of Jeep users liked the versatility and ruggedness of the CJ-5 yet found the short wheelbase limiting. The new 101" wheelbase CJ-6 was a full 20 inches longer, with sheetmetal body inserts forward of the rear wheel openings, and featured the conventional CJ-5 powertrain with the F-134 four-cylinder engine.

CJ-6 4x4 trucks targeted construction, mine, public utility and agricultural worksites. CJ-6 models closely followed the powertrain changes of the CJ-5. The Buick 225 V-6, 232 and 258 in-line AMC sixes and even the 304 V-8 have toiled admirably in the CJ-6 chassis. By 1975, however, the Jeep CJ image was that of a sporty recreational vehicle. Full-size 4x4 J-trucks met the majority of utility user needs. A declining demand for utility, shifting sales strategies and the 1976 introduction of a 94" wheelbase CJ-7 terminated AMC/Jeep's 104" version of the CJ-6.

As a utility workhorse and power source for PTO driven posthole diggers, hoisting equipment and cable winches, the 1956–71 CJ-6 became a utility legend. Offering pickup truck cargo space on a nimbler CJ chassis, the CJ-6 also served as inspiration for AMC/Jeep's short-lived CJ-8/Scrambler truck of the early '80s.

Most buyers perceive the '80s Scrambler as a sport-about light-duty hauler and recreational 4x4, unlike its predecessor, the spartan CJ-6. Lacking PTO capability and a firm identity, the CJ-8/Scrambler generated far less sales than AMC/Jeep anticipated.

Four-wheel drum brakes remained on the AMC/Jeep CJ models. The exceptionally strong, through-drive Spicer 20 transfer case replaced the side-drive Spicer Model 18. Dana's open-knuckle 30 front axle, phased into the '72–up CJ and final Commando models, serves both the CJ-5 and newly introduced 1976 94" wheelbase CJ-7.

The longer CJ-7 frame afforded room for the optional Warner Quadra-Trac full-time four-wheel drive system with a GM Turbo Hydra-Matic 400 transmission. The CJ-7 became the first CJ to offer an optional automatic transmission.

Upholding Jeep's Tough Image

AMC continued to improve each model. Fully boxed frames bolstered chassis strength on the 1976 CJ-5 and CJ-7. The addition of disc front brakes enhanced stopping on the late-'77 and 1978–up CJ models.

Full-size J-trucks also evolved. When AMC/Jeep assumed production of J-trucks, three wheelbases

F-134 Four Succumbs Under Emission Standards

Introduction of the larger 232/258 sixes and 304 V-8 engines into CJ models met tighter emission control regulations. Industry-wide engineering had grossly reduced the power output of most engines. Although the workhorse F-head 134 engine survives in parts catalog listings until 1974, the engine is virtually non-existent after 1971 models.

The more stringent emission standards of 1972, along with availability of high torque AMC 232 in-line six-cylinder engines, ended F-134 production abruptly. 1972–73 F-134 models are virtual carryovers from remaining stocks of Kaiser powertrain components.

Fig. 1-25. *Growing demand for an automatic transmission option and more rear passenger/cargo space prompted the 1976 introduction of AMC/Jeep's CJ-7 model. At a 94-inch wheelbase, the CJ-7 served a wide variety of user needs. When CJ-5 production stopped after 1983, the Jeep CJ-7 continued and became the chassis prototype for the 1987 YJ Wrangler model.*

Fig. 1-26. *The full-size Cherokee 4x4 entered the market in 1974. A standard 258 six and available 360 and 401 V-8 engines made this model highly competitive with the Blazer, Jimmy, Ramcharger, Trailduster and I-H Scout II. This clean '77, loaded with power options and a 401 V-8, has plenty of life left. Priced for resale at a reasonable $2995, the truck is a great multi-purpose vehicle.*

(110", 120" and 132") served 1/2-ton, 3/4-ton and one-ton capacity models. AMC introduced its 232 and 258 sixes and the 304 and 360 V-8s in 1972 Jeep trucks. By 1976, the AMC 401 V-8 appeared on the option list for full-size models. Torque and horsepower easily compete with Big Three truck engines of that era, and AMC's excellent reputation for powerplant reliability encouraged Jeep sales.

Despite heavy competition from the Blazer/Jimmy and Bronco, the early AMC/Jeep Wagoneers continued to attract suburban and rural buyers. AMC/Jeep trim and accessory options kept pace with those of luxury automobiles, and the reputation of the Wagoneer generated a large percentage of repeat buyers for the 110" wheelbase station wagons.

By 1974, the growing success of competitors' two-door sport/utility (SUV) models compelled AMC/Jeep to offer the full-size Cherokee. The wide track two-door Cherokee shared its 109" wheelbase with the Wagoneer Station Wagon. Full-size Cherokees, which

offered a standard 258 six and several V-8 options, rivaled Chevrolet's Blazer and similar SUVs.

AMC's Engine Options Battle For Market Share

By the mid-'70s, the AMC 304, 360, and 401 family of V-8 engines served throughout the Jeep J-truck/Wagoneer and Cherokee product lines. Lightweight CJ models used the milder two-barrel carbureted 304 V-8 option. Heavier, full-size truck models had the optional two-and four-barrel versions of the 360 and a four-barrel 401.

As federal and California regulations demanded lower exhaust emissions and better fuel mileage, the use of larger displacement engines became impractical. By the late '70s, AMC dropped the 401 V-8. The 360 assumed the role of heavy duty puller. Taller axle ratios (lower numerically) accommodated the stiffer

Fig. 1-27. *This 360 AMC V-8 in a fully equipped 1979 Wagoneer chassis offered ample power, despite the burden of a heavy emission control package. Trailer pulling was possible, as the J-trucks and original full-size Wagoneer offered a rugged chassis and geartrain.*

Fig. 1-28. *1979 Wagoneer offered some of the best powertrain components available in the light truck industry. AMC/Jeep used GM's Saginaw integral power steering and TH400 automatic transmission. Warner's Quadra-Trac or a Spicer 20 transfer case also contributed to the truck's quality reputation, as did Spicer/Dana front and rear axle assemblies with disc front and drum rear brakes.*

federal EPA/CAFE standards, and performance of carbureted full-size trucks declined steadily after 1979.

The 1979 U.S. four-wheel drive scene was a paradox. CJ-5 and CJ-7 models enjoyed wide popularity in a burgeoning off-pavement recreational market. At the same time, mandatory catalytic converters and a host of other emission control devices restricted the use of 4x4 vehicles. More four-wheelers than ever took to the hills despite U.S. Forest Service and B.L.M. warnings that catalytic converters could cause dangerous brush fires!

AMC Builds Superior Trucks

Through the 1970s, utility remained a strong theme in CJ development. The rugged T-18 Warner truck four-speed and Spicer 20 transfer case, coupled to a reliable 232 or 258 six, proved an unbeatable combination. The Spicer 20 transfer case also fit the three-speed T-15 transmissions found in V-8 CJs. (Unfortunately, the T-18 was only an option with 1979 and very rare 1980–81 V-8 CJs, although this rugged transmission appears regularly in V-8 powered J-trucks of that era.)

The combination of an improved frame, GM's Saginaw manual or power steering, disc front brakes, an open knuckle Dana 30 front axle and the optional T-18 four-speed placed the 1978–79 CJs among the best light duty four-wheel drive trucks ever built. The only weak link in the entire powertrain was the two-piece axle shaft/hub flange design of the AMC Model 20 rear axle, which Jeep CJs utilized from 1976–86. (From the late 1940s through 1975, Jeep CJ models employed the exceptionally durable and popular Spicer 44 rear axle.)

J-trucks, the full-size Wagoneer and the full-size Cherokee also reached their zenith by 1979. Despite

emission control constraints and a trend toward lighter weight components, these models benefited from hefty Spicer/Dana axles, disc front brakes and a Spicer 20 transfer case, frequently coupled to the T-18 truck type four-speed option on J-trucks and Cherokees.

Also available was GM's superior Turbo Hydramatic 400 automatic transmission with Warner Quadra-Trac, AMC/Jeep's challenge to Ford and GM sport/utility trucks equipped with the New Process full-time 203 transfer cases. The rugged and reliable THM 400 automatic, which GM ignored until the 1976 introduction of Chevrolet/GMC one-ton capacity K-model 4x4s, was on the Jeep J-truck/Wagoneer option list in 1965.

The 1980s: Years Of Technological Change

CAFE and EPA standards impacted light truck design, and by 1980, manufacturers introduced weight-saving body panels, lighter powertrain components and taller (lower numerical) axle ratios to meet tighter tailpipe emission standards and fuel economy regulations.

The strategy for CJ models was a major revision of powertrains. To comply with fuel mileage standards, AMC borrowed GM's Pontiac 151 four-cylinder engine. A durable, overhead valve pushrod design, nicknamed the "Iron Duke," this refined powerplant had a good record in GM sub-compact cars. Fifteen years earlier, with less emission hardware and lower (higher numerical) axle ratios, the 151 might easily have replaced Jeep's F-134 engine.

Restricted by a heavy burden of emission controls (especially in California trim), which included a catalytic converter system, the Iron Duke powered CJ labored under 3.73:1 and taller axle ratios. A close-ratio, aluminum cased four-speed transmission came on line in 1980, phasing out the far more durable and time honored T-18 truck gearbox used from 1972–79 in CJs and 1966–79 in J-trucks.

In high range, the 1980–86 Jeep CJ performed like an economy car. Aside from sluggishness, taller

The Last CJ-5

Beyond weight-saving measures, mismatched gearing and legislated engine constraints, Jeep CJ models suffered an even greater blow. The CJ-5, noted worldwide for its superior off-pavement prowess and tight access maneuverability, came under media scrutiny during the 1983 model year.

Recognized as the quintessential utility vehicle for back country travel, the CJ-5 offers superior ground clearance and a relatively high breakover angle (ground-to-skidplate clearance at the middle of the truck). The short wheelbase provides a tight turning radius and exceptional rock crawling capability. Approach and departure angles are ideal for rugged trail use and work in tight or awkward environments.

Such was the vehicle's design intent, and meeting these ends means the CJ-5 chassis geometry differs from most other autos and trucks. In particular, a somewhat higher center-of-gravity dimension results from the vehicle's off-pavement orientation.

An attack on the CJ-5's alleged vulnerability to rollover surfaced during a time of impassioned consumer advocacy and public resentment toward American motor vehicles and their manufacturers. Rather than subject the 28-year-old CJ-5 to a legal battle, AMC/Jeep Corporation removed the 84-inch wheelbase model from the marketplace. The ten inch longer CJ-7 and 104" wheelbase CJ-8/ Scrambler pickup (introduced in 1981) continued as Jeep's light utility 4x4 models.

axle gearing accelerated the clutch and driveline wear, especially with oversize tires. Fortunately, the all-new transfer case unit, Dana's iron case 300 design, had a redeeming 2.61:1 low range ratio to accommodate off-pavement rock crawling. Gone, however, was the rugged T-18 with its compound first gear ratio and iron case. A light duty aluminum cased transmission, with four closely spaced synchromesh gears, struggled in its place.

By 1982, AMC dropped the CJ's 304 V-8 option on 49-State (non-California) vehicles. (The V-8 ended years earlier in California models.) Fortunately, the 258 six, with its seven-main bearing design, survived both the EPA emission control standards and CAFE fuel economy requirements. As the sole carryover from quality '60s engine technology, the 258 would continue to serve Jeep trucks through 1990.

Pursuing fuel economy, Jeep introduced Warner's T-5 overdrive transmission in the early '80s CJ models. Although overdrive alleviated the need for ultra-tall axle gearing, Jeep continued using final drive ratios like 3.54:1 and 3.73:1. Both on- and off-pavement performance suffered. Worse yet, the light duty T-5's construction could not withstand the high torque loads and stresses of prolonged rock crawling or oversized tires. (See geartrain upgrades in later chapters.)

Downscaled powertrain components plagued all U.S. truck manufacturers in the early '80s. Jeep full-size J-trucks abandoned the rugged Spicer 20 gear driven transfer case units in favor of an all-new chain drive New Process 208 transfer case. Like other manufacturers, Jeep quickly discovered the NP208 weaknesses.

A failure-prone shift mechanism and other design flaws common to the NP208 transfer unit were unusual for New Process. Chrysler's New Process Gear Division had produced nearly two decades of extremely rugged geartrain components for four-wheel drive trucks. (The iron cased NP205 gear drive transfer case to this day boasts the best reputation of any light truck unit, and the durability of the NP435 four-speed truck transmission is legend.)

Although attempts to downsize and lighten major geartrain components ran counter to traditional American truck engineering, the trend proceeded. Jeep stamina and utility fell victim to an industry-wide switch to light-duty geartrain pieces.

Gone was the tough iron hardware that had characterized American 4x4 trucks for decades. Vehicle manufacturers adopted a new method, "torque rating," for assessing geartrain requirements. The marginal components selected were praised for their weight-saving advantages. Torque ratings became irrelevant as parts failed in service, and owners longed for the abandoned, earlier technology. 1980–86 was an awkward time for Jeep and all other U.S. truck manufacturers.

Time for the Compact XJ Cherokee: A Perfect Niche

The 1980s CJ-8/Scrambler, today popular and in demand, saw sales wane as consumers opted for 4x4 mini-trucks, compact pickups and the tighter access CJ-7 Jeep. The CJ-7 continued to prosper, especially after Toyota removed the 90" wheelbase FJ-40 Land Cruiser from the marketplace after 1983. International-Harvester's Scout II, the FJ-40 and Jeep's CJ-5 left the market in a span of four years! An epoch had passed.

AMC/Jeep Corporation abandoned the shorter wheelbase CJ-5 on the eve of the compact XJ Cherokee's introduction. Despite media rumblings and a rash of animosity toward the classic Jeep CJ-5, the 1984 XJ Cherokee 4x4 exceeded all sales and marketing expectations.

AMC/Jeep Corporation's decision to abandon the CJ-5 model proved wise. Further controversy would likely have detracted from the new XJ Cherokee. Instead, despite the impassioned pleas of hard-core back country four-wheelers who protested the CJ-5's passing, hordes of neophyte four-wheelers rushed to buy the new compact '84 Jeep Cherokee.

Abandoning the "driveable chassis" or ladder frame concept, AMC/Jeep developed a rugged unitized frame/body assembly for the compact Cherokee. In outward appearance, the styling of the new truck was bold and roguish, capitalizing on traditional full-size Wagoneer shapes and cues that were certain to create a truck image and readily foster brand identification. Interior appointments rivaled GM's new compact S-Blazer/Jimmy and Ford's Bronco II.

Consumers immediately liked the package, especially the option of four doors. American tastes and trends had changed dramatically, and practicality now held sway. Awkward rear seat entry had plagued two-door sport utility 4x4s for years. The Cherokee's four doors allowed easier interior access, and the new model could readily replace the traditional family station wagon. Buyers chose four-wheel drive for its added safety margin, protection under poor road conditions and comfortable transportation for winter recreation.

For the Cherokee's standard powerplant, the 2.5L/150 cubic inch AMC four-cylinder engine, which had first appeared in '83 Jeep CJs, was the logical choice. At a relatively light curb weight (less than 3000 pounds), the Cherokee could perform reasonably well with a four-cylinder engine.

Compact XJ Cherokee: America's First Unibody 4x4 Truck

AMC's successes with unibody autos provided the concept for the 1984 Jeep Cherokee. The first use of a unibody frame in a 4x4 domestic truck, the compact Cherokee offered a light curb weight, well suited to the standard 2.5L AMC four-cylinder engine. GM's 2.8L V-6 was optional, followed by the 1987 introduction of the AMC 4.0L fuel injected six.

The '84 Jeep Cherokee was a departure from all previous Jeep truck engineering. AMC, as an auto manufacturer, had practiced unibody construction for over three decades. While other manufacturers searched frantically for areas to reduce truck weight, AMC/Jeep had a ready solution.

Jeep/Eagle 4WD passenger cars had pioneered unibody four-wheel drive, although modest sales indicated that consumers clearly preferred 4x4 trucks to automobiles. (The demand for all-wheel drive cars was still years away.) 4WD Eagle experience gave AMC the much needed technology for building a 4x4 unibody truck.

Similar to the 232/258 sixes, the 2.5L four became the standard engine in CJs and the new '84 Cherokee. A pushrod overhead valve design, the 2.5L gained TBI in '86 Cherokees and served as the new '87 Wrangler's standard engine.

For broader market appeal, Jeep offered the GM 2.8L/173 cubic inch V-6 as an option. The compact Cherokee's automatic transmission, available on both four- and six-cylinder models, was a Chrysler 904 three-speed, coupled to a chain-drive, aluminum housed New Process transfer case.

Although modest horsepower satisfied many owners, the early 2.8L/173 V-6 had several drawbacks, including a marginal closed-loop carburetor system and a poor rear main seal design that led to chronic leaks. Worse yet, the main seal cure required engine removal and remachining of the rear block surface to accept an

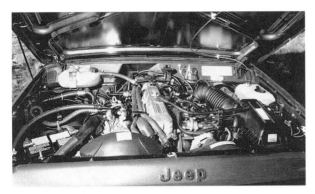

Fig. 1-29. *AMC's 1987 Cherokee 4.0L fuel injected engine proved extremely popular. Rated 177 horsepower, the healthy powerplant evolved from a twenty-two year legacy of Jeep success with seven-main bearing AMC in-line sixes.*

Fig. 1-30. *Compact XJ Cherokee proves its legitimacy in the off-pavement arena. Here, far from civilization and commuter chores, this '91 model doubles as an all-out recreational 4x4.*

upgrade seal. (This procedure was also common to early GM S-Blazer/Jimmy models equipped with the 2.8L V-6.)

Despite these setbacks, Jeep Cherokee sales reached unanticipated heights, outselling the competition and becoming AMC/Jeep's premier model. Recognizing the need for better performance, Jeep worked in-house toward a solution, and in 1987 introduced the 4.0L in-line six.

Building on a proven AMC design, Jeep changed the bore/stroke configuration of the 258 (4.2L) engine and added a bonus: multi-point electronic fuel injection. Delivering 177 horsepower, the new 4.0L in-line

six launched the Jeep XJ Cherokee ahead of all competition. Fuel economy improved dramatically, and the 4.0L engine easily met emission requirements.

The introduction of the 4.0L six became one of AMC/Jeep's most rewarding engineering and marketing decisions. Sales soared. The compact Cherokee and its counterpart XJ Wagoneer earned majority market share in the face of heavy competition from both GM and Ford. The all new 1987 Comanche pickup, built virtually on the same platform as the Cherokee, also received attention.

XJ Cherokee/Wagoneer to WJ Grand Cherokee/Grand Wagoneer

The compact XJ Cherokee immediately seized public interest, and, oddly, became an icon for the "Yuppie" generation of middle-class American society. America was ripe for a statement vehicle, one that helped define outdoor recreational interests, a youthful zeal for life and the North American spirit of adventure. Overlooked in the quest for image was the compact Cherokee/Wagoneer XJ's frequent ability to deliver 200,000 plus miles of service, even when driven regularly over the Alaska Highway.

As suburban and urban buyers flocked to Jeep showrooms and voted with their earned cash and good credit, the XJ grew more refined and added a roster of upscale features. By 1992, the demand for a more luxurious model with V-8 power spurred the introduction of the Grand Cherokee ZJ model and its counterpart, the mid-size ZJ Grand Wagoneer.

> NOTE —
> 1991 was the last year for the full-size Grand Wagoneer. The 1993 adaptation of the name "Grand Wagoneer" applies to a 'mid-size' model on the ZJ Grand Cherokee chassis. This unitized body vehicle is not the original ladder-framed, full-size Wagoneer/Grand Wagoneer.

Introduced as a 1993 model, the ZJ Grand Cherokee/Grand Wagoneer featured a 4.5" longer wheelbase than the 101.4" XJ Cherokee/Wagoneer, a slightly wider track width, nearly ten inches more overall length and nearly five-hundred pounds more curb weight in the 4.0L version. A 5.2L V-8 option quickly distinguished the ZJ Grand Cherokee/Grand Wagoneer from lighter Cherokee XJ models.

America's romance with the mid-size Grand Cherokee and compact Cherokee continues, and many owners have discovered the very real prospect of off-pavement access with these vehicles. Far roomier and better suited than the Wrangler for gobbling up commuting and highway miles, 4WD Jeep traction makes

Fig. 1-31. *The 1998 Cherokee XJ compact model carries forth an image and quality standard established by the late-1980s. A rugged geartrain, stout chassis, 4.0L six and 2.5L four have proven superior to all comers in this market. An XJ often delivers quality service well past 200,000 miles.*

Fig. 1-33. *1999 WJ Grand Cherokee offers bold, distinctive styling that reflects classic Jeep cues. Competing in a rapidly changing SUV market, the Grand Cherokee postures for success against stiff, World Class competition. Still a serious backcountry contender with wheel travel of 8.3 inches, axle clearance of 9.3 inches front, 8.3 inches rear, contemporary WJ Grand Cherokee will ford 19 inches of standing water.*

Fig. 1-32. *1993–98 ZJ Grand Cherokee captured the up-scale end of compact SUV market with terrific styling, Jeep 4WD tractability and the promise of fun with comfort. Last year for 5.2L and 5.9L EFI/MPI V-8 engines, this '98 model provided traditional American pushrod muscle and dependability from a rugged Chrysler LA powerplant. 5.9L V-8 rated 245 horsepower @4000 rpm and 345 lb-ft torque @3200 rpm.*

Fig. 1-34. *High tech 4.7L V-8 replaces traditional pushrod V-8s in new design 1999 WJ Grand Cherokee. 230 horsepower and 295 lb-ft of torque from a chain driven overhead camshaft design delivers top performance and fuel efficiency for the highly competitive and upscale SUV market. Along with maximum dependability, Jeep engineers achieved the goal of "most refined, quiet and best sounding Jeep engines" with the 4.7L V-8.*

an impression when those loose, steep or slippery grades arise.

The original ZJ Grand Cherokee enjoyed a half-dozen model years of refinement and definition. While the XJ Cherokee remained the quintessential Jeep "crossover" model between the Wrangler and more luxurious SUVs, the new Grand Cherokee 'WJ' model competes within the realm of upscale World Class SUV models. Despite dramatic shifts in styling, a Jeep 4x4 will always remain a Jeep, trusted and proven in a variety of terrain and challenges.

A WJ Grand Cherokee for the Next Millennium

In 1999, the Grand Cherokee reached new heights. While the popular 5.2L and 5.9L LA V-8s served many buyers needs in 1998, the '99 WJ Grand Cherokee in-

troduced a high technology overhead camshaft 4.7L V-8 gas engine. For non-U.S. markets a 3.1L five-cylinder turbo-diesel replaced the earlier 2.5L diesel. With further refinements, the 4.0L six continued as the standard WJ powerplant.

Distinguishing this milestone WJ were the five-speed automatic transmission and a Quadra-Drive four-wheel drive system. The Quadra-Trac II transfer case delivers power to Vari-Lok front and rear axles, each featuring speed-sensing torque transfer differentials. The torque and speed sensitive Quadra-Drive powertrain can provide traction under the most challenging conditions, including one-wheel only traction.

Vari-Lok challenges systems that rely upon electronic speed sensors and the brake system to stop a spinning wheel. With Vari-Lok, the differential readily transfers torque to the wheel with traction—without the hesitation and excessive wheel spin inherent to systems that use electronic sensors to measure wheel speed before applying the brakes.

Suspension improvements on the '99 WJ Grand Cherokee focus on bringing the roll center closer to

the center of gravity, thus reducing body roll and lean on corners. To accomplish this, Jeep engineers developed a three-link rear suspension that also lessens unsprung weight. Front suspension refinements complement the radically redesigned body of the newest Grand Cherokee.

In addressing the new WJ model, Tom Gale, Executive Vice President, Product Strategy, Design and General Manager/Jeep Operations noted, "We are well aware that in this extremely competitive segment, the battle for the best sport-utility vehicle is being fought on-road as well as off-road....We are not about to yield to anyone when it comes to delivering the best combination of capability and comfort. We plan to keep aggressively building on our strong history." Well said, Mr. Gale!

Fig. 1-1. *Progressive differential in '99–up WJ uses a gerotor type hydraulic pump and clutch pack for sending torque to fore and aft solid drive axles. Innovative, this torque sensitive transfer unit assures traction while minimizing wheelspin. 2.72:1 low range ratio and full lock-up of center differential in this mode mean traditional four-wheel drive use prevails.*

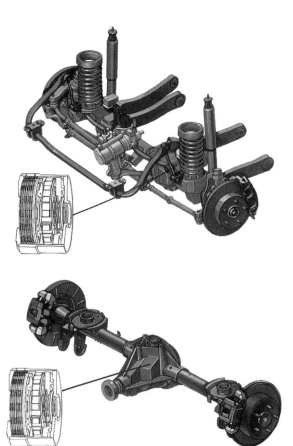

Fig. 1-3. *Progressive front (top) and rear (bottom) "Vari-Lok" axles feature a torque sensitive clutching mechanism within each differential that delivers torque to the wheel(s) with traction. WJ mechanical Quadra Trac II transfer case and torque sensitive axles require no driver input yet compete with other manufacturers' elaborate wheel-speed sensor and brake-application systems.*

Fig. 1-2. *In addition to Quadra-Drive system, the rear three-link suspension of '99–up WJ Grand Cherokee lowers body roll center and reduces unsprung weight. Improved cornering and reduced body lean have WJ handling at levels found only in World Class SUVs.*

Birth Of The Wrangler

As the trend toward multi-purpose 4x4s continued, AMC/Jeep recognized the need for a CJ-model facelift. For 1987, AMC introduced an all-new 93.4-inch wheelbase Jeep Wrangler YJ model. Replacing the eleven-year-old CJ-7, the Wrangler used nearly the same chassis layout, added distinctive front sheet metal changes and completely revamped the instrument panel and interior scheme.

The Jeep YJ/Wrangler appealed to an entirely new buyer. Relying on the image and off-pavement reputation of earlier Jeeps, the new Wrangler was as much a back country rover as a chic urban sportabout. One vehicle serving all transportation needs found an immediate following among active, youthful consumers.

There were limits, however. For reducing liability, AMC/Jeep had prioritized safety in the design of the Wrangler's wheelbase, track width, center-of-gravity and roll center. The CJ-5 controversy likely inspired the Wrangler's low-slung chassis design and relatively long wheelbase. Poor ground clearance resulted, inhibiting hard-core trail use.

As a consequence, the YJ Wrangler's sales appeal rested between the reputation of earlier, off-pavement oriented Jeep models and the multipurpose demands of contemporary buyers. Like the compact Cherokee, the YJ Wrangler's list of options offered far more than the austerity and stark styling found in earlier Jeep CJs. The new Wrangler's upscale interior, solid lower door sections, full instrumentation and a range of power options reflected the tastes of contemporary Jeep buyers.

Fig. 1-38. *1987 YJ Wrangler replaced the eleven-year-old CJ-7. Consumer demands for styling, luxury options and a more comfortable multipurpose vehicle encouraged the sportier Jeep YJ. Four-wheel drive and a two-speed transfer case provide off-road capability for the 93.4" wheelbase truck.*

The original '87 YJ Wrangler served well as a daily driver or off-pavement recreational vehicle and featured more comfort, security and style than earlier CJ models. In original form, the Wrangler YJ offered the indestructible 2.5L AMC four and 4.2L/258 in-line six engines. The four featured throttle body EFI, while the six continued use of a Carter BBD carburetor. A light duty import five-speed alloy cased manual transmission with overdrive came standard. Optional was a durable Chrysler three-speed automatic.

By 1991, the obsolescence of carburetion and need for improved fuel efficiency with cleaner tailpipe emissions encouraged use of the 4.0L EFI (multi-point fuel injected) Jeep XJ Cherokee engine in the Wrangler. Surely the longer-stroke, high torque 4.2L/258, revered by Jeep owners for two decades, had a die-hard following, but the newer 4.0L EFI engine promised better fuel efficiency, lower pollution levels, far more horsepower, trouble-free operation and instant adjustability to altitude changes.

The 1987–96 YJ Wrangler chassis remained a traditional Jeep ladder frame with a leaf spring at each wheel and hypoid (solid) driving axles. Refinements in spring rates, a semi-floating front hub arrangement, stabilizer bars and a Dana 35 rear axle stand out as significant differences between the YJ and last CJ models. The YJ chassis and geartrain lend themselves to the kinds of upgrades and off-pavement use so popular with the earlier CJ models. (See geartrain and chassis modification sections in later chapters.)

Wrangler TJ Advancements

1997 and the TJ model stand out as the largest singular chassis change in Jeep light utility truck history. The new Wrangler TJ preserved a time-honored ladder frame design, stouter than any earlier chassis, and introduced the first use of coil and link arm suspension. Similar to the proven late model Cherokee suspension, the new setup, in stock form, afforded *seven inches more wheel travel* than previous YJ and CJ models.

The TJ Wrangler immediately proved its worthiness and exceptional off-pavement suitability. Like all previous Jeep light utility trucks, the TJ features solid hypoid driving axles and a two-speed transfer case. By employing a stronger, more rigid boxed steel frame, the newest Wrangler has stamina that rivals any Jeep model built, readily serving on- and off-pavement chores. Refined, better handling and well matched for a wide variety of contemporary buyer needs, the TJ Wrangler platform postures Jeep light utility trucks for success well into the new millennium.

Wrangler: Carrying Forth a Tradition

The affordable ($8995) '89 Wrangler "S" entry-level truck provided a spirited 2.5L fuel injected engine with a five-speed overdrive transmission, plus all the 4WD features found on other Wrangler models. An affordable 4x4, the Wrangler S offered better handling and comfort than earlier CJ models.

Improvements in powertrain design and durability, plus attention to better suspension and handling, characterize Wrangler engineering. Despite significant advances in electronic fuel injection technology, 4.2L (258 cubic inch) Wrangler engines maintain carburetion through 1990, the last year of 258/4.2L engine production. The standard YJ and TJ Wrangler 2.5L four benefits from electronic fuel injection, and 1991 and newer Wranglers offer the Cherokee's fuel injected 4.0L in-line six as an option.

Several Wrangler theme models have appeared over the years. Mechanically identical, these trim and appearance packages satisfy various tastes. Imaginative visual effects are evident on '89 Sahara Edition (above), which featured a khaki cloth top and appealing canvas upholstery. 4.2L in-line six-cylinder engine was optional through 1990.

Wrangler Sahara Edition (top right) displays factory auxiliary lighting, tow hook and distinctive Jeep utility truck styling, although PTO-driven post-hole diggers and a three-harrow disc option were obviously missing from these late-'80s Wrangler themes!

Interior of Wrangler denotes convenience, comfort, quietude, performance and luxury. Power steering, an overdrive 5-speed transmission, carpeting, metal half-doors and fitted bucket seats offer dramatic contrast to the

original Jeep MB and CJ-2A. Ease of operation and improved ride quality make the YJ Wrangler and newer TJ very popular with first-time four-wheel drive buyers.

Above: Wrangler has all the spirit of earlier CJs. At a Pacific Northwest Jeep Jamboree, this Wrangler mixes it up with the CJs. Jeep 4x4 popularity and fun continue.

Jeep Joins the Big Three

Jeep truck products became the real success story of American Motors Corporation. Despite awkward mergers and foreign partnerships in the passenger car realm, AMC profited greatly from Jeep Corporation. Well accepted by American buyers and filling concise market niches, Jeep models brought AMC worldwide recognition.

The AMC/Jeep success owed much to Willys-Overland and Kaiser Jeep Corporation. The CJ's image, still visible in today's Wrangler, began with Willys' postwar civilian trucks. The full-size AMC/Jeep Wagoneer and J-trucks carried forth the foresight and innovative advances of Kaiser's Jeep Corporation.

Jeep products have always attracted success. Despite the decline of Willys automobile sales, Jeep provided Willys-Overland with a marketable business enterprise. Kaiser Corporation's effort to market Kaiser-Frazer, Willys and Henry J automobiles faltered, yet the Jeep truck line became Kaiser's long overdue success. When AMC/Jeep/Eagle went to the bargaining table with Chrysler Corporation in 1987, the popularity of Jeep trucks, and the very trademark, "Jeep," provided another substantial and marketable package. The compact XJ Cherokee's wide public acceptance, plus the obvious popularity of the new Wrangler YJ models, proved once more that Jeep was a valued product.

Chrysler Corporation gained much from the Jeep Corporation acquisition. Buyers worldwide liked the compact Jeep XJ Cherokee and Wrangler models. The full-size Grand Wagoneer provided Chrysler with a smaller volume, stable niche product, noted for its satisfied repeat owners dating to the 1960s. Jeep's new Comanche pickup showed promise, and Jeep had a well established reputation at highly visible off-road and SCCA compact truck racing.

American Motors Corporation sold all Jeep/Eagle interests to Chrysler Corporation on August 5, 1987. Following the transaction, Jeep Corporation joined Chrysler as a wholly new division.

Chrysler's commitment has secured the future of Jeep products. Jeep Corporation now has the support of a worldwide dealer network plus Mopar's highly advanced, computerized parts distribution system. In addition to parts stocks at Jeep outlets, Jeep owners can buy parts through other Chrysler, Dodge, and Plymouth dealerships.

Chrysler's Jeep Corporation also provides a vast service network. For four-wheel drive owners, availability of service is a major concern. Chrysler's huge service and parts network easily meets the needs of Jeep owners.

Jeep product engineering continually focuses upon transmission and transfer case durability. New Process Gear Division and New Venture now have direct access to Jeep geartrain development. AMC/Jeep's proven 4.0L in-line six and 2.5L four, plus several Chrysler-design engines including the LA 5.2L/5.9L V-8s and the high-tech 4.7L OHC V-8, provide ideal matchups for Jeep powertrains.

Since 1941, Jeep trucks have set the standard for four-wheel drive utility and off-road travel. Built for treacherous roads, remote work projects, extremes of

Fig. 1-39. *In late 1987, Chrysler assumed production of the full-size Jeep Grand Wagoneer, becoming the third manufacturer to build these stately trucks. Kaiser/Jeep Corporation introduced the original Wagoneer in 1962. AMC/Jeep continued to market these luxurious, upscale models until the Chrysler acquisition. Chrysler continued production of the full-size Grand Wagoneer through 1991.*

Fig. 1-40. *'88 Jeep Cherokee Limited displays the four-wheel drive emphasis of the late 1980s. Upscale buyers found the four-door XJ Cherokee ideal for urban commuting, vacation travel and young family needs. The phenomenal popularity of these trucks exceeded all market projections.*

weather, emergency service and adventuresome recreation, Jeep 4x4 products provide the prototype for all other multipurpose utility vehicles.

Worldwide, people recognize the trademark. Where work and play demand four-wheel traction, Jeep is there. A symbol of freedom, mobility and progress, Jeep remains the indomitable four-wheel drive marque.

Fig. 1-42. *1988 4WD Jeep Comanche Chief displays classic Jeep truck body lines. Preserving the rugged J-truck image provided the XJ-based Jeep Comanche with reasonable success. The Commanche stylizes the angles, shapes and four decade heritage of Jeep pickup trucks. Chrysler opted, however, to promote Dodge's Dakota pickup in lieu of the Comanche.*

Fig. 1-41. *The compact 1989 XJ-based Wagoneer Limited challenged the waning full-size Grand Wagoneer and offered luxury and power options that rivaled all competitors. Four-wheel anti-lock brakes, a 177-horsepower 4.0L EFI six-cylinder engine, Chrysler's durable automatic transmission, and Selec-Trac full-time four-wheel drive made an alluring package.*

Fig. 1-43. *Jeep's competitive spirit is legend. Amateur and professional racers benefit from the popularity, stamina, engineering and rugged image of Jeep trucks. In SCORE/HDRA racing, Walker Evans Racing and Jeep earned wide respect.*

Chapter 2

Buying a Jeep

Once upon a time, there was only one off-pavement civilian 4x4—the Jeep. Following the Second World War, the MB models shipped home to work and play. Battle scarred and tested, the GI Jeep gained a civilian counterpart in the 1946 CJ-2A 4x4, and the world of off-pavement travel has never been the same since!

Four-wheel drive light truck and utility vehicle sales have grown steadily. During the 1980s, four-wheel drive truck sales gained a large share of the light truck market, and today 4x4s are a common sight in all segments of American life. Jeep has played a substantial role in this trend, attracting loyal repeat buyers.

The brisk boost in sales in the late 1950s and early '60s of the CJ-5 Jeep, 4WD Pickups and Jeep 4WD Wagons, plus the introduction of the Wagoneer and J-truck lines, in 1962 and '63 respectively, increased the number of Jeep trucks available in the marketplace. Since the mid-'60s, sales of 4x4 trucks have proliferated, and if you cannot see your way to buying a new Jeep truck, a broad selection of used models can meet a wide range of needs.

Today, most Jeep owners see their 4x4 truck as multi-purpose transportation. Later AMC/Jeep CJs, the Jeep Wrangler, the compact XJ and ZJ/WJ Grand Cherokee, J-trucks and full-size Grand Wagoneer have

Fig. 2-1. *The boom in 4x4 sales of the last three decades has created a variety of quality used Jeep models. The roguish J-trucks evolved into highly attractive packages like this AMC/Jeep Laredo pickup.*

Fig. 2-2. *Parts are readily available for the Jeep L-134 four, also geartrain and chassis pieces back to 1941. Need a replacement Model 18 transfer case for a 1941–71 Jeep truck? No problem!*

Fig. 2-3. *Rumors circulated for years about huge stores of surplus Jeep trucks selling for $50 apiece! Many consumers dreamed of buying a military MB, M38 or M38A1 model Jeep in perfect condition.*

power and convenience options that rival many luxury automobiles. Even if you're on a tight budget, a higher mileage used Jeep 4x4 may have wear but still be restorable. Parts availability remains an attractive feature with all Jeep products, and you will readily find parts, even for a model MB surplus Jeep.

Buying A "Trail Wise" Four-Wheel Drive

As late as 1965, the main outlets for used four-wheel drive trucks were rural farms and ranches, oil companies, heavy construction and public utility companies and government agencies. Some Jeep vehicles also found homes with committed outdoorsmen, hunters and amateur geologists ("rockhounds") who steered their recreational 4x4s through remote deserts, dense forests and trails above timberline.

Restoring most of those used Jeep trucks required a confident mechanic and a lot of spare time. Sensible buyers stayed away from exasperated iron and dreamed of finding the mythical $50 military surplus Jeep that rested beneath a heavy coat of cosmoline, new and still in a shipping crate, at some U.S. Government G.S.A. sale.

Like a leather flier's jacket, the P-51 Mustang and other memorabilia, the MB Jeep will forever hold a place in America's history and national pride. Yet the original Jeep was anything but high technology. Designed with just enough power, largely through gearing, to carry a few fellows and a light trailer over some lousy roads, the WWII Model MB Jeep 4x4 has few components in common with the '87–up YJ Wrangler or newer TJ.

Because of model changes and improvements, your best bet when buying a used Jeep is plenty of facts

Fig. 2-4. *The WWII Model MB's GPW/T-84 transmission has several weaknesses, including the use of failure prone countergear bushings. Postwar and newer T-90 transmissions have needle countergear bearings, improved gears and synchronizer stamina plus a much stronger shifter mechanism.*

and lots of patience. Unless you want a prideful parade vehicle or enjoy nostalgia, there are better built Jeep models than the MB.

Willys-Overland eliminated some of the MB's shortcomings with the introduction of civilian CJ-2A models in 1946. The light-duty Spicer 23-2 rear axle soon gave way to a heftier Spicer 41-2 version. A T-90 Borg Warner three-speed transmission replaced the weaker GPW/T-84 unit. Even the L-head 134 four-cylinder engine saw refinements, in particular the solution to a valve timing chain and sprocket problem. 1946 and newer L-134 engines feature an improved timing gear set.

Other Jeep models also have strengths and weaknesses. Review the range of Jeep models, and decide which used Jeep is right for your needs.

1. The CJ Models

Jeep CJ-2As built after Serial #13453 have Spicer's Model 41-2 rear axle, similar to the highly regarded Spicer 44 design. The first Jeep with a one-piece windshield and the Spicer 44 rear axle was the CJ-3A, phased into the Jeep line as a 1949 model. Dealer-installed heaters became an option during this period, although any early CJ owner will testify that a dying campfire yields more BTUs than one of these heaters!

Be aware that early Jeep model changes lingered until parts depleted, so identifying a vintage vehicle often requires a look at the I.D. plate and serial number. Also, many models stayed in storage prior to sale, and it is not uncommon for a "1946–48" CJ-2A to have a "1949" or even "1950" official registration.

The CJ-3B sold from 1953–64, even though the CJ-5 came on line in 1955. Due to this kind of overlap, when buying a vintage Jeep or parts, you must accurately identify the chassis/serial number, engine, ignition distributor, axle housing(s), transfer case and transmission. Sleuthing the serial and parts identification numbers can help determine a Jeep's age and sequence in production.

CJ Engines

The most significant change for early four-cylinder CJ Jeeps is the introduction of the F-head 134 engine in 1953. This engine terminated the CJ-3A body style and summoned the flat-fendered, high hood CJ-3B.

Fig. 2-5. *Identification numbers play an important role with Jeep trucks. The serial number tells the build date for the truck and which design changes are effective. When restoring a Jeep, you will need the identification numbers from the ignition, axles, transfer case, engine block and electrical components.*

Fig. 2-6. *The Buick 225 V-6, found in 1966–71 CJs and 1967–71 Jeepsters, is an impressive engine. 160 horsepower is more than double the F-134's 75 horsepower rating. If you're after spunk, look here.*

CJ-3B, CJ-5 and CJ-6 models through 1971 use the F-134 engine as the standard powerplant. (Although the F-134 shows up in parts listings as late as 1973, AMC was simply using up remaining engines during the phaseout of Kaiser/Jeep Corporation parts.) The F-134 is a durable, fundamental engine, easy to work on and reasonably fuel efficient.

Jeep CJs adopted the Buick 225 V-6 in late 1965, and many V-6 models still exist from the 1966–71 model era. This is a tough, high torque engine, putting out a substantial 160 horsepower. The power-to-weight ratio of a V-6 powered CJ-5 is impressive. These trucks remain popular today and fetch a good price. When Kaiser sold to AMC, the Buick engine gave way to the AMC 232/258 in-line six and a 304 V-8.

Although most '40s and '50s CJs have 6-volt electrical systems, conversion to 12 volts is both simple and practical. The original 6-volt starter motor and wiring (if intact) can survive the changeover, and 12-volt bulbs will fit the 6-volt bulb sockets. When considering a Jeep CJ with a 6-volt electrical system, plan a 12-volt generator or alternator conversion as one of your first projects.

CJ Chassis and Handling

If you're looking for a Jeep with more stable handling characteristics, seek a longer wheelbase. The CJ-2A, CJ-3A, CJ-3B and CJ-5 Jeeps work exceptionally well on tight, twisty and rock strewn off-pavement turf, but a high center of gravity and roll center make these models more difficult to keep upright and on all four wheels.

The MB, CJ-2A, CJ-3A, M38 and CJ-3B stand on an 80" wheelbase. The CJ-5 and M38A1 are 81" until the AMC CJ-5 stretch to 84" in 1972. The CJ-6 began at 101" wheelbase and stretches to 104" in 1972. CJ-7 models boast a 94" wheelbase, while the CJ-8/Scrambler sets at 104".

> NOTE——
> Following the common industry practice, I've rounded wheelbase figures to the nearest inch. For example, the 104" wheelbase described may actually be 103.5". In building a Jeep chassis from scratch, consult your factory service guidebook for exact chassis measurements.

CJ Brakes and Axles

Jeep CJs have four-wheel drum brakes until late 1977. (All 1978–up models have disc front brakes.) An open-knuckle Dana 30 front axle appears on most AMC CJ models in 1972. Axles on full-size J-trucks and Wagoneers remain closed-knuckle Spicer 27, 30 (1972–73) or 44 types until the 1974 switch to the Dana 44 open-knuckle design.

Spicer/Dana axles have casting identifications, and a gear ratio tag attaches to the differential cover bolts. Axle gearing impacts your truck's uses, such as towing, back country travel and economy. Lower gearing (higher numerical ratios) are desirable for oversize tires, rock crawling or lugging heavy loads.

The earliest civilian CJ, M38 or M38A1 Jeep came with 5.38:1 axle gearing. With these axle gears, the L-134 engine whines to a feverish pitch at 50 mph. Beginning with CJ-3B models, horsepower increases

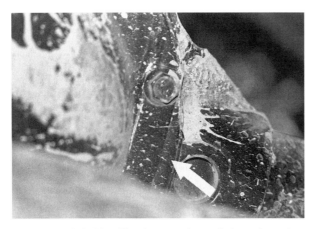

Fig. 2-7. *Axle identification tags (arrow) show the ratio for the differential. Lower gearing (higher numerically) means better pulling power and rock crawling ability. On a CJ, lower gearing is a 4.10, 4.27, 4.56, 4.88, 5.13 or 5.38:1 ratio. Tall gearing, for economy and primarily highway cruising, is a matched set of 3.07, 3.31, 3.54 or 3.73 ring and pinion gears.*

CJ Buyer's Guide

Among Jeep enthusiasts, I've seen more heated arguments around "the best year and model CJ" than any other topic. It's like discussing which breed of dog hunts best, whether fly fishing outshines ultra-light spin casting, or if Bushmills' Black Bush outclasses Jack Daniels.

The CJs span forty-one model years (1946–86). Pressed to rank bone stock CJs, my top choice overall is a 1978 or 1979 CJ-5 or CJ-7 with the T-18 four-speed option, 258 in-line six and power steering. (Wheelbase choice depends on your uses for the truck.) These models feature a stoutly boxed frame, Saginaw steering, an AMC seven-main bearing engine, and the open-knuckle Dana 30 front axle with disc brakes. One potential weakness in the truck is the Model 20 rear axle's hub design. (Aftermarket one-piece axle shafts are available to remedy this problem.)

My next choice is the 1976–early '77 CJ, again with the AMC 232/258 six and a T-18 four speed. Four-wheel drum brakes and the Model 20 rear axle are the only poor marks, although maintained properly, the large 11" drum brakes on these models serve fine.

While the 1966–71 Buick V-6 CJs are a classic marque, I like their performance but find the three-speed transmission and weaker steering system falls short. Of these CJ V-6 models, the best would be the rarer '70 and '71 Renegade models with boxed frames and full instrumentation.

Among the early L-head and F-134 powered CJs, I will always be partial to the T-98A four-speed truck transmission equipped models. Some later CJ-3B models have this transmission, but most show up in '60s CJ-5s and CJ-6s. From a safety standpoint, the '67–up dual braking system is a bonus, and this consideration applies to all Jeep models.

The CJ-2A and CJ-3A make fine off-pavement machinery, and the CJ-3B remains my favorite body style of all the Jeep CJs. If you plan to modify your Jeep truck's chassis or powertrain, the earlier models are popular. Avoid the use of an ultra high horsepower engine in any pre-'76 CJ with an unboxed frame. 1972–75 AMC/Jeep CJ models have a poor frame for hard off-pavement environments or the stresses of a high torque V-8. (See section on inspecting a Jeep truck.)

from 60 to 72, and the axle ratios become less drastic. 4.88:1, 4.56 and even 4.27 gearsets work well with the F-134. Kaiser/Buick V-6 powered CJs, unless sold with Warn overdrive, have 3.73 axle ratios, often too high geared (numerically low) for running oversize tires.

Emission control and fuel economy demands impact Jeep gearing from the mid-'70s until the present, and it's not uncommon for a truck to have gearing that is entirely too "tall" (high gearing, numerically low). Ratios of 3.07, 3.31 and 3.54:1 decrease performance but can improve gas mileage.

Also found near the differential housing is the tag for a Power-Lok or Trac-Lok limited slip differential. If maximum traction is your goal, consider this feature. Jeep trucks first offered optional limited slip differentials in the late 1950s. AMC/Jeep Model 20 rear axles, introduced in 1976 CJs, also offer a posi-traction/limited slip option.

CJ Steering Gears

A significant improvement with the AMC CJ Jeep was the Saginaw manual or power steering gear. Steering linkage changes eliminate the bellcrank and other obsolete features that plagued earlier Jeep models. (If you buy a pre-'72 CJ, an aftermarket kit is available to convert from Ross cam-and-lever steering to the Saginaw design. See the performance chapters.)

If you're interested in an early Jeep truck and it has a tow bar on the front, be wary of the condition of the steering gearbox. The already weak cam-and-lever gears wear prematurely when the Jeep is "flat towed."

Heavy Duty CJ Transmissions

If a pre-'72 CJ-5 or CJ-6 appeals to your tastes or pocketbook, a wise buy is the F-134 with a T-98A four speed truck transmission. On 1972–79 CJs, seek a T-18 four-speed truck box with the AMC 232 or 258 in-line six.

Nearly all Kaiser V-6 powered CJs and AMC/CJ 304 V-8 models use three-speed transmissions (unless you or a previous owner convert to a truck four speed). While these engines are fine, the three-speed transmission inhibits off-pavement crawling. As for transfer cases, the Spicer 20 through-drive unit found in 1972–79 CJs is a major design improvement over the earlier Model 18 side drive type.

CJ Engines for the Modern Era

Beginning with early 1970s Jeep models, economy and low tailpipe emissions are dominant themes. By 1980, the 151 Pontiac four makes the option list. Users find this engine spunky enough, but the transmission is a light-duty four-speed. These CJs have limited performance, offset somewhat by the newer Dana 300 trans-

Fig. 2-8. *A truck type T-18 four-speed transmission was an AMC/Jeep option in 1972–79 CJ six-cylinder models. Here, a cast iron cased NP435 truck transmission (top) replaces the original light duty aluminum housed four-speed in an '81 CJ-5.*

fer case with a greater reduction ratio in low range. AMC also added its own four to the option list in 1983, a 2.5L (150 cubic inch) engine.

Pontiac's Iron Duke 151 and AMC's 2.5L four, the 232 and 258 AMC sixes and the AMC 304 V-8 engines each have their place. Fours work fine for basic, economical transportation, sixes and V-8s add the prospect of pulling a lighter trailer. Off-pavement, due to low range gearing, any of these engines is usually adequate.

Don't assume that a V-8 can keep your Jeep from getting stuck. Driving technique and horsepower are separate issues. (See the chapter on operating your Jeep truck.) Determine your overall performance needs, then seek the right powertrain combination. Gearing can make a difference.

2. 4WD Pickups, Station Wagons, J-Trucks and Wagoneers

If performance is no concern, the earliest Jeep Station Wagon or 4WD Pickup model might suffice. The breakthrough year for station wagons and pickups is 1954. (Kaiser, upon buying Willys, introduced its re-

Fig. 2-9. *Oregon-based 1948 Jeep 4WD Pickup reflects the roguish appeal that Willys created with these trucks. A loyal following find the early trucks suited to a variety of uses. These models are strong candidates for a smaller V-8 conversion.*

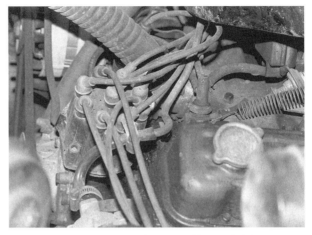

Fig. 2-10. *The Buick 350 Vigilante V-8 models have a special GM THM400 automatic or heavy duty truck four-speed option. 1970–71 Jeep Wagoneers and J-trucks represent the zenith for this Kaiser era marque.*

spected 226 L-head six.) Jeep trucks with the Hurricane 226 engine, built from 1954–63, have a good deal to offer. Some late 1962 and 1963 Utility Wagons have the 230 Tornado six. Most buyers of these vintage trucks have a strong appreciation for the body profile. Square, roguish and very solid, many Station Wagon and 4WD Pickup models are still on the road—and trail. Large numbers have V-8 conversions.

Kaiser's major renovation of the Jeep truck line came in 1962 and '63, with the introduction of the Wagoneer and J-trucks. Most J-trucks and Wagoneers are worthwhile buys at the right price, however, you should avoid some models. Pass on early Wagoneers with the optional 4WD independent front suspension, as these trucks have failure prone front suspension components and chronic troubles with front wheel alignment. Also have second thoughts about the innovative 230 cubic inch Tornado OHC Six. The design has caused a good deal of grief for mechanics and owners, despite the advanced technology.

For a stock Kaiser era Wagoneer or J-truck, my first choice is the refined '70 or '71 Buick 350 equipped 4x4 with either the THM400 automatic or a truck four-speed. These trucks offer top technology: Saginaw power steering, a dual braking system, a huge list of factory power options and quality axles. (Dana 44 front axle replaces the lighter Spicer 27 found on earlier J-series trucks.) By 1970, the Wagoneer led the industry in advancements and luxury options.

1972–79 AMC 360 and 401 V-8 powered trucks, including the rugged full-size Cherokee version of the Wagoneer, have tremendous value and appeal, with the Spicer 20 gear drive transfer case (part-time 4x4) usually having better stamina than trucks equipped

with Quadratrac (full-time 4x4). The late '70s full-size Cherokees with either the AMC V-8 or in-line 258 six make a tough package. These trucks have a strong chassis, better trailer pulling ability and plenty of power options.

> NOTE —
> Some owners convert Warner Quadratrac systems to part-time 4WD with an aftermarket kit. An added bonus with the Quadratrac conversion is overdrive.

By the 1980s, J-truck, full-size Cherokee and full-size Wagoneer sales declined. Powertrains are adequate, despite the use of an aluminum chain-drive transfer case. These trucks depreciate substantially, which often makes them exceptionally good used buys. You can get a lot of 4x4 truck for a modest sum! Aside from the marginal transfer cases, which also plague other 4x4 manufacturers' trucks of this era, there's every reason to consider such a Jeep.

3. The Jeepsters and Commandos

101" and 104" wheelbase layouts have shown up several times in Jeep 4WD models. Very early Station Wagons, 4WD Pickups and the Willys VJ Jeepster share the 104" wheelbase, while the 101" configuration first appears with the 1956 CJ-6. This chassis later encouraged production of the '67 Jeepster. These Jeepsters, with a Buick 225 V-6 option and an available GM Turbo-Hydramatic automatic, strike a great compromise between the CJ and full-size Wagoneer.

Fig. 2-11. *The vintage Willys 2WD VJ Jeepster inspired Kaiser's reintroduction of the Jeepster/Commando model in 1967 as a 4WD truck. AMC continued these popular models for a few years as the Jeep Commando. This original '49 VJ is today considered a collectible vehicle.*

Fig. 2-12. *The compact XJ Cherokee/Wagoneer was AMC/Jeep's marketing triumph. The truck's wide acceptance exceeded all industry predictions, boosting Jeep sales dramatically from 1984 onward.*

Fig. 2-13. *The Comanche is a stablemate of the compact XJ Cherokee, sharing many parts and features. Heavy competition in the compact truck market segment inhibited the Comanche's success. These trucks now attract the cost conscious used truck buyer.*

The Kaiser Jeepsters (C-101) have subtle improvements over the standard CJ, including the Spicer 27 front axle (which is also available on V-6 CJ models) and the Spicer 20 through-drive transfer case. Steering linkage is poor on early Jeepsters, as is the steering gear. The last few years of Kaiser production, improved Saginaw steering gears showed up on some Jeepsters, with power assist as an option.

AMC carried the Jeepster/Commando theme for a couple of years with the C-104, a slightly longer wheelbase to handle the 232/258 in-line six. Also available in 304 V-8 trim, with an optional T-18 four-speed truck gearbox and the Dana 30 front axle, these trucks are very rugged and versatile. The T-18 is a major gain over Kaiser's Jeepster with its three-speed manual transmission. (Tough automatic transmissions were options in both the Kaiser and AMC Jeepsters.)

If the AMC/Jeep Commando has any failing, it's in the looks department. The styling departs from Kaiser's image of the early VJ series, and the result is a bulkier, more awkward appearance. If you're looking for quality Jeep iron, however, this truck can be a good buy. Inspect the frame for cracks behind the front spring anchor ends, especially if the Commando has a V-8 or shows a history of hard-core rock crawling.

4. The Compact XJ Cherokee/ Wagoneer and Comanche Trucks

AMC/Jeep took a bold initiative at the mid-eighties. Aware of the demand for fuel efficient utility vehicles, Jeep designed a down-sized compact sport/utility model and a mid-size 4x4 pickup line. Sticking to basics, the XJ Cherokee/Wagoneer has generated a strong market following and attracts buyers with broad interests.

Be aware that the compact XJ Cherokee/Wagoneer or Comanche pickup has a unibody chassis rather than a ladder frame like a CJ, Wrangler or the traditional full-size Wagoneer/Grand Wagoneer, full-size Cherokee or J-truck. Care must be taken, including special undercarriage protection, if your plans include rough off-pavement use of the truck. As an all-season grocery grabber, family wagon and access to skiing, hunting or fishing, a compact XJ Cherokee/Wagoneer could prove a happy addition to your household.

While many tales exist of good service from 1984–86 compact Cherokees and the first Comanches, the 2.8L V-6 or carbureted AMC 2.5L four offers poorer performance than '87–up four and in-line six-cylinder models. Many Jeep owners actually prefer the four to a stock GM 173 V-6, although the carbureted 2.5L four-cylinder engine in an early XJ model or Co-

A Close Look at the XJ Cherokee Sport

In 1988, Chrysler's Jeep Corporation made an unusual move. While the four-door Cherokee models ran circles around the two-door competition, Jeep introduced its own two-door model. The Sport Cherokee 4WD captured the immediate attention of Chrysler's target: the "youthful market." Intended for "those in their early 30s, single or just married," this model gained quick success. Priced below the two-door Cherokee Limited and Laredo packages, sans the frills and built-in options, the Sport Cherokee is, simply, fun.

Bright color schemes, exterior graphics, and optional ten-hole OE aluminum wheels make the Cherokee Sport stand out. EFI on both the four- or six-cylinder engines, a five-speed transmission, power steering and floor carpeting enhance the Cherokee Sport package. Electronic fuel injection helps the engine start with ease, and altitude presents no problem.

Used Jeep buyers will rarely find the 2.5L four, although it's listed as standard equipment. Most XJ Cherokee owners drive the interstates, and the curb weight of the XJ Cherokee is near 3000 pounds. The 4.0L six (above) is more popular, with an impressive 177 horsepower @ 4500 rpm and whopping 224 ft-lbs torque @ 2500 rpm. This engine cruises well up on the torque curve in fifth gear overdrive, and throttle response is excellent. Performance is great from 2200 rpm upward. In 1991, Cherokee HO 4.0L horsepower jumps to 190. A 180-horsepower version of this engine replaced the traditional 4.2L six in the Wranglers.

You'll forego some of the power options with a Cherokee Sport. (A similar and even more austere version is popular with government agencies, including the U.S. Forest Service.) Manual window lifts and door locks suffice, giving the used truck buyer one less repair concern. If you find a Cherokee Sport with optional air conditioning, that package includes a valuable 100-amp alternator.

The Cherokee Sport has the same ergonomics as other XJ Cherokee models. Evident is the exceptional driving ease and handling—especially in tight access areas where a turning radius of 35.7 feet is useful. The truck rests on a firm 101.4" wheelbase.

An XJ Cherokee Sport's five-speed manual transmission alternates between the Peugeot and Aisin-Seiki designs. Either behaves far better than earlier Borg-Warner T-5 units. Shifts are strong, with a beefy synchronizer feel and positive gear engagement. Rpm drop under steady pulling is minimal, indicating well calculated gear ratios. The clutch is user friendly, just like the rest of the truck.

Leading link, coil spring front suspension and leaf rear springs have additional help from stabilizers and track bars. The truck handles well, steering stably on the highway, a place where most compact Cherokee trucks spend the bulk of their lives. A 3.5 turn Saginaw variable ratio power steering unit provides a 14.1:1 ratio (overall 15.2:1 when factoring the variable ratio)—quick enough by any standards.

With or without Bendix ABS braking, stopping a late '80s XJ Cherokee Sport under modest loads is usually no problem. Straight, predictable braking results from 10.98" diameter rotors in the front and 10"x1.75" rear shoe brakes.

As a hard-core off-pavement rock crawler, the bone-stock Cherokee Sport is out of its league. 15" OE rims and standard tires provide a minimum running clearance of approximately 9". Front view of '88 Sport Cherokee and Ty Tipton's '78 Jeep CJ-7 (right) shows the difference. XJ's rear axle to ground clearance is in the skimpy 7-1/2" range. Striving for safe handling on highway, however, the Cherokee Sport's roll center height is 14.17" front and 18.86" rear.

Despite widely publicized claims of "Rubicon Trail" off-pavement capability, the stock trim XJ Cherokee or a ZJ/WJ Grand Cherokee with similar unibody construction will not weather such a thrashing without at least some costly sheet metal damage. I would emphasize the difference between "surviving" or "making it" over the Rubicon versus being "well suited" for that trail, a wholly legitimate claim for the Jeep CJ, YJ or TJ Wrangler models.

For running over icy and snowy mountain passes en route to your favorite ski area, reaching the trailhead of a hiking path or towing a lightweight tent trailer over graded roads, an XJ Cherokee Sport will do admirably. These are the truck's best roles, and the very low 2.71:1 gearing of the transfer case means that the compact Cherokee has genuine Jeep climbing ability.

Adequate traction would take this vehicle to the top of any long, gravel driveway or over a roughly graded dirt road—with care, maybe even into some serious back country. Just respect the heavy gauge sheet metal of the unibody undercarriage. Take a good look at the "frame," such as it is, before flirting with rockpiles.

The XJ Cherokee's heating and air conditioning work wonderfully. Cherokee acoustics are superior to any of the lighter Jeep models. With the 4.0L six, power barely suffers when the air conditioning is on.

Rear seating is ample, but two-door models present a typical dilemma. Like other two-door SUVs, the gymnastics of tilting the front seats forward to admit rear passengers becomes old in a hurry. If you want to operate a livery service or ferry the Little League Team, get the four-door XJ Cherokee/Wagoneer model.

Overall, the Jeep XJ Cherokee is a great vehicle. Used for its intended purpose, these trucks will give years of quality service. The Cherokee model line's popularity reflects in sales figures. In 1990 alone, four-wheel drive XJ Cherokee/Wagoneer sales totalled 118,826, more than the combined totals for the Ford Bronco II, Chevy S-Blazer and S-15 Jimmy 4x4 models. This means plenty of well maintained pre-owned models in the marketplace.

manche will struggle with compound power options like air conditioning and power steering.

Impressive XJ Cherokee performance begins with 1987 models. AMC's 4.0L multi-point injected engine of 177 horsepower actually set the stage for a horsepower race among compact trucks. The racy, high-torque 4.0L jumped to 190 horsepower in 1991 and is still a winner after a dozen years. Considering the relatively light weight of these trucks, this is a substantial powerplant.

For light off-pavement use, economy and utility, consider a compact XJ Cherokee. 1984–86 models have soft (low) prices due to the engines. (These models make reasonable candidates for an engine swap. See later chapters.) For better stock performance and reliability, focus attention on an '87 or newer XJ Cherokee with the 4.0L six or EFI 2.5L four.

The Comanche pickup is built largely on the same platform as the unibody XJ Cherokee/Wagoneer. The powertrains and options are very similar. The unibody chassis is unique for a pickup, and in the fiercely competitive compact truck market, these models saw only modest success. At the right price, the Comanche's ride, options, performance and economy make the truck attractive.

5. The YJ and TJ Wranglers

In 1987, AMC/Jeep ended four decades of CJ Jeep production with the introduction of the 93.4" wheelbase YJ/Wrangler models. The following year, Chrysler/Jeep Corporation added a special edition Sahara model. By 1989, Jeep Wrangler had an Islander edition as well. Reminiscent of the specialized Jeep CJ packages from the late Kaiser and AMC eras (like the Renegade, Laredo, Levi and others), the Sahara took a visual theme to the limit.

The Wrangler YJ Sahara, Islander, Laredo and Standard models each offered a six-cylinder engine option. (Beginning in 1991, the XJ Cherokee's potent 4.0L EFI engine became available.) 1987–90 sixes are the traditional seven main bearing, 4.2L (258 cubic inch) in-line engine, one of the industry's all-time toughest designs. This engine served CJs from 1972–on and first appeared in 1965 J-truck/Wagoneers as a smaller 232 cubic inch version.

Owners rave about the torque, reliability, ease of service and reasonable fuel economy of 232 and 258 sixes. The weak link for a 258 six is the Carter BBD two-barrel carburetor found on late '70s to 1990 engines. This issue, and also the leaky valve cover troubles on CJ-era models, have aftermarket remedies. (See performance chapter for Mopar emission legal EFI retrofit kit.)

Fig. 2-14. *The 4.2L/258 cubic inch carbureted Wrangler engine has its roots in the AMC 232 that powered many 1965–70 Jeep J-trucks and Wagoneers. The 258 emerged in 1971 and fills many CJ and Jeep truck engine bays through 1990. 1991 and newer Wranglers use the 4.0L MPI/EFI fueled engine.*

The Wrangler's five-speed manual overdrive transmission shifts well, and hydraulic clutch linkage works smoothly. Transmission stamina under severe off-pavement use has been poor, however, for both the Peugeot and AX-series transmissions behind six-cylinder engines. (Four-cylinder transmissions have a higher survival rate due to less engine torque.) If you plan serious backcountry use, keep in mind the cost of retrofitting a gearbox like the rugged NV4500 transmission. (See geartrain performance chapter.)

The front axle disconnect and transfer case operate easily. Braking and steering control prove superior to earlier CJ models. A hefty front stabilizer bar, firm Bilstein shocks and short suspension travel lend a sports-car feel to the chassis. The 14:1 ratio Saginaw power steering ratio is very quick, fun for an experienced driver but often challenging for the unsuspecting neophyte.

In other respects, the Wrangler YJ delivers a stable, reasonably predictable road feel. Far less tipsy than the earlier CJs, both the YJ and TJ Wrangler handle much like a taut sports car, providing a secure feeling with either the torquey 2.5L standard four or a six-cylinder engine package.

Wrangler OE seats are great, with good form and cushioned to handle hours of driving. Ergonomics rate as high as most sport/utility models. Visibility, with or without the top in place, is adequate, and the truck parks and turns easily. The Wrangler is nimble in urban traffic, and the OE canvas top does a superb job of sealing. (Expect a higher noise level with canvas. If you want quiet, find a hardtop model or plan a retrofit.) The factory AM/FM/cassette system adds to the fun.

The Wrangler as a "Real" 4x4

AMC/Jeep created an image with the Wrangler YJ, continuing the Jeep legend of a truck that will go anywhere. The showroom stock rear axle clearance of only 8.14" and ramp breakover angle of a mere 25.19 degrees, however, substantially reduced the original Wrangler's rock crawling potential. As a hard-core trail runner, the stock YJ Wrangler falls short.

Manufacturers, including Jeep, now build vehicles for multi-purpose use. A relatively stable roll center height (16.1" front and 21.8" rear with stock tires) and a lower center of gravity than previous CJ models added a statistical margin of safety to the stock YJ Wrangler. In today's world of consumer advocacy and lawsuits, manufacturers must be conservative around safety engineering. In the Wrangler's case, the price was less ground clearance.

If the Sierra's Rubicon Run, Moab, Utah, or any other off-pavement hell hole suits your 4x4 plans, the Wrangler can provide a place to start. These trucks have the majority of powertrain and chassis ingredients for serious rock crawling. They need better (bigger and brawnier) wheels and tires, a set of aftermarket springs that will afford more travel plus ground clearance, and beefy shock absorbers to match the springs. For severe off-pavement rock crawling and the use of oversized tires, aftermarket chassis lift kits are available for leaf spring YJs and the link-and-coil spring TJs. (See performance chapters.)

So equipped, the Wrangler is better able to challenge rocky trails. Make sure, however, that you understand the handling changes, both on- and off-pavement, that result from raising your Jeep's chassis and body. Your safety and that of passengers is at stake.

The Wrangler YJ or TJ has a short rear driveshaft. Lift kit manufacturers warn of driveline vibration when you install a chassis/spring lift on these models. The fix for this problem is a transfer case output and yoke conversion kit from M.I.T. (See geartrain upgrades in later chapter.)

Before you purchase a Wrangler for hard-core off-pavement use, consider the cost of a mild chassis lift to achieve necessary clearance for larger wheels and tires. The larger tires will increase ground clearance, and the wider track width will help offset the raised center of gravity created by the lift. Always use discretion when altering a Jeep's chassis or body height. Installation of a lift kit changes the roll center, center of gravity and steering geometry of the vehicle. Select a respected kit and follow the manufacturer's guidelines and safety recommendations.

All Wranglers deliver traditional Jeep value. In stock form, however, be aware that the 2.5L EFI four

Special Edition Wranglers

For the Wrangler's market, image is all-important. Special edition models helped launch the YJ generation Wrangler, and many of the themes carry into the TJ era. Among the earlier models were the Wrangler Islander Edition, the Laredo and the Sahara, the latter surviving into the TJ era (shown below), with an additional SE and Sport edition.

Laredo began as the luxury hardtop, while the Sahara offered a khaki version for the wilds of Africa. Each package fit the same chassis, powertrain and body shell. The Standard S version became the traditional "utility" Jeep, just like the TJ's four-cylinder SE model.

On the paradisiacal Hawaiian Islands or the Coppertone beaches of California, the bright yellow, colorfully striped YJ Wrangler Islander fit well and promised instant gratification for many youthful buyers. Beneath the cosmetic exterior and interior appointments rested a refined chassis and powertrain with roots to the formidable CJ-7.

Personalized special edition Wrangler and Cherokee models have endless possibilities. How about a hardtop version of the Wrangler designated the "Mountaineer" for the backpacker? A freshwater fishermen's package, the "Angler," complete with rod and reel holders and a built-in tackle box? How 'bout a bird and game hunter's special edition, perhaps the "Woodsman," with an optional decoy bin and gun locker? Tired of waiting? Create your very own Jeep theme vehicle, built around your family's specific recreational interests.

and newer 4.0L EFI six-cylinder engines have more to offer than the 1987–90 carbureted 4.2L engine. On the rocks, CJ and early YJ Wrangler owners put up with carburetor flooding and engine stalling. The 258/4.2L six needs a Mopar Performance electronic fuel injection (EFI) conversion kit or an equivalent aftermarket fix.

6. Inspecting a Used Jeep 4x4

As a used Jeep 4x4 buyer, the fear of waking to a pile of scrap iron in your driveway is real. Gloomy repair expenses help fortify anxiety about buying any used vehicle. Insight, however, can help demystify your quest. Add to this the firm conviction that no matter how much you want a Jeep, you'll not allow desire to override good judgement. This is tough, as the search for a quality used Jeep often leads down blind alleys and into real junk. When you find what looks like a decent piece of iron, the impulse is to buy it—and that's when you really need to look closely.

Chassis

The condition of the frame is probably the most important aspect of a used truck. You can recondition cosmetic areas and mechanical assemblies, but a twisted, broken or fatigued frame is the ultimate nightmare. Several symptoms suggest that a Jeep's frame has sustained damage, and I always begin looking at a used 4x4 by crawling under the truck to check for the obvious signs of wear and abuse.

Damage is easy to spot: bent springs, spring hangers or frame crossmembers; torn cables or hoses; a twisted skid plate or damaged frame horns at the bumper attachment points. Axle misalignment shows as worn tires. If you have suspicions about the frame condition, suggest that the seller accompany you to a reputable frame and alignment shop. Have the Jeep's frame checked for straightness on a four-wheel alignment rack.

Critical measurements made between various points on the frame tell a frame specialist whether the

Fig. 2-15. *Some signs of frame damage are obvious, like this patchwork repair. Under hard trail running, 1972–75 CJs are notorious for cracking the frame just behind the front spring anchors. Shy away from trucks subjected to this kind of pounding.*

Jeep has sustained damage or suffers from fatigue and cracks. The specialist can check for wear at the steering linkage, the steering gearbox, spring hangers, bushings and all steering joints.

Inspecting Drivelines and Axles

Jack and support the Jeep safely off the ground and check the steering knuckle/kingpin bearings or ball-joints. Grab each front wheel at six and twelve o'clock and rock the wheel in and out. Play shows inboard of the wheels at the kingpin bearings or ball-joints. Check if the knuckle seals or axle tubes leak grease or gear lube. Check for wheel bearing looseness and any signs of water damage to the wheel bearings, front and rear axles or universal joints. Water is the number-one destroyer of wheel hub, steering knuckle and axle parts.

Any indication of water in the axle housings, transfer case or transmission assembly is cause for alarm. Geartrain pieces are expensive. Check for excess play at the ring and pinion gears by rotating each driveshaft back and forth. Distinguish U-joint looseness from gear problems. While driveshafts cost plenty, axle assembly overhauls are even more expensive.

When you test drive the Jeep, listen for whining, clunks or growling. Axle noises telegraph during acceleration, coasting and deceleration. You'll usually hear U-joint or driveshaft play as a metallic clicking or snapping noise when you change speed or jerk the throttle open and shut, especially at a steady road speed in a higher gear.

Checking Clutch and Transmission

The Jeep clutch is one of the more inaccessible components in the powertrain. Owners sell their Jeep rather

Fig. 2-16. *Water destroys 4x4 geartrain and chassis parts. Left alone, water ruins bearings, gears and very expensive machined parts. Axle assemblies and differentials can draw water through the housing vent and seals. Water left in a gearcase leads to a major overhaul.*

Fig. 2-17. *A U-joint is far less costly to replace than constructing a complete driveshaft or overhauling an axle. Isolate noises carefully. You're the one who will pay for the repairs or parts if you buy the truck.*

than replace a worn clutch! Official flat-rate labor to replace a clutch in a Kaiser V-6 Jeepster is 6.8 hours. Add clutch parts to this and the job costs as much or more than a good used engine.

Check the clutch by moving the transmission shifter to high gear at 20 mph. With the clutch pedal depressed, bring the engine speed to 2000 rpm and hold the throttle steady, then quickly let the clutch pedal go. Listen. If the engine speed drops immediately to a near idle, the clutch cover (pressure plate) assembly and disc are likely intact. A gradual decrease in speed most likely indicates that the clutch either slips or needs adjustment. Also make certain the clutch does not shudder during engagement.

When the clutch mis-adjustment is bad enough to allow slip, assume that major damage is already underway. Slippage generates heat and friction, which translates as rapid wear and fatigue.

Transmission woes have their own noises. While test driving the Jeep, listen for crunch and gear clash. In each gear, pull gently on the shifter while accelerating lightly. If the synchronizers and shifter detents are okay, you'll feel resistance at the lever. When the transmission immediately slides out of gear, suspect a weak synchro assembly. Synchronizer trouble also shows up on a steep downgrade under deceleration as the transmission jumps out of gear. Bearing or gear tooth wear can also cause the transmission to slip out of gear.

Automatic Transmission

An automatic transmission may slip or chatter on take-off. Harsh shifts can be another sign of trouble. A shuddering sensation, much like a bad manual clutch or weak motor mounts, also means big trouble. Burnt fluid, leaks or erratic shifts suggest that an automatic transmission is in bad shape. Repairs usually involve a

Fig. 2-18. *Synchronizer and gear problems have clear symptoms. These parts are very expensive, and accessing the transmission on a Jeep truck is a major task. Test the transmission and transfer case thoroughly, and if you have suspicions, understand the repair costs before buying the truck.*

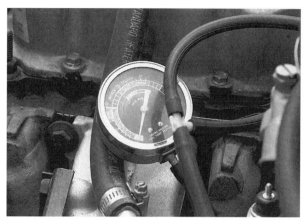

Fig. 2-19. *A manifold vacuum test can help pinpoint compression problems, incorrect valve or spark timing, weak valve spring(s), a clogged exhaust system or gasket leaks at the intake manifold. Without a scope or dyno, at least run a vacuum test on the engine.*

major overhaul, and again, the tough access to a Jeep transmission raises the cost considerably.

Get a transmission overhaul estimate before making an offer on the truck. Labor to remove, overhaul and install an automatic transmission in a Jeep 4x4 truck runs more than ten hours. Add the cost of hard parts, and a used Jeep buy takes on a whole new price perspective!

Engine

A common misconception about used vehicles is that the engine is most important. On Jeep 4x4s, an axle, transmission or complete brake system rebuild can easily exceed the cost of an engine overhaul. Installing a complete engine is often easier and less time consuming than removing and overhauling the transmission.

Before buying a used Jeep, you'll still want to make sure the engine is sound. An engine's basic requirements include: 1) normal and even compression, 2) accurate valve timing, 3) correct valve lift at each valve, and 4) normal bearing clearances and oil pressure. If you can borrow the Jeep, have the engine scoped or chassis dyno analyzed.

On a scope test, a quick check of "dynamic compression" can compare cylinder spark loads, which reflect as approximate compression. Now single out the weakest cylinder and test it with a compression gauge or, better yet, a cylinder leakdown tester. (You will find a complete explanation of engine troubleshooting in the service chapters.)

If you find signs of overheat, look further. Excess rust in the radiator or signs of chronic boil over suggest the seepage of cylinder gases or ambient air into the

Fig. 2-20. *A stethoscope or even a hollow tube can transmit engine noises. This is an automotive diagnostic tool that can help analyze and isolate knocks and rattles.*

cooling system. Causes range from a defective radiator cap or water pump (aeration) to a blown head gasket or cracked engine casting. Run a cooling system pressure test, and also check for normal coolant circulation. (See the cooling system chapter for troubleshooting details.)

Engine Oiling System

Engine bearing and lubrication problems are tricky to diagnose. On a Jeep with an analog oil pressure gauge, it's far easier to observe oil pressure under load. Check the consistency of the engine oil to make sure that heavy additives do not affect oil pressure. Warm the engine completely, watching the oil pressure the entire time. Drive the Jeep under load, up hills and such, and constantly monitor the oil pressure. Listen for knocks on cold start-up, after the engine has set for some time.

Try to isolate loose piston pin noise or a cracked piston by shorting or disconnecting each spark plug wire and seeing whether the knock is still there. Rod and main bearing noises may also decrease by eliminating spark. An automotive stethoscope or even a long hollow tube makes an excellent diagnostic tool for finding internal engine noises. Get used to the amplified sound, though, or the engine will resonate like a metallic thrashing machine. Learn to isolate normal noises like the clicking of a mechanical fuel pump.

Belts, hoses, wiring, the battery, filters and routinely serviced items speak for the truck's maintenance. Look thoroughly under the hood, and assess the quality of replacement parts. Ultra-cheap parts surely mean a neglected truck.

If you lack the equipment or skill to do a thorough inspection, consider paying a professional mechanic to check the engine, geartrain or cooling system. Should the mechanic find the truck in poor shape, you can either negotiate a better purchase price or walk away from a worn-out Jeep. Either way, the inspection fee pays off.

Telltale Signs of Wear

Sheet metal, body mounts and rubber seals also take abuse. The effects of sun, rain, snow and salted roads beat Jeep trucks mercilessly. Rubber rots, hinges twist and windows rattle in worn channels. The degree of wear can be a barometer of the overall abuse the truck has suffered.

Radio, heater and air conditioning systems are costly and time-consuming to repair. Don't accept suggestions that the air conditioner simply needs a recharge. Ask the seller to have the system charged before you agree to buy the truck.

Other signs of trouble are a broken speedometer and vague records of mileage. This isn't so important

Fig. 2-21. *The body mount cushions wear and fatigue. These parts of the truck indicate hard use and stress. Inspect all of the chassis mounts and bushings.*

on a 1946 CJ-2A, but it sure should color your thinking about a used '97 Cherokee! No lube stickers, missing pedal pads, bald tires and a poor paint finish each serve as warnings. You want a well kept Jeep that received regular maintenance.

Pollution Controls and Vehicle Registration

Since 1971, pollution controls on Jeep engines have proliferated. In the early '60s, the emission control era started with a PCV valve and closed crankcase. Then the smog pump emerged, followed by the exhaust gas recirculation (EGR) valve. Catalytic converters and unleaded fuel, evaporative systems for fumes and, more recently, electronic fuel and spark management have each become a part of the emission program. (See the chapter on emission controls.)

Smog laws, enforced by the states and federal government, mean that your used Jeep truck must have a functional and complete OEM emission control system. If equipment is missing, non-operative or malfunctioning, you will have a problem registering the truck. Inspection programs have become common, with California setting a model for the United States.

A Jeep 4x4 stripped by the previous owner of its emission hardware, or an engine transplant unauthorized by your state's smog program, means real trouble. Original Equipment intake and exhaust manifolds, a smog pump, electrical and vacuum controls, the catalytic converter, an EGR valve and the host of other pieces might run well beyond the cost of a good used engine. A modified engine with non-approved aftermarket headers, intake manifold, carburetor, ignition and other components is a prime candidate for failing the visual portion of an emission control test.

Make the seller responsible for the restoration of the smog system to meet legal demands. Otherwise, allow enough price reduction to cover the equipment necessary for compliance. If you have questions about necessary equipment or its cost, get an estimate from a licensed smog shop, Jeep dealership or your state motor vehicle pollution control agency before you buy the truck.

7. Buying a New Jeep

The Jeep 4x4, once regarded as a utility or work truck, has metamorphosed from a beast of burden into multipurpose transportation. Over the years, buyers and sales personnel have also changed. Years ago, Jeep and farm equipment sales often took place at the same outlet. Today, throngs of car people find themselves first-time truck buyers at Jeep/Eagle dealerships.

Fig. 2-22. *For sheer satisfaction, there's nothing more exciting than taking delivery of a new Jeep. This showroom stock TJ Sahara hardtop, with barely enough miles to wear the nubs off the Wrangler GS-A tires, ef-* *fortlessly pulled a USA VenturCraft Trailblazer trailer across Nevada's leg of I-80 to a remote hunting and fishing locale in northeastern Nevada. Rugged Mopar/Warn winch shown is a dealer-installed accessory.*

Whether or not you are new to four-wheeling and recreational vehicles, you should still take charge of selecting and ordering your new Jeep truck. "Buyer's remorse," mainly due to winding up with the wrong options and equipment, is not uncommon. Everyone wants to get a good deal. Yet many buyers shop 4x4 vehicles on the basis of price only, with just a vague idea of which equipment they need.

Dealer showroom literature sometimes does not explain the full range of options available, and further research is always practical. Jeep/Eagle dealers have detailed specification and equipment ordering books, and the fleet sales manager has expertise at how to "spec" out a new truck.

Such order books describe far more items than you will find in glossy point-of-sale materials. A complete, factory-tailored new Jeep always makes better sense than hastily selecting a random "nice color" truck on the lot. See the dealership's sales manager or fleet manager for details.

Selecting the Right Chassis

Veteran four-wheelers have learned equipment needs from dirt roads and sore forearms—places where stu-dio lamps and advertising props can't be found. For openers, you must determine whether a standard chassis has enough stamina for your needs. If not, the dealer's order and pricing book may describe heavy duty options that better meet your requirements. By researching equipment carefully, you can buy factory engineered and installed components that will work.

Understand Jeep chassis, suspension and powertrain ratings. While the compact Jeep XJ Cherokee frame and springs can support substantial weight, the 2.5L four with a lighter duty transmission certainly does not match the stamina of a classic full-size Cherokee chassis, a truck type T-18 four-speed gearbox and a 401 cubic inch V-8. A vehicle's toughness is not just load or tow capacity.

Factory Upgrades

Boost your load carrying capacity with a heavy duty spring option, heavy duty shock absorbers, a better wheel and tire combination and a trailer towing package. The cost of heavy duty OE springs is a fraction of what aftermarket springs will cost later: the manufacturer credits back the cost of standard parts when you order heavy duty factory installed upgrades.

When ordering springs, many buyers assume that if heavier is good, the heaviest available springs must be better. This is not always true in the case of 4x4s, especially full size trucks. Often, truck order books list snow plow front springs as an option. Without the massive weight of a snow plow, these springs can jar your bones! Unless you need snow plow equipment, order the regular heavy duty suspension package.

Always opt for the heaviest gear and axle components available. In the 1970s, simply ordering a four-speed transmission in a CJ was the difference between a passenger car type three-speed and a 2-ton capacity four-speed truck gearbox. The T-18 four-speeds were a bargain. When available, a heavier front or rear axle assembly (like the Dana 44 rear for TJs) is equally useful, and so is a heavy duty clutch or brake option. When you order these components, you buy years of extra service for your Jeep.

Heavy duty factory shocks are a must. Often, you will end up replacing worn-out standard shocks after 12–15,000 miles of normal on- and off-pavement use. Another practical item is an optional heavy duty anti-sway bar (front and rear if available). This will enhance highway cornering and stability. Often, the anti-sway bar, heavy shocks, heavy duty charging and factory cooling upgrade come with the trailer towing package.

Be aware that for hard-core rock crawling and trail running, traction suffers from sway bars that limit wheel travel. Consider where you'll use your Jeep, and choose your suspension options wisely, especially on Wrangler models.

Powertrain, Geartrain and Trailering Needs

One of the most miserable situations in the aftermath of a new 4x4 purchase is the discovery that the truck's pulling power cannot meet your needs. This occurs

Fig. 2-23. *Cherokee just keeps getting better! Intrinsic utility, comfort and nimble handling remain in 1998 model (shown). This is a highly refined multipurpose vehicle with an exceptional service record. Considering value and cost, the XJ is simply the best compact 4WD SUV available.*

Fig. 2-24. *1998 Grand Cherokee, last model with a push-rod V-8 option, offered Mopar's 5.2L and 5.9L MPI/EFI engines. Roguish 5.9L, a thoroughly modern version of a proven engine design, rated 245 horsepower and 345 lb-ft of torque. Such power made the '98 ZJ Grand Cherokee popular with performance enthusiasts. Standard high-torque 4.0L in-line six, fuel efficient and peppy, satisfied many buyers and carried forward to the re-styled '99 WJ model.*

when you pick the wrong engine, transmission and axle ratio combination or when the pursuit of fuel economy overrides all other considerations. Choosing the wrong axle ratio is a common and simple mistake: Today's "trailer towing" gear ratios were considered economy ratios before the mid-'70s.

A 2.5L compact Cherokee or Wrangler engine may work fine for commuting or breezing down a flat interstate, but attach your modest tent trailer and watch out for the slightest grades! You'll snail crawl up mountain passes and seriously stress the engine.

Any trailer over 1500 pounds requires a V-8 or larger six-cylinder engine. Towing a 2500-plus pound trailer requires the torque of a V-8. For my towing tastes, I have rigid standards that take into account the vehicle's wheelbase length and track width.

To the point, I will not tow a trailer weighing over 1500 pounds with a wheelbase shorter than a full-size Grand Wagoneer/full-size Cherokee. (These trucks rode on 109-inch wheelbases.) Such past models, and the even longer, wider 3/4-ton or one-ton rated J-trucks, offer adequate track widths for towing. For regularly pulling a trailer in the 2500–6500 pound range, my new vehicle choice would be a Dodge Ram HD2500 4WD pickup chassis.

For the Jeep purist intent on towing a heftier travel trailer, my choice would be a 1984 3/4-ton Model 27 Jeep J-20 Pickup with a 131-inch wheelbase and the optional 8400-pound GVWR rated chassis. If such a rig could be found in like-new shape or faithfully restored, this wheelbase length and chassis stamina would provide for safer towing.

NOTE —
Use of an equalizing hitch and sway control are must items for heavy towing. (See accessories chapter.)

In addition to handling and safety concerns, trailering demands ample suspension, a strong engine, heavy duty cooling, reserve braking capacity, stout axles and higher load range tires. If your new truck plans revolve around toting a hefty trailer, turn attention toward a full-size Dodge 3/4-ton (HD2500) model with a 131-inch or longer wheelbase and a robust V-8 or diesel powerplant.

Transmission Options

Automatic transmissions have become increasingly more popular. They sometimes fill special physical needs but most often satisfy drivers with no desire to work a manual transmission and clutch. Through the 1980s, 4x4 automatics with overdrive became increasingly more popular. Fuel savings have increased the popularity of overdrive automatic transmissions.

For a full-sized truck like Dodge's Ram 4x4 HD2500, the best, currently available manual transmission is an NV4500 iron-cased, heavy duty five-speed with a compound low gear and overdrive. This transmission can be retrofitted to a Jeep CJ, YJ/TJ Wrangler and even the XJ Cherokee using aftermarket components. (See geartrain modifications in later chapter.) In stock form, however, the Wrangler and XJ manual five-speed transmissions are lighter duty, closer ratio five-speed overdrives without a compound low gear.

Until the introduction of the 1999 WJ Grand Cherokee's five-speed automatic, an automatic transmission offered few advantages. Now, however, a four- or five-speed automatic can compete readily with a manual transmission in most instances. One exception is the advantage of a manual transmission and low (numerically high) axle gearing on steep or loose downgrades and when rock crawling.

Accessories for Survival

Look for factory extras that will increase your Jeep's life expectancy. For example, air conditioning or a heavy duty charging (electrical) system may include items like a heavy duty alternator, a larger battery and harnesses for trailer wiring. The factory-installed air conditioning option usually includes a heavy duty radiator and engine cooling upgrade. Again, factory options provide heavy duty service for just the cost difference between standard pieces and these heavier duty components.

Fig. 2-25. *1999 WJ Grand Cherokee introduced major refinements, dramatic styling changes and a new five-speed automatic transmission. High-tech 4.7L overhead camshaft V-8 signaled a new era in Jeep technology. Quadra-Drive traction system keeps Jeep at leading edge of fiercely competitive World Class SUV segment.*

Fig. 2-26. *Bendix pioneered four-wheel Anti-Lock Braking System (ABS) on Jeep's XJ Cherokee/Wagoneer 4x4 compact sport utility trucks. ABS reduces risk of skidding or loss of control in emergency and foul weather stops. Rear vehicle has ABS, while truck at front skids without ABS. ABS and heavy duty braking can enhance your new Jeep's performance.*

A heavy duty brake system may come as a stand alone option or with a towing package. Heavy duty brakes might include a heavier master cylinder, bigger vacuum booster, and even larger brake shoes, disc pads, drums or rotors. Factory equipment must meet high quality standards. Always consider factory-installed tow hooks, tow hitch assemblies and trailer wiring harnesses.

Look at available tire options. A few dollars extra can provide major improvements. Look over the factory tire options and compare them in the marketplace. Avoid getting stuck with useless or undercapacity tires. Match your new Jeep's tires to your turf.

Consider Special Ordering Your New Jeep

Check the dealer's inventory first. Your Jeep dealer may have just the truck you want—in stock. You might get lucky and drive home immediately with a new 4x4 truck. If, however, the inventory vehicles fall short of your needs, avoid buying someone else's truck.

If your local dealer does not have the Jeep you want, ask for a vehicle trade with another dealer or consider special ordering your Jeep. Although it's fun to get something new while you're in a buying mood, waiting for the right Jeep assures years of satisfaction and pleasure. The trade-off is worth the wait!

Fig. 2-27. *Even small items like factory-installed tow hooks are valuable. They fit properly and feature quality engineering. If you buy these pieces later, you'll pay as much or more and spend time fitting up parts.*

Chapter 3

Operating Your Jeep

The Sagebrush State has a mean elevation of 5,500 feet. Rugged peaks reach to 13,000 feet at northern Nevada. Harsh, 20-below winters, dry summer heat to 110 degrees and miles of open space characterize the places where I first four-wheeled a Jeep.

At Carson Valley, alfalfa fields stretch west to the Sierra and eastward to the base of the Pine Nut Range. There, sheep trails and BLM roads cross the scrub pine and juniper covered hills. Years ago, wild horses and old mine sites mingled with miles of remote sagebrush. The Basque-born sheep herders, their blue-eyed Australian Shepherds and wary coyotes were the few witnesses to a Jeep CJ-5 that whined up the primitive trails and climbed Sunrise Pass.

Behind the Wheel

Early June of '65, with summer looming ahead, I drove my father to Carson City in the CJ-5 Jeep. With a couple thousand miles on a learner's permit, I was ready for my driver's license exam. Practice included a trek through Tonopah and central Nevada's Smokey Valley, where a dusty alkali road stretched over a hundred miles across a desolate swath of semi-arid desert.

My license in hand, the CJ's ignition key never felt better. I immediately headed for the Pine Nut Range to hone my four-wheeling skills. When summer waned, the Spruce Green Jeep served as my companion for hunting and fishing, happily accessing places where first gear, low range became a must.

The T-98A four speed truck transmission, a wise option, lent a first gear ratio of 6.40:1. 4.27:1 axle gearing plus a low range ratio of 2.46:1 in the transfer case gave the truck an exceptional crawl ratio of 67:1—gearing so low that with the clutch engaged, the 12-volt starter could easily pull the truck up a steep incline while simultaneously firing the engine!

This was the ideal truck for four-wheeling. Ultra-low gearing, 7.00x15 mud-and-snow tires and a four-cylinder F-134 engine, the CJ-5 could snail crawl anywhere. The rugged and user-friendly powertrain encouraged sensible, minimal tire spin driving habits.

Fig. 3-1. *Old, abandoned minesites and wild horses characterized the Pine Nut Range east of Gardnerville, Nevada. At Sunrise Pass, I four-wheeled our family's new 1964 CJ-5.*

Fig. 3-2. *The Kaiser CJ-5 models had an 81" wheelbase and a standard 134 F-head four-cylinder engine. Our '64 model boasted the optional T-98A four-speed truck transmission (similar to later T-18), which provided an impressive 6.40:1 ratio in compound low gear. With 4.27 axle ratios and the Model 18 transfer case's 2.46:1 low range gearing, the '64 delivered a factory "crawl ratio" of 67:1. This was terrific gearing, especially with the stock 7.00x15 tire size.*

Past the Teething Stage

By 1969, far from Carson Valley at National City, California, I spied a stock appearing '50 CJ-3A Jeep with a FOR SALE sign on the windshield. When the title changed hands, the seller, a fellow truck mechanic, offered some sage advice, "Don't flat tow this truck for any distance! The cam-and-lever steering gearbox and the rear axle bearings will wear out fast if you do...."

The CJ-3A quickly won my respect. Parts for a vintage Jeep were very inexpensive, with great interchangeability and ready local sources. As I soon learned, the '50 model was a wise choice, as the truck featured 5.38:1 axle gearing, a reliable (gear drive camshaft) 134 L-head engine, a tough T-90 three speed transmission, the more reliable Bendix-type front axle joints, and a hefty Spicer 44 rear axle.

Those first months, the engine earned a new set of rod and main bearings, four new pistons, rings and a valve job. The flat oil pan and cylinder head made for an easy, in the chassis job. Next, I removed the radiator for recoring, upgraded the previous owner's 12-volt electrical conversion, installed a complete Walker replacement exhaust system and replaced the appallingly light duty OE clutch and worn clutch linkage parts.

Brakes, seals, front wheel bearings and a paint job put the Jeep in top shape. In low range, with low axle gearing, the CJ-3A tackled remarkably steep hills, wound confidently across the Anza-Borego desert, up Grapevine and Coyote Canyons and churned sand in the dry riverbeds of rural San Diego County.

Despite its formidable off-pavement performance, the CJ-3A's highway attitude was unnerving. The engine pitch sounded like a drone, screaming over 3200 rpm at 50 mph. The truck desperately needed an aftermarket Warn overdrive, but other priorities, like groceries, took precedence.

Best of the Bunch?

Since 1965, I have driven scores of 4x4 trucks. As a recreationalist, truck mechanic, heavy equipment operator and 4x4 magazine journalist, I've either driven or tested models built by Jeep, International Harvester, Chevrolet, GMC, Ford, Dodge, Nissan, Mazda, Mitsubishi, Toyota, AM General/Hummer, Land Rover, Mercedes-Benz and, yes, even Studebaker! Frequently asked which 4x4 truck I like best, my answer is simple: Many 4x4 trucks have a secure marketing niche. No make, however, becomes more a part of your family than a Jeep.

A four-wheel drive Jeep can complement your lifestyle. Suited to family recreation, foul weather security and off-pavement chores, your Jeep has special talents.

Fig. 3-3. *The modified powertrain of our '81 CJ-5 included a '90 Wrangler 4.2L engine and an NP435 truck four-speed conversion. I took my first driving exam in the stock '64 CJ-5. Three years later came the '50 CJ-3A. Our current semi-restoration project is an F-head powered '55 CJ-5. Each of our Jeep utility trucks provided room for personality and all wound up close members of the family. See how many times your Jeep shows up in the family photo album!*

Fig. 3-4. *Northern California's brutal Rubicon Trail is an adventure for folks of all ages. Singles, couples and families share the scenery, challenges of the trail and dry camps in spectacular forest settings. Safe vehicle condition and sober attention to driving is an imperative.*

Worked within its design limits, the powertrain and chassis will deliver years of dependable service.

Our children have grown up with various 4x4s, the family's access to hunting, fishing, hiking, firewood and North America's rugged back country. Jeep trucks hold a special meaning in our household. As a source of recreation and a cornerstone for wholesome family values, Jeep four-wheeling has served us well. The right Jeep truck model, whether new or preowned, can provide you and your family with a rich outdoor life and year around motoring safety.

1. Learning to Drive Your Jeep 4x4

Although technology has changed both the appearance and creature comfort levels of Jeep trucks, operating techniques remain much the same. Contorted road surfaces have always challenged four-wheelers. Although knowing your Jeep's equipment and controls is important, understanding the truck's handling characteristics proves an even greater asset.

The main difference between a Jeep 4x4 truck and a conventional rear drive truck or automobile is the live front axle and transfer case. In addition to the customary brake, accelerator and clutch controls, the Jeep's transmission has a shifter. Most Jeep transmission shifters come through the floorboard, although some Wagoneer and early Pickup/Station Wagon models (even the very first CJ-2A models) have column shift three-speed transmission controls. Automatic transmission equipped Jeep models have either steering column or floor console shift controls.

Most Jeep transfer cases provide high/low range selection and two- or four-wheel drive with either one or two levers reaching through the floor. Some early J-series models with an automatic transmission use a one-speed power divider instead of a two-speed transfer case.

In the 1960s, Jeep initiated the use of a single stick transfer case control, where one lever controls 2WD high, 4WD high, neutral and 4WD low. A variation is Quadratrac full time 4x4, which only requires low and high range positions but offers a four-lock mode.

For safety sake and powertrain survival, consult your Jeep owner's handbook or the 4WD instruction

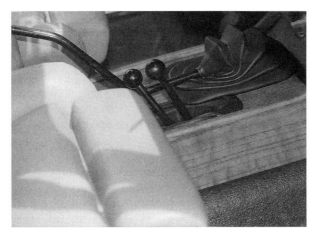

Fig. 3-5. *Although this '81 CJ-5 came originally with a single-lever transfer case, the system now boasts a Currie Enterprises aftermarket twin-stick conversion. Twin sticks provide mode variations that are not possible with the OE single lever control.*

decal for directions on operating the four-wheel drive system. This is a complex gear mechanism with very expensive components. Jeep Corporation knows best what your particular geartrain will tolerate.

High Range and Front Axle Drive

Two-wheel drive high range is much like driving any other truck. Power flows only to the rear axle and the transfer case operates at a 1:1 ratio. (The rear driveshaft spins at the same speed as the transmission output shaft.) When you move the shift lever into 4WD high range, both the front and rear driveshafts spin at the same speed as the transmission output shaft. High range 2WD is useful for hard surface highways and most civilized driving conditions.

In high range, the final drive ratios (front and rear axle gearing) determine the gear reduction. By shifting to four-wheel drive (4WD) high range, your Jeep truck offers substantially better traction, with the front axle pulling while the rear axle pushes the truck.

Jeep powertrains, with the exception of Quadratrac or full-time 4x4 systems, cannot tolerate four-wheel drive use on hard surfaced roads. Front axle pull and rear axle push never take place in perfect synchronization, and the result is gear bind. This condition, characterized by frozen transfer case levers and free-wheeling hubs, can damage the powertrain. (A differential within the transfer case of full-time 4x4 units prevents gear bind.)

Front axle engagement on hard surfaced roads also affects steering. The axle shafts transmit torque, which jacks the steering assembly as each front wheel strives for traction. On a loose surface road, these problems seldom occur. Dirt, snow or ice provide the necessary margin of slip.

All Jeep trucks with part-time 4x4 have a two-wheel drive mode. Preserving your powertrain means using four-wheel drive only when the road surface will allow some degree of slip. This also restricts the use of 4WD low range to ice, snow, mud and off-pavement surfaces.

Free-wheeling Front Hubs

Most Jeep 4x4s spend the majority of their lives on the highway or well graded dirt roads. The front axle assembly seldom needs to operate. Here, free-wheeling hubs can reduce wear at the front axle shafts, U-joints and the differential.

The first Jeep 4x4s had no free-wheeling hubs, and the front axle and axle shafts spun for the life of the truck. At one time an aftermarket accessory, then an OEM component, free-wheeling hubs reduce parts wear and increase fuel economy. Use 2WD and FREE hub mode whenever practical.

In the early 1980s, some Jeep models abandoned the use of manual hubs in favor of automatic locking hubs that engage when you shift to 4WD (high or low range). As torque flows to each front wheel, the hub assembly has an internal clutch mechanism that automatically locks the hub. In this mode, the hub functions much like a manual hub in the Lock position. (An exception is the automatic hub design that free wheels on downgrades and fails to provide vital compression braking.)

Although the automatic locking hub eliminates leaving your warm Jeep cab in a blizzard to lock the manual hubs, the automatic hub also requires backing

Fig. 3-6. *This set of fuel and wear saving OEM hubs on a CJ-5 is typical of the AMC/Jeep era models. A quality set of manual locking hubs offers reliable, predictable, sure engagement and disengagement.*

Fig. 3-7. *XJ Cherokee, followed by the YJ Wrangler, mid-size Grand Cherokee and the TJ Wrangler, introduced semi-floating front wheel hubs to Jeep trucks. There is no provision for manual hubs, and a front axle disconnect system reduces drag and wear. Owners have no need to lock hubs in wet or freezing weather!*

the truck up to disengage. Once road conditions allow a return to 2WD mode, you must stop the truck, shift the transfer case from 4WD to 2WD, then back the truck up several feet to disengage the automatic hubs.

Shifting the Transfer Case

When icy highway conditions are intermittent, you may leave your manual or automatic locking hubs in lock mode. During stretches of hard-surfaced road, simply disengage the front axle with the transfer case lever. When the mountain pass or snow zone is past, you can stop the truck, make certain the transfer case is in 2WD mode, and either manually unlock your front hubs or back your truck up if equipped with automatic locking hubs.

Some later model transfer cases boast shift-on-the-fly designs. These gear units allow the operator to move from 2WD high to 4WD high without effort. Under no circumstance, however, can you shift any Jeep transfer case to low range without stopping the vehicle. Although some transfer cases will tolerate engagement of low range gears at a very low vehicle speed, the safest method of low range engagement is at a complete halt.

For engaging the front axle drive at any speed, you will find that unloading torque from the gears helps ease the shift. If your Jeep has a manual transmission, leave the transmission in gear and depress the clutch momentarily as you move the transfer case lever from 2WD high to 4WD high. For automatic transmission models, leave the transmission in a drive range, but release the throttle as you pull the transfer case lever from 2WD to 4WD high range.

Consult your Jeep owner's handbook or instructional decals before engaging low range 4WD. An automatic transmission may require placing the transmission in Neutral or Park range before you move the transfer case lever. Otherwise, the transmission will spin the gears at speed as the transfer case shift lever passes through its Neutral mode. Severely abusive gear clash will result if you attempt to engage the low range gears while the transfer case input assembly spins at speed.

When to Use Four-wheel Drive

Faced with the perils of sleet and dropping temperatures, you'll cherish your Jeep's four-wheel drive system. When the highway shows wet surfaces, still a few degrees above the scourge of black ice, the time is right to lock your manual hubs.

Preparedness is your best hedge against disaster. As visibility decreases and traffic staggers to a crawl, the hazards and risks of stopping your truck to lock hubs rise dramatically. In some instances, leaving the pavement compromises your traction. When visibility drops, simply stopping your truck can cause a collision, as the driver of the next vehicle may react to your brake lamps and panic.

If the weather clearly calls for ice and snow, lock your manual hubs before you leave home. You can drive for miles with the hubs locked and the transfer case in 2WD high range without damaging the front axle system.

Once you have locked the hubs, you can engage 4WD high range while moving. As highway conditions worsen, or if a stretch of ice lies ahead, engage the front axle and leave the truck in 4WD mode until you're past the hazard. Then, simply shift the transfer case lever back to 2WD high mode. You'll likely repeat this procedure several times during long stretches of intermittent ice, snow and dry pavement.

If a dry, straight section of pavement lasts for a very short spell (1/8th mile or less), I leave the transfer case in 4WD mode, stay very light on the throttle to reduce torque application and work the steering carefully. As long as the truck steers straight, geartrain stress and risk of binding are minimal. I believe that under these conditions, shifting the transfer case in and out of 4WD places far more strain on components.

2. Off-Pavement Four-Wheel Drive

When the pavement ends and the dirt begins, consider your Jeep's traction needs. Since the softer roadway allows some slip and eliminates the risk of gear bind, it's wise to engage your hubs, whether you're in 4WD mode or not. Spinning the front axle system places a very slight load on the powertrain, and locking the hubs makes four-wheel drive available at a simple flip of the transfer case lever.

A common scene with off-pavement 4x4 caravans is the ritual of locking the hubs and "airing down." Lowering tire pressures increases traction and lessens bounce on irregular road surfaces. Lower tire pressures can also offset abrasion and rock damage to tires caused by stiff tread and sidewall surfaces.

Many four-wheelers, however, get carried away with airing down. Each tire design has a minimum safe inflation pressure. Lower pressures than this will risk unseating the bead. Unseating a bead or driving with severe sidewall flexing can ruin your expensive tires.

My rough guideline for airing down is that a tire with a 32–35 psi maximum load pressure will tolerate no lower than 20–24 psi pressure—and this for only short distances at slower speeds. As pressure drops, so does load capacity, and you're trading more traction

Fig. 3-8. *Locking the hubs and airing down is an off-pavement ritual. A portable air compressor can re-air tires after the run.*

for greater heat buildup and a higher likelihood of tire fatigue and failure. (See tire details in performance chapters.)

Concentrate on good driving habits and minimize wheel spin. Wheel spin loses traction, places tires at risk and causes environmental damage. Good driving technique will take your Jeep much further than low tire pressures.

A spinning tire is dangerous. How dangerous? General Tire suggests, "AVOID excessive tire spinning when your vehicle is stuck in snow, mud or sand. Never exceed 35 mph indicated on the speedometer. The centrifugal forces generated by a free spinning tire/wheel assembly may cause a sudden tire explosion resulting in vehicle damage and/or serious personal injury. Use a gentle backward and forward rocking motion to free your vehicle for continued driving. Never stand near or behind a tire spinning at high speed while attempting to push a vehicle that is stuck."

The number one cause of environmental damage, and the clearest sign of an inexperienced four-wheeler, is unnecessary tire spin. Your best traction is a tire tread surface that makes full contact with the road. You can minimize wheel spin by applying less throttle or shifting to a higher gear in the transmission. This will apply less torque to the wheels and lessen the likelihood of tires breaking traction.

The Terrain

Terrain dictates the use of four wheel drive. Experience teaches that it's always better to engage 4WD before entering a hazard than once you commit your Jeep. Mud and snow require a steady pulling traction, and stopping in the middle of a mud trail courts disas-

Fig. 3-9. *Lock your manual hubs and flip the transfer case lever into four-wheel drive before entering a water crossing. If in doubt about loose, slippery or muddy terrain, always use four-wheel drive.*

ter. Trying to regain traction may result in spinning tires and damage to a fragile environment. Wherever possible, keep moving with minimum tire spin and chassis bounce.

The Steepest Hills

If the trail gets rocky or steep and your Jeep begins bouncing, it's time for low range. Low range will reduce throttle effort and drastically lower the vehicle speed. The military MB and earliest civilian Jeep Model 18 transfer case has a 2.46:1 ratio. Late Jeep models reach 2.72:1 ratio. If your truck were idling through the rocks at 3 mph in first gear, placing the transfer case in low range would lower your idle speed to nearly one mile per hour. This allows far more control of the truck and reduces the risk of damage. If traction is good, stopping and starting become simple, with little, if any, throttle and no wheel spin.

When the top speed on a rough trail is 10–15 miles per hour, put the transfer case in low range 4WD and leave it there. You'll have plenty of transmission gears for keeping up with the crowd and also have the crawl speed to move slowly through rocky obstacles. This is the secret to safety and a long life for your Jeep truck.

> CAUTION —
> *Always slow down before you downshift transmission gears in low range. Low range gear reduction exaggerates the speed drop between gears, and the result feels like slamming on the brakes.*

Low range is a sensible braking mechanism. When facing a very steep decline, select the transmission gear that will control your Jeep's speed. Always minimize the use of your wheel brakes on slick or poor traction surfaces. If a wheel(s) lock up with application of the brakes (which they do readily on ice or sandy granite boulders), skidding will result. The best traction is a tire that continues to rotate. At the slowest imaginable speeds, in low range first gear, your Jeep's tires can provide traction over the full area of the tread. If possible, keep your tires rotating under engine compression braking to provide the highest percentage of traction.

The reduction ratio of low range also provides exceptional pulling power. Assuming that the Jeep can get traction, 4WD low range will permit a 75 horsepower, four-cylinder F-134 powered Jeep of 2500 pounds to move a stalled 8000 pound flatbed truck! Short pulls, like freeing a vehicle from a ditch, can easily be performed if your Jeep can get traction.

> CAUTION —
> • *If you need to move a heavy vehicle for more than a few feet, avoid using 4WD lock mode on a hard surfaced road.*
>
> • *Never hook the chain or strap to a trailer ball, driveshaft, spring hanger, steering components or an axle housing that has brake pipes or hoses running along its surface.*
>
> • *There are situations where four-wheeling is unsafe or will cause damage to the environment. When your Jeep totters on the edge of disaster, winching is far more practical than driving. A properly angled winch cable can function as both the motive force and a safety strap for your Jeep. If losing traction means poor vehicle control, use a winch. (See winching instructions in the accessories chapter.)*

Uphill and Downhill

Negotiating steep hills causes more adrenaline flow than any other Jeep maneuver. Angles, especially downslopes, appear distorted and ominous. This is just as well, as the real threat of losing control on a descent deserves all of your attention. Going uphill in four wheel drive, the front wheels claw for traction and tend to pull your Jeep into line. Downward, these same wheels want to skid, slip sideways and clutch frantically for traction.

On ascents, minimize wheel spin. When descending, use the correct gear to minimize skidding and the need to apply your Jeep's brakes. Moderation has never had a better mentor than four-wheeling.

Fig. 3-10. *Low range serves in rocky or dangerously steep terrain. Low range 4WD provides compression braking and far more control of the Jeep. Here's a typical place for 4WD low range and use of the lower transmission gears.*

In rough and angled terrain, excess movement courts disaster. Oversteering and understeering can cross the vehicle up at just the wrong moment. On both ascents and descents, if your Jeep loses directional stability, the risk of roll over increases.

> *WARNING —*
> • *Never drive sideways across a hill. If side tilt overcomes your Jeep's roll center, the vehicle is likely to turn over.*
>
> • *If your Jeep turns completely sideways on a steep sideslope, prepare to roll over. Always wear a seatbelt/harness and install a full roll cage if you intend to climb risky slopes. If you must get out of the vehicle, do so only on the uphill side.*

If you find your Jeep beginning to turn sideways on a loose traction downslope, keep your foot off the brake pedal. Steer into the skid, as if the vehicle were on ice or snow. If safe and timely, accelerate very gently to pull the vehicle straight. Either of these tech-

Fig. 3-11. *A winch can take over where four-wheel traction cannot do the job. Wherever wheel spin jeopardizes the environment, use a winch. As the TREAD LIGHTLY! philosophy spreads, expect wider use of winches and protective tree saver straps. Encourage fellow four-wheelers to stay on established trails and avoid damaging fragile eco-systems.*

Fig. 3-12. *Drive straight up and straight down hills. Never drive sideways across a hill face. Moving sideways on a hill, the risk of rolling your Jeep increases dramatically.*

niques require nerves of steel, acute sensitivity and your conviction that the Jeep cannot straighten out any other way.

Hair-raising Hill Climb Techniques

During the sixties, Jeep competitive events became popular. Organized hill climbs attracted large crowds, and the winning formula was traction, torque and solid driving skill. A Jeep needed enough muscle to claw its way up a rocky shale slope. Exotic traction tires and axle locking devices increased the chances of a win. Here, many of us learned the finer points of high-horsepower traction.

Most hill climb courses were remarkably steep. In some of my archival photos from that era, course-side judges stand with one leg a foot and a half higher than the other, leaning into the hillside to stay upright. Walking these hills was nearly impossible. Most slopes were simply crude cuts by a D-8 Caterpillar crawler tractor at its maximum grade angle. Some courses were even more primitive.

Modified Jeep F-134s, conversion V-8s, Buick V-6s, Pontiac slant fours and Chevy II four-bangers screamed at redline as these Jeep CJs charged the hill. The winner was the Jeep in each class (four-cylinder, V-6 or V-8 conversion) that reached the highest point on the hill.

The axles, clawing through paddle tires and spinning mercilessly, would grab whatever bite of traction the rocky hillside could furnish. Often, judges leaped out of the path of an airborne muscle Jeep that left the ground under full power and landed forty feet off the course with its nose end still aimed uphill and a wide open throttle jerking the frame into line again!

The risk of getting sideways was extreme. Jeeps would turn 90 degrees and promptly roll several times on their way down. Helmeted drivers, dazed and smiling through mouthfuls of gritty dirt, waved and signaled to the crowd that all was okay. Lowbed trailers lugged off the bashed and twisted Jeep, its frame tweaked and cracked, puking coolant and every other variety of liquid to the pavement.

> *WARNING —*
> *Competitive Jeep hill climbing is a hazardous sport. Damage to your vehicle and personal injury are real possibilities. Like other forms of competition, rules and safety regulations apply. Never attempt these competitive maneuvers without the benefit of a full roll cage, approved safety equipment, emergency medical personnel, close supervision and full acceptance of the risks involved.*

Fig. 3-13. *Competitive hill climbs and sand drags demand nerves of steel and lightning reflexes. Drag racing in loose sand requires four-wheel drive. Hill climbs prove equally challenging. Many hill climb 4x4s go home in pieces.*

Of all the driving techniques I gleaned from hill climbs, the most significant was the means for maintaining control of a tractionless Jeep on a steep slope. The trick is to reverse gears and back down, braking strictly by engine compression and avoiding the use of hydraulic wheel brakes. This is a critical maneuver that demands quick hands and feet. As soon as the truck reaches its furthest point on the hill and traction ceases, you must depress the clutch pedal quickly and simultaneously shift the transmission to reverse—then release the clutch pedal before the truck starts to roll backward.

Timing is critical. If you miss reverse and the transmission is in neutral, you will roll backward out of control. (The non-synchromesh reverse gear in a manual transmission will not permit a shift to reverse with the truck moving.) Stuck in neutral, the remaining option is to use the brakes, most often a disastrous move. Applied on a steep and loose slope, the brakes will lock up the wheels, which readily throws the Jeep into a skid. This can swing the truck sideways and cause a roll over.

The important steps are to: 1) shift your manual transmission to reverse just as the truck peaks its forward momentum, 2) release the clutch pedal immediately and steer straight backward with the engine idling, and 3) rely on engine compression braking with minimal, if any, application of the wheel brakes as you descend the hill. These steps must take place in rapid succession, and if your coordination and the engine tune are right, compression braking will provide a crawl speed in reverse.

Pitfalls of an Automatic Transmission

Jeep hill climbs teach another lesson. Trucks with automatic transmissions have extreme liabilities when hill climbing and in several other off-pavement environments. Although a torque converter helps multiply torque for hill and sand assaults, backing down slopes in reverse is a hazard. With the engine idling or stalled, the torque converter slips, acting much like neutral. This encourages use of the brakes as vehicle speed increases, and that's when trouble begins. Application of the brakes locks the wheels. When the wheels skid, the truck may turn sideways, and the Jeep could roll over.

Anyone who's witnessed a Jeep hill climb can appreciate the value of a manual transmission and quick reflexes. An automatic transmission has many advantages, including good throttle control and torque application in sand, predictable pulling in mud and tremendous torque for going up reasonable hills that don't require backing down. If, however, your plans include negotiating serious downslopes under compression or backing down hills with the engine braking in reverse, consider the superior control of a manual transmission and clutch.

Low Environmental Impact

The popularity of four-wheeling has an effect on the environment. TREAD LIGHTLY, Inc. and other organizations encourage low-impact four-wheeling and respectful use of public lands. Although the concept is new to some recreationalists, many of us have been treading lightly for decades.

In the summer of 1964, I attended Nevada Range Camp, a 4-H/USDA Extension Service project for high school students. Fifteen miles south of U.S. Highway 50 near Austin, Nevada, our base was the Reese River Valley at Big Creek. We studied erosion and other soil conservation matters, witnessed the planting of wild wheat over a vast semi-arid mountain range and discussed the fragile nature of desert environments.

If only the whole four-wheeling crowd could experience such a school! We drove forty additional miles of dirt road to the Reese River Reservation ranches and learned firsthand how Native American people apply their knowledge of the land to cattle ranching. (We also caught fourteen-inch untamed

Fig. 3-14. *Restore the soil when you've been stuck. Treading lightly requires back-filling holes to leave the path intact for future four-wheelers and other users.*

Fig. 3-15. *Should you cross? Not if there's a bridge nearby! Aware four-wheelers always take the easier route, the one that leaves the least impact on the land. There's plenty of opportunity for high adventure along more primitive trails. Save your Jeep for those places.*

Tread Lightly! Four Wheeling

TREAD LIGHTLY!, Inc. is a unique organization. Through the efforts of Clifford G. Blake, a U.S. Forest Service manager and long-standing advocate of multiple-use policy, TREAD LIGHTLY!, Inc. became the first joint public/private sector venture aimed at recreational use of public lands. As National Coordinator of the U.S. Forest Service Tread Lightly program, Cliff's vision encouraged the major manufacturers of motor vehicles and outdoor recreational equipment to take a direct role in promoting environmentally sound use of public lands.

Members of today's TREAD LIGHTLY!, Inc., a non-profit organization, include many domestic and import vehicle manufacturers, outdoor equipment manufacturers, 4WD aftermarket component suppliers, the outdoor and four-wheel drive media, tire producers, 4WD clubs and associations, environmental groups and interested individuals.

Chrysler's Jeep Corporation is a major TREAD LIGHTLY! sponsor, contributing funds and the sponsor/participation of creative personnel. Steven C. Klein, then head of Jeep Marketing, served as the first chairman of the non-profit TREAD LIGHTLY! organization.

TREAD LIGHTLY! works closely with the U.S. Forest Service and the BLM at promoting wise multiple use of public lands. It is the aim of members to use, and not abuse, the environment.

I, too, am a Charter Member of TREAD LIGHTLY! Like other concerned four-wheel drive enthusiasts, I devote energy to the low-impact advocacy programs of TREAD LIGHTLY!, Inc. Our aim is to preserve the environment and access to trails that generations of four-wheeling families can enjoy. As an active member, I encourage outdoor recreationalists to join TREAD LIGHTLY, Inc., and help make a difference! (In the United States, phone 1-800-966-9900 for membership details.)

The TREAD LIGHTLY Creed

T–ravel only where motorized vehicles are permitted. Never blaze your own trail.

R–espect the rights of hikers, skiers, campers, and others to enjoy their activities undisturbed.

E–ducate yourself by obtaining travel maps and regulations from public agencies, complying with signs and barriers and asking owners' permission to cross private property.

A–void streams, lakeshores, meadows, muddy roads and trails, steep hillsides, wildlife and livestock.

D–rive responsibly to protect the environment and preserve opportunities to enjoy your vehicle on wild lands.

Also, when it comes to trail etiquette, remember hikers and horses! Your Jeep kicks up dust, makes noise and raises terror in the eyes of unsuspecting people and horses. If you sense that hikers or horseback riders might be nearby, slow down. Show courtesy, pass with caution and be considerate. The only way we'll maintain access to the wilds is through shared cooperation. There's plenty of fun for everyone, and you know, sometimes it's okay to take a healthy walk!

trout from a yardstick wide feeder stream carrying spring snow melt into the Reese River.)

For my low impact four-wheeling habits, I am indebted to Nevada ranchers, the Bureau of Land Management, the USDA/U.S. Forest Service and Native Americans. Neither I nor any of my four-wheeling friends have ever torn up sagebrush, left livestock gates open or blazed our own trails across a fragile landscape.

Beyond the few bad apples who consciously destroy the environment by churning their tires on sensitive hillsides and fragile aquatic eco-systems, many 4x4 owners simply have no knowledge of how to four-wheel. Unaware of either the natural environment or their four-wheel drive trucks, naive recreationalists abuse their expensive equipment and our land.

3. Special Uses for Your Jeep 4WD

Your Jeep 4x4 system can perform a multitude of useful chores. One of the most gratifying aspects of four-wheel drive trucks is their utility value and ability to serve the community. In the wake of accidents, when weather strands motorists and where emergency vehicles are the only stock still rolling, a Jeep often leads the way.

You will undoubtedly enrich your four-wheeling experience by helping other motorists. A Jeep owner is duty bound to serve, much like a Canadian Royal Mounted Police officer. When the sleet and cold terrify lost motorists, or sheet ice has stacked passenger cars into ditches alongside the highway, your Jeep, a Thermos full of hot coffee and a toasty heater can be a welcome sight!

Many Jeep owners carry this responsibility even further, joining local Search and Rescue organizations.

Fig. 3-16. *Your Jeep 4WD is a serious emergency vehicle. Equipped with a C.B. radio, a winch, winch accessories, a Hi-Lift jack and a Max tool kit, your Jeep can assist stranded motorists. If you enjoy community service, consider joining a local Search and Rescue unit.*

Fig. 3-17. *A snow plow converts your Jeep into a versatile utility truck. Make certain your chassis has necessary modifications to handle the added weight of a snow plow.*

Volunteer firefighters who live in rough weather climates usually own 4x4 trucks, as their responsibilities demand readiness, regardless of weather conditions.

Snow Plowing and Utility Uses

Commercial users have always appreciated Jeep 4x4 trucks. A front-mounted snowplow is a common accessory for parking lot owners, ski lodges and even private residences where steep driveways become a hazard during the winter months. Today's TJ Wrangler equipped with a genuine Jeep Accessories snow plow kit carries forth a long tradition.

Jeep 4x4s spent the immediate postwar years building dams, accessing minesites and enhancing the productivity of American farms and ranches. In many of these environments, the Jeep became a standard piece of equipment, capable of moving materials into tight access areas along rough and hazardous roads. For modern society, the Jeep replaced the pack mule as a beast of burden.

Some of the more popular accessories that developed from the postwar boom in Jeep 4x4 use included PTO operated winches and posthole diggers, plows, harrow discs and auxiliary lighting. More recently, electric winches and on-board welders continue the Jeep's tradition as a workhorse.

The transition to recreational use has made the Jeep more manageable and comfortable. Today, aftermarket accessories emphasize handling, increased stowage, comfortable rear seating and personalized items that meet the recreational needs of owners. Despite the trend toward cosmetic appeal, the underlying Jeep 4x4 remains the same. When the wind howls, temperatures drop below zero and visibility shrinks, every motorist is glad to see a Jeep 4WD truck on the road.

Advanced Trail Running

Faced with temptation, a hill that rises into the pastel sky or a washed out trail that accesses a favorite fishing hole, my friend, Al Herndon, simply shrugs his shoulders and says, "You use two-wheel drive until you get stuck... Then you lock your hubs, shift into 4-wheel drive, and back out!"

Sage advice, Al. Four-wheelers, however, often scorn such practicality. Sometimes Nature provides surprises. Sand that appears hard suddenly sinks your Jeep to its frame. Nicely frozen tracks through a bog at dawn give no hint of the underlying mud soup that will churn like homemade butter by mid-morning. Last year's solid road, now ripped by torrential flooding and muddy rock slides, lies ahead—you still need to get through safely, with your cargo intact.

Veteran four-wheelers will agree, the easiest route through an area is the best one. Long before trails had difficulty classifications, four-wheelers scanned hillsides, washes, streams, and rock piles, sizing up the terrain. Many mountains from home, the challenge is to not get stuck. A C.B. radio, cell phone and a winch become logical companions for rough country travel.

Plan your trip in advance. Read road and trail conditions on a map or call the local Forest Service or BLM office for road reports. Aside from getting stuck, the number-one fear of all four wheelers, and justifiably so, is a roll over. Twisty, off-camber hillsides and slippery mountain trails have totalled many 4x4s, and the best means for avoiding a roll over is careful consideration of terrain.

Three conditions characterize most roll overs: 1) the vehicle faces too much side angle, which overcomes the truck's center of gravity and equilibrium; 2) a shift of weight upsets equilibrium on an otherwise negotiable sideslope; or 3) exaggerated speed, in any situation, compromises stability. This last point relates to off-camber side slopes, speeding around curves, or flirting with danger on casual 4x4 terrain by adding the element of excess speed.

Unfortunately, many four-wheelers, especially newcomers to the art of off-pavement driving, confuse "sport" with "speed." These two terms are not synonymous. Safe recreational trail driving is a far cry from desert racing. My writing colleague and friend, "Ironman" Ivan Stewart, is the master of fast desert travel on four wheels. He and other professional racers would

Fig. 3-18. *Plan ahead! What was solid frozen ground in the morning may be impassable mud by the time you return in the afternoon.*

Driving Through Sand Traps

Imagine a road, not just your ordinary fire road or graded gravel road, but a trail that winds through rugged high desert country. Ahead is the sandy wash, that dry riverbed of deep, loose sand. In flood season, a race of water tears through the steep walled canyon, swirling around tall rocks that now bake under the summer sun....

Since the ancients first rotated stone wheels, the number one obstacle to travel has been sand. Granular, loose and deceptive, sand operates by its own rules. When monsoons or summer rains saturate the ground, sand can be hard, packed, and tractable. In dry weather, however, the same material can defy even the best flotation tires.

For traveling loose sand, the best hope is steady forward momentum while keeping wheel spin to a minimum. The slightest amount of traction loss is sand's victory. Once wheels lose their grip, especially at both axles, the going gets tough.

Begin with basics. Lock your Jeep's hubs before entering the wash. Engage your four-wheel drive system, and if the load is great, use low range. High flotation tires also make a difference when negotiating sand. (See equipment chapter.)

Moving forward, you can feel the traction and load on the engine. (When I was an apprentice heavy equipment operator, old hands taught that you can feel the cutting depth of a dozer or grader blade in the seat of your pants!) Maintain a steady roll and concentrate on constant throttle pressure with a firm control of the steering wheel.

Suppose that your engine coughs as you bump a smooth rock, and the Jeep momentarily bogs. As the clutch re-engages, the truck strains forward. The tires begin to spin. In a few seconds, your Jeep 4x4 lies buried to the frame at the rear wheels and down to the springs at the front.

What now? If you're alone without a winch, the tool of choice is a "handyman jack," shown above. These tall, industrial strength setups can be used for a variety of chores: pushing, pulling or lifting. (In combination with chain or cable, a Hi-Lift jack can also serve as a "come-along.") A hefty board is usually necessary for a firm jack footing. Jack up each wheel and safely back fill the holes with sand. Place pieces of brush under and in front of the tires. Avoid spinning the tires and apply power smoothly.

quickly discourage fast driving in sensitive and uncertain environments, especially in a production vehicle.

For most recreationalists, safe and methodical trail driving proves challenging enough. This includes driving over rocky, slippery, sandy, snow-covered and mountainous terrain, safely getting your family, friends and 4x4s through tough trails.

4. Jeep Clubs

Bats darted through the treetops, silhouetted in azure-gold twilight. As our youngest son slept soundly in his bedroll, my wife stared warily across the campfire. "Moses," she asked, "why do we persist in traveling alone? Isn't there some way to have four-wheel drive fun short of re-enacting a Paleolithic vision quest?"

As the raccoon clan finished its unabashed parade past our campfire, my thoughts raced back to 1967. It was summer then, too, and nine rugged 4x4s rolled in a caravan from Miller Lake toward the trailhead leading into the Rubicon Springs. The formidable Sluice Box, rising westward above the Rubicon River, would be our Sunday morning run after a night's rest, campfire breakfast and an engine warm-up.

Without ceremony, our eclectic group of rugged individualists, nature lovers and 4x4 family fun-seekers were on a Rubicon Run. Ahead, in the makeshift back seat of a Jeep CJ-2A from Concord, California, two small children bounced happily.

For most of us, a Jeep four-cylinder engine was plenty, as none would leave low range for the next day and a half. Winches, four-wheelers with solid mechanical expertise and a full complement of survival equipment made that trip both fun and safe, with plenty of smiles and a steady trickle of adrenaline.

Those responsible four-wheelers, folks with scores of fireside tales to share beneath pine boughs and starlight at Rubicon Springs, were members of the Diablo Four Wheelers from Concord, California. Under the wise leadership of the club's president, Stan Johnson, we four-wheeled, camped, cooked, played, swam in icy lakes and turned our collective trail skills into a treasure of fine memories.

Why Go It Alone?

A lone driver attempting the Rubicon or other rough trails is always at risk. Such trails tax driving skill and vehicle stamina to the maximum. If the situation gets out of hand, a solo four-wheeler places himself, or herself, and passengers in real danger. Group travel provides vital safeguards and assurances.

Aside from safer passage, traveling as a group adds several other benefits: social activities, fun competitive

Fig. 3-19. *This Jeep owner faced a major crisis in the Rubicon. Alone, without a welder, he had no means except a makeshift chain bind for reattaching the truck's steering box to the frame! When we found him, he had driven only 150 yards in 2-1/2 hours! At this rate, imagine how much fuel and time it would take to go the rest of the six miles out.*

events and a place to build life-long friendships with those who share your appreciation for outdoor recreation. Additionally, many local, state, and national 4x4 groups serve as lobbyists for our access to public recreational lands.

What Does a 4x4 Club Do?

My wife, Donna, is a prolific reader who often shoves clippings and news briefs under my nose. "Look at this copy of IN GEAR that you grabbed at the SCORE Show. Every off road thing that we're interested in doing is covered here!" she exclaimed, rifling through the California Association of 4WD Clubs' periodical publication. "The calendar of events lists several runs and family outings that we've already talked about."

IN GEAR and publications like United's Voice, printed quarterly by the United Four-Wheel Drive Associations, Inc., brim with calendar events and news-worthy reports of 4x4 club activities throughout the United States. These and other four-wheel drive publications can broaden your Jeep contacts.

The regional publications include activities suited to entire families, off road survival tips, equipment ads, vehicle classifieds, accounts of trail rides, poker runs, 4x4 breakfast runs and group barbecues. A calendar of fund-raising benefits, public interest projects, social functions and future runs helps the members organize their time.

Fig. 3-20. *The 1988 Jeep Cup Championship near Toronto, Ontario ranks among my memorable Jeep experiences. Chrysler/Jeep sponsored the event, assembling the dozens of competitors from regional competitions in the U.S. and Canada. The camaraderie, spirit of competition and hospitality made a lasting impression.*

How to Find a Club or Regional 4WD Association

For newcomers to four-wheeling, clubs are an ideal way to learn safe driving skills and how to tread lightly on the land. Regional sanctioning associations promote family recreation, publish newsletters and encourage clubs to protect trails and sponsor local activities.

If four-wheeling with a group of outdoor enthusiasts is your kind of good time, contact your state or regional association of 4x4 clubs. Usually, better organized local clubs have membership in the association. The umbrella over all regional, state and locally sanctioned clubs is United Four-Wheel Drive Associations (UFWDA). UFWDA can provide guidelines for forming your own four-wheel drive group or provide referrals to regional associations and local clubs.

> NOTE —
> UFWDA
> 4505 W. 700 S.
> Shelbyville, IN 46176-9678
> Phone: 1-800-44-UFWDA
> Fax: 1-317-729-5930
> E-mail: www.ufwda.org

There are liabilities that accompany any vehicle owner's association, more yet for a group involved with 4WD activities. Charters and by-laws should follow established guidelines. State and regional associations or UFWDA can furnish advice to prospective clubs.

Anatomy of a Club Run

Sponsored by the Central District of CA4WDC, the Molina Ghost Run near Coalinga, California draws folks from as far away as Nevada and Oregon. Local legends and mining lore encourage a "Fright Night" run on opening night each year.

Most four-wheelers enter the dry camp (situated just below New Idria and halfway between Hernandez Reservoir and Coalinga) by way of Los Gatos Road. Some drive from the Highway 101 side of the mountains, winding down from Hollister, Ca. Those arriving early enough on Friday have a chance to join the Fright Night 4x4 trek through the surrounding hills.

Hundreds of participants arrive late Friday, setting up their camps after registering. Motorhomes and camper pickups serve as tow vehicles for the short wheelbase Jeep 4x4s. A trend has developed, with older Jeep CJs and military models outnumbering all other trail running rigs.

Friday night, as registrants fill up the dry camping area, a live band plays. This is not the night to party, though, and most campers prepare for the early run on

Mark Smith: Trailmaster of the Jeep Jamboree

Since 1952, Mark Smith has organized annual Jeep Jamborees along the Sierra's tough Rubicon Trail. Now an internationally recognized 4x4 event, the Rubicon Jeep Jamboree ranks as the most challenging of the many annual Jeep Jamboree runs sponsored by Chrysler's Jeep Corporation.

Mark Smith embodies the spirit of four-wheeling. In 1979, he and six other men headed out with seven stock CJ-7 Jeep trucks equipped with optional T-18 four speed transmissions and 258 in-line six-cylinder engines. The Jeeps and drivers triumphed over a gruelling route from Tierra del Fuego to Prudhoe Bay, Alaska.

En route, the Jeep 4x4s faced every conceivable obstacle, including the Darien Gap, a roadless hellhole of jungle that chokes off lower Panama. Within the Gap, a whole day's progress was as little as 500 feet!

A crew of machete-wielding road builders made it possible for Smith's group to cross the 200 mile Darien Gap in 21 days. Between Tierra del Fuego and icy Prudhoe Bay, Alaska, each Jeep's odometer clocked 21,000 miles.

Mark Smith brings many years of experience to the Jeep Jamboree events. Conducting classes, overseeing trail selections and making sure that participants have a good time, Mark promotes safe family four-wheeling.
For information on the Jeep Jamboree contact:
Mark A. Smith Off-Roading, Inc.
P.O. Box 1601
Georgetown, California 95634
Phone: (916) 333-4338

Fig. 3-21. *How do you feed 600 hungry four-wheelers? In style! CA4WDC/Central District clubs serve steak, corn on the cob, chili, beverages and—what? Haagen Daz ice cream in a dry camp? Hardly roughin' it!*

Saturday morning. Sleep proves elusive, as a steady procession of late arrivals rumble into camp until the wee hours. (Camping with many hundreds of people is hardly a place to catch up on your sleep!)

Saturday morning, staff lines the registered vehicles up for the day run. A "poker game" mixes with the travel. Each checkpoint en route provides a "card," with a poker hand building as the run proceeds. A long procession of vehicles eventually snakes the hills, yet everyone shares equally in the spectacular view and excitement.

As the scenes from higher peaks reveal a breathtaking California spring, the participants unwind. The Molina Run's main attraction is the Saturday tour into the hills west of the San Joaquin Valley. These same hills inspired the early California settlers and, later, the prose of John Steinbeck. Tall grass and brush sweep the region from February through mid-April. Traditionally, the Molina Run takes place in mid-March.

The last vehicles return to camp as the sky darkens. A major evening of fun will follow the best tasting dinner a herd of trail beaten and hungry four wheelers can imagine. Steak, beans, corn-on-the-cob, rolls, Haagen Daz ice cream and hot or cold beverages puts smiles on everyone's face.

The Central District's chefs and staff spend the whole day preparing this meal, and it shows. The horde of altitude-teased appetites really appreciate the effort. CA4WDC volunteers serve selflessly to assure the success of the Molina event. Certainly, anyone who's eaten a Molina Run barbecue dinner, or the hot eggs and sausage on Sunday morning, has gone home happy.

Saturday night is sheer fun and relaxation. After a long trip to reach Molina and pounding the ridgetops all day, four wheelers are ready for the live band. With liquor sanctions lifted for the evening, many adults imbibe the spirits, yet everyone follows the rules faithfully: NO DRINKING AND DRIVING ALLOWED!—just dancing and meandering back to your campsite when the night winds down.

Sunday breakfast precedes the vehicle show and a unique event—4x4 Trials Competition. The trials event is somewhat new to West Coast four wheelers and has begun to attract a following through the efforts of the Molina Run staff. The Central District

folks see that everyone remembers the contests, providing nice trophies, true mantelpiece stuff!

The Molina Run takes all ages into consideration. Each participant, including the smaller children, has plenty of fun. New friendships develop, campfire camaraderie runs high and the next year's event becomes the main topic of discussion before the weekend winds to an end. CA4WDC's Central District has earned wide recognition for its efforts.

Chapter 4

Working On Your Jeep

You will find your Jeep four-wheel drive truck easy to service. Quick access to components and sub-assemblies simplifies routine maintenance, while the Jeep's utilitarian design makes field fixes possible. Many owners learn the basics of automotive repair by working on their 4x4 Jeep.

Early CJ models and 4x4 Jeep trucks have uncomplicated chassis, powertrain and accessory assemblies. Although post-'71 4x4 Jeep trucks have more engine emission controls and power options, the basic Jeep design remains. Even later CJ or modern Wrangler models, despite boxing of frame rails, maintain a similarity to the early CJ-2A, CJ-3A and CJ-3B chassis.

Early Willys Pickup and Station Wagon models share many chassis and powertrain details with the CJs and 4x4 Jeepsters. Although the J-truck, full-size (Grand) Wagoneer and full-size Cherokee ride on larger frames and heavier axles, common Jeep engineering still applies.

1. The Jeep Chassis

Like the WWII Jeep, all CJ models, the Wrangler, J-trucks and the full-size Wagoneer/Cherokee feature

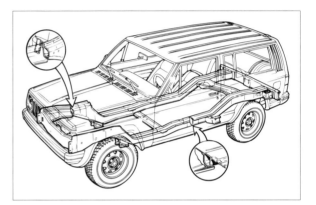

Fig. 4-2. *The compact Jeep Cherokee was AMC's ultimate success story. Unibody construction appeared for the first time in a domestic 4x4 truck. AMC's Eagle car laid the engineering groundwork.*

ladder frames. The compact XJ Cherokee/Wagoneer, Comanche pickup, ZJ/WJ Grand Cherokee and ZJ (mid-size) Grand Wagoneer have a unitized body/chassis, essentially a heavy gauge sheet metal frame made integral with the body.

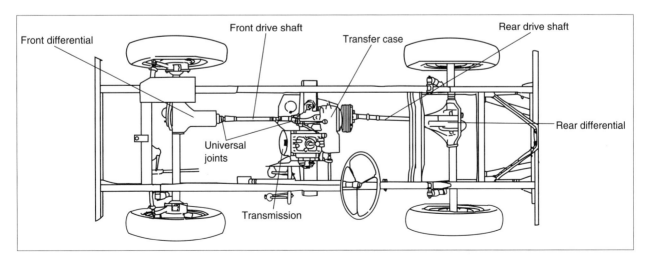

Fig. 4-1. *A conventional ladder frame has assured Jeep truck stamina on CJs, full-size trucks and Wranglers. De-scribed as a "driveable chassis" design, the rugged ladder frame supports the suspension, body and powertrain.*

Fig. 4-3. *All Jeep utility 4x4s from 1941 MB and early CJ-2A to the present TJ Wrangler have a ladder frame. Largest chassis change came with 1997 introduction of link-and-coil spring suspension. TJ chassis (foreground) still bears striking resemblance to YJ Wrangler and previous utility Jeep frame layouts. Leaf springs versus the TJ's coil springs/link arms serve as primary difference.*

Fig. 4-4. *Early Jeep trucks provide plenty of grease fittings. Use of bronze spring-shackle bushings requires periodic service with chassis lubricant. Newer models have rubber bushings and require less maintenance.*

Commonly described as a "driveable chassis," the ladder frame has several advantages. On most American trucks, these strong chassis help avoid the perils of body rust and fatigue. A restorer will often replace the entire rusty body tub of an older military or CJ model yet find the original frame intact and fully functional.

From a service standpoint, the ladder frame requires little maintenance. Support members, such as spring and shock absorber anchor mounts, attach solidly to the frame. Although early model Jeep spring shackles require periodic lubrication, the actual frame is maintenance-free. Aside from periodic power washing and/or brushing away the surface scale and debris, an undamaged frame seldom needs more than paint and undercoating.

Springs and Axles: All Models

All Jeep models prior to the compact Cherokee/Wagoneer and Comanche pickup feature a semi-elliptic leaf spring at each wheel. The XJ Cherokee/Wagoneer and Comanche, as well as the mid-size Grand Cherokee/Grand Wagoneer, have Quadra Link front suspension with coil springs and a solid axle. A TJ Wrangler has link and coil spring suspension with solid axles fore and aft. Hotchkiss-design rear axles are common on all Jeep 4x4 trucks. Every Jeep 4WD model, including the stylized '99–up WJ Grand Cherokee, has a live (solid housing) front axle.

A leaf spring anchors at one end and has a swinging shackle at the opposite end. During suspension movement, the shackle swings fore and aft. Early Jeep spring shackles feature grease fittings and replaceable bronze bushings. Later leaf spring models, with rubber spring bushings, require less periodic maintenance.

Live Axles

On all pre-XJ and Wrangler Jeep models, the live front axle is of full-floating design. Rear axles for various Jeep models are either full- or semi-floating type. (MB military models feature similar Spicer full-floating type axles front and rear, the front axle equipped with steering knuckles.) All civilian CJ models have semi-floating rear axles. Except for the heavier payload FC170 dual rear wheel model and the J-trucks equipped with a full-floating Dana 60 or 70 rear axle, every other Jeep truck has a semi-floating rear axle.

Full-floating front axles provide a distinct advantage for off-road and heavy duty service. If the axle shaft fails, the full-floating wheel hub continues to sup-

Fig. 4-5. *Full-floating axle provides wheel support in the event of an axle shaft failure. All earlier trucks and CJs boast full-floating front axles. MB military model was the only lightweight Jeep truck to offer a full-floating rear axle. FC170 dual rear wheel models and the heavier duty J-trucks also used full-floating rear axles.*

port the wheel and tire assembly. Although power delivery may be lost, the truck is usually driveable.

> *WARNING —*
> *Since a broken axle shaft or joint could impair steering and cause further axle damage, remove the axle shaft assembly before moving the vehicle.*

Jeep models feature three distinct live front axle designs. Early models boast closed-knuckle steering joints. Sealed, ball-shaped castings extend from the axle tubes and provide a cavity for oiling the enclosed axle shaft joint. Later models feature open-knuckle live axles, with ball-stud steering knuckle pivots. Here, the axle shaft, visible between the end of the axle tube and the knuckle, features a cross-type joint to permit steering.

The open-knuckle joint requires less maintenance, provides less trouble, and affords tighter turner angles.

Fig. 4-6. *Jeep 4x4s had closed knuckle front axles (top) for years. The CJ models changed to the open knuckle Dana 30 axle (bottom) in the '70s, following an industry trend. Wranglers use a semi-floating version of this axle with a part-time 4x4 axle shaft disconnect mechanism.*

Earlier, closed knuckle axles develop seal leaks and suffer chronic loss of grease. Also, the shimmed kingpin bearings on early axles require tedious adjustment, making service more complex.

Part-time 4x4 Axle Disconnect Systems

Wranglers and compact 4x4s feature an open-knuckle semi-floating axle with an axle disconnect system. Although energy flow between the wheels and transfer case ceases in the two-wheel drive mode, segments of the front axle shafts and differential still spin. Unlike the full free-wheeling mode of earlier manual locking hub models, this later design allows continuous parts movement within the front differential mechanism, axle shafts and axle shaft joints.

Overall, the hypoid (solid) live axle design and conventional chassis engineering have assured Jeep's high rate of reliability. Although Kaiser's Jeep Corporation used a troublesome independent front suspension (IFS) system on some early J-trucks and Wagoneers, all other Jeep 4x4s, including the compact XJ and mid-size ZJ/WJ models, have adhered to traditional solid axle engineering.

Steering Gear and Linkage

Early Jeep CJs feature very basic steering systems. A Ross cam-and-lever design steering gear, with a fore and aft pivoting steering arm, attaches to the frame. The drag-link connects this steering arm with a bellcrank. Prior to the CJ-2A models, the bellcrank attached to the axle housing, while four-cylinder and early V-6 equipped CJs have the bellcrank attached at the frame.

Beginning with the 4x4 Jeepster/Commando and later V-6 CJ models, a one piece tie-rod and forward

Fig. 4-7. *The steering bellcrank, common on all light military and CJ models, affects steering control. In restoring an early Jeep truck, check the bellcrank for excess play and replace parts as needed.*

mounted steering gear eliminate the need for a bellcrank. Much improved General Motors-built Saginaw steering gears also came into Jeep models during the Kaiser era, their recirculating ball design drastically reducing both wear and steering effort. The Jeep steering system continued to improve with the option

Fig. 4-8. *Early Jeep models have Ross cam-and-lever steering. Weakness of this design is high friction between lever studs and the spiral cam groove. These gears wear more rapidly, resulting in wander and reduced steering control.*

Fig. 4-9. *Key to GM's Saginaw success is the recirculating ball-and-nut design. The precisely machined worm shaft groove acts as an inner half of the ball bearing race, while the nut provides the matching groove. Reduced friction provides ease of steering and longer service life.*

of Saginaw power steering on Jeepster/Commando models and the AMC Jeep CJs.

Early J-trucks and Wagoneers benefit from Ross' worm-and-gear type steering units, a somewhat better design than the cam-and-lever gears found in CJ models. Full-size Jeep trucks also feature one piece tie-rods. By the 1970s, all models acquired the superior Saginaw manual and power gears. Saginaw steering gears have proven more reliable than any other system. These recirculating ball steering gears have, at one time or another, appeared in every make of American truck.

Fig. 4-10. *Saginaw integral power steering (shown here on a 1981 CJ) has a worldwide reputation for superior service and durability. Hoses run from the top of the gear to an engine mounted pump.*

2. Drum and Disc Brake Systems

Jeep braking systems consist of a hydraulic master cylinder feeding brake fluid through pipes and high strength brake hose to each wheel cylinder or disc caliper. Pedal pressure actuates the master cylinder piston (dual pistons on tandem master cylinders), causing brake fluid to flow.

Typical Jeep drum brake systems have one hydraulic cylinder per wheel. These cylinders have twin, opposing pistons that move outward as fluid under pressure enters the cylinder. Depending upon the model and brake type, Jeep drum brakes apply pressure via several methods, each design described generically as "self-energizing." (Self-energizing brakes, with shoes anchored at one end, utilize the rotational force of the drum to force a brake shoe, or the pair of shoes, more firmly against the braking surface of the drum.)

Overall, the earlier Jeep CJ brake systems are inferior to later designs. Weaker 9" double-anchor-pin brakes were common through the mid-'60s, with 10" x

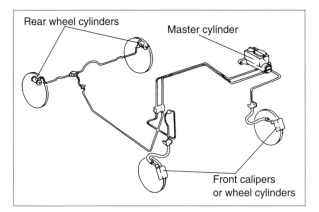

Fig. 4-11. *The Jeep braking system is similar to all American truck designs. A pedal actuated master cylinder forces fluid into each of the hydraulic wheel cylinders or front disc brake calipers. Brake shoes or pads act against the drums or rotors.*

Fig. 4-12. *Stopping on pre-'72 CJ Jeeps benefits from an 11" brake conversion. The 11" x 2" brakes at each wheel offer safer, fade-resistant braking action. Factory (OEM) 11" brakes on '72 to early '77 CJs worked well.*

2" brakes first appearing on model C101 Jeepsters and some '66 CJs. The tiny 9" x 1-3/4" shoes found on earlier CJs and military models provide little resistance to fade and a meager surface area for hard stops or carrying a load.

Until the early 1970s, all domestic 4x4 trucks featured drum brakes at each wheel. Disc front brakes found their way into Jeep Wagoneers and J-trucks by the mid-'70s. CJ models switched during the 1977–78 model runs. Disc front/drum rear braking provides superior control and a wider margin of safety.

Disc brakes offer several advantages, including resistance to fade, quicker recovery after exposure to water and ease of service. Easier maintenance and overhaul make disc brakes popular with Jeep owners.

American truck builders often rely on outside sources for brake parts. Willys, Kaiser, and AMC, due to small production volume, obtained brake hardware in this manner. Even Chrysler sources brake hardware from Bendix and other suppliers. For this reason, Jeep brake system layout and service are familiar and straightforward.

Emergency Brake

The Jeep CJ parking brakes also improved after 1971. On 1972 and newer models, the emergency/parking brake system activates the rear brake shoes and drums. Earlier models with the Spicer 18 transfer case depend upon an emergency brake assembly (drum type) mounted at the transfer case output flange. When applied, this brake prevents rotation of the rear propeller shaft, differential and axle shafts.

This kind of early Jeep parking brake, common to CJs and Willys Pickup/Station Wagon models, was no-

toriously vulnerable to damage from seeping transfer case oil and road debris. The limited surface area of the emergency brake drum and shoe lining provided marginal braking at best.

Jeep truck braking has improved steadily since 1967. From safer dual braking systems to disc front/drum rear brakes (even four-wheel disc brakes on some current models), Jeep has kept pace with the industry. By the late 1980s, compact XJ Cherokee/Wagoneer models pioneered the first four-wheel anti-lock braking system in the light truck industry. This Bendix system, designed to meet the broad needs of suburban commuter/light off-road users, brought Jeep substantial recognition.

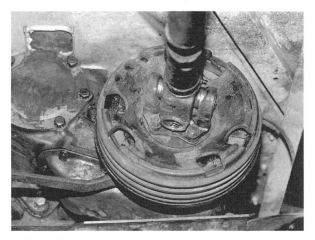

Fig. 4-13. *A mechanical shoe-and-drum mechanism at transfer case output flange provides emergency braking on early Jeep models. When wet, muddy, oil soaked or glazed, these brake mechanisms offer marginal service at best. Later Jeep trucks utilize rear wheel brakes, applied mechanically, for emergencies and parking.*

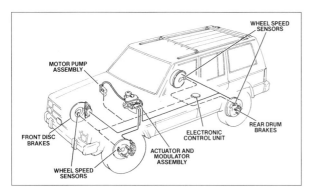

Fig. 4-14. *Jeep's compact Cherokee pioneered four-wheel anti-lock braking (ABS) on American trucks. The Bendix electronic sensor system gives trucks with disc front and drum rear brakes more steering control in a panic stop.*

3. Jeep Engines

Keeping pace with buyer demands, Jeep trucks have provided a wide range of engines, transmissions and powertrains. From the earliest 4x4 models, Jeep has provided users with high torque off-road performance, utility and reliability.

Fours, Sixes and V-8 Power

All Jeeps have liquid-cooled, forward mounted engines. The earliest engine, the four-cylinder L-head 134, appears through the CJ3-A model, with an improved F-head powerplant developed for the CJ3-B and CJ-5/military M38A-1. The F-head, in 72 and 75 horsepower forms, carried the CJ-5, CJ-6 and Jeepster into the AMC/Jeep era.

Early Willys Pickups and Station Wagons use L-head or F-head 134 fours and several L-head six-cylin-

Fig. 4-16. *F-head 134 four, found in CJ-3B, CJ-5 and CJ-6 models, offered larger intake valves in the head and L-134 size exhaust valves in the block. Later version of F-head engines boasts 75 horsepower, 15 more than the original L-head powerplants.*

der engines. Kaiser's L-226 in-line "Hurricane" six provided the best performance of the L-head Jeep six era.

The 230 Tornado Overhead Camshaft engine appeared in the first J-trucks and Wagoneers. A radical departure from previous American truck engine de-

Fig. 4-15. *The L-head 134 engine, a Willys design found in MB through CJ-3A models, positions all eight valves in the block. This painstakingly restored L-134 shows the massive oil bath air cleaner with long intake snorkel.*

Fig. 4-17. *Kaiser introduced the rugged Hurricane 226 L-head six, essentially a Continental design, to Station Wagons and Pickups. These Jeep trucks have provided great service.*

signs, this engine was troublesome and too complex for simple service and overhaul. By the mid-'60s, Kaiser replaced the 230 OHC engine with AMC's economical 232 in-line six. The AMC 327 V-8 became an engine option. (Do not confuse this AMC engine with a Chevrolet 327 V-8. Their only common feature is cubic inch displacement.)

J-trucks and Wagoneers also used the 350 Buick V-8 during the years prior to the AMC takeover. After the 1971 Jeep models, full-size trucks and Wagoneers use AMC 304, 360 and (later) the 401 V-8s. Versions of the durable, seven main bearing 232 and 258 AMC in-line sixes became standard powerplants in each Jeep model line.

Dauntless Buick V-6 And AMC Power

The CJ and Jeepster also utilized a Buick powerplant, the 225 odd-fire V-6. At the end of Kaiser's reign over Jeep Corporation, these powerplants provided ample power and a snappy performance level for smaller Jeep trucks. Following the 1971 models, AMC dropped the V-6, and CJ and Jeepster models offer 232 and 258 AMC in-line sixes, 304 V-8s, and a limited number of remnant F-head fours (through 1973).

Pontiac's 151 four launched Jeep CJs into the economy era of the '80s, followed later by the 2.5L AMC four. The AMC four has served as the CJ, Wrangler and compact XJ Cherokee base engine, with the 258/4.2L six available in all CJ models and Wranglers

Jeep Engine Evolution

Willys L-134 Four Cylinder (Introduced in 1941): Model MB version has chain driven camshaft. 1946 and newer design uses camshaft gears.

Willys F-134 Four Cylinder (1950–73): Introduced with 1950 Pickup trucks and Station Wagon, the 1951 Model M38A1 Military Jeep and 1953 civilian CJ-3B. AMC phased out the F-134 four after 1971 and replaced it with the AMC 232/258 in-line sixes.

Iron Duke (Pontiac-built) 2.5L/151 Cubic Inch OHV Four: Used as base engine in 1980–83 Jeep CJs. Iron Duke has two-barrel GM Rochester carburetion.

2.5L/150 AMC Four Cylinder: First used in 1983 with one barrel carburetor. With introduction of Wrangler in 1987, AMC 2.5L four gains throttle body fuel injection. 1991 and newer engines have multi-point EFI.

Willys L- and F-Head Sixes (1948–56): 148.5 and 161 cubic inch versions fit Station Wagon, Pickup and Jeepster VJ models. These small displacement, low horsepower Jeep engines change from L-head (valve-in-block) to F-head design beginning in 1952.

L-Head Hurricane Six: Originally a 115-horsepower version of Kaiser's 226.2 cubic inch engine. Introduced in 1954 4x4 Utility Truck/Station Wagon chassis. Better performance and reliability make these 1954–64 engines popular.

Kaiser/Jeep Corporation 230 Tornado OHC Six: Advanced in-line overhead camshaft engine used from 1962 through 1965 in Wagoneer and J-trucks. Produces 140 horsepower and 210 lb-ft of torque.

AMC In-line Sixes: Feisty seven main bearing 232 first used in 1965 J-truck/Wagoneer models. In 1971, Jeep trucks offer the 232 and a larger 258 (4.2L) six. 4.2L (carbureted) engine survives through the 1990 Wrangler models. 1987 and newer 4.0L multi-point EFI XJ Cherokee/Comanche

engine is also derivative of 232 design. 1991–up Wrangler benefits from this EFI/MPI 4.0L in-line six (shown).

Buick 225 Dauntless V-6 (1966–71): Officially on line with 1966 CJ models and the new Jeepster, these 160 horsepower engines deliver high performance in lighter utility Jeep models. Odd-fire, shaky idle did not detract from the torque and pulling power of this engine.

327 AMC/Rambler V-8: Introduced in 1965 J-truck/Wagoneer, this is the first V-8 to appear in a Jeep truck. Available through 1968, the 327 powers many J-trucks and Wagoneers. (Despite cubic inch similarity, this stodgy, reasonably torquey AMC 327 in no way resembles the nimbler Chevrolet 327 V-8.)

Buick 350 Vigilante V-8: The Buick 350, found in many 1968–71 J-trucks and Wagoneers, offers excellent performance and a high degree of reliability.

AMC 304/360/401 V-8s: The carbureted 360 AMC engine, available in 1971 and newer Jeep trucks, powers the last full-size Grand Wagoneer (1990). 304 V-8 option powers many 1972–81 CJs, some full-size Wagoneer/Cherokee models and J-trucks. Between 1974 and 1978, some J-trucks, Wagoneers and Cherokees benefit from the much larger 401 V-8 option.

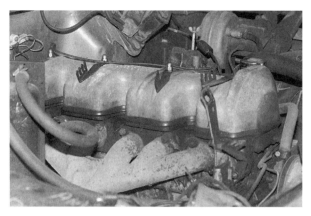

Fig. 4-18. *Kaiser's Jeep Corporation produced the innovative 230 Overhead Camshaft Tornado engine for the first J-trucks and Wagoneers. Too complex and years beyond its time, the Tornado six lasted from 1962–65 in civilian models.*

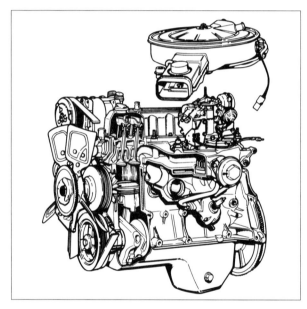

Fig. 4-19. *The eighties began with a shift to smaller displacement engines. Jeep CJ acquired Pontiac's Iron Duke 2.5L four. By 1983, AMC/Jeep provided its own 2.5L engine (shown here).*

through 1990. The XJ Cherokee, offering GM's 2.8L V-6 for a few years, introduced the new AMC 4.0L in-line six in 1987. The 4.0L powerplant provided the first application of multi-point electronic fuel injection in a Jeep truck.

American Motors switched to AMC sixes and V-8s following the purchase of Kaiser's Jeep Corporation. Chrysler, however, avoided the use of its own powerplants until the ZJ (mid-size Grand Cherokee/Grand Wagoneer) 5.2L and 5.9L V-8 options. (The 5.9L Dodge V-8 truck engine seemed a likely can-

didate for use in the last full-size Grand Wagoneers, but Chrysler had plans to phase out the model and left the AMC era features intact.)

The durable AMC 2.5L four and exceptional 4.0L AMC in-line six have proved ideal powerplants for the Wrangler and XJ Cherokee/Comanche models. ZJ/WJ Grand Cherokee models benefit from the base 4.0L engine as well.

4. Transmissions and Transfer Case Units

A wide range of manual and automatic transmissions have been coupled behind Jeep engines. For four-wheel drive, the transmission requires an additional member, a transfer case/power divider, which delivers power to both axles.

The standard Jeep clutch assembly is common to other trucks and automobiles. Spring-type clutch covers of several designs have been used in Jeep models. Each clutch provides the clamping force necessary to press the clutch disc between an engine-driven steel flywheel and the clutch cover face (pressure plate).

A pilot bearing at the rear of the engine crankshaft supports the nose end of a Jeep manual transmission input shaft/clutch gear. The clutch release or throwout bearing rides on the front bearing retainer of the transmission.

Clutch Linkage

Jeep trucks use a variety of clutch linkage types. Cable, cross shaft/rod, and hydraulic designs vary in reliability. Poor linkage design is a major weakness on several Jeep models, including early models with weak and failure-prone cable linkage and various mechanical linkages used on V-8 and six-cylinder CJ models of the AMC era.

The later CJ, Wrangler and compact XJ Cherokee trucks benefit from a hydraulic clutch linkage, a design far more compatible with chassis twist and engine torque flexing. Clutch linkage is an area where close periodic inspection is a necessity. Worn parts usually fail when your Jeep is in a remote, off-pavement environment. (See the service sections for preventive maintenance of Jeep clutch linkage.)

Rugged Automatic Transmissions

Jeep pioneered the use of an automatic transmission on a factory 4x4 truck. In 1962, with the introduction of the J-truck/Wagoneer, a Borg-Warner iron case 3-speed automatic came on line. Later, recognizing the merits of General Motors' new Turbo Hydra-Matic 400, Kaiser introduced the THM 400 to the light 4x4 truck

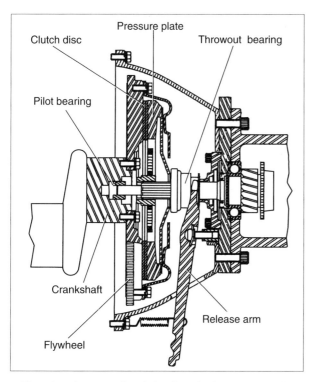

Fig. 4-20. *A conventional clutch and release mechanism characterize most Jeep trucks. The throwout bearing rides on the transmission front bearing retainer and presses against the clutch release fingers during disengagement. A crankshaft mounted pilot bearing centers and supports the input shaft.*

Fig. 4-22. *GM's Turbo 400 was a Jeep truck option for many years. From the mid-sixties to early eighties, Jeep employed this rugged automatic transmission in J-trucks and full-size Wagoneers/Cherokees—and even this lighter CJ-7 with Quadra-Trac.*

market. During each era, Jeep trucks have offered the most durable automatic transmissions available.

Jeep automatic transmissions meet the highest industry standards. Jeep is the only 1/4- through 3/4-ton

Fig. 4-21. *Jeep clutch linkage has been a traditional area of contention. Cable and mechanical linkage designs often fail under severe duty use. This '81 CJ-5 features more reliable OEM hydraulic linkage with a Girling clutch master cylinder. Such linkage came with Iron Duke engine.*

rated 4x4 truck to utilize the GM THM 400 transmission. Even General Motors overlooked this option, offering its lighter THM 350 in both Chevrolet and GMC 4x4s through 3/4-ton capacity.

Chrysler's famous three-speed 727A and lighter 904 and 999 Torqueflite transmissions have also seen service in the Jeep trucks. Earlier CJ-7s used GM's THM 400 transmission coupled to Warner's Quadra-Trac full-time 4x4. Other Jeep trucks have used similar combinations, with later models offering Chrysler's refined four-speed automatic overdrive transmissions. An advanced, high-tech five-speed unit first appears in '99 WJ Grand Cherokees.

Transfer Cases

Traditionally, Jeep transfer case units have attached directly to the rear of the manual or automatic type transmission. The common two-speed transfer unit serves as both a power divider (directing power flow to the front axle) and a means for achieving exceptionally low (Low Range) gearing.

With gear-type part-time 4x4 (the original Jeep transfer case design), the transfer case offers a distinct 2-Wheel drive mode. In two-wheel drive mode, power

Fig. 4-23. *CJ models use several part-time 4x4 transfer cases. The earliest, side-drive design (lower left) is the Model 18 Spicer (1941–71). Through-drive Spicer 20 (V-6 Jeepster models and all 1972–79 CJs) and iron Dana 300 (1980–86) transfer cases offer superior service (upper left and lower right, respectively).*

Fig. 4-24. *Aluminum transfer case for Wrangler is part-time design. Chain drive, lighter weight Command-Trac unit offers low range ratio of 2.72:1. Version shown here, coupled to automatic transmission, fits a '97 TJ.*

Fig. 4-25. *Warner's Quadra-Trac gave Jeep a full-time four wheel drive option in the '70s. Although most American trucks caught criticism for their full-time 4x4 systems, Jeep owners liked the comparatively reliable Quadra-Trac.*

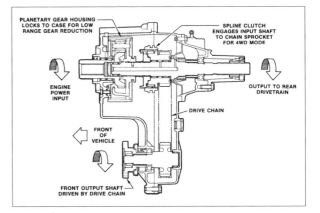

Fig. 4-26. *Command-Trac for the '80s compact XJ Cherokee/Wagoneer four-wheel drive system was actually the New Process 207 transfer case. The GM S-Jimmy/Blazer utilized a similar chain drive, part-time 4x4 system. NP231 transfer case also has similarities.*

flows from the engine through the transmission to the transfer case, then rearward to the rear axle. The front propeller shaft receives no power from the transfer unit.

In 4-Wheel-High or 4-Wheel-Low, power flows through the front and rear driveshafts to each axle. Low range provides a reduction gearset, with a ratio factor between 2:1 and nearly 3:1 (depending upon year and transfer case model application). The transfer case is a crucial part of the Jeep four-wheel drive system.

Jeep trucks have offered several transfer case designs, including gear and chain drive types. Chain drive emerged in the '70s, as full-time 4x4 popularity peaked. Chain drive, aluminum-housed transfer cases are currently popular for both full- and part-time 4x4 systems. Aluminum-housed transfer cases are lighter

and more energy efficient. Earlier through-drive gear units offer superior stamina.

On most 1972–79 full size Jeep J-trucks, Wagoneers and AMC CJ models with manual transmissions, the Spicer Model 20 transfer case was available. (The Model 20 first appeared in Kaiser's original J-truck/Wagoneer models.) These units offer tremendous stamina with minimal wear. Cast-iron cased, the Spicer 20's through-drive design handles loads to 3/4-ton truck capacity with ease. These transfer boxes often operate flawlessly for 200,000-plus miles in a well-maintained CJ. Their only drawback is the relatively light 2.03:1 low range ratio, which can be offset with the use of a truck-type transmission with compound low gear and/or lower (numerically higher) axle gearing.

Similarly, for many 1980–86 CJ Jeep owners, the Dana 300 transfer case has served well. The Dana 300 offers exceptional service with a cast-iron case and the quieter stamina of helically cut gears. An added feature on the Dana 300 is its 2.61:1 low range ratio, capable of superior off-road crawling ability.

The Model 18 Spicer transfer case, found in 1/4-ton military Jeep models, the 1946–71 CJs and Pickups/Station Wagons prior to J-Series/Wagoneer models, also proves rugged. A major drawback, however, is the side-drive design, which delivers all power via an intermediate gear and shaft. Unlike the straight-through power flow of later transfer cases, the Model 18 is subject to extra wear on gears and bearings plus a characteristic gear whine. A Model 18 asset is the P.T.O. outlet that permits installation of a Warn or Saturn aftermarket overdrive. (See performance chapters.)

All part-time 4x4 Jeep transfer cases have a power divider function. You can disengage power flow to the front axle by using 2WD mode. Warner's full-time Quadra-Trac and similar New Process designs, however, provide ongoing power flow to all four wheels, a concept first offered in mid-'70s Jeep models. Here, the rear and front wheels receive constant, differentiated power flow.

Driveshafts

Power flow between the transfer case and axles on Jeep four-wheel drive models is through conventional propeller shafts. Most often, Jeep trucks have Spicer cross-type U-joints with two-piece splined driveshafts. The slide couplers compensate for axle movement by expanding or contracting the lengths of the driveshafts.

Some earlier J-truck and Wagoneer models, and even a few later Jeep vehicles, feature ball-and-trunnion and/or Detroit-type propeller shaft joints. Ball-and-trunnion joints, prone to wear and vibration, have encouraged aftermarket driveshaft builders to fit new tube sections using Spicer cross-type U-joint companion yokes and flanges. For severe duty and steeper shaft angles, the use of heavy duty double-Cardan type joints has served some applications.

5. Repairs On Your Jeep

Your Jeep's serviceable components fit several subgroups. The typical chassis and powertrain layout provides an easy orientation. Once familiar with your Jeep's design layout, you can readily make repairs.

Unless you must remove the crankshaft, engine work is possible in the chassis. The engine bays of most Jeep trucks are broad and designed to facilitate service. An exception to this rule would be the V-8-powered full-size truck with a full complement of power accessories or a V-6 powered 1984–86 XJ Cherokee/Wagoneer or '86 Comanche pickup equipped with a host of power options.

Powertrain Orientation

You will quickly become familiar with your Jeep's features. Servicing propeller shafts, cables, the brakes, shock absorbers (commonly "airplane type" removable units) and wheels is fast and straightforward. The transfer case detaches from the transmission, making it easier to remove each of these units. Reducing the weight of the transmission/transfer case assembly permits safer handling of parts and reduced risk of damage.

Axle service, generally performed in the truck, follows standard guidelines for Spicer/Dana-type and AMC integral housings. Spicer/Dana axles have an excellent reputation for reliability.

Fig. 4-27. *Some J-truck/Wagoneers featured ball-and-trunnion driveshaft joints (top). Vibration and parts obsolescence encourage replacement with a conventional Spicer cross-type joint (bottom). This requires changing the transfer case U-joint companion flange and adding a slip collar.*

Fig. 4-28. *The Jeep CJ and Wrangler engine bays are readily accessible. Late models, however, with numerous power options and accessories, have a much busier profile.*

Like a trained Jeep mechanic, you'll find the factory service manual very valuable. By following factory recommended procedures for disassembly and installation of parts, you can perform professional level work. Your Jeep deserves the highest work standards and competency.

The Jeep Workplace

When servicing the Jeep truck, a clean and safe workspace is essential. Jeep geartrain and chassis parts are expensive. Losing parts can create lengthy delays, as many components have "special order" status.

By establishing neat work habits at the beginning of a repair or restoration project, you will speed up the work process and assure your success. Each part has its place. Before starting a repair, lay out labelled coffee cans or similar containers to hold the nuts and bolts.

Parts illustrations, either from this book or the detailed unit repair section of a Jeep factory service and repair manual, should accompany the job. Especially on older trucks, possibly with a history of mediocre repairs, you should account for each part shown in the guidebook.

Use Correct Tools

Review the required tools for the repair. Jeep vehicles, due to their special powertrain layout, often need specialty wrenches or other devices to complete a repair. You will find references to such tools in this book or your Jeep factory level overhaul manual. Avoid loss of time and knuckle tissue by using the proper tools.

Basics apply to work on any Jeep truck. Repairs to the undercarriage and wheel service frequently require chassis hoisting. The use of safe floor jacks and jackstands is a must. The ideal jackstands for your Jeep work have four- cornered platforms and a minimum five-ton rating per stand. Avoid the use of light duty, tube type stands. They provide too small a margin of safety for wrestling with a transmission or transfer case.

Jacks and Lifting

Quality hydraulic floor jacks are another safety requirement. Minimally, your floor jack must be of 1-1/2 ton or greater capacity. Whenever possible, avoid lifting the entire front or rear of the truck with a single jack. Never rely upon a hydraulic jack to support the truck while you work beneath the body or chassis. Install jack stands immediately to avoid overloading your jack. When lifting the Jeep for wheel and tire removal, take the extra time to install jackstands. Safety is primary.

To safely position your jackstands, note the design of the chassis. Common support points on the Jeep

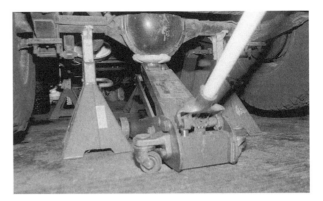

Fig. 4-29. *These 5-ton rated jack stands offer a huge safety margin for light Jeep truck work. The 1-1/2 ton rated floor jack offers features found in professional equipment. Invest in quality. Your safety is at stake.*

Fig. 4-30. *Jackstands allow safe positioning beneath the front and rear axle housings, or jacks can support the frame near the spring anchors. Consult your owner's handbook for safe hoisting points, especially on a unibody model.*

truck are the frame rails and beneath the axle housing tubes. Space jacks evenly, as near spring mounting points as possible. These are locations engineered to support the truck.

Avoid placing a jackstand in any area of the chassis where rocking might result. Never place a floor jack or jackstand under steering linkage, brake pipes/hoses, exhaust system parts or body sheet metal. On compact XJ and mid-size ZJ/WJ models with unibodies, note the reinforced chassis sections and appropriate axle points for safely supporting the vehicle. (Consult your vehicle owner's manual for factory-recommended support points.)

If you are uncertain about the lift points for your Jeep's chassis, talk with a local Jeep dealership service representative or refer to the factory repair manual covering your model. Especially while performing powertrain work, keep the jackstands well spaced and secure. Allow an ample and unobstructed space for work.

Hoisting Equipment

Powertrain and axle unit repairs involve very heavy sub-assemblies. If your service goals involve the removal and replacement of the axles, engine, transmission or transfer case, be prepared to handle these heavy units. Consider renting the correct hoisting tool or an engine "cherry picker" from your local rental yard. Rental firms often have transmission/transfer case jacks as well. When performing heavy work, always ask a robust friend or relative for assistance.

Hoists and specialty tools help prevent damage to your truck. Personal injuries are also less likely when hydraulic force takes the place of brute strength. The manhandling of parts, such as attempts to install a weighty transmission by hand, can lead to broken components and severe bodily injury. This is unnecessary and avoidable.

Failure to detach all hardware also leads to major damage. Take time to envision the entire sub-assembly. Check the shop manual's step-by-step service procedures and parts diagrams to make sure that you have disconnected all necessary hardware. Ask an assistant to watch progress from a different vantage point.

In the case of engine removal, always secure the engine with suitable chain or cables. Find balance points to assure the stability of the engine as you raise it, and also pay attention to the angle of pull. Use strong, high grade attachment hardware and an engine tilt cable that permits angle adjustments as you hoist.

Special Considerations

For work around coil springs, like those found on later model Jeep trucks, be extra careful. Unload the coil spring with a special spring compressor before attempting to remove it. Compressed coil force exceeds a ton, and an unrestrained spring can cause severe bodily injury, even death, or major damage to the truck.

Always account for the size of the transmission and transfer case assembly when placing the chassis on stands. If you intend to remove the transmission from beneath the truck, be certain that there is sufficient room. A disconnected transmission or axle, trapped beneath the truck, is much like the story of the man who built a boat in his basement.

6. The Jeep Owner's Toolbox

Jeep 4x4 service requires a full complement of tools. The off-pavement environment, full of hazards and mechanical threats, encourages an on-board complement of hand tools and simple diagnostic equipment. At home, for the Jeep owner who performs maintenance and repairs on his or her vehicle, a variety of tools make up the Jeep workshop.

Objectives and Tools for Your "Jeep Shop"

Above all else, an off-road 4x4 must provide optimal dependability. Hard-core trail running places major stresses on the chassis, powertrain, cooling and electrical systems.

Preventive maintenance is your best defense. Inspection, regular service, in-depth troubleshooting and light repairs are well within your reach. By accurately pinpointing problems, you have the option of either applying your mechanical skills or subletting repairs to a shop.

Fig. 4-31. *258 sixes are long and require care during removal. This cherry picker hoist provides the angle and control to safely lift the engine. Whenever possible, use an engine tilting device for safety sake.*

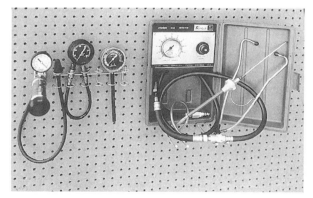

Fig. 4-32. *A vacuum pump or gauge tests ignition, carburetor and emission devices. A compression gauge and cylinder leakdown tester diagnose internal engine troubles.*

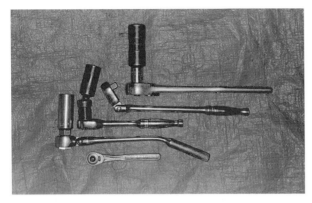

Fig. 4-33. *A variety of hand tools ease your Jeep work. These rachets and sockets serve specific needs, including spark plug changes and removal of wheel (lug) nuts.*

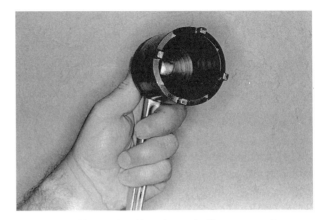

Fig. 4-34. *Front wheel bearing spindle nut wrenches are a must. This specialty socket, available through NAPA and other auto supply retailers, is for later model J-trucks. Such sockets are also available for earlier hex nuts. Never use a hammer and punch to remove or tighten spindle nuts.*

Reference Books: The Literary Tools

This book will serve as your orientation and reference guide for preventive care, tune-up and diagnosis of mechanical troubles. If your skill level and ambitions include sub-assembly repairs and overhaul, I highly recommend a Jeep factory service manual for such work. The factory level manual and your owner's handbook also offer tune-up specifications, fitup tolerances and fluid capacities.

When overhauling an engine, geartrain or electrical sub-assembly, a Jeep factory level service manual provides the details and specifications considered essential. For over three decades, my work has benefitted from the use of OEM factory manuals, MOTORS Truck Manual and Mitchell professional series (trade) service books. A factory shop manual, available through your local Jeep dealership, provides the most information, greatest detail and best illustrations.

Filling Your Toolbox

Tools for periodic maintenance and light repair work include troubleshooting and diagnostic equipment. Your Jeep garage requires a full assortment of U.S. size wrenches to cover all but the most recent metric hardware. Jeep, for the most part, has adhered to domestic tooling, despite U.S. auto industry attempts to shift toward the metric standard. Hand tools should include open and box ended wrenches, sockets in 1/4", 3/8" and 1/2" square drive sets and specialty sockets for spark plugs, wheel (lug) nuts and front wheel bearing nuts.

The wheel bearing nut wrench (for full-floating front axles) is a necessity. Many pre-owned Jeeps show signs of severely abused front wheel bearing nuts. Instead of using the correct socket, unequipped mechanics apply a hammer and chisel to the corners of the hex or slotted locking nuts. This not only ruins the nut but also

eliminates any chance of accurately measuring torque on either the bearing adjusting nut or the lock nut.

Jeep spindle nut wrenches are available in most retail auto parts stores and 4WD parts outlets. OTC, Snap-On, New Britain/NAPA and others produce flat-walled, 1/2" square drive hex sockets for precisely this purpose. The large nut size and small space between the nut and inner face of the hub makes use of a conventional socket or wrench impossible.

Later Jeep models utilize special wheel bearing nuts that require a special four-lug socket. Similarly, the steering knuckle upper ball-joint stud seat on many late Dana open-knuckle axles is adjustable. A special socket is available for accurately positioning these seats and setting correct ball-joint preload.

Additional Chassis and Powertrain Tools

The rest of your chassis tools should include tie-rod and Pitman/steering arm pullers, a pickle fork and those tools commonly used for working on domestic trucks. For the early Jeep owner, kingpin bearings and steering gear preload adjustments require a pull-type spring scale.

Cross-type U-joint service, a frequent Jeep repair procedure, may be performed successfully with a bench vise and some sockets, although more elaborate specialty tools are available. Driveshaft ball-and-trunnion joint service and several other service operations may demand access to a hydraulic press, bearing or gear pullers and fixtures. You can sublet these tasks to an automotive machine shop or rent equipment at a local rental yard. Cost and frequency of use will dictate whether you should buy a hydraulic press.

Fig. 4-35. *Specialty pullers will ease steering linkage disassembly. Use of the right tool prevents damage to expensive safety components.*

Fig. 4-36. *Many jobs require use of a hydraulic press. If a press is beyond your budget, sublet heavy bearing, gear or bushing work to an automotive machine shop. Attempts to improvise with a hammer are wasteful and dangerous.*

For transmission and clutch alignment work, a dummy input shaft is always a practical idea, as transmissions and attached transfer cases offer a major weight obstacle—especially on four-speed, iron-case truck transmissions. You can fabricate transmission locating dowels by removing the heads from long bolts.

Thread the bolts into the bellhousing's upper transmission mounting holes. These simple guide pin dowels will prevent clutch disc damage during installation of the transmission.

Spicer/Dana axle work may require use of a spreader to relieve tension on the carrier bearing cups during removal. In some cases, a spreader is not necessary if you pry and remove the carrier very evenly and carefully. Although axle overhaul is often a sublet repair, you can perform such work with the right tools.

Removing wheel hubs on tapered axle shafts requires a special puller. Rear brake work on many Jeeps also involves pulling the wheel hub/drum assembly.

Precise Measurements

Competent Jeep repairs require precise adjustments and measurements. A dial indicator and magnetic stand are valuable tools. Shimming bearings, checking shaft end float, adjusting backlash of gears, setting wheel bearing endplay and other chores require use of a dial indicator. The magnetic stand or a gooseneck holding fixture will help with awkward dial indicator measurements. You will also need a precision micrometer(s) for measuring shaft diameters and checking the thickness of shims.

Jeep service and overhaul work demand a wide range of torque wrenches: 1/4" drive inch-pound, 3/8" drive inch/foot-pound, 1/2" square drive foot-pound and even a 3/4" square drive heavy duty type. If cost is prohibitive, rent or borrow a quality torque wrench. Make sure the calibration is correct.

Nitty-Gritty Tools

Your basic hand tools should include a hacksaw, a variety of chisels, punches and drifts (both hard steel and

Fig. 4-37. *The dial indicator and a magnetic stand are very useful. For adjusting wheel bearing end play and runout on shafts, use a dial indicator. You can also detect camshaft lobe wear with a dial indicator.*

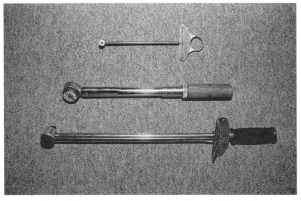

Fig. 4-38. *Torque wrenches come in a variety of sizes. This assortment serves every need from companion flange nuts to ultra-sensitive automatic transmission band adjustments.*

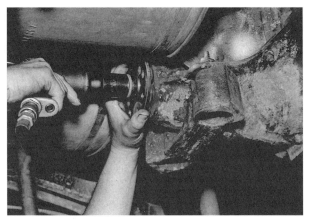

Fig. 4-40. *Air wrenches and other pneumatic tools save time and ease the heavier Jeep work, especially removal and installation of shaft nuts on the transmission, transfer case or axles.*

malleable brass), Allen hex wrenches, and in the case of later Jeeps, Torx-type drivers. Seal and bearing cup drivers are optional, as careful improvisation often works satisfactorily. Safety goggles should be worn whenever you work with air impact tools, sharp cutting tools, hammers, chisels or punches.

Brake Work Tools

For brake tubing nuts and fuel pipe fittings, a flare nut wrench set is mandatory. (Open end wrenches will damage compression nuts.) Other brake work tools include adjuster "spoon" wrenches, spring pliers, retainer/hold down tools, wheel cylinder piston clamps and bleeder hose. Disc brakes require a pad/caliper piston spreader and a micrometer for checking disc thickness/variance. There are special hones for wheel cylinder, master cylinder and disc caliper rebuilding.

Fig. 4-39. *The right tools assure a quality job. Both disc and drum brake systems require specialty tools. If you intend to perform brake work, invest in quality brake tools.*

Air Tools: Speed and Efficiency

Air wrenches are a major timesaver. A wide range of pneumatic tools quickly tame difficult repair jobs. In addition to time savings, air impact wrenches enhance the quality of work, especially those high torque, heavy duty repairs.

This is especially true with older sub-assemblies suffering from semi-seized hardware and rust accumulation. (Specially hardened, impact quality sockets should always be used with air wrenches.) Also, most Jeep transmission shafts, axle nuts and U-joint/pinion flange nuts require high torque settings. Air tools for the removal and installation of these large nuts eliminates the awkward use of a breaker bar and special holding fixtures.

> CAUTION —
> *Always check final torque with a torque wrench. Never use a pneumatic impact gun to fully tighten or torque fasteners. An inexperienced mechanic can easily over-torque or under-torque fasteners with an air impact tool. A safety hazard and/or damaged components can result.*

Engine Overhaul: Tools for In-Depth Repairs

In-the-chassis engine overhaul requires common tools like a valve spring compressor, cylinder ridge reamer, hone, and ring compressor. For a major out-of-chassis rebuild, you will sublet reboring the block, grinding the crankshaft and valves, fitting piston pins, installing cam bearings and other machine shop procedures.

Tune-up and Engine Diagnostic Equipment

The tune-up needs for your Jeep engine depend upon the model and engine type. Various fuel, spark and ignition systems have different tool requirements.

An early Jeep provides the debatable simplicity of a breaker point ignition, remote ignition coil and high tension spark cables. A common misunderstanding is that breaker points are easier to service. The contemporary Jeep electronic distributor is equally easy to troubleshoot and repair. (See discussion of repair and troubleshooting procedures in service chapters.)

Servicing your earlier Jeep's breaker point distributor requires traditional tune-up tools. A point feeler gauge set helps adjust the point gap. (Tappet feeler gauges are for engine valve stem clearance adjustments.) For accurate, parallel spark plug gaps, use a gapping pliers. Simpler wire-type feeler gauges work fine on used spark plugs and fit easily in your on-board tool kit.

A dwell-meter provides precise breaker point adjustment, while a timing light verifies timing after you have set the point cam/dwell angle. The volt/ohm meter is an ideal companion for your electrical troubleshooting and tune-up work, offering quick, concise diagnosis of everything from shorts and open circuits to testing alternator or generator current and battery voltage.

For precise performance, setting the breaker point spring tension assures accurate spark at all engine speeds while extending point life. (Today, this is rarely necessary. Modern, high quality replacement points have pre-set tension.) As a dedicated truck fleet mechanic and high performance enthusiast during the heyday of breaker point ignitions, I used my spring scale regularly.

Fig. 4-42. *A dwell meter, timing light and volt-ohmmeters contribute to tuning and troubleshooting. Volt-ohmmeter has become the single most useful electronic and electrical troubleshooting tool.*

Fig. 4-43. *Round out your tune-up tools with a fuel pump tester, vacuum gauge, float height gauge, needle/seat driver, assorted screw drivers, Torx sockets and a distributor terminal brush. During heyday of the Willys and Kaiser Jeep models, the breaker point spring gauge served as a high performance tuning tool.*

Carburetor tuning requires a float height gauge and needle/seat removal tool. A complete assortment of quality screwdrivers (straight slot, Phillips and Torx) is necessary for repairs and tuning chores on your Jeep.

Ignition wrenches are versatile for breaker point replacement and other electrical system repairs. A continuity tester is helpful, although the volt/ohmmeter surpasses the effectiveness of any test lamp. Although pinpoint tester probes allow testing through wire insulation, use a pinpoint tester sparingly. Avoid damaging insulation, which can lead to wire corrosion or shorts.

Electrical System Tools

When working alone, I find a remote starter switch handy. This permits cranking the engine from beneath the hood. A remote starter tool is very helpful for com-

Fig. 4-41. *Ignition tune-up tools should match your Jeep's requirements. This assortment results from more than three decades of exposure to Jeep engines. Ignition wrenches, point files, breaker cam lubricant and feeler gauges date to the breaker point era.*

Fig. 4-44. *Jeep starters with solenoid activated drive provide an opportunity to use a remote starter switch. For quickly aligning timing marks or checking compression, the remote switch is a major asset.*

Fig. 4-45. *Induction meters provide a quick view of starter current draw or generator/alternator output. Held over the starter cable or charge wire, the meter reads magnetic current flow.*

Fig. 4-46. *A leakdown tester exceeds all other methods of evaluating engine seal. Gauge is capable of pinpointing worn valves, defective piston rings, a blown head gasket or casting cracks.*

pression testing. With all spark plugs removed and the ignition switch off, you can hold the throttle open, crank the engine and watch the compression gauge—all from beneath the hood.

Regular battery maintenance, a critical need for Jeep 4x4 trucks, requires tools for cleaning the cable terminals and posts. A battery hydrometer test is useful when you suspect a dead cell. The simpler voltmeter test answers most battery questions.

Another quick diagnostic tool for starter and charging systems is the induction meter. These meters sense magnetic current flow through the starter or charge circuit cable, showing the approximate output in amperes. In seconds, you can determine current flow rate or draw.

Engine Compression Versus Cylinder Leakdown

Although the compression gauge registers cranking compression (a quick reference to overall engine condition), a more reliable test is cylinder leakdown percentages. The leakdown tester pressurizes a cylinder through the spark plug hole, with the piston at top-dead-center (TDC) of the compression stroke. If the valves, rings, head gasket or castings fail to seal normally, the tester indicates the volume or percentage of the leak.

The advantage of the leakdown test is two-fold. First, the piston rests at the point of greatest cylinder wear (maximum taper). With parts immobile, leakage and piston ring blowby show up readily. It is not uncommon for an engine to display normal cranking compression yet have 30% or higher leakdown due to poor ring seal. Eight to ten percent leakage is ideal. I'm comfortable with uniform leakage to 12% on a non-supercharged engine.

Secondly, the leakdown tester immediately indicates the area of the leak. If an intake valve leaks, air will blow back through the carburetor. A leaking exhaust valve sends an audible signal out the tailpipe. Piston ring wear telegraphs through the dipstick tube, oil filler hole or crankcase vent.

If a professional quality leakdown tester is unavailable or more costly than your budget allows, the traditional substitute is an air-hold fitting designed for changing valve springs. Screw the fitting into a spark plug hole. With the piston at exactly TDC on its compression cycle, adjust air line pressure to a point between 60 and 80 psi. Apply pressure to the fitting. Listen for leaks and pinpoint where leakage occurs.

Fig. 4-47. *Electronic ignitions have reduced service requirements. This late Jeep 258 Motorcraft unit, upgraded with several Ford DuraSpark components, is easily accessible and serviceable. The primary troubleshooting tool is a volt-ohmmeter.*

Electronic Ignition and Emission Control Service Tools

Later Jeep models bring computer-triggered electronic spark and fuel management (EFI) into play. Beginning with the XJ Cherokee's 2.5L and 4.0L in-line four and six engines, EFI has replaced the carburetor on all Jeep engines. Since the mid-'70s, all Jeep trucks have electronic ignitions, with a module eliminating the use of breaker points.

From a service standpoint, the electronic distributor has actually reduced Jeep maintenance. The compelling need for feeler gauges and a dwell meter has been eliminated. Instead, troubleshooting now consists of ohmmeter and voltage tests. Here, a precision digital volt/ohmmeter proves invaluable, a must tool for any contemporary Jeep toolbox and also a valuable troubleshooting tool for the older Jeep model.

Timing Light

The timing light has remained an important element of ignition tuning, as normal wear to the camshaft timing chain and distributor drive mechanism still require a periodic test of spark timing. The ideal timing light has a built-in advance, which allows testing the vacuum advance function and the mechanical (centrifugal) advance. Better timing lights are inductive variety. This means that you may hook the connector to the insulation of number-one cylinder's spark cable without disconnecting the cable from the spark plug.

Distributor machines, once popular for testing a distributor unit off the engine, have become obsolete. With built-in advance timing lights, the engine now acts as a test stand for spinning the distributor safely at

1000–1250 rpm (2000–2500 crankshaft rpm). The advance allows zeroing the timing to the factory TDC mark or any other degree setting within range. A distributor vacuum advance mechanism is common for the carbureted Jeep engines. Here, use of a hand held vacuum pump aids in testing ignition spark timing.

> *WARNING —*
> *When using the engine to increase distributor rpm, stay clear of the fan. Avoid standing above the fan, as fan separation or water pump shaft failure could cause severe bodily injury, even death. At speed, without normal air flow through the radiator, an engine-driven fan acts much like an airplane propeller. Attempting to pull forward, the fan creates high stress for the blades, fan clutch and water pump. Stay clear and limit engine rpm as much as possible. Most late model tuning specifications limit test speeds to a maximum of 2500 crankshaft rpm for a brief period.*

Tools for Checking Emission Controls

A vacuum pump/pressure tester also serves as a tune-up tool for emission control devices. You can test the exhaust gas recirculation valve (EGR), found on most Jeep engines since the early '70s, with a vacuum pump. Additionally, applying vacuum to various emission control parts, like the thermal vacuum switch and bi-metallic air cleaner switch, helps locate leaks and troubles.

As many emission switches rely on coolant temperature, an accurate temperature gauge is necessary. To test the opening point for a thermal vacuum switch, for example, requires both a thermometer and vacuum test tool. Troubleshooting emission controls becomes less intimidating when these tools are available.

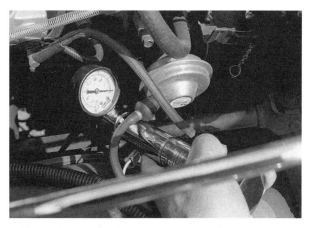

Fig. 4-48. *A quality hand vacuum pump/pressure gauge is valuable. Emission control devices like this 258 six's EGR valve test easily.*

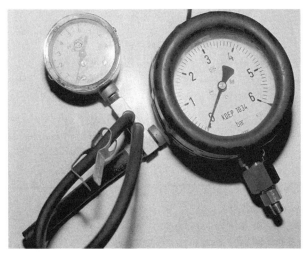

Fig. 4-49. *Fuel pump pressure affects carburetor needle and seat action. Electronic fuel injection systems require higher, precisely regulated fuel pressure. These gauges pinpoint trouble.*

On a pre-owned Jeep, emission control devices and hoses may be missing. For restoring the system, I strongly recommend Mitchell's Emission Control Manual or a Jeep factory shop manual. Either will provide diagrams and illustrations of the original equipment components. Your local Jeep dealership is the best source for emissions-legal replacement parts.

Cooling System Tools

Jeep engines depend on their cooling systems for survival. Traumatized by extreme climates, from scorching desert heat to sub-zero arctic gales, Jeeps must perform. Radiator cleanliness, the correct thermostat, proper coolant mixtures and a working fan provide the backbone of engine cooling efficiency.

The cooling system pressure tester is a versatile tool. For both radiator cap and cooling system tests, the hand pump tester provides quick results. Signs of head gasket seepage or a cracked engine casting are also within the scope of a cooling system pressure tester.

For anti-freeze and coolant protection, inexpensive radiator hydrometers are available. The reliability of your Jeep's radiator cap and the concentration of coolant/anti-freeze play a vital role in boil-over protection. Radiator cap pressure also raises the boiling point of the coolant mix. Therefore, it is essential to maintain a correct pressure constant in your Jeep's cooling system. STANT and other companies provide pressure testers for both radiator cap and radiator/cooling system diagnosis. When working around your Jeep's cooling system, first make certain that the engine has cooled completely.

CAUTION —
If you suspect a blown head gasket, be cautious. Starting the engine with the tester attached to the radiator neck may instantly cause the gauge to peg. When performing this test, be prepared to shut the engine off immediately.

"Soft" Tools

Conventional composition gaskets leak from the effects of heat (embrittlement), shrinkage or their inability to fill minute gaps and voids. The gap need not be very large, like a valve cover with a few thousandths of an inch of gasket gap. Such a leak, however, could easily spill an entire crankcase of oil along a remote four-wheeling trail. Over time, fatigue affects neoprene, rubber, cork and even steel gaskets.

Chemical products and sealants, known in the automotive trade as "soft" tools, make the ideal companion for your Jeep traveling toolbox. RTV silicone sealants are unlike conventional gaskets. Rather than deteriorate when exposed to corrosive oils, products like Permatex/Loctite's Ultra Blue or Black actually become more flexible, pliant and oil resistant.

During engine assembly, you should use silicone products at the oil pan gasket corners, especially between cork and neoprene junctions such as those

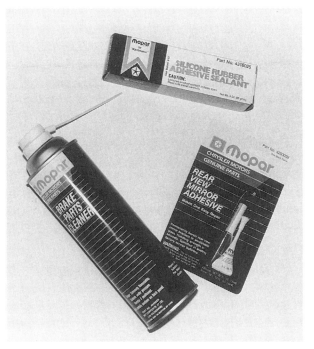

Fig. 4-50. *Mopar offers sealants and chemical "soft" tools that meet OEM guidelines for your Jeep truck. Specialized items, such as rubber bonder, mirror adhesive and brake parts cleaner, meet rigid standards and Jeep Warranty requirements.*

found with intake manifold gaskets. Along the trail, the Permatex Ultra sealants can create a thermostat housing gasket, valve cover gasket, oil pan gasket or timing cover gasket.

When selecting an RTV high temperature silicone for exhaust system joints and flanges, make sure the volatility of the sealant is correct. For applications involving emission control oxygen sensors, use low-volatility sealant. Higher volatility sealants can seriously damage the sensor. The Jeep factory warranty on emission hardware will not cover the replacement of an oxygen sensor damaged by the use of high-volatility RTV sealant.

> *WARNING —*
> *Never use a non-automotive silicone sealant, like bathtub caulk, on your Jeep engine or geartrain parts.*

On manual gearboxes and axle housings, the correct RTV silicone sealant provides a sturdy, permanent fit up of parts. For some parts assemblies, Jeep now uses anaerobic sealers that cure in the absence of air. Mechanisms like gasketless transfer cases and alloy transmission housings require anaerobic type sealants.

Many mechanics use silicone sealants to replace conventional gaskets, but there are Jeep geartrain parts that use a pre-cut gasket or shim(s) as a selective fit spacer. Unless otherwise specified in your factory service manual, avoid the use of RTV sealant in place of selective fit gaskets.

For axle differential covers and all oil exposed seals, automotive RTV silicone can help eliminate seepage. A Jeep will flex and distort paper gaskets, and the older transmission and transfer case cut gaskets are notorious for leaking. Late Jeep powertrains have discontinued the use of cut gaskets, substituting the more supple silicone products. RTV sealant allows a more direct fitup of parts, which reduces flexing, loose hardware and parts misalignment.

Neoprene-lipped seals serve on shaft surfaces. The outer jacket of these seals should be lightly coated with a product like Permatex Super 300 Form-a-Gasket before driving the seal into place. This includes timing cover seals, transmission or transfer case front shaft and output shaft seals and axle shaft seals. Although coating the jacket of a seal will not prevent the lip portion from failing, you can reduce the likelihood of housing bore-to-seal seepage.

Once you become familiar with the properties and proper uses of these sealants and adhesives, they prove as handy as your screwdrivers and wrenches. Often, soft tools provide faster, more permanent repairs than conventional gaskets—especially alongside a remote trail!

7. Miscellaneous Chores

There are other tasks that you may want to perform on your Jeep. In particular, front end alignment is a relatively easy job on a solid, hypoid driving axle. Adjusting toe-in may be within the scope of your service work. (The setting of caster and camber involves more skill, special tools and parts. A solid axle with springs in good shape, however, seldom requires caster or camber adjustment.)

Toe-in changes caused by normal wear of steering linkage take place over time. Inexpensive toe-set alignment bars, available through Eastwood Company and other outlets, serve home mechanics. These toe bars can be used on most Jeep 4x4 trucks, providing a savings in service costs, sublet shop time and troubleshooting effort.

A variety of miscellaneous tools serve your Jeep's needs. Body work and paint, detailing chores and repair of upholstery are often part of a complete restoration. With proper maintenance, your Jeep 4x4 will deliver years of rugged service.

For the serious restorer, many suppliers provide a wide range of tools. If you are the owner of a 1941–45 Model MB or a '71 V-6 CJ-5 model, serious restoration could increase the value of your truck.

Sourcing Jeep Truck Parts
Especially for AMC or Chrysler built Jeep models, your local Jeep dealer is a reliable parts source. Chrysler has incorporated OEM Jeep parts into the MOPAR network, resulting in broad parts access for customers.

A computerized parts system means that Jeep parts and accessories are also available through other Chrysler product dealerships. Chrysler/Mopar is the largest corporate manager of Jeep products to date. Parts availability now exceeds all previous OEM efforts.

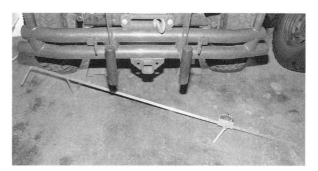

Fig. 4-51. *For front wheel alignment at home, Eastwood's catalog offers this inexpensive toe-set bar. Toe-in is easy to calculate and adjust on a solid Jeep axle.*

Jeep/Eagle dealers and other Mopar outlets find a very healthy aftermarket for quality engineered Jeep Accessories from Mopar. Other parts and accessories sources also serve the Jeep owner.

Due largely to the indomitable nature of early models, non-factory aftermarket sources continue to supply replacement parts for Jeep trucks. Despite the passing of Willys, Kaiser and AMC interests in Jeep, owners still need their parts. A variety of aftermarket outlets and vendors offer Jeep chassis, geartrain and engine components.

Several Jeep engines have popular automotive or industrial counterparts. These designs provide additional parts sources. Automotive parts outlets and machine shops throughout the U.S. and Canada are familiar with Jeep's progression of Willys, Kaiser/Continental, AMC, Buick, Pontiac, Chevrolet and Chrysler built engines.

Aftermarket Geartrain Sources

Axle, transmission, driveshaft and transfer case pieces are available from a number of sources. Many geartrain pieces have industry-wide use. Dana, Spicer, Borg-Warner (now Warner), General Motors, New Process, New Venture, Tremac and other manufacturers have produced a variety of components for Jeep and other American truck manufacturers.

In some instances, interchangeability of parts between makes is possible. Often, though, the Jeep version of a gear or powertrain component has enough differences to make parts sourcing more complicated.

For older models, aftermarket parts sources often have more insight than the modern Jeep dealership. There are several outlets for early geartrain, axle and other Jeep parts. Some specialize in accumulating parts for Jeep trucks ranging from the WWII MB through CJ models. (See appendix for parts sources.)

Outlets such as these specialize in gear parts, steering and hard-to-find Jeep items. For the restorer, an entire early Jeep could be constructed from parts in stock. Chassis, engine, electrical, fuel, suspension and even body panels are available.

Mail-Order Aftermarket

4WD Hardware and Four Wheel Parts Wholesalers offer a wide range of mechanical and body parts for the Jeep owner. 4WD Hardware, Ohio based, specializes in steel or fiberglass body panels for the restorer. Dick Cepek is also a huge mail-order and retail outlet that offers Jeep geartrain pieces, tires and accessory equipment to enhance any 4x4. Each of these outlets sell accessories and custom hardware for improving your Jeep.

These parts sources can keep a Jeep truck trail ready, while your Jeep dealer or a quality local auto parts store can help with tune-up and routine service parts. Choose the best available tune-up components for your Jeep 4x4. Your Jeep truck requires flawless ignition performance. Bargain hunting for replacement parts is unwise.

> NOTE—
> Water crossings and foul-weather driving conditions demand much higher standards of performance from a Jeep. Water-proofing should be a goal for your Jeep's ignition distributor, coil and secondary spark cables.

Quality Filtration

For consistent performance, use Mopar replacement air, oil and fuel filters. You will find high performance filtration systems in the Mopar Performance Catalog. For any Jeep exposed to poor fuel grades or water contamination, add-on fuel filtration is also essential. This includes water trap filters for driving in regions where gasoline has a high water content.

Chapter 5

Jeep Maintenance and Preservation

Off-pavement, your Jeep 4x4 faces many hazards. Reliability is essential, as trails often lead into isolated country, far from repair shops, Jeep dealerships, parts supplies and towing services.

Along Northern California's Rubicon Trail and its endless rock piles, a stranded vehicle is a serious problem. For hard-core four-wheelers who travel the Rubicon, regular Jeep maintenance is as important as a full complement of hand tools and spare parts.

The Rubicon Trail generates an endless stream of colorful stories. One harrowing tale describes a CJ Jeep, irreparably broken, that came out of the Rubicon atop a Trekmaster supply trailer. Another Jeep CJ towed the trailer. Most breakdowns are far less dramatic, though, and emergency field repairs often keep a 4x4 on the trail.

Engine tune, U-joint and cooling system failures can frustrate the off-road traveler. Rough terrain demands far more than basic transportation from your Jeep truck. When AAA towing or motoring club coverage is fifty rock-crawling miles away, "preventive maintenance" takes on new meaning!

Fig. 5-1. *Another day on the Rubicon Trail! Proper maintenance and driving finesse contribute strongly to your Jeep's survival.*

Although much of the maintenance on Jeep trucks is routine, preventive care has a direct effect on safety and survival. Even a simple fluid or filter change, common to any truck, helps ensure your passage through desolate back country.

1. "Full-service" Lubrication and Maintenance

Most modern gasoline stations fail to meet motorists' needs. Drivers at "Full Service" pumps pay up to two-fifths more per gallon for fuel, expecting genuine car care. Perhaps their windshield receives attention or the attendant will ask if the oil needs checking. After several minutes beneath the hood, the attendant might approach the customer sheepishly and inquire, "Where's the dipstick?"

When I was a high school student in the mid-sixties, there was Bud Berrum's Chevron, across the highway from the C.O.D. Garage, the Jeep dealership at Minden, Nevada. I worked after school and summers, and Bud ran a real service station. As attendants, we catered to customers' needs, and that meant service.

If you drove into Bud's Chevron while I was on shift, your cares were over! I'd pump 94–110 octane gas into the fuel tank, check the oil, drive belts, hoses, automatic transmission fluid, brake fluid, battery and windshield washer fluid. Without leaving a streak, I'd whisk away the summer bugs or January ice from your windshield, wipe your sideview mirror and even clean or polish the back window. If your tires were cool, I'd check air pressure all the way around, then the spare.

What did this cost? Nothing more than your gasoline business and, if you felt like it, you could say, "Thanks."

The lube room was always busy, with a grease job for two dollars and fifty cents and a "lube, oil and filter" running near five dollars, depending upon the filter's cost. A thorough wheel bearing repack, even on your Jeep, would be less than five dollars, including the price of new seals.

For these services, I'd take out Standard Oil's lubrication chart and look up your Jeep model. The guide listed each grease fitting, gear case and axle check points, and required fluid types. Safely on the chassis hoist, your Jeep would receive thorough treatment using Willys' or Kaiser's very own specifications.

All fittings greased, engine oil drained, oil levels checked, rubber bushings dressed with rubber lube, I would inspect the clutch free-play, exhaust system and chassis. After installing the oil pan drain plug with a new gasket, I'd lower your Jeep carefully and head for the hood latches.

Armed with special data for your early Jeep truck, I'd remove and service the oil bath air cleaner, check the coolant with a hydrometer, inspect the steering gearbox fluid level, and carefully check the brake fluid—but only after vacuuming the floorboard around the inspection plate and brushing all dirt away from the master cylinder fill plug. Next, I'd clean the battery case, check its water and wire brush the terminals.

Since vehicles like the early model Jeep had generators and wick-oiled distributors, a squirt can of motor oil was always handy. Careful not to overfill the wicks, I'd apply oil with a light squeeze of the trigger. Then, as the engine crankcase filled from the station's five-quart copper down spout can, I would test all lights and the turn signals (if your Jeep had them!).

Finally, I'd spray lube each hood, door and tailgate hinge, the parking brake handle mechanism and even the ball bearing in your aftermarket ash tray. Before the truck rolled out the door, I would vacuum the cab, clean all of the windows (inside and out), and check the air pressure at each tire—including the spare.

Was this all that our customers expected? Oh, no! A free wash job went with each lube and oil change. Winter or summer, searing heat or low 'teens temperatures (complete with a frozen water bucket and wash mitten), I'd wash your Jeep thoroughly and be thankful for the $1.50 per hour that Bud paid me.

Well, times have changed. In today's jiffy-fix world, few thorough, old-fashioned garages exist. I know of one such outlet: Dana Borda, a fellow alumni

Fig. 5-2. *Mini-Lube unit from MacNaught of Australia is a professional greasing system, ideal for the home garage. High pressure and durable, Mini-Lube makes a quick chore of lubrication. This unit came from CDU Services at Visalia, California, or try your local ag/industrial supply house.*

of Bud Berrum's Chevron, has operated a service facility at Carson City, Nevada, for nearly three decades, offering the level of vehicle care we practiced at Bud Berrum's Chevron.

Perhaps you know a shop like Dana Borda's or a Jeep dealership that provides this kind of service program. If not, I'd recommend you do your own Jeep maintenance. You'll be better off for it. Not only will you learn more about your favorite 4x4 truck, you'll also be better equipped to handle problems far afield.

Bud Berrum's training gave Dana Borda and me a darn good foundation. My first stint as a truck fleet mechanic yielded a "zero breakdown" record for the organization's twenty-two vehicles. I had entered that job with a thorough grasp of preventive maintenance. If you take preventive care half as seriously as Bud, Dana and I do, your Jeep will give its all. Knock on wood, I have never broken down on the highway or along a rough trail in any of my 4x4 vehicles. (I have, however, seen many poorly maintained rigs fail, often under the most precarious operating conditions.)

Chassis Maintenance and Trail Readiness

Your Jeep truck's chassis, though durable and designed for longevity, requires maintenance. Earlier CJs and the Willys-type Pickup/Station Wagon models demand more chassis service than later models. Early 4x4s have grease fittings at the shackle bushings, pedal pivots, steering linkage, transfer case linkage, rear axle bearings and other strategic friction points. Later models use zero-maintenance nylon and rubber bushings in several of these areas.

Non-serviceable, zero-maintenance pieces still require periodic inspection. These parts need replacement when they wear out. According to Willys and Kaiser schedules, earlier greaseable joints demand lubrication at 1,000-mile intervals. They, too, wear out, which means time for new bushings. Regular maintenance assures maximum life from any bushing.

Minimizing wear at friction points is the overall goal of chassis maintenance. In your Jeep factory service manual, you will find a chassis lubrication chart for your model. Pay close attention to the greases specified. The proper grease will meet both climate and severe service requirements for your Jeep truck.

As a home mechanic, you will likely use a hand grease gun, which minimizes risk of seal damage. U-joints, in particular, require hand gun lubrication. High pressure equipment can destroy delicate seals, leaving a U-joint exposed to debris and abrasive contaminants.

Selecting Lubricants

Various lubricants, oils, greases and fluids serve Jeep trucks. Proper oils and fluids are crucial to the safety and reliability of your Jeep 4x4. Compatibility of oils, correct fill quantities and proper viscosities are each essential to proper maintenance.

Earlier Jeep vehicles require conventional lubricants. Typically, 90-weight gear oil fills the differentials, manual steering gearbox, manual transmission and transfer case. Since the advent of chain-drive full-time 4x4 systems, automatic transmission fluid has become common for both the automatic transmission and transfer cases. Later model Jeep manual transmissions also call for lighter lubricants.

Mixing oil brands and types is a mistake. Even when viscosity and type (GL or API rating) are the same, producers add different chemical additives to their base stocks. Strange chassis/wheel bearing greases, engine oil and gear oils may react chemically with your Jeep's existing lubricants.

For this reason, the Jeep owner who maintains his or her own vehicle has a distinct advantage: the ability to assure consistent use of compatible fluids, greases and oils. When changing engine oil, select a brand and stay with it. Carry a spare can or bottle of this type oil to assure availability in the field. Likewise, when draining and refilling the gearboxes or differential, adhere to a specific type and brand of lubricant.

Synthetic oils have generated plenty of controversy. Synthetics lubricants tend to outperform conventional crude oil base stocks under heavy duty/severe service use. Regardless of your choice, beware of compatibility. Avoid mixing stocks of synthetic oil with either conventional oils or other synthetic brands.

Fig. 5-3. *Jeep trucks have specific lubrication requirements. Mopar offers special gear oils, power steering fluid and proper wheel bearing grease (Part No. 4318064)—a high quality, heat resistant grease well suited for disc brake models.*

When uncertain about the correct lubricant for a given area of your Jeep truck, refer to the owners handbook or a factory service manual.

Proper Greases

Lubrication greases have become simpler in recent years. Many vehicle manufacturers use a common, multi-purpose grease for all chassis, steering linkage and wheel bearing needs. I still prefer precise greases for each application: a specified chassis/steering linkage and U-joint grease or a specific wheel bearing lubricant. Use the highest grade grease (usually designated "wheel bearing grease for disc brake models") when servicing your Jeep's wheel bearings.

Wheel bearing greases and chassis lubes have various base stocks. The concern here is compatibility of greases.

> WARNING—
> *Do not mix brands or types of grease. If you have just begun servicing your wheel bearings, thoroughly remove all old grease before repacking with fresh grease. (See other service chapters for wheel bearing service details.)*

On steering linkage and chassis joint grease fittings, simply pump fresh grease through the assembly until only new grease squeezes out. Wipe away excess grease with a rag to prevent abrasive dirt from accumulating around the joint.

Gear Oil

For gear case lubricants and oils, use a slightly different strategy. Especially if your Jeep has higher mileage, the gear units should be drained and refilled with a high grade gear oil. Viscosity and oil type must correspond to the climate and your driving environment.

Once you select an oil brand/type, periodic inspection and topping off will be simple. If you drive your 4x4 Jeep on extended off-pavement trips, plastic squeeze bottles prove practical for dispensing oil.

From the earliest MB Jeep to the latest Wrangler, Jeep lubrication and service follow similar steps. Early Jeep 4x4 models require more details. Newer Jeep trucks have less grease fittings but still require routine chassis maintenance.

Service Intervals

Years ago, service intervals were more frequent. Industrial and agricultural Jeep users changed gear lube each 300 hours, flushed the cooling system twice a year and fussed constantly over the maze of chassis lube points. Tighter factory service intervals for early Jeep trucks, such as chassis lubrication each 1,000 miles, reflect heavy-duty use. Often subjected to severe environmental hazards, a traditional Jeep 4x4 demanded closer care than most other trucks.

Today's extended oil change intervals raise other concerns. The 7,500-mile oil change recommendations of many vehicle manufacturers mean that combustion contaminants continue to find their way into the crankcase oil for even longer periods. By this oil change point, with conventional motor oils, crankcase contamination can reach ten percent.

Few vehicles submerge their wheel hubs and axle housings in swift running streams. If, however, your Jeep sees this kind of use, regular wheel bearing service and axle housing inspection is mandatory. If you stall in a fast moving stream or suspect water seepage into the wheel hubs, repack the wheel bearings immediately.

Recognizing the superior quality of modern chassis and wheel bearing greases, you can usually extend the factory intervals between routine wheel bearing and axle service on older Jeep vehicles. Be certain, though, that wheel hub seals, gaskets and axle or gear unit one-way vent valves function properly.

If your early Jeep is likely to see water crossings, take additional precautions. Extend the axle housing or transmission and transfer case vents upward into the body. Using pipe thread nipples, oil resistant hose and insulated clamps, mount these vents well above the frame height. This reduces the risk of water entering important geartrain parts during stream crossings.

Your Jeep 4x4 truck demands the best. For maximum service life and performance, adjust oil and filter change intervals to 2,000–3,000 miles for premium grade conventional (mineral-based) oil.

Fig. 5-4. *Mineral and synthetic base lubricants include plastic squeeze bottles for gear oil and transmission fluid. Squeeze bottles are handy for field service.*

Fig. 5-5. *Vent hoses must be in good condition. Route these hoses well above the intended water line for your Jeep. This front axle check valve is halfway up radiator shell, a height beyond any normal stream crossing.*

Even with synthetic oil, Jeep driving demands call for oil change intervals at a maximum of 7,500–10,000 miles. (I change my synthetic oil strictly by coloration, not mileage. Under severe loads, the darkening of oil means time to change oil—regardless of mileage.) Install a new Mopar or other high quality oil filter at 3,500 miles or less and top off the oil level. Also replace the filter with each routine oil change. The goal is reliability. Superior lubricants and filtration are a Jeep's most basic need.

Severe Service Maintenance Schedule

Common sense should dictate your Jeep 4x4's service intervals. In industrial or farm work, service your oil bath air cleaner every 100–150 hours. (As always, dust conditions affect these figures.) If your Jeep has gone through 14 miles of dust along the Rubicon Trail, at a snail's pace in high ambient temperatures, clean your air filter (oil bath or dry paper element).

Stalling your Jeep for several minutes in a thirty-inch deep, fast flowing stream raises several concerns. Immediately inspect the hubs, wheel bearings, each gear unit and the engine oil. Grease all fittings.

Similarly, a day's hard play in dusty sand dunes begs a high pressure wash of the chassis, a complete chassis lube job and careful air cleaner service. (Keep sand away from the intake area during filter removal.)

The higher cost of today's replacement parts may tempt the use of inexpensive substitutes. For the urban commuter, the merits of higher quality filtration may

seem difficult to justify. As a serious four-wheeler, however, you must think differently. When a cactus laced trail winds for hours over blistering, knife edged rocks, you will appreciate a steady oil pressure reading. Here, high quality lubricants and Mopar/Jeep or equivalent filters offer cheap insurance.

Lubing Your Jeep 4x4

As you slide beneath the front bumper, the first grease joints come to view. If your Jeep is an early model, the leaf spring shackles and anchor pivots require grease. Wipe each fitting with a clean rag or shop towel, then apply fresh lubricant through the fitting. Watch for grease to exit the opposite end of the bushing. Wipe away the excess.

On leaf spring models with rubber or synthetic bushings, spray each bushing with rubber or silicone lubricant. This will reduce friction and surface oxidation while maximizing the life of these materials. Avoid use of lubricants containing petroleum distillates or other mineral-based solvents. They harm rubber, causing premature wear and parts failure.

Lube all other spring end pivots and shackles. If your Jeep has a stabilizer bar, use rubber lube on the

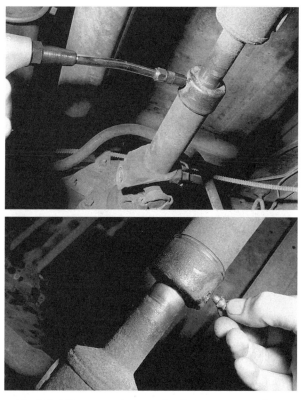

Fig. 5-6. *When greasing steering linkage, suspension or driveline parts, grease fittings sometimes fail. These fittings are replaceable. Take care not to overfill joints, as seals may rupture.*

Fig. 5-7. *Later vehicles have "zero maintenance" bushings. Your Jeep suspension and body grommets may last longer, however, when treated periodically with a quality rubber lube or protectant. Avoid use of any petroleum or mineral base products around rubber.*

Fig. 5-8. *There are many chassis lube points on an early Jeep. Some are difficult to find, like the rear axle bearing fittings (arrow, top), just inboard of the brake backing plates. These often get overlooked. Pedal, steering linkage and shift linkage fittings also require attention.*

bushings. Grease the steering linkage, tie-rod ends, the drag link, the bellcrank (if equipped) and Pitman arm joints. Remember to wipe each grease fitting before inserting clean grease.

Once you have greased the front spring ends and steering linkage, begin lubing all driveshaft components, including slip collars and U-joints. Avoid overgreasing joints, especially the splined slip collars. If the slip collar is extended, add grease modestly. Otherwise, compression of the driveshaft will displace grease.

> *WARNING—*
> *In extreme cases, overfilling a splined slip collar creates a hydraulic effect capable of damaging seals or squeezing a large amount of grease from the end of the driveshaft.*

Continue lubrication at the rear springs and driveshaft. On an earlier Jeep 4x4 model, you will find other grease fittings that need attention, including the clutch/brake pedal linkage, transfer case lever pivot, steering gear worm shaft upper bearing (on CJ-2A and CJ-3A models) and rear axle outer bearings on very early model CJs and trucks.

Rear Wheel Bearing Fittings

The often overlooked rear axle bearing fittings must be greased regularly. (Willys and Kaiser recommended 1,000 miles.) The originally specified grease was a No. 2 wheel bearing type. A high quality multi-purpose (chassis/wheel bearing rated) grease will serve well.

A "flat towed" (towed on the ground) early Jeep requires frequent lubrication of these rear axle bearings. For my CJ-3A, I carried a grease gun on long trips for this purpose. Grease exiting the axle bearing vent hole indicates when the bearing is full.

> *CAUTION —*
> *Overfilling can damage rear brake shoes and other parts.*

Steering Knuckle Joints

While still beneath the truck, check the closed-knuckle front axle shaft grease. (The fill hole appears much like a gear oil opening.) The steering knuckle cavity, however, contains an axle shaft joint requiring a light U-joint grease on Willys and Kaiser models. AMC/Jeep models recommend 140-wt. gear lube, but the light U-joint grease works fine and is less likely to leak from the inner seals. Here, a modern high grade, multi-purpose grease specified for chassis and U-joint use will work well.

Fig. 5-9. *Closed-knuckle front axles need periodic service. On earlier Jeep models, the knuckle cavities contain grease for the kingpin bearings and axle universal joints. Check seals regularly to prevent water damage.*

Fig. 5-10. *Contemporary chassis greases are generally lithium based with "moly" additives. Many greases have all-purpose ratings, although temperature and reaction to water (washout resistance) improve with the more specialized products.*

NOTE —
Steering knuckle lubrication serves two purposes: Both the axle shaft joints and kingpin bearings receive grease here. For this reason, periodic use of the front axle is necessary to assure adequate lube to the upper kingpin bearings. If your Jeep 4x4 model has manual hubs, engage the hubs' LOCK mode (two- or four-wheel drive will work) for a few miles each month. This will circulate sufficient grease to the axle shaft joints and kingpin bearings.

When lubing the steering knuckles, add enough grease to lightly fill the cavity. Avoid pressurizing the knuckle with grease, which would place stress on seals. Closed steering knuckles are notorious for seal leaks, anyway, especially at the large inner grease seal. This seal, exposed to road debris and ice, is especially vulnerable.

NOTE —
After running on slush or ice in freezing weather, always swing the front wheels to both extremes before parking your closed-knuckle equipped Jeep. The knuckle wipers will sweep away debris that could otherwise freeze and crack the large knuckle seal.

The early Jeep factory recommendation for steering knuckle/axle shaft grease replacement is 12,000 miles. Likewise, front wheel bearings call for a repack at 6,000 miles. If your Jeep is newer, you will find that Jeep Corporation extended these intervals. Modern greases lengthen periods between bearing and joint service.

Since disassembling a closed-knuckle unit is a considerable job, any means for extending service inter-

vals would be practical. Quality seals and superior lubricants serve beyond 12,000 miles if you avoid submerging the axles in streams or stalling in knuckle and hub height water.

Checking Fluids

On all Jeep 4x4 models, the axle differentials, transfer case and manual transmission each have oil fill plugs. The fill hole also indicates the oil full mark with the vehicle stationary and level. The recommended interval for changing gear and differential lubricant is 10,000 miles on early Jeep models. You should check fluid with each oil change (ideally, each 2,500 miles), more often if seepage is apparent.

The nature of operation, periods of idleness (which contribute to condensation and corrosion) and other factors will determine fluid change intervals. Modern gear lubricants are much more resilient, and many Jeep trucks go safely beyond 10,000 miles between gear lube changes.

Axle and Gearbox Lubricant

Your choice of gear lubricants will depend upon the Jeep's operating environment. Years ago, before multiviscosity gear oils, SAE 80-wt. was commonly recommended for Jeep front and rear differentials (except Powr-Lok units, which require special lubricant). SAE 90-wt. accommodated the typical manual transmission and transfer case fill. Cold weather operation demanded 80-wt. in all units except a Powr-Lok.

NOTE——
Powr-Lok is the Spicer trade name for a positive traction differential. The factory has optioned Powr-Lok and other limited slip axles for many years. The clutch units in positive traction differentials require special lubricants and/or additives. Cleaning requires special techniques to prevent clutch damage. Use only specified fluids in a Jeep limited slip differential.

Since the introduction of improved, multi-viscosity lubricants, 85/90-wt. and even 80/140-wt. gear oils (designed for both wide temperature range and limited slip use) have become popular. Later Jeep chain drive transfer cases, and even some manual transmissions, rely on lighter specified gear lubricants, including engine oils, automatic transmission fluids (ATF) and conventional or multi-viscosity gear lubricants.

NOTE——
For late model transmissions and chain drive transfer cases, including Quadra-Trac, Selec-Trac and Command-Trac types, consult your Jeep owner's manual for recommended fluid types.

Fig. 5-11. *Transmission and transfer case fill plugs double as check points for lubricant. With your Jeep on level ground, oil should just reach lower edge of fill plug holes.*

Fluid Levels

Before removing any fill/inspection plug, clean the surrounding area. Likewise, take special care when checking an automatic transmission dipstick. Keep debris and abrasive contaminants away from openings. These are expensive gear units, responsible for taking your Jeep into remote back country. Cleanliness assures reliability.

Fluid should never rest above a gearbox fill hole. If the gear unit is overfull on level ground, drain it back to the lower edge of the fill hole. (Always make sure your Jeep chassis is level before making this determination.)

Overfilled gear cases can raise havoc. A common example is the combination of steep vehicle operating angles and an overfilled early T-90 three-speed manual transmission. Excess oil, trapped between the shift rail ends and the control housing welch plugs, may actually drive a plug loose from the housing. When this occurs, a leak develops in the vicinity of the bellhousing, and gear lube can find its way to the clutch lining.

Engine Lubrication and Underhood Service

Put on a pair of handy latex mechanic's gloves, and place a container beneath the oil pan. With the oil still warm but not hot, remove the drain plug. Let the oil drain while you perform the engine bay lubrication chores.

NOTE——
Willys and Kaiser Jeep trucks demand more underhood attention than later models. The shift to dry paper air cleaners and throw-away canister fuel filters reduces the service requirements for AMC- and Chrysler-built Jeep trucks.

Fig. 5-12. *T-90 transmission, popular on a variety of 1946–71 models, is vulnerable to shift rail leaks. Overfilling can dislodge front shift rail plugs while shifting on a steep downslope.*

Although dry paper elements offer exceptionally good air filtration, they quickly fail when exposed to high dust levels. Jeep, recognizing the utility of oil bath air cleaners, stayed with this more expensive, earlier technology well into the 1960s.

Dry paper elements require frequent service and special safety precautions. During deep stream fording, water drawn through the intake snorkel can quickly pass through the paper element and into the engine's cylinders. If sufficient in volume, this water acts like a hydraulic ram, bending connecting rods or breaking other vital engine parts. Avoid use of an open faced paper filter air cleaner if water can reach the surface of the element.

Servicing an Oil Bath Air Filter

If your earlier Jeep engine has an oil bath air cleaner, service the unit every 2,000 miles. This is also a convenient time to change your engine oil. (Older engines with by-pass type oil filtration will benefit from such frequent oil changes.)

Fig. 5-13. *Oil bath air cleaner and sediment bowl fuel filters are common to earlier Jeep models. Although these filters require more service effort, they offer several advantages in the field.*

A very dirty oil bath-type air filter, unlike a paper element, will still permit reasonable engine performance. This can create the impression that the filter is okay. For maximum performance and economy, however, you must service the oil bath unit more frequently when driving in dusty conditions.

Remove the oil bath air cleaner assembly completely from the engine, then separate the filtering element from the oil cup. Clean both of these components thoroughly in a suitable solvent and allowed them to air dry. Avoid use of compressed air, as it may damage the element.

On CJ models, the oil cup fills with just over half a quart (U.S.). On early J-trucks and other models with oil bath filters, you will find an oil fill line in the oil cup. Use clean, fresh engine oil (no need for an expensive synthetic type here), and take care not to spill oil during re-installation of the bulky assembly.

Make certain that your Jeep's air cleaner seals properly. Abrasive dust, seeping into the engine through an air cleaner mounting gasket leak, can quickly destroy piston rings. If the air cleaner seals look weak or seat poorly, replace them immediately.

Dry Paper Air Filtration

Your Jeep will likely see more dust exposure than most other vehicles. A clean, adequate intake air supply is crucial to your engine's survival.

Any late model Jeep has dry paper air filtration. For such a Jeep to perform well, you must service the dry paper element regularly. Once impacted with dirt, the dry paper element starves the engine for air. The effect is like running your engine continuously with the choke on.

In extreme cases, you must replace the element immediately. If you are uncertain whether the air cleaner will flow enough air, perform a simple field

Fig. 5-14. *An exposed dry paper air filter is cause for concern. If enough water splashes against the filter surface, your running engine could draw water. Bent connecting rods have resulted from large doses.*

Synthetic Versus Mineral Oil Products

When Jeep L- and F-134 fours and the Hurricane 6 engines reigned, few oil choices existed. Viscosity and detergent levels were the sole concerns. Until the 1960s, multiviscosity oil was virtually non-existent.

The fundamental difference between one brand of mineral based oil and another is the additive package. Generally, we accept that a modern, multi-viscosity, high-detergent, high-dispersant oil offers broader engine protection under the widest variety of engine operating conditions. Over the last two decades, a newer debate has surfaced around mineral versus synthetic based oils and greases. Based upon currently available information, the higher quality synthetic oils and greases appear far superior to conventional mineral or crude stock products.

Sludge kills engines. Poor oil circulation always accompanies sludge, and a plugged or restricted oil screen means scored bearings and engine failure. Although changing oil is the best way to resist sludge buildup, other factors also play a role. The composition of an oil, regardless of the oil drain intervals, can build sludge, and high temperatures encourage sludge buildup.

The traditional gasoline automotive engine, for each 100 gallons of fuel burned, produces a horrifying 1/4 to 4 pounds of nitrogen and sulfuric acid, 1 to 2 ounces of hydrochloric acid, 90 to 120 gallons of water, and 3 to 10 gallons of unburned gasoline. For the once popular lead-additive gasolines, add 6 to 10 ounces of lead salts to this medley of pollutants. At the typical 3,000-mile drain interval, petroleum oil in the crankcase has reached a contamination level of four percent.

How, then, do synthetic oil manufacturers extend oil change intervals to 15,000 miles or more? Mobil and others claim that longer term viscosity stability (due to superior control of hydrocarbon volatility), plus greater resistance to sludge formation, contribute to these longer service cycles. Superior ingredients reduce engine heat, friction and oxidation. Higher film strength and lower volatility lead to claims that quality synthetic oils will last longer and protect an engine far better than any mineral base oil currently available.

The lubrication quality, engine cooling and cleansing action of synthetics is exceptional. Even at -40° F (pictured) Mobil Delvac 1 still pours. Typical mineral based oils have already solidified. Test results also show Mobil 1 operating an engine 50° F cooler than a premium mineral based oil.

Under laboratory tests, high grade synthetic oils drastically reduce sludge, piston varnish, wear of metal parts and oil consumption. Importantly, the piston ring sealing properties of an oil largely determine the amount of contaminants that will find their way into the crankcase, and high grade synthetic oils claim exceptional ring sealing capability and cylinder wall protection.

Prominent race engine builders confirm the merits of synthetic oils. Notably, Smokey Yunick, quoted from a *Popular Science* interview, commented about his Indianapolis 500 race engine and polyol synthetic. Upon teardown after the race, Yunick observed, "When you disassemble an engine that's been run on petroleum oil, if you examine the rings and cylinder bores with a glass, you'll see ridges and scratches—that's wear going on. With polyol [a variety of synthetic], when you take the engine apart, everything has the appearance of being chrome plated. In the engine we ran at Indianapolis, we used a polyol synthetic. When we tore the engine down, you could still see the original honing marks on the bearings...no wear at all. I've never seen that before."

Is such protection necessary for your Jeep? Recognizing the stresses of off-road driving and harsh climates, any oil product would face hard work in a Jeep engine.

On the downside, many owners switching to synthetic oil on high mileage engines have trouble. Worn, varnish-coated seals and gaskets, suddenly faced with the high cleansing action and superior lubricity of synthetic oil, begin to leak. The synthetic oil has washed away the "false sealing surfaces" of built-up varnish and deposits. Seals and gaskets may require upgrading, but once seals meet normal standards, a synthetic oil will likely increase seal and gasket life.

Service Footnote:

Based upon my research and experience, I will not use any other oil than a high grade synthetic in my 4x4 gasoline engines. As for change intervals, I go exclusively by oil coloration, typically running synthetic oil between its new, honey color and a medium mocha. Dark brown is the furthest wear point for my oil. Near-black would be way too much wear. Using this formula, my oil lasts anywhere from 2,000 to 10,000 miles. In my experience, a Jeep carbureted engine will require more frequent oil changes than a later model, cleaner-burning EFI powerplant.

Whether or not the oil gets changed, I replace a full-flow oil filter each 2500–3000 miles. I use a shorter interval of 1500–2000 miles for my restored F-134 Jeep engine with a by-pass filtration system. When there's no need to change the oil, I simply replace the oil filter and top off with synthetic oil.

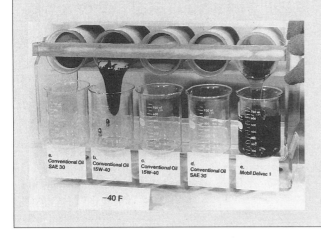

a. Conventional Oil SAE 30 b. Conventional Oil 15W-40 c. Conventional Oil 15W-40 d. Conventional Oil SAE 30 e. Mobil Delvac 1

–40 F

Fig. 5-15. *Dry paper air filter element held toward sunlight reveals degree of clogging. Light should be clearly visible around the entire cleaner. If not, replace the filter.*

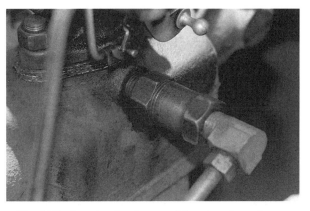

Fig. 5-16. *Jeep trucks pioneered the closed crankcase ventilation system. Even the earliest MB and CJ models feature an orificed ventilator valve, the predecessor to modern positive crankcase ventilation (PCV) valves.*

test. Remove the filter and gently tap its base on a clean, flat surface until all debris has fallen free.

It is virtually impossible to thoroughly clean a dry paper element. Reverse blowing (inside to outside) with compressed air will not extend element life. Most manufacturers caution against such cleaning methods, emphasizing that damage to the paper will result.

You can quickly test the paper air filter's condition by the sunlight method. Aim the filter toward bright sunlight or a similar source. (Even a lantern or flashlight will do, but keep a safe distance from any flame—the air cleaner element emits highly flammable gasoline fumes!)

Tilt the element and look from the center toward the light source. Rotate the cleaner slowly. A new or functional dry paper filter will reveal light through its wafered layers. If no light is visible, or light seems scarce and intermittent, assume that the element needs replacement.

When planning a long trip over dusty roads and trails, carry extra air cleaner elements. A clogged air filter drastically reduces fuel economy and performance. Carbon buildup and internal engine damage result from long-term neglect. A fresh air filter is cost effective.

> NOTE —
> Engine service includes the fuel, spark and emission control systems. For details on tune-up and servicing these areas, refer to the service chapters.

Closed Crankcase System

Jeep pioneered closed crankcase ventilation. Two decades before the positive crankcase ventilation system became a mandatory California pollution control device, Willys engineered a sealed crankcase for the MB Jeep's L-134 engine. The goal, however, was to water-

Fig. 5-17. *Jeep power steering is an asset. With the engine stopped, check fluid at the power steering reservoir fill cap. Keep debris from entering the reservoir. Use correct type ATF or power steering fluid specified for your truck.*

proof the engine. Eliminating an open road draft tube and carefully locating the air cleaner helped keep moisture from the engine's crankcase and cylinders.

A crankcase ventilation valve or "PCV" requires periodic service. For details, see the emission control and tune-up chapters.

Attention to Details

While beneath the hood, check the manual or power steering gear fluid. Begin by clearing away debris from the inspection plug (manual steering gear) or the power steering pump dipstick. Remove the plug or dipstick, check the fluid level, and top off fluid as necessary. If you find the fluid very low, look for leaks.

Manual steering gears use conventional gear lubricant. SAE 80-wt. or equivalent is the standard for an earlier Jeep. (In a temperate or hotter climate, 90-wt.

works fine in a manual steering gear.) Power steering requires the fluid type recommended on the power steering reservoir or in your Jeep owners manual.

By-pass Cartridge Oil Filter

Older L-head and F-head Jeep engines have cartridge type engine oil filters. If your filter mounts separately from the engine, with oil lines connected to the engine block, you have a by-pass oil filter. The steel canister has a removable top.

A replacement cartridge fits securely within the canister. As you remove the top and disassemble the filter, note the parts layout. Discard the cartridge and wipe sludge and debris from the interior of the housing. A clean rag or shop towel, dampened lightly with solvent, will help here.

Install a new cartridge, making certain that the oil seals are intact. Install the new lid gasket, and replace pieces in the reverse order of disassembly. Assuming you drained the oil, install a new crankcase drain plug gasket and tighten the plug securely.

Refill the engine crankcase with fresh oil, adding enough oil beyond the FULL mark to fill the new oil filter. (If the filter canister sets level, you can fill the filter before installing its lid, then fill the crankcase to the dipstick's FULL line.) Run the engine for several minutes; check for leaks; stop the engine; allow oil to drain into the crankcase for several minutes; check the oil level, and top off if necessary.

Jeep introduced spin-on oil filters with Kaiser's revolutionary 1962 Tornado 230 engine. If your Jeep engine has a spin-on filter, replace the unit with each oil change. Fill the crankcase to FULL and add enough

additional oil to fill your new oil filter. (Some filters take a full U.S. quart, while smaller units take half a quart.) Run the engine and check for oil leaks. Shut off the engine; wait a few minutes for complete oil drain down; check the oil level, and top off if necessary.

Often Overlooked Items

On the earlier Jeep trucks, the generator, ignition distributor and even the starter motor (CJ-2A models) require periodic oiling. Several drops of oil, applied regularly to the oil wicks, assure long service. Look for spring-loaded oil caps at these locations and add clean engine oil with a squirt can. Jeep recommends oiling every 1,000 miles. Avoid excess use of oil. Simply saturate the oil wicks.

Several other service points require attention. The battery case should be kept clean, with distilled water added as necessary. Manifold heat riser valves, found on many Jeep engines, need regular service. Apply penetrating oil to the shaft. Make sure the weight and valve move freely.

Remove the speedometer cable, wipe it down and dress with speedometer cable lubricant. Treat all early Jeep control cables (steel conduit sleeve type) with a penetrating oil such as WD-40. Some lithium sprays work equally well. (With penetrants, always wipe off excess to avoid attracting dirt.) If cables still balk, remove and clean them thoroughly, then lubricate with a suitable graphite or lithium base grease.

Jeep clutch control cables have always been a serious point of wear and contention. The cable ends, cable and pivots require regular attention. Although Jeep originally called for engine oil as a lubricant, a white lithium grease that dries after contact works far better and lasts longer.

White lithium and silicone sprays work well on hood and tailgate hinges, latches, strikers and locks.

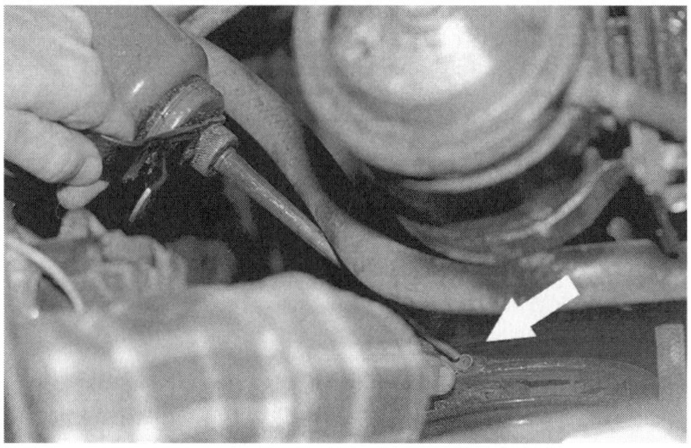

Fig. 5-18. *The by-pass oil filter has a removable cartridge. This element requires replacement every oil change. Put on a pair of mechanic's latex gloves and thoroughly clean the canister with a fresh, solvent dampened cloth.*

Fig. 5-19. *Oil wicks (arrow) are common to early Jeep generators, distributors and some starter motors. Add motor oil cautiously, just enough to soak the wick.*

Fig. 5-20. *The heat riser valve must move freely. Engine performance and the cold-start system rely on this valve working properly. Mopar has a special penetrating oil (Part No. 4318039) formulated specifically to loosen and lubricate the shaft.*

Lithium acts more like a grease, while silicone penetrates exceptionally well and frees up sticky mechanisms. Use a quality silicone spray (without petroleum solvents or distillates) around rubber parts. Read the label carefully to understand each product's intended use. Choose a lubricant that will dry quickly. Wipe off any excess to avoid dirt accumulation.

Keep these products away from painted surfaces.

2. Long-term Storage Of Your Jeep Truck

Many Jeep 4x4s see only seasonal use and park for the rest of the year. Some Jeep trucks are strictly for snowplowing, while others collect dust until the fall's big game hunt. An arctic Jeep might hibernate through chilling winter gales, immobile from early fall to the beginning of summer.

Proper storage of a Jeep vehicle takes various factors into account. Temperature and humidity require certain precautions. You must protect the engine, geartrain, cooling and electrical systems, body, fuel system, tires and brakes.

Body and Upholstery

Preserving the body and upholstery of your Jeep involves many of the same chemicals that you use for detail work. A heavy coat of wax, preferably buffer applied for even distribution, is always advisable. For extreme climates and long storage, cosmoline helps.

For upholstery, if vinyl, along with the dash pad and all other plastic and rubber areas of the Jeep, I apply a coating of 303 Protectant. This product also helps preserve tire sidewalls and canvas tops.

Protective Anti-oxidation Coatings

Professional rustproofing treatment, hot wax, and spray undercoatings help protect the underside of the body and chassis. You can apply some products at home, like rubberized spray undercoating. Whenever your Jeep faces exposure to salt air, every precaution must be taken to eliminate oxidation of bare metal.

Once the body, frame/chassis, wheels and tires have been thoroughly protected, you should blanket the Jeep with a fitted cover. An enclosed garage, barn or storage shed would further protect your Jeep from elemental damage. Prevent exposure to bird droppings, tree sap and other corrosive hazards that impair wax protection and destroy paint. In a humid climate, allow the covered vehicle to "breathe" sufficiently, or moisture damage may occur.

Engine Protection During Storage

Before storing your Jeep, change the engine oil and install a new oil filter. (With fresh oil, run the engine to warm up. This will assure clean oil flow throughout the system.) The air filter element (paper-type) should also be new and sealing properly. If your older Jeep has an oil bath air cleaner, thoroughly clean the unit and change the oil. Belts and hoses must be in top condition. With the engine shut off, apply a quality belt dressing to each drive belt.

If the engine will set for a very long period, or if high humidity and varied temperatures are a factor, protect the cylinder walls, valve guides, valve seats, valves and piston rings. Remove the spark plugs and squirt approximately two tablespoons of Marvel Mystery Oil or a similar lubricant into each cylinder.

Re-install the spark plugs, and with the coil wire disconnected or ignition rotor removed, crank the engine very briefly. This will coat the cylinder walls and other bare metal in the upper cylinders with a film of highly refined oil. You may want to leave the ignition inoperative as a safety and anti-theft measure during storage.

After the storage period, before attempting a start up, crank the engine over. This will pump the excess oil from the cylinders. Remove and clean the spark plugs or install a fresh set. Reinstall the ignition rotor or coil wire and start the engine, maintaining the lowest possible rpm. Oil pressure should appear immediately upon start-up and quickly register normal.

Protect Dormant Fuel System

If water contamination in the fuel is a concern, run a can of fuel system de-icer through the fuel tank before storage. Carburetor cleaner with alcohol or other water bonding dispersants may be sprayed directly into

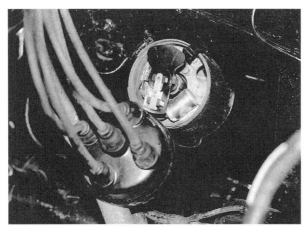

Fig. 5-21. *Removal of the coil wire and rotor during storage discourages theft and allows engine cranking without a start-up after long dormancy.*

the float bowl through the carburetor vent opening (either externally or at the air horn, depending on carburetor design). A teaspoonful would be plenty.

Cooling System and Storage

The cooling system requires fresh antifreeze/coolant (ethylene glycol type or a newer, environmentally friendlier equivalent) with a 50/50 mixture that tests

Fig. 5-22. *Radiator hydrometer tests specific gravity of coolant/anti-freeze. Weak concentrations allow freeze-up and also lower the boiling point. Excess concentration adversely affects the expansion rate.*

minimally to -34 degrees Fahrenheit on a hydrometer. Add a quality water pump lubricant/anti-rust agent. An alternative to water pump lubricant is traditional "soluble oil," a vegetable based, non-mineral (non-petroleum) oil that also preserves rubber parts. Run the engine, with the heater on, to thoroughly mix coolant and lube/anti-rust.

Unless the storage area will be subject to temperatures below -34 degrees Fahrenheit, avoid heavier concentrations of anti-freeze. Pure anti-freeze has an insufficient expansion rate and can actually allow engine parts to expand and break at cold temperature extremes. This is also the reason why a "boil over" results from over-concentrations of coolant. Follow the mixture chart and manufacturer's recommendations on the anti-freeze/coolant container.

Tighten all hose clamps, inspect hoses for cracking or weather checking and consider installing a new thermostat if the system requires flushing or draining. When running the engine and circulating new coolant, be certain to operate the heater. Coolant/anti-freeze of proper mix must fill the heater and all hoses, or damage from localized freezing could result.

Chassis and Powertrain Preservation

Several powertrain items require attention. Lubricate the U-joints and all other grease fittings on your Jeep. Force old chassis lube from the joints and make certain new grease squeezes from the joint. To prevent surface oxidation and dehydration, dress rubber bushings at the shock absorbers, springs and sway bars with a specified rubber lubricant or 303 Protectant.

If you haven't repacked the wheel bearings recently, buy new front wheel seals and fresh grease. Remove

Fig. 5-23. *Rubber bushings at shackles, sway bar and shock absorber ends require protection from oxidation and friction. Special rubber lubricant (non-mineral based) or silicone helps protect these vulnerable parts.*

the wheels and hubs, and inspect for any signs of moisture damage. Thoroughly clean, closely inspect and re-pack the bearings with fresh, quality grease. Fit new seals during installation. (For details on how to repack front wheel bearings, see service chapters.)

Check fluid levels in each gear case and the axle/differential units. Note the cleanliness, smell and appearance of the gear oil. (A burnt, acrid odor indicates older, likely worn gear lube.) Moisture will give a milky, greyish appearance either in the fluid or around the housing cavity.

If moisture appears, drain and flush the gear unit with a light engine oil or a specified flushing oil, then drain completely and refill with fresh, appropriate grade gear oil. (During flushing, drive the Jeep, at a minimal load, for only a very short distance.)

Major damage to expensive bearings, gears and shafts will result from unchecked water in the gear cases. Inspect all gearcase and axle housing vents. One-way check valves must be clean and seat properly.

If you are storing an automatic transmission equipped Jeep for a lengthy period, change the transmission fluid and filter. Operate the truck long enough to fully circulate clean fluid. ATF is a high detergent oil, and fresh fluid purges older, acidic lubricant that would otherwise act on seals. Fresh fluid also helps flush varnish from the sensitive valve body.

Preparing the Electrical System For Storage

Before you place your Jeep on furlough, the electrical system requires attention. Disconnect the battery to eliminate any drainage from the clock or other items. Clean the outer battery case thoroughly with a solution of baking soda and an inexpensive nylon paint

Fig. 5-24. *One-way check valve (arrow) allows transfer case, transmission and axle housings to vent pressure. Make sure these valves are clear and seating properly to prevent moisture from entering the gear unit.*

brush. If you remove the battery, make sure it rests on a non-conductive surface with a full charge at the time of storage. Remember, a fully discharged battery, one with low enough specific gravity, can freeze and crack.

> *WARNING—*
> *Avoid splashing battery cleaning solution on painted surfaces or into your eyes. Wear protective goggles. Make certain that the cleaning solution does not enter any of the battery cells. Rinse away all solution with a stream of clean water, and allow to drip and air dry thoroughly.*

Many battery specialists recommend storage of the battery at a moderate temperature. If possible, avoid exposing the battery to extreme heat or cold, and always store away from spark or flame sources. After storage, bring the battery up to full charge with a trickle charger. (Make certain that the charger has a built-in voltage regulator to prevent overcharging.)

Brake System and Storage

Hydraulic brake fluid has an affinity for moisture. On all Jeep trucks built prior to 1967, the master cylinder vents directly to atmosphere. These systems are vulnerable to moisture contamination. Eventually, especially if you store the vehicle for long periods, moisture seeps into the system, causing oxidation damage and pitting of the hydraulic brake cylinders.

As a minimal precaution, especially with these older braking systems, you should routinely flush fresh brake fluid through the hydraulic system. (A power bleeder speeds up this procedure.) The aim is to force old fluid, and any contaminants held in suspension, from the system.

The traditional, more involved method is to flush the system with denatured alcohol, then disassemble each wheel cylinder and the master cylinder. Air dry the lines and cylinders; replace all rubber seals; then reassemble and fill/bleed the entire system with clean, DOT 3 or higher grade fresh brake fluid. (See service chapters for details on brake work.)

When you have flushed and cleaned the system thoroughly with denatured alcohol, a third alternative is available. Silicone brake fluid, although expensive, virtually eliminates the water absorption problem. When converting from conventional brake fluid to silicone, however, the system must be entirely purged of conventional brake fluid. If you store your Jeep truck on a regular basis, silicone brake fluid is practical.

Fortunately, since 1967, most Jeep brake systems
are far less prone to absorbing moisture. Master cylinder covers with a bellows-type seal offer reasonably
good protection against atmospheric contamination.

Tires and Final Comments

If your Jeep will be dormant for over a few months,
place the truck on jack stands. Tires suffer from longer
storage periods, with sidewall distortion and undue
belt/ply stress.

Jeep storage precautions directly relate to local
climatic conditions. Desert environments pose concerns about ultraviolet damage and dehydration of
rubber seals and bushings. Arctic regions demand protection from freezing. Moist and salt air regions call
for anti-rust measures.

Fig. 5-25. *Rubber bushings and tires succumb to dehydration, oxidation and embrittlement. Inspect your Jeep
for bushing, cushion, body mount and tire fatigue.*

Chapter 6

Troubleshooting

Your Jeep 4x4 takes plenty of abuse, especially on primitive trails. While routine maintenance and inspection will enhance the truck's overall reliability, your talent at making emergency field repairs could mean the difference between walking or driving back to civilization.

After more than three decades of exposure to Jeep 4x4 trucks, I cannot overstate the need for preventive care, those service steps that turn up potential problems. In most cases, parts provide ample warning before they fail. Your best tactical advantage for preventing trouble is periodic inspection of the chassis and powertrain.

Each time you lube or tune your Jeep, take a thorough look at the chassis, axle and driveline components. After a hard day on the trail, kneel under the truck and take a physical inventory of the chassis.

1. Aftermath of Hard Four-wheeling

Stretching over rocks and logs stresses your Jeep's chassis to the limit. Springs and shackles twist in every direction, while bushings and joints battle awkward angles. As the dust settles from a day on the rocks, your Jeep needs a thorough inspection for damage.

Look beneath the front bumper at the axle, steering linkage, leaf or coil springs and the front shackles or link arms. Vulnerable items include the tie-rod assembly, steering stabilizer shock and axle housing. Look for oil seepage and cracks along the axle unit, especially gear lube leaking where the axle housing tubes press into the center member. Extreme jarring and twisting can dislodge, bend or crack these tubes and injure the housing.

Fig. 6-1. *Far from the pavement or your home garage, troubleshooting skills are vital. Regular, preventive care pays off in these situations.*

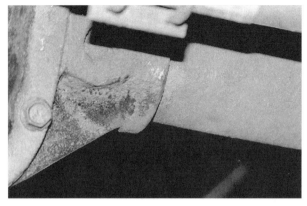

Fig. 6-2. *Nearly all Jeep trucks have solid, Spicer-type live front axles. Severe off-road pounding can loosen the axle tubes at the housing center section.*

Fig. 6-3. *Spring flex loosens U-bolts and clamps. Look for misaligned leafs, broken plates and spring sag.*

Note the condition of the springs. Look for broken or out-of-line leafs and bent U-bolts. If a leaf spring appears offset from its axle perch, suspect a broken center bolt. Leafs out of alignment mean loose U-bolts or distorted spring clamps.

The tie-rod and steering damper are especially vulnerable on Jeep trucks. Due to available space and the necessary position of the front driveshaft, the steering linkage must mount forward of the axle housing on a solid axle vehicle. This makes steering parts susceptible to damage. Setting near the centerline of the axle housing, a long tie-rod and hydraulic stabilizer face unseen rocks, tree stumps and debris.

Veteran Jeep operators know where this tie-rod rides. Aware driving involves a sense for low hanging and vulnerable chassis parts. When knocking around on boulder-strewn trails, protect your Jeep's axle housings, suspension, steering, driveshafts, brakes, fuel system and other chassis/powertrain components.

Check the stabilizer bar (if so equipped), support links and bushings. These parts really flex, especially off-road. Look closely at the brake hoses and other brake hardware. Brush, tree limbs and loose rock can damage sensitive safety items. Learn to scan along brake and fuel lines; watch for kinks or rock damage. In the worst cases, it is possible to rip whole sections of brake pipe loose from the frame or rear axle housing. Accidently backing into a rock or tree stump can crush the rear axle housing pipes and impair braking action.

Before finishing your inspection, pay close attention to the steering knuckle joints. Earlier closed knuckle joints have kingpin bearings. Later models with open knuckles use ball joints. A broken or loose joint will impair steering. Severe impact can break a kingpin bearing race, crack a knuckle casting or damage a steering knuckle ball joint. On closed-knuckle front ends, especially earlier Jeep trucks and CJs, also

Fig. 6-4. *Steering linkage, stabilizer shock and tie-rod require close inspection. Mounted in front of the axle housing, the tie-rod is vulnerable to rocks, stumps and debris.*

watch for spindle separation from the knuckle casting and for cracks in the spindle.

Inspect the rear axle housing for leaks, cracks or broken welds. Springs and spring supports demand close attention. Look for emergency brake cable damage, signs of water in the axle housing and evidence of mud or sand in the brake drums. Inspect the exhaust system for leaks, dents, kinks or any other damage that might impair flow or generate unsafe fumes.

The driveshafts, flexing and moving constantly, are also susceptible to damage. On rocky trails and creek bed travels, keep U-joint flanges and driveshaft tubes away from rocks and stumps. It is relatively easy to spring (bend) a driveshaft tube.

Memorize the safe, original appearance of your Jeep undercarriage. When inspecting the chassis, use that image as a standard. Subject to off-pavement hazards, Jeep reliability depends on smart driving habits, the willingness to pick sensible travel routes and unrelenting chassis inspection. Skid plates are not enough.

Fig. 6-5. *Brake hoses and brake or fuel pipes require close inspection. In rough terrain, these safety items face many obstacles.*

Fig. 6-6. *Steering knuckles and kingpin (pivot pin) or ball-joint pivotal supports are vulnerable to impact damage. Inspect these safety components regularly.*

2. A Guide to Troubleshooting

Engine failure is the most intimidating aspect of remote travel. Earlier Jeep engines have skid plate protection to prevent an oil pan rupture, yet your engine can quit for far less reason than loss of oil. Unprepared, you'll burn as much shoe leather over a shorted ignition module as a seized connecting rod bearing.

> CAUTION —
> *Later model Jeep engines have no oil pan skid plate. In severe rock-crawling, some owners have ruptured the oil pan, punctured the oil filter or torn loose the drain plug. Know your oil pan's location and protect it. If necessary and practical, install a skid plate to protect the pan and oil filter. Good driver skills and prudence can prevent most of these problems.*

Maintaining your Jeep requires troubleshooting savvy and the means to remedy common problems. Whether you perform repairs or sublet the work to a qualified shop, troubleshooting skill increases self-sufficiency and heightens understanding of your Jeep. (For additional details, see service chapters.)

> NOTE —
> Overhaul of model-specific powertrain and chassis components is beyond the scope of this book. For additional overhaul and repair guidelines, refer to your Jeep factory shop manual or a professional-level service manual.

2.1 Engine and Electrical Problems

Lack Of Power

Low Compression results from a pressure leak at one or more cylinders. Loss of compression suggests several defects. Leaking or misadjusted intake or exhaust valves, worn or defective piston rings, a blown head gasket or casting cracks can each lower compression. So does a severely worn camshaft and timing chain or gear set. Coolant loss into the engine oil (turning it milky) indicates a cracked cylinder head or engine block—or a leaking head gasket.

Diagnosing low compression requires a compression gauge or cylinder leakdown tester. (See other chapters for test procedures.) A field testing method involves shorting each cylinder's spark lead and noting engine rpm drop.

Internal Friction indicates major engine trouble. A Jeep engine that will not crank easily requires close inspection. First, rule out the obvious starter/electrical problems. Place the transmission in neutral. Remove

Fig. 6-7. *A compression test reveals loss of cylinder pressure. When only two adjacent cylinders show low pressure, suspect a warped cylinder head or a head gasket failure. General wear to the valves and piston rings has caused low compression in this 258 AMC/Jeep six.*

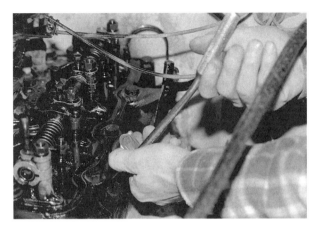

Fig. 6-8. *Remove the spark plugs and rotate the crankshaft. High resistance indicates internal damage.*

all spark plugs and rotate the crankshaft with an appropriate socket and ratchet. The engine should turn freely, with only moderate resistance from the valvetrain.

To eliminate transmission damage as a possible cause, have a helper disengage the clutch (depress the pedal) while you rotate the crankshaft. If the engine will not turn freely, suspect bearing, piston, connecting rod or valve damage. When water (either drawn through the intake system or originating as an internal leak) prevents engine rotation, removing the spark plugs allows the liquid an avenue of escape. Water in sufficient quantity can cause severe damage, including bent or broken connecting rods.

Overheat/Seizure means serious trouble. If the engine will not crank or rotate after a severe overheat, major damage has likely occurred. Pistons can distort from the heat and gall the cylinder walls. Lubrication deteriorates, compounded by the severe load of seizing pistons, and the crankshaft bearings fail. (A connected rod may break as well.) Valve stems can seize in their guides, and the camshaft may even seize in its bearings. Casting cracks are common, especially around exhaust valve seats and cylinders.

The least gloomy prospect is that a cylinder head, or even both heads on a V-8, has warped, permitting head gasket failure. Coolant has filled the cylinders, locking up the engine. Here, however, the risk of bent connecting rods and other crankshaft assembly damage remains.

Fuel Starvation results from low fuel supply pressure or volume. In addition to fuel pump malfunctions and restrictions in the supply or return lines, EFI-equipped engines suffer from pressure regulator defects or fouled/defective injectors. A sticking carburetor float needle, although rare, is another source of

Fig. 6-9. *Radiator damage, overheat and loss of coolant are more than an inconvenience. Piston/cylinder wall galling and engine bearing damage result from extreme heat. Amount of heat involved will determine the extent of damage.*

Fig. 6-10. *A fuel pump pressure gauge quickly determines pressure output. Before condemning the pump or other expensive items, look to the simpler causes, like a plugged fuel filter.*

trouble for carbureted engines. Also check for a clogged fuel/gas cap, especially on earlier vented-type fuel systems.

Testing fuel pump pressure requires a special gauge. Pump flow volume is easier to determine. Before suspecting the fuel pump volume, flow rate or carburetion/injection troubles, consider the fuel filter(s) or the fuel line inlet filter in the gas tank. Especially with a paper fuel filter, a single fill-up with watery gasoline can stop fuel flow.

Weak Ignition creates hard-starting problems and a lack of power. Breaker point rubbing block wear retards ignition timing and points resistance increases with pitting and arcing. Condenser, rotor, distributor cap and spark cable defects each weaken spark output. Check the distributor shaft for excess runout (sideplay), a common cause of erratic spark output and ignition timing. Dwell angle variance of more than two degrees is a sign of distributor defects.

> NOTE —
> Mechanics often condemn the coil, although a coil is less likely to fail than a condenser, breaker points or an electronic module.

Breaker point and electronic ignitions are vulnerable to wire failures and poor connections (due to corrosion or dirt) that cause poor ignition performance. Check carefully for insulation breakdown and shorts to ground. Especially on early Jeep models with cloth-wrapped wire, insulation failure is a very common source of trouble. Test wires at suspected junctions.

You will find a wiring diagram for your Jeep in a factory or professional level shop manual. If an electrical or ignition problem is not readily apparent, diagnose the problem further with either your volt-ohmmeter or take your Jeep to a local service garage.

Vacuum Leaks, if severe, will prevent the engine from running. A sufficient leak creates low manifold

Fig. 6-12. *A low-volatility spray solvent or penetrating oil helps detect engine vacuum leaks. With the engine idling, spray toward the intake manifold sealing edges and the carburetor base. If a leak exists, rpm will change.*

pressure, stalling, a lean air/fuel mixture and backfire. Even small leaks can lean the air/fuel mixture, cause idle speed to drop and prevent smooth performance.

A sudden inability to idle indicates a vacuum leak. Check the PCV valve, all vacuum hoses, the distributor advance diaphragm and transmission vacuum modulator, if so equipped. Intake manifold bolts loosen over time, resulting in poor gasket sealing and vacuum loss. Torque manifold bolts and the carburetor mounting nuts. As the engine idles, spray a mist of low-volatility penetrating oil along the gasket sealing edges. Listen for a change in engine speed. This indicates a leak.

Clutch Slippage and related troubles are relatively easy to detect. Before testing, check and adjust the clutch at the release arm. (See service chapters for clutch adjustment methods.) Make certain that the clutch disengages and engages properly. Through the release arm opening in the bellhousing, observe whether the throwout bearing actually moves the

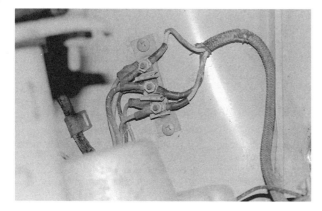

Fig. 6-11. *Wiring shorts, fraying and bad grounds cause the majority of field failures. Look closely at routed wires and connections.*

Fig. 6-13. *Always check clutch adjustment at the release arm. Pedal play alone is misleading, as linkage wear can masquerade as clutch free play.*

clutch release fingers (levers). Have an assistant depress the clutch pedal.

If the clutch release arm has insufficient movement, check the linkage from the pedal all the way to the release arm. Note excessive play and correct the cause. In the case of a hydraulic linkage system, inspect the fluid level and bleed any air from the system. Repair or replace defective parts.

Now drive down a deserted road at 15–20 mph. Depress the clutch pedal, and place the transmission in high gear. Raise engine rpm to 2500 and rapidly release the clutch pedal. Engine rpm should drop immediately. If rpm decreases gradually, the clutch unit is probably weak. Sources of trouble could include worn clutch cover springs, a worn or glazed clutch plate or oil on the clutch unit.

Engine Will Not Run

My 'Three Essentials' for optimal engine performance are normal compression, correct valve lift and proper valve timing. When troubleshooting reaches beyond spark timing adjustment, changing a fuel filter or basic tuning, make certain your engine meets these three requirements. Measure compression with a compression gauge or cylinder leakdown tester. (See tune-up/service chapters.) If compression registers normal for each cylinder, verify valve lift by removing the valve cover (side cover on L-head Jeep blocks and F-heads).

Measure the height of each valve from a closed position to fully open. This is the total (gross) valve lift produced by each camshaft lobe. Compare this to specifications found in your Jeep factory service manual. (Some procedures call for lobe or valve lifter lift instead of gross valve lift.)

In addition to valve lift, make note of valve timing variances that result from a severely worn timing chain mechanism or gearset. If ignition timing has suddenly become retarded, yet the distributor housing remains securely clamped to the engine block, suspect excess slack in the timing chain or bad sprockets, which can allow valve timing to jump one or more teeth.

Tune-up Problems include faulty ignition, inadequate fuel supply, flooding or vacuum leaks. On breaker point ignitions, verify point dwell angle and resistance. Both breaker point and electronic distributors require spark timing adjustment. Fuel system troubles involve dirty filters, plugged carburetor passages, a sticky needle/seat assembly in the carburetor, a defective float or a defective fuel pump. (See service chapters for details on ignition timing procedures and other tune-related tasks.)

Isolate problems. Verify the strength of the ignition spark, check timing and ensure that the engine has

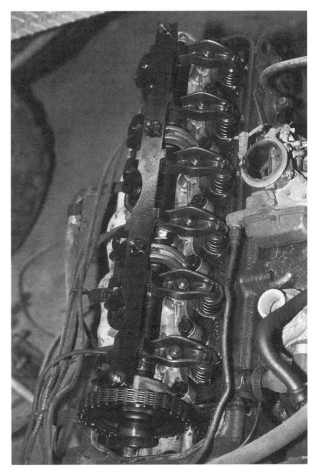

Fig. 6-14. *A worn camshaft lobe or improper valve adjustment will affect valve lift. Always check valve adjustment or tappet clearance before testing valve lift.*

Fig. 6-15. *Tune troubles include spark timing, fuel supply and emission control components. A Jeep engine cannot idle or run properly with a defective EGR or plugged PCV valve, shown here on F-134 engine.*

an adequate fuel supply. Check vacuum circuits. Make certain that the emission control system is functional, especially the PCV and EGR valves. If indicated, re-

Fig. 6-16. *Exhaust system restriction is a possible cause of power loss. Off-road use leaves tailpipes, mufflers and catalytic converters vulnerable to damage. Tap muffler with a rubber or sand filled plastic hammer to test for loose baffles.*

Fig. 6-17. *Battery maintenance is the best preventive care for the starting circuit. Don't buy a new starter, generator or alternator before thoroughly cleaning the battery and cables.*

move and overhaul the carburetor with a quality rebuild kit. You will find instructions for the carburetor overhaul within the kit or professional service manual.

Exhaust System Restriction has vexed more than one Jeep troubleshooter. Check the exhaust system. Off-road pounding can flattened the tailpipe or muffler. Restricted exhaust can prevent the engine from starting or developing full power. A muffler or catalytic converter may show no external damage yet have broken baffles or internal restrictions. Include the exhaust system on your engine performance checklist.

Engine Will Not Crank

Poor Battery Maintenance/Charge Circuit Troubles remain the primary sources of starting problems. The simplest cause is dirty or corroded battery posts. Regular cleaning of the posts and battery case prevent hard starts and a stranded Jeep. Make certain that cables are clean and connections tight, especially on an early 6- or 12-volt electrical system with high amperage demands and a low output generator.

Generator or alternator troubles are quick to identify. A charge current induction meter or a simple volt-ohmmeter offers the best testing results.

WARNING—
Begin with the voltmeter OFF. Take care not to generate a spark near the battery. Securely attach the negative (black) probe on the battery negative post and the positive (red) probe on the positive pole. Do not allow leads to touch each other or a conductive ground. Away from the battery, insert the other end of each lead in its proper slot on the voltmeter. Set the voltmeter on DC.

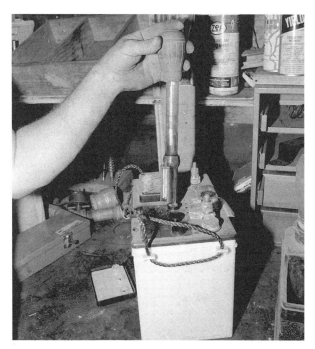

Fig. 6-18. *A safety precaution, even for a battery that shows no sign of weakness, is the hydrometer test. Specific gravity of a fully charged battery should read uniformly at each cell. Perform this test before cold weather begins.*

Measure voltage across the battery posts before cranking, during cranking and after starting the engine. Make certain that the maximum charge voltage reads within the regulator's normal charging range as listed in your Jeep's factory service guidelines or a professional manual.

Dead Battery Cell(s) present a difficult diagnostic problem. A high capacity battery can limp along with a dead cell for months. It takes a deep overnight freeze to bring out the worst in a battery. To avoid walking home from a chilly mountaintop, test each of your battery's cells with a battery hydrometer. Specific gravity should be uniform.

Starter Motor Problems generally give warning. A solenoid switch or starter drive unit often shows signs of weakness before failing. Run-on, clicking and erratic cranking are signs of starter and solenoid troubles.

Jeep engines use a variety of starter and solenoid designs, but starter principles remain universal: The solenoid acts as a relay to handle heavy amperage flow. In some designs, the solenoid actually moves the starter drive. On all but the later Jeep engines, starter motors are a series-wound design with brushes. Periodically inspect for water damage, clutch drive fatigue and brush wear.

Poor cranking when hot is often due to worn brushes or armature bushing wear that allows drag on the field coils. Exhaust headers passing too close to the starter may also cause hard starting when hot. To diagnose whether your starter draws too much amperage, test the draw with an induction meter on the starter cable or measure the voltage drop across the battery while cranking the engine.

Geartrain Friction Or Drag can prevent cranking. (Also see section on Lack of Power.) Among the geartrain items that prevent engine cranking is seizure of a transmission input shaft bearing, the gearsets or the crankshaft pilot bearing. A seized pilot bearing on a manual transmission will not allow power to disen-

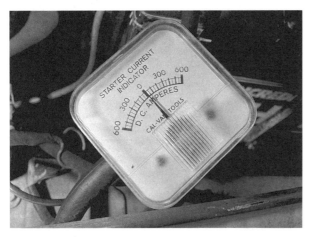

Fig. 6-19. *Starter defects often give warning. A clicking solenoid or erratic, dragging starter motor indicates trouble. An amperage draw test helps determine the condition of the starter.*

gage between the engine and transmission. However, the engine will crank in neutral.

Seized transmission components also allow the engine to crank with the clutch disengaged, but the engine will stall when you engage the clutch. (Before suspecting a damaged transmission, check the clutch adjustment and operation.) A seized transmission can result from poor lubrication, severe parts stress or excessive wear.

2.2 Cooling System Troubles

Jeep engine cooling presents a challenge, especially with high horsepower conversion engines or trips through hot desert environments. Rock crawling in the desert at high noon is the ultimate test for any Jeep cooling system.

Before troubleshooting common cooling system problems, let's clarify your Jeep's needs. For years, the two most common buzzwords around Jeep cooling system upgrades have been "four-row" and "cross-flow" radiators. These terms, however, are meaningless without understanding that horsepower equals BTUs. The more horsepower, the more heat your radiator and fan system must handle.

The best illustration of this principle is my friends' Arizona based CJ-7 Jeep with a hybrid V-8 engine transplant. The original 258 six ran very cool with a custom four-row radiator and aftermarket electric fan. With the V-8 conversion, however, the engine ran hot at rock crawling speeds.

What was wrong? Well, the radiator had plenty of flow capacity, tube size and fin surface area, but the electric fan could only draw so much air through the core. With an in-line six at 8.5:1 compression ratio, the light CFM air flow was adequate. An extra one-hundred horsepower, however, proved too much.

The cure in this case was a mechanical, engine driven fan. Well-pitched blades and a shroud solved the cooling problem completely. (Had the radiator core surface been too small, both a larger radiator core and a mechanical fan would be necessary.) Heavy-pitched truck type and aftermarket mechanical fans draw far more CFM air flow than the typical aftermarket electric fan.

When addressing your Jeep's cooling needs, begin with an ample radiator and cooling fan. Make certain a shroud captures the fan's air draft—without creating an air block. (See the cooling chapter for details.) Jeep CJs and Wranglers have relatively small grill openings, leaving the fan with a greater responsibility.

A factory air conditioning-type radiator provides a good design for the basically stock Jeep engine. For

Fig. 6-20. *This CJ-5 features a late 4.2L Wrangler engine and a factory (OEM) "air conditioning" radiator with shroud. Aftermarket stainless steel flex fan keeps engine within 5° F of thermostat setting, even under load in the hottest climates.*

Fig. 6-21. *Pressure tester checks hoses, water pump, engine block, gaskets and heater core. Radiator pressure cap must also seal properly, or boiling point will drop.*

higher horsepower transplant engines, evaluate the heaviest duty radiator available for the engine in its chassis of origin. Have a comparable flow (and surface area) radiator built, complemented by a hefty engine driven fan. A fan clutch unit, which lessens the engine load at speed, is optional.

Engine Overheat At Low Speeds suggests an undercapacity or restricted fan or radiator. Overheat can also result from insufficient water pump volume, cavitation or aeration problems. Air, either trapped within the cooling system or siphoned through a pinhole leak or defective water pump seal, can cause cavitation (air gaps and blockages). Cavitation drastically lowers cooling efficiency.

Another source of air in the cooling system is a mild head gasket leak that allows pressurized combustion gases to seep from a cylinder into an adjacent cooling port. This rapidly creates rust or oxidation, visible in the upper radiator and coolant recovery tank. As preventive care, you should periodically check torque of the cylinder head bolts, tighten all hose clamps, watch the water pump bleed hole for seepage and pressure check the cooling system.

> *CAUTION —*
> *Restrictions in air flow through the radiator core, such as a tall winch or plugged bug shield, will cause overheating.*

Engine Overheat At High Speeds involves incorrect coolant flow (either too fast or too slow) through the radiator, restrictions in the radiator core or an undercapacity water pump. Many of the symptoms for low speed overheat apply, so first follow those trouble-

Fig. 6-22. *A relatively inexpensive item like the thermostat can cause major heating problems. Replace the thermostat during your periodic flush and refill of the cooling system.*

shooting guidelines. Always check the thermostat, which regulates the coolant flow rate and temperature.

If coolant actually pushes from the radiator overflow at higher speeds, the water pump generates more coolant than the gallon-per-minute (GPM) capacity of the radiator core. (The core is either too small or plugged with scale.) Freeze plug failure and hose leaks are not uncommon under such conditions, as excess pressure backs through the entire cooling system.

Coolant Boil-over requires careful diagnosis. Is the coolant erupting from extreme engine heat? This means the radiator and fan cannot cool the liquid sufficiently—or that the engine/powertrain produces very high temperatures due to abnormal friction, spark timing error, improper air/fuel mixtures or other defects.

> NOTE —
> An undercapacity radiator flow rate will cause coolant overflow from the radiator— even at normal engine temperatures.

Note when the overflow occurs. Monitor the temperature gauge closely. If the engine runs consistently hot, suspect a sticky thermostat, plugged radiator core, obstructive block "mud" (accumulated rust and scale in an older engine), a defective water pump or any other factor that could raise coolant temperature.

2.3 Clutch and Manual Transmission

Clutch Noises mean trouble. Fatal clutch noises include the abrasive, metallic whirring of the throwout bearing during disengagement, the grinding of clutch plate rivets as the clutch engages, or the rattle of broken clutch disc torsion springs. Any new, persistent sound from the clutch is cause for concern.

A defective pilot bearing makes noise with the transmission in gear and the clutch disengaged. Clutch disc or cover assembly noises occur during engagement and disengagement. (Broken clutch cover springs cause uneven engagement and severe chatter.) Throwout or release bearing noise becomes apparent with light pressure against the clutch pedal, just enough pressure to start the bearing spinning.

> *CAUTION —*
> *Continued operation with a defective clutch can damage motor mounts, the flywheel and components of the transmission.*

Gearbox noises grate and amplify according to load on the gear teeth. Coast and acceleration noises differ. Transmission bearing troubles give distinct cues, with countergear or counter bearing noises evident in the lower gear ranges. Input or output bearing noises correspond to shaft speeds. Any unusual clutch or transmission noise requires immediate repairs.

Gear Clash in a Jeep manual transmission or transfer case has several possible causes. Before con-

Fig. 6-23. *Clutch plate (disc) torsion springs and rivets make distinct noises. Rivets grind against the flywheel or clutch cover face while torsion springs rattle in the hub.*

demning the transmission, check the clutch adjustment at the release arm and note any slack in the linkage. Complete travel of the linkage is necessary for disengagement of the clutch. A partially disengaged clutch causes difficult shifting and rapid wear of parts.

Another source of clash is hasty shifting to a non-synchromesh first or reverse gear. You must allow gears to quit spinning before engaging gear teeth. (An exception is the careful, precise, slow vehicle speed, "double-clutch" downshift to first gear. Maturing Jeep owners remember this as the common method.)

A defective synchromesh assembly will also produce a metallic clashing noise during gear shifts. Similarly, the use of the wrong gear lube can cause synchronizer balkiness and also make shifting difficult under various climate conditions. Gear clash and hard shifting will occur when using an overly stiff gear lube viscosity in winter months.

Long before the advent of multi-viscosity and synthetic gear lubes, a well-driller friend from Idaho attested that STP Oil Treatment allowed his surplus "deuce-and-a-half" (2-1/2-ton capacity 6x6) to operate in -40° F weather. Prior to adding STP to the gear cases, the engine would stall as the clutch engaged in neutral—even while revving the engine at high rpm.

Heavier gear and engine oils become rigid in extremely cold environments. Today, multi-viscosity synthetic motor and gear lubricants virtually eliminate these kinds of cold weather problems.

Synchronizers, which act much like a friction brake mechanism, wear over time. A patterned gear clash or jumping out of gear (especially first or second on a Jeep three speed unit) indicates a defective pilot or transmission bearing(s), a worn shift housing, damaged shift fork(s) or synchronizer troubles. Such problems most often require a transmission overhaul.

The Vehicle Will Not Move means several possibilities with a Jeep powertrain. A failed clutch is the first consideration. A clutch permanently disengaged (linkage extended and binding, disc worn completely or clutch cover springs broken) may still allow shifting of gears.

> NOTE —
> A clutch that will not disengage indicates damaged clutch linkage or bad contact between the throwout bearing and clutch cover fingers. With the engine shut off, place the transmission in low range, low gear. Click or crank the starter. This should move the truck. Check the clutch linkage and release mechanism.

> *WARNING*—
> *When cranking the engine with the transmission in low gear and clutch engaged, make sure nothing is in the Jeep's path. The engine may start and cause the truck to leap forward. Be ready to immediately shut off the ignition switch.*

If the clutch works, check the transmission and transfer case. Begin by locking the front hubs and engaging four-wheel drive. Now shift gears and try to move the truck. If your Jeep still will not move, power flow has stopped at the transmission or transfer case input. If the truck moves in four-wheel drive mode, suspect a broken rear transfer case output, a failed rear driveline or rear axle troubles.

When power fails to reach the axles, defective transfer case shift linkage is a common cause. The linkage may bind or catch between gear ranges, creating a neutral effect and preventing power flow. As an emergency repair, shut off the engine, block the wheels carefully, crawl beneath the vehicle and shift the transfer case manually.

> *WARNING*—
> *Stop the engine and place safety blocks at each wheel before attempting this repair. The vehicle could roll with the transfer case in neutral.*

Poor Traction/Erratic Wheel Spin is a differential problem. On Jeep full-time Quadra-Trac systems, the transfer case's differential mechanism is much like an axle differential. Before condemning a differential-type transfer case or the axles, however, rule out the possibility of a defective front wheel hub or a balky front axle shaft disconnect system (found on many Wranglers, XJs and ZJs).

Check the front hubs or axle disconnect first. Engage the wheel hub or axle lock mechanism, and jack

Fig. 6-24. *Shift linkage binding or failure can prevent power flow. In an emergency, it may be necessary to free linkage by manually moving the transfer case shift rails beneath the floorboard. Before moving shift rails, turn off the engine and block all four wheels to prevent vehicle from rolling. Stay away from scorching hot exhaust system!*

Fig. 6-25. *Power flow includes front hubs that work properly. While the engine, clutch, transmission, transfer case, driveshafts, differentials and axle shafts may work fine, a defective free-wheeling hub can prevent front axle traction.*

each front wheel, one at a time, safely off the ground. By hand, rotate the raised wheel assembly with the opposite wheel still on the ground. The axle shaft should spin the front differential and cause the front driveshaft to rotate. (If your Jeep has a front axle positraction unit, the wheel assembly will rotate only slightly in each direction.)

If your Jeep has a limited slip or Powr-Lok differential, erratic handling and odd traction are often caused by wear in the differential clutch unit. Lurching, clicking and snapping noises indicate trouble here. A failing limited slip delivers poor traction and makes noise, most notably as the vehicle negotiates a turn.

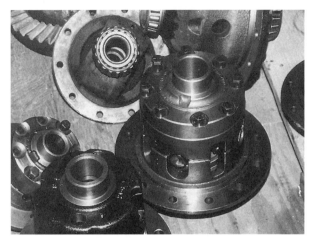

Fig. 6-26. *Limited slip, like Jeep's Spicer Powr-Lok traction unit, features multi-plate clutches. Wear occurs over time, and traction effectiveness diminishes.*

Fig. 6-27. *U-joints fail at inopportune times. Off pavement and on trails, radical driveshaft angles and high torque loads place maximum stress on these components.*

Gear bind is a common phenomena with any 4x4 vehicle. If you attempt to operate your Jeep on a dry, hard road surface with the front hubs locked and the transfer case in either 4WD high or low range (or Lock mode on full-time 4x4 systems like Quadra-Trac), the rotational speed differences between the front and rear axles will create a reactionary counterforce in the geartrain.

As such, gear bind prevents disengagement of the transfer case. To overcome the binding force, gently rock your Jeep forward and in reverse while maintaining gentle, steady pressure on the transfer case lever. There is a point of free load, somewhere between forward and reverse power flow, at which the bind loosens. At that moment, the transfer case lever will slide into the two-wheel drive position.

CAUTION —
Never apply excess force to the transfer case lever.

2.4 Driveshaft and Axle Woes

A common driveline problem on Jeep 4x4s is U-joint and constant velocity joint failure. Especially in rough and rocky terrain, the radical change angles of the driveshafts place major loads on U-joints and steering joints. Massive torque applied under high stress driving conditions can destroy a U-joint.

The loud, metallic snap of a breaking U-joint is hard to forget. Back country veterans of hard-core trails generally carry spare U-joints for such occasions. Although proper driving habits prevent the majority of mishaps, U- joint failure is still a concern.

Another source of driveshaft trouble is torque-twisting the tubes. A properly built driveshaft, operating at normal angles and in correct phase, will withstand tremendous abuse. If, however, a shaft sustains impact damage or operates at an abnormal angle, the tube and welds may fail.

Inspect your Jeep's driveshafts regularly, and note any shake or vibration at road speeds. A bent or "sprung" driveshaft will create havoc, most apparent as vehicle speed increases.

If your Jeep truck has conventional, non-positraction differentials, an axle shaft or joint failure means an immediate loss of traction. Although your four-wheel drive system may still permit movement when the rear differential fails, if a rear axle shaft breaks, you must not drive the truck. (The exceptions are Model MB military Jeep and very early CJ-2As with the full-floating Spicer 23-2 rear axle or those 3/4-ton to one-ton Jeep trucks with full-floating rear axles.) A broken semi-floating axle shaft can cause the tire and wheel to separate from the axle housing.

Front axle shaft or steering joint failure is another safety risk. A broken shaft, cross-type joint or constant velocity joint may wedge in the housing or steering knuckle cavity. This could prevent rotation of the steering knuckle and wheel spindle, causing loss of vehicle control. If the axle shafts are still safely supported, you may place the transfer case in two-wheel drive mode and turn the hubs to FREE. Drive cautiously and make certain that the steering knuckles continue to pivot freely.

Raise each wheel/tire from the ground and rotate the wheel (with both front hubs engaged) to determine whether the axle shafts and joints are intact. Watch at

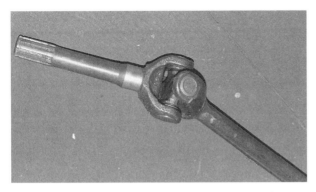

Fig. 6-28. *Front axle joint failure is a dangerous situation. A broken shaft or joint can wedge in the steering knuckle and prevent the wheels from turning. Before driving the Jeep, check closely for such damage. In an emergency, you can remove a full-floating front axle shaft found on all Willys and Kaiser models, AMC CJs, full-size Grand Wagoneers and J-trucks.*

Fig. 6-29. *Ring and pinion gears, side gears and differential pinions can each fail. Remove the axle inspection cover to check these parts. Excess play at the pinion shaft or axle shafts suggests trouble.*

the open steering knuckle (axle) joint and check for driveshaft rotation.

If your Jeep is a late model without a full-floating front axle and has no provision for free-wheeling front hubs, axle shaft damage poses several driving threats: steering impairment, risk of losing a wheel assembly, loss of braking or the possibility of increased damage to the truck. If an inner component in the axle breaks, exercise extreme caution if you must move the truck at all.

> *WARNING—*
> *Do not attempt to drive a semi-floating front axle model if the steering knuckle, outer axle shaft, wheel hub or wheel bearing carrier have become damaged.*

> *CAUTION —*
> *If you must operate your Jeep with failed axle components, understand the extent of damage. If necessary, remove the inspection cover from the differential to locate the source of trouble. (In the field, catch drain oil and save for a refill as needed.)*

On CJs, full-size Grand Wagoneers and J-series trucks with Quadra-Trac, the full-floating front wheel hubs will still permit removal of a broken front axle shaft in an emergency. If you must move a CJ or full-size Quadra-Trac truck that has an unsafe, broken front axle shaft or joint, first remove all pieces of the broken axle shaft, then the front driveshaft assembly. Set the transfer case in 4-Loc. (See your Jeep factory service manual for step-by-step details on front axle shaft removal.)

During axle oil changes, with the differential cover removed, clean and inspect all parts. Look closely for abnormal tooth contact patterns on the ring and pinion gears. Check the pinion shaft for any end play or radial movement. Inspect the seals, observe side gear/pinion backlash (play) and note the condition of the carrier bearings that support the ring gear and differential carrier housing. Preventive maintenance and careful inspection remain your best safeguards against axle troubles.

Common differential troubles include clutch failure on positive traction units, broken differential side gears or small pinions and the stripping of teeth from the ring and pinion gears. Bearing failures, seal leaks and thrust washer wear are other trouble areas.

2.5 Steering and Tire Troubles

Wander, the tendency for steering to either drift or follow road irregularities, is a common complaint with four-wheel drive vehicles. The usual causes are front end misalignment, cupped tires with bias-plies, a loose steering gear, defective steering linkage or suspension wear.

When aligning the front wheels, service should include a caster check. Insufficient positive caster angle causes shimmy and loss of steering control. If your Jeep needs coaxing to steer straight after a turn, check caster and toe-in. Suspension sag, spring lifts and shackle kits affect caster angle, too.

For a solid front axle, camber is only a concern if the steering knuckle/spindle, axle housing or axle tube(s) have become damaged. If slight caster and camber correction is necessary and no safety problem exists, adjustment shims are available.

Fig. 6-30. *Use of a quality tire gauge is essential. Your Jeep requires specific pressures for on- or off-highway use. Off-highway pressures below 18–20 psi will reduce load capacity drastically and possibly damage the tires. Always check tire pressures cold, and follow the manufacturer's recommended inflation rates for your Jeep model.*

NOTE —
Properly adjusted wheel bearings, secure spindles and correct tire inflation pressures are crucial to safe handling. For backcountry use, a Jeep 4x4 requires ground clearance, which means a higher center of gravity than vehicles designed for the highway. This translates as more sensitive handling characteristics, especially for the shorter 80"–94" wheelbases of military, CJ and Wrangler models. Safe suspension and steering are crucial.

Loose steering gear and linkage result from wear and the rigors of off-pavement pounding. Excess play translates as wander. Depending upon your Jeep's front end design, inspect for wear at tie-rod end(s), the steering gear, spring bushings and shackles, link arms, the bellcrank assembly, draglink, steering arms, kingpin bearings and all ball-joints.

Front End Shimmy usually results from looseness in the steering knuckle (kingpin) bearings or ball-joints. An additional factor is looseness in the steering linkage, front wheel spindles or wheel bearings. Sagging springs and improper wheel alignment (especially caster angle) can also cause front end shimmy. Oversize tires or severe tire imbalance will exaggerate a shimmy. The slightest shock or vibration can set off this potentially violent shaking of the front wheels. With manual steering, kingpin shimmy is a wrist-wrenching experience.

Perform a quick check of spindles, wheel bearings, kingpins or ball-joints by raising front wheels safely from the ground and installing jack stands beneath the axle housing. Grab each front wheel and tire firmly at

6- and 12-o'clock. Rock the tire in and out with a lifting motion. Note the amount of movement.

If play exists, have a helper watch the backside of the wheel and steering knuckle. Determine whether the play is at the wheel hub (loose wheel bearings or spindle) or the knuckle support (kingpin bearings or ball-joints). When wheel bearing play is excessive, adjust the wheel bearings to specification, then repeat the inspection. (See service chapters for further details.)

Wheel Run-out and Tire Imbalance is another area of concern. Especially with oversize mud-and-snow tires, the weight mass at each wheel becomes excessive. Cleated truck tires, unlike conventional passenger car types, readily fall out of balance with normal wear. Periodic re-balancing and rotation are essential for good wear and ride quality.

NOTE —
Unless otherwise specified by the tire manufacturer, rotate front to rear, rear to front with radial type tires; switch "in cross" with bias ply, non-radial tires.

Hard-core Jeep rock crawling can dislodge wheel weights or cause them to rotate on the rim. Tire damage, including internal belt separation of radial tires, creates vibration and shake. Bent wheel rims (runout) cause a wide range of handling and tire wear problems. As part of my preventive care, I periodically spin balance each tire and wheel, paying close attention to rim run-out and distortion. Always replace rims that show excess lateral or radial run-out.

Traditionally, the heavy duty bias-ply tires have benefitted from truing, a procedure that trims out-of-round material from the new tread surface. Radial

Fig. 6-31. *Spin balancing is the best safeguard against vibration and abnormal tire wear. In some cases, tires require truing, matching or balancing on the truck. Rotate tires every 5,000–7,500 miles and check balance as needed.*

Tire Rotation Tip: The Imbalanced Brake Drum or Rotor

On occasion, a Jeep truck has an imbalanced wheel hub, brake drum or rotor. Rather than continually balancing the wheels and tires on the vehicle, I use this technique:

Begin by precisely balancing each wheel/tire assembly on a spin balancer. Now mount and spin (floor) balance the wheel/tire assembly on the Jeep. If additional weight is needed, note the amount of weight necessary to compensate for brake drum or rotor imbalance.

Now find a wheel stud near the valve stem. Dab some durable, fast drying paint on the end of the stud to indicate where the wheel's valve stem indexes with the brake drum or rotor. Now place the valve stem at six o'clock and note the exact clock location (relative to the valve stem) where you added weight to the wheel.

At future tire rotations, you can simply remove the extra weight before installing this wheel/tire at its new location. The wheel/tire moving to the imbalanced rotor or drum will require the same amount of weight as the first wheel/tire. Before mounting the wheel, place the right amount of extra weight in exactly the same clock position as required for the first wheel/tire. Once again, the paint-marked wheel stud will indicate where to place the valve stem when you install the tire/wheel at the out-of-balance hub/drum or rotor.

If you keep a record of required weight and clock positions relative to the valve stem holes, future wheel balancing can take place solely on a spin balancer. For the imbalanced hub/drum or rotor, you'll simply add the right amount of weight, in the right position on the wheel, before mounting the assembly on the Jeep.

Fig. 6-32. *Master cylinder pushrod clearance is crucial to safe braking. Insufficient clearance at the tip of the pushrod will prevent the piston from retracting completely.*

tires sometimes require tread and sidewall matching, a procedure that contributes to uniform tread pressure over the full circumference of the tire.

Tire imbalance is usually noticeable between 45 and 55 mph, sometimes higher. Occasionally, a set of Jeep tires and wheels will balance perfectly, yet the symptoms of imbalance remain. This situation calls for balancing the tires on the vehicle, with the brake drum or rotor and hub included in the rotating mass.

2.6 Brake Problems

Brake Pull and Grab occur when you apply the brakes. Defects in the hydraulic or mechanical parts of the brake system cause these problems. A pitted or corroded wheel cylinder or disc caliper piston bore can cause erratic piston action, while a sticking piston prevents normal movement of the brake shoes or disc pads.

An incorrectly adjusted master cylinder pushrod or dirty and corroded fluid reservoir can affect brake performance. If brake fluid cannot return to the master cylinder reservoir through the compensation port, fluid trapped in the system will keep pressure on the brakes. This can cause drag, fade and erratic braking action.

Several mechanical factors contribute to brake pull and grab. Oil on the brake lining, binding linkage, a broken shoe return spring, warped brake shoes and drums (bell mouthed or out-of-round), distorted rotors and pads, hard spots on drums or rotors and excessive lining wear can each cause erratic braking. Poor lining quality, which leads to fade and undercapacity braking, is another source of trouble.

Slipshod brake jobs, without turning drums and rotors or rebuilding hydraulic cylinders, can lead to problems. With exposure to water, mud and drastic climate changes, your Jeep brakes deserve quality care. Restore your brakes properly, then protect the brake system by periodically cleaning debris from shoes, backing plates, brake drums or rotors. Inspect the dust boot seals regularly.

WARNING—
All older brake lining contains harmful asbestos. Brake vacuum equipment and special parts washers are available to prevent exposure to harmful asbestos brake dust. If you cannot safeguard yourself from asbestos, leave brake work to a professional shop. When performing brake work, inquire whether an appropriate non-asbestos lining is available for your Jeep model.

Failure to Stop has two symptoms: no pedal pressure or an extremely hard pedal. No pedal pressure generally means a hydraulic system failure, especially on a pre-'67 Jeep with a single master cylinder system. Also, as an off-pavement vehicle, your Jeep faces environmental hazards that can damage brake pipes or hoses. If fluid loss has occurred, carefully repair the hydraulic system, bleed air out and check for leaks before driving the vehicle.

In rare instances, mechanical problems such as a broken brake shoe, drum or actuating linkage will cause the master cylinder piston to fully exhaust its stroke before the brakes apply. (Actually, this too is a hydraulic failure, although a mechanical cause underlies the problem.)

Under extreme circumstances, misadjusted brake shoes, combined with major lining wear, will create the same effect. The brake pedal reaches the floor before lining reaches the drums. If your Jeep's brakes have no self-adjusters (such as early models), you must periodically adjust the shoe-to-drum clearance and note lining wear.

Normal lining wear lowers the level of fluid in the master cylinder reservoir. Check brake fluid at regular intervals to assure an adequate reserve. The master cylinder must displace a full stroke of fluid to actuate the wheel brakes. (See chapters on maintenance and brake service.)

An extremely hard pedal is usually the result of contaminated lining (oil, dirt or water), glazed brake lining or warped drums and/or rotors. Poor brake shoe seating, a consequence of improper shoe arc, can prevent lining from making full contact with the drums. Binding of linkage, actuating hardware or hydraulic cylinder pistons will also increase pedal pressure.

If your Jeep (especially an earlier CJ with through the floor pedals) will set up for long periods of time, make certain that pedal linkage and pivots receive adequate lubrication. When stored in a damp climate or exposed to icy road debris and corrosives, the pistons in the master cylinder, wheel cylinders and disc calipers sometimes rust and corrode in their bores. In freezing weather, always check your brakes before driving the truck. Wet hardware may ice up—another cause of hard pedal.

Additionally, hard pedal can result from overheated lining or fade. There are several causes of fade: improper fitup of brake parts; hydraulic fluid trapped in the lines (due to a misadjusted master cylinder push-

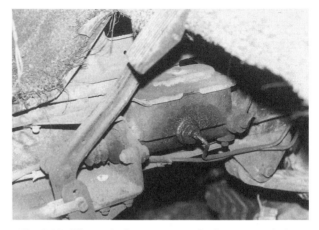

Fig. 6-33. *The early Jeep master cylinder mounts below the floorboard. Exposed to moisture, debris and ice, the master cylinder's dust boot must seal properly. Otherwise, rust and corrosive road salts will attack the cylinder.*

Fig. 6-34. *Glazed or contaminated brake lining, rotors and drums will increase pedal pressure. A defective outer axle shaft seal permits gear lube to saturate and ruin the brake lining.*

rod, bent pipe or kinked brake hose); extensive use or abuse of the brakes; excess load on the brake system; a misadjusted wheel-type emergency brake system; incorrect brake shoe-to-drum clearance (too tight); and glazed or contaminated lining.

Chapter 7

Engine Tune-up

Tuned correctly, a Jeep 4x4 can carry its full payload over primitive trails above 14,000 feet elevation. Late model Jeep engines with electronic fuel injection, oxygen sensors and computer regulated air/fuel ratios will adjust readily to any driving environment. Earlier conventional ignition and fuel systems require some tuning changes to meet the challenge of high altitude four-wheeling.

I consider my Jeep's needs much the same as my own. Living at a thinner air elevation of 4,400 feet, I condition for hiking, hunting and fishing at even higher elevations. Similarly, I prepare my CJ-5 for a vigorous four-wheel drive workout at 9,500 feet elevation.

For breaker point or conventional electronic ignition CJs and the 4.2L YJ Jeep with carburetion, precise engine tuning can make your 4x4 far more versatile. Understanding your Jeep's tune-up needs, including the fuel, spark and emission control systems, will also improve your troubleshooting and field repair abilities. Tune-up skills provide a cornerstone for off-highway survival.

Back country reliability begins with an ignition and fuel system tune-up. Emission control service, which has played an increasingly larger role in engine maintenance, also affects your Jeep's performance. (See chapter on emission controls.) For basic tuning, however, the exhaust gas recirculation (EGR) circuit and closed crankcase ventilation (PCV) system become your main concerns.

> **NOTE —**
> Jeep pioneered the closed crankcase ventilation system. Always service or replace your positive crankcase ventilation valve (PCV) when tuning your Jeep engine. Idle, manifold vacuum and general performance depend upon a functional crankcase ventilation system.

Properly tuned, your Jeep engine will deliver miles of rugged service, maximum utility and peak fuel economy. Far from a paved road, in rough backcountry, you'll be grateful for a reliable, quick starting engine.

Fundamental Engine Requirements

The best tune-up cannot compensate for internal engine defects, wear or damage. As an Adult Education automotive and diesel mechanics instructor, I fielded many thoughtful questions about engine needs and tuning.

Reflecting upon the race engine builder's credo that a naturally aspirated internal combustion engine is essentially a "vacuum pump," I devised a simple formula: 'The Four Basics.' An engine must meet these requirements before any kind of tuning can be successful:

1. Normal Compression
2. Correct Valve Lift And Opening Duration
3. Correct Valve Timing
4. Normal Oil Pressure and Parts Tolerances

Additionally, the engine must operate at normal coolant temperature.

Proper ring, valve and gasket sealing produces normal compression. The valvetrain condition determines proper valve lift, valve opening duration and valve timing. Valvetrain troubles include wear at camshaft lobes, the timing chain, timing sprockets or gears and the valve springs. Oil pressure relies upon good engine bearings, polished and true bearing journal surfaces and a sound oil pump.

For tuning purposes, you can add stable vacuum to the checklist. If your engine meets the four basic requirements and has no vacuum leaks, tuning efforts will be successful.

1. Jeep Engine Types

L-Head and F-134 Engines

The Willys F-134 four-cylinder engine, built from 1950 to 1973, shares many features with the L-head (flat head) 134 engine. I still find these two engines refreshingly fun to work on. Tuning steps are very similar.

L-head engines came in MB, CJ2-A, CJ-3A and M-38 models. The F-134 engine first appeared in the 1950 station wagon and pickups, CJ3-B and M38-A1

Fig. 7-1. *The F-134 engine design evolved from Willys' success with the L-head powerplant. This engine serves more than two decades of light Jeep trucks.*

Fig. 7-2. *1987 marked a milestone year for AMC engine development. 4.0L Cherokee powerplant features multi-point fuel injection (MPI) and electronic spark management. Routine maintenance consists of periodic spark plug changes and filter replacement.*

Jeep models. In 1955, the F-head 134 was the engine choice for Willys/Kaiser's new CJ-5.

A 134 engine provides the perfect training ground for a budding mechanic. Such a basic design is simple to understand. Routine tune-ups take minimal time. Of all the Jeep engines, the 134s remain among the simplest and least expensive to tune and repair.

2.5L GM and AMC Engines

Two distinctly different 2.5L four-cylinder engines, built by Pontiac (1980–83) and AMC (1983–present), have powered Jeep trucks. AMC/Jeep used the Pontiac engine in CJ models, while the AMC engine powers many compact Cherokees, Comanche pickups, later CJs and Wranglers.

These 2.5L (151 GM and 150 AMC) engines each serve well, despite a heavy dose of emission controls on carbureted models. Each design is an overhead valve, pushrod type. The Pontiac 151 "Iron Duke" features common GM components. AMC's 2.5L four is a member of the 4.0L and 4.2L six-cylinder engine family. The 2.5L fours offer ease of service and minimal tune-up requirements.

Kaiser's OHC "Tornado Six"

The 1962 introduction of Jeep Corporation's Wagoneer and J-truck line was a technological milestone. Highly innovative and advanced for its time, the new models' overhead camshaft in-line six-cylinder engine made an immediate sensation.

Although technicians and owners have mixed sentiments about Kaiser's short-lived Tornado engine, many of these engines still deliver service in civilian and military surplus Jeep trucks. For Tornado six owners who have stubbornly resisted a modern V-8 transplant, this chapter contains guidelines for servicing your trusty, four main bearing Kaiser hybrid.

AMC's 232/258 and 4.0L Sixes

In 1965, Kaiser's Jeep Corporation acquired AMC 232 sixes as a replacement for the 230 OHC Tornado engine. Few realized the significance of this move. The rugged seven main bearing engine, increased in displacement to 258 cubic inches by 1971, became the AMC/Jeep engine of choice, eventually providing the foundation for AMC's advanced Cherokee 4.0L engine, a dutiful offering to this day.

Why is this in-line six so popular? Simplicity of design and seven well laid out main bearings make the difference. Where the four-main 230 Tornado engine offers an advanced cylinder head design, the 232/258 and 4.0L simply outlast most other engines in the industry. By 1969, even International-Harvester used AMC's 232 and, later, the 258 in-line six.

Tuning for all 232 and 258 engines is basically the same. None of these AMC/Jeep engines require valve adjustment. Hydraulic lifters and non-adjustable rocker arms eliminate this. A fundamental workhorse, the Jeep 232 and 258 sixes have both breaker point (1965–74) and electronic ignitions ('75–up).

The 4.0L Cherokee/Comanche/Wrangler engine has electronic spark and fuel management. Multi-point fuel injection gives the Cherokee and '91–up Wrangler a major performance edge over other engines. These engines require scant attention during routine service. (If you plan to service or troubleshoot your electronic fuel and spark management system, consult a factory service manual or a reference source outlined in the Appendix.)

For the 4.0L engine, fuel and ignition system maintenance means periodic fuel filter, air cleaner element and spark plug changes. I find the intervals for these services, prescribed in your owner handbook, overly optimistic.

Off-pavement stresses and carrying cargo will increase the load on your engine and increase spark plug wear. Fuel quality (including water content) and other factors reduce the longevity of disposable fuel filters. In the interest of reliable service and impressive performance, I change spark plugs at 15,000–20,000 miles with electronic ignitions and 8,000–12,000 miles on breaker point systems. I replace the fuel filter(s) at the same time.

Jeep V-6

Twice in Jeep history, General Motors V-6 engines have made the option list. In the mid-'60s, the feisty Buick 225 was the powerplant of choice for the CJ and Jeepster trucks. Nearly two decades later, the Chevrolet 173 V-6 engine powered the earliest compact Cherokee trucks.

Ironically, each of these V-6 engine designs gave way to an AMC powerplant. The V-6 Buick, replaced by in-line 232/258 sixes, lasted through 1971. GM's 173 V-6 yielded to the far more powerful AMC 4.0L multipoint fuel injected engine found in 1987 Cherokees and Comanche pickups.

The 225 Dauntless (Buick) V-6 made legends of Kaiser's CJs and Jeepster. This engine provided more

Fig. 7-4. *Buick's iron block 225 V-6 engine made a legend of 1966–71 CJ and Jeepster models. These 160-horsepower engines launched lightweight Jeep models into America's Muscle Era.*

than double the horsepower of the standard F-134 powerplant and brought "high performance" status to the lighter CJ Jeep. Today, an original V-6 powered CJ in good condition still fetches a strong price.

Jeep V-6s are very basic. Tune-ups place little demand on either your time or wallet. The Dauntless/Buick 225 V-6 has breaker points and a simple two-barrel carburetor. AMC's Cherokee/Comanche 2.8L (Chevrolet) V-6 has a closed loop, computer regulated fuel and spark management system.

Jeep V-8

AMC began providing engines for Kaiser's Jeep Corporation in 1965, and five years later, Jeep Corporation handed the Toledo, Ohio, Jeep plant keys to American Motors. Except for the brief period from 1968–71 (when Kaiser utilized Buick's healthy 350 V-8 for the Wagoneer and J-trucks), AMC provided the bigger muscle for Jeep trucks until the Mopar V-8 in the late 1990s.

The first Jeep V-8 option was AMC's 327. Although this engine shared bore and stroke with the popular 327 small block Chevrolet V-8, there is no real similarity. The AMC 327 is representative of earlier American Motors V-8 technology: strong engines with cumbersome valvetrains and heavy block castings.

Subsequent 304, 360 and 401 AMC V-8s employ thinner walled block castings, much like the successful designs of industry "small-block V-8" competitors. The 304 engine proved so versatile that AMC placed it in 1972 CJs and Commandos.

In 1972, the 360 V-8 became a mainstay for the Wagoneer and J-truck lines. The 401 V-8s gained some prominence in full-size trucks from 1974–78. Unfortunately, the 401 never had a chance to display its per-

Fig. 7-3. *The Chevrolet 173/2.8L V-6, although small, adequately powers many 1984–86 compact Cherokees.*

Fig. 7-5. *AMC 304, 360 and 401 V-8 family share many components. Introduced in 1971 Jeep full-size J-trucks and Wagoneers, 360 engine served well for more than two decades.*

formance potential, as emission constraints drastically reduced horsepower.

Although used for only a few years, the Buick 350 is also a formidable powerplant. The same engine found in many Buick passenger cars of the 1968–71 era, this powerplant is both powerful and reliable. As the rugged GM Turbo 400 transmission was already a mainstay option for J-trucks and Wagoneers, the 350 Buick V-8 was a natural choice.

Today, an original 350 Buick V-8 powered Jeep still brings a good price. These trucks have excellent powertrain stamina and classically good looks. The final full-size Grand Wagoneer held a striking resemblance to the last Buick-powered model of 1971.

Emission controls demand a good deal of attention with the AMC V-8 engines. Big displacement means more pollution per mile—unless pollution controls do a proper job. These engines are harder to bring into emission compliance than the fours, in-line sixes and V-6s. Only at the expense of much horsepower have '72 and newer AMC/Jeep V-8s stayed within federal and California emission requirements.

You will find the chapter on emission controls useful when tuning your Jeep V-8 engine. Refer to the emission control chapter before attempting a major tune-up on a late '60s or newer Jeep V-8 engine.

2. Ignition Tune-up

Spark plugs, the distributor cap, rotor, coil and plug cables make up the secondary ignition circuit. The rotor requires periodic replacement, along with spark plugs, the breaker point set and condenser (if so equipped).

When testing the output of a GM HEI ignition, use a commercial tester plug or fabricate a similar device. The idea is to keep the plug shell grounded to the engine block and not allow any spark wire to arc directly to ground. This tool is also handy for back country troubleshooting, enabling a quick assessment of spark output.

> CAUTION —
> *When testing spark, the misfire of one cylinder creates a rich mixture in the exhaust stream. This sends a confusing signal to the oxygen sensor and also loads up the catalytic converter and/or muffler with raw fuel. Do not test ignition spark for lengthy periods.*

2.1 Spark Plugs

I always begin an engine tune-up by cleaning debris from the area around the spark plugs. Then I remove the wires and use a clean plug socket to avoid dripping grit into the cylinders. A flex handle spark plug ratchet serves well with odd-shaped or difficult to access cylin-

Fig. 7-6. *This commercial tester plug is a necessity for GM HEI ignition. Never create a spark arc to ground. Ignition damage could result.*

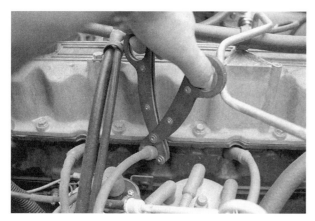

Fig. 7-7. *Use of a spark cable pliers is always wise. Grip the plug insulator firmly. Avoid tugging on wires. Carbon-core can separate easily.*

Fig. 7-8. *Spark plug cleaning machines were once very popular. However, you need a spark plug tester or engine oscilloscope analyzer to verify a used spark plug's ability to fire. Avoid trouble. Replace spark plugs at each tune-up.*

der heads (especially the Tornado six with its hemispherical combustion chambers).

> CAUTION —
> • *On models with carbon-core spark plug wires, Jeep recommends the use of a spark cable pliers to prevent damage when removing the wires.*
>
> • *Wearing protective goggles, use compressed air and a nozzle to blow debris away from the base of the spark plugs. Remove spark plugs carefully.*

Read spark plugs closely. Fouled spark plugs provide valuable insight. Oily plugs generally mean worn valve guides or piston rings. A sooty black or wet plug surface indicates gasoline fouling, unless ash from burnt oil is also present.

Gasoline fouling is less ominous than oil fouling. Gas fouling of one cylinder usually indicates a worn spark cable or ignition system problem (a defective rotor, distributor cap, breaker points, condenser, coil, electronic ignition module or wiring).

> NOTE —
> Oily plugs on L-134s usually mean worn piston rings, since valve heads face upward (valve stems face downward), and all eight valve guides are low in the block.

If all spark plugs appear gas fouled, yet the ignition tests okay, suspect a carburetion or fuel injection problem. The plug tips may also show other kinds of damage, including broken porcelain. When this occurs, check for detonation or pre-ignition. Severely advanced timing or the use of poor fuel can also cause plug damage.

Fig. 7-9. *Detonation (ping) is always a symptom of engine stress. Worse yet is pre-ignition, which burns up pistons, shatters rings and even breaks connecting rods.*

> NOTE —
> 134 Jeep engines have a bad habit of burning holes in pistons. Low octane gas and a high rate of piston travel take their toll.

Before installing new spark plugs, verify that each plug has the correct part number and heat range for your engine. A slightly hotter (stick within one heat range) spark plug may work better during extremely cold weather, when long warmup periods, especially with carbureted engines, tend to carbon foul the plugs.

> CAUTION —
> On engine designs with high-energy ignition systems and stringent emission standards, the correct spark plug is crucial to engine survival. The emission control decal on the radiator core support provides tune-up data for your engine.

Check each plug gap carefully. I prefer a plug gapping tool that provides a flat and parallel gap surface.

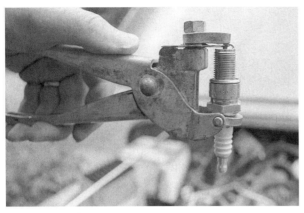

Fig. 7-10. *The spark plug gapping tool assures a parallel firing surface.*

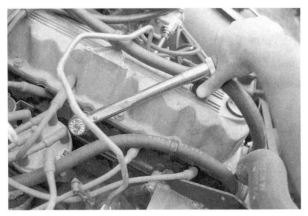

Fig. 7-11. *If you have limited experience with tightening spark plugs, use a torque wrench. Over-tightening can distort spark gap or damage the plug or cylinder head threads.*

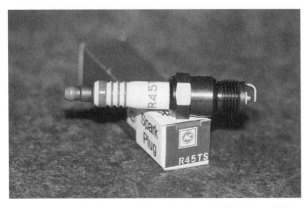

Fig. 7-12. *AC plugs work best in Jeep's GM V-6 and V-8 engines. Note tapered seat on this V-8 plug, which needs no sealing gasket. Smaller hex head requires 5/8" plug socket.*

Many home mechanics, however, achieve good results with a round wire gauge. Bend the side electrode strap carefully. Never attempt to move the center electrode.

In the heyday of the 134 engines, it was popular to clean and re-use spark plugs. Most mechanics have abandoned this practice. Clean plugs may look good, but have usually lost their firing capability. The only way to test a used plug is by running the engine on an oscilloscope or with a plug tester. New plugs eliminate costly troubleshooting.

If you have limited experience at tightening spark plugs, use a torque wrench. On 134s, 30 ft/lbs of torque is plenty; further tightening may distort the spark gap or damage the plug.

For the 2.5L Pontiac Iron Duke engine, AC/Delco spark plug boxes indicate proper torque settings. Underhood emission decal describes plug gaps.

On Tornado OHC engines, gap each plug carefully to 0.030 inch. Torque in place at 20–30 ft/lbs.

All 232/258 engines require a 0.035" spark plug gap. From early Delco-Remy breaker point systems to later Motorcraft solid state electronic ignitions, plug gap remains the same. Simple. Spark plug tightening torque is 25–30 ft/lbs.

173/2.8L V-6 engines require a 0.045" gap. The 225 Buick V-6, with its breaker point ignition, uses a 0.035" gap. Tapered-seat 173 plugs torque to 7–15 ft/lbs, while earlier 225 V-6 plugs torque to 30 ft/lbs.

Jeep AMC V-8s, the lone 327 and the 304/360/401 family require a 0.035" spark gap. (Some late '80s and newer 5.9L/360 engines call for a 0.033" gap. Check your underhood decal.) 30 ft/lbs of torque will properly seat the V-8 spark plugs. Torque smaller tapered seat, gasketless spark plugs to a maximum of 15 ft/lbs. Use a 5/8" plug socket.

2.2 Wires and Distributor Cap

Because modern spark cables have a carbon core, your Jeep ignition wires require periodic testing for ohms resistance and shorts. The simplest volt-ohmmeter comes in handy here, providing a quick means for checking resistance between the ends of each spark cable. Typically, the longest leads (15" to 25" on 232/258 engines for example) require a minimum resistance of 4,000 ohms and maximum of 15,000 ohms.

As you check the spark cables, twist and coil each wire gently. This will reveal opens or defective segments of wire. Also look at the insulation. Carefully route wires to prevent nicks and melted insulation.

WARNING—
Never puncture or use a pinpoint probe on carbon core wire insulation.

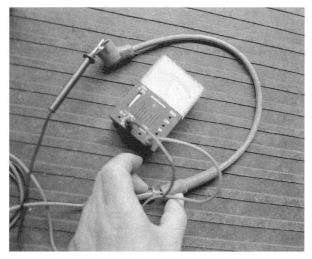

Fig. 7-13. *Check plug wires with a volt-ohmmeter. Attach leads to each end of the wire and read resistance.*

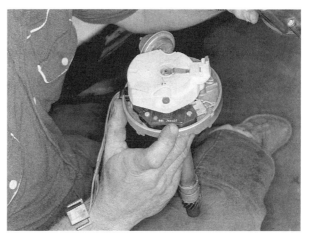

Fig. 7-15. *Rotor on GM HEI or EST ignition often burns a hole from center contact to top of distributor shaft. Spark arcs to ground, shorting out ignition. Periodically check rotor.*

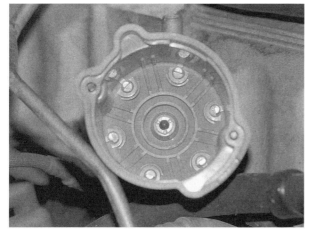

Fig. 7-14. *Aluminum contacts on Motorcraft 4.2L distributor cap oxidize and corrode. Replace this cap when heavy corrosion, arcing or carbon tracking becomes evident.*

A quick, preliminary test of plug wire condition is possible with a strobe timing light—preferably the induction type. Hook up the timing light lead to one spark cable at a time. With the engine idling, observe the consistency of the light flash while also listening to the smoothness of the engine. Ideally, the spark should appear steady, without misfire, pause or interruption.

There are other causes of misfire, including lean or rich fuel mixtures, a fouled spark plug, a defective distributor or a worn ignition coil. Remove the suspected wire and test it with your ohmmeter before investing in an expensive set of spark cables.

The spark plugs and cables are part of the secondary ignition circuit. In addition to these components, the distributor cap and rotor require attention. Re-

place the distributor cap when you see wear, cracks, carbon tracking (a cause of cross-firing between cylinders) or badly corroded electrical contacts. I inspect the cap for cracks, examine the rotor contacts and clean the cable sockets with a distributor brush.

> **NOTE —**
> On GM HEI or EST ignitions, high voltage erodes the rotor. If not corrected, electricity goes to ground through the distributor shaft. Inspect the rotor carefully. Replace the rotor if arcing or wear is evident.

2.3 Primary Ignition System

On non-electronic ignition systems, the points and condenser require periodic replacement. Intervals between breaker point set replacement depend upon several factors: point misalignment, severe rubbing block wear, pitting, arcing, blue discoloration or contact surfaces showing a peaked buildup of metal on one side (which usually means condenser trouble).

When I entered the field of automotive mechanics, ignition point service was still popular. Light filing, spring pressure tests and readjustment were routine procedures.

Today, we regard points as disposable. At routine intervals, usually 8,000–12,000 miles, most mechanics simply install a new set of points and a condenser.

Years ago, if the condenser tested okay and the points wore evenly, re-use of the condenser was acceptable. In fact, if the condenser tested within specification, it was likely better than most new ones out of the box.

Fig. 7-16. *This breaker point spring tester was once a popular tool. Proper spring tension is crucial to long point set life.*

Fig. 7-18. *Loose, frayed or broken primary wires will cause ignition trouble. On earlier 134 engines with cloth wire insulation, shorts to ground become common as wires age.*

Better engineered breaker point sets have eliminated the need to adjust point spring tension. Setting the breaker point cam angle or dwell, however, remains crucial to peak performance. (Dwell is the number of distributor cam degrees between the time that the points close and re-open. Proper dwell allows coil saturation for a hot, crisp spark.) Proper dwell angle assures good engine starts, smooth performance and long point set life.

A major source of ignition trouble on older engines is defective primary circuit wiring. Cloth wire can fray and short to ground against the engine block or distributor housing. Insulators on the distributor wire terminal block also wear, allowing the stud or wires to short. Take care when installing the points and condenser. Failure to correctly insulate the points

spring from the distributor housing can cause hard starts, misfire or a total short-out of the ignition.

Route and attach primary wires and spark plug cables securely. Imagine your Jeep jostling in rough terrain. Will the wires stay in place, come loose or short to ground? Before condemning your coil or other parts, look for wiring problems.

Remove the distributor cap to service the primary ignition parts. The centrifugal advance mechanism is in the base of many Jeep distributors, below the breaker point plate. If timing tests reveal a sluggish or erratic advance, remove the distributor for disassembly and overhaul. (Consult your Jeep factory service manual for overhaul procedures.)

Fig. 7-17. *Wire leads through the distributor housing wear and deteriorate. Shorts cause engine misfiring and ignition failure. Check leads whenever you service the distributor.*

Fig. 7-19. *Place cam lubricant against correct side of rubbing block. As distributor cam rotates, grease should press against the rubbing block. Grease applied to the opposite side of the rubbing block will pull away, possibly fouling the points.*

During breaker point installation, use a point rubbing block lubricant, applied to the side of the rubbing block that faces the distributor cam rotation and thrust. (This will push grease against the block rather than pull it away.) Wipe old grease from the distributor cam and apply a thin film of fresh lubricant.

> NOTE—
> Always check and, if necessary, re-set ignition timing after you install new points or make a dwell angle/point set adjustment.

Dwell Meter and Setting Points

Dwell meter point adjustment assures adequate coil saturation for high speed operation plus enough spark for easy starting. Use of a dwell meter will also extend breaker point life.

With the 134 Jeep engine turning at cranking speed or an idle, correct dwell is 42 degrees on Auto-Lite distributors and 25–34 degrees on Delco-Remy units.

When servicing your ignition, use a dwell meter to set the points. For initial start-up, if your 134 engine has an Auto-Lite distributor, set the points at 0.020" maximum gap (highest spot on the lobe). Delco-Remy units require 0.022" gap.

For OHC Tornado engines, gap points to 0.020" to start the engine. Re-set the point gap to achieve 38 degrees of dwell angle, measured on the six-cylinder scale of your dwell meter. This will provide optimal starts, good high speed performance and reasonable point life.

For initial start-up, the 232/258, 225 V-6 and V-8 Delco-Remy distributors require a 0.016" maximum

point gap. With the engine cranking or at an idle, dwell is 31–34 degrees for the 232/258 in-line sixes and 30 degrees for V-6 and V-8 Delco-Remy distributors.

The 225 V-6 engines use two distributor types: a GM Delco-Remy window cap style or a Prestolite design. On the Prestolite unit, watch carefully for distributor shaft bushing wear.

If your distributor shows a dwell variance of more than 2 degrees, check the shaft bushings. With the rotor removed and points open on a cam lobe, press gently against the shaft. Note the point gap. Now pull on the shaft lightly. Again measure the point gap. The difference between these figures indicates distributor shaft bushing wear. When a Buick 225 V-6 Prestolite distributor shows wear, many owners replace it with the more dependable Delco-Remy unit.

> NOTE—
> When converting from a Prestolite to a Delco-Remy distributor, you must replace the coil and ballast resistor with the correct Delco-Remy type.

The window on the side of the Delco-Remy distributor cap provides valuable access for setting points. With the engine running and a 1/8" Allen hex wrench inserted lightly into the adjuster screw head, dwell set is quick and easy.

> WARNING—
> *Accidentally inserting the hex wrench into the area of the point contacts can result in a strong electrical shock.*

Prestolite 225 V-6 distributors call for 29 degrees dwell and a 0.016" point gap for initial adjustment. As with other non-GM distributors, dwell setting requires removal of the distributor cap and careful re-

Fig. 7-20. *A dwell meter measures cam angle from breaker point closure to re-opening. 38 degrees of dwell is right for the Tornado six distributor, measured on dwell meter's six-cylinder scale. Always set meter to match number of cylinders!*

Fig. 7-21. *Many 225 V-6 Jeep owners have converted from the OEM Prestolite distributor to the superior Delco-Remy window cap unit.*

gapping of the points. This is very time consuming, another good reason to find a Delco-Remy distributor.

On the Delco-Remy ignition, a surprisingly accurate field adjustment is to slowly turn the point adjuster screw clockwise until the engine begins to misfire. Back the hex wrench counterclockwise exactly 1/2 turn. When you have the opportunity, verify the setting with a dwell meter.

If you use a Delco-Remy or equivalent point set and carefully place it in position, the engine will usually start with no adjustment of the point gap. Yes, without the use of a dwell meter or feeler gauge, you will find that the engine will at least run, enough to proceed with a dwell setting. (If the engine will not start immediately, either check the cranking dwell with a meter or remove the distributor cap and set the point gap with a feeler gauge.)

Fig. 7-22. *GM window cap distributor is ideal for an off-highway trail 4x4. Dauntless 225 V-6 engines with Delco-Remy ignition enjoy the benefit of quick, external point/dwell adjustment.*

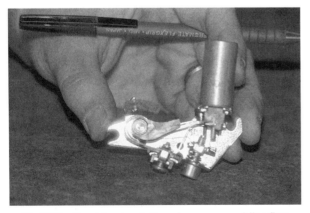

Fig. 7-23. *Combined point/condenser assemblies first appeared in the early 1970s. These easy to install sets eliminate fumbling with a condenser lead and clamp. Assemblies retrofit to earliest window cap distributor.*

Fig. 7-24. *Place point/condenser set carefully on the breaker plate. Properly positioned, a quality replacement point set for window cap distributors has a pre-set gap that usually permits initial engine start-up.*

A dwell meter point adjustment assures adequate coil saturation for high speed operation plus crisp spark for easy starting and longer point life. With the engine cranking over or at an idle, dwell angle is approximately 30 degrees for V-6 and V-8 Delco-Remy distributors. I like to set new points at 29-1/2 degrees. By the time the rubbing block wears in, the dwell will be 30 degrees.

Electronic Primary Ignition System

On the 173 V-6 and 151 Pontiac engines, removing the distributor cap provides access to the electronic ignition parts. Several components are replaceable. These include the HEI module, rotor, pole piece/pickup coil, capacitor with connectors, distributor cap and the ignition coil. On conventional HEI ignitions, vacuum and centrifugal advance units are also accessible with the distributor cap removed.

Testing electronic ignition components requires use of a sensitive digital volt-ohmmeter and other equipment, including an oscilloscope. For service and repairs beyond basic tuning, refer to your factory shop manual section covering the ignition system.

Electronic ignition modules are the contemporary equivalent of breaker points. The two 2.5L Jeep engine designs have different ignition modules. Pontiac 151 Delco-Remy HEI distributors have an internal module, accessible with the distributor cap removed. AMC/Jeep 2.5L distributors rely upon an external module/coil assembly. On the AMC design, ignition spark timing is a computer (Electronic Control Unit or ECU) function, and the distributor lacks a conventional timing advance mechanism.

Before condemning a module or any other electronic ignition component, check the wiring circuits. Wires can fray, short and develop loose connections. Module lead wires often fail on vacuum advance

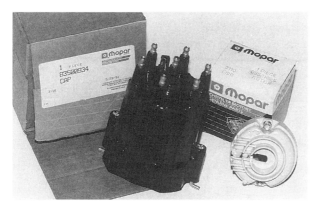

Fig. 7-25. *173/2.8L V-6 ignition and other service parts are available through your local Jeep dealership. Mopar offers this high quality distributor cap and rotor for Cherokee and Comanche 2.8L V-6 applications.*

equipped GM distributors. Check your Jeep's wiring carefully, and replace defective wires or plug connectors as needed.

Once you remove the HEI distributor cap, the module is not difficult to replace. Apply the special silicone heat insulating gel supplied with the new module. An even coating on the back of the module helps isolate this sensitive component from engine heat.

2.4 Spark Timing

Precautions: Before you start the engine to verify spark timing, check the tightening torque on fan and water pump mounts. Make sure the water pump shaft and bearings do not have play or wobble. When timing your engine, stay away from moving parts. Do not race the engine, as the fan is more likely to come loose on a stationary vehicle than when air is moving through the radiator. Make sure your hands, clothing and tools are well away from moving parts. Never operate the engine beyond 2,500 rpm during service work.

L-134 and F-134

Initial spark timing for all 134 engines is 5 degrees advance at an idle speed. Use your stroboscopic timing light for best results. If you need to service your engine in the wilds, I have a static timing technique that can prove very useful:

Begin by locating the distributor wire lead to #1 cylinder. Remove the distributor cap and spark plugs. Manually turn the engine over in its normal direction of rotation. Watch the rotor as it approaches the #1 cylinder firing position. (The firing order for all 134 fours is 1-3-4-2.)

Rotate the crankshaft slowly, and stop exactly where the timing marker indexes with the 5-degree ad-

Fig. 7-26. *Timing lights with built-in advance will check performance of the spark advance mechanism. Add initial timing degrees to the specified distributor advance degrees for a given engine rpm. Strobe light should index with "0" (TDC) mark.*

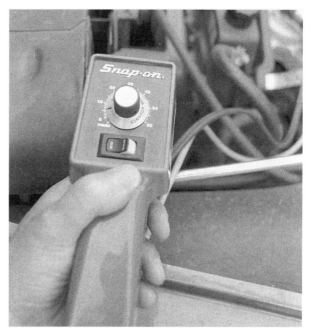

Fig. 7-27. *To static time a 134 engine, rotate distributor housing with the ignition switch ON. Rotate in direction of shaft rotation first, then reverse (clockwise) towards #1 cylinder firing position. Keep hand away from primary wire and points/condenser to avoid a shock!*

vance mark. On 134 engines, the marks and pointer are either visible at the flywheel (CJ-2A and some CJ-3A models) or at the timing cover and crankshaft pulley.

Turn the ignition switch to the ON position. With the distributor clamped loosely, move the housing in the direction of shaft rotation (counter-clockwise), well past the #1 cylinder distributor lobe. Now, very slowly rotate the housing clockwise toward the #1 cylinder firing position. Watch the point contacts carefully.

> CAUTION —
> *Avoid electrical shock by keeping your hand away from the primary coil wire. When the condenser unloads, the primary wire receives a strong voltage spike. Make sure your hand isn't the prime source to ground.*

At the exact moment the points arc, you will have set the timing to 5 degrees advance. A running engine may show a slight variance (due to camshaft and distributor/oil pump gear lash). For start-up and emergency purposes, however, this is a highly accurate method.

A variation on this static timing method also works well. With spark plugs removed from the engine, rotate the crankshaft to locate the timing marks as before. Now, reinstall the distributor cap. Place an old spark plug on #1 plug wire and ground the plug's metal shell. Loosen the distributor housing clamp.

Turn the ignition switch to ON. Rotate the distributor housing counter-clockwise a few degrees, then slowly rotate the housing clockwise until a spark fires across the test plug. If you tighten the distributor at this exact point, accurate static timing will result.

Rotating the distributor first counter-clockwise and then clockwise prevents the advance mechanism from distorting the static timing. If you overshoot the firing point, repeat the procedure by first rotating the housing counter-clockwise, then clockwise.

2.5L Spark Timing

You will need an induction timing light to set your 2.5L engine's ignition spark timing. Since the magnetic current signals in the distributor require that you crank the engine, it is impossible to static time your electronic ignition system.

If you plan to remove the distributor, carefully mark the rotor position and scribe the distributor housing location before pulling the unit. Upon reinstalling the distributor, immediately verify timing with your induction timing light.

Perform base timing adjustments on GM 151 HEI ignitions with the vacuum advance line disconnected, its open end taped. Move the distributor housing to set the initial timing advance to the degrees specified on the underhood decal.

On later 2.5L AMC engines with TBI, the spark timing is electronically controlled. The ECU (fuel and spark management computer) receives signals from the flywheel speed sensor and several other engine sensing devices. Once you establish the correct initial

Fig. 7-28. *A distributor wrench allows easier access to adjuster clamp nut. Moveable distributor housing allows for timing corrections.*

(idle) timing setting, there's no other timing adjustment.

OHC "Tornado Six" Spark Timing

Once the dwell is correct, set the ignition timing. Disconnect the vacuum line and plug the open end. Make certain idle speed is normal, at 590–600 rpm. With the marks clear on the crankshaft pulley, attach the timing light to #1 cylinder spark lead. Start the engine and check for timing at 5 degrees BTDC (before top dead center). If the timing is off, loosen the distributor adjusting nut with a distributor wrench. Rotate the distributor housing until the 5-degree pulley mark indexes with the timing cover reference line.

An easier approach is possible with a timing light that has adjustable advance. Simply dial the advance until you index the timing cover line with the "0" or TDC mark on the crankshaft pulley. Read the scale on the timing light. If the reading is more or less than 5 degrees, rotate the distributor housing accordingly until you reach a setting of 5-degrees advance. This type of timing light is also ideal for verifying the performance of a spark advance mechanism.

You can quickly test the vacuum advance unit with a vacuum pump. With the engine idling, disconnect and plug the vacuum line and read the timing advance. Now apply 12 in./hg. of vacuum to the advance unit. 15 degrees of additional crankshaft timing advance should appear at the crankshaft. (Vacuum advance should just begin to move at 5 in./hg. of vacuum.)

CAUTION —
The maximum centrifugal advance is 30 crankshaft degrees at 2800 crankshaft rpm. Although a timing light with built-in advance could verify this setting, running the engine to 2800 rpm while leaning toward the fan is very dangerous.

If you suspect an inoperative centrifugal advance mechanism, mark the distributor housing and rotor location. Remove the distributor. Overhaul the unit and have the advance tested in a distributor test machine. Although these machines have become rare, they were very popular when the 230 Tornado six was in vogue.

232/258 Sixes Spark Timing

The 232/258 has a very mild centrifugal advance pattern or "curve" and relies heavily upon its vacuum advance for extra spark timing. At a hot idle speed of 550 rpm, early 232 engines require 5 degree initial spark timing (vacuum line disconnected and plugged). Use a timing light to verify timing.

The crankshaft pulley has a notch mark. A timing scale, cast into the front timing cover of the engine, provides marks from TDC (top-dead-center for #1 cylinder) to 12 degrees advance. Each line equals two advance degrees.

Use of a timing light is faster and more accurate than static timing. However, you can use the F-134 static timing technique when a light is unavailable. (The firing order for all 232 and 258 sixes is 1-5-3-6-2-4.)

Fig. 7-29. *Timing marks on 232/258 show 2-degree increments. At an idle with vacuum line disconnected and plugged, the pulley mark should index between 4- and 6-degree lines. 5 degrees BTDC is shown here.*

WARNING—
Avoid electrical shock by keeping your hand away from the primary coil wire. When the condenser unloads, the primary wire receives a strong voltage spike. Make sure your hand isn't the prime source to ground.

225 V-6 Spark Timing

225 V-6 engines have both vacuum and centrifugal spark advance. The Delco-Remy mechanical (centrifugal) advance is accessible beneath the rotor. The vacuum advance moves the breaker plate. The Prestolite distributor has its mechanical advance mechanism beneath the point breaker plate.

These engines rely upon a ported carburetor vacuum source for low-speed vacuum advance. Centrifugal advance takes over as engine speed increases. When setting the initial (base) spark timing, the engine should idle at 550–650 rpm. Disconnect the vacuum advance line and plug it.

There is some debate around the 225's base timing. Prestolite models call for "0" (zero) degrees initial advance. Buick 225 engines with Delco distributors call for 5 degrees initial spark timing (vacuum line disconnected).

As regular gasoline was typically 94 octane when these engines were new (high test or Ethyl rated 102–110 octane), let detonation or ping be your current guide. Begin with the 5 degree advance figure and retard the timing as necessary.

If available, use a timing light to verify timing. The crankshaft pulley has a notch mark. A timing scale, attached to the front timing cover of the engine, indicates from TDC (top-dead-center for #1 cylinder) to 15 degrees advance. Each line on the tag equals 2-1/2 crankshaft degrees.

Fig. 7-30. *Disconnect and plug or tape off 225 V-6 vacuum advance hose (arrow) before verifying base timing.*

Fig. 7-31. *Timing marks on 225 V-6 show either 2 or 2-1/2 degree increments. Set timing with vacuum advance disconnected and engine at idle. Pulley mark should index between "0" and "5" line, depending upon fuel octane requirements. 4 degrees BTDC is shown here.*

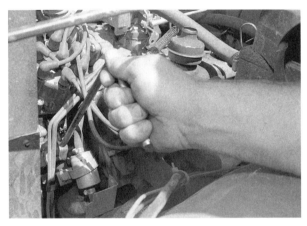

Fig. 7-32. *225 V-6 distributor housing clamp is easy to reach with a special offset distributor wrench. Loosen bolt slightly, just enough to move housing.*

Use of a timing light is always preferable to static timing. However, you may want to static time the engine if installing a replacement Delco-Remy distributor. You can use the same method described earlier for the F-134 engines. (The firing order for the 225 V-6 is 1-6-5-4-3-2. Cylinders number 1-3-5 on the driver's side/left bank and 2-4-6 on the right bank.)

> WARNING—
> *Avoid electrical shock by keeping your hand away from the primary coil wire. When the condenser unloads, the primary wire receives a strong voltage spike. Make sure your hand isn't the prime source to ground.*

V-8 Spark Timing

All Jeep V-8 engines have both vacuum and centrifugal spark advance. The Delco-Remy mechanical (centrifugal) advance mechanism is beneath the rotor. The vacuum advance moves the point breaker plate. On later Motorcraft electronic distributors, the mechanical advance mechanisms are beneath the electronic coil pickup plate.

The V-8 engine relies upon vacuum for low speed spark advance. Centrifugal advance takes over as engine speed increases. When setting the initial (base) spark timing, the engine should idle at the factory recommended hot idle speed. If available, the underhood decal specifies base timing and hot idle rpm for your particular engine.

An early 327 engine in a J-truck or Wagoneer should warm idle at 550 rpm (manual transmission) or 500 rpm in drive with an automatic. By 1972, the 304 and 360 AMC engines require 700–750 rpm (manual) and 650 rpm (automatic in drive). The increased speed is due largely to emission control requirements. Before setting base timing, disconnect the vacuum line and plug or cap it.

The 327 AMC and 350 Buick V-8s call for 5 degrees BTDC (before-top-dead-center) initial spark timing with the vacuum line disconnected. Since regular gasoline had an octane rating around 94 in the sixties, let detonation or ping be your spark timing guide. Begin with 5 degrees advance and, if necessary, retard the timing slightly to eliminate ping.

> NOTE —
> Manifold vacuum decreases as altitude increases. Additional spark advance compensates for the altitude change. I have found that most engines will tolerate from 1/2 to 1 degree of extra initial advance per 1000 feet of elevation. For safety sake, limit extra spark advance to a maximum of 3–5 crankshaft degrees. Remember, detonation is your best guide to octane and timing needs. Restore the original timing setting when you return to a lower elevation.

If available, use a strobe light to verify timing. On AMC 327 V-8s, a fixed pointer attaches to the timing cover. The pulley has three notches: TDC, 5 and 10 degree advance. Buick 350 V-8s have a timing tab on the front cover and a single notch on the pulley. Zero (0), 4, 8 and 12 degree advance, plus 2-degree increment lines, are visible on the timing tab.

The 304, 360 and 401 AMC powerplants also use a single timing notch on the crankshaft pulley and a tab on the timing cover. On earlier versions, the timing tab shows TDC and advance/retard in 5-degree increments. Later engines dispense with the advance marks, showing TDC, 5 and 10 degree retard only.

> NOTE —
> All Jeep V-8s except the 327 have clockwise rotation distributors. The AMC 327 V-8 distributor rotates counter-clockwise.

A timing light, if available, is always quicker and more accurate than static timing. However, you may need to static time your V-8 breaker point ignition, especially if you have removed the distributor for service. You can use the same method described earlier for the F-134 engines. (The firing order for all Jeep V-8s is 1-8-4-3-6-5-7-2. Cylinders number 1-3-5-7 on driver's side/left bank and 2-4-6-8 on the right bank.)

> WARNING—
> *Avoid electrical shock by keeping your hand away from the primary coil wire. When the condenser unloads, the primary wire receives a strong voltage spike. Make sure your hand isn't the prime source to ground.*

Fig. 7-33. *Clean timing tab and notch thoroughly before starting engine to verify timing. A dab of white or yellow indelible paint helps locate the mark with a timing light.*

3. Fuel System Tune-up

Carburetor adjustment is another aspect of your tune-up. Before setting the idle mixture, make certain that the fuel pump provides an adequate supply of gasoline. Change disposable filter(s) on later models and clean the fuel pump's sediment bowl filter on earlier Jeep engines.

A plugged fuel filter will restrict fuel flow and affect engine idle. If carburetor flooding, starvation or other problems exist, you will find overhaul procedures in your Jeep service guidebook or a "carburetor kit" instruction sheet.

Correct idle mixture and float settings contribute to a smooth idle and stable engine performance. Altitude changes alter the idle mixture. If you plan to operate your Jeep at a higher or lower altitude for any length of time, expect to adjust the idle mix.

> WARNING—
> *During many fuel system procedures fuel will be discharged or exposed. Do not smoke or work near heaters or other fire hazards. Have a fire extinguisher handy.*

3.1 134 Fuel System

When your 134 engine floods with gasoline or bucks during high speed runs, check the float setting. You can find float specifications in your factory or professional service manual. Also use the manual for checking the float drop setting.

The mechanical fuel pump on the earlier 134 L-head engines is a single diaphragm type. This pump serves only as a fuel supply for the carburetor. On F-134 engines, a dual-diaphragm fuel pump functions as both the fuel supply and as a vacuum source for the windshield wipers.

Before condemning either the carburetor or fuel pump, check the bolts that secure these parts to the manifold and block. Also check the manifold mounting edges for vacuum leaks. Look for kinks in the fuel pipes and hoses.

> CAUTION —
> *When servicing the fuel pump or its filter, tighten the bail nut carefully to avoid breaking the glass bowl.*

Float Setting

134 engines use various Carter Y-series carburetors. To set the float, loosen the fuel pipe and carefully remove the carburetor air horn. Check the float height setting with the air horn inverted and held level.

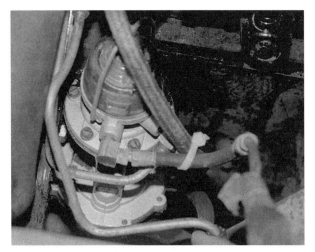

Fig. 7-34. *Early 134 engines feature a sediment bowl on the fuel pump. The serviceable sediment screen traps debris and functions much like a contemporary fuel filter. During service, avoid exposure to gasoline. Disposable mechanic's (latex) gloves are now available for these tasks.*

Fig. 7-35. *Carter W- and YF-series (shown) carburetors served a host of earlier Jeep engines. To check float setting on YF, remove and invert air horn.*

CAUTION —
Take care not to press the needle into its seat. Damage to the needle/seat and erratic performance could result.

WARNING—
When testing fuel pump volume, make certain that your container is safe and able to catch all of the gasoline. Route gas away from spark sources or hot engine parts. Spark from the ignition or engine heat could ignite fuel and cause a serious fire.

If the float level is correct and fuel starvation persists, check the fuel pump output. Correct pump pressure varies between models and pump designs (from 2-

1/2 to 4-1/2 psi). Verify your engine's requirements in a factory-level service manual.

An older, fatigued fuel pump diaphragm will stretch or rupture. Look closely for fuel dilution in the crankcase or leaks around the pump. If the cause of low pressure/volume is unclear, remove the pump and check the fuel pump arm and the camshaft lobe or eccentric that operates the arm.

Idle Mixture

Before adjusting the carburetor, look down its throat for carbon and debris. Spray carburetor/choke cleaner can remove accessible varnish and carbon. Short of an overhaul, these solvents work well for periodic cleaning. (If dust or grime is present, suspect an inadequate air cleaner seal, and correct the problem.)

The preliminary idle mixture setting for the Carter YF carburetor ranges from 1/2 to 2 turns open. Warm the engine completely. Make sure the heat riser valve works properly on L-head engines and that the thermostat brings coolant to normal operating temperature. Make certain that the choke valve is fully open.

Begin the idle adjustment by turning the idle mixture screw slowly clockwise. A noticeable lean misfire should occur. Stop here. Slowly back the idle mixture screw out (counter-clockwise). When a smooth idle occurs, the setting is correct. If the idle speed is incorrect at this point, reset the throttle stop screw, then repeat the idle mixture adjustment.

Fig. 7-36. *Many items wear to excess. If your early Carter carburetor has a warped or corroded body, or a loose throttle shaft, consider a new or rebuilt replacement.*

Turn the needle in gently. Over-tightening the mixture screw can seriously damage the needle end. If no lean misfire occurs as the mixture screw reaches its closed position, suspect dirty carburetor air bleeds.

Other Carburetor Troubles

If your 134 engine runs roughly or responds poorly under acceleration (flat spot), check for dirty jets or a defective accelerator pump. Either of these symptoms require a carburetor overhaul or replacement. Some wear is impossible to correct, so consider the age of the carburetor. A replacement unit is often practical.

Early Jeep fuel pumps are rebuildable. Repair kits were once a common item at the local retail auto supply. Today, however, rebuilt or new replacement pumps are available. For extended trips into the backcountry, it's wise to carry an extra fuel pump, a needle/seat kit and a carburetor float.

Fuel Pump Installation

Fuel pump installation on your 134 engine begins with cleaning the area around the fuel pump. Carefully detach the fuel lines at the pump. Safely cap the fuel inlet line to prevent fuel leakage during service.

Loosen the fuel pump mounting bolts evenly and remove the pump and gasket. Look closely at the cam lobe that operates the pump arm. Make certain a worn lobe is not the problem.

Clean the gasket surface on the engine block thoroughly. Use a suitable gasket sealant, applied to each side of the new gasket. Set the pump in place. Put sealant on the mounting bolt threads. Insert the bolts into the pump.

Rotate the crankshaft to place the pump camshaft lobe on its low or "heel" side to reduce pressure. Carefully place the rubbing surface of the pump arm against the lobe. Start the bolt threads with caution, pushing the pump squarely toward the block surface. Tighten the bolts evenly until the pump is secure.

Make certain the fuel pump arm remains in place and straight during installation. Wedging the pump to one side can damage the pump lever or housing.

3.2 2.5L GM and AMC Four Fuel System

Emission controls make later model carburetors difficult to adjust. Qualified technicians use elaborate equipment and procedures to adjust the idle mixture and other settings. For your routine service, the 2.5L Jeep carburetors prove restrictive.

An overhaul and staging of the 2SE or E2SE (California) carburetor on 2.5L GM engines involves numerous adjustments. For most Jeep owners, this is a carburetor better left alone. Overhaul requires exper-

Fig. 7-37. *2SE and E2SE Rochester carburetion provide fuel mixtures for 151 GM 'Iron Duke' engine. E2SE, found on California Jeep models, has a closed loop, electronically controlled main metering system.*

tise and special gauges, an accurate vacuum pump and exacting service data. Only with professional service guidelines will an experienced technician overhaul such a carburetor. Unless you have a strong background in carburetor overhaul, either sublet your carburetor to a specialist or purchase a new or rebuilt (exchange) unit.

> NOTE —
> Routine service of the fuel system helps prevent problems. Before considering a carburetor overhaul, change the fuel filter and air cleaner. Spray clean the carburetor. Make sure that spray carburetor cleaner does not damage the sensitive oxygen sensor. Read labels and use these products sparingly.

Refer to the emission control chapter for insight into the many emission control defects that cause rough idle and poor running. An EGR valve that doesn't seat properly can create symptoms just like carburetor trouble—so can a defective PCV valve, an inexpensive and routinely replaced item. If flooding, starvation or rough running persist, consult your factory or professional service guidebook for carburetor overhaul procedures.

Fuel Pump and Supply System

When fuel supply is weak, indicated by starvation, check the fuel pump. Although a common design, the GM 151 fuel pump produces a relatively high pressure of 6.5–8.0 psi. This pump should displace a minimum of one pint fuel in 30 seconds.

Before suspecting either carburetor or fuel pump trouble, check the bolts securing these parts to the manifold and block. Also check the intake manifold-to-cylinder head gasket for possible leaks. Look for kinks in the fuel pipes and hoses, and replace all fuel filters. Don't forget the sock filter at the fuel pickup in the fuel tank. If you have proof of a clogged sock filter, remove the fuel tank and gauge sender. Replace the filter.

> *WARNING—*
> *When testing fuel pump volume, make certain that your container is safe and able to catch all of the gasoline. Route gas away from spark sources or hot engine parts. Spark from the ignition or engine heat could ignite fuel and cause a serious fire.*

Idle Mixture

Idle mixture on carbureted 151 engines is considered non-adjustable. However, there is a provision on the 2SE/E2SE carburetors for idle mix changes. The adjusting screw has a plug cover, and access requires modifications to the carburetor. By law, this procedure is permissible if the engine fails a tailpipe emission test.

California carburetors (the E2SE version) have a closed loop C-4 (Jeep Computer Controlled Catalytic Converter) system. An electrical solenoid activates the carburetor main metering system to change the air/fuel ratio. Closed loop carburetion was a transitional step toward electronic fuel injection. Service of closed loop carburetion involves a thorough knowledge of the computer system.

If your 151-powered California Jeep has this system, repairs must follow the procedures outlined in your Jeep factory or professional service manual. There is nothing simple about the C-4 system, and the close relationship of the components means that any changes or modifications affect the entire system. Modifying or tampering with this fuel system is also illegal and usually results in poor overall performance.

Mechanical Fuel Pump Installation

Mechanical fuel pump installation on your carbureted 2.5L Jeep four-cylinder engine is essentially the same as for the 134 four-cylinder engines described earlier. EFI systems use electric fuel pumps.

3.3 Kaiser's OHC Tornado Six Fuel System

The Tornado sixes used two carburetors: Holley's 1920 series one barrel and the 2300 series two barrel. Each has provision for idle adjustment; the 1920 uses a single screw for mixture, while the 2300 has two screws.

To adjust idle mixture, warm the engine completely and make certain that the choke (automatic or manual) stands straight up. The exhaust manifold heat

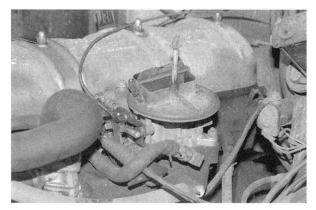

Fig. 7-38. *Most Holley 2300 idle mix screws are at sides of the main metering block. This is a rugged and easy to repair carburetor type with parts readily available.*

riser operation plays a key role in automatic choke operation. (See the exhaust/emissions chapter.)

Set the curb idle to 600 rpm. Turn the mixture adjusting screw(s) clockwise until the engine just begins to misfire. (On two barrel types, do one screw at a time.)

Back the screw out slowly until the engine idle smooths out. The smoothest idle point is the correct setting. Re-adjust the curb idle speed. If necessary, repeat the idle mixture adjustment until you achieve both correct idle speed and mixture. Here your 230 Tornado six will give optimal performance and fuel economy. If the automatic choke needs adjustment or the carburetor needs an overhaul, refer to a professional service guide.

Float Setting

Checking float settings on either the 1920 or 2300 model Holleys is very simple. On the 2300, correct fuel height is within 1/16th inch of the check plug's lower edge with the truck on a level surface.

Fig. 7-39. *Measure 2300 series fuel level at sight plugs. Have truck level and engine idling as smoothly as possible. Fuel should just reach lower edge of the plug.*

2.5L TBI/MPI Four and 4.0L MPI Six Fuel Injection

The 2.5L/150 AMC four first appeared in some '83 CJs, and since 1984 this engine has provided standard power for all Jeep CJs, Wranglers and Cherokees. This is basically the Cherokee 4.0L six minus two cylinders.

Early versions of the rugged AMC 2.5L four have carburetion. By 1986, AMC began fitting TBI electronic fuel injection and spark management systems on Cherokee models with the 2.5L four. The Wrangler's 2.5L engines had TBI in 1987. By 1991, the 2.5L engine gained multi-point EFI (MPI).

Jeep's introduction of throttle body injection to the Wrangler and Cherokee/ Comanche 2.5L fours improved off-road performance. The system is relatively simple, although troubleshooting and service require a professional level guidebook. You will need a digital volt-ohmmeter and basic tools for most TBI or MPI troubleshooting. Follow the step-by-step diagnostic procedures in your Jeep shop manual.

Beyond base spark timing, the 4.0L MPI six and 2.5L TBI or MPI engines time their spark through the

A full complement of sensors feed constant data to ECU computer. Air/fuel mixtures depend upon oxygen sensor signal. Oxygen sensor and manifold pressure signals help adjust for altitude changes, a significant gain with EFI.

ECU (computer). All timing changes result from engine sensor input. Spark and fuel injection problems range from irregular battery voltage, to wiring or connector faults, to defects in a variety of switches and sensors: the closed throttle switch, coolant temperature switch, engine speed sensor, oxygen sensor, gear selection switch, the knock sensor, manifold absolute pressure sensor, manifold air/fuel mixture temperature, starter motor relay, or wide open throttle switch.

Before condemning expensive electronic parts, check the simpler possibilities. Wiring, ground leads and vacuum hose leaks cause a variety of problems. Make a systematic check of the wire leads. The fuel pump mounts in the fuel tank. During start-up, you should hear the pump operate. If the pump is not active, check the fuel pump relay or wiring.

Most fuel and spark components on the TBI or MPI engine are very reliable. The least likely item to fail is the ECU computer. If you suspect sensor, fuel injector or other problems and want to perform your own service, a Chrysler/Jeep factory shop manual provides answers. Mitchell's Electronic Fuel Injection manual also devotes excellent space to Jeep engines.

Troubleshooting Jeep electronic fuel and spark management system requires a precise digital volt-ohmmeter. Tenths and hundredths of a volt make a difference.

The 2300 series float adjusts externally. With a large, straight blade screwdriver, loosen the fuel valve seat lock screw. Using a box end wrench, turn the adjusting nut clockwise to lower fuel level or counterclockwise to raise the fuel height. Tighten the lock screw and again check the fuel level at the sight plug. The 2300 is popular for its tuning flexibility and quick field service.

On 1920 carburetors, remove the economizer diaphragm and measure the fuel level with a depth ruler. The correct fuel level is 3/4 inch below the machined surface. (Set the gauge's cross rail just flush with the opening in the casting.) The engine should be level and idling.

To reset the float requires removal of the float bowl and careful bending of the float adjusting tab. Refer to your service manual for float adjustment specifications.

Tornado Fuel Pump Replacement

If the fuel pump output tests less than 3.5 to 5.5 PSI, or one quart flow per minute at engine idle, rebuild or replace the pump. Before condemning the pump, make certain that the sediment screen is clear and that there are no air leaks into the fuel supply line.

The earliest Tornado six has a difficult fuel pump installation. The pump pushrod must stay against the camshaft lobe as you align the pump. Later versions of the 230 engine have a spring to hold the pushrod in place. For all engines, rotate the engine until the pump pushrod is in its highest position before installing the new pump.

Clean the gasket surface and apply sealant to each side of a new gasket. Coat threads with sealant, too. On early engines, remove the valve cover. This enables holding the pushrod in position as you fit the pump into place. Tighten bolts evenly to prevent distortion of the fuel pump. Replace worn fuel hose as necessary, and tighten fittings with a flare nut wrench.

3.4 AMC 232/258 Six Fuel System

Earlier 232/258 tune-up includes carburetor adjustment. Before setting the idle adjustment, make certain that the fuel filter(s) permit an adequate supply of fuel. If flooding, starvation, a frozen automatic choke or other problems exist, it's time for a carburetor overhaul. (Consult your Jeep shop manual or other professional service guidebooks for choke service and carburetor overhaul procedures.)

When the fuel supply is weak, indicated by starvation and lean misfire, suspect fuel pump trouble. The mechanical fuel pump is a single diaphragm design. This pump draws fuel from the tank to the engine, then pumps gasoline to the carburetor.

Before condemning either the carburetor or fuel pump, check the bolts securing these parts to the manifold and block. Tighten fuel pipes and check for air leaks between the tank and fuel pump. Also check the intake manifold-to-cylinder head gasket for possible

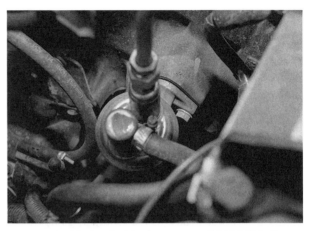

Fig. 7-40. *Mechanical fuel pump on all 232/258 in-line sixes mounts forward of right motor mount on side of the block.*

leaks. Look for kinks in the fuel pipes and hoses, and clean the sediment screen on early 232 fuel pumps.

Light Carburetor Service

Low speed and idle performance rely on a correct idle mixture. Substantial altitude changes require re-adjustment of the idle mixture. If you plan to operate your Jeep at a much higher or lower altitude for any length of time, re-adjust the idle mix for that elevation.

When your 232 or 258 floods on steep slopes or bucks during high speed runs, suspect the float setting. You can find specific float settings in your factory or professional service manual. Also refer to the manual for float drop settings.

Float settings for most 232/258 carburetors begin with loosening the fuel pipe and removing the carburetor air horn. 232/258 engines use various carburetors, including some Holley units during the Kaiser years. The Carter YF type (one barrel) and BBD (two barrel) are most common. These models require float height setting with the air horn inverted and held level.

Before adjusting the carburetor, turn off the engine. Look down the throat for carbon and debris. A spray type carburetor/choke cleaner will remove accessible varnish and carbon. Short of a carburetor overhaul, these cleaners work well. (If dust or grime is present, look for an inadequate air cleaner seal.) Restart the engine and allow the loosened debris and cleaner to run completely through the engine.

Fig. 7-41. *A quality spray carburetor cleaner will remove accessible debris. Try to wash exposed bleed holes. Spray cleaner into air horn vent. This will allow cleaner to work inside the float bowl.*

> CAUTION —
> *Make sure that carburetor cleaner will not damage the sensitive oxygen sensor. Read labels and use these products sparingly.*

Before condemning the carburetor settings or any other part of the fuel system, make certain the inlet fuel filter and air cleaner element are clean. On some 232/258 engines, a polyurethane pre-cleaner element also requires service.

Clean this pre-cleaner element in solvent; wrap it in a rag to draw out excess solvent; allow to air dry, then re-oil with 10/30 motor oil and gently squeeze out excess oil. Install the pre-cleaner over a new dry paper element.

> NOTE —
> A defective carburetor float loses buoyancy. Flooding and poor fuel economy are symptoms.

Idle Mixture

Idle mixture setting for YF carburetors range from 1/2 to 2 turns open. (Consult your underhood emission decal.) Warm the engine completely. Make sure the heat riser valve works properly on engines so equipped and that the thermostat brings coolant to normal operating temperature.

Begin the idle adjustment by turning the idle mixture screw slowly clockwise. A noticeable lean misfire should occur. Stop here. (If no change is apparent and the screw reaches a closed position, suspect dirty carburetor air bleeds.)

Fig. 7-42. *BBD carburetors found on late CJs and Wranglers through 1990 feature closed-loop computer circuits. Designed for strict emission compliance, these fuel systems provide limited room for adjustment.*

Slowly back the idle mixture screw out (counterclockwise). When a smooth idle occurs, the setting is correct. If the idle speed is more than 30 rpm off the factory recommendation, re-set the throttle stop screw. Repeat the idle mixture adjustment.

> NOTE —
> Always make certain the choke is fully open before attempting a carburetor idle mixture adjustment.

Later YF and earlier BBD equipped engines have idle mix limiter caps. These are removable, but adjustment requires discretion. Adjust the engine to the "lean best" setting to help meet clean air standards. (See your factory or professional service manual for guidelines.)

The later BBD carburetors have stepper motors for main metering fuel mixture control. These carburetors are part of a computer system that relies upon engine sensory data. Idle mixture is non-adjustable unless emission standards cannot be met. There is a professional service procedure for accessing the factory-set adjuster screws.

Consult a factory or professional service book before adjusting or servicing the late BBD carburetor. (Note that the vacuum actuator and idle solenoid interact with your truck's electrical accessory circuits.) The curb idle speed and fast idle are adjustable. Use the underhood decal as a guide for these rpm settings.

If your 232/258 six runs roughly or responds poorly under acceleration (flat spots), check for emission control defects, dirty carburetor jets or a defective accelerator pump. Carburetor troubles require either an overhaul or costly replacement of the assembly. Be sure of your diagnosis.

> NOTE—
> The two-barrel BBD carburetor has proven problematic for Jeep CJs and YJs. Poor gasket sealing and quirkish vacuum leaks plague many of these carburetors. I reason, however, that 258/4.2L sixes ran well when new. If you're willing to buy a carburetor tune-up kit and fresh carburetor (dip) cleaner, then sit at the workbench for hours painstakingly cleaning, inspecting for wear and casting flaws, making factory adjustments and carefully torquing screws, the rebuildable BBD can work. Many opt, however, for an EFI retrofit kit like the Mopar Performance 50-State legal alternative. (See performance chapter.)

Fuel Pump Troubles

When the fuel supply is weak, check the fuel pump output. Pump pressure varies between 232/258 applications and pump designs, but the range is 4 to 5 psi. Volume tests at the carburetor inlet line should produce one pint per 30 seconds at a slow idle speed.

> WARNING—
> *When testing fuel pump volume, make certain that your non-glass container is safe and able to catch all of the gasoline. Route gas away from spark sources or hot engine parts. Spark from the ignition or engine heat could ignite fuel and cause a serious fire.*

If pump pressure or volume is inadequate, remove the pump. Look closely at the camshaft lobe that operates the pump arm. Make sure wear at the lobe is not the problem. Rebuilt or new replacement pumps are available.

Fuel pump installation on a Jeep 232 or 258 engine is similar to that described earlier for 134 four-cylinder models.

3.5 225 and 2.8L V-6 Fuel System

225 V-6 tune-up also involves carburetor adjustment. Before setting the idle adjustment, make certain that the fuel filter flows an adequate supply of fuel. If flooding, starvation, a sticking choke or other problems exist, your carburetor needs an overhaul. (For overhaul procedures, consult a professional service guidebook or instructions furnished with a quality rebuild kit.)

> NOTE—
> The 2.8L V-6 uses the 2SE or E2SE carburetor. See the section on 2.5L GM fuel system for details.

When fuel supply is weak, indicated by starvation and lean misfire, look for kinks in the fuel pipes and hoses. Change fuel filter cartridge(s). If trouble still exists, suspect fuel pump trouble. The pump mounts at the left front of the 225 engine (on the timing cover). Watch for external fuel leaks or gasoline dilution of the crankcase oil.

Before condemning either the carburetor or fuel pump, check the bolts securing these parts to the manifold and engine block. Tighten fuel pipes and check for air leaks between the gas tank and fuel pump. Also check the manifold to cylinder head mounting edge for possible leaks. Re-torque 225 V-6 intake manifold bolts to 45–55 ft/lbs. Work from the center bolts toward each end "in cross."

Carburetor Float Setting

The 225 Buick/Jeep engine receives fuel through a model 2G (manual choke) or 2GC (automatic choke) Rochester carburetor. When the 225 floods on steep slopes or bucks during high speed runs, check the float setting. As 1966–71 models used different versions of these Rochester two-barrel carburetors, you will find specific float settings in a quality service manual or the instructions within a quality overhaul kit. Also use these sources to determine float drop settings.

> NOTE—
> You will need the carburetor seven-digit tag number when setting up your Rochester carburetor. When you adjust the float, take care not to press the needle against its seat. Excess pressure could cause damage and erratic performance.

For setting the float, loosen the fuel pipe and remove of the carburetor air horn. In the 2G and 2GC Rochester, the float hangs from the air horn. Once you invert the air horn, you can measure the float height

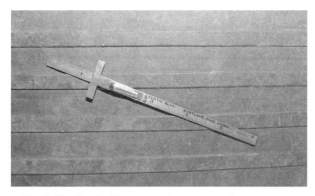

Fig. 7-43. *Quality T-gauge rule serves carburetor overhauls. Better carburetor kits come with detailed instructions for each model and a plastic or cardboard 'throw away' gauge for setting float height, drop and linkages.*

Fig. 7-44. *Idle mixture screws are easy to access on Rochester 2G, 2GC and 2GV carburetors. Clockwise leans mix. Counter-clockwise enriches. Adjust one screw at a time.*

with a T-gauge. Holding the air horn upright, you can read the float drop setting.

225 V-6 Idle Mixture

Low speed and idle performance rely upon correct idle mixtures. A large altitude change will require re-setting the carburetor's idle mixture. If your 225 V-6 Jeep CJ or Jeepster/Commando will operate at a significantly higher or lower altitude for any length of time, plan on adjusting the idle mix.

Before adjusting the carburetor, turn off the engine. Look down the twin bores for carbon and debris. A spray carburetor cleaner can clean accessible varnish and carbon. Short of an overhaul, these cleaners do a good job. (If dust or grime is present, check the air cleaner base seal.)

Re-start the engine and allow the loosened debris and cleaner to run completely through the engine. This can temporarily foul the spark plugs and mimic erratic performance. Clear the engine of foreign matter before attempting to adjust the carburetor.

> CAUTION —
> *Before condemning the carburetor settings or any other part of the fuel system, make certain the in-line fuel filter is fresh. Also service the air cleaner. (See lubrication and maintenance chapter.)*

When adjusting the carburetor, first warm the engine completely. Make sure the heat riser valve works properly and that the thermostat brings coolant to normal operating temperature. Be certain that the choke valve stands upright.

Begin the idle adjustment by turning either idle mixture screw slowly clockwise. Stop just as you notice a distinct lean misfire. (If no change is apparent

and the screw reaches a closed position, suspect a carburetor internal leak or vacuum leaks.)

Slowly back the idle mixture screw out (counterclockwise). When the smoothest idle occurs, the setting is correct. Repeat this step with the other idle screw. If the curb idle speed is more than 30 rpm off the factory recommendation, re-set the throttle stop screw, then repeat these idle mixture adjustment steps.

Service Advise: Always make certain the choke remains fully open while attempting a carburetor idle mixture adjustment. Do not allow the engine to idle for long periods during adjustment, or the spark plugs will foul and distort engine performance. If you have difficulty judging the engine's smoothness, use a tachometer while you set the carburetor mixture screws. Adjust the engine to a "lean best" setting to help meet clean air standards.

If your Jeep's 225 V-6 engine runs roughly or responds poorly under acceleration (flat spots), suspect dirty carburetor jets, a low fuel supply (incorrect float setting, clogged fuel filter or weak fuel pump) or a defective carburetor accelerator pump.

Fuel Pump Service

If fuel starvation is still apparent after adjusting the float level, check the fuel pump output. Pump pressure on the 225 V-6 should vary between 4.25 and 5.25 PSI. Volume tests at the carburetor inlet line should produce one pint per 30 seconds at an idle speed of 500 rpm.

> WARNING—
> *When testing fuel pump volume, make certain that your non-glass container is safe and able to catch all of the gasoline. Route gas away from spark sources or hot engine parts. Spark from the ignition or engine heat could ignite fuel and cause a serious fire.*

If pump pressure or volume is inadequate, remove the pump. Look closely at the eccentric lobe that operates the pump arm. Make certain wear at the lobe is not the problem. Rebuilt or new replacement pumps are available.

Steps for fuel pump installation on your Jeep's 225 V-6 engine is similar to that described earlier for 134 four-cylinder models.

3.6 Jeep Carburetor V-8 Fuel System

Before setting the idle adjustment, make certain that the fuel filter(s) and pump provide an adequate supply of fuel. Replace the paper air filter element if dirty. Make sure the choke is not frozen or sticking. If your engine has symptoms of flooding, fuel starvation, lean misfire or cutting-out, check the carburetor float setting or consider a complete carburetor overhaul. (Consult your Jeep shop manual or other professional guidebooks for carburetor overhaul procedures.)

Before condemning either the carburetor or fuel pump, check the bolts securing these parts to the intake manifold and engine front cover. Tighten fuel pipes and check for air leaks between the gas tank and fuel pump. Also check for loose manifold mounting hardware, a common cause of vacuum leaks. Look for kinks in the fuel pipes and hoses, and change the fuel filter cartridges.

When testing fuel pump pressure (5–6.5 psi) or volume, disconnect the fuel pipe at either the fuel pump outlet or carburetor (whichever is easier). Safely route fuel from this point to a safe, non-glass container, far from any spark or engine heat. Idle the engine at 500 rpm and expect a one pint volume in 30 seconds.

> **WARNING—**
> *When testing fuel pump volume, make certain that your non-glass container is safe and able to catch all of the gasoline. Route gas away from spark sources or hot engine parts. Spark from the ignition or engine heat could ignite fuel and cause a serious fire.*

V-8 Carburetor Types

The Jeep V-8s have used various OEM carburetors. 327 AMC engines feature either a 2209 two barrel or 4160-type Holley four barrel carburetor. Buick 350 V-8s use GM's reliable Rochester 2GV two barrel. AMC 304/360 V-8s have used the F-2100 and 2150 series Ford Motorcraft two barrel carburetors.

Some mid-'70s 360s and all 401 V-8 AMC engines use the 4350-series Motorcraft/Ford carburetor. This carburetor is a "square flange" four barrel unit. Holley's list #0-9626, a 4160-series unit, is a bolt-on re-

Fig. 7-45. *Holley end-float type carburetors have an external float adjustment for each float bowl. Sight plugs on the bowls permit quick fuel height checks without removing the bowl.*

placement. High performance Holley units also fit this manifold pattern. (See high performance chapter.)

In the 1980s, AMC met V-8 emission requirements with elaborate closed loop or "feedback" carburetors. These computer-regulated fuel systems have no simple provision for idle mixture adjustment, although tune-up includes idle speed and related settings. If you suspect a carburetor or fuel system problem with your later V-8 engine, consult the Jeep factory shop manual or equivalent professional guide. Do not attempt to adjust any part of the system without professional service guidelines.

Float Settings

When your V-8 floods on steep slopes or bucks during hard acceleration or high speed runs, the float setting could be at fault. You will find specific float height and drop settings in your factory service manual or the instructions found in a quality overhaul kit. Verify your carburetor list or tag number before re-setting the float or adjusting linkages.

> **WARNING—**
> *When adjusting the float, take care not to press the needle into its seat. Excess pressure could damage the needle and seat. Erratic performance results.*

Motorcraft float setting procedure involves loosening the fuel pipe and removing the carburetor air horn. (Except for Holley 4160 carburetors, all Jeep V-8 carburetor floats hang from the air horn.) Once you invert the air horn, a T-gauge can measure float height. Hold the air horn upright to read the float drop setting.

Idle Mixture

Smooth low speed and idle performance depends upon correct idle mixture settings. If you intend to operate your Jeep V-8 at a much higher or lower altitude, plan to adjust the idle mixture. (Idle mixture adjustment does not apply to later engines with closed loop feedback carburetion and oxygen sensors. The closed loop engines may, however, require idle speed adjustments.)

Before adjusting your V-8 carburetor, turn off the engine. Make certain the air cleaner is clean and not restrictive. Look down the carburetor throats for carbon and debris. A spray carburetor cleaner can clean accessible varnish and carbon. Short of an overhaul, these cleaners do a good job. (If you find dust or grime in the carburetor throats, check the air cleaner seals and correct the problem.)

Re-start the engine and allow the loosened debris and cleaner to run through the engine. This debris can foul spark plugs and cause a rough idle. Before you adjust the carburetor, run the engine at a fast idle to clear out debris.

> CAUTION —
> *Read the carburetor cleaner's instructions. The product may be harmful to catalytic converters or oxygen sensors. Use cleaner sparingly, and keep spray away from heat sources and the truck's paint finish.*

Warm the engine completely. If your engine has a heat riser valve, make sure that it works properly. Al-low coolant to reach normal operating temperature. Make sure the choke valve stands upright.

Begin the idle adjustment by turning an idle mixture screw slowly clockwise. Stop when you hear a noticeable lean misfire. (If no change is apparent and the screw reaches a closed position, there may be carburetor internal leaks, vacuum leaks, a loose carburetor base gasket, or clogged air passages.)

Slowly back the idle mixture screw out (counterclockwise). When you reach a smooth idle, the setting is correct. Repeat this step with the other idle screw. If the curb idle speed is more than 30 rpm off the factory recommendation, restore the idle speed by re-setting the throttle stop screw, then repeat the two-step idle mixture adjustment.

Make certain the choke stands fully open while you adjust the carburetor idle mixture. Avoid idling for long periods, as this will foul spark plugs and distort your idle settings. Adjust the engine to a "lean best" setting, your contribution toward cleaner air.

> NOTE —
> If a Jeep V-8 engine runs roughly or responds poorly under acceleration (flat spots), suspect dirty carburetor jets, a defective accelerator pump or an inoperative distributor spark advance. Check the spark timing advance, both centrifugal and vacuum. If okay, consider a carburetor overhaul.

V-8 Fuel Pump Replacement

If fuel pump pressure or volume is inadequate, you need to replace the pump. Rebuilt and new replacement pumps are available for Jeep V-8 engines. Fuel pump installation on your Jeep's V-8 engine is similar to that described earlier for 134 four-cylinder models.

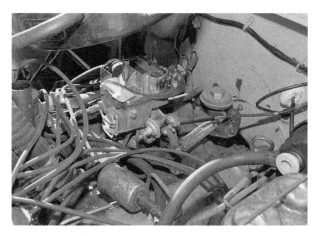

Fig. 7-46. *Both two and four barrel V-8 carburetors have twin idle mixture screws. Clockwise leans mixture; counter-clockwise enrichens. Adjust one screw at a time. Shown here is a Motorcraft two-barrel carburetor on a '74 Jeep Renegade 304 V-8.*

Fig. 7-47. *Loosen and tighten V-8 fuel pump bolts evenly to prevent binding of a long fuel pump arm. This will prevent damage to pump or misalignment with cam lobe or eccentric.*

4. Major Engine Diagnosis

If you suspect major engine trouble or your fuel and spark tune-up has little effect on performance, perform further diagnosis.

On later engines such as the 173 V-6 engine, or the Buick 350 and AMC 304/360/401 V-8s, emission controls can cause trouble. A defective EGR valve, for example, often mimicks symptoms of carburetor and fuel supply trouble. (Electronic closed-loop carburetion or fuel/spark management can be another source.)

The 225 Buick V-6 and 327 AMC V-8 engines were products of a different era. Although PCV and air injection came on some of these engines, the emission control packages were simple and not likely to cause trouble. (See emission control information in other chapters.)

Trouble may brew deeper in the engine. After years of exposure to tune-up and engine overhaul needs, I use a compression gauge solely for quick referencing. A low reading typically requires squirting clean motor oil into the cylinder to distinguish piston ring wear from valve troubles. Skirting this archaic procedure, I move to a leakdown tester for pinpoint diagnosis.

A leak of more than 10–12% in any cylinder raises questions of wear, although most Jeep engines will still offer reasonable service to 20% leakage. High performance demands, such as turbocharging, however, require 10% or less leakage at any cylinder.

4.1 Compression Testing

For quick diagnosis, a compression gauge is very handy. I prefer a threaded hose gauge, which allows one-person operation. Clean spark plug areas, then remove all of the spark plugs. Screw the gauge end into #1 cylinder's spark plug threads. With the gauge secure, visible and lying away from rotating engine parts, open the throttle wide

Crank the engine several revolutions, until the highest stable reading occurs. Record the reading, and repeat these steps for each cylinder. See the table for general compression guidelines. Consult a factory manual for exact specifications.

> NOTE —
> According to contemporary factory guidelines, engine balance depends upon a maximum variance of 25–30% between the highest and lowest cylinder. I believe this is too great for satisfactory performance and fuel economy. Smooth operation, especially in an off-highway rock crawling situation, demands far better balance. The traditional factor, 10% difference between the highest and lowest cylinder, remains my standard.

Fig. 7-48. *A cylinder leakdown test of this freshly rebuilt engine reveals normal seal. Compression gauge reading is nowhere near as accurate. Leakdown tests foretell trouble long before a compression gauge.*

Table a. Typical Compression Specifications

Model	Compression (psi)
L-134	90–110
F-134	120–130
2.5L GM/AMC	120–130
AMC 232 Six	145
AMC 258 Six	140
OHC Tornado Six	120–130
173 V-6*	135–145
225 V-6/350 V-8 (Buick)	150–165
327 (AMC) V-8	150–165
AMC 304/360/401 V-8	120–140

*The 173/2.8L V-6 has an 8.5:1 compression ratio. Factory recommended cranking compression must be a minimum of 100 psi or produce no more than a 30% variance between the highest and lowest cylinder pressures. I believe that 100 psi is very low, and optimal performance will require 135–145 psi figures. Balance is not as crucial on the 173 V-6, however, as the 60-degree "V" design runs much smoother than the inherently imbalanced 90-degree V-6.

Analyzing Compression Readings

Higher than normal compression means carbon build-up. Excess carbon is very hard on the piston rings and valves. At its worst, carbon buildup contributes to deadly "pre-ignition," the premature ignition of fuel by glowing material in the cylinders. Unlike very mild detonation or "ping," pre-ignition can break pistons and connecting rods—so can severe detonation.

NOTE —
Low compression readings indicate either worn rings, valve wear, a blown head gasket or cracked castings.

Improper valve clearance also causes low compression readings. Although most service guidebooks list valve adjustment as a possible cure for low compression, this is very seldom the case.

After thirty years' exposure to engine repair and machine shop work, I believe that running an engine with valves that do not seat completely will cause permanent damage to valve faces and seats. A valve adjustment cannot remove hard carbon buildup, pitting and burnout of valve faces and seats. For these problems, only a valve grind or cylinder head rebuild can restore performance.

Tight valve clearance generally results from normal wear on engines without hydraulic valve lifters. As the valve faces wear into their seats, a process called "valve seat recession" occurs. Unleaded fuel aggravates this wear, especially in engines designed during the leaded gas era.

Hydraulic valve lifters should have enough built-in clearance to run between engine overhauls without the need for a valve adjustment. Unless valve seat recession is excessive, the valve clearance should remain stable between engine overhauls on a 232/258 six and other hydraulic lifter Jeep engines.

Unleaded Fuel Woes

Leaded gasoline once helped lubricate valve seats, faces and stems. Complete phase out of leaded fuel is well underway, and nearly all U.S. pump gasoline has no lead. This leaves valves and valve seats of older, leaded gas era Jeep engines at greater risk.

The problem of unleaded gasoline and valve seat recession has a remedy. An automotive machine shop can retrofit hardened steel (replacement) exhaust valve seats into the head(s) or block of a Jeep engine. Hardened exhaust valve seats will prevent heat damage and valve wear caused by unleaded fuels.

Octane requirement for all 232/258 engines is 91 or better. Under current fuel standards, this means such an engine needs high test fuel. If you must run your Jeep truck on 90 or lower octane, retard the timing a few degrees to reduce harmful detonation. Power may suffer some, but the engine will survive longer.

NOTE —
When overhauling or performing cylinder head work on a 232 or 258 Jeep six, consider the use of slightly lower compression pistons or, simpler yet, use a thicker than OEM head gasket to lower compression. If milling/decking the cylinder head, be sure to use a thicker head gasket.

Re-torque The Cylinder Head

When you find a low compression reading, re-torquing cylinder head bolts may help remedy slight gasket seal or head warpage problems. Re-check cranking compression when finished. (See illustrations for tightening sequence.)

L-Head/F-134: Torque the head bolts to 60–70 ft/lbs. On F-134 blocks, one head bolt, #5, is beneath the carburetor in the integral intake manifold. Remove the carburetor to access this bolt.

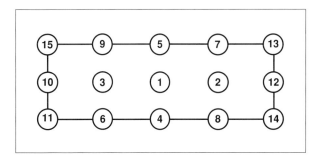

Fig. 7-49. *Cylinder head torquing sequence for L-134 and F-134 engines. On F-134, access to #5 head bolt requires carburetor removal.*

2.5L GM/AMC: Tighten the GM 151 bolts to 92 ft/lbs. 150 AMC bolts require 110 ft/lbs on all bolts except #8, which calls for a 100 ft/lbs setting.

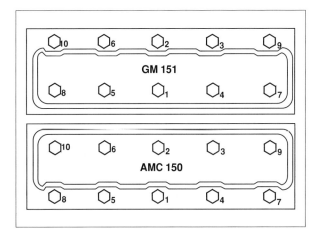

Fig. 7-50. *Iron Duke GM 151 (top) and AMC 150 (bottom) cylinder head bolt tightening sequence. Note location of bolts relative to valve cover gasket cutout in head.*

230 Tornado OHC: Torque head bolts in the sequence illustrated to 80–95 ft/lbs. When all bolts are tight, the three nuts in the center of the head require re-tightening to 15–20 ft/lbs.

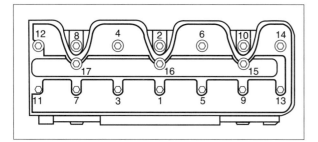

Fig. 7-51. *Torque sequence for 230 Tornado OHC cylinder head.*

232/258: Record the compression readings for each cylinder. If you find low readings, re-torque the cylinder head bolts. 232/258 engine cylinder head bolt torque is 85 ft/lbs, tightened in sequence.

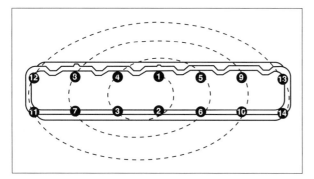

Fig. 7-52. *232/258 cylinder head bolt tightening sequence.*

V-6: 225 V-6 head bolts torque to 65–80 ft/lbs in sequence. Torque 173 V-6 head bolts to 65 ft/lbs.

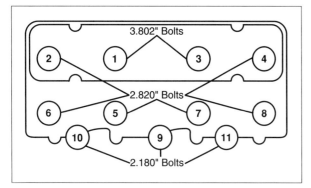

Fig. 7-53. *225 V-6 head bolt tightening sequence.*

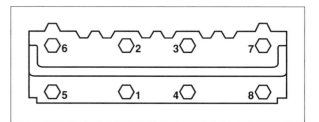

Fig. 7-54. *173/2.8L GM V-6 head bolt tightening sequence.*

V-8: 327 V-8 head bolts torque to 60 ft/lbs in sequence. Torque 350 Buick head bolts to 75 ft/lbs. AMC 304/360/401 engines require 110 ft/lbs torque.

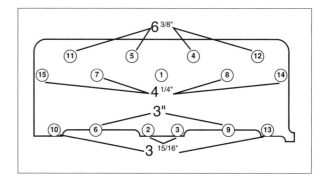

Fig. 7-55. *327 AMC V-8 head bolt tightening sequence.*

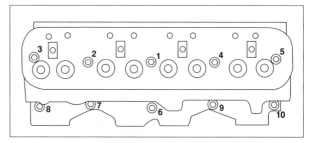

Fig. 7-56. *1968–71 350 Buick/Jeep V-8 cylinder head bolt tightening sequence.*

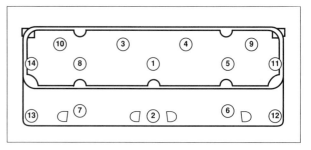

Fig. 7-57. *1971–up AMC 304/360/401 V-8 cylinder head bolt sequence.*

For all engines, after torquing each head bolt in sequence, let the bolts rest for a few minutes. Re-check torque a final time. I find that when frictional forces subside, one or more of the bolts might yield slightly.

4.2 Valve Adjustment

If the camshaft lobe profiles are normal, a valve adjustment of just a few thousandths of an inch will restore valve lift and opening points. Valve adjustment usually reduces noise and improves engine performance. (Generally, hydraulic lifters eliminate the need for valve adjustment between engine or cylinder head overhauls.)

> NOTE —
> On 2.5L, 232/258, V-6 or V-8 engines, valve clearance and adjustment problems are highly unlikely as each of these engines use hydraulic valve lifters. A sufficient range of plunger travel compensates for normal valve face and seat wear. If you hear noise from the valvetrain or valve lifters, suspect defective hydraulic lifters, a worn rocker shaft or rocker arms, bent pushrods, flat camshaft lobes or a malfunctioning lubrication system. On the 225 V-6, check for oil pump and pump housing wear, a common problem with earlier Buick V-6s.

L-Head and F-134

All 134s have valve adjusting mechanisms. The exhaust and intake valves are in the block of L-head engines. F-134s have exhaust valves in the block and intake valves in the cylinder head. Periodic valve adjustment protects the valves and maintains peak performance. Before you adjust the valves, allow the engine to cool completely, then remove the tappet side cover (either engine design).

Fig. 7-58. *On F-134 engines, valve adjustment requires removal of both top valve cover and side (tappet) cover. Periodic valve adjustment decreases likelihood of burning a valve.*

Fig. 7-59. *For 134 fours, number 1 and 4 cylinders each reference from TDC mark on crankshaft pulley or flywheel (earlier L-heads). Number 3 and 2 cylinders reference from a mark 180 degrees past this point.*

On F-134 engines, remove the valve cover as well. This provides access to the intake valves and rocker arms. Remove spark plugs to make engine rotation easier.

You must index the camshaft during valve adjustment. I find that using the crankshaft timing marker eliminates guesswork. Begin with #1 cylinder, setting the pointer on the TC (top-dead-center) mark. If #1 cylinder is ready to fire, both the intake and exhaust valves will have clearance. (This is how you determine that #4 cylinder is not up to fire.) As an alternative, remove the distributor cap and view rotor position.

Now, mark the crankshaft pulley or flywheel 180 degrees from the TDC or TC mark. To do this, scribe a straight line across the center of the crankshaft pulley. On a clean pulley surface, dab a spot of white or yellow indelible paint. This reference will allow faster adjustment of #3 and #2 cylinders' valves.

On early L-134 engines with flywheel reference marks, carefully rotate the crankshaft 180 degrees from the flywheel's TDC or TC mark. In this position, dab a spot of paint on the flywheel surface adjacent to the reference pointer.

Hold the exhaust valve tappet with a special tappet wrench. These are very thin open ended wrenches sold through professional tool sources. Turn the self-locking adjuster while sliding the feeler gauge between the valve stem end or rotator cap (Roto Cap) and the tappet adjuster. A 0.016" blade gauge should fit this gap with just the slightest amount of drag. (Some early F-134 engines have no rotator caps. These Eaton "free" exhaust valves adjust to 0.012" clearance.)

Adjust the #1 intake valve of L-head engines in exactly the same manner. (If you have trouble distin-

Fig. 7-60. *Both L- and F-134 engines and Willys sixes require special tappet wrenches for valve adjustment.*

guishing the intake valve from the exhaust valve, simply note the location of the intake and exhaust ports at the manifolds.) The gap for the intake valves of L-head 134s is also 0.016".

If your engine is an F-134, you may now adjust the clearance between the intake rocker arm and valve stem for #1 cylinder. This gap is normally 0.018", measured with a blade feeler gauge. If the gap requires adjustment, make certain that you first re-torque the cylinder head and also the rocker shaft pedestal nuts. (Torque pedestal nuts evenly to 36 ft/lbs.)

Set the rocker-to-valve stem clearance by loosening the lock nut and rotating the adjuster. Tighten the lock nut securely, and re-check the clearance. Often, you must compensate for the thread pull-up caused by tightening the lock nut.

Turn the crankshaft in the direction of normal rotation. Align your new mark (180 degrees from the TC position). This readies the next cylinder in the firing order (#3) for valve adjustment. Set the #3 cylinder intake and exhaust valves.

Again turn the crankshaft, in the normal cranking direction, until the TC mark aligns. This time, #4 cylinder is ready to fire, and you can adjust these intake and exhaust valves.

Rotate the crankshaft 180 degrees more, in the direction of normal rotation, aligning your painted mark with the timing pointer. In this final position, repeat the adjusting procedure for #2 cylinder's intake and exhaust valves.

> NOTE —
> Although valvetrains on the Willys six-cylinder L- and F-head engines are similar to the 134s, you must use a different approach when positioning the crankshaft. See your shop manual before attempting a valve adjustment on these early six-cylinders.

L- and F-134 Valve and Side Cover Gaskets

When you have adjusted the last pair of valves, clean the valve cover on the F-134 and side cover on both the L- and F-head engines. Carefully remove old gasket material from the engine castings.

> CAUTION —
> *Do not allow gasket material to fall within the engine. Stuffing clean rags inboard of the gasket edges and around pushrod holes on an F-head engine is helpful. A shop vacuum makes an effective clean-up tool.*

If you use an original equipment type cork gasket on the side cover, soak the gasket in water for some time (preferably overnight or at least while adjusting the valves). Once saturated, the gasket is more pliant and less likely to tear. Using Permatex High-Tack or an equivalent adhesive, coat one side of the gasket thoroughly. Allow the sealant/adhesive to set up, then attach the gasket to the side cover surface.

Carefully place the gasket and cover in position and secure the bolts. On F-134 powerplants, perform this procedure with the valve cover gasket as well. After starting the engine, check closely for oil leaks.

Kaiser's OHC Tornado Six

The overhead camshaft in the Tornado cylinder head has mechanical rocker arms that follow the camshaft lobes. This innovative head design has advancements not found in other U.S.-built truck engines until the late 1990s.

> NOTE —
> Six cam lobes open and close the Tornado's twelve valves, each cylinder operating from one lobe. Valve lift and duration match at each intake and exhaust valve.

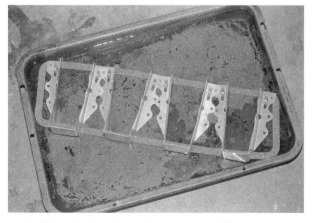

Fig. 7-61. *Cork gaskets often shrink and distort in storage. To restore a side cover gasket and avoid risk of tearing, soak in water until completely pliant.*

You can adjust these valves either hot or cold, with a hot running clearance preferred. Some mechanics avoid hot settings due to uncomfortable temperatures and the knuckle busting moving parts. Frankly, I prefer hot valve settings for their accuracy. The drawback is the oily mess that results, which may require engine cleaning.

The main advantages of hot adjustments are: 1) a better look at valve action and lift under actual operating conditions, and 2) an end to tedious hand rotation of the crankshaft while setting the valves. Since the 230 six allows for hot running clearances, I'll share the procedure. Begin by removing the valve cover with the engine warmed thoroughly and shut off.

Valve clearance is 0.008" for both intake and exhaust valves. Have your flat blade feeler gauge ready, and start the engine. At the slowest smooth idle setting possible (perhaps as low as 400–450 rpm if you're careful), insert the clean feeler gauge flatly and squarely between the valve stem tip and the rocker arm end.

Correct settings allow a very slight drag as you gently pull and push the feeler gauge. You are actually feeling the precise moment of the widest tappet clearance. Setting hot, running clearance requires practice.

Tighten or loosen the moving adjuster nuts with a deep, six-point socket and ratchet. Move each nut slightly and re-check. When you achieve correct valve clearance settings at all twelve rocker arms, shut off the engine. Install the valve cover, start the engine and set the hot idle speed to 590–600 rpm.

Fig. 7-62. *Flat blade tappet gauges have various thicknesses. The 230 Tornado intake and exhaust valves call for 0.008" clearance. Make certain blade lays flat and squarely between rocker arm end and valve stem tip.*

If this is too much effort or you don't like whirring parts and a bath in oil, static valve setting on the 230 six is simple.

Thoroughly warm the engine and turn the ignition off. Place the transmission in park or neutral (with the parking brake set and wheels blocked). Remove the spark plugs, and rotate the engine with a socket attached to the crankshaft pulley bolt. (Stay away from the fan blades and radiator core with the socket and ratchet or breaker bar.) Turn the crankshaft bolt in a clockwise (viewed from the front) direction.

For each cylinder, you will turn the engine over until the camshaft lobe's peak faces downward, toward 6 o'clock. In this position, you can adjust both the intake and exhaust valve clearance as described. Rotate the crankshaft to position the camshaft for each cylinder's valve adjustment.

This is the simplest way to learn valve lash adjustment. You can even get a "feel" for the running adjustment. With all twelve valves statically adjusted and the engine still warm, start the engine and test the running clearances as described.

Jeep V-6 Engines

173/2.8L V-6 engines have a provision for valve lifter adjustment, although the factory settings usually last until overhaul. Generally, valve noise means defective parts, but on rare occasions, lifter adjustment may solve the problem.

The valve adjustment method is much like the Chevrolet V-8 engines. Completely warm the engine, shut it off, then remove the valve cover. Install oil deflectors to prevent an oil bath. Run the engine at a slow idle, and loosen one rocker nut until noise is heard clearly. Slowly remove the excess valve lash. At exactly zero rocker arm to valve stem lash, very slowly (1/4 turn at a time, letting the engine stabilize after each twist) rotate the nut 1-1/2 turns down for proper lifter pre-load. Repeat the procedure at each valve.

For further details on 173 V-6 valve adjustment or service, consult your factory level manual. You will also want to use oil stopper clips for preventing an oil bath during valve adjustment. These clips are available through professional automotive tool sources.

Fig. 7-63. *Valve lash on Dauntless 225 V-6 is non-adjustable. Adjustment on 173 V-6, similar to a Chevrolet V-8 engine, is zero lash, then an additional 1-1/2 turn preload on the lifter plunger.*

Tune-up Specifications For My Jeep Engine

Idle Speed:_____

Initial (Low Speed Or Idle) Spark Timing @
_____RPM:_____-Degrees.

Higher Speed (2500 Crankshaft RPM) Spark Timing
_____-Degrees.

Carburetor Idle Mixture Adjustment
Procedure (If Adjustable)

_____

Air Filter Part Number_____

Fuel Filter(s) Part Number_____

Spark Plug Type And Number_____

Breaker Point Or Module Part Number

_____

Distributor Cap Part Number_____

Rotor Part Number_____

Drive Belt Part Number(s)_____

Fig. 7-64. *Sample quick reference chart for tuning your Jeep engine. Keep a clean, dry copy of these specifications in your on-board tool kit.*

Chapter 8

Emission Controls

All manufactured motor vehicles must comply with federal and state tailpipe emission standards. Since the 1960s, Jeep truck engines have required factory installed emission control devices, designed to combat air pollution. Some emission control devices help the engine achieve more complete combustion, while others work directly at reducing tailpipe pollutants.

Emission control components vary, depending upon the model year and requirements. Your Jeep's emission control package may include the ignition spark timing, the carburetor or EFI and a series of devices to reduce three major exhaust pollutants: 1) the poisonous gas, carbon monoxide (CO), 2) raw, unburned hydrocarbons (HC), and 3) oxides of nitrogen (NOx), a prime ingredient in visible smog.

Many Jeep emission controls focus on peak performance, fuel efficiency and longer engine life. The care and maintenance of these devices remains an important part of servicing your truck. Even minor engine tuning requires a working knowledge of emission control components. Proper idle, acceleration, gas mileage and overall performance depend upon a fully functional emission control system.

1. Emission Control Basics

L-134: The First Emission Control Engine

Jeep engines can claim the very first pollution control device, a positive crankcase ventilation (PCV) valve. Although Willys simply wanted to seal the military Jeep's engine from moisture, the concept of a closed crankcase would later serve as the first motor vehicle anti-pollution device.

In the early 1960s, other U.S. vehicle manufacturers began installing Positive Crankcase Ventilation (PCV) systems on engines. The simple principle aimed at purging the engine crankcase of combustion blow-by and fumes.

Prior to 1961, most engines vented blow-by to the atmosphere through a "road draft tube." These devic-

Fig. 8-1. *Jeep four-cylinder engines pioneered the closed crankcase. The motive in 1941 was to seal the wartime model MB crankcase for water crossings. Clean air concerns were still two decades away. Left of oil filter assembly is the closed oil filler tube on this '48 L-134 four.*

es were simply open pipes with their tips cut on an angle toward the rear of the vehicle.

The road draft tube relies on low pressure vacuum, created as the vehicle moves forward, to purge the crankcase. Primitive and inefficient, especially at slow road speeds or when the engine idles with the vehicle parked, a road draft tube pollutes the environment and permits condensation and corrosive agents to build up sludge in the crankcase.

The modern Jeep PCV system allows manifold vacuum, regulated by a spring-balanced valve, to draw crankcase blow-by back through the intake manifold. This closed crankcase system continuously removes and recycles harmful combustion by-products. A PCV valve and closed crankcase contribute to better performance and longer engine life.

The Air Injection System

The most visible emission control device is the air injection pump. Found as original equipment on many Jeep truck engines since the mid-1960s, the smog pump's ungainly physical features and maze of plumbing have attracted unwarranted criticism.

Fig. 8-2. *Simple PCV valve on your Jeep engine contributes to engine longevity by actively fighting sludge and crankcase condensation. Additionally, a closed crankcase prevents water from entering the engine during stream fording. A modern PCV system requires the simplest of maintenance: periodic valve replacement. Also make sure that hoses and grommets seal properly.*

Fig. 8-3. *This clean-air filter lies just inside the air cleaner cannister on most closed crankcase engines. Manifold vacuum through the PCV valve creates low pressure in the crankcase. Clean air enters the engine from the filter. Without an adequate source of fresh air through the breather filter, PCV vacuum could damage engine seals and gaskets.*

Fig. 8-4. *Many Jeep owners have mis-labeled the air injection pump as a power robbing device. This relatively passive system requires only a fraction of a horsepower to operate. The benefit is a cleaner environment through lower tailpipe emissions.*

Fig. 8-5. *The diverter/bypass valve directs air away from the exhaust stream during deceleration. This prevents an over-rich mixture of unburned fuel from igniting and damaging the exhaust system.*

Fig. 8-6. *One-way or anti-backfire check valves prevent hot exhaust from reaching the air injection pump and hoses. Hazardous, charred hoses and a burned pump result from a defective check valve.*

Air injection is an external emission control. It has no effect on the fuel/induction or ignition system and creates a negligible amount of exhaust back pressure. Although the engine drives this pump, power drain is less than one-half horsepower—hardly noticed by a V-8, six cylinder or even a torquey four-banger. Since the air injection system is basically passive, removal of the pump system does not improve performance.

CAUTION —
Tampering with the air injection system can prevent cool air from reaching the exhaust valves, manifolds and air injection tubes. Heat damage to your Jeep engine can result.

Fig. 8-7. *Distribution tubes direct clean air into the exhaust manifold(s) or the cylinder head exhaust ports. Jeep emission control systems follow typical AMC, GM and, more recently, Chrysler passenger car and light truck designs.*

Fig. 8-8. *An EGR valve can lower upper cylinder temperatures—as much as 2000° Fahrenheit. Lower temperatures reduce oxides of nitrogen (NOx) emissions, a key component in visible smog. 258 Jeep EGR valve, effective from off-idle through cruise rpm, operates from ported vacuum.*

The principle of air injection is simple: Inject oxygen into the exhaust stream near the engine exhaust ports and/or directly into a catalytic converter. Given this fresh source of oxygen, the combustion of unburned hot hydrocarbons and carbon monoxide can continue.

Your Jeep engine's air injection system requires little maintenance. Pump bearings are permanently lubricated, and the drive belt seldom requires adjustment. The rest of the air injection system consists of a diverter/bypass valve, anti-backfire check valves, and manifold distribution tubes.

Air Bypass Systems

The diverter or bypass valve receives a high manifold vacuum signal during engine deceleration, when carburetor "venturi effect" causes an over-rich fuel mixture. The valve opens, allowing pump air to vent into the atmosphere. Without a diverter valve, air pumped into rich, unburned exhaust stream gases would cause spontaneous combustion. The exhaust system could be severely damaged.

Additionally, in some applications the engine's exhaust valves, manifold(s) and even the air injection tubes rely on pump air for cooling. When an air injection system is defective, or a mechanic disables the engine's emission devices, the side effect can be melted injection tubes, damage to exhaust valves or a cracked exhaust manifold.

Exhaust Gas Recirculation

Lean fuel mixtures reduce CO and HC emissions. These lean fuel mixtures, however, also increase combustion temperatures and raise NOx emissions. In the

early 1970s, engineers discovered a simple, effective means for lowering combustion temperatures: recycling exhaust gases. Simply recirculating exhaust through the intake stream dilutes fresh air/fuel mixtures yet has little effect on the air/fuel ratio. These cooler combustion temperatures reduce NOx while enhancing performance.

The exhaust gas recirculation (EGR) system permits the use of leaner air/fuel ratios without compromising cylinder temperatures. EGR valves serve a useful function on any engine that runs low octane fuel, requires a mild spark advance curve or operates with lean air/fuel mixtures.

Unfortunately, ill-informed mechanics see EGR as a source of trouble or a horsepower thief. This false reasoning overlooks the EGR system's ability to lower scorching combustion temperatures (which run as high as 4800° F without an EGR system) to below 2500°. Operating properly, the EGR system helps eliminate detonation (ping).

If, after tossing the EGR valve in the dumpster, your Jeep engine now suffers severe ping, look here for the problem. Lean burning, low-octane fueled engines need their EGR system to prevent detonation, poor combustion and damage to internal engine parts, including the pistons, rings and cylinder walls.

The Catalytic Converter

Found on most Jeep engines since 1975, the catalytic converter is an anti-pollution device. Simply a muffler-like component, the converter operates a chemical processing plant in your exhaust system.

Fig. 8-9. *Catalytic converters resemble a muffler. These miniature chemical processing plants reduce output of carbon monoxide, hydrocarbon and oxides of nitrogen. Always consider the ultra-high temperatures generated by a catalytic converter. To avoid starting a brush fire, never park your Jeep truck in tall, dry brush!*

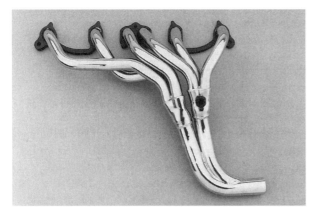

Fig. 8-10. *An aftermarket high performance exhaust system can reduce back pressure. Contribute to clean air, even if high performance is your goal. Be sure your exhaust system complies with federal and state emission regulations. This Mopar Performance exhaust component is "50-State legal" for use on a 4.0L Cherokee.*

Oxidizing catalysts (usually platinum and palladium) in the converter react with carbon monoxide and hydrocarbons. The by-products of this catalyzing process are harmless carbon dioxide and water. Reducing catalysts also take oxygen out of NOx, leaving harmless free nitrogen to pass out the tailpipe.

While some complain about sulphuric acid and a "rotten egg smell" during rich fuel conditions, the catalytic converter's only negative performance effect is exhaust system back pressure. Aftermarket high performance catalytic converters are now available to reduce this back pressure. (See the performance chapters.) They reduce pressure yet still contribute to clean tailpipe emissions.

Cold-start and Warm-up Devices

All gasoline engines require cold start systems. For a Jeep truck engine, which operates in the most extreme climates, our survival depends on proper start-ups. A carburetor's choke or EFI engine's cold start enrichment cycle must meet both cold start-up and emission control needs.

For low tailpipe emissions, the choke should open as quickly as the engine can accept leaner air/fuel mixtures. To accomplish this, a number of devices come into play. The air cleaner assembly doubles as the thermal air system to direct heated air from the outside surface of the exhaust manifold into the intake inlet of the air cleaner.

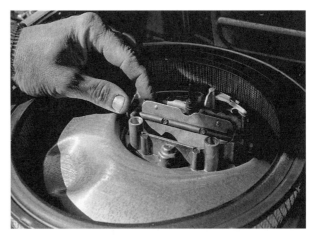

Fig. 8-11. *The conventional choke, either manual or automatic, must open quickly to maintain low tailpipe emissions. Adjust your Jeep choke for safe driveability and lower pollution levels. (See a factory or professional service guide for proper setting.)*

Fig. 8-12. *Some automatic chokes operate as manifold heat reaches a bi-metallic coil spring. Others open via a heated electrical coil, activated as the ignition circuit opens. Still another method is an opening signal received from engine coolant temperature.*

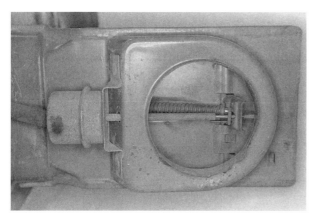

Fig. 8-13. *A vacuum motor opens the hot air passage. For faster warmup, heated air is available to the air cleaner. This allows more complete combustion on a cold engine, reducing tailpipe pollution levels.*

Fig. 8-14. *The heat riser valve plays an important role during engine warmup and choke operation. A heat riser stuck shut creates severe back pressure, reducing engine power. A heat riser stuck open causes the choke to stay on too long, decreasing performance and fuel economy.*

Carbureted Jeep engine chokes come in a variety of shapes and sizes. Early models rely on manual, cable controlled choke valves. Later carbureted engines feature both electric and bi-metallic spring (engine heated) automatic chokes. Fuel injected (EFI) engines benefit from a computer controlled cold start enrichment system that maintains precise air/fuel ratios and driveability during the entire engine warmup cycle.

Additionally, many carburetors rely on a vacuum signaled choke pull-off to allow quicker vehicle operation during warmup. The typical choke pull-off unit consists of a vacuum diaphragm and choke release linkage, usually operated by ported vacuum. (Ported vacuum originates just above the carburetor's throttle valve to provide high vacuum just as the throttle opens, with very slight vacuum at an idle.)

On many Jeep emission engines, a thermal air cleaner (TAC) provides a vacuum-actuated warm air valve. The vacuum motor receives signals from a thermal vacuum switch and/or bi-metallic valve. The vacuum motor opens and closes the warm air door at the air cleaner intake. When the engine warms sufficiently, the vacuum motor closes the warm air door, permitting cooler, fresh air to enter the air cleaner. A thermal air cleaner allows quicker choke opening and better driveability as the engine warms.

Exhaust Heat Riser

The heat riser, often eliminated with the installation of aftermarket exhaust headers, also serves a vital function. During cold start-up, the riser valve stays closed, which re-directs hot exhaust to the base of the intake manifold. On some Jeep engines, this heated section of the manifold provides a stove well for the choke. For many Jeep engines, a heat passage warms the area un-

Fig. 8-15. *Later Jeep 258 in-line sixes eliminate use of an exhaust heat riser. An electric heating unit mounts in the plenum area of the intake manifold. During cold engine operation, this heater aids combustion and permits better driveability, much like a conventional heat riser.*

der the carburetor. This permits better atomization of fuel and more thorough combustion.

Some riser valves open with a vacuum diaphragm/motor, while others rely on a heated bi-metallic spring. It is important that the manifold heat passage remain clear. Often, especially on V-8 engines, the passage clogs as carbon builds up.

Switches, Valves, and Vacuum Controls

Your Jeep engine's emission control devices must know when to work and usually require energy to work. A variety of electrical and vacuum switches help meet those requirements. The ignition switch often serves as the trigger for a fuel shut-off solenoid.

Other switches, such as the thermal vacuum switch (TVS), control vacuum to the distributor spark advance or an EGR valve. Most TVS switches rely on rising engine coolant temperatures to expand an enclosed wax pellet. This, in turn, opens or closes one or more vacuum ports in the TVS.

On your Jeep engine, vacuum serves as a very powerful and economical source of energy. Vacuum switches, valves, and motors, like those that open and close the thermal air cleaner intake flap, serve quickly and efficiently.

Vacuum- or electrically-operated throttle positioners serve a variety of roles. Some raise the idle speed to compensate for extra loads like the air conditioner. Others serve as a dashpot, relying on a spring and resistance diaphragm to slow the throttle return. On carbureted engines, a dashpot helps reduce over-rich fuel flow (venturi effect) during deceleration.

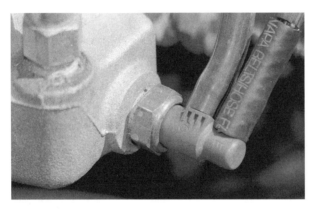

Fig. 8-16. *Thermal vacuum switches are very useful. On many Jeep engines, they activate the thermal air cleaner and the EGR valve. At a pre-set temperature, the valve opens ports, directing vacuum to various devices. Check your Jeep's vacuum circuit diagram to determine the role of any TVS switches.*

Fig. 8-17. *Vacuum powers a number of engine devices. Many later Jeep carburetor designs rely on a vacuum-actuated throttle positioner. Vacuum often provides ignition spark advance. Emission service always includes inspection of vacuum hose circuits.*

Fuel Tank and Carburetor Fumes

Raw fumes from gasoline are another source of air pollution. To contain these vapors, Jeep trucks have benefitted from evaporative emission control devices since the early 1970s. Although storage methods vary, vacuum helps capture float bowl, crankcase and fuel tank fumes, eventually recycling them through the engine's intake system.

When servicing or repairing your Jeep's fuel system, you must route vacuum and ventilation hoses very carefully. Follow a factory or professional level guide for your Jeep model.

> *CAUTION —*
> *Gasoline fumes are highly volatile. Use extreme caution when working with the evaporative emission control system. All parts must fit according to design, including the gasoline cap.*

Conversion Engines and Emissions

Many Jeep 4x4 trucks have conversion engines. The low horsepower output of early four and L-head six-cylinder engines has encouraged swapping to larger, more powerful powerplants. Since the late 1950s, a number of manufacturers have produced parts for engine and transmission swaps into the Jeep chassis.

Engine conversions come under emission control compliance laws in many states. Whether your Jeep truck now has a conversion engine or you plan such a change, be certain of your state's emission control laws. (You will find further information on engine conversions and emission control compliance in the performance chapters of the book.)

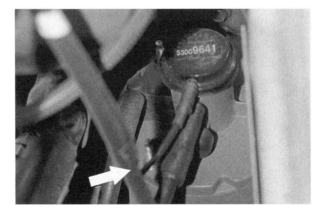

Fig. 8-18. *Jeep evaporative emission controls include a vapor canister. The replaceable canister is plastic with a granulated carbon element inside. The fuel tank, carburetor vent and other gas vapor sources each feed the evaporative emission system. Correct hose routing is critical to performance and safety.*

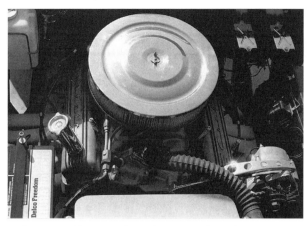

Fig. 8-19. *V-8 transplants into early Jeep chassis became a popular practice in the 1960s. An entire industry developed around improving the performance level of Jeep 4x4 trucks.*

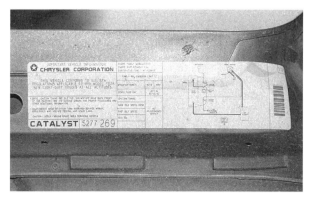

Fig. 8-20. *The underhood emission and tune-up decal is important. It describes the standards for tuning your Jeep engine and also the emission control package assigned to the vehicle. This decal often describes smog devices while mapping out vacuum hose circuits.*

Passing An Emission Test

Although California has the strictest motor vehicle pollution laws in the United States, many vehicles that fail California's smog tests have sufficiently low tailpipe emissions. They fail the visual inspection portion of the test. Here, before the engine has a chance to show how cleanly it burns, the inspector takes a close look at the emission control system and vehicle chassis. Any missing or modified parts are cause for failure.

This is a tough test. All vacuum hoses, flexible heat tubes, the smog pump drive belt, vacuum switches, the EGR valve (if required) and closed crankcase devices must be intact and function properly. The inspector, using a detailed guidebook and the emission decal found under your Jeep's hood, checks closely for each OEM engine and chassis device—including the unleaded fuel restrictor if your Jeep was so equipped from the factory.

The vehicle can fail visual inspection for something as simple as a missing section of aluminum flex hose at the thermal air cleaner. Although aftermarket performance parts often fail the visual test, a growing number of components now comply with California Air Resources Board (CARB) standards.

Increasing numbers of aftermarket high performance engine components, including intake manifolds, a number of ignition devices and many exhaust system pieces, also meet CARB standards. (Lists of these devices are available from the California Department of Consumer Affairs, Bureau of Automotive Repairs.) Other aftermarket components, generally described as "not legal for use on California highways," hold a good chance of getting your engine an "F" on the smog inspection test.

Fig. 8-21. *Nearly all '75 and newer U.S.-sold Jeep vehicles require unleaded gasoline. Note that this CJ Jeep's filler neck has a restrictor. A California smog inspection will include a look at the fuel filler.*

NOTE—

For your Jeep to be inspected at a regular smog station, 50-State legal parts must bear a special CARB-assigned number. A pioneer component under this certification process was the retrofit supercharger built by K.F. Industries for the Jeep Cherokee 2.8L GM V-6. More recently, Mopar Performance received California (50-State) approval under an executive order (E.O. #D265-7) for the EFI retrofit kit that replaces carburetion on 1981–90 258/4.2L in-line Jeep sixes. See engine performance chapter for details.

The cold start circuit is among the many items checked on the visual inspection. Although this system operates for only minutes during warmup, every component is essential. A hand choke retrofit kit to replace an automatic choke, a missing vacuum hose or a discarded thermal air cleaner each cause failure. Even raising the air cleaner bonnet with a thicker filter element results in an "F," as the canister opening compromises both the cold start and closed crankcase systems.

Well tuned and running properly, your engine will meet hydrocarbon, carbon monoxide and NOx standards at both an idle and the required 2500 rpm. Bonafide defects, such as vacuum leaks, carburetor flooding, bad ignition cables, fouled spark plugs or a defective EGR valve, will result in a tailpipe test failure. Ignition timing must match OEM specifications for the engine.

When a California Smog Chek inspector suspects that the wrong engine is in the chassis, he or she may examine the block and/or cylinder head casting numbers. If determined that your engine is not original for the truck, you'll receive a non-compliance certificate and referral to a referee.

The referee station identifies the engine by casting or serial numbers, determining the age and OEM emission requirements for both the engine and the chassis. (You may need sales documentation for the engine.)

The referee compiles a list of necessary emission control devices for both your truck's chassis and the conversion engine. A visual engine and chassis inspection confirms whether the needed devices are in place. If not, the referee recommends which device(s) will bring your Jeep into compliance.

After meeting compliance, the vehicle receives a certification tag noting the required emission control

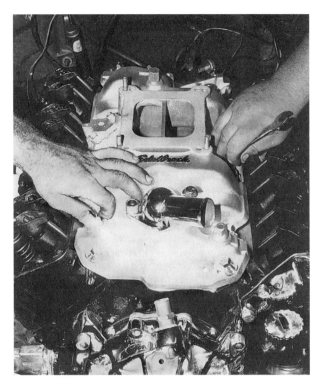

Fig. 8-23. *Use of this Edelbrock Performer intake manifold is acceptable. The dual-plane design, provision for an EGR valve and no increase in tailpipe emissions helps determine compliance. A leader in the aftermarket industry, Edelbrock has California-certified many components in recent years.*

Fig. 8-22. *By California and U.S. EPA standards, this CJ Jeep engine, despite a closed crankcase, EGR valve, enhanced ignition and precise tuning, is not legal. Handsome aftermarket performance air cleaner, open and missing a thermal air system, would immediately fail visual smog inspection. (Note: K&N offers emission legal air filtration elements that fit stock/OEM air cleaners.)*

devices. This enables the owner to take the truck to any California 'Smog Chek' station for a biennial or change of ownership inspection. If the truck complies, you only need to see the referee once.

For emission compliance under California-legal criteria, your engine must fit a given range of years (be the same year or newer than your Jeep truck chassis) and display only OEM or state-approved aftermarket parts. If so equipped when sold new, your Jeep chassis may need a catalytic converter(s) and gas tank unleaded fuel restrictor. After such scrutiny, the engine must pass a tailpipe emission test, meeting standards equal to or cleaner than those set for the original Jeep engine in good operating condition.

The Jeep Exhaust System

The Jeep exhaust system is subject to severe abuse. Off-highway debris, harsh climates, corrosion, freezing and scorching temperature extremes, and a variety of other hazards impact your truck's exhaust system. Aside from emission related components, like the catalytic converter, the system has several other replaceable components.

Your truck's exhaust system begins at the exhaust manifold flange and heat riser (if so equipped). The exhaust pipe leads from the manifold to either the catalytic converter or a muffler. (Pre-'75 trucks have no catalytic converter.) If the truck uses a catalytic converter, a pipe exits the converter and connects to the muffler. After the muffler, a tailpipe continues to the rear of the Jeep.

Jeep V-6 and V-8 engines with a single exhaust system use a Y-shaped exhaust pipe that leads to the catalytic converter or muffler. These single exhaust systems restrict the flow of gases on V-type engines, and many owners of V-6 and V-8 Jeep trucks have converted to dual exhaust—which now raises legal issues.

It was once acceptable to split the exhaust system and install a second catalytic converter. U.S. EPA law then ruled that any conversion to dual exhausts is illegal, whether both pipes have a catalytic converter or not. Since the OEM chassis may determine whether your vehicle can legally have dual exhausts, it may not be possible to install dual exhausts on a Jeep originally equipped with a catalytic converter.

Example: If you swap an emission legal V-8 into a catalytic converter-equipped CJ chassis, you may be legally required to use a large, single exhaust system with an appropriate and functional catalytic converter.

> *WARNING—*
> *Dual tailpipes can always exit the rear of the truck—even if both pipes must move along the same side of the chassis. Your health and safety, and that of passengers, depends upon a leakproof, rear exiting exhaust system.*

> CAUTION —
> *Check Federal and State emission requirements before swapping engines or modifying a catalytic converter exhaust system.*

> NOTE —
> Dual exhaust conversions are legal on any pre-catalytic converter era Jeep chassis. Laws apply only to dual exhausts on a catalytic converter chassis.

A defective muffler can restrict exhaust. When inspecting your Jeep's muffler(s), look beyond the outer jacket. While rust, corrosion and holes are obvious, more subtle damage, like broken baffles, may lie just beneath the surface. With a rubber mallet, tap on the reinforced end seams to rattle the muffler. Loose baffles will shake in the canister. Listen carefully.

Always replace any worn or damaged parts. On your Jeep, inspect the exhaust with each lube job. A leakproof system is a necessity. Backflow of exhaust

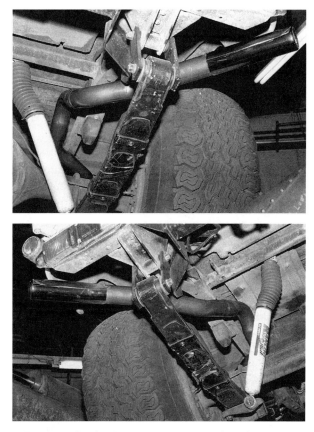

Fig. 8-24. *Dual exhaust system conversions for V-6 and V-8 engines help reduce back pressure for better economy and performance. A correct installation has tailpipes exiting at the rear of the truck, just like original equipment. Keep exhaust fumes away from the cab and bed areas. Check current state and federal requirements before converting to dual exhausts—especially on a catalytic system.*

and seeping fumes present a health hazard to vehicle occupants. Open and cloth tops, and short wheelbase models aggravate the problem.

By design, Jeep tailpipes have always exited to the rear of the truck. This is important to health and safety, as fumes can flow away from the truck's body. Some owners, however, choose to shorten their exhaust systems, thinking that less length will improve performance. Such pipes usually exit just forward of the rear wheels. This is a significant health hazard, as exhaust fumes roll upward from the sides of the truck and into the cab.

If a muffler shop suggests short dual exhaust pipes that exit out the truck's sides, insist that the tailpipes continue to the rear of your Jeep. An experienced muffler technician can bend and twist pipes to fit the contours of your Jeep chassis while making sure the pipes adequately clear the rear axle movement.

2. Routine Emission Control Service

At regular intervals, your Jeep emission control system requires attention. Individual Jeep emission systems differ. For details on a specific engine's equipment or step-by-step testing/troubleshooting, see your Jeep factory shop manual.

My illustrations provide an overview of common emission system components. These captioned photos should clarify some of the emission control issues covered in this chapter.

Fig. 8-27. *The air pump drive belt requires periodic adjustment and replacement. Relatively light load of this device assures long belt life.*

Fig. 8-25. *Inspect vacuum hoses. Vacuum provides a principal energy source for emission control switches. Hose routing and condition are critical to peak performance. Vacuum leaks reduce performance and create tuning problems.*

Fig. 8-26. *Replace the PCV valve at routine intervals. Change the PCV valve with each spark plug replacement (30,000 miles maximum for late engines). On some engines, the interval maximum is 12,000 miles. Engine idle, a clean crankcase and other vacuum related functions benefit from periodic PCV valve service.*

Fig. 8-28. *EGR valve inspection is simple. Attach a vacuum pump to the valve. With the engine idling, unseat the valve by apply vacuum. Idle should get rough, even stalling the engine. Watch vacuum pump's gauge to be certain EGR valve diaphragm holds vacuum.*

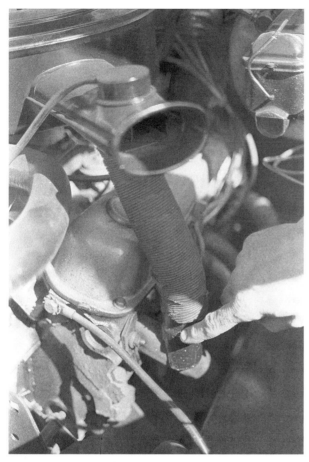

Fig. 8-29. *Inspect warm air vacuum motor on the thermal air cleaner. Make certain this device works properly. If the heat tube shows evidence of leakage or poor fitup, replace the tube.*

Fig. 8-30. *Observe choke operation and timing. Spray all carburetor linkages with a quality cleaner. Clean the choke valve, choke housing and vacuum piston or brake if there is any evidence of choke sticking. Choke should move freely when unloaded.*

Fig. 8-31. *On a cold engine, spray the heat riser valve with a suitable penetrant and oil. Make certain that the valve moves freely and the bi-metallic spring or vacuum diaphragm is intact and functional.*

Fig. 8-32. *Many Jeep chokes open electrically. Several later Motorcraft and Carter BBD carburetors feature electric choke units. Check the current flow to the choke unit with a voltmeter. Chokes quickly become too hot to touch. Take care not to burn your fingers!*

Fig. 8-33. *Examine the rubber air injection hoses for signs of charring. Check the vacuum line to the diverter. On a fully warmed engine, snap the throttle open and shut and observe whether air exits the by-pass/diverter valve under deceleration. If the valve functions properly, air should bypass.*

Fig. 8-34. *Inspect the evaporative canister and hoses. If the canister smells heavily like gasoline or feels weighted with liquid, safely drain the gas and replace the canister with a new unit. Evaporative canisters have check valves and require careful routing of hoses from the carburetor/EFI unit, vacuum source and fuel tank.*

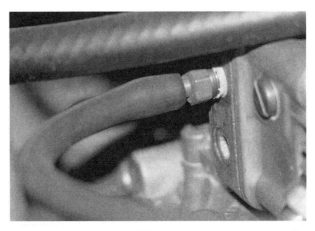

Fig. 8-36. *The modern OEM or aftermarket carburetor is plumbed for emission devices. Several vacuum sources (manifold or ported) may be built into a carburetor.*

Fig. 8-35. *Check electrical connections at switches and solenoids. Watch the solenoid as someone activates the ignition switch and air conditioning. An idle control solenoid has been popular on Jeep engines since the 1970s.*

Fig. 8-37. *A popular tool with emission control specialists is the basic hand vacuum pump/pressure tester. Use the tester to check an EGR valve, vacuum diaphragms, vacuum hose circuits and thermal vacuum switches.*

Chapter 9

Cooling System Repairs

Your Jeep truck places high demands on its cooling system. The engine must maintain normal operating temperatures, whether the air outside is -60° F or 125°. Dusty roads pack dirt and abrasive material into the radiator's core, and rock from the tires of caravaning vehicles attacks the radiator core along with the windshield. Twisting trails, where tires hang suspended in air, attempt to tear the radiator core supports loose, while hoses flex precariously and stress the radiator's inlet and outlet tubes.

Many Jeep owners consider creature comfort a valid part of four-wheeling. Why suffer with 120° desert heat inside your vehicle? Add to the cooling system's burden an air conditioner. The installation of a factory or aftermarket air conditioner heaps another challenge onto the cooling system, as the air conditioning condenser restricts air flow through the radiator core.

Naturally, as Jeep vehicles became more popular, many buyers expected an automatic transmission option. Jeep's Borg-Warner, GM and Chrysler-built automatic transmissions each cool from the engine's

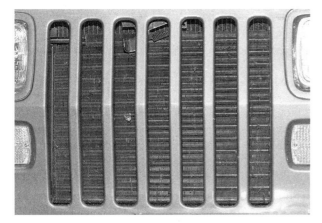

Fig. 9-1. *An automatic transmission and air conditioning place an added load on the engine's cooling system. The air conditioning condenser and auxiliary transmission cooler each block some air flow through the radiator core.*

radiator, placing an even greater load on the radiator and cooling fan system.

The final cooling challenge for many Jeep vehicles has been the conversion engine. A higher horsepower engine places a tremendous load on the radiator and fan system. CJ models are the most likely candidates for a V-6 or V-8 conversion, and they have small grille openings for air flow. This factor increases the risk of overheat, especially when a winch assembly or other accessories mount forward of the grille.

> *WARNING—*
> • *Never remove the radiator cap when your Jeep's engine is hot. Hot coolant under pressure leaves the radiator with force and could scald you severely.*
>
> • *Coolant is poisonous to pets. Use extreme care when draining and disposing of engine coolant.*
>
> *CAUTION —*
> • *Coolant can damage painted surfaces. Rinse spills with water immediately.*
>
> • *Avoid adding coolant to the engine when it is hot or overheated. If you must add coolant, do so only with the engine running and the coolant/water pump turning.*

1. Cooling System Basics

A chronic engine cooling problem is usually traceable to the radiator. Often, especially with transplant engines, an under capacity radiator creates trouble. Several rules apply when choosing the correct radiator, but the main issue is horsepower. Higher horsepower equates to a greater need for heat transfer, your Jeep radiator's principal job. Engineers see horsepower output as the main variable when determining the capacity of a radiator or fan system.

Your Jeep engine loses approximately one-third of its thermal energy as heat radiation from the radiator, the heater core and surfaces of the engine. Another one-third of the thermal energy goes out the tailpipe as hot exhaust. (This valuable energy, when harnessed to

Horsepower Equals Heat

For those who like engineering formulas, here's the equation for engine cooling: Draw off 42.5 BTUs of heat per minute for each horsepower. Sufficient cooling requires maximum transfer of heat from the engine to the air. The radiator, comprised of coolant tubes and fins, handles the majority of this task.

Since BTU heat dissipation relates directly to the area of radiator tube and fin exposure, a radiator's surface area and the number and size of the tubes each play a major role in cooling. Fan draw and ambient air flow help determine how quickly heat will dissipate from the radiator.

Fig. 9-2. *Here is the difference between a late model Chevrolet V-8 cross-flow radiator and the early Jeep down-flow unit. Overall size, number of tubes and the core surface area for a V-8 is substantially larger than that required by a 134 four.*

power an exhaust turbocharger, produces considerable horsepower.) The final one-third of this thermal energy drives the pistons downward and rotates the crankshaft.

Matching Cooling System Components

There are several cooling system concerns. Whether you are restoring an earlier model or increasing your truck's off-pavement performance, you must accurately determine horsepower. Obviously, it's better to guess high than low, as a thermostat can regulate coolant temperatures if you install a slightly oversize radiator. Too little radiator core, and the engine will never run cool.

Consider the engine's water pump volume and coolant flow rate. If the engine pumps more water into the radiator than the tubes can flow, the coolant will overflow the filler neck as engine speed increases. This is a common symptom of an inadequate radiator flow.

The radiator's thermal efficiency, or BTU rating, must be sufficient. The formula stands as an absolute minimum and assumes a low to medium air flow rate (approximately 725 to 1150 feet per minute) through the radiator core. Excess loads, high ambient temperatures, air restriction or unusually slow road speeds require additional capacity. Slow speed crawling on scorching hot days is a way of life for many Jeep 4x4s.

For proper heat transfer, your Jeep engine requires the right radiator flow rate. Maintaining normal engine temperatures requires a sufficient radiator surface area, adequate tube and tank size and a matching water pump circulation rate. The volume of engine fan air flow must match the radiator size and amount of coolant circulation.

Flow rate is the amount of coolant that can move through the radiator in a given interval of time. The industry standard of measurement is gallons-per-minute flow or gpm. If your Jeep's original radiator won't cool

a larger transplant engine, the cause is likely inadequate gpm flow or a shortage of radiator surface area.

The usual cure for flow rate weaknesses is a larger radiator or radiator core. Popular four-row radiators offer a thicker core with four rows of tubes. If you must adhere to the original radiator's height and width dimensions, and that radiator has two or three rows of tubes, the addition of a four-row core may provide the needed gpm flow.

Fan Air Flow

If, despite adequate coolant flow and proper thermostat action, your Jeep engine overheats, air flow or fan shrouding could be at fault. Slow speed operation places a greater demand on the fan. Especially with a narrow grille opening, fan draw is a critical element of cooling. Correct air flow across the radiator's cooling fins and tubes assures adequate heat transfer. Incorrect fan location, a defective fan clutch, or an improperly shaped shroud can prevent air from passing through the radiator core.

Many Jeep owners have removed the fan clutch unit and attempted to run a non-flexing metal fan. This can actually create a blockage of air flow at high road speeds. Here, air moving through the grille and radiator can travel much faster than the draw speed of the fan. For this reason, and to reduce horsepower drain, either a fan clutch assembly or flexible-blade direct drive fan are frequently found on high performance engines.

The proper diameter fan blade assembly, the correct shroud and an adequate air opening in front of the radiator will round out your cooling fan needs. The

Fig. 9-3. *Here a Flex-A-Lite aftermarket flex fan and spacers replace a factory fan clutch and fan. Stainless steel blades will flatten at higher engine speeds to prevent air blockage. Note reverse fan rotation, required on late Jeep 4.2L and 4.0L engines with serpentine drive belts.*

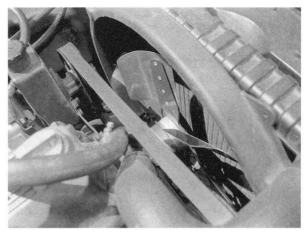

Fig. 9-4. *Location of fan and shroud are important to cooling. Fan blade lies halfway within shroud opening. Shroud captures air from the entire radiator core. '90 Wrangler engine in an '81 CJ shows reverse rotation fan.*

Anti-freeze/Coolant and the Jeep Cooling System

Late model Jeep engines operate hot. More thorough combustion, better fuel economy, and lower CO and HC emissions result from lean fuel mixtures; the side effect is more heat.

Years ago, Jeep engines came from the factory with 180° "winter" thermostats. It was common practice to install a 160° thermostat in summer months. Today, cooling system constraints and emission restrictions have engines running at 195–205° F thermostat settings. Normal operating temperature ranges to 240° F—well past the boiling point of water.

A radiator pressure cap of 15 psi can raise the boiling point of a 50/50 anti-freeze and water mixture to 265° F, while a 60/40 coolant mix is good for 270°. Each pound increase in radiator cap pressure raises the boil-over point by approximately three degrees.

Your Jeep cooling system works best when the coolant ratio is correct and the radiator cap seals properly. The slightest drop in cooling system pressure will compromise the system's resistance to boil-over. Make sure the cap's pressure rating is right for your engine.

Also, while anti-freeze/coolant seems the cure-all for raising the boiling point, there's a limit to its use. The expansion rates differ between water and anti-freeze/coolant. Excess ethylene glycol limits the solution's ability to expand within itself. Running pure anti-freeze will cause a boil-over—expansion right out of the system!

Too much anti-freeze/coolant also affects the freezing point. At -8° F, pure ethylene glycol anti-freeze will actually freeze, resulting in broken engine castings and/or a cracked radiator core.

> *WARNING—*
> *Never mix ethylene glycol solutions richer than the 68% maximum ratio recommended by Jeep. (Minimum recommended mix is 44%.) A 68% anti-freeze/32% water solution usually provides engine protection to -90° F.*

A mix of at least 40% water is practical in an ethylene glycol anti-freeze/coolant solution. This can be confirmed by either mixing the solution from scratch or testing the cooling system with an anti-freeze hydrometer. Make sure that the coolant has circulated (through the heater system, too!) before you attempt to check its specific gravity with a hydrometer.

ZEREX
Antifreeze Coolant
For Extreme Conditions

ZEREX Antifreeze Coolant has been designed to prevent freeze-ups, boil-overs and corrosion year-round even under extreme conditions. ZEREX Antifreeze Coolant has demonstrated its effectiveness under the worst conditions in torturous performance testing.

- Prevents Cold Weather Freeze-ups
- Prevents Hot Weather Boil-overs
- Prevents Over-heating In Traffic Congestion
- Prevents Corrosion And Rust Damage
- Protects All Cooling System Metals

ZEREX PROTECTION CHART

Freeze-up/Boil-over Protection	Protects against freeze-ups down to	Protects against boil-overs up to
For Extreme Conditions Install a 70/30 Mix of ZEREX and Water	-84°F	276°F*
For Year-Round Operation Install a 50/50 Mix of ZEREX and Water	-34°F	265°F*

*Using a 15 PSI radiator cap

CAUTION: COMBUSTIBLE MIXTURE

N.Y.F.D. C. of A. No. 2413. Container Approved By Bd. of Stds. and Appeals Cal. No. 58-84-A

DIRECTIONS:

1. DRAIN
Caution: Do not remove radiator cap when engine is hot. To drain radiator, open drain valve at bottom of radiator. Turn drain valve counterclockwise while exerting even pressure. Caution: Do not exert heavy or uneven force.

2. FLUSH
Flushing helps remove sediment and sludge built up under normal conditions. Flush radiator with water and start engine with heater control on high. Run engine to normal operating temperature to open thermostat. Stop engine and drain again. For a complete back-flush of the entire cooling system use a ZEREX Flush Kit.

3. INSTALL
Add required amount of ZEREX to radiator (Refer to ZEREX Protection Chart). If necessary, add water to fill radiator. Do not use more than 70/30 mix of ZEREX and water. Run engine with heater control on high to normal operating temperature to fully mix the ZEREX and water. Let engine cool and recheck level. Drain and flush cooling system recovery tank and install required amount of ZEREX. Periodically, check the antifreeze coolant level and condition. For an accurate test use a ZEREX Antifreeze Coolant Tester.

WARNING:
HARMFUL OR FATAL IF SWALLOWED.
Do not drink antifreeze coolant or solution. If swallowed, induce vomiting immediately. Call a physician. Contains Ethylene Glycol which caused birth defects in animal studies. Do not store in open or unlabeled containers.
KEEP OUT OF REACH OF CHILDREN AND ANIMALS.

GUARANTEE
SATISFACTION GUARANTEED OR YOUR MONEY BACK

ZEREX is a registered trademark of BASF Corporation, Parsippany, NJ 07054

0 26223 47035 2

shroud must capture the entire core area of the radiator. Ideal fan location will have half the depth of the blades inside the shroud, the other half just rearward. This allows the fan to draw under all circumstances and prevents turbulence or air blockage within the shroud.

A final area of concern is coolant or air blockage within the cooling system. Beware of improperly installed thermostat or engine gaskets, especially the head gasket(s)! When performing a valve grind or complete engine overhaul, follow gasket instructions carefully.

> CAUTION —
> *Always be certain a replacement water pump has vanes that rotate in the same direction as the original pump. Later Jeep engines with serpentine belts use reverse rotation water pumps. Do not interchange pump types.*

Finding Leaks

Coolant leaks can ruin a good day of four-wheeling. As a safeguard, check your cooling system regularly with a pressure tester. External leaks are easiest to find. Simply pump the tester to the cooling system's normal pressure, and watch the gauge. It should not drop. If it does, look for leaks at hoses, the intake manifold, the thermostat housing, freeze plugs or the radiator core.

If no external leaks are present, suspect an internal engine leak such as a seeping or blown head gasket, casting cracks, or an interior intake manifold/cooling passage leak. A blown head gasket or cracked casting will either leak coolant into a cylinder or create low compression in two adjacent cylinders.

When coolant can enter a cylinder, compression gases also leak into the engine's cooling ports. High pressure cylinder gases entering the cooling system will cause a rapid overflow at the radiator filler neck or the coolant recovery tank.

Intake manifold gaskets leaking at the coolant crossover passages on Jeep V-6 and V-8 engines will drain coolant into the crankcase. So will a leaking timing cover casting or gaskets. Block or cylinder head cracks cause coolant leaks into the upper cylinders and/or crankcase, depending upon the crack's location in the casting.

There are several tests for an internal coolant leak. Securely attach a pressure tester to the radiator fill neck. Have someone start the engine while you watch the gauge. If pressure rises rapidly and pegs at the high side of the gauge, shut the engine off immediately. This indicates that cylinder pressure has entered the cooling system and pressurized the radiator. A casting crack or blown head gasket is the cause.

> WARNING—
> *Be careful. Cylinder gases in the cooling system will create an abrupt and dangerously high rise in pressure. (Imagine 100-plus psi of pressure within a cooling system designed for 17 psi!) Protect your tester by shutting the engine off immediately.*

The appearance of bubbles in the radiator often indicates the presence of cylinder gases and a head gasket or casting leak. This can be deceptive, though, since other causes of such "aeration," including water

Fig. 9-6. *Strange place for an exhaust gas analyzer probe! With engine idling at normal temperature, an exhaust infrared tester can sniff cylinder gases just above the radiator filler neck. Combustion gases will enter cooling system through a blown head gasket(s), a cracked cylinder head or a crack in the block. Carbon monoxide (CO) gas is detectable here.*

Fig. 9-5. *Cooling system pressure tester is quickest check for leaks. Pump the tester to normal cooling system pressure, then watch gauge. Sealing properly, no drop should occur.*

pump malfunctions, can also introduce air bubbles into the cooling system.

An infra-red exhaust analyzer can quickly confirm whether bubbles in the radiator are from leaking combustion gases. With the engine idling, hold the probe just above the open radiator fill neck or coolant recover er tank. A reading of carbon monoxide and hydrocarbons indicates that combustion gases are present in the cooling system.

> *WARNING—*
> *Use extreme care when working around an open cooling system. Do not remove the cap if the system is pressurized or if the engine has warmed up.*

Automatic Transmission Load

A more subtle means for overtaxing your cooling system comes from the automatic transmission. Automatic transmissions operate hot, well in excess of normal engine coolant temperatures—and your Jeep's radiator is the means for cooling the transmission. As a result, a heavily worked transmission can actually cause an engine overheat.

Your Jeep's automatic transmission must run at normal temperatures, as heat is the number one cause of parts deterioration in an automatic transmission. Oddly, hot engine coolant is responsible for cooling the transmission.

Even the Borg-Warner automatics used in the first J-truck and Wagoneer models had fluid lines that ran to the radiator for cooling. On these Kaiser-era Jeep radiators, the lower tank contains a cell through which hot automatic transmission fluid (ATF) passes. Engine coolant, circulating around this cell, draws heat from the scorching ATF. On later cross-flow radiators, the cell is within a side tank of the radiator.

Fig. 9-7. *An add-on auxiliary transmission cooler takes a tremendous load off the engine's cooling system. Install an auxiliary transmission cooler if your Jeep plans include trailer pulling or rock crawling.*

One of the best solutions for better engine and transmission cooling is an auxiliary transmission cooler. Some Jeep trucks feature an optional OE transmission cooler (usually part of a heavy duty, air conditioning or trailer pulling package). Aftermarket manufacturers build cooler units that either mount near the radiator core or alone in a steady air stream.

The auxiliary transmission cooler resembles an air conditioning or refrigeration condenser. Air, either from vehicle movement or from the engine's fan draw, moves past the fins on the transmission cooler, drawing away transmission fluid heat.

Position your Jeep's aftermarket transmission cooler carefully. Since so much heat passes from its surface, placing the unit in front of the radiator core is not always wise. Pre-heated air can raise the temperature of the radiator fins and tubes. Often, a better approach places the cooler safely behind the radiator or somewhere in the vehicle's air stream, without restricting the flow of radiator air.

Electric Fans: A Controversy

It takes far less to cool a low compression in-line four or six-cylinder engine than a robust V-8. The earliest L-134 Jeep engines cranked out a modest 60 horsepower. Later F-134s boasted 72–75 horsepower, while the 225 (Buick) V-6 raised the figure to 160 hp. Later EFI 4.0L Cherokee engines produce 190 horsepower, Grand Cherokee 5.9L V-8s put out 245 horsepower, and V-8 conversion engines range from 250–500 horsepower!

There's a temptation to use an auxiliary electric fan. On many V-8 conversions, the engine's mechanical fan rides off-center of the radiator core. Even with a custom built, thick and narrow cross-flow radiator, the engine-driven fan may miss the radiator centerline. Here, many builders believe that a heavy electric fan unit will solve the problem.

> *CAUTION —*
> *For off-highway pounding, avoid the use of electric fans that rely on the radiator fins for support. 4x4s bounce hard, too hard for radiator fins to support a weighty fan. Fin mounted fans can permanently scar your costly radiator core and also damage the coolant tubes.*

A mechanical, engine driven fan, if centered reasonably well and shrouded properly, proves superior in all cases. Heavy-duty "truck" fans or an aftermarket flexible cooling fan will provide far more pitch and draw than the typical electric fan.

Fig. 9-8. *Hybrid Flex-A-Lite electric fan installation is based upon a heavier truck application. This fan assembly mounts safely outside radiator core area. High temperature crawling, however, requires greater air flow than even the best electric fan can offer. In rough and rock crawling desert terrain, Flex-A-Lite's heavy duty, stainless steel blade mechanical fan (shown earlier) offers superior protection from overheat.*

Fig. 9-9. *Even a defective spark advance mechanism or vacuum unit can cause engine overheating. The State of California once advocated a retrofit smog control that eliminated vacuum spark advance under most driving conditions. Engine overheat damage was so prevalent that California abandoned the measure.*

Where an electric fan may provide adequate cooling for highway use, the real test of Jeep cooling is a high noon rock crawling episode on an August trip through the desert. Here, a heavy duty mechanical (engine driven) fan serves better than any electric fan currently available.

Tenacious Overheat Problems

Cooling problems go beyond the radiator and fan. If the engine is suspect, consider several items. A dirty or corroded block, obstructions in the block, the wrong cylinder head(s) (or an improperly installed head gasket) and excessive internal friction can each cause overheating. Some other overheat sources include faulty ignition timing or spark advance, excess carbon in the combustion areas or on the piston crowns, valves ground too thin, a defective thermostat, the wrong intake manifold, cross-firing spark plug wires and an overly lean or rich carburetor mix.

Water pump defects are a common cause of trouble. The most obvious pump problem is a leaking seal. Worn pump bearings allow pulley and fan blade runout, usually visible when looking sideways at the idling engine. Improper gaskets, corroded impeller vanes or a missing water pump backing plate can also cause coolant circulation problems.

A plugged exhaust system or a stuck heat riser valve will quickly overheat an engine. Pinched or air-blocked cooling hoses, excessively hot spark plugs or a loose fan belt(s) can also cause grief. Too much com-

pression, common after milling cylinder heads, and low octane fuel can lead to destructive, chronic detonation and overheating.

An older radiator may need "boiling and rodding." This process involves removing the top and bottom tanks, boiling the radiator in caustic, then running rods through the scaly tubes. Re-assembly and pressure testing complete the job. Pressure testing the radiator assures a margin of safety as late model Jeep trucks operate at higher pressures. Higher pressures and adequate anti-freeze/coolant raise the coolant boiling point.

A clean, pressure tested radiator, with adequate flow rate and proper fan cooling, should keep your

Fig. 9-10. *Most radiators that test leak free at 20 psi in the shop will offer long service. A 17 psi cap raises the boiling point. When combined with a 50/50 mixture of high grade anti-freeze/coolant and water, boiling point exceeds 260° F.*

Jeep engine running at normal temperatures. An exotic engine, however, may require a special radiator. Especially challenging are small military and CJ grille openings and big V-8s. Although a cross-flow radiator may offer the only solution, down-flow radiators work fine and, depending on the chassis, often far better than a cross-flow unit.

As for specialty radiators, off-pavement crawlers sometimes suffer from overly exotic radiators. Don't rush to buy a NASCAR or SCCA aluminum road racing radiator. The unit may rely on high speed air flow for cooling, a nonexistent commodity when you're sharing crawl speed desert floors with the lizards.

Whatever your off-highway or load plans, cooling is top priority. Do your homework when installing a bigger engine. If you're planning a high performance overhaul of your Jeep's original engine, consider a heavy duty OE replacement radiator. Often, a radiator specialist can mount your original radiator tanks and brackets to a much larger core.

When constructing a radiator, the catchy term "four-row" core is sometimes as unreliable as "cross-flow." The size of each tube is actually more important than the number of rows. Many three row cores, with larger tubes, offer higher BTU dissipation ratings than a four-row core with small tubes. When in doubt, consult flow and BTU charts at a local radiator shop. Once properly installed, the correctly engineered radiator and fan assembly should work well under all driving conditions.

2. Changing Your Water Pump

Eventually, every Jeep water pump will fail. Although water pumps often last between engine overhauls, the typical load and stress placed on a Jeep 4x4 can cause earlier failure. However, if you periodically pressure check the cooling system, maintain an adequate amount of coolant/anti-freeze and keep proper tension on the belts, the water pump should not leave you stranded.

> **NOTE —**
> Old timers taught that water-soluable oil (non-petroleum, non-mineral base) could help preserve water pump bearings and rubber hoses. Modern "water pump lubricant" liquids serve a similar purpose and can help reduce risk of oxidation damage.

Pressure check your cooling system regularly. Sometimes, the water pump will only leak when hot and under pressure. Also, with the engine shut off, rock the fan blade to test the water pump shaft bearings. (Caution: Be extremely careful when handling an aftermarket stainless steel fan, as the edges are often sharp as a knife. Wear a leather glove.)

Fig. 9-12. *A four row core is not always "bigger" than a three row. Tube size also contributes to flow rate and surface area. Pay close attention to gpm flow ratings and engine application when selecting a radiator. Recyclers are a source for ideas.*

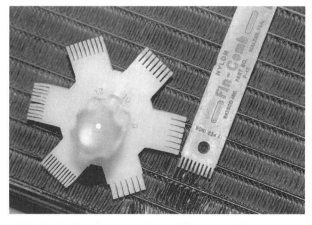

Fig. 9-11. *Fin design makes a difference, with serpentine-type fins generally better for the off-pavement environment. Overall, whether your oversize radiator is a down-flow or cross-flow design, quality construction and adequate air flow are more important than whether coolant moves horizontally or vertically.*

Fig. 9-13. *Water pump failure seldom occurs instantly. Signs of weakness, like coolant seepage or a wobble to the shaft bearing, give some forewarning. Watch the bleed hole at the base of the pump. When the seal fails, coolant will leak from here.*

At the first sign of water pump seepage, replace the pump. Don't take chances or attempt a permanent fix with a liquid or powder stop leak. A weak pump will surely fail when you need it most.

WARNING—
• Never remove the radiator cap when your Jeep's engine is hot. Hot coolant under pressure leaves the radiator with force and could scald you severely.

• Coolant is poisonous to pets. Use extreme care when draining and disposing of engine coolant.

CAUTION —
• Coolant can damage painted surfaces. Rinse spills with water immediately.

• Avoid adding coolant to the engine when it is hot or overheated. If you must add coolant, do so only with the engine running and the coolant/water pump turning.

2.1 To Replace Water Pump

The early Jeep engines are easy to service. For later models, depending upon equipment and how many engine accessories stand in the way, water pump replacement can be complicated. Power steering and other engine driven accessories make later engines much busier than the early Willys fours and in-line sixes.

Jeep CJs with a 151 Pontiac engine or 2.5L AMC four have wide open engine bays and easy access to the radiator. Water pump access is relatively straightforward. By contrast, a Jeep V-8 engine with an alternator, power steering, air conditioning and an air

injection pump requires considerable time to replace the water pump.

Begin by placing a large pan beneath the radiator drain cock. With the engine cool, loosen the petcock and allow coolant to drain into the pan. (You may find that removing the radiator cap allows faster draining.) Unless this coolant is relatively new and very clean, discard it at your local recycling outlet.

Disconnect the negative battery cable if your engine requires removal of the alternator and its mounting bracket. With the negative battery cable disconnected, loosen the alternator belt, whether serpentine or V-groove type. Unbolt and carefully lay the alternator aside with its wires still attached.

CAUTION —
On serpentine belts, make careful note of belt routing.

Loosen the upper and lower radiator hoses at the radiator inlet and outlet. Remove the radiator fan shroud, then loosen the fan belt or serpentine belt. On serpentine belts, make careful note of belt routing. Remove the fan and fan clutch (where applicable).

NOTE —
If you are not removing the radiator on later models, re-install one radiator support screw at each side to support the radiator as you detach the fan shroud. On the CJ Iron Duke or 2.5L AMC four, the space between the radiator and the engine is enormous, so you can replace the water pump easily, with just the removal of the shroud.

Remove the lower hose from the water pump. You may need to remove the upper hose to allow more work room. Now loosen all other hoses attached to the water pump.

On AMC in-line fours and sixes with air conditioning, it may be necessary to loosen the air conditioning pedestal slightly and unbolt it from the water pump. (Don't remove the mount completely, as installation is awkward.)

On AMC V-8 engines with air conditioning, you must remove the compressor bracket stud that attaches to the water pump. (Jam a pair of nuts on the stud and turn the inner nut counter-clockwise to remove the stud.) You will also need to carefully disassemble those portions of the power steering pump bracket that prevent removal of the water pump.

If you need to remove the radiator, do so now. Simply unbolt the unit from the core support and lift it out carefully to avoid damaging the core fins.

Fig. 9-14. *Serpentine belts have many routing configurations. Note your engine equipment and compare with Jeep workshop manual charts. Many later fans are reverse rotation design.*

Fig. 9-15. *This pedestal supports the air conditioning compressor or an idler pulley on in-line AMC/Jeep engines. If the air conditioner interferes with pump removal, loosen the bolts holding the pedestal to the engine. Don't remove these bolts completely, as they are difficult to install.*

CAUTION —
If the radiator is left in position, be very careful not to damage the radiator core with fan blades, hardware or your tools.

NOTE —
On many 4.0L Cherokees with heavy accessory options, you must remove the auxiliary electric fan before unbolting the radiator. Loosen the auxiliary fan and its electrical connection, and lift the unit from the radiator support.

Now unbolt the water pump. The number of mounting bolts or nuts vary. Once you have removed all of the bolts, the water pump will come loose with very gentle prying. (The gasket is all that holds it in place at this point. Some newer models use an anaerobic sealer, so pay close attention.) Never force parts, and pry gently against the iron castings. Avoid prying or damaging softer metals like aluminum.

If the hoses show any wear at all, replace them and install new clamps as well. This is also time to replace the thermostat.

Once the water pump is out of the way, carefully scrape old gasket material from the engine block or timing cover mounting surface. Take care not to scrape gasket material into the cooling ports, as this material may find its way to the radiator tubes and restrict coolant circulation.

Examine the radiator for rust and scale, seepage at solder seams and signs of corrosion. Consider sending the unit for boil out cleaning and pressure testing, even if no leaks are apparent. You only want to do this job once, so consider any parts that might fail soon in service.

Years ago, water pump rebuilding kits were available. Today, the local parts outlet supplies complete new or rebuilt replacement pumps. Make certain that the new or rebuilt pump is identical to the pump you have removed, and inspect the new gasket. Jeep engines have either forward or reverse (serpentine belt) rotation water pumps. Be certain that the new pump's impeller vanes match the original pump.

Use an appropriate sealant on each side of the gasket. Take care not to apply more than a thin, even coat. Excess sealant finds its way into the radiator tubes. On the 2.8L Chevrolet V-6 and other late engines, a 3/32" bead of anaerobic sealer takes the place of a conventional gasket.

Fig. 9-16. *Check radiator solder seams and joints for coolant seepage and repair weak or loose brackets.*

Fig. 9-17. *Use correct gasket sealant when installing a water pump. Place a thin coat on each side of a cut (paper) gasket. (Permatex's traditional Form-A-Gasket and High Tack products serve well on cut gaskets.) Clean threads of bolts and pipe fittings and apply thread sealant. Some later water pumps do not use a gasket and require anaerobic type sealants. Jeep shop manual for your model or a Permatex-Loctite catalog describes which sealant to use at certain locations.*

Fig. 9-18. *These bolt markings represent different grades of USS and SAE hardware. Three marks is Grade 5. Six marks is a Grade 8 bolt, a much higher tensile strength than the general purpose Grade 5.*

Carefully wire brush bolt threads to remove rust, old sealant and surface scale. If electrolysis or oxidation has weakened these water pump bolts, discard them and replace with new, properly graded hardware.

Torque bolts according to their thread size and grade standards. Many service manuals neglect the torque settings for water pump hardware. See the appendix of this book for a general purpose torque/tightening chart and an explanation of grade markings.

CAUTION —
• *Use hardware grading equal to or better than that indicated on the heads of OEM bolts. Install new lock washers, and apply sealant to the bolt threads. The fan and water pump impeller contain a lot of energy. One of the worst possible accidents is a fan coming loose and either driving through the radiator core or flying in lethal fashion from the engine bay.*

• *Aluminum and other soft alloys tolerate far less tightening torque than cast iron. (Example: On 230 Tornado sixes, the seven nuts that secure the water pump to the alloy timing chain cover call for 20 ft/lbs torque. Secure the Tornado fan and pulley capscrews to 15 ft/lbs. Tighten all bolts gradually and in cross sequence.) Always check torque settings described in your Jeep shop manual.*

On AMC in-line fours and sixes, torque water pump to block mounting bolts to a maximum 15 ft/lbs. Tighten fan blade to hub screws to a maximum of 20 ft/lbs and fan clutch to water pump hardware at maximum 20 ft/lbs. Tighten bolts gradually and in cross sequence.

On 304, 360 and 401 V-8s, torque water pump-to-engine block mounting bolts to a maximum of 25 ft/lbs. Tighten the water pump-to-timing cover screws to 48 in./lbs. Secure fan blade to hub screws to a maximum of 20 ft/lbs. (Also torque fan clutch unit to water pump bolts to 20 ft/lbs.) Tighten bolts gradually and in cross sequence.

NOTE —
For tightening specifications on the mid-'60s 327 engine, consult a factory or professional guide for the Jeep or AMC/Rambler 327 V-8.

For some trucks, it's easier to remove the power steering pump pulley during disassembly. Re-install and torque the pulley retaining nut to specifications in your factory or professional level shop manual.

On Buick 225 V-6 engines, tighten the water pump cover to timing chain cover bolts to only 7 ft-lbs. The larger bolts that reach through the timing cover to the block require 29 ft-lbs of tightening torque. Secure the Buick fan blade to water pump hub screws at 20 ft-lbs. Tighten all bolts gradually and in cross sequence.

Torque 2.8L V-6 water pump mounting bolts gradually and in cross sequence as follows: 6mm stud size bolts to a maximum of 9 ft-lbs; 8mm stud size bolts to a maximum of 18 ft-lbs; and 10mm stud size bolts to a maximum of 30 ft-lbs.

On the GM Iron Duke 151 four, tighten all bolts gradually and in cross sequence. Final torque for the Iron Duke's water pump to block mounting bolts is 25 ft-lbs. Secure the fan assembly to water pump hub screws at 20 ft-lbs.

Once you've safely secured the water pump, pulley and fan, install a new fan or serpentine belt and tighten securely. Avoid damaging your new water pump or the alternator/generator by following the factory belt tightening procedure. In some cases, a special belt tensioner or a torque wrench is necessary to meet OE requirements.

If no data or special tools are available, a V-groove belt should deflect about 1/2" when you apply heavy thumb force midway between the pulleys. (The alternator or generator pulley should rotate very slightly as you press firmly on the belt.) Serpentine belts require a large amount of tightening force. Adjust by factory guidelines.

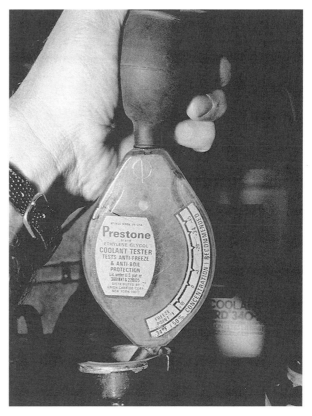

Fig. 9-20. *Cool the engine, remove the cap carefully, then check coolant mix with a hydrometer. Strive for at least a 50/50 ratio, which translates as -34° F protection when using popular ethylene glycol solutions.*

Install the radiator, making certain the draincock is shut snugly. Put a light coat of sealant on the hose connections and install with new clamps centered carefully. (Where applicable, make sure the coil of wire is in place within the lower radiator hose if so equipped. This prevents the hose from collapsing.) Making sure screws remain accessible, tighten the clamps securely.

Pour anti-freeze/coolant and correct water mix into the radiator. Allow coolant to seek its own level, then top off as necessary. On closed systems, fill to the top of the filler neck, then seal with the radiator cap. Add coolant to the overflow bottle's COLD line.

Install the radiator cap, turn the heater controls to HOT and start the engine. Let it reach operating temperature. Turn the engine off and allow it to cool completely, then slowly open the radiator cap.

Assuming that the coolant has circulated thoroughly with the heater on, you may want to check the mixture with a hydrometer. This will help you decide whether to top off with straight coolant, water or a mixture of both. Unless your climate has arctic tem-

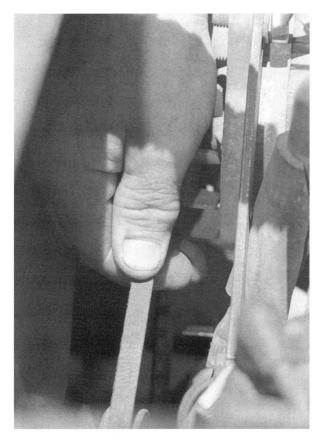

Fig. 9-19. *Follow factory belt tightening procedure whenever possible. If data is unavailable, adjust a V-type belt to 1/2" deflection midway between the generator/alternator pulley and fan pulley. Measure this deflection while applying firm thumb pressure to the belt. Correct tension will rotate alternator pulley very slightly as you apply pressure.*

peratures, strive for a 50/50 ratio, which will read as minus 34° F protection with an ethylene glycol anti-freeze solution.

You will also want to re-check torque on all hardware. At this time, re-torque the hose clamps and look closely for leaks. If you suspect a leak, pressure check the system.

Chapter 10

Clutch and Transmission Service

Clutch and transmission problems are sometimes difficult to separate. The high cost of a clutch replacement or transmission overhaul makes diagnosis very important. Transmission wear is often mistaken for a bad clutch and vice versa. As troubleshooting skill is the best mechanical resource you can muster, I'd like to help you understand various clutch and transmission problems.

First signs of trouble usually appear while driving your Jeep. As an accurate troubleshooter, you must isolate each symptom and determine its cause.

1. Clutch and Transmission Troubleshooting

> *WARNING—*
> *The clutch disc may contain asbestos fibers. Asbestos materials can cause asbestosis. Always wear an approved respirator and protective clothing when handling components containing asbestos. Do not use compressed air, do not grind, heat, weld or sand on or near any asbestos materials. Only approved cleaning methods should be used to service the clutch disc or areas containing asbestos dust or asbestos fibers.*

Clutch "Chatter"

You release the clutch pedal, and the powertrain shudders, sometimes violently, as clutch engagement begins. If the problem has developed suddenly, especially after an unusually hard day of pounding a rocky trail, examine the engine mounts and transmission/transfer case mount. On many models, a torque arm, complete with cushion mounts, helps limit engine torque twist. Check this mount along with the others. Examine the clutch linkage as well.

Some Jeep models have a brace rod that helps minimize powertrain torque flexing. Examine any braces for damage or loose hardware, as this is another source of chatter. If none of these problems exist, look

Fig. 10-1. *Defective motor and transmission mounts can create clutch chatter symptoms, especially on suspended pedal models with mechanical clutch linkage. This brace on a Dana 300 transfer case limits torque twist. Inspect all mounts before condemning your clutch.*

to the clutch unit. Disc wear, clutch damage or oil on the disc arc common causes of chatter. Especially in a Jeep 4x4, operated at odd and steep angles, an engine oil leak from the rear main seal or pan gasket can find its way into the clutch assembly and saturate the disc.

An attempt to burn off the oil by "riding the clutch" to generate friction is generally a waste of time and could prove dangerous. Clutches can explode under extreme stress or from over revving. There's no sure way to clean the disc in the truck, either. Oil entering the clutch housing in any quantity will ruin the disc.

Another source of oil on the clutch is from the transmission. The front bearing retainer seal is responsible for keeping oil within the gearcase. These seals wear, and on rare occasions, the retainer may crack or leak around its sealing gasket(s). Gear oil, acidic and tenacious, has a devastating effect on a clutch disc.

A common cause of clutch chatter is a distorted clutch cover or broken springs. Excess heat and overworking the clutch can warp a clutch cover. Springs break from fatigue or abuse. Heat also weakens springs, making them exert uneven force. Simply put, clutch chatter results from uneven application of pressure. Loose clutch cover bolts, broken torsional springs in the disk hub or a warped disc will cause chatter.

Clutch slippage symptoms are obvious. In gear, the engine revs up, yet the truck does not accelerate. Slippage and chatter often have common causes. In either case, clutch cover apply pressure cannot hold the disc firmly. Slippage results from oil saturation of the

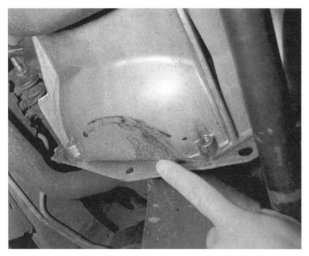

Fig. 10-2. *An engine oil leak at the rear main seal or pan gaskets can cause clutch damage. Oil saturates the clutch disc and causes chatter, slippage and failure. The only cure is a new main seal and clutch replacement.*

Fig. 10-3. *As the clutch disc wears thin, clamping force decreases. (The clutch cover springs compress less, which reduces their apply pressure.) This is why a high mileage OEM-type clutch, even in good condition, cannot deliver the same performance as a new assembly.*

disc or extreme wear of either the friction disc or clutch cover springs. The faintest sound of rivets grating on the flywheel face or pressure plate is a sure sign of major wear. Replace the clutch before irreparable damage to the flywheel results.

Unwanted Clutch Noises

Jeep owners become accustomed to particular powertrain noises, those rhythms and pitches of whirring machinery that accompany us along the trail. An abnormal sound from the clutch area immediately draws attention.

A defective clutch sends a clear message. A warped or severely worn disc will grate or transmit a metallic sound as the disc engages. Broken torsional springs around the disc hub also transmit noise. The more common "clutch noises," however, are often bearing defects.

The pilot bearing supports the forward end of the transmission input shaft. Pressed into the center bore of the crankshaft flange or flywheel, the pilot bearing allows the clutch or input gear to rotate independently of the crankshaft during clutch disengagement. The typical Jeep pilot bearing is a needle caged bearing, ball-type bearing or a bronze bushing. While some bearings have permanently sealed cases, others require lubrication at time of installation. (See your Jeep shop manual for lube details.)

A pilot bearing or bushing should only need service during clutch replacement. A dry pilot bearing, however, is common with a Jeep that performs submarine duty. Running in surf, deep stream crossings and other water traps can wash grease from the pilot bear-

Fig. 10-4. *There are three types of pilot bearings and bushings used in various Jeep applications: the solid bronze bushing, a needle bearing assembly and a caged, permanently lubricated ball bearing. In some Jeep applications, you will have a choice of types. Needle and ball bearings offer less friction. Bronze bushings have a reputation for long, trouble-free service.*

ing. Dry, the bearing wears quickly and sets up a howling noise distinct from any other. With the clutch disengaged and the transmission in a gear, pilot noise is obvious.

> CAUTION —
> *A needle or ball bearing should never be used with an input gear designed for a bronze bushing. Heat treatment of gears differ. Hard needle bearings will damage an input end designed for use with a bronze bushing.*

> NOTE —
> In the worst cases, the pilot bearing seizes on the clutch/input gear nose end and mimics symptoms of a clutch disc and pressure plate that won't disengage properly.

Another oddity that occurs with back woods four-wheeling is debris from the trail entering the clutch housing. (Protective plates, tinware and rubber boots help prevent this from happening. The phenomenon usually occurs with a modified Jeep or at an exposed opening, such as a missing clutch fork boot.) In rare cases, gravel becomes embedded or trapped in the clutch disc and mimics the symptoms of chatter, slippage and metallic grating. More common are the twigs or rocks that rake or rattle against the spinning clutch assembly.

A time-honored clutch noise is the release (or throwout) bearing. These bearings often fail before the disc and clutch cover, and the noise is easy to distinguish. First, make certain that the clutch is adjusted properly, as described later in this chapter, and that free-play exists between the clutch release fingers and the throwout bearing. At this point, with the engine

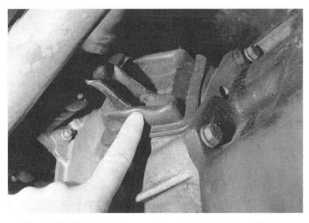

Fig. 10-5. *The dust boot at the clutch fork is a vital part. Water and debris entering your Jeep clutch housing can damage parts. Keep seals, plates and tinware in good condition.*

running and the pedal fully released, the throwout bearing cannot make noise.

Now apply very light pedal pressure, just enough to bring the bearing against the fingers. The bearing will begin spinning, and here noise may develop. (It may require firmer pressure before the bearing transmits sound.) To avoid confusing throwout bearing noise with pilot bearing noise, leave the transmission in neutral with the clutch engaged. This way, the clutch/input gear can turn at the same speed as the pilot bearing.

With the transmission in neutral, the clutch fully engaged and the throwout bearing clear of the release fingers, you will not hear a clutch pilot or throwout bearing noise. If you hear bearing sounds now, look to the transmission for trouble.

Difficult-to-shift Gears

The simpler causes of hard shifting are a mis-adjusted clutch or insufficient clutch linkage travel. Begin troubleshooting by adjusting the clutch properly and examining linkage from the release fork all the way to the pedal. You need full pedal travel and proper fitup at the various links.

If your Jeep clutch linkage has a pivoting bellcrank, replace worn bushings and eliminate any excess play. Each link must provide full, steady movement when you depress the clutch pedal.

Any obstacle to complete clutch disengagement will cause hard shifting. Aside from mechanical or hydraulic clutch linkage problems, this includes a warped disc or pressure plate, a clutch disc bound on the input gear splines, a seizing pilot bearing or debris wedged between the clutch disc and pressure plate or flywheel.

> NOTE —
> For smooth shifts and complete clutch disengagement, the clutch pressure plate must move away from the disc and allow the disc to rotate freely and independently of the flywheel.

On Jeep trucks with hydraulic clutch linkage, look first to hydraulic system troubles. Aside from proper pushrod and pedal height adjustments, the hydraulic system requires a full stroke of fluid to release the clutch completely. This means that the master cylinder piston must retract completely, and the clutch slave cylinder piston must have ample travel in its bore.

The clutch master cylinder piston must return to its stop when you release the pedal. Adjust the pushrod and/or pedal height to achieve correct piston-to-pushrod clearance and travel. Assuming that the master cylinder has a full fluid reservoir (check fluid first!), check pushrod and pedal height adjustments. (See adjustment section of this chapter.) If the fluid has run low, the system may require bleeding. Like a hydraulic brake system, the hydraulic lines can trap air, causing a loss of piston movement at the slave cylinder.

Flush and bleed the system periodically with clean brake fluid to purge sludge, accumulated moisture and any air. If the system draws air regularly or looses fluid, overhaul the master cylinder and slave cylinder units. (See brake section for tips on hydraulic cylinder overhaul, or refer to a factory level service manual.)

In good operating condition, bled properly and full of fresh brake fluid, the hydraulic system will move the clutch release arm enough distance to disengage the clutch. If your clutch still drags, consider other causes.

Manual Transmission Troubleshooting

Jeep models have used a variety of manual transmissions. Rather than elaborate on each design, let's focus on universal transmission troubles. If you have the skill and tools necessary to overhaul your transmission, a factory level service manual provides an excellent, in-depth guide for rebuilding the unit.

> NOTE —
> With a proper instructional guide, manual transmission work is gratifying and straightforward. Jeep and other professional service manuals provide excellent step-by-step procedures for repair and overhaul.

Never work on your Jeep transmission without first reviewing a professional level service manual. Subtle differences between synchronizer assemblies and other parts make each Jeep transmission unique. Follow a professional guide to assure correct procedures, clearances and use of tools. Done by the book, the job can prove rewarding and a great confidence builder.

As hard shifting is a symptom shared with clutch troubles, take the time to distinguish causes. Begin by adjusting the clutch and transmission linkage. Check torque on transmission and transfer case mounting hardware. Although most Jeep transmission shifters are within the control housing and inaccessible to adjustment, some three-speed transmission trucks have column shift linkage. On these models, the neutral gate and shift linkage alignment are crucial to shifting ease. (Refer to the shift linkage adjustment section of this chapter.) Periodically clean away all debris and lubricate the shift linkage.

Hard Shifts, Jumping Out of Gear and Other Woes

Binding shift linkage is always a concern. Your Jeep truck is subject to twisting and off-highway stress, and the effects are often felt at linkages and pivotal supports. Eliminate any binding conditions in the shifter or clutch linkage. Also, before disassembling the transmission to pursue a shift problem, take gear lubricant into account. In many late model trucks, lighter oils, including ATF, have replaced traditional 80- or 90-weight gear lube.

If your manual transmission has the wrong gear lubricant and the weather gets cold, expect trouble. The braking action and movement of synchronizers becomes difficult, and in some cases, the effect is so severe that gear clash makes cold shifting impossible.

> CAUTION —
> *Perfectly good clutches come under suspicion because a transmission won't shift into the lower gears when cold. The cause is often an improper viscosity lubricant which prevents normal synchronizer action.*

Refer to your Jeep's lubrication specifications when selecting correct lube—summer and winter. In extreme climates, it may be necessary to change oil in the fall and spring. If the linkage, lubricant and clutch check okay, look to possible transmission problems.

Hard shifting is rarely a transmission shift fork problem, although you cannot rule out this defect. Broken shift rail detents and other shift mechanism troubles are possibilities, although that likelihood is again slim. The most common hard shift problem is a defective synchronizer assembly.

Synchronizers wear over time. The balky second-gear shift common to high mileage Jeep T-90 transmissions is usually a synchronizer problem. The tendency of a transmission to slide out of second, third or any other synchronized gear is often a synchronizer assembly problem, although there are other causes as well.

Loose transmission bearings, worn synchronizer parts and excessive clearances can cause a transmission to slip out of gear. (Before condemning the transmission on column shift models, check shift linkage adjustment for full travel and smooth operation.) Worn or chipped gear teeth, excessive shaft end play, and drive gear pilot bearing wear are causes of hard shifting and jumping out of gear. Other causes include a loose or mis-aligned clutch housing, worn motor or transmission mounts, a broken torque brace, or a severely worn crankshaft pilot bearing.

Fig. 10-6. *Oil viscosity affects shifting. Mobil's synthetic 75W-90 weight gear lubricant replaces traditional 90-weight. Mobil claims easier shifts. This multi-viscosity lube will work at -50 degrees Fahrenheit, allowing one oil to serve year round in extreme climates.*

Synchronizer interlock springs, detent keys and shift rail poppet springs each help keep the transmission in gear. Wear or defects here require a transmission teardown. If you have isolated trouble to the transmission, prepare for considerable expense. An overhaul must be thorough, replacing all worn pieces. If severe growling or gear whine noises have developed, you may wish to compare the cost of a major overhaul to that of a recycled or new transmission. (See geartrain performance chapter for upgrade transmissions that could provide better service than the OEM Jeep unit.)

Burnt gear oil is a sign of major trouble. If fried oil and various metals come from the drain hole, expect to find costly heat-discolored shafts, damaged gears and failed bearings.

Transmissions contain hard steel gear and shaft parts, bronze thrust washers and in some later units, nylon shift fork slippers. When you service your transmission, examine the drain lubricant carefully for the presence of these materials. Bronze thrust washer material in small quantities is normal. These washers wear very slowly over time. A high degree of bronze or the presence of harder metal pieces, however, means trouble.

2. Clutch Service

Each Jeep clutch eventually fails. Fortunately, a clutch rarely breaks without warning. The key to getting the most from your clutch is to exercise reasonable driving habits, avoiding severe powertrain shock loads or ongoing clutch slippage and overheating.

Although several modifications speed up clutch wear, oversize tires have the heaviest impact. Jeep trucks are popular candidates for large tires, as greater ground clearance and improved traction improve the vehicle's off-pavement capability. On the downside, big wheels and tires have the same effect as installing taller (numerically lower) axle gearing. Unless you change axle gearing to offset the new tire diameter, bigger diameter tires will cause the clutch to work much harder.

Clutch Wear

A variety of problems lead to clutch slippage. Mis-adjusted clearance between the throwout bearing and pressure plate, overloading, slipping the clutch and other bad driving techniques each speed up the pro-

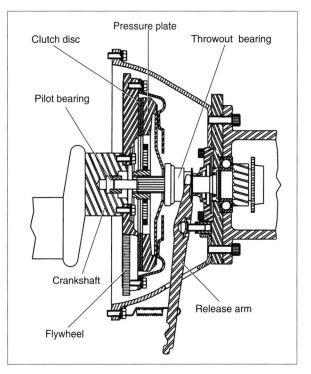

Fig. 10-7. *The spring loaded clutch pressure plate sandwiches clutch disc face against flywheel. As disc's friction material wears, spring apply pressure weakens. This accounts for slippage common with higher mileage clutch units. Shown is cross-section of diaphragm type clutch.*

cess. Even under optimal circumstances, the clutch disc wears, becoming progressively thinner and weakening the clutch cover apply pressure. In each case, slippage results.

> NOTE—
> The best safeguard against premature clutch wear is to reduce the time interval that the clutch plate slips during engagement. Beyond this, proper use of the gears can help. (See chapter on operating techniques.)

Jeep clutch wear is obvious. Slippage will occur as you release the pedal, when the truck climbs steep inclines and during low speed lugging of the engine. If your clutch isn't noticeably weak, you can push the test further: Place the shifter in high gear at 10–15 mph. Disengage the clutch, and, as you hold the clutch pedal to the floor, bring the engine speed to about 2000 rpm and quickly release the clutch pedal.

Assuming that clutch freeplay has been adjusted correctly, one of two things will happen. When the clutch is in good condition, releasing the pedal will cause an immediate and noticeable drop in engine rpm, sometimes enough to nearly stall the engine. If the clutch has excessive wear, such as glazed friction lining or weak pressure plate springs, the engine speed will either remain high for several seconds or drop slowly.

Sooner or later your Jeep clutch will fail this test. When it does, a variety of rebuilt and new clutch assembly options exist to restore or improve your truck. Improved aftermarket clutch designs work with no

modifications to your truck's existing flywheel, clutch linkage or other clutch-related parts. (See the performance chapters for details on aftermarket clutch parts.) Jeep clutch replacement presents an excellent opportunity to improve your truck.

Identifying Your Clutch

There are several clutch types used by Jeep trucks: Rockford, Auburn, Borg & Beck, Long-type (rarely), and several diaphragm designs. All clutch discs have torsional springs and composition friction materials.

The earliest Jeep models used Auburn and Rockford clutch assemblies. Auburn clutches have a three-spring clutch cover design, while the Rockford type offers a more conventional six-spring layout. Each of these oddly configured clutch types served adequately on postwar models, but by the early 1950s, as more horsepower and the need for higher clamping force developed, Willys added the more popular Borg & Beck design for heavier duty applications. The Borg & Beck clutch offers nine springs for broader clamping force.

Willys and Kaiser four-cylinder trucks use the Auburn or Rockford type clutch. 8.5" and 9.25" diameters are interchangeable. For clutch replacement, always consider the optional larger or heavier duty clutch.

Kaiser/Jeep J-trucks have Auburn or Borg & Beck direct-pressure type clutches, except for later Buick V-8 models. V-6 CJs and Jeepster V-6s came with various clutch types.

Fig. 10-8. *Replacement clutch assemblies range from OE types to aftermarket high performance designs. Midway's Centerforce II and Dual Friction designs provide an option. In my varied tests, Centerforce clutches have delivered exceptional clamping ability, quality and service.*

Fig. 10-9. *Earliest Jeep models use the Auburn clutch with three springs. CJ-3A and later Willys and Kaiser CJs have an improved Rockford style clutch with six springs (shown). You can upgrade an early Jeep 8-1/2" diameter clutch to a 9-1/4" diameter 'heavy duty' replacement.*

Fig. 10-10. *Borg & Beck clutches are common to Jeep trucks. This original '81 AMC/Jeep CJ-7 clutch on a 258 six is a Borg & Beck unit.*

Fig. 10-11. *In addition to clutch diameter, the spline configuration must match the transmission input gear. It's good practice to take your complete clutch unit to the parts house. Warning: Keep parts safely contained to avoid inhalation of asbestos fibers from the disc.*

Clutch diameter increases with larger displacement engines. Late Kaiser and AMC/Jeep trucks use 10-1/2" and 11" diameter clutches. Generally, torque and horsepower demands determine the size of your clutch. When you increase the engine performance level, a heavier duty clutch is often necessary.

NOTE—
One exception to the clutch diameter rule is Midway's Centerforce II or Dual-Friction aftermarket clutches. These exceptional designs offer superior clamping force without the need for a larger-than-OEM diameter clutch unit. (See performance chapters for details.)

AMC engines use direct pressure, semi-centrifugal and diaphragm type clutches. When buying a new clutch assembly, you will need to match your clutch disc diameter, the hub splines configuration and the clutch cover design. Jeep trucks use a variety of manual transmissions, and clutch splines can vary between designs. Identify your transmission before ordering parts.

2.1 Clutch Adjustment

Periodically, an older manual transmission Jeep truck will require clutch adjustment. On later Chrysler and AMC models, clutch adjustment is automatic, as hydraulic clutch linkage compensates for wear. Other models use mechanical linkage and/or cable controls to actuate the clutch.

NOTE—
Jeep hydraulic clutch linkage dates to early Kaiser J-truck/Wagoneer models. These applications, however, do require periodic clutch adjustment.

Of all Jeep OEM linkage designs, hydraulic linkage has worked best. Early light duty Jeep trucks suffer from clutch cable failures. Later AMC-era CJ cable type (brief use) and mechanical linkage can be troublesome: Engine torque twist has been known to pull mechanical linkage loose from the engine! Aftermarket retrofit parts address these problems. (See the performance chapters.) Overall, especially for off-pavement use CJs and Wranglers, hydraulic clutch linkage gives less trouble.

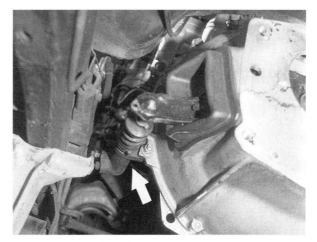

Fig. 10-12. *AMC equipped this '81 model CJ with hydraulic clutch linkage (arrow). Slave cylinder mounts firmly to the clutch housing, providing steady, accurate clutch action under all operating conditions. Mechanical linkage models cannot make such a claim.*

Fig. 10-13. *Always check clutch free-play at the release arm (arrow). Note relationship of throwout bearing and clutch release fingers. Linkage wear can make free-play measurement at the pedal inaccurate.*

Whenever service needs take you beneath your Jeep, inspect clutch linkage and its adjustment. Always begin clutch adjustment by checking freeplay at the release arm. Although proper clutch operation also demands sufficient pedal travel and play, the release arm provides the only true measurement of the throwout bearing to clutch finger clearance. Maintaining the required gap between the clutch cover's release fingers and the throwout bearing's face will assure full engagement of the clutch and a long life for the throwout bearing.

On all models with adjustable clutch linkage, normal clutch wear will decrease the clearance between the clutch release fingers and the throwout bearing. When clutch wear grows to excess, the throwout bearing will actually ride on the fingers. This will cause premature failure of the clutch release bearing or damage to the clutch release fingers.

If such wear goes beyond the point of contact, the throwout bearing will not allow the clutch to engage completely. Slippage occurs, resulting in heat buildup and possible glazing or damage to friction material. Adjusted too tightly, the clutch will wear rapidly and ruin a perfectly good clutch assembly and release bearing.

> CAUTION —
> *Your Jeep clutch is costly, difficult to access and involves many hours of labor to replace. Avoid trouble. Inspect linkage and check the clutch adjustment regularly.*

Minor Adjustment: Early Models

Early Jeep 4x4s have through-the-floorboard pedals. CJ-2A and CJ-3A models call for 1-1/2" free-play at the clutch pedal. This assumes the linkage is in good condition and return springs pull the pedal to the top of its travel. All L-head six and CJ-3B and newer Willys or Kaiser models with through the floor pedals call for 1" free-play.

These pedal free-play figures strive for 1/16" of clearance between the pressure plate fingers and throwout bearing face. Despite these pedal travel specifications, make sure that 1/16" of free-play exists between the release bearing and clutch release fingers.

Check release arm movement within the bellhousing, specifically at the throwout bearing. Many Jeep designs attach a return spring to the throwout bearing collar. Correct adjustment eliminates risk of the release bearing dragging on the clutch fingers with the clutch pedal released.

On cable linkages, make the adjustment at the cable and clevis. The 4WD Station Wagon and Pickups (L-head six and F-134 powered models) feature a mechanical linkage that adjusts at the release rod nearest the clutch fork. In either case, you will need to crawl under the truck with appropriate wrenches. Loosen locknuts before attempting the adjustment. Secure locknuts after the adjustment, and always re-check the release bearing to clutch finger clearance.

> WARNING—
> *Be sure to set the parking brake and block the wheels/tires before attempting a clutch adjustment. If you happen to disengage the clutch during clutch adjustment, this would be the same as placing the transmission in neutral—On an incline, the truck could roll.*

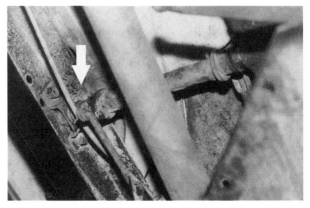

Fig. 10-14. *Clutch linkage on this early CJ-5 has a through-the-floor pedal and pivot (arrow). A mechanical bellcrank link and cable make up the linkage. Watch for wear at pivots and look closely for cable fatigue.*

Minor Adjustment: Early Kaiser J-trucks

Early J-trucks with hydraulic clutch linkage also require clearance between the throwout bearing and clutch fingers. Disconnect the clutch arm return spring and push the release rod into the clutch cylinder until the piston bottoms in the bore. Check the free-play between the clutch release arm and the pushrod end. This play must establish a 0.050" to 0.060" clearance between the clutch fingers and throwout bearing.

The correct throwout bearing adjustment is equal to approximately two turns of the pushrod shorter than zero clearance. Simply, if you're not sure whether the 0.050" minimum clearance has been established, loosen the pushrod's lock nut and turn the pushrod until obvious play exists. Now, lengthen the pushrod with your fingers until you eliminate free-play at the release fork. (The pushrod piston must remain bottomed in the slave cylinder bore during the adjustment.) Back the rod off two full turns, and tighten the lock nut.

> NOTE—
> Properly adjusted, the release fork outer end will move freely for more than 0.050" to 0.060". The arm is a lever, which multiplies the distance traveled by the throwout bearing.

Only rarely does the pedal height of a hydraulic clutch J-truck need adjustment. When you have adjusted the clutch properly, the clutch master cylinder piston retracts completely in its bore, and there should be zero clearance between the pedal pushrod and the master cylinder piston. Normal height for the clutch pedal, with the release rod fully retracted, is approximately 1/2" above the brake pedal. Install all return springs and make certain spring tension is ample enough to hold the retracted clutch release (throwout) bearing away from the clutch fingers.

Minor Adjustment: AMC/Jeep Models

All 1972 AMC models have cable-actuated clutches. Unlike earlier models that use sections of cable plus mechanical linkage, the '72 models feature fully housed cables from the pedal to a cable stop near the clutch release arm. The design eliminates the mechanical linkage troubles that result from off-pavement twisting and engine torque movement.

Adjustment is simple: Begin by lifting the pedal to the top of its travel, then disconnect the clutch release fork return spring. Loosen the cable ball adjuster to make sure play exists. Tighten the adjuster slowly until you just remove play. Now loosen the adjuster nut 3/4 turn and secure the lock nut. At the release fork, check for play between the release bearing and clutch fingers. This should approach 1/16" at the bearing end of the lever. Re-install or replace the return spring.

Pedal height is adjustable. If you need to adjust the pedal height, dimensions are available in your Jeep factory service manual or a professional service guide. Rarely is this service necessary. However, if you need to make this adjustment, check and re-set clutch free-play as required.

Fig. 10-15. *Kaiser's J-truck introduced hydraulic clutch linkage to Jeep trucks in 1962. These 230 Tornado six powered models require periodic clutch adjustment.*

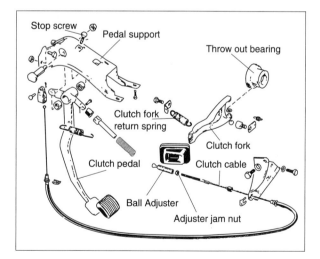

Fig. 10-16. *1972 AMC/Jeep features a housed clutch cable from pedal to release arm. Design eliminated effects of chassis and body twist. AMC/Jeep used housed cable linkage briefly.*

Minor Adjustment: Later AMC and Chrysler Clutch Linkage

AMC returned to both mechanical and fully hydraulic clutch linkage designs. Adjustments for post-'72 vehicles vary, and you will need to consult your factory level service manual for model-specific details. One rule applies with all Jeep trucks: Always make certain enough free-play exists between the clutch release/throwout bearing and the fingers of the clutch.

Some later hydraulic clutch linkage designs omit the use of heavy release arm springs. This design relies on the rotational force of the clutch to thrust the release bearing slightly away from the clutch fingers when the driver releases the pedal. (A small spring inside the clutch housing keeps the release arm in position and provides very slight assistance.) These systems "self-adjust," requiring no adjustment between clutch replacements.

Assuming that pedal height is correct and the clutch cylinders work properly, this type of hydraulic clutch linkage provides enough piston travel to compensate for normal wear of the clutch disc and other parts. The system simply compensates for wear, providing correct pedal play for the normal service life of the clutch. Aside from regularly checking the hydraulic (brake-type) fluid level, this is a maintenance-free system.

Another design found on later Jeep manual transmission models is the hydraulic throwout (clutch release) bearing. This clutch release mechanism has completely eliminated linkage, depending on a hydraulic piston within the throwout bearing assembly to move the bearing into the clutch fingers. The throwout bearing operates the clutch in the traditional manner.

Like the later release fork hydraulic systems, the hydraulic throwout bearing requires no adjustment whatsoever and relies on clutch force to throw the bearing slightly away from the fingers upon release of the pedal. In theory, the system works fine. In service, however, the design presents a major problem if a hydraulic leak develops at the throwout bearing seals. Repair or replacement of this hydraulic release bearing requires the same effort as accessing the clutch.

Despite the economy of parts and efficiency of a non-linkage design, the hydraulic throwout bearing leaves the truck vulnerable to a major repair. If your Jeep truck has a hydraulic throwout bearing, prudence calls for the overhaul or replacement of this assembly at each clutch replacement. For that matter, one should replace any type of throwout bearing during a Jeep clutch replacement—This is cheap protection against unnecessary work later.

Fig. 10-17. *Simple Girling hydraulic clutch design first appears in early '80s four-cylinder CJs. A self-adjusting hydraulic linkage system, these models require no clutch maintenance other than topping off fluid.*

To bleed air from this late hydraulic clutch linkage system, a bleeder tube exits the clutch housing alongside the hydraulic pressure line. Always use fresh DOT 3 or better grade brake fluid and maintain cleanliness. Keep contaminants out of the system, as damage to the release unit could result. Make every effort to protect this release mechanism from premature failure.

3. Clutch Replacement Tips

Replacing your Jeep clutch is a major job. Before condemning your clutch, try a simple adjustment first. Remember, too, that clutch wear or failure symptoms are similar to other troubles, like loose or broken motor mounts, a worn axle limited slip unit or binding clutch linkage. If a clutch failure diagnosis seems premature, consider all other possibilities first.

> *WARNING—*
> *The clutch disc may contain asbestos fibers. Asbestos materials can cause asbestosis. Always wear an approved respirator and protective clothing when handling components containing asbestos. Do not use compressed air, do not grind, heat, weld or sand on or near any asbestos materials. Only approved cleaning methods should be used to service the clutch disc or areas containing asbestos dust or asbestos fibers.*

When your Jeep truck requires a clutch replacement, a factory service manual for your model will clearly outline the steps. Rather than provide step-by-step instructions for the clutch replacement, this section provides those "footnotes" that factory workshop manuals often omit when speaking to a "knowing" professional mechanic.

Fig. 10-18. *Examine motor mounts and other areas before condemning the clutch. Mounts sag, break, loosen and become oil saturated. A Jeep 4x4 clutch job is a major task, done only when necessary.*

Fig. 10-19. *Jeep clutch replacement calls for transfer case and transmission removal. On four-cylinder models and some V-6 and V-8 chassis with extra radiator to fan clearance, it may prove easier to remove the radiator, move the engine forward, and leave the rest of the powertrain in place.*

Like other vehicles, the clutch in your 4WD Jeep lies between the engine and transmission. Unfortunately, the removal of the transmission involves far more work than the typical two-wheel drive truck. The front and rear driveshafts attach to the transfer case. You must remove the transfer case and the numerous components that connect directly to the transfer case and transmission.

Although the common procedure for a clutch replacement is to remove the driveshafts, transfer case and transmission, I've often found it easier to move the engine forward, leaving the rest of the powertrain in place. This is particularly true of four-cylinder models, where engine weight and length are less difficult to handle. The approach involves unbolting the engine and either suspending it far enough forward to replace the clutch or completely removing the engine from the chassis.

Obviously, if you have any good reason to remove the engine, consider a clutch replacement at the same time. Likewise, if your radiator needs repair when the clutch begs attention, do both jobs simultaneously by partially removing the engine.

The choice is yours. First read the factory procedure for removing the engine, then the steps for replacing the clutch. Depending upon the model, you may spend a lot less time on the cold ground by removing and installing the engine than if you remove the driveshafts, transfer case and transmission. Assess your particular truck. Often, the late model engine's accessories and confusing plumbing/electrical maze make engine removal less tempting.

When removing and installing powertrain components, understand that they are very hefty and cumber-

Fig. 10-20. *A massive truck four speed, coupled to an iron transfer case, can easily weigh 250 pounds. Separate these components and use a special transmission jack to remove and install the sub-assemblies. Here, transfer case has been removed with a transmission jack. Floor jack shown supports engine/transmission.*

some. Use appropriate jacks and any other safety equipment to protect yourself from injury. If you cannot afford a transmission jack, rent one. This will save time, make the job easier and prevent damage to vital parts. Aligning the transmission and transfer case with the clutch is an awkward job, even with a special jack.

A T-18 truck four-speed gearbox and Spicer 20 iron transfer case weigh nearly 250 pounds—enough to pin you to the garage floor permanently! Use extreme caution with this type of bulk, as no clutch job is worth a permanent injury. Use a hoist, hydraulic transmission jack or special lifting devices and safety stands.

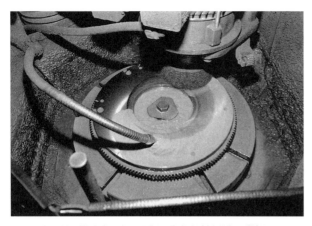

Fig. 10-21. *Flywheel must be free of heat cracks, blue discoloration and glazing. If any of these symptoms are present, sublet the flywheel to an automotive machine shop for closer inspection and service.*

For saving time and protecting vital parts, always use clutch aligning tools. More trouble occurs during attempts to align the transmission with the clutch hub than any other operation. Never hang weight off the clutch hub, or damage will result.

Take care to tighten clutch cover bolts gradually, evenly and in cross sequence, following factory guidelines. Warping a brand new clutch cover can ruin the whole job and require a teardown to correct clutch shudder.

Inspect the flywheel surface for heat cracks, glazing and possible warpage. Again, with the magnitude of this task, don't try to cut corners. Mark the flywheel's location on the crankshaft and remove the flywheel. Sublet the flywheel to a quality automotive machine shop. Let them inspect the flywheel and resurface its face. If the starter ring teeth show any damage, either replace the ring or the entire flywheel.

Remember, these are the toughest parts to access on your Jeep. Repair or replace any component that shows a questionable degree of wear.

> CAUTION —
> *Proper flywheel thickness is important for normal clutch operation and correct positioning of the release bearing. Make sure flywheel thickness is within factory specifications.*

The Parts List

The job is tough, and you don't want to do it over. When you make your list of necessary parts, begin with the clutch cover (pressure plate), clutch disc and throwout or release bearing. Closely inspect the crankshaft pilot bearing and clutch release arm for wear. If in doubt, replace these parts.

On most Jeeps, weather and age have taken their toll. The release arm sealing boot has disappeared or is in rough shape. Replace it now. Any saggy return springs need replacement. Look closely at the clutch linkage; inspect for wear, fatigue and life expectancy. Inspect the transmission front bearing retainer that supports the throwout bearing. If galling or wear exists, toss this part and replace with a new one. The retainer helps maintain release bearing alignment and must be straight and true.

Replace all seals that are leaking or could leak. This includes the front bearing retainer seal, control housing shift rail plugs on early T-90 transmissions and felt wick seals used with early Jeep front bearing retainers. Use your imagination; visualize where a leak could develop and which parts would be especially hard to access.

Toss out any worn fastening hardware and replace with equivalent grade bolts, nuts and locking devices. Know your grading (see appendix charts) and upgrade if necessary. If you remove the flywheel, install new original equipment (OE) type replacement flywheel bolts. The same with the clutch cover. Replace all locking hardware and/or washers, and clean or chase threads to assure proper torque settings.

> CAUTION —
> *Use properly graded hardware, identical to OE design. Engineers often design bolts to serve a particular function. Match hardware perfectly, and do not install generic hardware in place of specially configured bolts. Always replace hardware with identical parts. Match bolt shoulder length, thread pitch, grading, lock washer design and other details. Never replace specialized hardware with generic fasteners.*

Tools

For a quality job, you'll need several specialty tools. Removal of the pilot bearing generally requires a special puller. For solid bushing type pilots, here's a CJ-2A era mechanic's alternative: Pack the pilot cavity with grease. Find a steel shaft or old transmission input gear with the same diameter nose as the pilot bushing bore. While wearing eye protection and cushioning your blows with a block of wood or a plastic hammer, tap the shaft into the pilot bore.

The effect is like a hydraulic ram. As you tap, grease will create impact force at the back side of the pilot bushing and, presumably, drive the bushing out. This only works with thicker-shouldered bushings, not bearings, and the shaft must fit somewhat snugly into the bore.

Fig. 10-22. *Some type of clutch disc aligning tool is a must when fitting a new disc. Always install a new pilot bearing/bushing and clutch throwout bearing when replacing the clutch disc and pressure plate.*

Fig. 10-23. *The transmission front bearing retainer also supports the throwout bearing. Galling or a rough surface can cause erratic clutch operation, including chatter during engagement. If wear is obvious, replace the retainer.*

A clutch aligning tool is a must. An old input gear with the same splines serves well, aligning the clutch disc as you secure the clutch cover to the flywheel.

Over the years, I have accumulated a drawer full of alignment dowels for the two upper bolt holes of various clutch/bellhousings. Simply cut the heads off long bolts of the proper thread size. For simpler removal of these locating dowels, make a screwdriver slot at the end of each dowel. Keep threads clean.

By using these alignment dowels, you can keep the transmission centered as you slide the assembly into position. Once you've installed the lower transmission bolts, unscrew the dowels and replace them with transmission mounting bolts. Tighten all bolts in sequence. Establish final settings with a torque wrench.

> *CAUTION —*
> *Prevent damage to the transmission case, bearing retainer, clutch hub and pilot bearing. Carefully maintain transmission alignment during installation. Always support the transmission with a jack until all upper and lower mounting bolts are secure.*

You will want some high melting point grease for the groove inside the collar of the throwout bearing. (Some manufacturers package the bearing with grease.) Also, make sure you have proper sealant if you intend to remove the front bearing retainer. Unless the retainer requires sealant only and no gasket, a new gasket is a good idea, too.

Make sure you have plenty of parts cleaner and shop towels. This can be a very messy job, especially on a Jeep. (Before starting, thoroughly pressure wash the chassis and powertrain.)

> *CAUTION —*
> *On some transmissions, like the NP435 four-speed, be careful. Front bearing retainer gaskets are selective fit shims for adjusting the end-play of the input gear and bearing. Don't alter the thickness of these /gaskets!*

In recent years, I have taken a cue from modern automotive "technicians." (In my era, we apprenticed, reached journey status, then eventually earned the right to call ourselves "master mechanics.") I now use mechanic's latex gloves, and my industrial strength hand cleaner has a citrus base and no ammonia. Knuckle tissue and hands appreciate this measure of concern, and, frankly, those "grease monkey" tasks have become downright enjoyable!

> *WARNING—*
> *Use whatever means necessary to protect yourself from asbestos. All but the more recent motor vehicle clutch discs contain asbestos. Asbestos is harmful to your lungs and respiratory system. Special filtration is necessary to protect yourself from asbestos fibers.*

Clutch Linkage Repairs

Mechanical clutch linkage requires periodic service, as bushing wear leads to unwanted free-play. Rods and levers that actuate the clutch tend to wear and fatigue at pivot points. Nylon bushings wear out, along with pedal stops and return springs. You must replace parts when wear develops.

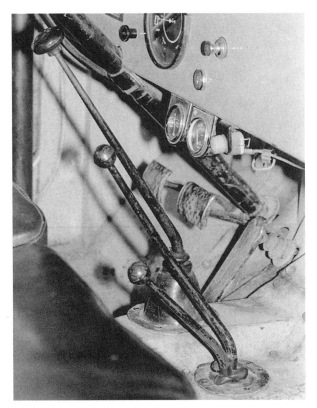

Fig. 10-24. *Mechanical clutch linkage requires regular inspection for wear and excessive play. Models with through-the-floor pedals have the advantage of chassis mounted linkage. This reduces the tendency to flex, distort and bind.*

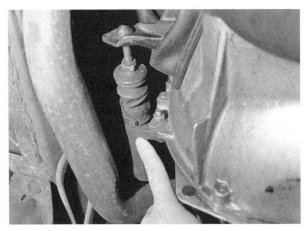

Fig. 10-25. *Jeep hydraulic clutch system eliminates many problems. Twisting and body/frame flex off-pavement raise havoc with mechanical clutch linkage, especially models with suspended, cab-mounted pedals. Here, hydraulic cylinder mounts solidly to the bellhousing and moves with the powertrain.*

Jeep hydraulic clutch systems consist of a master cylinder, a hydraulic pipe and/or hose, and either a clutch slave cylinder or hydraulic throwout bearing (later models). Like your braking system, cleanliness and fresh fluid assure longer service.

When performing work on the hydraulic clutch system, you need clean hands, free of grease, oils or abrasive contaminants. Repair kits are available for the master and slave cylinders, or you can replace these parts if they show excess wear. Any repairs must follow brake system standards.

Look closely at the hose. Again, like brake hose, this is a wear item. If embrittlement or dehydration has occurred, replace the hose. Use DOT 3 or better brake fluid, and repair the system in accord with factory service manual guidelines. (See the brake section of this book for further details on hydraulic system repairs.)

4. Transmission Adjustments

On Jeep manual transmissions, linkage adjustments are limited to three-speed column shift models. Other gearboxes feature removable levers and control housing assemblies considered part of the transmission assembly.

> NOTE —
> Rarely does a control housing require overhaul, although this service is often possible without removing the entire transmission unit.

Jeep column shift linkage will wear, stretch and fatigue. This requires periodic adjustment. Worn parts require replacement. Periodic cleaning of parts and thorough lubrication are also important. (See the lubrication chapter.)

Unknown to many Jeep buffs, the earliest CJ-2A had a column shift mechanism. To serial No. 38221, the CJ-2A had a column shifter and linkage. Apparently, Willys wanted civilians to enjoy column shift, which was popular on U.S. automobiles and a few postwar pickups.

Some early Jeep Pickups, Station Wagons and the Forward Control models also had column shift linkage while most Jeep trucks and CJ models use a cane floor shifter that rises from the transmission. The first Jeep trucks to use column shift linkage in large numbers were the three-speed equipped J-trucks of the early '60s.

Column shift linkage adjustment follows a basic procedure. Two rods reach from the transmission control levers to pivoting arms at the steering column. The column shifter moves fore and aft in a neutral gate, aligning the shifter with one pivoting arm or the other. One rod links to the first/reverse control lever, while the other attaches to the second/high gear control lever.

Adjustment consists of aligning the two pivoting arms so that the shifter moves smoothly from the first/reverse gear path, through the neutral gate and into the second/high gear shift path. You will find specific adjustment procedures in a Jeep factory or professional level service manual.

Linkage adjustment must serve three purposes. Become familiar with each: 1) the rod adjustments should place the steering column pivot arms in perfect alignment during neutral movement; 2) for driver convenience, the column shifter must move through a comfortable range of motion; and 3) rods must move freely in each direction to permit complete engagement of reverse, first, second and third gears.

This last point is crucial. The only place to verify proper gear engagement is to crawl beneath the truck. Make sure the engine is turned off and cold so the exhaust system won't scorch your hands. Set the parking brake and block wheels to prevent the vehicle from rolling.

Have an assistant move the shift linkage. Make sure the control lever moves freely and completely through the neutral gate and into each gear position. If you are uncertain, remove the shift rod at the transmission control lever and note whether the lever is completely in gear. Simple—despite more elaborate service guidelines and adjustment measures, these are the goals. Pursue them.

Automatic Transmission Adjustments

Your Jeep automatic transmission requires periodic service. Look for fluid leaks, the condition of vacuum hoses to the module, if so equipped, and perform periodic fluid and filter changes. Cleanliness in the service of your transmission cannot be overstated, as guidelines call for lint-free shop towels when working around the automatic transmission's valve body.

There are two controls involved with your automatic transmission. Later trucks have sophisticated electrical and electronic controls, yet the cues remain similar.

First, the manual (shift) valve requires proper adjustment. This measure cannot be overstated. A manual valve out of adjustment may direct an inadequate flow of hydraulic fluid within the transmission. Incorrect manual valve adjustment can cause weak shifts, incomplete apply pressure, slipping clutch packs and weak band application. Damage or complete transmis-

Fig. 10-26. *When servicing your automatic transmission, cleanliness is crucial. Dirt, even lint, in the valve body can cause shifting irregularities and other problems that lead to an overhaul. When changing the filter, use extreme care.*

sion failure can result from incorrectly adjusted shift linkage.

The second automatic transmission adjustment is the kickdown or downshift linkage. The mechanical linkage found on early Borg-Warner transmissions, or the electrical switch used on THM 400 and other transmissions, takes a message from the throttle to the transmission. The electrical switch or mechanical linkage causes a downshift to second gear at full throttle (if speed range is less than 55–70 mph, depending upon the Jeep model and axle gearing).

A vacuum modulator also affects shifts. This diaphragm helps determine upshift and downshift points. If your transmission shifts erratically, either the governor or vacuum modulator could be defective. Of these two devices, the modulator is much easier to replace.

Before condemning your automatic transmission, perform a full service. Change the fluid and filter. Adjust the manual linkage, centering the shift indicator for neutral and park. Readjust the neutral safety/start switch, if necessary, to assure that the engine will start only in neutral or park.

Adjust carburetor linkage on models with manual detent/kickdown controls. Check the adjustment of electrical kickdown switches on THM400 and later transmissions. Change the vacuum modulator, if suspect, and make certain that correct and sufficient vacuum signals reach the modulator.

Your factory level service manual details each of these services, or you may prefer to sublet the work. If none of these measures improve your automatic transmission's performance, accept the likelihood of in-depth repairs. Like a manual clutch, the automatic transmission parts wear over time.

Be aware that you have overhaul options with the GM-built THM 400 and newer Chrysler transmissions, including heavy duty replacement parts. High performance torque converters and internal pieces are also available. (See later chapters for performance details.)

Fig. 10-27. *A full service on your automatic transmission includes a fluid and filter change, adjustment of the shift and kickdown linkage or electric switch, and adjustment of the starter circuit's Neutral/Park safety switch.*

Chapter 11

Transfer Case, Driveshafts, Axles and Hubs

WWII Jeep MBs moved briskly along hard-sur-faced roads, grappled with mud and snow, inched up steep grades and sloshed through swamplands. Such a wide variety of chores required auxiliary gearsets, and the Spicer Model 18 transfer case provided just the solution.

1. Transfer Cases

The Jeep transfer case attaches at the rear of the transmission and divides power between the front and rear axles. A two-speed transfer case also offers low range, the extra gearset available for four-wheel drive use and heavy chores.

On Jeep powertrains, the transmission output shaft drives the transfer case input. On Spicer Model 18 transfer cases, the rear output yoke is opposite the front driveshaft output. Power flows downward to the output shafts. Known as a "side-drive" design, power first travels through a pair of transfer case drive gears. When the driver shifts the 2WD/4WD lever, a sliding fork moves a clutch mechanism that engages the front output shaft and activates four-wheel drive.

Fig. 11-1. *The Borg-Warner T-90 three-speed transmission (pictured) and Spicer Model 18 transfer case served a variety of Jeep trucks from 1946 to 1971.*

For rock crawling (low range), the Model 18 Jeep transfer case reduces speed through engagement of a gear on the intermediate shaft. When the operator shifts to low range, a sliding gear first releases the high-range gear, then moves further to engage the low-range gear.

For the original MB or a Willys/Kaiser era CJ, the Model 18 transfer unit serves very well. It easily met the requirements of Willys-style 4x4 Pickups and Station Wagons, too. Extra friction, gear noise and bearing wear, however, make a side-drive transfer case less attractive than the Model 20 Spicer unit that superceded the Model 18.

Through-drive Transfer Cases

As Jeep four-wheel drive trucks evolved from utility trucks into multi-purpose vehicles, the transfer case design also changed. As 4x4s spent more time on the highway than off, Jeep reduced two-wheel drive wear and tear by directing power straight from the transmission output shaft to the rear driveshaft.

The early Jeep's Model 18 transfer case gave way to the Spicer Model 20 unit, introduced in the original Kaiser/Jeep Wagoneers and J-trucks. (As an aside, early Wagoneer models with automatic transmissions offered a single-speed Model 21 power divider without low range.) The Kaiser Jeepster also used this "silent" transfer case.

These rugged Spicer 20 transfer cases feature a single control lever for easier operation, though they still use a sliding gear to engage low range. After AMC assumed the Jeep Corporation, all 1972 models (including CJs) used the iron cased Spicer 20 through-drive transfer case.

Full-time Four-wheel Drive

During the seventies, a series of unique transfer case systems appeared. Warner's Quadra-Trac, found in many Jeep models, competed with the chain-drive, full-time New Process 203 equipped Dodge, Ford and GM 4x4 trucks.

A full-time four-wheel drive transfer case prevents use of front locking hubs and provides four-wheel traction at all times. Jeep/Warner Quadra-Trac uses an internal differential system which allows proportional power flow. The differential system, similar to a spider gear arrangement in an axle, continuously delivers power to both the front and rear axles. A hefty chain connects the two drive outputs, while a gearset provides low range. High and low range lock modes override the differential system for off-pavement or loose traction driving.

Excess parts wear and poor gas mileage encouraged most light truck manufacturers to abandon full-time four-wheel drive by the early 1980s. The return to part-time four-wheel drive, however, did not signal Jeep's change back to the rugged Spicer 20 unit. Although the Jeep CJ acquired the durable and versatile Dana 300 transfer case in 1980, the full-size Wagoneer/Cherokee and J-trucks switched to a New Process 208 chain drive unit.

The NP208 transfer case is a lightweight aluminum transfer box. The NP208 design allows quick, easy shifting (on-the-fly) between 2WD high and 4WD high ranges. Although drive chain life might be an assumed weakness with these designs, chains and sprockets are in fact very durable. On NP208 transfer cases, wear is more often seen in the shifting forks and nylon fork channels.

Lightweight "Part-time" Systems

For high performance usage and hybrid Jeep buildups, OEM chain drive transfer cases seldom replace the earlier iron-cased Spicer 20 transfer case or the highly regarded Dana 300. Shift mechanism failures and leaks have plagued many aluminum chain drive transfer case units. A major overhaul is necessary to correct these problems.

The 1962–79 Spicer 20-equipped Jeep trucks and 1980–86 CJ models with the Dana 300 transfer case offer the best stamina. (Advance Adapters' Atlas transfer case is rapidly gaining stature as a "bulletproof" retrofit unit for Jeep use. See performance chapters.) Iron cases and durable gear drives have proven superior to other designs.

Some of us have railed against the use of lighter duty transfer cases with chain drive. The industry argues that weight savings and reduced friction encourage the use of these light duty units. A Dana 300 or New Process 205 prototype gear-drive transfer mechanism could easily fit within a high strength, lighter weight alloy case.

Most four-wheelers are fully capable of pulling a lever, twisting a manual hub or reading an instruction

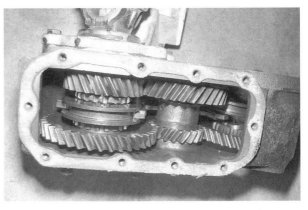

Fig. 11-2. *Later CJ Jeep's rugged Dana 300 transfer case uses helically cut gears. These 1980–86 units are ideal for V-8 conversions.*

decal. Overall reliability and off-pavement survival suggest the need for heavy duty factory options—choices like a bulletproof part-time 4x4 Dana 300 prototype or New Process 205 transfer case that can give trouble-free service for more than 150,000 miles. Perhaps the Atlas transfer unit could become an upgrade option for the TJ Wrangler.

Fig. 11-3. *These New Process transfer case units serve Jeep and other truck makes. They are lightweight, easy to shift and feature chain drive.*

Chain Drive Transfer Case Troubles

Failure of a fork or shift mechanism can leave your 4x4 stranded. From the NP208 chain drive transfer case forward to the current part- and full-time units, trouble symptoms include jumping out of gear, failure to engage low, high or neutral range, or noisy operation. These signs generally call for an overhaul or at least a teardown and repairs.

Before tearing into your transfer case unit, check the easier possibilities. Fluid deserves a look. (Various applications use ATF or special lubricants, so check your Jeep's requirements.) Leaks develop at seals, case halves, and castings. Pay close attention. Shift linkage sometimes needs adjustment or alignment. Make certain the linkage does not bind or interfere with the body parts. When these simpler cures fail, plan to remove the transfer case unit for overhaul.

The chain drive transfer cases are usually simple to remove. General procedure includes placing the shifter in 4H and draining the fluid. Disconnect all cables, linkages and driveshaft joints. Drain all fluid, then separate yokes from the input and output shafts. See whether the exhaust pipe or brake cable interferes, and check the top of the transfer case for switch wires.

Once you have disconnected all external parts, place a transmission jack beneath the transfer case. Now unbolt the case from the transmission adapter. In minutes, with the use of a floor jack or the help of a stout friend, you can free the transfer case from the adapter. Keep all parts level until the input shaft completely clears the transfer case.

Place the transfer case on your workbench. Level the ends, and lay the unit with the case split lying parallel to the benchtop. Remember to replace all seals, including yoke seals. Always refer to your Jeep factory level service manual for detailed procedures on the removal, teardown, rebuilding and re-installation of your transfer case.

Transfer Case Troubleshooting

Overhauling your Jeep transfer case is a job much like a transmission overhaul. If such work is necessary, you will find step-by-step overhaul procedures in the factory or professional level service manual for your Jeep. Within the scope of this book, I will share general troubleshooting guidelines for common transfer case problems.

The most frequent transfer case trouble is hard shifting. Often, the remedy is really simple, requiring nothing more than cleaning linkage and properly lubricating these parts. Sometimes the problem is bent or damaged linkage, the result of off-pavement abuse.

If external linkage is not the problem and your transfer case slips out of gear or front wheel drive, an-

ticipate more serious trouble. Before condemning the transfer case unit, however, I'd suggest that you check the transfer case to transmission attaching hardware. A loose transfer case housing can cause gear binding and internal pressure on the gears.

Deeper Troubles

Service manuals list the shift mechanism among the possible causes of transfer case problems. Poppet balls and springs are an area of concern in earlier transfer case shift mechanisms, but noises, jumping out of gear and difficult shifting usually indicate more serious troubles.

Before removing the transfer case from your Jeep for overhaul, it's always prudent to check the condition of the springs and poppet balls. There are instances when a worn or broken spring does cause trouble, but bearing damage, a bent shift fork or other internal defects are more likely the culprit.

If your high-mileage transfer case has never been through an overhaul, suspect bearing fatigue at the very least. Worn bearings mean excess gear clearances and poor tooth contact, the primary causes of expensive gear failure. A factory or professional level shop manual will provide proper guidance for your transfer case overhaul.

2. Driveshafts

Jeep 4x4 driveshafts take tremendous punishment. Excess suspension travel, weighty loads, radically changing driveshaft angles and modifications like suspension lift kits can tear your U-joints and driveshafts to pieces.

Often, the cause of a U-joint failure is miscalculated. Although wear racks up quickly on trucks that ford streams, flex their springs to the maximum and crawl through tortuous rocks with massive torque applied through low range gears, driveshaft failure often results from poor fitup. Shafts pieced together out-of-phase or badly angled are the worst culprits.

> NOTE —
> Wear in the rear driveshaft slip yoke and stub spline can produce an unusual vibrating sound at "float" condition. This is especially noticeable on a Jeep with driveline-mounted parking brake, as the brake drum amplifies the noise and shake.

Your driveshafts' U-joints must be in phase with each other. Observing proper grease intervals and grease gun pressures contribute to driveshaft longevity. Beyond these factors, driveshaft survival depends mostly on torque loads. These include the weight

Fig. 11-4. *U-joint failures have many causes. A loss of grease or worn seals allows moisture into joints, resulting in brindling of the bearings. Bad driveshaft angularity can break the yoke or bearing.*

Fig. 11-5. *Trent Alford at M.I.T. in El Cajon, California aligns hefty replacement parts for a heavy duty rear driveshaft that will increase the stamina of a CJ-5.*

Fig. 11-6. *Long wheelbase Jeep trucks use a mid-shaft bearing. Wear here will cause severe vibration.*

placed on the vehicle, the amount of engine torque applied to the joints, and the departure and receiving angles between the two yokes of the driveshaft.

A common problem for a lifted Jeep is too much angle on the joints. This results from the radical difference in height between the axle pinion shafts and the transfer case output shafts. Rotating the axle pinion shaft upward is a shoddy method for reducing U-joint angles. This approach can lead to another crop of problems, those caused by different U-joint angles at each end of the shaft. U-joints rotating on widely dissimilar arcs can create enough rotational vibration and stress to break a gear case housing.

Driveshafts Under Construction

Jeep driveshaft survival depends upon joint size, tubing diameter and wall thickness, plus the ability of the assembly to compensate for speed, length and angle changes. Often, a driveshaft that would work perfectly well in its original mode cannot handle a chassis lift or increased horsepower loads. Here, a custom heavy duty driveshaft is necessary.

Fig. 11-7. *Use of a hefty custom built driveshaft assures resistance to torque loads. With a truck-type four speed and low gearing, reduction ratios in excess of 70:1 are common. Such torque is tremendous. Shown is custom rear shaft on an '81 CJ-5. If you want an ultra-low crawl ratio, consider driveshafts that can handle the torque.*

Fig. 11-8. *Although they look similar, replacement U-joint at left fits one-ton trucks. Middle joint is size found in most CJs, Wranglers and full size 1/2-ton Jeep trucks. At right, smaller sized joint found at front driveshaft of Kaiser-era Jeepsters often leads to trouble.*

Fig. 11-9. *Dramatic difference between OEM Jeep CJ front driveshaft tube section and new 0.188" tube under construction is obvious.*

Fig. 11-10. *This step is critical during driveshaft construction. Proper driveshaft "phasing" requires that U-joint cross yokes are absolutely in line. Before welding, a spirit level and a perfectly flat benchtop assure alignment. Some shops square up shafts in a custom fixture.*

Fig. 11-11. *Before MIG wire-feed welding, the shaft is carefully tapped into alignment. The builder will work this section until total runout is less than 0.005". Such tolerances are necessary for vibration-free results and illustrate the importance of protecting your driveshafts from off-pavement bashing.*

Proper Lubrication

U-joint survival depends upon regular lubrication. Stream crossings, wintry highways and sandy deserts take their toll. Assuming that U-joint dust seals are in top shape, you can follow Spicer's on/off highway lubrication guidelines: 5000–8000 miles or every three months (far more often if your Jeep is subject to either severe service or exposure to water). A high-quality lube gun and clean grease are prerequisites for preserving U-joints and their delicate seals.

When selecting U-joint and driveshaft greases, follow Spicer's guidelines. For regular service, use National Lubricating Grease Institute (NLGI) Extreme Pressure Grade 1 or 2 greases. Avoid heavier greases. Severe service requires lithium soap base or EP grease with a temperature range of +325 to -10° F.

Driveshaft Angularity

Angles and rotational arcs make or break U-joints and driveshafts. While torque load determines the proper size U-joint to use, engineers design driveshafts for an 85% efficiency factor. (For the highest load to place upon your driveshafts, the formula is: Lowest Gear Torque (First Gear/Low Range) = Net Engine Torque X Transmission Low Gear Ratio X Transfer Case Low Range Ratio X 0.85.)

Two angles affect a driveshaft: side-view drop and plane-view shift. Side view is simply the angle that the driveshaft slopes downward from the transfer case to each axle's differential. Plane view is the lateral angle of the driveshaft, viewed from directly above the frame.

For your Jeep's driveshafts to live, the angles on each end of the driveshaft (the side-view drop combined with the plane-view shift) must create as little non-uniform motion as possible. U-joint angles, in simple terms, must rotate on nearly identical arcs, with the vertical faces of the U-joint flanges nearly parallel. (Spicer/Dana recommends that the limit of inequality must not exceed that of a single U-joint operating at a 3-degree angle.)

The included U-joint angles should remain identical on each end of the driveshaft. When the shaft rotates, joints should move in similar arcs, with bearing cross shafts each running at the same tilt.

Speed dictates maximum allowable driveshaft angles. A driveshaft rotating 5000 rpm (somewhat obscure for a Jeep 4x4 unless flat out in a desert race) tolerates no more than 3 degrees, 15 seconds of operating angle, while the same shaft spinning 1500 rpm will work at an 11-degree, 30-second angle. Driveshaft length affects this formula, too, with longer driveshafts tolerating more operating angle.

Owners who lift their trucks with shackle kits or springs must also consider that a 3/4-degree change in the differential pinion angle will change the U-joint operating angle about 1/4 of a degree.

Shimming the axle housing at the spring perches is a common method for restoring the pinion angle and U-joint operating angles. Driveline specialists insist that appropriate hard steel shims be used or, if the angle is radically off, cut the spring perches from the axle housing and re-position the perches at the correct angle. Brass and aluminum shims tend to pound out during off-road bashing.

Before modifying your engine, transmission or transfer case angles, take accurate measurements of the shaft angles. When lifting a 4x4, the side angles of the driveshafts also change. Small changes are acceptable, as long as the axle swings up and down on its original arc of movement. Problems begin when the side angle or drop becomes excessive.

An excellent source of information, including formulas and professional driveshaft service tips, is Spicer/Dana's Trouble Shooting Guideline, available through Spicer distributors or Dana Corporation, Drivetrain Service Division, P.O. Box 321, Toledo, Ohio 43691. This quick reference guide and the Spicer Universal Joints and Driveshafts Service Manual offer professional insights on driveshaft service, maintenance and proper fitment.

Looking upward from directly below the rear driveshaft, the line between the U-joint flanges is evident. A short shaft demands precise side and plane angles.

Side view angle shows the relationship between the sloping driveshaft and the U-joint flanges. Note that flange centerlines are parallel.

CJ Jeeps and Wranglers boast long front driveshafts with very slight slope (side view angularity). As length reduces torque load, this heavy duty replacement shaft will easily handle the chores.

U-joint Service and Repair Tips

A U-joint failure is serious, either on- or off-highway. Driveshaft breakage on an out back trip in the Colorado Rockies or California's Rubicon tests your survival skills to the limit. Learning to replace your own U-joints will drastically reduce the risk of becoming stranded.

U-joint replacement begins with driveshaft removal. Before loosening a driveshaft, mark the shaft's order of assembly. Drivelines must be in-phase, with couplers kept in line with their original splines. If your driveshaft has two pieces, scribe an indexing line on each section. Reassembly in the original position will assure satisfactory service, alignment, and balance.

Cleanliness is essential, regardless of the locale in which you make the repairs. (I've replaced U-joints on the tailgate of a pickup and atop a granite boulder.) If the work area is particularly gritty, beware. New U-joints, freshly coated with grease, attract dirt like a horseshoe magnet draws pig iron from beach sand.

Assuming that the shaft isn't damaged, you can make a permanent U-joint installation in the field. Approach the job with "professional" expectations. Spend a few extra minutes to ensure your trip home and prevent the need for a second teardown and parts replacement.

The tools needed to remove and replace a U-joint are minimal. In the field, a good mechanic's hammer, solid punch, blade screwdriver, a variety of sockets and a set of pliers can handle the job. Specialty or homemade tools ease the job further, although the principles remain the same.

If your technique is correct, even the most trying environment will not prevent a quality job. Find a solid surface to work on, preferably steel plate like a step bumper, a front winch mounting plate, or a hefty board in a pickup bed. Get out of the weather if gale winds prevail, and plan on several minutes of painstaking work.

U-joint Installation

Although an arbor press or specialized U-joint tools are helpful, don't be misled. Some of the best craftsmen in the automotive repair industry still replace U-joints with basic hand tools. The reason? U-joint bearing caps fit precisely into their saddles and bores, and the slightest cocking of a cap during installation can ruin a driveshaft. Presses and hefty tools eliminate the "feel" of the cap moving into its bore. Hand tools often sensitize us and provide a safer fitup.

Fig. 11-12. *Coupler types and U-joints vary. Double Cardan (constant velocity) joints appear on heavy duty and shorter 4x4 driveshafts. Joint to yoke attaching methods also vary.*

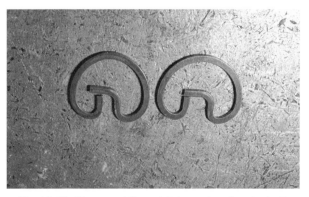

Fig. 11-13. *Disassembling a joint requires few tools. On Spicer-type U-joints, you must remove two external snap rings.*

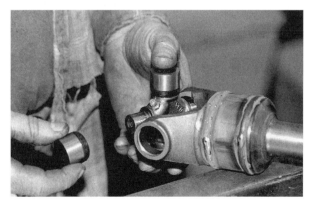

Fig. 11-14. *Once both bearing caps are free of the driveshaft, you can separate the U-joint.*

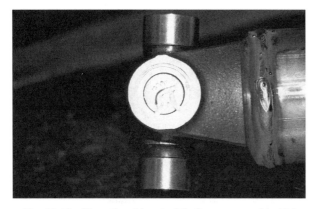

Fig. 11-15. *Clean the driveshaft before reassembly. This will assure proper fitup of parts.*

Fig. 11-16. *Protect these snap ring grooves during service. Striking a groove flange with a hammer or punch could cause permanent (expensive!) driveshaft damage. Here, I find an old socket that will fit inside the bore, then tap on the socket with a plastic head hammer or use the socket and a bench vise to simulate a simple "press."*

Fig. 11-17. *Install the first bearing cap. Use the hammer carefully and support the bearing needles with the cross section of the U-joint. If you doubt your hammer skills, use a socket to drive the bearing cap into its recess. Install the cap far enough to insert the snap ring. Install the second cap. Again, carefully keep the cross section centered to hold needle bearings in place. If all needles remain intact, the second bearing cap will just clear its snap ring groove. Install the snap ring. Make sure snap rings seat completely.*

Fig. 11-18. *New U-joints come with snap rings and a grease fitting. Make sure needle bearings stay in place during assembly. Always align the grease fitting to permit easy access and service. Field lubrication of double Cardan joints requires special grease gun tip.*

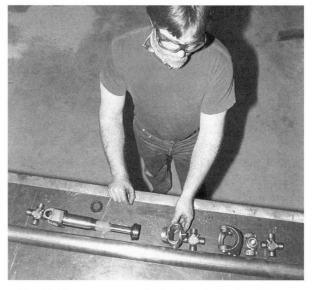

Fig. 11-19. *A constant velocity, double Cardan U-joint has a precise assembly sequence. Note and mark alignment of parts before disassembly. Be aware of the spring, which must be in place when installing the new joints. Re-assemble in exactly the reverse sequence of disassembly.*

Once you have completed the U-joint replacement and re-installed the driveshaft in the truck, grease the U-joints. Caution: Do not grease a U-joint before bolting it into the yoke, as you will force the bearing caps out of position. (Specifications for tightening bolts or nuts are found in your factory-level service manual.)

Fig. 11-20. *Detroit type U-Joints utilize internal snap rings. Straps hold the joint to the yoke.*

If you left the grease gun home, new joints usually contain enough grease for the drive back. "Permanently sealed" (solid-cross, no grease fitting) joints, in fact, have high quality grease and seals that require no further greasing. Other joints, equipped with grease fittings, require periodic service.

3. Axle Assemblies

The mysteries within the axle housing, the maze of gears and bearings, are responsible for turning horsepower into motion. How that happens is as significant as any other function of your Jeep's powertrain. Although axle overhaul is beyond the scope of this book, your knowledge of tell-tale wear signs could prevent serious trouble or the risk of increased damage and higher repair costs. Let's begin with some axle basics.

As the driveshaft rotates, the pinion gear turns. The pinion shaft/gear, attached to the U-joint companion flange, carries power into the axle. Supported by bearings in the axle housing, the pinion shaft's spiral bevel gear transfers power to a matching ring gear, which changes the direction of the power flow by 90 degrees.

The ring gear bolts to a case, generally called the differential carrier. Bearings support the differential carrier in either the hypoid axle housing or a removable third member housing. (Nearly all Jeep models use integral-type hypoid axle housings, the exception being a few very early trucks with oddball spiral-bevel rear axles featuring two-piece, vertically split axle housings.)

Together, the ring and pinion gears serve two functions: changing the power flow direction and re-

ducing speed. If the axle shafts connected directly to the ring gear's case, both wheels would spin continuously at the speed of the ring gear. Such a locked rear end or "spool," although maximizing traction, is incapable of adjusting for the vehicle's left or right turns.

Like all other four-wheeled vehicles, Jeep trucks have unequal wheel speed when making a turn. The inside wheels rotate slower than the outside wheels. If all four wheels turned at equal speed, serious trouble would result. Tires would skid and axle shafts would work against each other.

Here the differential becomes important. When turning, we need to vary the speed of the right side wheels from those on the left. In a straight ahead mode, the ring gear turns both shafts at equal speed, that speed determined by the axle ratio and engine rpm. For turns, individual axle shaft speeds must adjust for smooth traction at each wheel.

Imagine your Jeep's driveshaft(s) rotating at 2000 rpm. With ten teeth on the pinion gear and forty teeth on the ring gear, the axle shafts will each spin at 500 rpm when the vehicle drives straight ahead.

> NOTE —
> Although useful for illustration purposes, the 4-to-1 axle ratio I just described would cause the pinion gear teeth to continuously "find" the same ring gear teeth, an undesirable trait. Instead, engineers devise ratios like 4.10, with a 41/10 tooth arrangement that constantly renews tooth contact for better gear life.

Differential Action

As the Jeep enters a corner, the inside wheel turns slower than the outside wheel. The speed at each wheel must differ. To allow for the speed change, the differential contains sets of gears inside the rotating carrier case. While ring and pinion speeds are constant, the differential gears allow axle shaft speeds to vary.

The differential carrier housing is hollow, and the axles slide through the space in the housing, entering from each side. Splines on the inner ends of the axle shafts engage the differential side gears. These side gears, in non-locking differentials, also have bevel teeth that mesh with two smaller gears, called pinions or spider gears.

The spider gear teeth, facing inward toward the center of the carrier case, engage with the side gear teeth. The spiders float on a shaft, which mounts rigidly through the center of the carrier case. Effectively, the four gears can move independently of the carrier.

The result: 1) If road speed at both wheels remains the same, the gears all rotate like a solid unit in unison

Traction on Icy Roads and Off-Camber Trails

If your Jeep has a limited slip or positive traction differential, use extreme caution on icy or muddy roads, off-camber trails and side-slope situations. Here, any four-wheeled vehicle can go sideways or spin out if both wheels at an axle lose traction and spin simultaneously. Unless you remain light on the throttle, a limited slip or locked rear axle is a prime candidate for a spinout.

Both wheels spinning will typically send the vehicle toward the low side of the road or trail. On an icy highway at speed, a shorter wheelbase vehicle is more likely to spin out than a longer wheelbase, wider track truck. To reduce risk of a spinout, lower your speed gradually, maintain a light throttle to keep from spinning the tires, and do not over-react.

If possible, I order 4WD vehicles without limited slip axles. I opt for aftermarket manually locked differentials like the ARB Air Locker. I will leave the axle "open" (in conventional, non-locking mode) on an icy, off-camber highway. This provides the truck with more directional stability and reduces risk of spinout. When I'm in need of "Rubicon" rock-crawling traction, the manual locker is a useful tool.

with the differential carrier case; 2) when turning a corner, the four gears can rotate at the speed necessary to apply more rpm at the outside wheel and proportionately less at the inside wheel; and 3) at times, unfortunately, the conventional differential mechanism directs power to the wheel with least resistance or traction. This last point remains the primary shortfall of conventional, non-locking differentials.

When watching a Jeep crawl in rocks, sand and loose terrain, it's easy to distinguish a conventional axle: The wheel without traction will spin futilely, while the opposite wheel, with better traction, stands still!

Controlling Wheelspin

Traction loss is a serious problem. The other extreme would be damage caused when no differential action takes place. A Jeep's handling with a permanently locked rear axle would be very dangerous. For this reason, we depend upon systems that provide more positive traction but still allow differential action.

Jeep limited slip differentials enjoy a variety of trade names. Several aftermarket, performance systems have also been developed, many suited for street, rock-crawling and racing use. (See the performance section of the book for detailed information on aftermarket traction devices.)

Typically, a limited slip unit is built around a clutching mechanism within the differential. Simply put, the clutching device enables torque delivery to the

axle and wheel with traction. The basic difference between factory limited slip and aftermarket "locker" differentials is the design of the clutching or lock-up mechanism.

By design, the clutch type limited slip unit can still allow variance of wheel speed on corners. The differential behaves in much the same manner as a conventional unit, permitting the inner wheel to rotate slower.

Spicer-Dana and Other Jeep Axles

Although integral housing hypoid axles require more tools for disassembly, they generally provide substantial ring and pinion support. Spicer's integral-type axles serve most Jeep trucks. (The AMC Model 20 rear axle, also integral style, appears in Jeep's lighter duty models from 1976–86.)

Semi-floating axles offer less safety margin than full-floating axles. On the semi-floater, a single outer wheel bearing supports the axle shaft, while the splined inner end of the axle shaft relies on the differential side gear for support. A broken axle shaft can cause real trouble.

Many semi-floating Jeep axles rely upon bearing retainer plates at the outer bearing to hold the axle in place. Other types use a C-lock at the inner (differential) end of the axle shaft. If the axle shaft shears in the

Fig. 11-21. *Comparison of ring and pinion gears says it all. Top row, left to right, is the earlier Jeep/Spicer 27, a light duty Dana 28, and a WWII vintage Spicer 25. Bottom row of Dana gears shows the 60, 44 and 70 sets. The 44 is a popular front and rear axle on full-sized Jeep 1/2-tons and at the rear of pre-'76 and 1986 CJs. 44 is also an available heavy duty option on TJ Wrangler. Two larger gearsets fit 3/4-ton and one-ton trucks.*

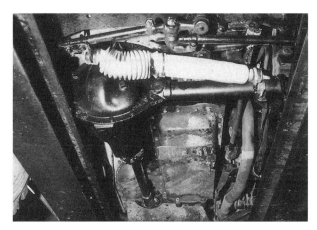

Fig. 11-22. *This early Jeep/Spicer integral front axle housing features pressed-in and welded axle tubes and closed steering knuckles. An integral axle overhaul generally takes place in the chassis. The job calls for a special spreader to remove the differential carrier from the axle housing.*

Fig. 11-23. *Compare the Dana 70 differential side gear with that of the 44. Note size of axle splines inside each gear, which indicate difference between a one-ton truck's axle shaft diameter and that of a full-sized 1/2-ton, an earlier CJ or the TJ's heavy duty option.*

wrong place, or if a C-lock should break, the remaining axle shaft, hub, brake drum (or rotor) and the wheel/tire can slide out the side of the vehicle!

A full-floating rear axle shaft, by contrast, is simply a power link. The wheel and hub ride on bearings much like on the front end of the full-size Jeep 4x4 trucks or a CJ model. A retaining washer and nut (typically backed by an additional lock nut) provide for wheel bearing adjustment and keep the hub in place. The machined spindle is an integral part of the rear axle housing. At the full-floating front axle, the spindle attaches to the steering knuckle. The axle shaft fits through the spindle's bore.

Engaging the side gear at the inner end, the rear axle shaft's outer flange bolts to the wheel hub. On full-floating Jeep front axles, the axle shaft has outer

splines that engage a drive plate or free-wheeling hub. If a full-floating axle shaft breaks, the hub and wheel continue to rotate on the spindle.

Although all CJs and full-size conventional Jeep trucks feature full-floating front axles, most Jeep trucks have used semi-floating type rear axles. (Two exceptions are the WWII military MB model with its Spicer full-floating front and rear axles and the later AMC-era J-20s equipped with Dana 60 full-floating rear axles.) While Detroit's Big Three used full-floating rear axles on all 3/4-ton and larger trucks, Jeep only applied such stamina to one-ton trucks. Many "heavy duty" J-trucks have weaker semi-floating rear axles.

Distinguishing Front Axles

Two significant changes occurred in Jeep 4x4 front axles: The shift to open steering knuckles, which began in the early '70s, and a shift away from conventional full-floating front axles, which accompanied the late model change to vacuum disconnect axles. Free-wheeling hubs, and even the provision for hubs, vanished with the compact Cherokee/Comanche models and the YJ Wrangler.

Until the 1970s, Jeep axles featured closed front steering knuckles. Fully enclosed front axle shaft joints (Rzeppa, Bendix and Spicer types) receive grease from the sealed knuckle cavity. Later, open knuckle axle joints are Spicer-type U-joints, most often permanently sealed with grease. (Permanently sealed joints are easy to distinguish. They have no grease fitting.)

> *CAUTION —*
> *If axle shaft joint is of permanently sealed type, always replace with a similar design. U-joints drilled for grease fittings are not strong enough for this application.*

Vacuum disconnect axles have no need for wheel hubs. A vacuum operated "shift motor" couples and uncouples a section of one front axle shaft. This prevents front wheel rotation from turning the propeller shaft to the transfer case. The differential gears still rotate, however, and at considerable speed. The result is a reduction of some drag, although the earlier full-floating front axles with free wheeling hubs provide the only means for completely eliminating front axle and driveline friction or wear.

Axle Troubleshooting

Before suspecting trouble with your Jeep's axles, check the fluid levels and also the type of gear lubricant required. On limited slip differentials, special lubes prevent multi-plate clutches from sticking together. If you introduce a non-specified oil to these axles, symptoms of differential trouble can result.

Try to isolate the noise. Tire sounds, front or rear wheel bearing noises, engine and transmission troubles and even the type of road surface can confuse the situation. Especially with large tires, a Jeep often develops alleged axle noises that have nothing to do with the differential or any other axle component. Check each of these other possibilities before condemning your axles.

A clicking or patterned ratcheting noise at the rear wheels is a possible wheel bearing problem. By supporting the rear axle safely on jack stands, you can rotate each wheel by hand and feel for bearing roughness. (See other chapters of the book for front wheel bearing inspection and service.) If you detect an actual wheel bearing problem, consult your Jeep or professional level service manual for axle shaft removal and wheel bearing service.

Differential side gear and small pinion (spider) gear noises are most likely heard when the vehicle turns. If your Jeep has a conventional or limited slip rear axle that makes noises as the truck negotiates a corner, suspect differential trouble. Such front axle noises, especially with the hubs engaged and the transfer case in 4WD, also suggest differential trouble, although a defective axle shaft joint can create similar sounds.

A continuous grating noise that varies with vehicle speed suggests pinion bearing failure. A Jeep that runs in deep water without immediately changing gear lubricant is vulnerable to failure of the ring gear, pinion gear and bearings.

Ring and pinion noise is distinguishable under various driving conditions: coast, drive or float. Deceleration creates coast noises. Drive noises are detectable as you accelerate the Jeep. Float noise occurs under light throttle situations and easy loads that keep the ring and pinion gears spinning but with the least amount of gear tooth contact pressure.

When your Jeep's axle gear lubricant smells badly burned, remove the inspection cover and examine the gear teeth and bearings. Blue discoloration usually indicates extreme heat, fatigue and poor lubrication. If lubricant is very low for any length of time, Jeep axles are subject to severe parts damage. Always watch for seal leaks or other symptoms of fluid loss. Proper fluid levels are crucial to axle survival.

Seal Leaks

Axle seal failure is a primary cause of fluid loss on Jeep trucks. Look closely for fluid loss at the axles whenever you service your Jeep, and watch for oil drips when you park your truck. The locations for axle seal leaks

Fig. 11-24. *A pinion seal leak is easy to spot. Loss of lubrication can lead to expensive parts damage.*

are easy to monitor, beginning with the pinion shaft seal, the ventilation valve (if so equipped) and the axle shaft seals.

The pinion shaft seal is easiest to locate. Follow the driveshaft to the U-joint flange, then note the point at which the pinion shaft enters the axle housing. The seal that surrounds the shaft at the entrance to the axle housing is the pinion shaft seal.

Axle shaft seal leaks appear as oil dripping from the bottom of the rear brake backing plates or at the steering knuckle on an open-knuckle front end. Spindle bushing wear on closed-knuckle front ends can dilute wheel bearing lubricant. (See brake section for more details on parts damage from leaking axle seals.)

Whenever a seal leak occurs, check for proper lubricant levels. Overfilled steering knuckles or differentials will cause leaks and can even dislodge a seal by hydraulic pressure. A common leak on all closed-knuckle front ends is the large inner oil seal. Wear at this seal will leak grease from the knuckle cavity. Fortunately, with careful steps, you can replace the inner knuckle seal without removing the entire steering knuckle.

Seal Installation Tips

Jeep axle seals are difficult to replace. You'll want to do the job right the first time. Axle seal replacement requires a holding tool to keep the U-joint flange from rotating while you loosen its nut. (Mechanics usually use an air impact gun when performing this work.)

Before installing the seal, clean the housing bore thoroughly. Be certain to apply a thin film of gasket sealant to the outer edge of the seal. Coat the inner lip of the seal with light grease. (Early Jeep leather seals require soaking the seal in oil before installation. Neoprene replacement seals are now available.)

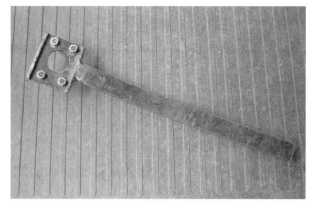

Fig. 11-25. *This tool, fabricated over twenty-five years ago with simple materials, holds the U-joint flange. Pinion shaft nut torque is very high, and heavy leverage is necessary. Today, most mechanics simply use a precise air impact gun to perform this kind of job.*

Fig. 11-26. *An early Jeep trait: the spindle's six bolts have ripped cleanly from the threaded holes in the steering knuckle casting. This generally results from bolts loosening and pounding out the threads. Bolts pull loose, often taking hunks of thread material and casting with them.*

Tap the seal gently and evenly "in cross." I like to use a rubber or plastic sand head hammer to avoid damaging or distorting the steel portion of the seal. Although I've always had access to special seal drivers, I feel that carefully placed hammer taps can produce the same results or better. You can maintain the feel for what you're doing with a soft headed hammer and a light touch.

Coat the backside of the flange washer with a thin film of gasket sealant, and install a new self-locking nut if required. Torque the nut to factory specification.

Other seals, including those for the front and rear axles, are more difficult to access. Many Jeeps have rear brake drums that press onto the axle shaft. You will need a special puller to remove the drum. If your Jeep's front or rear axle seals leak, consult a factory or professional service manual before tackling the job.

> NOTE—
> On 1976–85 Jeep CJs with the Model 20 AMC rear axle, do not remove wheel hubs when performing brake work. The drums can be separated from the wheel hub flanges.

Front Axle and Knuckle Seals

You can replace the closed-knuckle inner seal by carefully cutting the felt seal on a diagonal (see a factory-level manual for details) and sliding the seal, wiper and retainer over the axle housing tube. With careful seal placement and use of sealant, you can achieve results equal to completely removing the steering knuckle.

The sealing gaskets at the front spindles are another area of concern. Early Jeep spindles have a nasty habit of loosening on the steering knuckle and pounding the gasket to pieces. Once loose, a very unsafe con-

dition exists, with the risk of shearing the bolts or threads that attach the spindle to the knuckle casting.

Some remedies for this chronic spindle bolt problem include: 1) drilling and wire tying the bolt heads to aircraft standards, 2) replacing the bolts with Grade 8 studs secured with thread locking compound, then using aircraft Grade 8 self-locking nuts to secure the spindle, or 3) installing special aftermarket "buttonhead" studs that have either a full-length thread or serrated shoulder and compact, rounded head—The high tensile strength buttonhead studs pass from inside the knuckle through the thread holes and face outward to receive the spindle. The spindle attaches with self-locking aircraft grade nuts.

> NOTE—
> If threads in the knuckle casting have become slightly damaged (not unusual), the buttonhead stud approach can salvage a knuckle casting. Make certain these studs seat securely and have enough support to remain in place and properly aligned. Use Loctite 271 or equivalent where studs pass through casting.

4. Locking Hubs

Free wheeling hubs stretch drivetrain life by thousands of miles. Manual or automatic locking hubs eliminate front axle shaft rotation during two-wheel drive operation. Hubs save wear on front axle joints, seals, the differential assembly, and front driveshaft components. Drag, especially in cold weather, translates to added engine and geartrain wear, increased clutch effort, and loss of fuel economy.

On most Jeep full-floating front axles, you can install retrofit manual or automatic locking hubs. (An exception is a Jeep truck equipped with the stock Warner Quadra-Trac system.) A full-floating axle's front spindle and hub design allows use of free-wheeling hubs.

Full-floating wheel hubs, supported by inner and outer wheel bearings, ride on the spindle. The axle shaft fits through the hollow recess of this spindle, and the spindle attaches to the steering knuckle. At the splined outer end of the axle shaft, a drive flange attaches to the wheel hub casting, much like the systems found on 3/4-ton and larger truck rear axles. Here, the axle shaft delivers its rotational force to the wheel hub, drum/rotor, wheel and tire.

> NOTE —
> Compact XJs, ZJs, WJs and all Wranglers
> do not have full-floating front wheel hubs.
> You cannot install free-wheeling hubs on
> these stock front axles. (See performance
> chapter for upgrades and hub conversions.)

Earlier Jeep locking hub systems were manual. Highly dependable, manual hubs remain a popular retrofit item to this day. Although locking front hub mechanisms differ between manufacturers, each design disengages the wheel hub flange from the axle shaft. Free-wheeling hubs allow the wheel hub, brake drum/rotor, wheel and tire to rotate freely as an assembly—in a fashion similar to a 2WD wheel hub.

Automatic locking hubs were part of the move away from troublesome '70s full-time four-wheel

Fig. 11-28. *This very early Warn system was clearly manual. The "hub caps" bolted in place of the Jeep factory drive flanges and permitted the wheel hubs to rotate without turning the axle shafts.*

drive systems. (Those full-time systems increased maintenance costs, taxed fuel economy and did not use free-wheeling hubs.) Many Jeep owners had liked the convenience of hubless driving. Bridging the gap, automatic hubs provide easier operation for part-time four-wheel drive systems.

Maintaining Your Locking Hubs

Many four-wheelers struggle with their front locking hubs. Some go to extremes, fabricating special "tools" for muscling a stubborn manual hub knob. Whenever you need more than light hand force to rotate a free-wheeling hub, there's something wrong with the hub mechanism or its installation.

A series of parts make up the locking hub. Laid out, these pieces can include gears, springs, locking clips or drive plates. Manual hubs utilize sleeve bushings, needle bearings, ball or roller bearings. Periodic bench stripping and service of the front hubs will assure free movement and proper lubrication of all parts.

Free-wheeling hub bearings and bushings are not intended to tolerate the rotational loads of parts running at speed. If pressed into such service, as when one hub is accidently left in LOCK while the other is on FREE, a free-wheeling hub assembly will quickly fail. Periodic disassembly and cleaning of the hubs will help reduce risk of dragging and binding.

Servicing hubs is relatively simple and should accompany every front wheel bearing re-pack. Repeated or prolonged submersion of your Jeep 4x4 in deep, fast-running water requires immediate hub disassembly and inspection for water damage. The sealing areas of hubs deteriorate over time, another reason for periodic inspection and service.

Fig. 11-27. *Aftermarket free-wheeling hubs have existed for nearly as long as the civilian Jeep. Hubs come in many shapes and sizes to fit various axle splines and wheel hub flanges.*

Service Work

Servicing front wheel locking hubs is well within a competent home mechanic's ability. Hub disassembly requires basic handtools, including a torque wrench and snap ring pliers. As always, seek out a service guidebook before attempting hub work. A detailed schematic of the hubs will eliminate guesswork as you inventory parts. Service kits contain details for disassembly and assembly work.

Servicing hubs requires cleanliness and order. Remove parts carefully, noting their relationship to each other. Lay pieces on clean newspaper or shop towels. Clean pieces carefully in solvent. (Avoid harsh cleaners that affect plastic parts.) Clean grease will not adhere properly to solvent coated parts. Rinse away solvent with a dish detergent solution and clean water rinse, then air dry (preferably with compressed air) before greasing parts.

> *WARNING—*
> *Never spin bearings with compressed air. High speed, friction and stress could score the bearings or cause the assembly to explode.*

Use a grease recommended for your hubs. If wheel bearing type is acceptable, use the same grease that you use for your front wheel bearings. This often falls into the category of high temp wheel bearing grease, recommended for disc brake equipped applications. Such greases have excellent heat resistance yet afford the viscosity needed for free hub movement on those -40 F degree mornings in North Dakota. One way to avoid mixing unknown grease types is by performing wheel bearing service at the same time.

> *NOTE —*
> Be sure to use correct grease(s) on a hub mechanism. Automatic locking hubs require special grease types, or they will not function properly. Manual hubs accept a broader range of lube types.

Service kits are inexpensive and provide cheap insurance against hub sealing problems. The O-ring or paper gasket that looks marginal is a risk. For a few dollars, new seals and other hardware will keep water out of your hubs and wheel bearings.

Properly and sparingly applied, a silicone compound like Permatex Ultra-Blue or Black can provide additional protection in areas that benefit from sealant. As with any mechanism, inspect parts carefully. Look for bushing wear, galling, scoring and binding of parts. Include emery cloth in your service tools for light touchup of rough or scratched pieces. (Clean thoroughly after sanding, and dry before re-packing.)

Fig. 11-29. *First step in overhaul of Warn hub is removal of free-wheeling hub unit from the wheel hub flange.*

Fig. 11-30. *Disassembly begins with clutch mechanism flange screws.*

Fig. 11-31. *Drive hub rides in needle bearings on this early Warn hub design. Watch out for falling needle bearings!*

Fig. 11-34. *Now remove the spring clutch mechanism.*

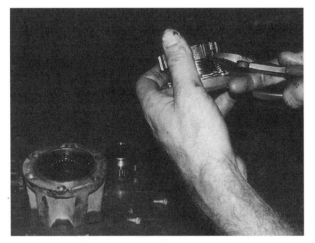

Fig. 11-32. *Spring roll pin locks clutch unit to flange...*

Fig. 11-35. *Snap ring holds hub knob to flange.*

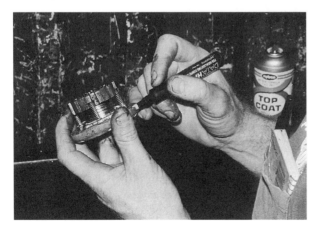

Fig. 11-33. *Mark or scribe location of plate to flange.*

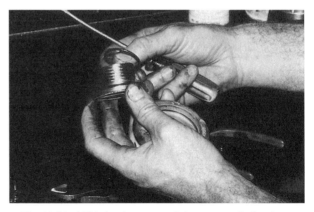

Fig. 11-36. *With knob removed, important O-ring is accessible. Here's where water often seeps into hub units.*

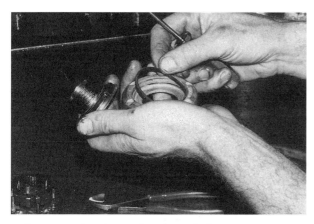

Fig. 11-37. *Another critical O-ring is found here.*

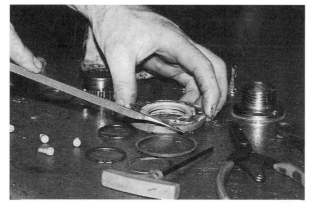

Fig. 11-38. *Scrape gasket material from surfaces before thoroughly cleaning parts.*

Fig. 11-39. *After a washing cabinet dip, thorough rinse and air blow drying, these clean pieces can go back together.*

Fig. 11-40. *Pack cavity of needle bearing bore with a compatible wheel bearing grease. Needles are carefully replaced. Last bearing holds set together by "keystone effect."*

Fig. 11-41. *Drive hub, with proper spacer/thrust washers in place, goes easily into bearing bore.*

Fig. 11-42. *Snap ring secures drive hub.*

Fig. 11-43. *Install new O-rings, greased lightly, to base of brass knob assembly and to cover.*

Fig. 11-44. *Install hub knob and place in FREE position.*

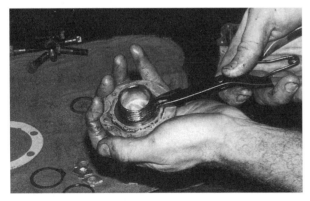

Fig. 11-45. *New snap ring, provided in Warn service kit, fits at base of knob.*

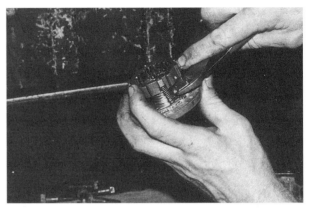

Fig. 11-46. *With clutch spring mechanism screwed into place, re-install spring roll pin.*

Fig. 11-47. *Check clutch movement by rotating hub knob to LOCK, then slide clutch mechanism into the clean, lightly greased hub body bore. Careful fitup, torquing bolts, and bending lock tabs will help assure proper operation.*

nal splines, check for debris, rough edges or galling. Clean, check and lightly grease the axle shaft splines. Be sure the locking hubs fit up smoothly.

High-grade fasteners, specified for this installation, are necessary. The mounting bolts are subject to tremendous stress, so tighten them in sequence. Recheck final torque before securing new lock tabs. Some bolt applications require wire tying, Loctite or special lock tabs/washers.

> **NOTE ——**
> The hub mounting bolts on late CJ Jeep models with five-bolt flange free-wheeling hubs are notorious for loosening and/or shearing. One remedy is the installation of Grade 8 studs set with thread locking compound, using aircraft grade self-locking nuts. This has prevented many hub and casting failures.

Once clean, the hubs re-assemble easily on the workbench. After putting each unit back together, make certain that the finger control works freely and smoothly. Hubs that test friction-free on the bench should provide easy operation on the vehicle.

Before installing the hubs, carefully inspect the wheel hub mounting flange. On hub flanges with inter-

Fig. 11-48. *For ease of maintenance, most hub manufacturers offer service kits for their hubs. Warn's kits consist of paper gaskets, snap rings, O-rings, new Allen head screws, and bolt lock tabs when required.*

Lastly, especially if your Jeep truck was purchased used, be certain that all parts are present. Often, after several services, small pieces get lost. Find a blowup schematic in a service guide, parts catalog or manufacturer's literature. Compare your pieces with those required, and restore the hubs accordingly.

Retrofitting New Hubs

Eventually, your Jeep's free-wheeling hubs will wear out. The effects of weather, age and abuse take their toll. Later-model automatic locking hubs may simply fail to meet your requirements. Fortunately, you can retrofit a set of quality manual hubs. I always install manual hubs for severe duty four-wheeling or regular off-pavement use.

A variety of hubs are available through aftermarket suppliers. When selecting new hubs, consider your driving habits and intended use of the Jeep. Although price often influences our decisions, weigh cost against the prospect of walking home from a remote mountain range or the desert.

Since free-wheeling hubs require the same stamina as the differential, transfer case or transmission, consider upgrading your equipment. The controversy around automatic locking hubs continues. I have only one view on the subject: Unless you need automatic hubs to offset a physical challenge or other medical problem, forget them!

Whenever possible, I request new test vehicles with manual hubs or a delete-automatic-hubs option. I nearly always retrofit manual hubs to a used 4x4 purchased with automatic hubs. Stepping from the truck to twist manual hubs into LOCK is worth it. At least I'm certain the hubs have engaged. Uphill or down, I know that positive engine power and compression braking will assure safe four-wheeling.

Hubs are your lifeline in rough terrain and foul weather driving. When working properly, your Jeep's locking hubs provide economy and a margin of security. Appreciate their contribution and treat them with respect.

Chapter 12

Suspension and Steering

Several years ago, I interviewed Jim Sickles at Downey Off-Road. When my questions shifted to worn suspension parts, Jim commented, "Springs are a perishable commodity." No vehicle proves this point better than a Jeep 4x4!

Fatigue, owner upgrades and modifications limit the life-span of springs, shock absorbers, shackles, bushings and steering linkage. Changes in tire diameter or the need to carry an extra load often call for more body/chassis clearance and a suspension lift kit.

1. Springs

Three criteria govern your Jeep's spring height and rates: 1) the necessary eye-to-eye length of the spring, 2) arch of the spring, and 3) plate thickness for each spring leaf. Coil springs (found on the XJ Cherokee/Comanche, ZJ/WJ Grand Cherokees, and the TJ Wrangler) have specific wire diameters and free length/height. Leaf spring arch or coil spring length determines your truck's ride height, while leaf spring plate thickness or coil spring wire diameter determines load capacity and spring rate.

For hard off-pavement use, special spring heights and rates offer advantages. Although inexpensive

Fig. 12-1. *Rear leaf springs are common on Jeep trucks. Note support for working on the truck, a set of 5-ton (per stand) rated jackstands. Don't compromise here. Your life and limbs are at stake.*

modifications meet some tire clearance and ride height needs, the right springs offer a much better solution. A properly arched lift spring eliminates the need for lengthened shackles. (Long shackles are less costly but often compromise OEM engineering.) Carefully designed springs can also raise chassis/body height without axle caster changes or pinion and driveshaft angle problems.

Aftermarket springs can meet most OE engineering requirements for your Jeep and still provide a safe, moderate amount of lift. A traditional spring/blacksmith shop will fabricate stock-type replacement springs for improved ride quality and longer service life.

Installing Jeep Leaf Springs

Jeep leaf spring replacement is relatively simple. Unlike torsion bar and coil spring installations, there is no threat of a loaded spring flailing out of its socket like a lethal missile. If you keep the axles safely away from the springs until all parts are attached, there's an even lesser risk of injury. Although awkward, the Jeep truck leaf spring replacement is reasonably easy.

When aligning the parts, mount the spring's single frame eye first, then secure the shackle assembly. On models with the axle above the spring, place a jack somewhat near the spring center to bend out a slight amount of arch. Compress the spring just enough for the axle's spring pad to drop into place at the spring center bolt.

> NOTE—
> Especially with new lift springs, spring compression is necessary to achieve spring conformation at the original axle center point. Use a safe garage floor jack for this purpose.

Attach the U-bolts carefully, tightening U-bolt nuts uniformly. Watch the exposed thread lengths to determine equal tightening. Torque nuts in sequence to specifications. (See your Jeep service manual.) Gradually tighten each nut until you have reached full torque value and the bolt threads extend past the nuts evenly. Properly installed springs often live for 60–100,000 miles or more, depending upon how and where you drive your Jeep.

> NOTE—
> After driving a few miles, or whenever your Jeep has faced a twisty challenge, re-torque these nuts.

Shackle and Bushing Service

Jeep leaf springs move in a shackle. Early models use U-shaped supports that pivot in a replaceable threaded bushing. Later Jeep models use low-maintenance rubber bushings. Eventually, either type of shackle bushing will wear out.

Always replace the U-shackles and their threaded, hex-head bushings as sets. Even with proper lubrication, the bushings and load-bearing threads wear. CJ models built before early 1957 use both right- and left-hand threaded bushings.

> NOTE—
> Always check the frame and spring eye bushings for right or left thread types. Avoid cross-threading the hex-headed bushings.

When assembling U-shackles, align the hex-bushings about halfway through the frame hanger and spring. Install the grease retainers and seals on the shackle, and carefully start the bushing threads. Screw the upper and lower bushings on evenly to help the upper hex-head bushing seat firmly against the frame. The lower spring eye bushing must have slight (1/32") clearance between the spring eye and the hex head. Make certain that the shackle moves freely. Spring breakage can result if bushings bind.

Jeep spring bushings and frame hanger designs vary. Each type requires specific torque settings for both the pivot bolts and shackle nuts. Refer to your Jeep truck manual for further details on spring assembly methods and torque settings.

Frame Damage

Off-pavement pounding in the rocks can damage your Jeep frame. The early pickups and station wagons, CJs, J-trucks, full-size Wagoneer, full-size Cherokee and Wrangler models feature a "driveable chassis" or ladder frame. Subject to severe twisting and overload, frame damage is possible.

Compact Cherokee/Comanche and Grand Cherokee models have a heavy gauge sheet metal body pan with sub-frame assemblies attached front and rear.

These vehicles are vulnerable to both undercarriage sheet metal damage and distortion.

During routine service, inspect your Jeep's frame. Look closely for tears, cracks, wrinkles, loose rivets or damaged fasteners. Inspect axle housing mounts and spring hangers. All pivot bolts and other friction points require a close look. Make certain crossmembers are intact. Consider the skid plates and transmission crossmember an integral part of the frame. Structural support and frame stiffness depend on the crossmembers.

A common area of frame fatigue on '75 and earlier CJ models, especially trucks with heavy off-pavement histories, is just behind the front spring anchor points. The anchor (rear) end of the springs receives a great deal of punishment, as trail obstacles want to drive the front axle from beneath the Jeep. The frame, sadly, receives the brunt of the punishment and often cracks.

Likewise, spring shackles on later CJs tend to break, along with the front spring shackle upper frame brackets. The brackets that hold the upper end of the shackles fit flush against the frame. A hole in the bracket, designed to clear factory frame rivets, creates a weak zone. When a 1976–86 Jeep CJ twists in the off-pavement environment, the push and pull at the front shackle brackets can break them loose from the frame. (See Chapter 19 for suspension upgrades.)

> WARNING—
> Fatigued or stress damaged spring shackles, frame brackets, spring hangers and shock absorber brackets pose a safety hazard. Inspect your Jeep frame, spring and shock supports regularly.

Fig. 12-2. Later CJ spring shackles and shackle frame supports fail under severe service. OE bolt-on frame bracket breaks at this hole designed to clear frame rivets. Inspect these brackets frequently, especially after hard off-pavement operation. Detached bracket reveals emergency weld repair made on the trail.

2. Shock Absorbers

Single shocks, dual shocks, gas shocks and more...The market is rife with shock absorbers. What does your Jeep need? Which shock works best? Is there a formula for choosing the right shock absorbers? You bet!

Shock absorbers play a large role in your Jeep's handling, ride, braking and safety. As shocks wear and fatigue, they lose their effectiveness. On most off-highway vehicles, the original shock absorber set fails before any other chassis item. Shocks deteriorate rapidly under excess heat, friction and overwork. On some Jeep 4x4s, the shock absorbers fail fast. Why? Shocks deteriorate from high heat, excess friction and overloading.

Most Jeep shock absorbers look similar, and despite different designs, they each meet the same goals: Damping the oscillating motion of the vehicle's springs, controlling frame and body bounce, limiting the effects of uneven loads placed on each wheel, and attempting to keep the wheels safely on the ground when the suspension moves violently.

Off-pavement, your Jeep's suspension travels constantly, often to full extension with equally pounding compression. Damping such forces, the shock absorbers pay severely, frequently succumbing to leaks or ineffective performance. Driver discomfort and unnecessary squeaks and rattles quickly follow.

Shock Absorber Design

Many original equipment shocks concentrate on highway ride and driver comfort. The two common shock absorber types, single-tube and twin-tube, offer entirely different operating characteristics, yet most truck builders have traditionally installed hydraulic single-tube shocks, shying from the more expensive and rugged twin-tube, gas-cellular and gas-charged shocks.

> NOTE—
> Jeep original equipment shocks concentrate on highway ride and driver comfort. For overall good performance, mid-'80s and newer Jeep models, including the XJ Cherokee, ZJ/WJ and Wranglers, have offered gas-charged shocks.

Single tube oil-type shock absorbers consist of a machined steel cylinder and a rod/piston assembly. The body of the shock absorber holds oil to resist the force of the moving piston. Precise valving in the piston controls the flow of oil, which in turn regulates the movement of the shock absorber piston and rod.

If resistance against the piston is too great, the suspension cannot move freely. Too little damping, and

the road forces cause serious handling and ride problems. Therefore, the most critical ability of a shock absorber is to sense road forces and continually work to control them. The heat generated during rapid movement of the piston compounds that job, weakening the damping ability of both the hydraulic oil and gas. Fluid fade results from high piston velocities.

When your Jeep truck tackles a washboard road, the valving within the shock absorbers is put to the test. A quality shock absorber may boast as many as ten stages within its valving mechanism, each stage addressing a specific fluid velocity and load.

Better: Twin-tube and Gas Shock Absorbers

Twin-tube shock absorbers provide the added benefit of a second valving and reservoir system. Beyond the valves in the piston head, these shocks provide a bottom check valve, permanently attached to a machined inner cylinder. Although the valving in the piston head allows fluid to bypass under the compression and rebound of the shock absorber, the second fixed valve enhances damping sensitivity. This valve enables fluid or gas pressure in the reservoir (located between the inside cylinder tube and outer shell of the shock absorber body) to act as an added damping force.

Foaming (aeration) of fluid prevents proper shock absorber action. Foaming creates gaps in damping, which cause erratic and ineffective shock behavior. Many measures have been taken to offset this problem. The best current solution is the use of a gas like nitrogen. Compressed gas or a gas cell pressurizes the fluid and eliminates many troubles associated with hydraulic oils—including aeration, fade and heat buildup.

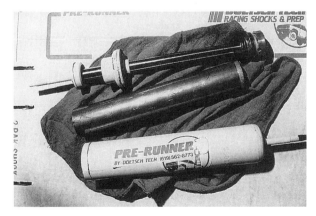

Fig. 12-3. *Laid out, twin tube shock absorber components consist of outer tube, inner tube and cylinder, and the rod and valve assembly. Fluid fills the reservoir of sealed Doetsch Tech unit.*

Gas-operated shocks promise more consistent, thorough damping rates. When high performance and constant pounding demand real shock action, gas shocks perform. Non-gas shocks, vulnerable to oil thinning, operate best under moderate piston velocities. By contrast, nitrogen gas shocks stay cooler and foam-free, allowing valves and fluid to continue working, even at high piston velocities.

Popular nitrogen gas shocks come in low- and high-pressure designs. Since the rod and piston of a gas-charged shock takes real punishment, most users prefer low-pressure types. Although racing or high performance driving may demand high-pressure (200 psi or greater) nitrogen gas damping, many quality shocks fit within the low pressure category.

NOTE —
Jeep has offered Bilstein's low pressure gas shocks as OEM equipment and options. These shocks offer high resistance to heat and prove better suited for heavy duty, multi-purpose driving.

Due largely to their off-pavement superiority, gas-charged and gas-cellular shocks have become popular aftermarket items. Hours of jarring through desert washes or pounding along rutted washboard roads will convince most non-gas shock users to make the switch.

NOTE —
Note: "Gas-cellular" and "gas-charged" shocks are not the same. A popular gas-cellular shock has a gas-filled cell inside the shock's fluid reservoir. This cell expands with heat, compressing oil to help prevent foaming and aeration. By contrast, gas-charged shocks have pressurized gas (typically nitrogen) constantly applying force against the fluid. While both shock types resist aeration, foaming and fade, the true gas-charged shock (low- or high-pressure variety) exerts a prescribed pressure on the piston and pushrod. Under certain driving conditions, this can help keep a wheel/tire on the ground. For washboard or bouncy terrain at speed, many users and racers prefer the more costly gas-charged shocks.

Choosing the Right Features

When buying replacement shock absorbers for your Jeep, consider a twin-tube shock, preferably a gas-cellular type, or a bonafide gas-charged design. Piston head size, rod diameter, seal types and valving design determine the strength, reliability and performance of a shock absorber.

WARNING —
Even low-pressure gas charged shock absorbers can place stress on shock absorber brackets. If you use a gas-charged shock, select a pressure that will not break a bracket or cause a safety hazard. (See OEM Jeep Bilstein types for factory offerings and pressure ratings.) Early Jeep models with washer and cotter pin shock fasteners are not candidates for gas pressurized shock absorbers. If the stamina of shock bracketry is questionable, use an oil-type twin-tube or twin-tube gas-cellular shock absorber.

Most OEM telescoping shocks offer meager 1" to 1-1/8" piston diameters. Replacement shocks should have pistons of 1-5/16" or larger size. Popular for many years, the 1-3/8" piston head has satisfied all but the most brutal off-pavement Jeep maulers and heavyweight haulers.

Typical higher performance shocks are Rancho's RS7000 twin-tube types with a 1-5/8" piston diameter. Adjustable ride setting RS7000 shocks have ten-stage, velocity sensitive valving and a chrome-hardened 17.3 millimeter pushrod. For practical all-around use, the popular twin-tube RS5000 or tri-tube/mono flow RS9000 (five-position adjustable valving) units offer quality service. Each of these three shock types are gas-cellular designs.

The Perennial Question: My Choice of Shocks

For a hefty full-size truck chassis, the RS7000 works well. However, lighter weight vehicles do not generally require such damping. While there are many quality shocks in the marketplace, I prefer Rancho's RS9000 over other multi-purpose shocks. Using these shocks with Rancho's RC9700 remote cab control system for added versatility, I have tested one set of shocks for seventy-plus thousand miles on a 3/4-ton 4x4 chassis with a curb weight of 5,800 pounds.

The RS9000 shocks have held up without a glitch and offer a setting range that spans five shock damping profiles. (Position #3 of the five settings is approximately an RS5000.) These shocks accommodate widely varied driving conditions and tire types, and settings have been so reliable that tire tests with this vehicle have used the RS9000 settings as a criteria for judging a tire's ride quality and relative stiffness. (See performance suspension chapter for further details.)

There are many shock absorbers that satisfy consumers. I would emphasize, too, the value of high-pressure gas type shocks if Jeep recommends such a design for your vehicle. If you find OEM shocks satisfactory and your Jeep chassis is essentially stock, consider staying with OEM or equivalent shock absorbers.

Fig. 12-4. *Piston head and cylinder have valves and precisely metered orifices. Doetsch Tech's Pre-Runner shocks boast "progressive valving."*

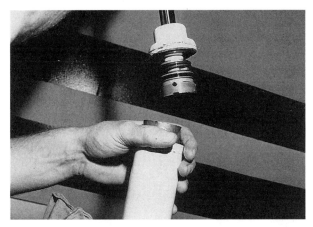

Fig. 12-5. *O-ring sealing on these valves is a sign of better quality.*

Fig. 12-6. *Rancho's RS5000 shock absorbers and suspension packages are popular. Gas cellular type, these shocks are of twin tube construction and offer ten-stage, velocity sensitive valving. RS5000s have satisfied Jeep owners for many years*

Sealing ability contributes to the life expectancy of shock absorbers. Pistons should be O-ring sealed, and the cylinder requires a tough, double wall. Oversize fluid reservoirs provide better cooling and more resistance to fading. Refinement of the valve mechanism, that ability to "sense" terrain and load demands, will determine a shock absorber's worth. Proper shock damping is a primary element of your truck's suspension system.

Lastly, shock mounting grommets and eyes must hold up to road demands and off-pavement pounding. A shock absorber is useless when detached or loose, while a weak set of eye grommets allows wasted movement and undamped travel.

3. Jeep Steering and Front End

Off-highway driving punishes your Jeep's steering and suspension components. The live front axle design, especially with full-time 4x4, adds extra wear to the steering knuckle ball joints (later models) or kingpin bearings (earlier models). Replacing a steering knuckle ball joint is a major job, requiring removal of the wheel hub assembly, spindle, axle shaft and steering knuckle. (For repairs on your Jeep front axle unit, including axle shaft removal, refer to your factory-level service manual.)

Rebuilding a Battered Steering Knuckle

Greg Williams is a veteran race truck suspension mechanic with a wealth of front end and suspension experience. At his East County Alignment "day job," Greg rebuilds Jeep and other popular 4x4 steering and suspension systems regularly. As an enhancement for this chapter, Greg helps illustrate repairs on a Dana 44 open-knuckle front axle.

A U-joint had blown apart, and Greg's work includes straightening the frame before making axle repairs. After removing the automatic locking hub and the rotor/wheel hub and bearing assembly, Greg tackles the steering knuckle removal. These illustrations provide insight.

> *WARNING —*
> *Do not re-use any fasteners that are worn or deformed in normal use. Many fasteners are designed to be used only once and become unreliable and may fail when used a second time. This includes, but is not limited to, nuts, bolts, washers, self-locking nuts or bolts, circlips and cotter pins. For replacement always use new part(s) of OEM grade and quality.*

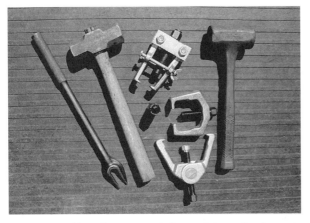

Fig. 12-7. *Use of proper tools is crucial to safe, dependable work. Steering knuckle replacement requires each of these tools. A spring scale is also necessary.*

Fig. 12-8. *This Dana 44 front axle provides an excellent example of U-joint failure. The steering knuckle now needs replacement as a result of the damage.*

Fig. 12-9. *Loosen tie-rod nut, leaving a few threads in place to prevent tie-rod from falling. As joint will not be re-used, insert a pickle fork between tie-rod joint and steering arm to separate the ball stud from its tapered seat in the arm.*

Fig. 12-10. *Alternate method for loosening tie-rods is a pair of hefty hammers. Place one at the back of the steering arm's tie-rod seat and rap the other hammer on the front of the arm. A sharp rap will dislodge the tapered ball stud from its seat. Take care not to damage the steering arm or tie-rod threads.*

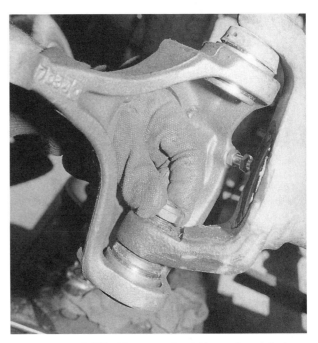

Fig. 12-11. *Self-locking nuts should be replaced during re-assembly. Nuts that hold spindle to knuckle and lower ball joint nuts are self-locking type and should be replaced with new self-locking nuts during assembly.*

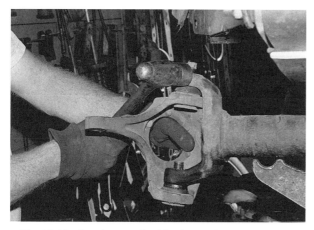

Fig. 12-12. *Another method for loosening ball stud is to simply strike the flange near ball stud. With a few solid blows directed at flange, ball joint drops. (Lower ball joint nut is loose, but still in place to prevent spindle from falling to the ground.) Follow by removing upper ball joint adjusting sleeve using a specially keyed socket.*

NOTE—

As an option to Greg's approach, Jeep suggests loosening the upper and lower ball joint nuts until the top of the nut is flush with the end of its stud. Rap the top of the upper stud/nut squarely with a lead, brass or sand head hammer to unseat both joints.

Fig. 12-13. *Installation of a new steering knuckle and adjuster sleeve is straightforward. Install adjuster sleeve loosely to allow tightening of lower ball joint.*

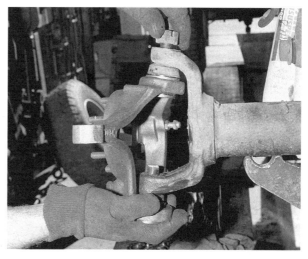

Fig. 12-14. *Finger tighten the castellated upper nut to hold the knuckle in position while torquing the lower self-locking nut to specification. Now set the adjuster sleeve for proper pre-load on the ball joints, followed by final tightening of the upper nut. The castellated nut requires a new cotter pin. Replace self-locking nuts with new and identical OEM grade hardware.*

Fig. 12-15. *Axle shaft seals must be placed in order on the new axle. Use original pieces as an example, or better yet, consult your Jeep service manual's illustrations. Before installing the spindle, repack the needle bearing with fresh grease.*

Fig. 12-16. *Once spindle is secure on the steering knuckle, proceed with wheel bearing service and assembly. (See next chapter and your Jeep factory manual.) With wheel hub/rotor assembly installed, mount disc brake caliper and tie-rod. Torque bolts and tie-rod nut to specification, then install new cotter pin at tie-rod nut.*

Knuckle Assembly and Tie-rod Footnotes

The tapered and threaded upper ball joint seat is a critical part, responsible for setting a slight load on the ball joints for steering control and proper wear. Upon re-assembly, adjust the new sleeve slightly loose until the lower ball joint is secure. While supporting the knuckle, torque the new self-locking nut to the lower ball joint stud.

Now, torque the adjusting sleeve at the upper ball joint to specification. (Find specs in your Jeep service manual.) Lastly, torque the castellated ball stud nut to spec, completing the job with the installation of a new cotter pin.

Re-assemble the remaining parts in the reverse order of disassembly. This is also a good time for a wheel bearing re-pack. Assemble wheel bearings carefully and adjust to spec. Include new inner wheel grease seals with the bearing pack. Follow the procedures outlined in your Jeep factory-level service guide.

Always use new self-locking nuts, new lock tabs or retainers and new cotter pins. Clean assembly methods during fit-up of parts, proper use of tools, and correct procedures for cleaning, re-packing and adjusting bearings will assure a safe job. If you intend to re-use parts, don't bang directly on the ball joints, tie-rod ends or their studs. Aim your sharp hammer blows carefully and protect the dust boots from damage.

> CAUTION —
> *When adjusting wheel alignment or installing new steering linkage pieces, always center the tie-rod ends. The ball studs and their sockets should line up evenly before you tighten the sleeve clamps. Make sure each tie-rod end has its full range of motion.*

Kingpin Bearings

Early closed-knuckle Jeep axles use kingpin bearings rather than ball joints. At the bearing caps, metal shims adjust and set the steering knuckle preload. When your Jeep has high mileage, the bearing clearance may increase enough to cause looseness at the knuckles. If inspection reveals kingpin bearing play, replace the bearings and their races.

> CAUTION —
> *Caution: When a large amount of kingpin play appears suddenly, suspect that kingpin bearing race or knuckle damage has occurred. Immediately repair the problem.*

Front End Maintenance

Whether your truck serves utility needs or playfully roams the backcountry, safe vehicle control depends on a reliable steering system. Jeep steering layouts and engineering differ widely in design and function.

Suspension type and steering linkage design dictate the location of the steering gear, while driving requirements determine the speed or ratio of the gear. Nimble handling results from correctly matching the suspension, steering linkage and steering gear.

Caution: In an attempt to "personalize" a Jeep's use, owners often alter the chassis engineering by installing "lift kits" and other suspension modifications that can compromise the original steering geometry.

Fig. 12-17. *Shims beneath the upper bearing caps on CJ3A and newer closed knuckles control the steering knuckle preload (models through CJ2A use shims at both upper and lower caps.) If these bearings need adjustment, use a spring scale and follow guidelines found in your factory level service manual.*

Bump steer and other anomalies result from the mis-alignment of suspension and steering linkage. See performance chapter for further details on safe approaches to lift kit installations.

Production 4x4s generally feature milder steering and suspension reaction. Issues of safety and liability enter the steering and suspension equation, and manufacturers de-tune suspension for a wider audience of drivers. (One exception is the later Jeep CJ and Wrangler owners' complaint about the factory's overly responsive power steering ratios.)

Types of Steering Gears

By the mid-'60s, the success of ball-and-nut steering gears, pioneered at General Motors, began spreading to other manufacturers. Jeep 4x4s had traditionally used the more primitive Ross cam-and-lever steering gears.

Within these early Jeep steering gearboxes, a machined, spiral groove runs along the steering or worm shaft. This gear meshes with a perpendicularly mounted cross-shaft and its cam. (The crude relationship of these parts create high friction and encourage wear.) The Pitman arm attaches at the outer end of the cross-shaft (sector). Clockwise and counterclockwise rotation of the cross-shaft translates as fore and aft swing of the Pitman arm.

> *CAUTION —*
> *A common cause of steering parts damage is from towing your Jeep. The Ross cam and lever type gear cannot tolerate this reverse flow of energy, where the road surface and turning of the front wheels cause the tapered pins on the cam to force rotation of the worm shaft.*

By contrast, Saginaw recirculating ball-and-nut steering gears drastically reduce friction. A square block (nut), machined internally to form the top half of a ball race, rides on ball bearings. These ball bearings run in the worm shaft's groove. The precisely machined groove serves as the inner half of the ball race.

Machined teeth on the outer surface of the nut engage teeth on the Pitman (cross/sector) shaft. As the worm shaft moves the nut, the nut's teeth rotate the sector shaft. Service adjustment, although rare with ball-and-nut gears, focuses solely on the mesh between the ball nut teeth and the Pitman shaft's teeth. (Worm shaft bearing preload is also adjustable.)

The largest difference between the older Ross cam-and-lever gears and the Saginaw recirculating ball-and-nut designs is the reduction of stress and friction. Gliding motion of the ball nut, up and down the worm shaft, takes place with ball bearing smoothness.

Fig. 12-18. *Saginaw ball-and-nut steering is both rugged and low-friction. A recirculating ball bearing design, these steering gears outlast all others when pounded in the off-pavement environment.*

Wrist wrenching steering gear kickback also proves far less likely with Saginaw's ball-and-nut design. In severe four-wheel drive use, these gears survive. Chrysler, Jeep, I-H and Ford have used GM's Saginaw steering gears.

The earlier Jeep cam and lever gears suffer from tooth chipping and, in the worst cases, seizure from jammed tooth debris. Friction and shock loads translate to wear that requires periodic adjustment. Unseen damage often follows hard use or abuse; experience suggests that any steering gearbox with excessive play demands disassembly for inspection and replacement of defective parts.

Power Steering Option

Power steering, once considered a horsepower-robbing accessory for lazy drivers, is now a 4x4 norm. Major design breakthroughs, especially the switch to integral power steering gears, popularized power steering by the late 1960s. GM's Saginaw gearworks again provided the superior unit, a rugged and comparatively compact gear assembly.

Before integral power steering gearboxes, Jeep power steering was a cumbersome affair. Linkage-type power assist, with a hydraulic power ram and an awkward network of hoses, first appeared on the early J-trucks and Wagoneers. The design centers around a conventional steering gearbox. A control valve, mounted at the drag link/Pitman arm socket, senses the driver's apply pressure. Hydraulic force directs ram pressure to the left or right. Linkage type power steering is an add-on device that simply reduces steering effort. Beyond attracting debris and becoming

Fig. 12-19. *Saginaw's ball and nut technology carries to the integral power steering gears. Every U.S. truck manufacturer has benefitted from using these rugged power steering gears.*

damaged from trail obstacles, linkage power steering offers some benefit.

By the early 1970s, the popularity of power steering encouraged AMC to offer Saginaw power units as an option on all models. The J-truck and Wagoneer were already several years into the use of Saginaw gears, and now CJ and Jeepster models acquired the system. AMC also adopted Saginaw manual steering gearboxes as standard equipment. The reliability found in Saginaw manual and power gears is legend.

Saginaw Steering Gears: Here to Stay

Saginaw integral power steering gears employ a rotary valve that opens ports and directs high pressure fluid to help during turns. The degree of assist corresponds to the driver's steering wheel effort.

Some Saginaw integral units offer a unique variable ratio, produced by using unequal length teeth on the Pitman shaft and rack piston. As you steer full left or right, the Pitman shaft speed increases, quickening the steering. Straight ahead, steering is very stable, with a slower ratio giving more road feel.

Jeep's Saginaw power steering gears are sensitive, precise mechanisms operating under close tolerances and very high fluid pressures. Service on a power gear is rare, but when necessary, requires intricate preloads and special assembly tools. Safety depends on proper fit-up of parts. Despite basic similarities between recirculating ball-and-nut manual gears and the Saginaw integral power units, you need much more skill to service a power gear.

Jeep owners often retrofit Saginaw integral power gears to their early 4x4 chassis. Even the Saginaw re-

circulating manual gearbox provides a drastic improvement for the early Jeep truck. Advance Adapters and others make conversion kits for retrofitting Saginaw gears to the earlier 4x4 chassis. (See performance chapters of the book.)

In the off-pavement environment, the few horsepower lost running a power steering pump are well spent. Quicker steering and ease of handling provide desirable gains.

Steering Linkage and Safe Four-wheeling

Although lock-to-lock ratios affect turning quickness, the true blueprint for off- and on-highway handling is the precise delivery of a driver's steering intentions. Front wheels must respond instantly to steering linkage movement.

Later model steering linkage includes a stabilizer shock designed to eliminate severe road kickback. Although an OE or aftermarket stabilizer is a definite asset, it's not a substitute for worn steering components. Before masking steering wander with a stabilizer, look for worn or dangerously loose linkage.

If your Jeep wanders, inspect the wheel bearings, knuckle joints and steering linkage for excess play. The Pitman arm, draglink, tie-rod ends, steering knuckle ball joints and the kingpin bearings are acute areas for wear.

Fig. 12-20. *The best procedure for checking steering linkage, ball joint and wheel bearing play is to shake the tire and wheel assembly. Jack and secure the front end safely off the floor. Grip each front tire at 6 and 12 o'clock to check ball joints and wheel bearings. Lower one tire to the floor, then shake the raised tire from a 3 and 9 o'clock position to note steering linkage wear. Have a partner watch for play at each tie-rod end and other joints while applying shaking, back-and-forth force.*

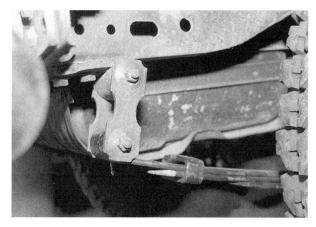

Fig. 12-21. *Excess spring movement contributes to wander. New springs require replacement of spring bushings. Here, a mild lift includes use of both OE-type hard rubber upper bushings and urethane lower bushings that came with aftermarket spring package.*

Fig. 12-22. *Sway bar bushings are also perishable. On a later Jeep, inspect these pieces for wear, looseness and deterioration. Too loose, the bar serves no purpose. Control in corners benefits greatly from the sway bar. Here is bushing wear at sway bar link.*

Begin your inspection with the wheel bearings and knuckle joints. Next, check the steering linkage. Worn tie-rod ends and other joints cause steering looseness, road wander, and the risk of losing steering control. On a 4x4, this is even more crucial, as off-road pounding stresses steering parts to their limits. Despite their exposure to the worst kinds of abuse, Jeep steering linkage components are much the same as those used on any other American truck.

Rear spring and axle position affects steering control. Check for damaged or misaligned springs, loose U-bolts, broken spring center bolts, and worn or defective spring bushings. Wander, "rear wheel steer" and "dog tracking" can result from frame or rear suspension misalignment and defective parts.

Worn steering linkage parts are generally not serviceable. When defective, you must replace them. (The early Jeep draglink is rebuildable.) Parts removal requires care and should follow professional service guidelines. You may need special tools, including pullers. Cleanliness is essential. Debris must not interfere with the tight fitup of tapered ball studs on tie-rod ends and ball joints. You must torque self-locking and castellated nuts to factory specs. (Install a new cotter pin on castellated nut.)

> *WARNING —*
> *Always replace bent steering linkage components. Straightening a bent tie-rod compromises safety. Stretched one way, then the other, tie-rod tubes and hard steel rods will weaken, and can snap under load.*

Periodic steering linkage maintenance is simple, consisting of wiping dirt from fittings then greasing

Fig. 12-23. *Inspect ball joint supported steering knuckles. Excess play here causes "kingpin" shimmy, characterized by a violent shake of the steering wheel and the front end. Kingpin bearing shims on early models and upper ball joint adjustment sleeves on open knuckle axles allow for preload settings and minor adjustment.*

joints with clean grease. Safety inspection, however, must include dust boots, joint wear, and rod straightness.

The Bellcrank

A common wear point on early Jeep models is the steering bellcrank. The bolt, spacer, bearing assemblies and seals are available as a service/rebuild kit. Bellcrank wear and looseness cause wander and poor front wheel alignment. Steering tie-rods drift up and down with the loose bellcrank, altering toe-set and preventing safe vehicle control.

Fig. 12-24. *Bellcrank bearings on pre-AMC CJ steering linkage are a wear item. Loss of precise steering, tire wear and wander are common signs of bellcrank problems.*

NOTE —
Always check the bellcrank for play when tire wear or steering looseness and wander occur. The bellcrank is a ready source of steering system trouble on an earlier Jeep.

Inspecting the Steering Gear

Restoration of steering linkage, knuckle joints and wheel bearing tolerances usually eliminates steering play. If looseness remains, make certain that the frame, spring bolts and spring attachments are intact and that hardware is secure. Tires and front end alignment are also a concern, as wander often occurs when tires have abnormal wear patterns.

NOTE —
Jeeps with solid front axles make wheel alignment simple. Unless you've bent the axle housing or frame, alignment should consist only of toe-set.

If steering play still exists, suspect the steering gearbox. For a quick check, carefully rotate the worm or steering shaft, and note the movement necessary to move the Pitman arm. On later trucks with exposed steering shafts, this operation is easy. Park your Jeep with the wheels straight. Turn the shaft at the input end of the steering gear while holding the Pitman arm with your other hand.

It's easy to detect Pitman movement by gently rotating the steering shaft. Be sensitive to the exact point at which the Pitman arm responds to the steering shaft movement. Rotate the shaft in the opposite direction to determine the degree of play. If wear or play is evident, either a steering gear adjustment or overhaul is necessary.

NOTE —
The steering gear must be in its center position when checking play. Steering gears have a "high point" in the exact center position that creates a very slight pre-load in the straight ahead driving position. This is the zone where play should be tested.

If you suspect a mis-centered steering gear, disconnect the linkage at the Pitman arm and very gently rotate the steering to one extreme. Rotate gently and count the exact turns back to the opposite extreme, then divide that number by two. Turn the wheel back this amount, and your steering gearbox will be on center. Check for play, over-center preload and the steering wheel/spoke location at this point.

WARNING —
• *Never turn the steering shaft hard against its extremes, as damage to ball races could occur.*

• *The steering wheel/spokes must be centered at the steering gear's center or high point. It is a dangerous mistake to re-position the steering wheel away from the steering gear's center in an effort to "straighten" the steering wheel.*

NOTE —
Nearly all Jeep steering linkage types have been designed to permit re-centering of the steering wheel (and steering gear) without re-positioning the steering wheel from the factory/centered position. The rare exception is a solid type front axle with a one-piece tie-rod and a non-adjustable draglink: Such models as the early Willys/Kaiser Pickup and Station Wagon fit this description.

Always begin a front end set-up with the steering gear's center point and steering wheel in true alignment. You can then use the adjustable draglink sleeve or tie-rod sleeves (depending upon model year and linkage type) to center the steering wheel—without changing the steering wheel's alignment with the steering gear's center point. By following this procedure, you know that the steering wheel and steering gear are on center when the front wheels are in the straight ahead mode.

Signs of Steering Gearbox Trouble

Sudden development of steering gear play or symptoms of wander, clicking noises or binding imply internal damage to the gear. Although quality Saginaw steering gears have great resiliency, hard-core four-wheeling can break even the best steering unit. I've seen California's Rubicon trail rip an OE power steering gear loose from the frame rail of an AMC era Jeep

CJ. The unsuspecting driver looked with disbelief at his immobilized truck.

> NOTE —
> Especially with power steering gears, driving technique is an important element in preventing such misfortunes. When bound up in the rocks, tires put up tremendous resistance. A Saginaw power steering gear has so much torque that an ignorant driver will wrestle with the steering wheel until the steering brackets snap loose or crack. This happens most frequently with 1972–86 CJs. Use discretion and size up the trail obstacles and resistance before applying full power steering force.

Unless high mileage dictates a minor adjustment to compensate for wear, any more than slight steering gear play suggests internal damage. Since the gear's inner workings are invisible without a teardown, you must make a judgement call. Never adjust a gear that has substantial play. Here, the removal and teardown of the gear is mandatory.

Before considering a steering gear teardown, review your factory-level service guidebook. Understand the complex tools, close tolerances, and sequence of disassembly and re-assembly. Power steering gears, in particular, require special care, cleanliness and safe work habits. Consider a new, factory rebuilt or undamaged (low mileage) recycled gear. Sometimes a rebuilt/exchange unit proves cost effective. Individual power steering pieces get very expensive.

> CAUTION —
> *The Saginaw power unit is a very intricate and sophisticated gear. As with any Jeep steering gear, the worm shaft bearing preload, cross shaft mesh and centering are crucial concerns.*

Fig. 12-25. *Coupler above the steering gear (arrow) is a wear point. An open column and coupler enable a quick check for steering gear damage and excess backlash.*

> NOTE —
> Early CJs or the M38/M38-A1 military Jeep with frame-mounted steering bellcranks suffer from constant front wheel toe-in and toe-out changes as the axle housing moves with the spring action. This creates tire wear and stress on the entire steering system. Road feel and steering control suffer as well. (See Chapter 19 for steering upgrades.)

Steering Linkage and Suspension Damage

Four-wheeling involves a variety of terrain—and obstacles. Rocks, stumps, slick mud, and streambeds each threaten the chassis and wheels. Damaged steering and jarred wheel alignment can ruin a brand new set of tires in just a few miles.

Exposed chassis and suspension parts are vulnerable. Especially sensitive are the leaf spring centering bolts and spring U-bolts, which shear or break and allow the axle to shift out of alignment.

Jeep models with link-and-coil spring suspension fare slightly better. Coils ride above the solid axle, and even though stressed to the limit, they seldom break, even under tight off-pavement twisting. Coil springs can dislodge, however, from serious chassis impact. Also, you must protect the suspension link arms and their frame brackets.

Steering linkage is a crucial area of concern. On Jeep straight axles, the linkage must move with the axle to maintain wheel alignment. Tie rods lie near the axle centerline, making tie rods the most vulnerable linkage component. The drivetrain layout, with the driveshaft angling from the transfer case to the backside of the front axle, dictates this tie rod position.

Tree stumps can easily damage the tie rod or steering stabilizer. If the stabilizer shock becomes bent, steering bind is possible. If obvious damage exists, remove the stabilizer shock. Other than some wander and possible "shakiness," the truck can get home without this unit. Once home, immediately replace the stabilizer with a new one.

3.1 Wheel Alignment

Subjected to off-pavement pounding, your Jeep demands regular steering system inspection and front wheel alignment. The longevity of expensive tires and your safety depend on proper front wheel tracking.

Front end misalignment hints of defective or worn steering and suspension parts. Consider wheel alignment an important part of your Jeep's preventive maintenance program. Watch for wear and damage.

Steering Geometry

For the Jeep truck, a periodic front end alignment includes checking/setting toe-in. Toe-in is the measurement between the centerlines of the tire tread at the tires' horizontal midline. Imagine lines scribed at the center of your front tire treads that run the full circumference of the tire. Each line references 360 degrees of tire tread surface and offers an easy measurement at the front and rear of the tire. The object when setting toe-in is to properly space these two points.

Vehicle manufacturers establish toe settings on the basis of rolling resistance and chassis geometry. Generally, bias ply tires require a slight (1/32" to 1/8") toe-in. Modern radial tires have less rolling resistance and need only minimal inward (front side) toe. They often call for a zero toe set, which means exactly parallel tires when in the straight ahead mode.

Normal steering and reasonable tire wear also depend upon correct caster and camber. Camber is simply the upright angle of the tire. The camber angle can change when an axle housing, steering spindle, or steering knuckle becomes bent. All three steering angles can suffer from a hard four-wheel drive bashing.

Some IFS and control arm suspensions allow caster and camber adjustments by tilting the top of the wheel inboard (negative camber) or outboard (positive camber) from a vertical axis. Solid axle housings common to Jeep trucks require the installation of eccentric offset bushings at the upper ball joints, installation of

Fig. 12-27. *Note use of a special tie-rod sleeve wrench. After rain, slush, mud, and water crossings, joints require fresh chassis grease to displace water and foreign matter.*

Fig. 12-28. *Caster and camber gauges clamp to the wheel. Once on a center line with the wheel spindle, levels indicate steering angles and wheel tilt.*

Fig. 12-26. *Toe-set is a regular part of Jeep 4x4 chassis service. Especially on vehicles subjected to off-pavement pounding, tire life depends on periodic checks of front wheel toe-set. Radial tires have different toe-set requirements than bias-ply types. Adjust toe-in when installing new tires. On solid front axles, toe-in is normally the only adjustment required. Caster or camber changes result from axle, chassis or suspension damage and normal spring and suspension wear. Link-and-coil suspension offers a provision for caster adjustment on XJ, ZJ/WJ and TJ Wrangler models.*

wedge-shaped shims at the spindle mount or, when safe, slight bending of the axle housing.

Caster is trickier to define. The caster angle is the tilt of an imaginary line drawn through the centerline/axis of the steering kingpins. On ball joint front ends like Jeep open-knuckle axles, we draw this line through the orbital centerline of the upper and lower ball joints.

If this line tilts rearward, we call this positive caster. Tilted forward, we have negative caster. Caster angle's purpose is to encourage straight ahead orientation of the wheels. Correct (positive) caster causes the steering wheel to center itself as we leave a turn. Caster also helps prevent kingpin shimmy, the violent back and forth shaking of the front wheels.

On leaf-sprung solid front axles, caster can be set by placing shims between the axle perch and main leaf of each front spring. Accurately degreed, these wedge-shaped shims restore proper tilt of the kingpin or ball joint centerline. Solid front driving axles with link arm designs (like coil sprung XJ, ZJ/WJ or TJ models) have factory provisions for rotating the axle housing slightly to adjust caster during alignment.

The last front end geometry issue is steering axis inclination. Effectively, steering axis inclination is two angles (caster and camber) in one, with the steering spindle angled to maintain a specified arc during turns. Steering axis inclination depends upon the condition and integrity of the steering knuckle and spindle. If axis of inclination has changed yet caster, camber and toe-in remain correct, suspect a bent or defective steering knuckle or spindle.

Field Fix to Get Home

What does any of this have to do with getting home from a bone jarring assault on a rock pile? A front end alignment is a good idea after any serious off-highway bout. In an emergency, you can restore toe-in in the field—at least closely enough to keep your precious tire rubber from peeling away like an apple's skin!

> *CAUTION —*
> *Back woods straightening of the tie rod could save a long walk out of remote mountains or desert and allow your Jeep to track reasonably straight. As for the permanence of such a fix, realize that any straightened steering linkage part should be replaced as soon as possible. A straightened steering link is prone to fail in service, a highly hazardous safety risk.*

> NOTE —
> Many frame and axle specialists can skillfully straighten a slightly bent I-beam or solid axle (and even pull out several degrees of frame kink). No professional, however, will re-use a bent piece of steering linkage.

In an effort to drive your damaged truck, be very cautious not to break a bent tie-rod as you attempt to straighten it. Use care to distribute force over a broad area while centering the pull at the bent section. If the kink is at the threaded portion of a tie rod, leave it alone. Threads respond badly to stretching, and breakage is very likely.

Attach a tow strap to an immoveable object—like the tree stump that caused all this trouble! Use the truck's power to lightly pull the tie rod straight or, preferably, use your Jeep's winch, a tree and a snatch block. Park the truck in low gear or 'Park' with the brake set.

Run the cable forward and loop it 180 degrees at the snatch block. Attach the hook to the tie-rod.

Use your winch remote control to operate the winch while watching the tie-rod from a safe distance. Straighten the tie rod enough to provide safe clearance for moving parts and approximate wheel alignment. Once you straighten the tube or sleeve, adjust toe-in as required.

> *CAUTION —*
> *When adjusting wheel alignment or installing new steering linkage pieces, always center the tie-rod ends. The ball studs and their sockets should align before you tighten the sleeve clamps. Make sure each tie-rod end has its full range of motion.*

> NOTE —
> See the steering knuckle section earlier in this chapter for tie-rod end removal.

A Wooded Backdrop for Your Alignment Shop

Temporary toe-in can be set with a few hand tools, a tie-rod sleeve wrench, a tape measure, and an axle or frame jack. Center the steering (Pitman arm) before beginning. Set the steering wheel for normal, straight ahead driving, then jack one front wheel slightly off the ground. Without a toe adjusting bar and pinpoint scribe for drawing lines around the tire centerlines, the next best tool for a primitive alignment is a piece of chalk.

Carefully note the tread pattern of your front tires. Find reference notches that are easy to identify. Hold the tape measure level, close to the horizontal

Fig. 12-29. *After straightening the tie-rod with a tow strap, the "Lantern Alignment Shop" opens. Raise the driver's side wheel slightly from the ground and reference mark the front tire tread. Keeping the steering wheel straight ahead, measure between front side and rear side reference marks. This indicates the degree of misalignment.*

Fig. 12-30. *Loosen the tie rod clamps and stabilizer mount, then turn the tie rod to adjust its length. The adjusting tube, often stubborn from rust and scale at the tie rod threads, may require a pipe wrench(s) to rotate.*

Fig. 12-31. *Safely position the sleeve clamps after confirming the final measurement. Clamps must not interfere with the axle or hamper steering linkage movement.*

Fig. 12-32. *Make sure plenty of tie rod thread remains within the sleeve/tube ends. Tighten clamps and make certain that parts move freely as you turn the steering wheel.*

mid-point of each tire's diameter. Make sure that the tape does not interfere with suspension parts, and pull it snugly from the opposite tire's mark. If you encounter an obstacle, drop the level of the tape, re-match the tread pattern, and try again. Once the tape is level, make note of the length between your two marks.

Perform the same procedure at the rear of the front tires. Again, attempt to draw a level line, close to the tires' horizontal midline, without parts interference. Note the length between these tread pattern points. (Make sure your patterns match those at the front.)

These two measurements make up a rudimentary field toe-in alignment. For simplicity, you might use an emergency toe-in spec of zero. Here, both front and rear measurements read the same. (Were our goal 1/8" toe-in, the rear measurement would be 1/8" longer than the front. Simple? Well, with practice it gets easier.)

A bent tie rod shortens the distance between the steering arms. On a solid axle Jeep, this toes the front wheels inward. If bend remains, expect a long measurement at the back side tread. To compensate, the tie rod needs lengthening.

Loosen the tie rod end clamps to allow rotation of the adjusting tube/sleeve. Note the left-hand and right-hand threads at each end of the tube, and also the amount of thread screwed into each sleeve end. If you must lengthen the tie rod, be careful not to unthread the tube so far that the tie-rod thread fitup becomes too shallow and unsafe.

The tube may not rotate easily. Moisture, rust, and scale cause seizure of tie-rod end threads. A rust penetrant will sometimes help. Rotate the tube, checking

the fore and aft tire measurements often. When the measurement is correct, tighten the clamps securely.

Many of us have been fortunate enough not to hit tree stumps or rocks. It's wise, however, to travel prepared. Whether we experience trouble or need to help others, survival skills help. A slow drive to pavement with a temporary field fix sure beats walking! Success can sometimes be a twelve-mph trip to civilization—with your Jeep's heater humming, windshield wipers swishing and headlights leading the way.

Chapter 13

Brakes and Wheel Bearings

P roperly functioning wheel bearings and brakes are essential to safe driving. Inspect your Jeep's wheel bearings and brakes regularly. Perform all brake work with careful attention to cleanliness, correct specifications and professional work standards.

> *WARNING—*
> *• Brake friction materials such as brake linings or brake pads may contain asbestos fibers. Do not create dust by grinding, sanding, or cleaning the pads with compressed air. Avoid breathing any asbestos fibers or dust. Breathing asbestos can cause serious diseases such as asbestosis or cancer, and may result in death. Use only approved methods to clean brake components containing asbestos.*
>
> *• Brake fluid is poisonous. Wear safety glasses when working with brake fluid, and wear rubber gloves to prevent brake fluid from entering the bloodstream through cuts and scratches. Do not siphon brake fluid with your mouth.*

1. Wheel Bearings

Jeep front wheel bearings are tapered roller type. Tapered roller bearings provide for float. While maintaining the vehicle load, properly adjusted rollers can still move laterally (axially) within the margins of the roller guides. Ball bearings, by contrast, cannot tolerate axial play.

Any type of rolling bearing will microslip (slide or scuff) slightly, and all bearings suffer chronic wear at their rollers, balls, and races. The most common bearing race, roller or ball steel is a chromium-alloy, usually SAE 52100 bearing race steel. This is tough, pure stuff (ranging between 60–68 on the Rockwell C scale tests for hardness). These materials furnish high rolling mileage, but the hardness makes races vulnerable to impact damage and pitting from abrasive contaminants. For this reason, thorough cleaning, inspection, and periodic bearing re-packing with a suitable grease is necessary.

Front Wheel Bearing Fundamentals

Although wheel bearing service procedures and exact adjusting specifications differ among models, some general points apply to all Jeep vehicles. (Adjustment standards and methods for your Jeep are available in the factory shop manual or professional service guide.)

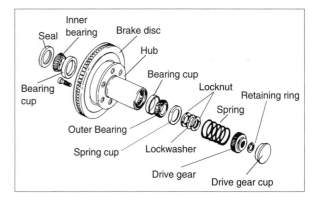

Fig. 13-1. *On Jeep full-floating front axle, tapered roller front wheel bearings require end play adjustment. A specified in and out movement of the bearing assembly provides proper tolerance.*

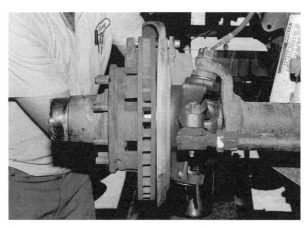

Fig. 13-2. *Disc rotor and wheel hub act like an integral unit. Correct disc brake rotor lateral runout is critical. Trueness of rotor and proper adjustment of the wheel bearings provide acceptable runout.*

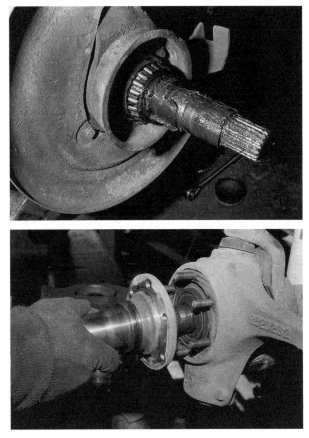

Fig. 13-3. *Inspect spindle surface where wheel bearings ride. Wear, galling or play here will affect the adjustment of bearings. Check closely for cracks, especially if your Jeep has wide aftermarket wheels and oversize tires. Make certain spindle-to-knuckle attaching fasteners are not loose. Always replace worn parts and self-locking fasteners.*

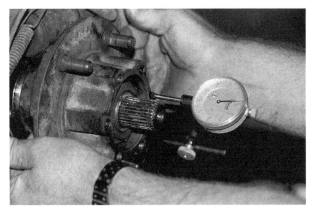

Fig. 13-4. *Dial indicator on magnetic stand measures wheel bearing end play. This measurement addresses the acceptable range of bearing roller movement (axially) on the races. Holding the hub flange at 9- and 3-o'clock, push the hub straight in and pull straight out while measuring end-play. Check your Jeep factory service manual for proper end-play specifications.*

Precise wheel bearing adjustment takes end play into account. End play is measurable with a dial indicator attached to the wheel hub, outer brake drum face or rotor. Push the brake drum or rotor straight inward with both hands. (Push evenly to avoid cocking the hub to one side). Take a dial indicator reading, aiming straight toward the spindle.

The dial indicator measures end play when you pull the hub straight outward. Do not rock the drum or rotor, or a false reading will result. End play is the straight inward and outward (lateral) movement of the hub along the spindle axis.

Bearing Survival

The two most common causes of bearing failure are poor maintenance and abuse. Poor maintenance includes neglecting periodic cleaning or failure to re-pack and properly adjust the bearings. For Jeep 4x4s, abuse takes on several additional forms. A Jeep may

sport oversized custom wheels and tires—or perhaps a change in weight on the front end, the result of a V-8 transplant. Operating the truck with either too much load on the bearings or excessive lateral stress can cause damage. Often, failure results from using radically offset ("reversed") wheels.

Shifting the tire centerline outboard from the stock location causes vehicle weight to act as leverage against the wheel hub and bearings. With a front mounted winch and a hefty V-8 engine, imagine 800 or more pounds loaded directly on each wheel hub. Apply that same weight with the tire centerlines located further outboard. In addition to supporting the weight, the bearings must now resist additional leverage force.

Wheel Bearing Service Notes

Always service wheel bearings with the correct grease. All wheel bearing greases are not the same. Mixing grease types severely damage parts and compromise your safety. (See the lubrication section of this book.) When re-packing your Jeep's front wheel bearings, begin with a thorough solvent cleaning. Make certain that no solvent residue remains on the bearings before re-packing them with fresh grease.

> CAUTION —
> *Wash bearings and other parts in clean solvent. Remove all old grease and any solvent residue. Drying with compressed air is acceptable, however, never spin the bearings. Severe bodily harm could result from a bearing assembly flying apart at speed.*

Also clean the spindle, inner wheel hub and races. Wash, wipe and dry parts thoroughly to remove any traces of solvent before re-packing the bearings. Use the recommended wheel bearing grease for your model. Disc brake equipped vehicles demand exacting wheel bearing adjustments and highly heat resistant lubricant.

Always replace grease seals. Do not attempt to re-use them. Installing new front or rear wheel seals lowers the risk of contamination and parts failure. At the front, seals prevent moisture and dirt from entering the hub assembly. Rear axle seals prevent grease or gear lubricant from ruining brake lining and causing failure of the rear brakes.

Use proper tools, refer to your factory or professional repair guidebook, and take your time when servicing your wheel bearings. On early models with a bendable locking washer between the two spindle

nuts, install a new washer whenever fatigue is obvious. Done properly, a wheel bearing re-pack and seal replacement will last for many miles. Precise steering, handling and braking result, assuring your Jeep's safety and reliability.

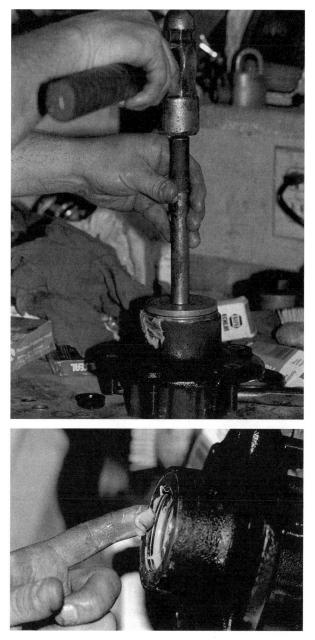

Fig. 13-6. *After cleaning and thoroughly drying the hub and rotor assembly, swab clean grease against the walls of the hub's inner cavity. Grease should fill the hub's grease recess and provide a dam to prevent hot grease from leaving the inner sides of the bearings. Install the freshly packed inner wheel bearing and a new grease seal. Wipe outside of hub casting to keep grease away from brake linings. The hub is now ready for installation on the spindle.*

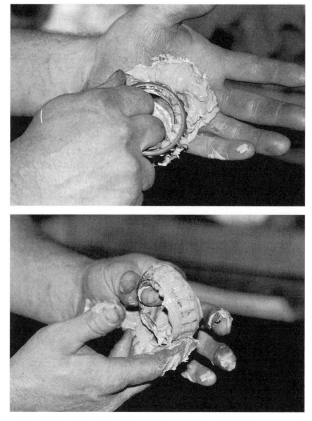

Fig. 13-5. *Wheel bearing packers make this job easy and assure complete grease penetration of the rollers. When hand packing a bearing, squeeze the grease between the wider end of the bearing cage and the inner bearing race. Make sure grease flows out the opposite end of the rollers. Go around the entire bearing assembly at least two full times to assure thorough saturation. Once grease fills all spaces between the rollers, spread a generous film of grease around the outer face of the bearing and cage.*

Fig. 13-7. *Install the re-packed outer wheel bearing, then the thrust washer. (On later 44 front axles found on J-trucks and full-size Wagoneers, the inner/adjuster nut doubles as the bearing thrust surface. This nut is round, not hex, and requires a special four-lug spindle wrench.) Build a dam of additional grease around outer side of bearing and thrust washer.*

Fig. 13-8. *With outer bearing and thrust washer in place, thread the adjuster nut carefully onto the spindle with the correct spindle nut wrench. (Consult your Jeep service manual or a professional level guide for adjustment procedure and torque figures.)*

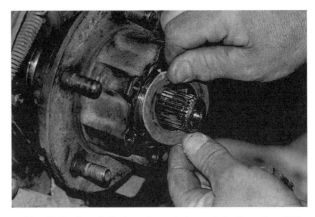

Fig. 13-9. *Carefully install retaining tab lockwasher (CJ and early hex nut style) or indexing lock plate washer (later 44 style), then install and torque the outer lock nut to specification before measuring hub end play with a dial indicator. (Confirm parts assembly order in the Jeep service manual for your model.)*

Fig. 13-10. *Once bearing end-play is correct and hex lock nut has been torqued to specification, bend the CJ/earlier truck style lockwasher tab (shown here) to secure the nuts. (Those Jeep axles that use two hex-style nuts have these bendable lock-tab washers.) I bend one tab inward over an inner nut flat, another tab outward over an outer nut flat.*

2. The Braking System

Jeep 4x4s depend on engine compression and quality braking to negotiate treacherous terrain and survive under harsh weather conditions. Inclement weather, barely passable roads and rough trails carpeted with jagged obstructions are home to many Jeep trucks. These perils and hazards challenge the brake system.

All Jeep brakes actuate by hydraulic pressure. The basic hydraulic system is a brake pedal and master cylinder. Pre-1967 Jeep brake systems have a single master cylinder. On Willys Station Wagons, Pickups and

CJs, the master cylinder mounted beneath the floorboard. J-trucks and Wagoneers were the first Jeep models to mount the master cylinder forward of the firewall. (FCs were the first Jeep trucks to offer suspended brake and clutch pedals, followed by Kaiser's J-trucks and Wagoneers.)

In 1967, the U.S. Department of Transportation invoked safety standards requiring dual hydraulic circuits on the master cylinder. All U.S. Jeep trucks from that year forward have separate hydraulic brake circuits for the rear and front brakes. If either end of the system should fail, brakes still operate at the opposite axle.

For Jeep 4x4s, the dual brake system was a significant advancement, eliminating the risk of brake loss in the event of a fluid leak. For a truck chassis exposed to fallen trees, jagged rock and raw terrain, the pre-'67 single braking system offers little protection. If a brake hose snaps, a hydraulic wheel cylinder ruptures or a steel pipe tears, the whole hydraulic system loses pressure and the brakes fail completely.

Pedal Signals

A spongy brake pedal is caused by air in the hydraulic system. This leads to poor braking action and rust within the system. Check for leaks and bleed air from the system.

A brake pedal that drops gradually to the floor under pressure, with or without accompanying loss of brake fluid, indicates a leak. If the master cylinder, wheel cylinders, hoses and pipes reveal no signs of fluid leakage, suspect an internal leak within the master cylinder.

> NOTE —
> The primary seal/cup can leak and allow brake fluid to by-pass. Although unable to maintain hydraulic pressure within the system, a primary seal/cup leak does not cause a loss of fluid yet the pedal will drop under pressure. Fluid seepage at the pushrod end of the master cylinder indicates a secondary cup/seal leak.

Another sign of trouble is the pulsating brake pedal, characterized by a rhythmical pumping action during braking. On your Jeep 4x4, possible causes include warped drums or rotors, defective brake hardware, a bent front spindle or rear axle shaft and loose wheel bearings. These symptoms can occur suddenly, often following an off-road pounding or water submersion.

High pedal pressure accompanied by increased stopping distance is fade. Fade suggests poor lining quality or materials that have fatigued severely. Brake pull, another common symptom, results from contam-

Fig. 13-11. *On earlier Jeep models without self-adjusting brake mechanisms, you must periodically adjust the drum brake lining to avoid a low pedal. An early Jeep also has the parking/emergency brake at the rear driveline. The emergency brake drum has openings for inspection and adjustment of the brake. Watch for oil, grit and contaminants that will make your parking brake ineffective. Also check and lube the parking brake cable periodically.*

inated brake lining or mis-adjusted shoes. If brake pads or shoes require replacement, change lining at both wheels of that axle.

Other Brake Woes

Metallic brake noise signals danger. Generally, metal-on-metal sounds imply total loss of lining and the dragging of shoes or pad backs against a drum or rotor. These symptoms quickly degenerate into damaged rotors or drums, often beyond the point of repair. Periodic inspection of your Jeep's brakes can help prevent this trouble.

Check for leaks, worn lining and heat damage. Look closely at hoses and brake pipes, especially in those areas exposed to debris and trail abuse. Periodically, remove the front and rear brake drums to assess lining wear.

> *WARNING—*
> *Brake friction materials such as brake linings or brake pads may contain asbestos fibers. Do not create dust by grinding, sanding, or cleaning the pads with compressed air. Avoid breathing any asbestos fibers or dust. Breathing asbestos can cause serious diseases such as asbestosis or cancer, and may result in death. Use only approved methods to clean brake components containing asbestos.*

Brake Fluid Precautions

Safety is at stake when you replenish your Jeep's fluids. Accidental use of mineral-based oils in the hydraulic brake or clutch system can cause swelling of rubber seals and complete failure of the brakes or clutch.

> *WARNING—*
> • *Brake fluid is poisonous. Wear safety glasses when working with brake fluid, and wear rubber gloves to prevent brake fluid from entering the bloodstream through cuts and scratches. Do not siphon brake fluid with your mouth.*
>
> • *Always use DOT 3 or higher rating brake fluid in the master cylinder/braking system or hydraulic clutch system of your Jeep truck. Never add motor oil or any substance other than brake fluid to a hydraulic brake system. Do not mix silicone brake fluid with conventional brake fluid.*

Clean, moisture-free brake fluid is fundamental to brake safety. The master cylinder cover must seal tightly. When topping off fluid, use clean brake fluid with the DOT rating Jeep has specified for your vehicle.

Exposed to the atmosphere, brake fluid has a short shelf life. Keep lids sealed snugly and never store fluid in an open container. DOT 3 fluid, fresh out of a new can, boils at 401° Fahrenheit or higher, while the absorption of only 3% moisture reduces the boiling point to 284°. This is ample justification for an annual brake fluid flush and replenishment with clean brake fluid.

As braking is essential to your safety, apply special care when handling brake service parts and brake fluid. Brake fluid has an affinity for water. Store a tightly resealed brake fluid container in a dry location. The need for cleanliness cannot be overstated, as brake parts will fail when exposed to abrasive debris or mineral/petroleum based oils, solvents and greases.

Brake Fluid Service

Your Jeep's brakes require regular attention. Routine concerns include checking the hydraulic brake fluid, inspecting hoses and steel pipes for damage, and noting the lining left on disc brake pads and brake shoes. Check the brake fluid level at each lubrication interval.

Dusty trails, stream crossings, slush and snow expose various brake parts to water, abrasive dirt and road salts. An older Jeep, with its master cylinder mounted beneath the floorboard, has an atmospherically vented filler cap. These models face the constant risk of contaminants and moisture entering the reservoir.

Take care when checking the fluid. Especially on models with floorboard inspection covers, make cer-

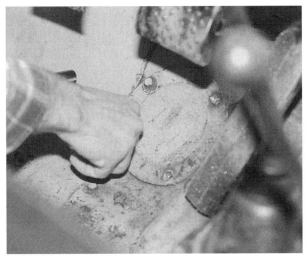

Fig. 13-12. *Before checking brake fluid on an early Jeep truck, vacuum or brush dirt away from the inspection plate hole and the master cylinder fill plug area. Carefully remove the plug to verify the correct fluid level, 1/2" below the top of fill hole.*

tain that debris and grit cannot fall from the floorboard into the open brake fluid reservoir! Before removing the master cylinder fill plug, clean the area thoroughly.

The early master cylinder design also raises other service issues. The air vent in the master cylinder cap often draws dust and moisture into the master cylinder reservoir. It is common for abrasive "mud" to accumulate in the base of the master cylinder reservoir. A complete system flush and overhaul of each hydraulic cylinder is the only remedy for this kind of contamination.

Conventional brake fluid, with alcohol as a component, has an affinity for water. Atmospheric moisture, passing through a cap vent, mingles with brake fluid. Even more frustrating for earlier Jeep 4x4s, submerging the master cylinder in running stream water raises havoc with the hydraulic braking system.

Most Jeep owners and mechanics ignore flushing of the hydraulic system. Years ago, brake parts manufacturers recommended pressure feeding a special flushing compound (usually denatured alcohol) or clean brake fluid through the system annually. Replacement of all rubber cups, seals and boots would follow. For an early Jeep that passes through streams regularly, this is still a good practice.

Newer Jeep braking systems have much less trouble with atmospheric contamination of brake fluid. The later master cylinder covers with rubber bellows type seals can accommodate pressure changes without the need for an open vent between the reservoir and atmosphere. Despite these measures, moisture still en-

Fig. 13-13. *1967–up U.S. Jeep trucks feature tandem master cylinders, although CJ models maintained through-the-floor pedals for several years. AMC and Chrysler mount the Jeep master cylinders high on the firewall, a sensible distance from debris and water. Still, always clean around the master cylinder before removing the cap or cover.*

ters the hydraulic system at approximately 3% volume per year.

For servicing, flushing or bleeding the brake system, consult your factory-level service manual. Jeep brake systems vary, and modern brake designs, especially the newer Anti-lock Braking Systems (ABS), call for different procedures than earlier models.

NOTE —
At the very least, pump fresh brake fluid through the system annually and bleed out all air. Make certain that fresh fluid passes through all the lines. If your Jeep has an under floorboard master cylinder with a cap that vents the reservoir to atmosphere, periodic inspection and service of your hydraulic system is especially important.

Brake Service and Overhaul Tips

Avoid introducing contaminants or abrasive foreign material into the hydraulic reservoir(s). Such debris damages sensitive rubber parts within the master cylinder and hydraulic system, and late Jeep aluminum master cylinder bores are especially vulnerable to scoring.

During brake system overhauls, check the labels on brake parts cleaners. Many contain petroleum solvents or distillates. These cleaners work fine as metal parts de-greasers. However, petroleum-based or mineral-based solvents and oils can cause rubber parts in the wheel cylinders, disc calipers and master cylinder to swell up and fail.

Always inspect hydraulic brake cylinders for pits and corrosion. If in doubt, replace the cylinder. If rebuildable, remove the cylinder from the system and

hone its bore lightly (with a suitable brake cylinder hone). Hone just enough to break the glaze. Be certain not to leave debris or abrasive material in the cylinder. Check the bore diameter. If within tolerance, bath the cylinder in a dishwashing soap (like Ivory Liquid), scrub with a toothbrush, rinse thoroughly in clear water, and dry with clean, compressed air. Assemble new rubber parts with clean brake fluid or special brake rubber parts assembly lube.

CAUTION —
When servicing your hydraulic brake system, never use mineral or petroleum-based solvents or oils around rubber parts. Denatured alcohol and automotive brake fluid are among the few substances that will not destroy rubber. The traditional cleaner for critical brake parts is denatured alcohol. Allow alcohol to evaporate completely before filling the system with brake fluid.

When servicing disc brakes, make certain that floating (self-centering) caliper assemblies and pistons slide freely. If signs of friction exist, overhaul or replace the caliper.

If four-wheeling has caused damage to your Jeep's hydraulic brake lines or fittings, replace parts only with D.O.T.-approved brake components. This includes brake tees, junction blocks and valves, which must meet or exceed your truck's original equipment brake standards.

Use pre-formed steel brake pipe. This tubing, cut to length and double-flared at each end, comes complete with flare nuts and ready to install. Once you have shaped the new tubing with a tubing bender, use a flare nut wrench to remove and replace the brake pipes. Torque nuts to manufacturer's specifications.

Fig. 13-14. *Disc caliper piston scoring resulted from the severe heat generated as a rotor disintegrated. Piston seizure can cause brake lockup or severe brake pull.*

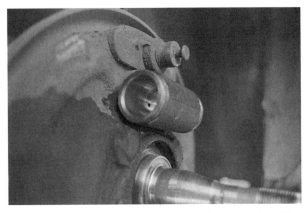

Fig. 13-15. *Wheel cylinders cannot tolerate scoring. If honed, this cylinder will lose too much material. Pitting and scoring result from moisture and wear. Periodic flushing could have prevented this problem.*

Fig. 13-16. *Late model master cylinders have aluminum housings. Most shops regard these assemblies as throw away items, finding them ill-suited for overhaul. Scratches and scoring are common and render the cylinder useless.*

Fig. 13-17. *Overhauling disc brake calipers requires cleanliness, care and proper tools. Here, a new seal seats in a reconditioned, safely sized bore.*

CAUTION —
Avoid introducing debris or contaminants into the hydraulic system when changing brake hoses or pipes. Always bleed the system and check for leaks before driving your Jeep.

While servicing your brakes, inspect the wheel bearings and axle seals. A leaky rear axle seal can quickly ruin new brake lining. Preserve your Jeep's braking system. Apply preventive care wherever possible. This is your best safeguard against losing your brakes.

Brake Linings

Whether your Jeep is bone stock or highly modified, performance is important. Although we refine our engines, transmissions and axles, brakes often get overlooked.

WARNING—
Brake friction materials such as brake linings or brake pads may contain asbestos fibers. Do not create dust by grinding, sanding, or cleaning the pads with compressed air. Avoid breathing any asbestos fibers or dust. Breathing asbestos can cause serious diseases such as asbestosis or cancer, and may result in death. Use only approved methods to clean brake components containing asbestos.

Improving your Jeep's brake system begins with brake lining. Organic friction materials use asbestos, usually in a phenolic-resin compound. Asbestos, an environmental hazard, places the brake mechanic at risk. Respirators and protective wear are common tools for asbestos and brake industry workers.

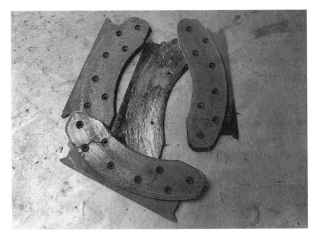

Fig. 13-18. *Age, fatigue and overheating cause brake lining failure. Thinner lining loses heat resistance, as witnessed by these heat-cracked disc brake pads.*

Fig. 13-19. *Thinned brake lining shows heat crack formation. Replace parts now to avoid the risk of lining separation.*

Fig. 13-20. *New brake lining has code marks. Many states require edge coding to help a consumer determine lining type and quality.*

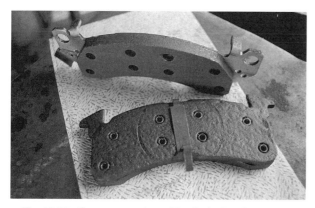

Fig. 13-21. *Coat new pad steel backs before installation. The special silicone grease dries quickly and helps prevent brake squeal.*

The brake and clutch industry attraction to asbestos has been its exceptional heat resistance, low wear and minimal noise. Asbestos health risks outweigh benefits, however, and asbestos-bearing organic friction materials are bordering extinction.

Bendix, a respected industry supplier of quality brake parts, advises several precautions when purchasing new brake lining: 1) If your truck has OEM semi-metallic brake pads, always refit with semi-metallic lining; 2) Replace asbestos/organic pads and shoes with comparable lining; and 3) Don't replace OEM organic or organic/asbestos lining with semi-metallic lining—unless sanctioned by the vehicle manufacturer.

NOTE —
As of this book's publication, asbestos is still legal in some applications. Vehicle manufacturers, however, now follow guidelines to phase out asbestos as suitable non-asbestos products become available. Stay informed on this issue. For health sake, avoid asbestos brake and clutch products if you can find a safe, acceptable alternative.

Semi-metallic brake lining, well suited for front disc pad material, provides cooler operation. Under severe braking conditions and heavy loading, semi-metallic lining rapidly draws heat away from the rotors. Excessive heat, the cause of fade and pad/rotor damage, is less likely with semi-metallic brake lining materials.

Manufacturers recommend that replacement brake lining match the OEM materials. Poor braking, short pad life and rotor scoring or warping can otherwise result. From a safety standpoint, fade leads to complete brake failure. If you have questions about your Jeep's original equipment lining, consult your local Jeep dealership or a reputable brake parts supplier for guidelines.

If your Jeep can use semi-metallic disc pads, special preparation of the rotors is necessary. When resurfacing your rotors, Bendix recommends a satin-smooth final cut, followed by a non-directional finish. Correct rotor finish will eliminate squeal and hard pedal action.

Semi-metallic pad replacement always includes rotor re-surfacing—even if very minor work is necessary to true the rotor and condition the surfaces. The final non-directional finish assures quieter operation and quick seating of pads. Before installing rotors, clean them thoroughly and wipe their faces with denatured alcohol

Fig. 13-22. *Non-directional finish of rotors assures semi-metallic lining break-in. Some manufacturers recommend a brake lathe grinder for this task, while others find a hand-held drill motor and disc sander acceptable. Wear a particle mask and safety goggles.*

Semi-metallic Brake Break-in

Like engines and other automotive components, brakes require break-in. For semi-metallic brake pads, Bendix recommends light use of the brakes for the first 150–200 miles. For new brakes, avoid panic stops if possible. Instead of hard burn-ins, Bendix suggests 15 to 20 slow stops from about 30 mph. Use light to moderate brake pedal pressure and allow at least 30 seconds recovery between stops.

As another consideration, semi-metallic lining requires heavier pedal pressure when cold—or wet. Some disc brake trucks, with heavier (solid) front rotors, dissipate heat so effectively that a semi-metallic retrofit lining cannot work at peak efficiency. Reciprocally, less expensive organic lining will overheat and wear rapidly when installed on a late model, lightweight rotor system designed for semi-metallic lining. This is one more reason to stick with original equipment brake lining recommendations.

Drums and Rotors

The trueness of a rotor or drum is essential. Drums and rotors should be checked for scoring, hard spots, warpage and proper inside diameter (drums) or thickness (rotors). Micrometers for this task are common to brake and automotive machine shops. If the rotor or drum surface is at all suspect, re-surfacing on a brake lathe is necessary.

A common cause of disc brake rotor damage is over-torquing the wheel nuts. Wheel nuts too loose or tight, or tightened out of sequence, can warp a rotor. Use of an impact gun is the easiest way to over-tighten

Fig. 13-23. *Before disassembly, check your Jeep hub/drum and disc rotor for lateral runout, warpage and rotor thickness variance.*

wheel nuts. Aside from the risk of breaking wheel studs, over-tightening enlarges wheel holes and warps disc rotors. Improperly torqued nuts can warp a rotor enough to cause premature pad wear and pulsation of the brake pedal.

Rotors, drums and lining are expensive. Care should be taken to tighten each set of wheel nuts gradually and "in cross." Whenever possible, use a torque wrench for final tightening.

> **NOTE —**
> Always re-check air gun tightened wheel nuts when you have new tires mounted commercially. If too tight, jack up the wheel, loosen the whole set of nuts, and re-tighten properly. If too loose, bring nuts to specification—tightening in cross sequence.

Fig. 13-24. *Read the thickness and wear of the rotor with an outside micrometer. Determine whether to cut the rotors or buy a new pair. Better ventilated, lightweight rotors are often candidates for semi-metallic pads. Your local Jeep dealer's parts department can verify which type of lining is acceptable.*

Fig. 13-25. *Hazardous heat and rotor scoring to the extreme! This rotor separated from its hub. Note condition of brake lining before final failure. Caliper piston scoring and likely seizure are evident. All of this could have been avoided by periodic inspection of brake parts and proper maintenance. This time, remarkably, no deaths resulted.*

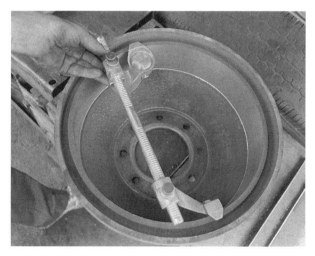

Fig. 13-26. *Re-surfaced rear brake drum assures a quality brake job. Lining will wear-in better and offer complete contact with the drum surface.*

Fig. 13-27. *Professionals install hardware kits with every brake overhaul. Old springs and retainers fatigue from heat. New pieces contribute to proper shoe alignment and longer service life. Hardware kits are cheap insurance.*

Fig. 13-28. *Specialty tools used for brake work include seal drivers, piston removal tools, adjuster spoons, bleeder wrenches, spring pliers and retainer/removal tool. Seen also is a set of master cylinder bench bleeding hoses.*

Fig. 13-29. *Wheel cylinder cups and dust boots are available in a variety of sizes. Replace these parts at each brake overhaul. For the older trail Jeep's periodic brake system flush, you will replace these cups and the dust boots.*

Fig. 13-30. Other damage, like these over-torqued and broken wheel studs, adds to restoration cost. Broken studs are usually the result of over-torquing during wheel installation or from rusty, seizing wheel nuts.

Fig. 13-31. Here is a common cause of premature rear brake lining failure: This semi-floating axle's bearing seal has leaked. Gear oil saturated and ruined the brake shoes and rubber wheel cylinder dust boots.

Fig. 13-32. Re-surfacing the brake drums is an important part of a brake job. Jeep factory manuals suggest safe machining limits. Rivet heads, steel pad backings and metal shoe backs cause severe damage to drums and rotors. Periodic, preventive maintenance and brake inspection can help avert such irreparable damage.

Fig. 13-33. New wheel cylinder boots protect against moisture and debris. Once the cylinder overhaul is complete, new brake shoes and hardware fit into place.

Chapter 14

Body and Detailing

Harsh climates, brush scratches and off-pavement bashing tear unmercifully at your Jeep's body. Over years, a 4WD Jeep also accumulates its share of oxidation. The battle against rust is a vigil. You must watch constantly for fresh scratches and exposed metal. In salt air regions, including areas with corrosive salt spread on winters roads, Jeep bodies are especially vulnerable. In such environments, the bright metal, chrome and painted surfaces oxidize rapidly.

1. Battling Rust

Rust is a persistent problem for any off-pavement 4x4. Sadly, tens of thousands of otherwise restorable Jeep trucks have wound up as rusty hulks at recycling yards. In addition to environmental hazards, some Jeep bodies have weak sheet metal or a design that provides very poor water drainage. Mid-'80s and newer models, with more extensive use of galvanized (zinc treated) metals, plastic and rubberized trim, resist rust much better than older trucks.

The worst Jeep models for rust are the CJs, military, and early (Willys-style) Station Wagon/Pickup trucks. Aftermarket vendors do a substantial business around complete replacement body tubs for the CJs and military MB, M-38 and M38-A1 vehicles.

More persistent rust areas are tailgates, the windshield frame, floorpans, door sills and, of course, any place that holes have been drilled in the body—including holes for aftermarket roll bar mounting plates. Rust forms at hood hinges and other places where paint can wear thin. Inner fender panels, the cowl, grill shell and front fenders rust quickly in corrosive air or on salty roads.

> NOTE —
> Rust often lies beneath the front floor (OEM) carpeting of later model CJs and Wranglers. Floorboard rot is common with CJ aftermarket roll bar installations.

With the body and chassis thoroughly clean, inspect your Jeep for rust. Pay close attention to areas with add-on accessories. Look for poor sealing and exfoliation (bubbling), which indicates rust formation beneath the paint. If you suspect rust, remove the accessory and treat the area with thorough sanding, primer/sealing and paint as needed. When damage is excessive, consult a local body shop.

The flat panels on a CJ or military body are a good place to enhance your metalwork and painting skills. Restoration and maintenance include sealing, priming and painting your Jeep.

Jeep frames, although made of metals which resist rust perforation, build up surface oxidation. Wear a particle mask and safety goggles, and clean rust with a drill-powered wire brush. Prime and paint surfaces to prevent further problems. (Use a rust inhibiting primer or paint.)

Fig. 14-1. *When carpet rolls back, so does metal! The small bulge at outer body surface never suggested this severe rust. Aftermarket roll bar extensions mount to front floor of CJ models. Unless you seal properly around drilled metal, carpets may hide an area where water can accumulate. Here, menacing rust will form. Always take rust bubbles ("exfoliation") seriously.*

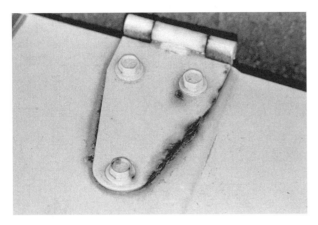

Fig. 14-2. *Hinge joint shows surface rust. A professional body worker sees this as salvageable. Separate the hinge from the hood and sand blast all surfaces to restore metal.*

Fig. 14-4. *This is insidious rust. Hidden behind an after-market trim panel on the CJ-5, rust now presses through sheetmetal. Watch for high spots like this—especially when considering a used Jeep buy.*

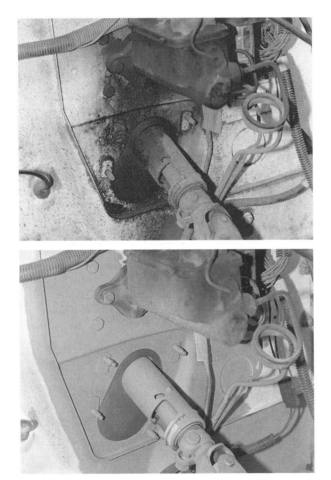

Fig. 14-3. *Surface rust on firewall, although unsightly, does not effect the integrity of base sheetmetal. Sandblasting reveals that underlying metal is strong and serviceable.*

Fig. 14-5. *Sandblasting at this metal bulge reveals a broader problem. Hidden between an aftermarket trim panel and interior carpet, severe rust damage resulted from inadequate metal priming/sealing job when owner drilled holes through sheetmetal to install an aftermarket roll bar.*

Rust Repairs

Louie Russo, Jr., is a body and paint master. If your Jeep restoration includes body work, Louie's step-by-step rust repair on this CJ-5 serves as a good lesson. Consider these procedures carefully before tackling your Jeep's rust. Techniques shown here provide a like-new fix and prepare the Jeep for a quality paint job.

Fig. 14-8. *Remove or treat all rust-effected metal. At this point, wire brushing and sandblasting will determine strength of metal and uncover any pinholes to fill.*

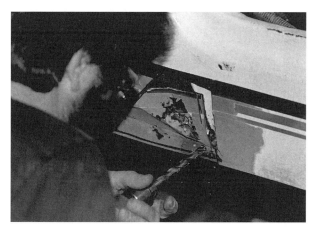

Fig. 14-6. *Factory rivets drilled, Louie Russo separates floorpan from the interior body brace. Extent of rust is still illusive, even at this point.*

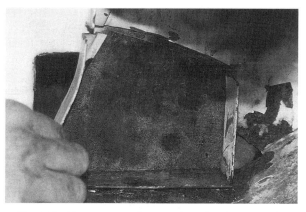

Fig. 14-9. *Heavy-gauge flat metal section from a hefty 1930s car fender has become a replacement piece for the original tub brace. Louie welds the handformed repair section into place. Note use of salvageable segment of the original brace. This small portion of metal helps maintain alignment and contours.*

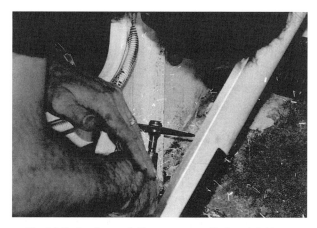

Fig. 14-7. *Louie carefully removes rotted metal. Here, a carbide disc cuts quickly through the sheetmetal brace. Structural integrity of the body tub is a consideration with this repair. Caution: Wear a particle mask and safety goggles when grinding with carbide discs!*

Fig. 14-10. *MIG welded into place, section now fits against the cleaned floorpan. Heat applied to lower bracket flange allows shaping with a body hammer until new brace matches OE fit perfectly. Louie also welded pinholes in floorpan. Surface grinding of welds will restore original appearance.*

Fig. 14-11. *Louie cuts and forms flat piece of sheetmetal to fit cutout. He purposely keeps the original lower roll of body lip to avoid re-shaping edge. Drilling and spot-welding outer panel to inner brace duplicates OE engineering. MIG confines heat. Louie strategically lays down welds while carefully quenching hot sheetmetal to maintain shape.*

Fig. 14-12. *Surface grinding reveals Louie's careful handling of metal. Masterful heat isolation, shrink/stretch control and correct heat diffusion results in near perfect surface straightness.*

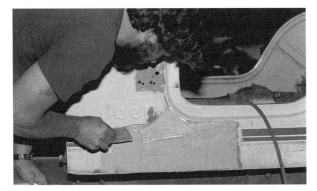

Fig. 14-13. *Louie applies a light coat of plastic body filler to sanding scratches and very slight depressions. Once shaped and sanded, only a tiny amount of plastic will remain. Louie Russo prefers the challenge of metal working to the simpler, plastic fill approach. His work shows "good-as-new" quality.*

2. Body Detailing

As a Jeep owner, you'll get to know your local self-service car wash. Here, the combination of soap and high pressure spray can transform a mud caked 4x4 into respectable suburban driveway material. In minutes, pounds of mud and debris will stream from the body, wheel wells, frame, axles and suspension.

Detailing your Jeep begins with a thorough wash. 4x4s face as much dirt, sun and abrasive wind as a desert camel, yet there's no protective hair or hide to seal the elements from your Jeep's paint finish. Magnetic abrasives cling tenaciously to the paint pores, while scorching sun and road salts oxidize the trim and rubber. A cleaner must be gentle enough to leave healthy paint intact, yet still cut and flush the grit from the paint.

There are many commercial car wash solutions on the market. The main objective with any good car soap is to dissolve road oils and gently flush dirt away. Although dishwashing liquids work well, commercial products might be part of a "system," chemically engineered to work with specific waxes or polishes.

Even more important is your washing technique. For a safe wash job around grit and abrasives, avoid scratching the finish. A sponge or wash cloth is hazardous. Special car wash mitts work much better, but hand pressure can still cause grit to press into the paint or drag across the surface.

Eastwood Company at Malvern, Pennsylvania, offers specialty detail supplies for auto and truck restorers. I find that Eastwood's tools can protect a Jeep's finish and extend good looks for years.

Fig. 14-14. *Local coin-op pressure washer can remove debris and pre-clean your Jeep's finish after a hard day of off-pavement use. Never hand wash a mud-coated vehicle! Avoid commercial car wash brushes.*

For hand washing, the gentle bristles and cushion provided by a horse hair brush reduce the risk of scratches yet still massage foaming soap into paint pores. Your Jeep's panels will cleanse easily, followed by a gentle rinse with clean water. Use a quality, rubber-nosed faucet nozzle, capable of controlling pressure while protecting the vehicle's finish.

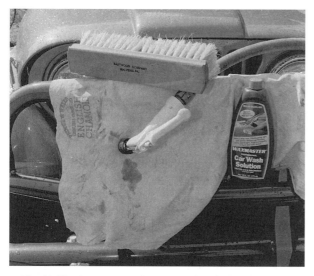

Fig. 14-15. *A spray nozzle, car wash solution, horse hair brush and a genuine English chamois are tools for a safe wash job.*

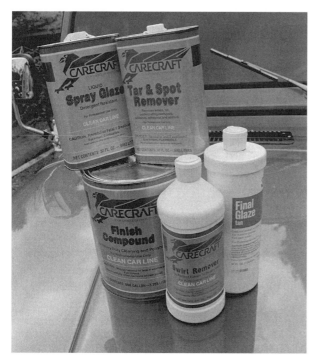

Fig. 14-16. *Eastwood Company's mail order catalog features products for a show-winning appearance.*

CAUTION —
If there is thickly encrusted mud or dirt on your Jeep, begin with a trip to the local high pressure (or "brushless") car wash. Use pressurized cleaning to remove this abrasive material. Avoid rubbing or brushing the surface, as this will scratch and mar the paint finish.

Why Fight Your Paint Finish?

Most four-wheelers can find better things to do with their weekends than wash and polish a truck. The backwoods and seasonal four-wheeling spots hold a lot more fun than performing a wax job. In recent years, professional detailers have taught us how to drastically speed up detailing work. Shifting away from disc-sander type buffers, the orbital polishers appear everywhere—and for good reason.

Traditional buffing methods, especially hand or disc polishing, can leave the paint finish full of swirls. Worse yet, the risk of buffing right through the paint edges scares most non-professional detailers from even attempting to use a disc-type buffer. The gentle orbital buffers, as an alternative, offer the first-time user a chance to do a professional polishing job without ruining an expensive paint finish.

Your First Orbital Buffing Job

When your new paint finish turns dull from road film and caked mud, don't panic. Armed with the right detailing chemicals and a quality orbital buffer, you can produce a professional wax job in less than an hour. Park your Jeep in a cool, shady area, then wash and chamois the finish. Now apply wax to cool metal.

The body contours and bolt-on accessory hardware of a Jeep CJ or Wrangler can prove difficult for buffing. Steep sides, hinges mounted above the hood, and devices sticking out everywhere create a real challenge for an orbital buffer. Still, the promise of uniform buffing action, as opposed to sluggish, ineffective hand waxing, spurs the job forward.

Carnauba based semi-paste wax, mixed with a liquid polish, works best with the orbital buffer. Although the buffer easily handles other chemical products, the combination polish and wax allows a faster, more thorough job. Carnauba based waxes provide better paint breathing and protection from atmospheric hazards.

NOTE —
I've had good results with waxes such as Eagle 1 and Mothers. Look for a carnauba product, the more natural the better. Paint is like our skin: subject to damage from oxidation. Carnauba wax allows paint to breathe.

Fig. 14-17. *This buffer bonnet's grey debris came from a fully cured new paint job after a thorough wash. An orbital buffer, used with a wide range of detailing chemicals, can strip/clean, apply wax or polish and buff the finish to a high luster. Uniform results with orbital buffer make hand or disc-type polishing obsolete.*

Fig. 14-18. *A random orbital waxer/polisher is your best investment, an incentive for performing detail work. Chamberlain/Waxmaster and other units are available from retail suppliers.*

Apply the wax and polish simultaneously to the terry cloth buffing bonnet. Operating much like a floor polisher, movement of the orbital buffer is easy to master. The application of wax/polish will take approximately twenty minutes on a CJ or Wrangler, and an extra fifteen minutes on a Jeep pickup, Cherokee or Wagoneer.

The buffer will lay down a uniform blend of wax. Hand applied areas rub easily with the wax/polish that remains on the polishing bonnet. Install a clean cloth and begin buffing. In minutes, the surface will glisten from every angle. Gentle hand rubbing and detailing with a terry cloth towel brings the less accessible areas to a high lustre.

Fig. 14-19. *An orbital buffer works with any number of specialized products. Shown are Waxmaster and Mother's brands of waxes and polishes.*

Orbital buffing leaves your Jeep finish with a protective, penetrating coat of Carnauba wax. Surface oxidized material has transferred to the buffing pads. As for the risk of paint removal from orbital buffing, years ago, I interviewed Loren E. Doppelt, Senior Product Manager for Waxmaster/Chamberlain. Loren noted, "I've buffed and polished a sample hood at car shows. The hood receives 1000 buffings before we re-paint it...Frankly, even then, there's no evidence that the paint is damaged."

Conventional hand waxing, a tedious, unfulfilling task, is passe. An orbital buffer produces professional results, the first time out. For a sharp appearance that lasts for years, treat your Jeep to quarterly polish jobs with a random orbital buffer and a quality carnauba wax/polish.

Weather-beaten Paint

A grossly oxidized finish may still respond to a finishing compound buff out. Follow buffing with a careful polish and wax job. Seek a quality compound that lifts dead paint by chemical action, not abrasion, and leaves no swirl marks.

Badly oxidized finishes may take a full morning and several orbital buffer pads to fix. (Bonnets are washable and re-usable if you keep them wet after use.)

Finishes raked by disc buffer swirls respond impressively to an orbital buffing with a quality swirl remover. Applied directly to the buffer pad, this non-scratching substance is more like a polish than a rubbing compound. I've played with ultra-fine sanding scratches left by 1200 grit wet-sanding paper and found that an orbital buffer can remove all traces in minutes—without cutting deeply into the clearcoat or finish.

The Rest Of the Details

When your Jeep's paint finish comes back to life, a sparkling surface with deeply colored lustre, there's a real incentive to complete the detailing chores. Here, too, I recommend fast, high quality chemical products for highlighting the interior and exterior trim. Flat stainless steel and chrome moldings respond readily to the gentle buffing action of the orbital machine, and the balance of the stainless hardware will polish easily by hand. Rubber and vinyl, the two most vulnerable materials after paint, require a hand-applied combination cleaner/protectant product that will counter oxidation.

The principal cause of oxidation on your Jeep paint and rubber is sunlight. Use of a protective UV-blocker agent on vinyl, leather and plastic trim extends the life of these materials. I heartily recommend 303 Protectant for this job. A gentle cleaner, 303 claims to provide a protective barrier against oxidation without damaging the vinyl topcoat chemistry. Sensitive vinyl surfaces must flex and breathe. Any coating that either draws away the special surface chemistry or seals the topcoat from breathing will eventually cause embrittlement. Avoid silicone oils and other chemistry that leave a "wet" look on vinyl.

> NOTE —
> According to Orvis, the fishing tackle company, 303 will also lengthen your flyline cast as much as 30 feet.

Wheel cleanup is simple on a Jeep. Painted steel rims respond readily to a light coat of Carnauba wax. If wheels are chrome and dull, hand rubbing with a

Fig. 14-20. *Boating industry highly recommends 303 Protectant for vinyl and fiberglass. 303 helps protect plastics, rubber, vinyl, leather and canvas. I use 303 Protectant for each of these automotive needs and for outdoor gear as well....Acme, a distributor for BesTop canvas Jeep tops, offers specialty product at right.*

Quick Tips to a Better Detail Job

1. Wash your Jeep thoroughly. Use bug and tar remover and other specially formulated chemicals to treat problem areas.

2. When using a buffer, make sure your polish and waxes are compatible. Chemical bases differ, and some chemicals react adversely with others.

3. Use several terrycloth towels for hand or orbital buffing. Avoid spreading road oxidants and corrosives from the lower body panels onto the upper body panels: Towels used for buffing the sides and rocker panels must not be used on upper body surfaces.

4. Always wax your Jeep in the shade. Many polishes and waxes have chemistry that will evaporate rapidly in direct sunlight. A hot paint surface is more vulnerable to damage.

5. Apply polish to the cloth or bonnet. Pouring it onto the painted surface may cause uneven chemical action, including stains.

6. Avoid use of any product that seals paint permanently. Such materials may prevent normal expansion and contraction of paint and seldom offer protection against UV radiation. Auto painters lament the "fish-eye" effect that results when repainting finishes sealed with permanent protectants.

7. Invest in the miracles of modern science. Special detailing chemicals not only leave more time for four-wheeling, fishing and fun, but they often provide superior results.

8. Allow vinyl surfaces to breathe. Most vinyl has a chemically engineered topcoat that needs protection. Choose your vinyl treatment carefully. I use '303' Protectant.

9. Use a small detail brush to reach difficult areas. A freshly polished finish draws attention to those small crevices and crannies that you miss. Extra minutes make the difference between a show-stopper and a shoddy job.

10. Pay attention to quality. There's a reason for higher priced products, and all waxes are not the same. The longest lasting stuff may not serve your paint finish best. Look for breathable carnaubas and anti-oxidants. They can extend the life of your Jeep's finish.

metal polish such as Simichrome does the trick. If the wheel surface has oxidized, polish on a die grinder powered buffer pad will restore the surface. A light coat of Carnauba-based wax will allow porous surfaces to flex and breathe.

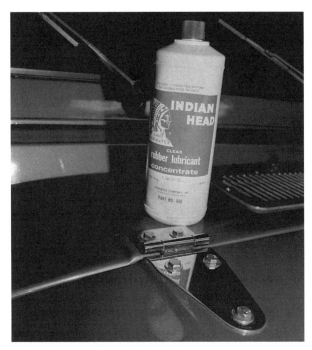

Fig. 14-21. *Permatex Indian Head Rubber Lubricant has a long history. Claimed harmless to vinyl and canvas tops, this substance has many uses around your Jeep—including emergencies like mounting tires along the trail. Used regularly on shock bushings, sway bar bushings and other chassis rubber, Indian Head Rubber Lubricant enhances off-pavement service and parts life.*

The final step in detailing your truck is interior clean-up. Professional shampoos, cleaners and specialized chemicals work quickly on the interior. Carpet stains and other tough challenges respond best to professional cleaners.

Stripping Film and Wax Buildup

Improperly applied waxes and polishes, particularly those which seal the paint surface, will permit oxidation and yellowing. ("Yellow" simply means that oxidation has occurred.) The worst example is a truck with a clear coat finish that has become sun-bleached, dulled or cracked.

Some aftermarket paint sealant/protectant products also pose a threat to paint. Claiming long term paint protection and ease of maintenance, many of these products actually smother the original paint. Sealed and unable to breathe, the treated paint or clear coat surface succumbs to weather checking, cracking and other damage caused by ultraviolet sunlight.

The most common cause of wax buildup is poor application technique. The paint finish likely had untreated surface oxidation, and uneven hand rubbing has built up successive layers of wax. Although most

Chemistry 101 for Detailers

Effective detailing means knowing which chemicals to use on a given surface. When washing your Jeep, look for solutions that prevent streaking. Professional car soaps remove very little wax and allow several cleanings between re-wax jobs. Tar and spot removers are actually high-grade cleaning solvents designed for safe work around interior and exterior finishes.

> CAUTION —
> *Before trying any detailing product, read its label closely for proper use and application. You could ruin an expensive paint finish or leather upholstery by simply applying the wrong chemicals.*

Although tar and spot remover safely removes grease, gum, most stains, adhesives and undercoating, it may affect the topcoat of some vinyl and plastic items. Read labels carefully. When safe, these chemicals are useful for removing wax and silicone before painting stripes or applying touchup.

Rubber dressing and protectants generally have a polymer or silicone base. Renewing tires, moldings, floor mats, pedal pads, dashpads, vinyl tops and other items is often as easy as applying the right chemistry to the surface. Some materials require slight hand buffing.

Rubbing and finishing compounds meet several uses. Cleaning or cutting into the painted surface, these materials remove dull paint, orange peel and corrosive water spots.

Often, new paint or even clear coatings require color sanding, which leaves a mildly scratched, dull surface. Power (orbital) buffing with a non-abrasive chemical compound can make the finish smooth and shiny.

Carecraft's Swirl Remover fits a special niche. Carecraft calls its product a buffing cleaner capable of removing fine scratches and oxidation. Swirl Remover contains no wax or silicone, yet it lubricates the buffer pad. As a follow-up to rubbing compound or a poor detail job, Swirl Remover has no harsh abrasives and can be a mild, effective alternative for restoring a slightly oxidized finish. Though not at ease with abrasive rubbing compounds, I have pulled off professional quality "magic stunts" with Carecraft's Swirl Remover and an orbital buffer.

Additionally, there are treatments and cleaners for upholstery, rugs, chrome, stainless steel and every other material found on Jeep trucks. The concern here is chemical compatibility. For questionable materials, always test chemicals first. Discoloration and damage can result from improper use or mixing incompatible chemicals.

Let modern tools and chemistry do the work. Save your time and energy for recreational pursuits!

one-step waxes and polishes employ a cleaner to cut through and loosen the old layer of wax, such chemistry often fails.

After using a random orbital buffer and professional chemical products, it's obvious why hand polishing leads to wax buildup. A truck waxed regularly by hand will turn a terrycloth buffer bonnet blacker than the tire sidewalls. Successive layers of wax simply seal off the paint. Paint cracking or severe fade then develops. A proper wax job should lightly and evenly coat the surface.

Use a chemical finishing compound and an orbital buffer to reverse the damage of wax buildup. (Wherever possible, avoid the use of rubbing compounds. They are abrasive and remove paint.) The goal is to eliminate old wax and gently lift oxidized, dead paint from below the wax.

Once the finishing or cleaning compound has removed wax and oxidized paint, the surface will regain its luster. The fresh finish can receive a coat of quality polish or wax.

3. Pickup Bed and Tub Liners

Did your Jeep Pickup, Comanche, Gladiator or CJ Scrambler go off to work, only to return with its bed all bashed and battle scarred? Does your cargo bed rattle with tools, jacks and other menacing items? An aftermarket slide-in or sprayed bed liner can prevent utility bed damage. Both the looks of your Jeep and its resale value will benefit from bed protection.

Permanent Installations

Many Jeep truck owners want ongoing bed protection. The multi-purpose use of these vehicles create a never ending hazard to the paint and sheet metal in the bed. Loading firewood, hauling parts or moving construction materials often mixes with your recreational chores.

The traditional plastic tub liners now compete with durable spray-in bed liners. A slide-in plastic tub liner is replaceable (or removable on re-sale of the truck). Current spray-in materials are permanent. Spray-in liners offer valuable rust-proofing benefits, as the tough polyurethane spray adheres to every square inch of the pickup bed or a CJ/Wrangler tub.

This last point is important. A large concern with slide-in bed liner installations is that moisture can creep beneath the liner. Once there, collected water waits patiently for bare metal to appear. Hidden rust forms, spreading beneath the bed liner. Often, rust perforation through the bottom of the bed is the first clue that oxidation has occurred.

Paint Scratch Repairs

Four-wheel drive vehicles have close scrapes with trees, limbs and brush. Scratches detract from the appearance of your Jeep, and brush-on touch up paint often leaves ugly scars. Armed with a random orbital buffer, some brush touch-up paint, a sheet of 1200-grit color sanding paper, a 3M Soft Hand Pad and some Carecraft Swirl Remover, here's my formula for a super-fast, professional repair:

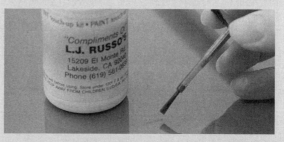

9:00 a.m.—Slight scratch in hood surface is carefully cleaned and filled with touch-up paint. (5 minutes)

11:00 a.m.—Left in direct sunlight, touch up is completely dry. Move the Jeep into the shade.

11:30 a.m.—Gently color sand with 1200-grit paper and 3M pad: Confine sanding to the crown of the touch-up paint. Sanding stops when adjacent paint finish shows signs of ultra-fine, uniform discoloration. (10 minutes)

11:40 a.m.—Swirl Remover applied to orbital buffer pad. Buffing the discolored area, action concentrates directly on the repair. Light use of the buffer edge will focus the polishing effort. (2 minutes or less buffing time)

11:48 a.m.—Wipe away excess. Treat the beautifully matched surface to a new coat of wax/polish. (6 minutes)

12:00 p.m.—Load fishing poles, reels and gear into the Jeep. Try not to grin too broadly. Drive a few hours to hot angling spot. Set up camp, then head for pools and ripples on creek. As sun gets low, catch limit before returning to camp. (Time involved depends on fishing action.)

If a bed liner is installed in a new truck, the odds of rust formation can be drastically reduced. Most rustout develops when owners install bed protection after scratches and seam spreading have already scarred the bed. For a bed liner installation in a used truck, first eliminate all rust, caulk or seal each seam, and prime any repaired surfaces.

Tub or polyurethane spray-in bed liners offer protection against chemicals, corrosives and denting. For loading and handling materials, however, another factor should also influence your choice of a liner: anti-skid protection. Some liner surfaces become so slick when wet that they create an actual hazard. Others of-

fer no-skid surfaces that keep a cargo handler from doing the Russian splits—often with a heavy load in each hand!

An alternative to the permanent tub or spray foam installation is a bed mat. Bed mats, custom fitted to cover the entire floor of your truck, provide substantial protection. Better mats offer skid resistance and a cushioned cargo surface. Mats insulate the bed or floor from cargo damage. Additionally, you can remove a quality mat periodically to thoroughly clean and wax the bed to reduce the risk of rust formation. Better mats are resistant to oil, chemicals and marring, providing years of service.

Chapter 15

Electrical System Basics

Jeep restoration and maintenance include the electrical system and wiring. Repair work and routine service frequently mean the renewal of wiring and changing connectors. Often, the frame-up restoration of a Jeep chassis requires wiring the truck from scratch!

A successful wiring job is gratifying. Your Jeep works dependably when the lights glow, turn signals flash, starter spins, wipers swish, spark plugs fire, alternator charges and electric fuel pump pulses. Understanding the dynamics of a Jeep electrical system can enhance your troubleshooting skills, a vital asset when traveling off the pavement.

1. The Electrical System

Jeep electrical systems vary in voltage layouts. Until the late 1950s, civilian Jeeps were all 6-volt designs. Military Jeeps before the M38 were six-volt, while the M38 (flat fender) and later M38-A1 (CJ body style) had 24-volt electrics. All Jeep civilian models from the late 1950s forward have 12-volt negative ground electrical systems.

System Overview

Depending on the chassis year, a 6-volt or 12-volt wet storage battery supplies current for the electrical system. Jeep trucks have used a variety of starter motor types, including spring Bendix, overrunning clutch drive, Bendix Folo-Thru Drive, Delco-Remy and Auto-Lite designs and, more recently, Chrysler's permanent magnet motor types.

Generators served Jeep battery charging needs for several years into the 12-volt era. The first models to use alternators were early '60s J-trucks and Wagoneers.

Early Jeep wires and looms were cloth-wrapped, supplanted by plastic in the 12-volt era. Either insulation type deteriorates over time. The Jeep 4x4 used off-pavement, in agriculture, around corrosive industrial settings or at a minesite will eventually be a candidate for electrical wire restoration.

What Is An Alternator?

Although alternator designs have evolved since the early '60s, their operation remains much the same. Typically, as the ignition switch turns ON, a wire lead with 12-volt current feeds to the alternator or external regulator. Through transistor and diode switching, current reaches a field coil. While the engine cranks, a high field current is generated to increase available voltage. This is the pre-charging mode.

Once the engine starts, the alternator's rotor spins at speed, with alternating current produced within the stator winding. The stator sends AC current to an internal rectifier bridge and diodes, which convert the AC current to usable 12-volt DC current. Diodes also prevent battery current from draining at the alternator.

The battery (BAT) pole on the alternator or regulator performs two roles: 1) a route for charging current returning to the battery, and 2) as an information source for battery state of charge or load.

During normal operation, any amperage drains on the battery send a voltage reading to the alternator's regulator. (Later trucks feature voltmeters on the instrument panel. The voltmeter illustrates a relationship between battery drain and volts.) During engine cranking, a 12-volt battery reads approximately 9 or 10 volts. At times, winch operation mimics this load. Headlights, air conditioning or any other electrical demand also drops voltage at the battery.

How the Alternator Charges the Battery

The alternator maintains full battery voltage under a range of loads. When your Jeep's battery has a low state of charge, the alternator returns high amperage current to the battery. Although this current flowing from the battery is actually a quantity of amperage, the battery and regulator interpret the flow in terms of voltage.

Charging a 12-volt battery requires meeting a range of voltages at various temperatures. At very low temperatures, for example, the regulator may test at 14.9–15.9 volt current. The same regulator at 80° F may operate between 13.9 and 14.6 volts, while 140° ambient temperature produces 13.3–13.9 volts. Above 140° F, the same regulator may offer 13.6 volts.

Since a fully charged battery reads approximately 12.6 volts, the charging circuit must at least maintain that voltage. This requires enough current flow to recharge the battery plus the amperage needed to operate the entire range of electrical devices...How odd that 13.5 or greater volts serve the charging needs of a 12-volt electrical system.

Routine Service

Battery condition and state of charge are very important to your Jeep's performance. Later models with electronic fuel and spark management systems depend upon precise voltage readings and strong current supply. Any Jeep, regardless of the environment in which it operates, requires a quality battery in premium condition. The new generation of high cold cranking amperage (CCA) batteries exceed older OEM requirements by a good margin. (For details on battery service, see the lubrication/service chapter.)

> NOTE —
> Alternator/generator drive belt condition is crucial. Always carry a spare belt on remote backcountry trips.

Jeep generators require periodic bearing lubrication. Generator systems use an external voltage regulator which is adjustable.

"Polarity" is a concern when servicing or replacing either the generator or generator regulator. You must "polarize" the generator/regulator to prevent damage and permit charging. As the regulator adjusts current flow back to the battery, correct wiring of the charging system is essential.

Polarizing the generator is important when you replace the generator or voltage regulator. The two types of regulators (either internally or externally grounded field) require different procedures. Make certain which regulator your Jeep has, and consult your Jeep service manual before attempting to polarize the generator/regulator.

Jeep lighting is basic, with current simply flowing through switches and relays to the headlights, tail lamps, turn and brake lights, warning lights and interior lamps. To avoid shorts and unreliable service, your Jeep lighting system requires safe wire routing, correct wire size and secure connections.

Aftermarket accessories pose a challenge. Sound systems, add-on lighting, auxiliary fuel pumps and other additions to your Jeep's electrical system de-

mand careful consideration. Where should components source their current supply? What wire gauges are suitable? How do you route wires safely? (See "Accessories" chapter for additional details.)

The factory Jeep electrical system follows a layout common to other U.S. trucks and cars. Early CJ and military Jeep electrical systems are very simple, built around common components available at most auto supply houses. Jeep Corporation's early J-trucks and Wagoneers boasted more stylized instrumentation, distinctive manual switches and more modern electrical systems. These vehicles introduce model-specific electrical parts and power accessories.

The busiest, most complicated Jeep electrical systems emerged between the late 1970s and mid-'80s. Air conditioning, closed loop emission controls and electronic fuel, spark and automatic transmission systems create a maze of wires.

> NOTE —
> Work on any Jeep electrical system involves use of accurate wiring diagrams. You must understand wire gauge requirements and have a practical sense for where to route wires and avoid electrical shorts.

Relays

Relays begin to appear with the 12-volt models. Relays have two basic designs, each with a different function. The electro-thermal relay receives and delivers current to a bi-metallic contact set. After exposure for a given interval of heat, the switch opens, stopping current flow. As the contacts cool down, the switch closes. The common turn signal switch is this type of relay.

Fig. 15-1. *Relays and fuses come in a variety of sizes and meet various needs. Circuit or reset breakers work well with vehicles that are temporarily exposed to shorts or grounding (like your Jeep 4x4 submerged in a running stream).*

Fig. 15-2. *This unique fuse/relay holder, available through Wrangler Power Products, features popular ATO-type fuses and circuit breakers that fit ATO sockets.*

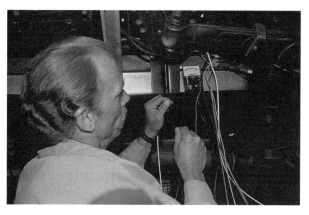

Fig. 15-3. *Grounds are as important as hot sources. Ohmmeters take the guesswork out of testing your Jeep's engine, chassis and body grounds.*

The main advantage of relays is that minor amounts of current can control major power flow. For heavy amperage (a measurement of electrical resistance), this is useful. Systems like the horn and starter motor can use lighter wiring over several sections. The horn button activates a relay, which directs current from a higher amp battery pole to the horn. Starter solenoids, which deliver very high battery current directly to the starter motor, activate from much lighter gauge wires.

An electro-magnetic relay directs current to most Jeep starter motors. Some Jeep starter solenoids also engage the drive teeth with the flywheel teeth. Similarly, fuel cut-off solenoids and similar devices use electrical current to magnetize and move a plunger. This is a practical, safe way to perform mechanical tasks.

Volt/Ohmmeter: The Perfect Troubleshooting Tool

An ohmmeter can read circuit continuity levels and ohms resistance. A volt meter reads the actual voltage available at a given circuit. Adjusted for alternating current (AC) or direct current (DC), volt meters measure line voltage between any two points. For automotive electrical troubleshooting, either function can provide a wealth of useful information.

Ohms, a measurement of electrical resistance, follows an engineering formula: 1 ohm = 1/siemens = 1 volt/ampere. Simply, each ohm is a precise increment of resistance for current flow. Conductive liquids or solids (such as electrical wiring) serve as mediums through which we measure ohms resistance.

Aside from testing alternator diodes or components in a fuel injection or electronic ignition system, most Jeep electrical troubleshooting centers around continuity of current flow and availability of voltage.

The ohms segment of a volt/ohmmeter will quickly satisfy a wide range of continuity checks, including efforts to find shorts and partially or fully "open" circuits.

An inexpensive needle meter can handle basic voltage and resistance tests. For less than twenty-five dollars, you can buy a quality pocket-size tester. (My Radio Shack tester, purchased in 1982 for $10, still functions flawlessly. The compact volt/ohmmeter has survived travels over a variety of rough terrain.) Designed for light use, these units offer a wide range of effective tests and fit neatly into your Jeep toolbox. For testing fuel injection and other electronic components, however, you must use a digital meter.

> *CAUTION —*
> • *Connect or disconnect multiple connectors and test leads only with the ignition off. Switch multi-meter functions or measurement ranges only with the test leads disconnected.*
>
> • *Do not use a test lamp that has a normal incandescent bulb to test circuits containing electronic components. Use only an LED (light emitting diode) test lamp.*
>
> • *Do not use an analog (swing-needle) meter to check circuit resistance or continuity on electronic (solid state) components. Use only a high quality digital multi-meter having high input impedance (at least 10 megohm).*

1.1 Electrical Troubleshooting

Four things are required for current to flow in any automotive electrical circuit: a voltage source, wires or connections to transport the voltage, a consumer or device that uses the electricity, and a connection to ground. For trouble-free operation, it is very important that the ground connections, including the negative battery cable and the body ground strap, remain clean and free from corrosion.

Most problems can be found using only a multimeter (volt/ohm/amp meter). These include checks for voltage supply, for breaks in the wiring (infinite resis-

Fig. 15-4. *Trailer connectors demand more than a test lamp check. You can detect insufficient current flow or resistance at a ground lead with your volt/ohmmeter.*

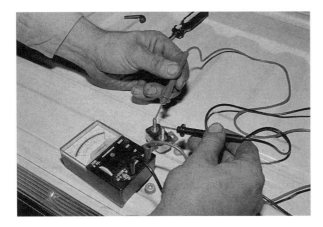

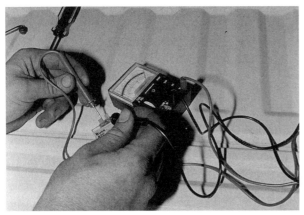

Fig. 15-5. *This 20 amp breaker and a late ATO style Buss fuse each pass the ohmmeter test. Test any suspect circuits and switches for resistance readings.*

tance/no continuity), or for a proper path to ground that completes the circuit.

D.C. electric current is logical in its flow, always moving from the voltage source toward ground. Keeping this in mind, electrical faults can be located through a process of elimination. When troubleshooting a complex circuit, separate the circuit into smaller parts. The general tests outlined here may be helpful in finding electrical problems. The information is most helpful when used with the factory wiring diagrams.

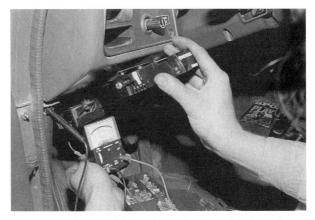

Fig. 15-6. *Test variable voltage devices with the volt meter. Although most trailer brake controllers are now electronic, they still send voltage signals to the trailer brakes, much like with earlier rheostat-type controllers.*

Testing for Voltage and Ground

The most useful and fundamental electrical troubleshooting technique is checking for voltage and ground. A voltmeter or a simple test light should be used for this test. For example, if a parking light does not work, checking for voltage at the bulb socket will determine if the circuit is functioning correctly or if the bulb itself is faulty.

To check for positive (+) battery voltage using a test light, connect the test light wire to a clean, unpainted metal part of the Jeep or a known good ground. Use the pointed end of the light to probe the positive (+) connector or socket. To check for continuity to ground, connect the test light wire to the positive (+) battery post or a battery source. Use the pointed end of the light to probe the connector or socket leading to ground. In either case, the test light should light up.

WARNING —
Never create electrical sparks at the battery. A hot or defective battery emits explosive gases.

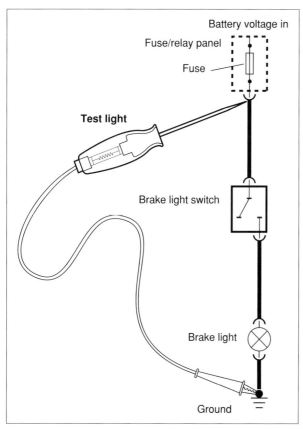

Fig. 15-7. *Test light set-up for checking voltage. A test light is the quickest way to check for voltage and ground.*

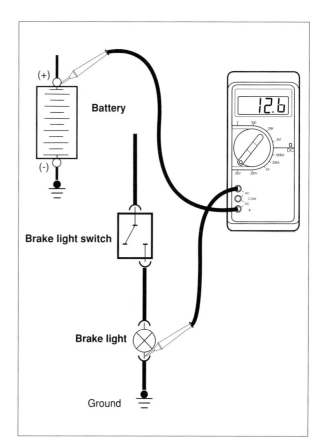

Fig. 15-8. *Voltmeter being used to check for ground.*

CAUTION —
Do not use the pointed end of a test light to pierce through a wire's insulation. This could permanently damage the wire or insulation. For the Jeep used off-pavement or for launching a boat, piercing an exposed wire leads to "wicking action." Here, corrosion migrates within the wire and shorts some distance away. This creates a difficult troubleshooting problem common to boats and boat trailer wiring.

NOTE —
A test light only determines if voltage or ground is present. It does not determine how much voltage is available or the quality of the path to ground. If the voltage reading is important, such as when testing a battery, use a digital voltmeter. To check the condition of the ground connection, check the voltage drop on the suspected connection as described below.

To check for voltage using a voltmeter, set the meter to 'DCV' and the correct scale. Connect the negative (-) test lead to the negative (-) battery terminal or a known good ground. Touch the positive (+) test lead

to the positive wire or connector. To check for ground, connect the positive (+) test lead to the positive (+) battery terminal or voltage source. Touch the negative (-) test lead to the wire leading to ground. The meter should read battery voltage.

CAUTION —
When using an analog (swing needle) voltmeter, be careful not to reverse the test leads. Reversing the polarity may damage the meter.

Continuity Test

The continuity test can be used to check a circuit or switch. Because most automotive circuits are designed to have little or no resistance, a circuit or part of a circuit can be easily checked for faults using an ohmmeter or a self-powered test light. An open circuit or a circuit with high resistance will not allow current to flow. A circuit with little or no resistance allows current to flow easily.

When checking continuity, keep the ignition off. On circuits that are powered at all times, disconnect the battery. Using the appropriate wiring diagram, a

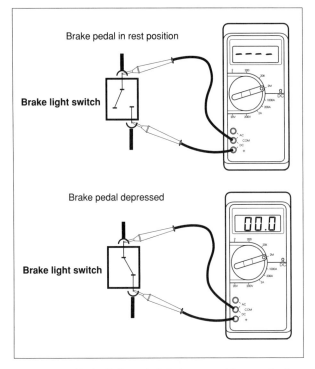

Fig. 15-9. *Brake light switch being tested for continuity. With brake pedal in rest position (switch open), there is no continuity. With brake pedal depressed (switch closed), there is continuity.*

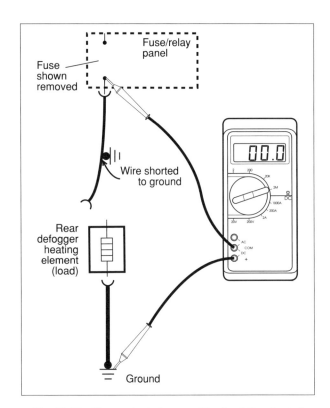

Fig. 15-10. *Ohmmeter being used to check for short circuit to ground.*

circuit can be easily tested by checking for continuity. In this way, you can locate faulty connections, wires, switches, relays, and engine sensors.

Short Circuit Test

A short circuit is exactly what the name implies. The circuit takes a shorter path than it was designed to take. The most common short that causes problems is a short to ground where the insulation on a positive (+) wire wears away and the metal wire becomes exposed. If the exposed wire is live (positive battery voltage) and contacts a ground source, a fuse will blow and the circuit may possibly be damaged.

> *CAUTION —*
> *On circuits protected with large fuses (25 amp and greater), the wires or circuit components may be damaged before the fuse blows. Always check for damage before replacing fuses of this rating. Always use replacement fuses of the same rating.*

Shorts to ground can be located with a voltmeter, a test light, or an ohmmeter. Short circuits are often difficult to locate. Therefore, the correct wiring diagram must be available. You can find short circuits using a logical approach that follows the current's path.

> *WARNING —*
> *When disconnecting battery cables from a Jeep negative ground system, disconnect the negative (ground) cable first. When re-attaching the battery cables, attach the negative/ground cable last. This reduces risk of creating a spark that could cause the battery to explode.*

To check for a short circuit to ground, remove the blown fuse from the circuit and disconnect the cables from the battery (negative/ground cable first). Disconnect the harness connector from the circuit's load or consumer. Using a self-powered test light or an ohmmeter, connect one test lead to the load side fuse terminal (terminal connected to the consumer's wiring circuit). Touch the other test lead to a quality ground. If the test lamp lights or the ohmmeter shows continuity, this circuit/wiring has a short to ground.

A wire open, not shorted to ground (fuse not blown), can be located using a test light or a voltmeter. Battery cables attached, remove the fuse for the circuit being tested. At the fuse block, connect one of the test instrument's leads to one fuse terminal, the other lead to the opposing terminal. Switch on (power up) the open circuit. (If necessary, check the wiring diagram to determine when the circuit is live.)

Working from the wire harness nearest to the fuse/relay panel, move or wiggle the wires while observing the test light or the meter. Continue to move down the harness until the test light blinks or the meter displays a reading. This is the location of the short/open.

Visually inspect the wire harness at this point for any damage or defects. If no faults are visible, shut off the circuit and disconnect the test lamp or voltmeter at the fuse terminals. (If wire in question is a continuously hot or battery lead, disconnect the battery cables, negative cable first.) At the suspected harness section, carefully slice open the harness cover and/or the suspected wire's insulation. Inspect closely and repair any faults found.

Voltage Drop Test

The wires, connectors, and switches that carry current are designed with very low resistance so that current flows with a minimum loss of voltage. A voltage drop is caused by higher than normal resistance in a circuit. This additional resistance can decrease or stop the flow of current.

A voltage drop appears as problems ranging from dim headlights to sluggish wipers or rapidly flashing

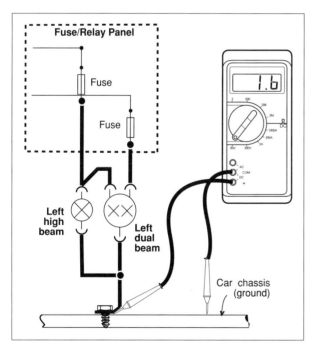

Fig. 15-11. *Example of voltage drop test. Symptom: dim headlights. Voltmeter showed 1.6-volt drop between ground connector and chassis ground. After removing and cleaning headlight ground, voltage drop returned to normal and headlights became bright once more.*

directional signals. Some common sources of voltage drops are faulty wires or switches, dirty or corroded connections or contacts, and loose or corroded ground wires and ground connections.

Voltage drop can only be checked when current is running through the circuit, such as by operating the starter motor or turning on the headlights. Making a voltage drop test requires measuring the voltage in the circuit and comparing it to what the voltage should be. Since these measurements are usually small, a digital voltmeter should be used to ensure accurate readings. If you suspect a voltage drop, turn the circuit on and measure the voltage at the circuit's load.

> *WARNING —*
> *To avoid risk of creating a spark at the battery and a possible explosion, take voltage readings away from the battery. The starter solenoid or a similar main junction/terminal block can serve here and provide nearly the same readings as battery voltage.*

> NOTE —
> • A voltage drop test is generally more accurate than a simple resistance check because the resistances involved are often too small to measure with most ohmmeters. For example, a resistance as small as 0.02 ohms results in a 3 volt drop in a typical 150 amp starter circuit. (150 amps x 0.02 ohms = 3 volts).

> • Keep in mind that voltage with the key on and voltage with the engine running are not the same. With the ignition on and the engine off, fully charged battery voltage should be approximately 12.6 volts. With the engine running (charging voltage), voltage should be something like 14.5 volts. For more precise measurements, measure voltage with the ignition on and then with the engine running.

> • The maximum voltage drop, as recommended by the Society of Automotive Engineers (SAE), is: 0 volt for small wire connections; 0.1 volt for high-current connections; 0.2 volt for high-current cables; and 0.3 volt for switch or solenoid contacts. On longer wires or cables, the drop may be slightly higher. In any case, a voltage drop of more than 1.0 volt usually indicates a problem.

Testing Battery and Charging System

When checking the battery and charging circuits, be careful and considerate of battery hazards. High amperage applied to a defective battery is, literally, a potential bombshell. When you know the Jeep's charging system is functional but the battery acts dead, proceed with extreme caution.

Fig. 15-12. *The solenoid junction block and other points well away from the battery provide alternate battery testing sources. Avoid direct voltage checks at the battery, especially after heavy charging from the alternator or a battery charger. Explosive hydrogen gas can surround the battery and ignite from the slightest spark.*

WARNING —
Always unplug your battery charger before connecting or disconnecting the clamp leads. A minute spark near an overcharged or defective battery is a hazard. Avoid the risk of igniting explosive hydrogen gas. If in doubt, make volt/ohmmeter tests well away from the battery, at the alternator, a factory wire junction or the breaker panel.

Find a good ground, and attach the negative probe. Attach the positive probe to the hot wire source and read battery voltage. If you get a reading of 12.30 or less volts, with all known current drains (including lights, ignition and accessories) shut off, the battery's state of charge is at 50% capacity or lower. This indicates poor electrical connections, weak alternator output, excessive current drain from accessories or a defective battery.

You can check for each of these with the volt/ohmmeter. Start the engine and begin at the alternator. The battery signal to the voltage regulator should say, "I'm low on voltage, flow some current my way." In response, the normal charge circuit will call for a heavy amperage flow. Use the voltmeter mode of the tester, and probe the charge wire at the alternator with the positive lead. Attach the negative lead to ground.

Charging properly, the alternator should now read well over 12.6 volts. With current flowing toward the battery, voltage could read 14.8 volts or higher, depending upon the parameters of the voltage regulator. If you see no increase in voltage beyond your static battery test level, the alternator or regulator is not per-

forming properly. Before condemning these expensive parts, however, troubleshoot further.

Shut the engine off and leave the meter set for a precise reading in the 12–15 volt range. Touch the heavy (BATTERY or BAT) lead at the rear of the alternator with the positive (red) meter probe. Using a quality engine ground for the negative probe, again read available voltage at the alternator. This should be approximately the same as the battery's voltage.

If you cannot read voltage here, a wiring or fusible link problem exists. Trace the route of the alternator BAT lead. At the first junction between the alternator and the battery, your ohmmeter test can begin.

Zero the meter and set for DC-Ohms and K-Ohms. Check the wire for continuity and conductivity by holding a probe at each end of the wire and reading the scale. If no opens or shorts exist, the meter will set at the zero line. If there is too much resistance, as with a slight open in the lead or a poor connection, the needle will read upward on the scale. An actual open in the wire prevents the needle from moving at all.

Repeat this procedure along the wire path toward the battery. Eventually, you will locate the short or open. Resistance readings help locate corrosion within wire leads and at connections, too. Battery cables or terminal clamp connections often develop such problems. Unseen in a visual inspection, a current blockage cannot fool your ohmmeter. The energy needed to keep current flowing is measurable.

NOTE —
When the alternator unit is defective, your Jeep shop manual will provide test information and overhaul procedures.

Most bench tests of alternators, generators, starters, coils and ignition modules involve a volt/ohmmeter. You can also test headlight and dimmer switches, relays, breakers, fuses, and turn signal switches with the meter. Tracing poor ground wires, repairing faulty gauges, finding nuisance shorts, isolating worn spark plug cables and most other electrical tests are well within the volt/ohmmeter's ability.

Getting A Charge Out Of Your Alternator

Concerns around alternator output should begin with checking the drive belt tension. Next, inspect all wire connections. To test the alternator and regulator output, test the current flow from the alternator with an induction ammeter. Compare the ammeter flow to Jeep factory specifications, beginning at an idle, then 1500 rpm and 2000 rpm. Perform the induction meter test with the battery charge low. You want the alternator near maximum output.

NOTE—
Alternator and generator output tests are similar. For simplicity, I use the term "alternator" for this section. If your earlier Jeep truck has a generator, you will find many of these troubleshooting and testing suggestions useful and applicable.

An induction ammeter, although not as accurate as more expensive test equipment, provides a quick sense for alternator output. These handy tools fit easily in your trailside Jeep tool box. Since the meter simply fits over the cable or wire insulation, you can test without removing any electrical component. (Make certain that magnetic interference from adjacent wires does not influence the readings.)

My alternator (charging) and starter (draw) induction meters have served for over twenty-five years. If your equipment includes inexpensive magnetic field induction meters and a volt-ohms-resistance meter, you can perform a variety of field tests.

NOTE—
When you suspect alternator troubles but cannot find the source, sublet the alternator and regulator to an automotive electrical repair shop. The shop can separate regulator troubles from alternator defects.

Factory or professional service manuals detail bench testing and additional troubleshooting guidelines for your alternator and regulator.

NOTE—
Most public libraries maintain a reference section with automotive service manuals. If you intend to perform professional level work on your Jeep, I recommend investing in a Jeep shop/service manual for your model. See 'Appendix' for sources of reprint OEM manuals that cover earlier Jeep models. Assure professional results by using such guidelines. I do.

Shorts and Voltage Leak-off

If starter and alternator circuits check okay and the battery cells read normal specific gravity at a full charge, chronic low battery voltage is still possible. Accessories like the clock or the improper hook-up of an aftermarket sound system can cause the battery to go dead. (Be sure to wire your sound system through a fused and key-switched 'Accessories' source.)

A defect in the ignition switch, air conditioning clutch, lighting equipment, the turn signal switch, a ra-

dio, tape deck or hazard lamp can each draw excess current from the battery. The dome, underhood and hazard lamps operate without the ignition switch on, so check these areas first. When an aftermarket accessory taps directly to a battery source, disconnect the accessory and see if the problem resolves.

If a current drain persists, suspect the ignition switch. A shorted ignition switch can deliver current, even when the key is in the off position. Current may be passing to the coil, ignition module or computer (on later Jeep models). You can confirm current flow at each of these areas by probing for voltage readings with your volt-ohmmeter.

Testing Ignition and Fuel System Components

Most Jeep tool boxes include test lamp type continuity and hot lead testers. The volt/ohmmeter serves far beyond these tools, giving precise readings about the underlying condition of your Jeep electrical system. Spark plug misfires or engine balking under load are often the result of excessive resistance in the primary or secondary ignition circuits. Here, the volt/ohmmeter provides the ideal tool for diagnostic work.

Many late Jeep ignition and fuel system parts rely on electrical switches, relays and electronic components. Given the ohms-resistance values for these pieces, you can easily test them with a meter. (Be aware that tests on electronic EFI/computer components require a digital volt-ohmmeter.) Troubleshooting and service guidelines in a factory-level service manual provide test criteria.

Ballast resistors, spark plug wires and electronic ignition modules each have specified tests. Voltage and ohms-resistance readings of a ballast resistor can determine whether the unit works properly. Likewise, an

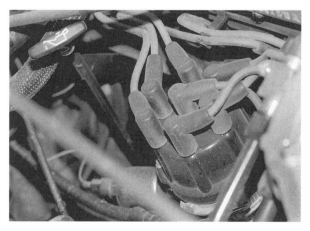

Fig. 15-13. *Check your ignition cables periodically with an ohmmeter. Electronic ignitions with higher firing voltages place more stress on high tension carbon cables.*

ignition coil has a specified resistance in its winding. Ohms resistance tests of a coil can identify most shorts and internal defects. An inexpensive volt-ohmmeter can even find fraying, weak primary wires in an older breaker point ignition.

You can also test spark plug cables with an ohmmeter. Read resistance and identify defective wires or those that will demand excessive firing voltage. Continuity/ohms tests can quickly identify a rotor short or a cross-firing, carbon tracking distributor cap.

> NOTE—
> When worn excessively, GM HEI ignition rotors short to ground through the distributor shaft. You may experience this problem with Jeep's Iron Duke (Pontiac) four or 2.8L V-6 engine.

Used imaginatively, volt/ohmmeter tests often serve the same purpose as diagnostic analyzers that cost thousands more. Although fancy oscilloscope patterns and digital electronic readouts are valuable, the volt/ohmmeter's simple, pragmatic answers outweigh the limitations of much more elaborate diagnostic equipment—you can't tow an oscilloscope engine analyzer through the Rubicon!

2. The Starter Motor and Cold Cranking Chores

Starter motors must overcome engine compression, valve spring tension and spinning belt-driven components. Toss in some ignition spark advance, and it's clear why some starter drive housings break.

12-volt starters are high torque electric motors, some aided by internal gear reduction drives. Very heavy lock test amperage draw, well in excess of 450 amps on some V-8 engine applications, is normal. Such a starter may demand over 100 amps just to spin freely on a bench test.

> NOTE—
> A defective starter motor may draw over 500 amps while cranking the engine, enough to melt both the battery and its cables. The typical engine with a modest compression ratio requires a starter cranking draw of only 150 to 210 amps.

A 12-volt automotive starter motor can spin as high as 8500 rpm on the bench. However, while cranking the engine at 160 crankshaft rpm, with an 18-to-1 flywheel-to-starter drive tooth ratio, this same starter motor might spin 2900 rpm. Considering the amperage necessary to rotate the crankshaft, the starter motor has a major job.

Brush-type starters consist of typical electrical motor components: an armature, field coils and brushes that ride on the armature's commutator. From a service standpoint, these motors require nothing more than periodic brush changes and replacement of the armature end bushings. There are other wear factors, however, that can also retire the starter motor from service.

The Starter Solenoid
For massive current flow to reach the starter, without cooking the wiring circuits, the starter utilizes a solenoid switch. Simply put, the solenoid is an electrical switch that handles heavy current flow. The switch receives its signal from the ignition/starter switch via a small wire. Ignition switch current magnetizes the load switch inside the solenoid.

Once the load switch closes, heavy battery cable current flows to the starter motor. This sequence works in tandem with a starter drive gear. The gear engages the flywheel or flexplate ring gear teeth during starter operation. To prevent severe clash of teeth, starter drives have a clutch mechanism.

The Starter Drive
There are two types of starter drives. One design engages when the solenoid switch moves a shift lever. The other starter drive, found on the earliest Jeep starter motors, is a Bendix spring drive. The Bendix unit has a spring on the head of the starter drive. As the starter spins, centrifugal force launches the drive gear toward the flywheel ring gear. The spring absorbs shock. These Bendix drives were popular on Ford products for years, and they require no shift lever fork.

The very popular GM (Delco-Remy) starter utilizes a fork attached to the solenoid's magnetic plunger. When ignition switch current flows to the solenoid (mounted astride the starter motor), two events occur. The plunger moves the starter drive toward the flywheel teeth. Just upon engagement, a second phase begins as the solenoid closes the heavy amperage switch; battery current now flows to the starter motor.

All starters must compensate for drive gear shock. One source of starter nose end breakage, especially on big V-8s, is poor bracing at the rear of the starter. On many high performance GM applications, an angle bracket bolts between one of the starter through-bolts and the engine block. The bracket helps withstand the torque required to spin an LS-6 454 V-8. It alleviates starter flexing and prevents the drive gear from climbing up the flywheel teeth. The brace also reduces the risk of breaking the aluminum starter nose housing.

Fig. 15-14. *Release lever relationship is clear here. The solenoid's magnetic core draws the lever and also closes a high amp current switch. Forward of lever is clutch and drive gear.*

Fig. 15-15. *Induction ammeter can check starter or generator (shown here) current flow. Without removing the starter or any other parts, place the meter over the battery cable insulation. Used in conjunction with a volt-ohm meter, the induction ammeter can help pinpoint defects and malfunctions by showing excessive current draw while the engine cranks over.*

Troubleshooting the Starter Motor

Assuming that your Jeep engine won't crank over, you need to answer a few questions. Does the starter solenoid click? Is the starter motor turning too slowly? Can you hear the starter motor spin, but the engine isn't cranking?

If the battery and cables check okay and the solenoid simply clicks, the trouble is either 1) a defective solenoid, or 2) a defective starter motor (bad brushes, armature, or internal windings). Also check the starter drive shift lever or fork.

> NOTE—
> Check the neutral safety or clutch pedal switch before condemning the starter or solenoid switch.

When the starter motor turns too slowly or not at all, you must also consider internal engine problems. Two exceptions are a jammed starter drive or water in the cylinders, called "hydro-lock." Either condition will prevent the engine from rotating. If you suspect water in the engine, remove the spark plugs and crank again.

If you suspect internal engine problems, turn off the ignition switch and disconnect the coil high tension lead. Rotate the crankshaft by hand and observe any friction. If the crankshaft turns okay, the trouble is in the starter motor.

Attach a starter motor induction meter to the heavy starter cable, and observe the amount of current flow necessary to crank the engine. If an abnormally high amp draw is evident (above 150–210 amps), remove the starter motor for a bench test to determine the damage. Should the starter motor spin quickly and loudly, without rotating the crankshaft, suspect a defective starter drive.

On starters with the solenoid mounted at the motor housing, the starter drive or the starter shift lever could be faulty. Noise also suggests teeth missing from either the starter drive, flexplate or flywheel ring gear. The latter prospect is costly and difficult to repair. Fixing a damaged starter ring on a flywheel or flexplate requires removal of the transmission and either the clutch or torque converter.

In ranking order of cost, solenoids are the least expensive item next to brushes and armature bushings. Rebuilt starter motors are available and inexpensive, although a high performance engine may require a specialty aftermarket starter. Often, a generic rebuilt starter will not handle the load of a modified engine. You may need an aftermarket high-torque type starter.

If the field coils and armature are intact, your starter's overhaul includes new end bushings, properly installed and reamed to fit. New brushes, re-dressing (cleaning and re-surfacing) of the commutator, replacement of the starter shift lever/fork, a renewed solenoid and general clean-up of components will complete the job.

Review your factory-level service guidebook before attempting a starter motor overhaul. Sublet the services that exceed your capabilities or tool capacity. If your starter is not salvageable, consider a new or rebuilt unit, or consult an auto electric overhaul shop that specializes exclusively in bench repairs and the overhaul of electrical components. Jeep dealers and auto supply houses can furnish rebuilt/exchange starters for Jeep engines.

Overhauling Your Starter Motor

Off-pavement survival depends on an engine that will crank and start. Especially with an automatic transmission, starter performance is crucial. Depicted in the photos is a unique starter motor with features common to a variety of Jeep starters. For specific details on your Jeep's starter and electrical system, refer to a factory-level service manual.

Fig. 15-16. *A worn solenoid welded its contacts and kept the drive and starter motor engaged. The motor winding unraveled—not a healthy prospect for back-country travel.*

Fig. 15-18. *On this starter design, overhaul begins with the solenoid switch removal. This particular starter shares features with GM Delco-Remy units. The solenoid mounts to the nose section.*

Fig. 15-17. *Crumbliss test bench at North County Rebuilders tests this V-8 starter motor. If you suspect trouble with your Jeep starter, an auto electric shop can assess the unit's performance.*

Fig. 15-19. *Brushes are easily removed once you move this shield.*

Fig. 15-20. *Brushes removed, the end plate comes off.*

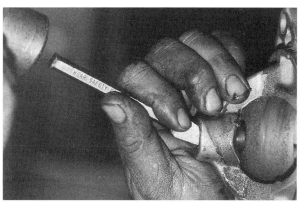

Fig. 15-23. *End bushing replacement is a standard procedure.*

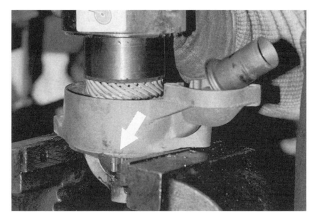

Fig. 15-21. *The commutator and armature show wear. Note the angle of the shaft (arrow), an indication of end bushing wear.*

Fig. 15-24. *Loosening brushes precedes field coil removal. An impact driver is necessary for removing field coil screws (arrows). These screws are seated very firmly and should only be removed if field coils require service.*

Fig. 15-22. *These two armature/commutators are identical—except for the diameters of the commutators. Smaller diameter is the result of re-surfacing/dressing.*

Fig. 15-25. *Bench tester charges armature. Time-honored hacksaw blade test indicates shorts or opens.*

Fig. 15-26. *Commutator receives re-surfacing in a metal lathe. This operation requires professional skill. Sublet the work to a local rebuilding shop.*

Fig. 15-27. *A new or rebuilt drive is a must. This item wears over time.*

Fig. 15-28. *Some starters require soldering new brushes into place. Once-common replacement brush sets have become rare, often available only through rebuilders.*

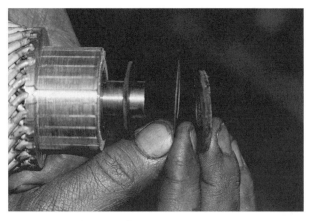

Fig. 15-29. *Selective fit thrust washers control end play of the armature.*

Fig. 15-30. *Release fork wear is evident in fork on right.*

Fig. 15-31. *Rebuilt solenoids are not all the same. On the right is a cheap replacement item of approximately 80 winds. 140 wind wire at left is a high quality rebuild, similar to a new OE unit.*

Chapter 16

Accessories

The American public's enthusiasm for the Jeep began when the first WWII MB 4x4s hit the surplus auction blocks. Former military rigs and a civilian CJ2-A counterpart quickly found their way to ranches, construction sites, utility company fleets and the homes of outdoor enthusiasts.

Struck by the primitive nature of the Jeep utility truck, enterprising owners and entrepreneurs began enhancing the vehicle's versatility. By the late 1940s, free wheeling locking hubs, cloth tops, engine-coolant heaters, auxiliary electric wiper motors, spare gas can holders and a host of power take-off driven accessories helped broaden the uses and improve the driveability of Jeep trucks.

Aftermarket and Dealer Installed Accessories

When Kaiser introduced the V-6 Buick engine option in 1965 CJ-5A and CJ-6A models, Jeep dealers were enjoying brisk profits from the sale of aftermarket products. Roll bars, spare tire carriers, draw hitches, front locking hubs, Warn's overdrive and front mount-ed winch products were popular accessories for the Jeep four-wheeler. Lighting and safety equipment had gained popularity, and extra traction was a constant topic. Factory limited slip and aftermarket locking differential designs were subjects of interest among hardcore off-pavement Jeep users.

Remote camping, rock collecting, searching ghost towns, fishing, hunting, hill climbs and assaulting rocky terrain were already commonplace Jeep roles. For the more competitive four-wheelers, off-road racing offered a new challenge. By the late 1960s, the Mint 400 and emerging Baja off-road races attracted large numbers of Jeep enthusiasts and celebrity drivers.

Aftermarket accessories have personalized Jeep 4x4 trucks since the late 1940s. While many items have become original equipment on Jeep trucks, other components remain specialty aftermarket products. As a Jeep owner, you can choose from a huge array of aftermarket upgrades, including safety enhancements, high performance components, wheels and tires, utility products and cosmetic accessories.

Fig. 16-1. *As the aftermarket grew, even Sears Roebuck offered Jeep parts. After thirty-five years, this original 1956 CJ-5 still has its "Allstate" free-wheeling hubs in place.*

Fig. 16-2. *CJs through the mid-'60s came from the factory without a right side wiper. This 1956 truck has an auxiliary electric motor conversion, a very popular item, easy to install.*

1. Winches

More than any other product, the power winch has expanded the versatility of Jeep 4x4s. Pioneered by Claude C. Ramsey, front mounted power take-off (PTO) winches were the first designs. By 1948, the Ramsey winch earned Willys' "Jeep Factory-Approved" status, expanding the Ramsey winch market to every Jeep dealer.

These early winches relied upon engine power. Jeep's Model 18 transfer case has the unique advantage of a power take-off access. By tapping into the transfer case at the PTO source, each of the transmission's forward speeds and reverse is available. PTO power flows from the transfer case to the front mounted winch gearbox via a driveshaft.

Koenig Iron Works also offered PTO winches. In the 1930s, Emil Koenig had furnished oil field trucks with power drive winches. Koenig's entry into the postwar power winch field targeted both commercial and recreational users. Koenig's "King" winches were suitable for front, rear and bed-mounted use. This gave Koenig, like Ramsey, access to the commercial hoisting and tow truck markets.

As U.S.-built light trucks shifted to 12-volt electrical systems, the Koenig/King and Ramsey PTO product lines drowned in the wave of electric winch sales. By the early '70s, bulky PTO winches, with scores of moving parts and complex installation tasks, made the PTO winch far less attractive than the growing number of versatile electric winches. Ramsey Winch Company made a successful transition to electric winches. The respected Koenig Iron Works, however, disappeared from the Jeep accessory market.

Fig. 16-3. *Model 18 Spicer transfer case has a PTO access. This convenient feature became the power source for Ramsey's early winch units. Different versions of Model 18 transfer case served from earliest MBs through '71 model CJs.*

Electric Winches

Since the late 1960s, a warm debate has waged between PTO winch advocates and electric winch users. More recently, hydraulic winch users have taken the place of PTO advocates. Hydraulic winches, powered by the power steering pump, have similar drawbacks to the PTO winch. If the engine stalls in the middle of a stream crossing, the winch is non-operative.

PTO and hydraulic winch buffs argue that battery power limits use of electric winches. Stranded in a stream, will the battery last long enough to pull the truck free? Electric winch advocates counter that a stalled engine can't spin a PTO shaft or power steering pump pulley. Either way, the operator is in trouble.

Dual battery installations, isolators and high output alternators have virtually eliminated the shortfalls of electric winches. Today, better electric winches furnish the quality—and quantity—of service that users demand. The notable manufacturers in the truck mounted electric winch market include Ramsey, Warn and Superwinch. Consumer preferences relate to gear and motor designs, stamina, amperage draw, utility and longevity.

Determining Your Winch Needs

Electric winches have a variety of ratings. Speed, or feet-per-minute (fpm) spooling, results from the gear reduction ratio and motor speed. Most electric winches feature worm, spur or planetary gear systems. The vehicle's battery (and/or an auxiliary battery) powers the winch motor, which resembles the motor portion of an automotive starter. In turn, the winch motor spins either a drive gear, worm shaft or sun gear.

Worm-and-gear systems rotate the worm gear inside a bull gear. Typically, the bull gear attaches to the cable spool drum. An advantage of the worm drive is its ability to stop abruptly or "load-reverse" when power flow ceases. Planetary and spur gear arrangements, by contrast, require a brake mechanism to prevent reverse rotation when the winch stops.

Worm gear systems, due to their low efficiency factor (the ability to transmit energy from one gear to another), require no brake. By contrast, if a winch gear system could develop 100-percent efficiency, it would spool in either direction with equal ease, whether loaded or unloaded.

> NOTE —
> Gear efficiency of less than 45% creates a self-locking capability. Here, the relationship and ratios of the gears create a weak incentive for free-spooling, even with a load on the cable. Worm gear systems, although extremely strong, offer only 35–40% efficiency.

Fig. 16-4. *Mopar/Warn winches include electric planetary types XD-9000i (9,000 lb. rating) and MD8000 (8,000 lb. rating). Available through your Jeep dealer, kits have all installation hardware and necessary wiring. You can also order a Mopar/Jeep Accessories mounting plate and Grille Guard. Compact, low profile MD8000 winch, shown on 1998 Wrangler TJ, can single-line pull more than two times curb weight of a CJ or Wrangler.*

Fig. 16-5. *Mopar/Ramsey Pro Plus 8000H, 8000HX and Pro 9000H winches are available through your Jeep dealer. Mopar/Jeep Accessories can provide a Grille Guard, mounting plate and all hardware for winch installation. Like Warn, Ramsey offers a full line of planetary and worm gear winches.*

Spur gear drives like Warn's Model M8274 work at 75% efficiency. This requires a braking mechanism to prevent load-reversal. Similarly, the popular planetary gear systems offer 65% efficiency. One variation, the compound planetary gear, produces 40% efficiency. This provides for self-braking action. The compound planetary gear system requires a high speed motor, generally in the 4000–5000 rpm range.

The planetary systems provide both strength and smooth operation. Compact planetary winches respond well to torque loads. Direct power flow to the sun gear permits lighter weight, a low profile and high output/load ratings.

Winch Motors

At present, the heaviest duty winches feature series wound motors. These motors provide maximum torque with a price: maximum amperage draw. The series wound brutes demand a heavy duty battery or use of an auxiliary battery.

Permanent magnet motors require far less amps, draw less battery power, and save weight. On light and medium load winches, these motors work fine. Many newer autos and trucks feature permanent magnet starter motors. These motors serve well, as engine cranking takes a short time and seldom generates excess heat.

The arguable disadvantage of permanent magnet motors is overheat. Under sustained, heavy loads, the permanent magnet motor tends to overheat. The operator needs to monitor the winching effort and time involved, allowing time outs for cooling the winch motor.

> CAUTION —
> *Most winch motors have circuit breaker protection to prevent extreme overload. Heat can weaken the motor. Proper winch use does not tax the winch motor for extended periods of time.*

Winching Batteries

Modern batteries offer higher cold cranking amperage (CCA). These are far more practical for series wound motors. Dual batteries, once mandatory for high output winch systems, are now optional. If your Jeep's battery rates 650 CCA or higher, the normal needs of a

Fig. 16-6. *Mopar's Sure-Start battery provides a "battery within a battery" for starting if you leave the lights on or if there is an electrical problem. By flipping the switch, you activate the back-up portion of the battery for reserve power.*

high output, series wound winch motor could be met with a single battery. (I seek ratings of 850 CCA or higher for a single battery that serves both a winch and the Jeep's electrical system.)

If you anticipate extreme duty use or lengthy winch pulls, consider a second battery and an automatic battery isolator. The isolator prevents draining your main battery below the level necessary to start the engine.

Selecting A Winch

Determine your truck's gross vehicle weight (GVW) before choosing a winch. This is the combined weight of the truck, your cargo, fuel, oil and any other items on board. Include your spare tools, the mounted winch and any accessories attached to the truck. Also account for other motorists. If you travel with a group, your winch is a welcome device. As a rescue or emergency vehicle, your Jeep may have a wide range of uses. Consider not only your Jeep's GVW but also the weight of other vehicles and motorists you might assist.

Engineers compute the winch safety factor at 1.5 times the working GVW of your truck. Working GVW is the real world, loaded version of your vehicle. If in doubt, weigh your fully loaded Jeep at a local truck scale. Add the winch weight and multiply this working GVW by 1.5. (Example: If your fully loaded truck and winch weigh 4000 lbs., the minimum winch capacity should be 4000 x 1.5, or 6000 lbs.)

Many buyers, even Jeep CJ owners, seek winches of 8000 lbs. capacity or higher. The added margin of safety is obvious with a high output winch. Effects of load and long pulling times will place far less stress on a heavier duty winch motor.

Also be clear of a winch's rating method. Single-line pull or double makes a critical difference. Applying the physics of a snatch-block (making a 180-degree turn of the cable and coming back to a tow hook near the winch) provides almost twice as much pulling strength and far less strain on your winch unit.

> CAUTION —
> *Although physics shows nearly a doubling of pulling power, engineers advise a 15% safety factor. If your winch's single line pull rates 6000 lbs., the 180-degree turn of the cable should increase pulling power by 85% or 5100 lbs. This provides a total pull rate of 11,100 lbs. It's important to realize that any deviation from the 180-degree pull angle will reduce the load capacity. Also, consider the cable rate (load limits) when using a snatch/pulley block. Although doubling and even tripling the cable is possible, you must always consider cable limits and safety.*

Fig. 16-7. *A snatch block and 180-degree reversal of the cable can reduce load on the winch motor by nearly one-half. Always allow a 15% safety margin.*

Always strive to minimize loads on the winch and cable. Even with a high output winch, reducing load to well below safety limits is a smart, prudent strategy.

Mounting A Winch

Winch mounting position is important. Winches that mount above the frame/bumper height are better suited to off-pavement use. Often, when you most need a winch, the front of the truck is low to the ground. Above bumper height, the cable and spool will still be easy to reach.

In the worst instance, a below bumper mount could actually become buried in snow, mud or a creek. As with any front bumper extension, the truck's approach angle may also suffer from a below-the-bumper mount. A winch near the ground also increases the likelihood of dragging the cable during pulls.

Many 4x4 owners, however, prefer hiding a winch behind the bumper. On CJs and Wranglers, an open grille front area is important. In very hot climates, under severe loads, a high mount winch may compromise the Jeep's cooling system. Decreased air flow over the radiator core reduces radiator efficiency. Here, the modern low-profile winch serves best.

Options are another factor when selecting your winch. Winch manufacturers frequently offer extra equipment. A roller fairlead, winch cover, remote controls, a portable/receiver mount, handtools or a wiring harness may be items you'll want—either when you purchase your winch or later.

Mechanical engineers design winches and winch mounts. As life, limb and expensive property are at stake, proper installation is a necessity. Your safest strategy is a manufactured winch mount kit from the winch builder. Such installation kits fit the frame and vehicle requirements of your Jeep. Mount kits address load points, the strength of frame attachments and ease of access to the winch. Engineers take the rated load capacity of the winch and apply that force safely to the truck's frame.

Kits include proper hardware and instructions. (If your Jeep has modifications that make a kit difficult to install, consult the winch manufacturer for possible solutions.) Eliminating any part of a winch installation package could compromise safety and the load capacity. Likewise, use only the graded and designated hardware included in the kit. Bolts, nuts, spacers and sleeves each aim for safety.

Sadly, operators often underestimate the load forces involved with winching. A cable draw to maximum load capacity must transfer force safely to the frame. This concern goes beyond the winch mount and hardware. If the winch attaches to the OEM bumper or brackets, that hardware must also be at factory standards. If the bumper has been removed, make certain that the attaching bolts and nuts meet or exceed OE Jeep standards. Winch kit engineering assumes that the truck meets OEM engineering guidelines.

Portable Winches

A more recent development in winch mounting is the portable winch receiver. Recognizing the versatility of a detachable front or rear mount winch, manufacturers now build winches and winch frames to fit Class III (2" square) trailer receivers. Using a quick disconnect cable and pin-type receiver, these winches install and disconnect in minutes.

The main advantage of a quality portable winch is storage. Protected from theft and foul weather, the winch may stow in a covered pickup bed or within a hardtop. Ready for an emergency, the winch assembly is free of ice, mud or rusted cable. Additionally, the portable winch is useful at either end of the vehicle.

Portable winches rely on the safety of your truck's receiver mount. Commercially made, frame mounted hitches have class ratings. Most rate 'Class III,' which means the hitch/receiver has safety engineering for proper frame attachment, including all hardware. Graded bolts and reinforcement plates accompany the hitch kit.

Unfortunately, many homemade and poorly installed hitches fall short of Class III standards. If you

Fig. 16-8. *Portable winches allow for quick installation and removal. A Class III or stronger frame mounted receiver can serve at either end of your Jeep. (You need a custom-built, Class III strength hitch for front installation.) The portable winch is versatile for recovery work.*

find that a portable winch suits your needs, have your hitch inspected by a specialist or install a frame mounted hitch with the correct class rating recommended by the winch manufacturer.

CAUTION —
• The load capacity of a properly installed Class III hitch is typically 5000 lbs., with a maximum tongue weight of 500 lbs. If a portable winch rates 8000 pounds, you cannot safely use the winch to its limit without compromising the receiver's rating. Also overlooked is that the receiver's 5000 pound trailering capacity applies to a trailer with wheels and tires. By contrast, some winching can be a dead pull, which creates far more load and stress than a trailer rolling on wheels and tires.

• Failure to install a safe hitch is hazardous. Under heavy load, a bumper mounted hitch could break away, causing personal injury or damage to your truck. Be aware: Cosmetic tube bumpers seldom rate even Class II hitch status. A portable winch requires a frame-mounted Class III (or higher) rated receiver/hitch assembly.

Winch Controls and Installation

Winch installation kits offer either direct or remote controls. The remote cable allows control of the winch feed from twenty or more feet away, well away from the cable, spool and gearworks. This gives an optimal view of the pull without the operator standing in line with the load.

When mounting the control box, follow the suggestions of the manufacturer. Since distance equates to amperage loss and resistance, many control units have

Carry-on Winch Accessories

Mounted safely and wired, your new winch is ready for work! A few accessory items, stowed properly, will help your winch perform at peak capacity. These devices enhance performance and provide a greater safety margin.

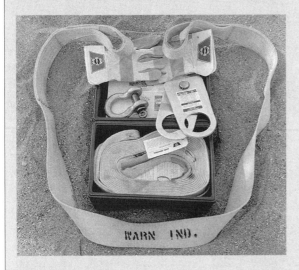

Accessory kit bags offer compact storage for important winching gear. Warn's kit includes a snatch block, forged steel shackle, tree protector, leather work gloves and a carrying bag. Ramsey and other manufacturers also offer winch accessory kits.

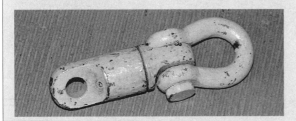

An industrial or logging supply provides an excellent assortment of high grade snatch blocks, pulleys, shackles and swivels. Swivels protect cable from twisting under load, a common source of damage. Load-rated hooks are also available. Watch for rough inner edges on hooks. Protect your nylon tree saver and recovery straps by carefully beveling forging scars with a grinder or file.

Recovery Strap—Often, you can free a stuck vehicle with a tug rather than setting up your winch. Many strap designs provide controlled stretch, which reduces shock.

Snatch Block—Known in other circles as a pulley block or block and tackle, the snatch block is an anchor plate with a pulley inside. Attached in front of the truck with a 180-degree return of the line, the snatch block offers 85% (with safety factored) load reduction when you attach the cable hook near the winch.

Choker Chain—A term familiar to woodsmen and loggers, the choker is a high tensile strength link chain with hooks at each end. The chain is highly versatile, acting as a vehicle recovery tool or reinforcement between two anchor points. You'll find it handy for wrapping around huge rocks, truck frames or other anchor points. You can easily store a six- to ten-foot choker in your Jeep.

Tow Hooks—Factory or aftermarket front and rear frame-mounted tow hooks require high tensile strength bolts and self-locking aircraft quality nuts. Attaching points and hardware must meet OE frame requirements. Never mount a tow hook directly to the bumper. Hooks are available with spring clips to prevent straps from slipping off. These are especially useful for one-person operation. Mounted upward, downward or sideways, tow hook bolts should align in the direction of pull. Mount the hook(s) at frame height and remember that the safest pull is a straight line. Avoid welding tow hooks into place, since they may need replacement at some time.

"D-Shackle"—This is a versatile device for attaching and joining straps, rings, chain and even cable. When using a D-shackle with straps, make certain that strap material rubs against the inside of the looped end. Otherwise, the strap may fray or be damaged. In assembling the shackle, tighten threaded pin all the way, then back off 1/4 to 1/2 turn to prevent seizing the pin when straps apply tension.

Gloves—Every accessory kit should include a pair of hefty leather work gloves. These gloves must resist weather, cable friction burns, scraps and abrasions. Frayed cable and sharp sheet metal edges can cut fingers to the bone.

Tree Saver Strap—For attaching a winch cable or anchoring your vehicle to a tree, the tree saver strap protects the bark and live sections. The eyes of the saver strap provide an attachment point for your D-shackle, which in turn serves as the snatch block anchor.

Shovel and Hand Items—A simple, often overlooked tool is the folding shovel. Many winch mounts provide a frame for building a shovel/axe/jack mount. Carry along strong wire cutters, as a broken cable can raise havoc with the winch or a truck chassis. Bring pliers, screw drivers, wire, a crimping tool, some electrical connectors and the basic wrenches to access your winch solenoids.

The MAX Multi-Purpose Tool Kit and a Hi-Lift Jack—These make must items for serious off-pavement Jeep adventures.

Fig. 16-9. *Remote winch control is a must. Never stand in the line of a winch cable. If the cable breaks and recoils under load, severe bodily injury could result.*

Fig. 16-10. *A heavy duty ground system for the engine, alternator, frame and winch assures full power. Here, 1/0 welding cable supplies both positive and negative battery cables and the complete ground circuit.*

a specified location. A switch box should be easily accessible, in an airy space, preferably out of the weather—or at least shielded.

Modern electric winch controls include solenoids, breakers or relays. In most instances, the control box is a plastic case, sealed from the weather. Since relays and/or solenoids flow constant battery current, you must isolate them from moisture. If ice, snow or sleet were to freeze inside the switch box, a current drain could sap your battery. Similarly, a short could occur if you operate the winch.

A properly grounded electrical system is essential. The issue becomes even more critical with a winch. A 600 amp resistance load, even for a brief time, will tax your Jeep's electrical system to its limit. Poor grounding is a fast way to lose current.

> CAUTION —
> *Check engine and battery grounds to the frame, cab and winch. Paint can act as an insulator between a ground terminal or bolt and the grounding surface. This creates a voltage drop. Make sure each ground terminal makes thorough contact. For winch and dual battery installations, I use 1/0 gauge cable with crimped battery cable ends on both the ground (-) and hot (+) lead circuits.*

Winch Wiring

As a guideline, the best ground system takes the battery negative cable directly to the engine block. Next, the alternator housing or its ground post connects to the engine block, with a ground strap from the engine block to the frame completing the circuit. (A ground strap should also go from the frame or engine block to the cab/body.) The winch system may now ground directly to the engine block or frame.

Each manufacturer furnishes specific electrical requirements for its winch models. Consult your kit in-

structions for details. As an additional item, consider an accessible master disconnect switch. Mount the switch in an easy to reach place, out of line from the winch cable path. Under extreme load, winch motors and the electrical system can overheat; an accessible master switch allows shutting the system down completely—without placing your limbs in jeopardy.

> CAUTION —
> *If your winch electrics interface with a complex electrical system (sound system, auxiliary lights, an extra battery and high output alternator), you need heavy gauge, high amperage battery hot lead and ground circuit cables. Ground cables must be as stout as hot leads.*

Using A Winch

A broken winch cable is potentially lethal and could easily break your Jeep's windshield. For this reason, brush/grille guards make smart additions to a winch mount. Make sure that the cable can spool evenly onto the drum. Attach the cable's hook to a substantial anchor point.

> CAUTION —
> *A breaking cable and loose hook can snap back with enough force to easily pierce the windshield. Many winching instruction booklets suggest that before operating a winch, you should raise the hood. I have always done so. Stay clear of the cable's path at all times. Snapping winch cables and hooks traveling at high velocity have killed or seriously injured people. The Jeep's grille, radiator and windshield are vulnerable. Use extreme caution when winching.*

If possible, stand far to the side when winching, well outside the cable's path. Many operators lay a blanket over the cable, assuming that this will reduce recoil if the cable breaks. Although a cover may help contain the cable, no cloth blanket can absorb the immense force of a snapping cable. Visualize the path a broken cable might follow, and stay out of that space!

> *WARNING—*
> *Always assume that a loaded winch cable is dangerous. Imagine the path a snapped cable might follow. Never stand in that space.*

> *CAUTION —*
> *• Always winch/pull as straight as possible. Wear leather work gloves whenever you handle wire cable.*
>
> *• For safety sake, always leave a reasonable length of cable on the winch spool. Your winch manufacturer has guidelines for the necessary length. Paint the cable red from the starting spool wrap to the length specified. When spooling out cable, the sight of red cable will indicate that the maximum safe length has spooled out.*

Fig. 16-11. *Loads on cables are fully capable of launching a tow hook, clevis, snatch block, bumper section, bumper bracket or frame piece through the windshield of a vehicle. Never stand in line with a loaded cable. Many Jeep owners raise their hoods to protect the windshield in the event of a cable failure. Use your remote winch control to keep clear of the cable.*

Fig. 16-12. *A sensible anchor point for your tow chain or strap is the receiver of a safely mounted hitch. A Class III hitch/receiver rates 5000 lb. load capacity and should withstand the stress of moving another light vehicle. Caution: Avoid use of elastic or "bungie cord" recovery straps. The load of a stretched cord can place far too much stress on tow hooks and frame attachment points.*

Freeing a vehicle often requires two full runs of cable. If the vehicle wants to roll faster than the cable spooling rate, apply slight brake pedal pressure. Many winches operate at both a minimum and maximum operating load. Proper cable spooling depends upon working within this load range.

Pull-Pal Anchor Device

Often, we need a winch but no tree or appropriate anchor point is within sight. This is typical for desert country and sand washes. Here, an anchor device like the Pull-Pal is ideal.

Fig. 16-13. *Pull-Pal works much like a backhoe arm, angling its broad shovel blade downward and into the ground as winch cable load applies. In a barren landscape, this device proves as valuable as your winch. Used properly, a winch and Pull-Pal will reduce environmental impact.*

Preventive Maintenance For Your Winch

Your winch is a safety device and lifeline. When a four-wheeling trip requires winching, a secluded box canyon or muddy creekbed is no place for error—or a poorly maintained winch.

Unlike PTO winches, with their oil-filled transmissions and mechanical driveshafts, the modern electric winch requires simple service.

Cable Inspection—The major wear item is the cable. Properly used, the wire winch line will last for years. One careless moment, however, can weaken or kink the cable. If a nighttime or blizzard winching episode leaves your winch cable coiled wrong, free-spool the cable entirely and check for damage. Kinks, broken outer strands and twists that leave the cable distorted are each signs of weakness. Clean the cable thoroughly to allow close inspection.

Lubrication—Your winch may have grease fittings and require periodic lubrication. If you have an oil bath drive (usually on 'PTO' winches), the gear oil must be clean and up to the full level. Check for seal leaks. If your winch operates in a dusty and wet environment, always clean the grease fittings before greasing. Use the manufacturer's recommended grease or a water-resistant chassis/bearing lube. Cable friction leads to fatigue and unnecessary stress. Many users lube the cable.

Mounts, Hooks, Pulleys and Straps—Inspect hooks and straps. Make certain clevis pins are free of moisture and lubricate them lightly. Dry out your nylon straps before storing them. Check tow hook and winch mount bolts and nuts for tightness and signs of fatigue. Inspect parts closely for bending or possible fatigue cracks. Periodically clean and lubricate pulleys and the snatch block.

Electrical System—Inspect your remote control cable, control box and all cable leads to the winch. Insulation on these leads must be in good condition and free from nicks.

CAUTION —

• As greases often attract unwanted dirt and dust, special lubricants are available for use on cables. (Some types cure like cosmoline.) This reduces messy handling and resists dirt accumulation. Such lubes also work well on clevis pins, hook pivots and the snatch block. They provide a good moisture barrier against rust.

• Amperage passing through the winch motor cables is high enough to weld metal. If a hot cable shorts to ground, a fire or severe damage might result. Inspect the cable routing to make certain no cable lays across sharp metal edges. You can reduce the effects of moisture through the use of silicone sprays and dispersing agents. Make certain that the control box, plug and remote connector pins are free of mud and debris.

The Pull-Pal's unique engineering causes the shovel to dig into the ground as the load applies. I have tested the Pull-Pal in hard pan, firm mud, hard-packed snow and wet beach sand—each with favorable results. Capable of staying upright as tension applies and the shovel's point takes a set, my Pull-Pal has worked in one-person winching scenarios.

While there is no anchor device that can meet every situation, the Pull-Pal has served me well. Any time I anticipate using a winch, the Pull-Pal comes along. I will not travel to remote, rough country without this device.

NOTE —
When winching with a Pull-Pal anchor device, use the same safety precautions as you would under any other winching conditions.

2. Electrical System Upgrades

Automotive electrical wiring must meet a variety of load requirements. Amperage demand determines the proper wire gauge for each electrical device on your Jeep truck. Since resistance increases with distance, longer runs of wire require heavier gauge sizes. OEM wire sizing reflects the amperage demand and specific distance between a current source and electrical device/consumer.

NOTE —
Wire for 6-volt accessories and components is substantially heavier than that for later 12-volt systems. This is an advantage when converting an early Jeep 6-volt system to 12 volts. Most often, OEM wiring is more than ample for the job.

For re-wiring and repair work, safety standards apply. As a rule, a 12-volt system's ignition draws between 1.5 and 3.5 amps. A pair of horns draw 18–20 amps, while electric wipers demand 3–6 amps. A pair of back-up lights drain 3.5–4 amps, while an air conditioning compressor clutch drains 13–20 amps. Headlights demand 8–9 amps on low beam and 13–15 additional amps for high beam operation. (This is for a four lamp, 12-volt system. Assume slightly less draw for Jeep two-headlight systems.)

The cigar lighter, often used for plug-in accessories, drains 10–12 amps from the battery. A radio draws up to 4 amps (tape decks and CD-players draw more), while power antennas drain 6–10 amperes. Instrument lamps, engine gauges, a clock or dome light each pull from 1–3 amps, a comparatively mild load. Wire type ranges accordingly, the gauge size increasing with wire length.

> *CAUTION —*
> *Heavy duty add-on devices and aftermarket accessories have specific amperage draws. Make certain wire gauge can handle these current demands. Consider distance, and increase gauge size for longer wire runs. Upgrade wire size where necessary.*

By contrast, the 12-volt starter motor, with its arc welder size battery lead, draws 150–450 amps during cranking. (This is a generalized range for modern automotive engines, with a lower compression 12-volt Jeep F-head four leaning toward the bottom end of the scale.) Such amperage requirements, just like a winch, demand heavy wire sizing.

When wiring from scratch, always consider distance. A device demanding 10 amps of current requires a minimum 18-gauge wire for a seven-foot run. At 75 feet, the same device needs a 10-gauge wire. Under capacity wire creates an excess voltage drop (loss of current due to the wire's resistance), and lights will burn dimly. If the wires are grossly undersize, resistance and heat rise to the point that the insulation melts, followed by a short to any available ground.

> *NOTE —*
> When choosing wire, the higher the wire's AWG number, the smaller (lighter duty) the wire size.

For auxiliary lighting (lightbars, emergency lights, KC floods, halogen lamps and such), look closely at the Watt ratings. Manufacturers indicate the Watt or amperage demand for a device, and there's a simple formula for converting watts to amperage: wattage divided by voltage = amperage. Example: On a 12-volt electrical system, a 100W lamp equals 100W divided by 12, or 8-1/3 amps. Therefore, an exotic string of ten 100 Watt lamps draws 83.3 amps.

> *NOTE —*
> For determining your Jeep's electrical system needs, consider the typical amperage draws for various accessory and OEM items. Add up the on-line components, and build your charging and battery system around these demands.

Matching Amps to Wiring

When selecting the right wire gauge for your add-on accessories, make note of the relationship between amperage draw, watt ratings, candle power and length of the wire runs. Resistance increases over distance, and many accessories set far from the battery current source.

Auxiliary lights, a sound system or a winch each have an assigned amperage draw. Add to that rating a safety margin. You can always go bigger with wire size and be safe. Wherever possible, use fuses or circuit breakers. Protect higher amp items with reset breakers. Protective devices are available from 1.0 amp to 250 amp ratings and higher.

The winch current draw is similar to a starter motor. Route cables very carefully to avoid high amperage shorts and possible fire. Review the winch manufacturer's guidelines for circuit protection and cable routing.

Consider distance, as wire span equals resistance. Resistance raises amperage. Note the length of wire feeding each accessory. Select the recommended amperage ratings from an automotive wire manufacturer's guidebook, and match wire size accordingly. For safety sake, account for the entire distance that current will flow, from the battery source to the accessory.

If your Jeep has an aftermarket fiberglass body or panels, add the ground wire lengths that return from each accessory. Choose a wire gauge for the total length of the power lead and ground wire. Ground leads must always match the amperage requirements of power leads.

Multi-strand automotive wire, available at local auto supplies, typically comes in spool lengths of 25–100 feet. Determine the amperage draw for each electrical component in your Jeep's system, and select the correct gauge sizes. Consider normal amperage draw when choosing fuses and relays. These safety devices must prevent wires from frying in the event of an overload or short.

When matching fuses to electrical components, each fuse should allow slightly more amperage flow than the device requires. Allow this margin for upstart surges and hot operation (when amperage draw increases slightly).

> *CAUTION —*
> *When an OE electrical circuit suddenly requires more amperage than the factory fuse type, there's trouble. Never install a high amp fuse as a cure for an OE electrical circuit that keeps blowing fuses. Find the reason for the overload, perhaps a wire short or bad connection, and fix the problem.*

Fuses blow for valid reasons: a defective electrical component, a bare wire short or open in the circuit, a weak ground, loose connections, or a charging circuit defect. Resolve the problem and install the correct fuse. A small volt-ohmmeter makes the ideal tool for troubleshooting resistance and the continuity of wiring circuits. (See chapter on "Electrical System Basics.")

The backside of a CJ or early Jeep truck dash is readily accessible. Later J-truck, Wagoneer, Cherokee, Comanche, Grand Cherokee and even Wrangler electrical systems have become increasingly more difficult to access. On the newer Jeep models, a wire repair, switch replacement, radio removal or other under-dash task can be as difficult as working on a passenger car.

> CAUTION —
> *Do not attempt electrical troubleshooting or repairs without a factory shop manual(s) for your Jeep model. You will find wiring diagrams and wire color codes in the electrical section of a Jeep service manual.*

High Work Standards

The longer runs of wire from the front to the rear of your Jeep require close watch. Safe routing of these wires is essential. A quality wiring job ensures that vibration and road shake will not separate or damage wires.

> CAUTION —
> *Improperly installed plastic wire ties, clamps and straps have a nasty habit of wearing through wire insulation.*

A yardstick I like to apply is the "worst case scenario." (Some call this "Murphy's Law.") Assume that the wire you're routing will face tension, heat and friction. Are there sharp metal edges just waiting to whittle at your vital wiring loom? Can engine heat melt the plastic off wires? Will chassis movement tear a crucial connection apart? You must depend on your wiring in blizzards, on remote desert moonscapes, atop craggy, windswept mountains and even in the fast lane of the freeway during rush hour. Take the time to route, shield, tape and secure all wires.

Wire Looms and Connections

Use plastic shielding looms (convoluted sleeves), quality wire connectors, ties and straps. Re-wiring often involves use of insulated, solderless connectors. These connectors must match wire gauge sizes. Use a quality crimping tool on wire connectors.

Color coded, solderless connectors have become popular over the last three decades. They are easy to fit, quick to secure in tight places and offer long service

Fig. 16-14. *Wrangler Power Products offers this crimping tool for the do-it-yourselfer. These crimps in heavy duty copper battery terminals offer maximum conductivity and a long-lasting cure for resistance and voltage drop problems.*

life. A special crimping pliers is necessary for installation. Don't cut corners when buying this tool. Tight, neat connections depend on professional caliber tools.

> NOTE —
> A new generation of electrical connectors with heat-shrink insulation is now available. For weatherproof connections, consider these more expensive butt and terminal connectors. (A hair dryer will shrink the thick insulation.) These connectors resist water "wicking" and offer additional insurance against wires pulling apart.

Expect to waste a few connectors practicing your crimping skills. Too tight or loose won't do. On connectors and crimp terminal ends with seams on the sleeves, make certain your crimp is on the solid side, not the seam.

Factory (OE) wire connections are often solder type, with molded insulation. In some cases, aftermarket pigtails are available to restore OE integrity at electrical connections. Some fitups, however, benefit from the use of an entire OE wiring harness, tailored for your Jeep. Pre-formed harnesses, insulated properly, provide the best connections possible.

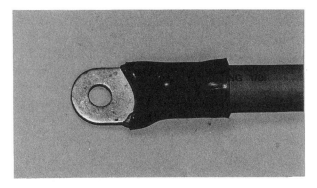

Fig. 16-15. *This is a quality wire connection. After crimping, the copper terminal receives a coating of special adhesive-lined heat shrink tube.*

Fig. 16-16. *These are quality battery attachments, two crimp type terminals and a unique compression nut clamp. Each meets high industrial/automotive standards and features rugged copper construction.*

NOTE —
Genuine Mopar/Jeep Accessories wiring harnesses meet OEM standards for safety and integrity. You will find that these harnesses properly match and interface with your Jeep's wiring. When buying accessories for a Wrangler, XJ, ZJ or WJ model, consider this Mopar advantage. (See your Jeep dealer for details and catalogs.)

Some forethought and a factory schematic of your Jeep's electrical system will contribute to a quality wiring job. Electrical work, done correctly, is very gratifying. It also provides a better understanding of how your Jeep operates. Armed with this knowledge, you'll gain confidence about traveling to remote places.

Consider the Electrical Load

When amperage load rises, so does the need for a high performance electrical system. Four-wheel drive

trucks offer more room for accessorization than any other vehicle—and four-wheelers press their electrical systems to the limit.

Installation of an aftermarket high output alternator can serve your high amperage charging needs. Along with high amps from the alternator, you must also consider the wiring and safety devices needed to support a high output charging and accessories system.

Protecting Your Electrical System

Once you've selected the right alternator to meet your amperage needs, plan on upgrading the wiring. In external regulator systems, wiring starts with the alternator-to-regulator harness. Needs here include proper wire sizing and use of quality terminals. If the alternator has an integral regulator, an adequate charge wire, routed directly to the battery, is essential.

If your alternator delivers 130 or less amps, the appropriate requirement for a 10-foot or less length alternator lead is 4-gauge wire. A positive battery cable with the proper ring size end for the alternator output stud would be adequate. (Protect this lead with a 150 amp circuit breaker or fusible link.) For the battery cable, premium 1/0 size copper welding-type cable is best.

The fine strands of the welding cable, with quality crimped or compression clamped ends, will handle high resistance loads. Unlike battery cables, which are relatively rigid and of lower grade, welding wire meets the highest industrial standards for carrying amperage. Fine-strand wire permits oversizing the cable without excess resistance, voltage drop or false battery/current signals to the voltage regulator.

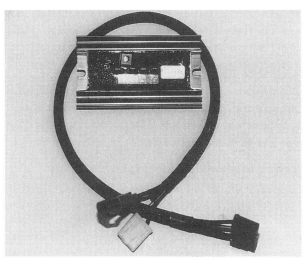

Fig. 16-17. *Aftermarket voltage regulator and wire harness for Wrangler Power Products' high output alternator shows attention to detail. Note terminal ends, sheathing and insulation.*

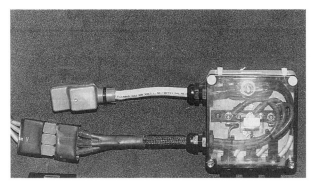

Fig. 16-18. *This setup from Wrangler Power Products offers terminal protection and a high quality appearance. Imagine these junction boxes beneath the hood of your Jeep.*

When building the charging/battery wiring with 1/0 welding cable, make sure you also use 1/0 cable for all grounds, including the engine-to-frame and battery. The 12-volt battery system is direct current (DC), and this means the ground circuit wire gauge must match the charging and starter demands.

> NOTE —
> Use an ample ground lead between the frame or engine and the body/cab. Check ohms-resistance between ground terminals and ground wire ends to assure adequate grounds and no voltage drops.

Dual-battery Electrical Needs

Many Jeep owners with heavy duty electric winches add an extra battery to their system. For electrical systems with auxiliary batteries, I heartily recommend the use of a battery isolator.

The "Autosave" is one type of automatic battery disconnect designed to stop the current flow from the auxiliary battery when voltage drops to 9.6 volts. This prevents abuse of your Jeep's expensive accessories and also protects the auxiliary battery from severe discharge. Upon recharging the battery to a full 13 volts, the Autosave automatically reconnects the circuit.

"Battery Separator," by contrast, performs two functions: 1) deliver maximum current for starting, and 2) provide charge system protection. In the event that the chassis (main) battery is low, Battery Separator reads the voltage level of the auxiliary battery and brings that current on line to help start the engine. The Battery Separator also monitors the two batteries once the engine starts. The separator applies current only to the main battery until it reaches a 13.2 volt charge. The separator then reads the auxiliary (winch) battery and feeds current to both batteries as needed.

Other battery isolators and devices are also available. Additionally, electronic and magnetic/mechanical relays, ranging in amperage limits from 100 to 200 amps, can handle high amperage current flow chores. Hefty 250 amp battery shut-off switches also meet heavy current requirements.

Circuit breaking relays, gaining popularity over traditional fuses, work very well on Jeep 4x4s. In environments where temporary shorting is likely, such as submersion in a running stream, a circuit breaker will reset when the hazard passes and the components dry. This is helpful. Circuit breakers range from high-amp cutouts to smaller two-spade ATO fuse size relays that conveniently fit in place of original fuses.

Assessing Your Electrical System's Reliability

Building a first class wiring system involves use of high grade copper terminals and wire products. Judge switches by two criteria: amperage load capacity and the switch's designated number of service cycles. Better quality switches have amperage load and service cycle ratings. You will find these switches in automotive electrical or industrial parts catalogs.

If you want maximum performance from your Jeep's electrical system, each component, including crimped and compression terminals, should bear either a military, commercial or industrial (UL) rating. The switches found at discount outlets seldom have these ratings. For the sake of your Jeep's reliability, be suspect of any electrical component without a recognizable rating.

> NOTE —
> When in doubt, seek out an industrial/commercial supplier or high quality automotive source like NAPA's premium Belden/Echlin lines or Wrangler Power Products. For OEM replacement components, you can rely upon genuine Mopar/Jeep parts.

Protect the electrical system from battery acid and the corrosion of salty winter roads. Guard against the effects of squelching summer heat and arctic weather. Underhood heat and desert climates can gnaw away at wire insulation and tax the voltage regulator and other relays. Here, quality electrical hardware is your best preventive measure. High grade electrical pieces, including both brass and copper battery attachments and wire terminals, help prevent trouble on a heavily worked Jeep electrical system.

Some Unusual Electrical Hardware

Wrangler Power Products and Warn Industries offer a number of specialty items for Jeep use. One is a battery

Fig. 16-19. *This is the best way yet to jump batteries, with special quick-connect system that terminates at front bumper.*

jumper system that mounts permanently to the front or rear of your truck. Quick connect cables serve easily in emergencies. You can park directly in front of a stalled vehicle, avoiding the hazard of hanging your Jeep out in the road—or running over a cliff!—while trying to pull alongside. Wrangler's system features 1/0 welding cable, copper terminals and industrial grade connectors.

Selecting A Battery

Each battery has an ampere hour rating and cold cranking capacity. The engine and electrical system dictate battery requirements, with air conditioning, power options, the engine size and compression ratio determining the necessary battery group size.

If your Jeep is a hybrid with an engine transplant, battery selection should favor the engine. Find a listing

An On-board Welder

We were five tortuous, rock crawling hours into the Rubicon. In our whole group, only one rig had given us mechanical trouble. Compared to the two guys now standing in the trail, our trip was a breeze!

A Saginaw power steering gear and two burly arms had ripped apart the frame brackets that support the steering gearbox. In three hours time, the Jeep CJ-5 had moved only a couple of lengthy stone's throws.

As much as we wanted to help these guys, our tools fell short. What we really needed was a welder. An on-board frequency welder is just the tool for such scenes. An alternator powered frequency welder takes a fabrication welder wherever your Jeep truck goes. Mounted either underhood or in the bed, such a compact unit is powerful stuff.

The Premier Power Welder (shown here) can do serious welding, easily running 1/8" rod on steel plate or making professional repairs on a broken Jeep chassis member. Since the principle is frequency, not amperage, cable length to the worksite is no barrier.

A high-output alternator is at the core of the frequency welder system. At a fast engine idle, the alternator reaches beyond 120 amps, levels suitable for welding. Typically, frequency welder's have alternators that operate in the 130–160 peak amperage range.

Some mobile welders also provide a 110-volt DC outlet with enough wattage to run brush motor power tools or a string of camp lamps. A "battery booster" mode can start a stranded vehicle in minutes.

Mobile welder kits come complete with all mounting hardware, the alternator and wiring. Options include your choice of welding cables, all welding accessories and even TIG (heli-arc) or MIG (wire weld) equipment. From my view, this is the ultimate tool for the serious outback Jeep.

CAUTION —
Read welder's instructions carefully before welding on a Jeep chassis. Improper polarity can cause damage to wheel bearings and other parts. Use necessary precautions to assure successful repairs.

for a car or truck equipped with your swap engine and approximately the same accessory package. Note its battery size. Select a similarly rated battery that will fit your battery box, if possible, or change boxes to an adequate size. Secure the battery safely, and use the best battery cable connections available.

> **NOTE—**
> An under-capacity battery will discharge quickly and require excessive, high amperage recharging. Such recycling leads to short battery life.

A 12-volt battery operates best above 12 volts. When you crank the engine for a minute or the headlights have burned without the engine running, the battery voltage actually drops below 12 volts. A healthy battery will recover some voltage if left alone for awhile, however, to completely restore the battery's charge, the alternator must flow amperes.

Earlier Jeep charge systems (both generator and alternator versions) have external voltage regulators. These devices act as electrical current monitors, directing charge flow to the battery. The regulator receives battery voltage signals and adjusts current to achieve a full charge.

The later Jeep has a volt meter instead of an ammeter. The older ammeters read the actual amperes of electrical current that flow toward or away from the battery. If the regulator functions correctly, an ammeter tells us the flow of current necessary to restore battery voltage. Volt meters, by contrast, show the battery's actual state of charge.

A battery with bad cells loses even more voltage while spinning the starter motor. This could bring the battery reading down to 8 volts or less. When this occurs, the alternator floods the battery with heavy amps of current, and a vicious cycle begins. The already tired battery suffers from this fast charge, which heats the battery and further reduces its life. Soon, the worn battery is nothing more than a source of recyclable lead.

Likewise, your old six-cylinder's battery that now strains to spin that larger V-8 transplant will soon exhaust itself. Rapid voltage depletion and the need for a maximum charge rate after each start-up will quickly ruin a battery. Use of heavy lighting and a winch has the same impact.

High Performance Charging Circuit

A high output alternator can restore the battery's state of charge in minutes. A higher output OE alternator usually accompanies power options like air conditioning, electric door locks and power window lifts. Even with a high output OEM alternator, four-wheelers find

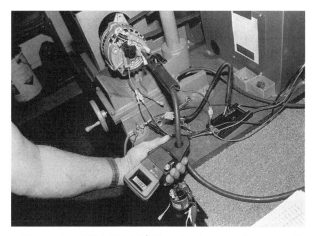

Fig. 16-20. *OEM GM CS-130 style alternator is potent. If your Jeep has a GM engine transplant, consider this OE unit. Capable of 100 amps at an equivalent of 1500 crankshaft rpm, top end output of this popular post-'85 alternator is 103 amps. Characteristic of many late model alternators, the CS-130's most impressive attribute is 61 amp output at an engine idle.*

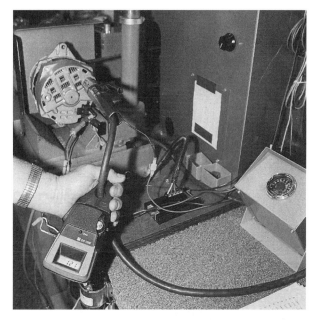

Fig. 16-21. *Wrangler Power Products tests a GM factory CS-144 alternator, which stormed to a 121 ampere output by 5000 rotor rpm. Idle speed amperage read 61. Wrangler builds the GM CS-133 or CS-144 alternators into even higher output 140 and 160 amp systems.*

ways to overwhelm their electrical system. Auxiliary lighting, high watt sound systems, and dual-battery installations leave the alternator with a heavy burden.

The alternator's strongest advantage over older generator designs is the ability to produce a higher charge rate at slower speeds. Since auxiliary lighting and your winch frequently operate with the engine idling or stopped, this factor is critical. Alternators meet the demands of vehicles that idle in traffic with air conditioning and other luxury accessories drawing on the battery.

Late OEM alternators have outstanding charge rates at an idle. By comparison, Jeep trucks built before the '80s, even with high output factory alternators, lag at lower rpm. A typical high output alternator of early '70s vintage might produce 55 amps @ 6500 alternator/rotor rpm but only 9 amps at an engine idle. In fairness, this alternator at 1500 engine rpm jumps to 44 amp output. Still, the message is clear: At a curb

Fig. 16-24. *Here are high quality components for building longevity into a charging system. Your new alternator is just the beginning. Shown is a junction block for high amperage, battery size leads.*

Fig. 16-22. *Upgrade your wiring system when you install a high output alternator. A heavy duty solution is 1/0 welding wire with custom crimped ends. This CJ-5 boasts a 140-amp Wrangler Power Products alternator system.*

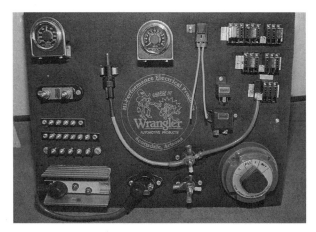

Fig. 16-23. *Wrangler Power Products display hints that electrical system integrity goes well beyond the alternator installation. Industrial-strength switches, cables and other hardware assure safety and the maximum benefit from a high output alternator.*

idle, or when you're rock crawling in the desert, the older alternator has limited output.

When considering an OE alternator retrofit, consider later units. By 1982, an 80 amp Delco-Remy alternator produced 55 amps at 2000 engine rpm. The newest Delco high output units produce in excess of 60 amps at a 675 rpm idle. Now, that's progress!

Always increase battery size when installing a high output alternator. Running a winch from a single, low ampere hour battery is dangerous. Completely draining a battery then forcing massive current back into it (which is the voltage regulator's normal response to a fully discharged battery) will heat up the battery plates and cause their failure. Weakened batteries can actually explode under such conditions.

3. Roll Bars

It is always unnerving when a trail shifts off-camber and your Jeep's tilt meter runs off the scale. On hazardous trails, where risk of a rollover runs high, your best protection against bodily injury and severe vehicular damage is a roll cage and ample seat belt/harnesses.

Product liability concerns have encouraged aftermarket manufacturers to classify cab and other steel bars. There are bonafide roll bars (chassis or cab mounted) and also a class of lighter weight, largely cosmetic tube or bed bars.

Cab cages, built for Jeep trucks and multi-purpose sport/utility 4x4s, resemble race truck protection. The critical differences between a hard-core Baja desert racing cage and a manufactured cab cage are the bracing and mounting methods.

A Racing Roll Cage

Off-road racing is the best test for roll cages. The standards set by the High Desert Racing Association (HDRA) and SCORE say a lot about our safety needs. Whether you are building your own cage or shopping for quality aftermarket rollover protection, racing requirements offer the highest standards.

For racing, the minimum tubing size for a 2000–3000 lb. truck is 1-3/4" diameter for open cockpits and 1-1/2" for closed cabs. Tubing wall thickness is minimum 0.120". A 3000–4000 lb. race vehicle requires 2" x 0.120" for open cockpits and 1-3/4" x 0.120" for a closed cab. In trucks over 4000 lbs., tubing size increases to 2-1/4" x 0.120" for open cockpits and 2" x 0.120" for closed cabs.

Materials and construction follow strict guidelines. HDRA/SCORE recommends CRW, DOM, WHR, or WCR mild carbon steel or 4130 Chromoly steel. Light weight and high strength make 4130 popular.

According to official rules, "All welded intersections should be stress relieved by flame annealing. Welds must be high quality with good penetration and no undercutting of the parent metal. No oxy-acetylene brazing on roll cage tubing is permissible. No square tubing is permitted. Use of other materials is subject to prior HDRA/SCORE approval."

Along with these minimum material standards, HDRA/SCORE has strict construction guidelines. The cage must mount securely to the frame or body. All intersection points must have gussets and bracing. "Cab or body mounted cages must not be attached to the body structure by direct welding, but must be bolted through and attached by the use of doubler plates (one

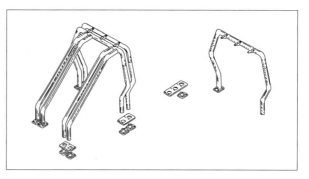

Fig. 16-26. *Hobrecht, Grizzly, Smittybilt and others make attractive truck bars for pickup beds. These bars provide mounts for lighting and minimal protection. Mounted to the bed sheet metal, they do not qualify as bonafide roll bars. Hobrect and Smittybilt also offer more protective cab cages for Jeep CJs, Wranglers and some pickups.*

on either side) with a minimum thickness of 3/16"...Roll cage terminal ends must be located to a frame or body structure that will support maximum impact and not shear..."

The required tubing sizes apply to front and rear hoops, front and rear hoop inter-connecting bars, rear down braces and all lateral bracing. Minimum bolt size for any attachments is 3/8", with Grade 5 or better strength.

A minimum requirement for HDRA/SCORE racing is a roll cage with one front hoop, one rear hoop, two inter-connecting top bars between the hoops; two rear down braces and one diagonal brace. Gussets are mandatory at all welded intersections on the main cage and down braces. Fabricators must also use gussets at any single weld where a fracture could reduce safety.

Triangular gussets at the top corners may be halves of a 3" x 3" x 1/8" flat plate. Another approach is "split, formed and welded corner tubing, or tubing gussets the same thickness as the main cage material." When making the rear down braces and diagonal bracing, the angle cannot be less than 30 degrees from a vertical plane.

HDRA/SCORE rules provide another valuable insight. If a race truck has no steel doors to protect the driver and co-driver (like the typical soft top Jeep CJ), side bars are mandatory. A minimum of one bar per side, as near parallel with the ground as possible, must provide protection yet allow the driver and co-driver (i.e., passenger) to get in and out of the vehicle quickly.

The side bars, formed from the same tubing as the roll cage, must attach to the front and rear hoops of the cage. Gussets and other such braces are also necessary. For a cloth top vehicle with canvas doors, side bars make sense. Sure, it may be tougher to crawl in and out

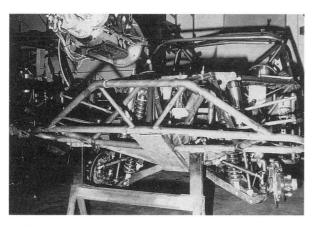

Fig. 16-25. *Where does the roll cage/frame end and the suspension begin? On desert race trucks and Jeep stadium race trucks, the line is thin. Bracing angles reflect Nature's strongest design: the triangle. This shape repeats itself throughout the chassis and cage.*

of your truck, but if city traffic is part of your game plan, the added protection could prevent severe injury in a "T-bone" accident.

Racing rules also state that the roll cage bars must be at least 3" in any direction from the helmets of the Driver and Co-driver in their normal driving and riding positions. Safe and proper bar padding applies.

> NOTE —
> Poorly constructed cages have many back-country four-wheelers knocking themselves silly against their roll bars. Secure and fitted seat harnesses, a properly aligned roll cage and adequate bar padding are a must to help protect the driver and any passengers.

In addition to the roll cage requirements, HDRA/SCORE requires head and neck restraints to minimize whiplash. The restraint is usually 36 square-inches with at least 2" of padding. Rules also call for padding at all areas of the roll bar or bracing that the occupants' helmets might reach. For an off-pavement Jeep truck, full padding of the entire interior cage is sensible.

Practical Alternatives

Few Jeep drivers will ever experience a rollover at high speed or the catastrophic impact forces that regularly threaten desert racers. For a reasonable margin of safety, short of a racing-specification cage, manufactured cab cage systems will often suffice.

Better manufactured kits have the advantage of pre-fabricated pieces with all necessary bends in place. Manufacturers like Smittybilt and Hobrecht work hard to assure proper fitup and ease of installation.

Fig. 16-28. *A popular approach with CJs that feature a single hoop or factory roll bar is the "front cab extension kit." These weld-on extensions offer full cab and windshield height protection, although attaching a cage or roll bar to sheet metal floor panels has obvious limitations. This system does not match a desert racing cage, which welds directly to the frame. Shown is an Oregon-based sand drag flat-fender with a nicely fitted trail type cage.*

While HDRA/SCORE standards assure maximum protection, less elaborate designs can serve most off-pavement situations. At lower speeds, especially rock crawling, rollover is generally the less extreme matter of slowly laying a Jeep 4x4 on its side. Here, a quality roll cage with side protection, proper seat mounts and secure seat belts/harnesses will meet most needs.

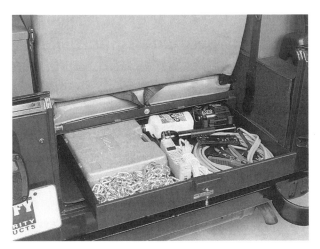

Fig. 16-29. *A sensible way to secure items is with Tuffy Security lock boxes. Intended as a first-rate theft deterrent, Under Seat Security Drawer is a lockable box for beneath rear seat of CJs and YJ/TJ Wranglers. Tuffy Security boxes provide good places for valuables, tools and items that could become hazards in the unplanned event of a roll-over.*

Fig. 16-27. *Roll bars require padding. If your bars are shaped oddly or you want a custom pad, Bar Glove by the Off-Road Factory is one such accessory.*

4. Seat Belts and Safety Harnesses

Rough terrain driving means odd angles and plenty of bouncing. Vehicles can roll over, even at a snail's pace. With few exceptions, occupants are better off when safely seat belt/harnessed within the truck.

The Racing Harness

HDRA/SCORE racing standards provide an excellent yardstick for measuring seat belt and harness quality. The minimum standard for racing is a five-point, fast release seat belt and shoulder harness assembly. Buckles must be metal-to-metal, with the single anti-submarine strap attached "as close to the front edge of the seat as practical so that it will exert maximum restraint to the upward movement of the belt and harness."

Seat lap belts are 3" width, the submarine belt 2", and shoulder straps must be 2"–3". Harness materials must be Nylon or Dacron Polyester and in "new or perfect condition with no cuts or frayed layers, chemical stains or excessive dirt." HDRA/SCORE recommends that belts be changed after one year of use. They must be changed three years from the date of manufacture.

The mounting position of the shoulder harnesses is approximately 4" below the top of the driver and co-driver's shoulders. This issue is critical, as severe injury can result from poorly positioned belt anchor points. "Lap belts should be kept at a minimum at least 2-1/2" forward of seat and backrest intersection.

All belts must be mounted directly to a main structure member with the strength at least 1-1/2" x 0.090" tubing with gussets." HDRA/SCORE also recommends keeping adjustment buckles a minimum distance of 1-1/2" from the seat to prevent accidental loosening or chafing.

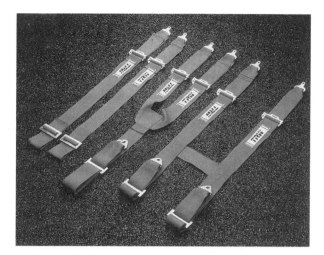

Fig. 16-30. *TRW shoulder harnesses demonstrate two popular styles: 'H' and 'Y' types. TRW is popular in off-road and other forms of sanctioned racing.*

Avoid Submarining!

Submarining is your body sliding beneath the lap belt during a frontal impact. In desert racing, submarining also occurs when a truck or buggy flies over a rise and lands nose first in a silt bed or the edge of a streambed.

Spinal and head injuries can result from submarining. By sliding down into the seat, the body's alignment during the recoil-phase (when the body slams rearward after impact) is awkward. Your head may hit the space between the headrest and seat back. This can cause severe neck injury.

Several factors cause submarining: poor design of the safety-belt, bad location of the belt's attachment points, and the wrong seat configuration. Many shoulder belt designs actually pull the lap belt up during a collision. Schroth, a producer of rally and racing seat belts, discovered that evenly distributed loads on the shoulder belts were more likely to pull the lap belt up and cause submarining.

As a remedy, Schroth's ASM (AntiSubMarining) system is designed to allow one shoulder belt to re-adjust very slightly on impact. This turns the body a few degrees. The slight shift in body position causes the lower body to press into the lap belt earlier (approximately 20 milliseconds sooner). This tiny delay before the shoulder belts begin to pull allows just enough time for the body to tighten against the lap belt.

Using a pre-calculated energy change also cushions head and shoulder force as the belts begin to tighten. An additional benefit, Schroth notes, is that the design prevents hard pressure on the sternum and breastbone.

Once the ASM shoulder belts have experienced a heavy frontal impact shift (enough force to lengthen the Schroth belt), the belts require replacement. Similarly, it is advisable to replace any other type of seat belt that has been subjected to substantial impact force.

Filler Safety Products, very popular with racers, also stresses the importance of proper seat belt mounting. On 5- and 6-point harnesses, Filler recommends that lap belts angle 45–55 degrees to the tangent line of the thigh. Filler shoulder harness tail straps require a 45-degree angle from the seat top, tying to a roll bar cross brace located 4 inches below the shoulder line.

The lap belt anchors 2" forward of the point where the driver's back line and the floor intersect, or 2-1/2" forward of the intersect point of the seat and

backrest. Belts should attach to the floor at the same width as the occupant, with brackets aimed in the direction of belt pull. The crotch strap should anchor in line with the driver's chest. Filler's guidelines comply with HDRA/SCORE rules.

Engineers work continuously to improve seat belt and roll bar systems. If your Jeep truck has an appetite for the rough stuff, give yourself a fighting chance.

5. Trailering With Your Jeep

For towing, shorter wheelbase Jeep models can be troublesome. In my estimation, the 80" to 94" CJ and Wrangler wheelbases should not pull more than a tiny military/utility trailer, a tent trailer, a very light boat trailer or an occasional cement mixer from the local rental yard.

As a rule, short wheelbase vehicles don't track well in front of long framed trailers. Even without a trailer, a 94" or less wheelbase vehicle is a handful on ice, slick pavement or when turning at excess speed. The shorter the wheelbase, the tighter the turning radius, though, and that's where CJs and Wranglers reign. These 4x4s are perfectly suited for tight, twisty off-pavement trails—sometimes even with a tiny utility/tent trailer in tow.

Steering control is the primary drawback for short wheelbase tow vehicles. Most 4x4s under 104" wheelbase have insufficient frame length for absorbing the side sway and whip of a trailer. Additionally, a lightweight CJ or Wrangler chassis could be easily overrun

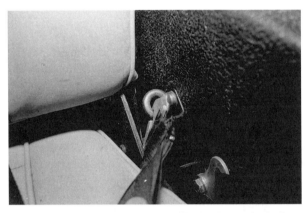

Fig. 16-31. *Grade 8 or better quality hardware, including this eye loop anchor from Filler Safety, assures safe seat belt and harness attachments. A 3" square steel reinforcement plate backs up sheet metal where harness strap attaches.*

Fig. 16-32. *Factory seat belt anchors provide quality attachment points for custom lap belts. OE engineering strives for high strength and proper angles.*

Fig. 16-33. *U.S.A. VenturCraft's TrailBlazer tent/cargo trailer proves ideal for any Jeep. TJ Wrangler safely pulled this trailer through crosswinds, up grades and at 75 mph interstate speed limits. In backcountry, TrailBlazer's 16" ground clearance, 21 cubic feet of sealed cargo space and an easy-to-assemble tent with a queen-size bed made for a perfect camping companion. We will tote this 465 pound fiberglass bodied trailer behind our '55 CJ-5 with an F-head four engine.*

Fig. 16-34. *Another product from U.S.A. VenturCraft's is tailgate "tent" conversion for models like XJ Cherokee and Grand Cherokees. Cargo area of most Saves is ample enough for camping out. This tent enclosure provides the seal and weather barrier needed. Smart idea!*

by a bigger trailer, especially during braking. A higher center of gravity further hinders short wheelbase 4x4s; risk of a rollover increases with a trailer in tow.

Obviously, a two-ton load pushing at the rear bumper centerline of a 2500 lb. CJ-5 would tax both the vehicle's design and intent. Once directional control ceases, the next move could very well be a rollover, surely a poor way to end a vacation or outing. Although terrific off-pavement vehicles, these goatlike Jeep models have no place in front of a twenty foot trailer!

For those Jeep models better suited to towing, a set of beefier springs, heavy duty shock absorbers, sway controls and an increased tread width can help stabilize the truck. A wider-than-stock tread width, accomplished with the correct width wheel rims and reasonably oversized tires, can lend directional stability.

> *WARNING —*
> *Once a short wheelbase vehicle crosses up or skids sideways on a firm roadway surface, expect big trouble. When a short wheelbase Jeep starts to skid, with steering out of control, the directional stability has usually been lost. The truck has over-committed to the maneuver. Events happen very quickly with a short frame and higher center of gravity. Expect a full spin—or worse—in most cases. Towing an oversized trailer can readily induce this behavior.*

> NOTE —
> Pulling a two-horse trailer with an 81" wheelbase V-6 CJ-5 begs disaster. The best Jeep models for this kind of trailering each have ladder frames: the J-trucks (preferably a late AMC-era J-20 with heavy duty chassis option), the full-size Wagoneer/Grand Wagoneer and the full-size Cherokee.

> NOTE —
> • If your plans include a trailer beyond the shortest military-style or stubby utility/tent unit, consider a Jeepster/Commando, Comanche pickup, full-size or compact XJ Cherokee, a ZJ or WJ Grand Cherokee or a J-truck/Wagoneer for the job. The larger the trailer, the longer wheelbase and wider track width your tow vehicle should be. I will not tow a car hauler or tandem axle travel trailer with any vehicle under 110-inch wheelbase. My preference for such trailers is a 129-inch or longer wheelbase. For pulling a 3500-plus pound, 20 foot or longer trailer on a regular basis, I want an HD2500 Dodge Ram 4x4 with a Cummins diesel engine.

> • The Jeepster/Commando and CJ-6 have 101" to 104" wheelbases; the Scrambler (CJ-8) sets at 104"; the XJ Cherokee is 101.4 inches. In my view, the modest tread widths, light curb weights and modest wheelbase lengths limit these Jeep models to a 1500 pound maximum trailer weight. Always use proper hitch equipment that matches the trailer and tow vehicle's requirements. If required or advised, be certain that trailer brakes function properly.

Use A Stable Hitch Assembly and An Equalizer

The equalizer (load distribution) hitch has dramatically increased trailer towing safety. Essentially a tensioned torsion bar set, the equalizer helps neutralize weight on the tow vehicle.

An equalizer assembly is basically two unassuming bars that trail rearward from the ball mount. They swing in their hitch bores, attached by chain to brackets mounted on the trailer frame. Here, the lengths of the adjustable chain become significant. Chain settings determine the torsion bar force applied between the hitch and the trailer frame.

Fig. 16-35. *Drawtite equalizer and EAZ-Lift Sway Control provide ingenious means for stabilizing a trailer in tow. The trailer frame and truck chassis move in unison, offsetting road forces while distributing the load.*

The theory is ingenious. As the bars load, the tongue weight that formerly pushed downward on the rear of the truck is now "equalized" by the torsion bars and distributed over the trailer frame. Incredibly, your Jeep truck can set nearly at its unloaded ball height with the trailer attached.

Visualize pulling a trailer without the equalizer. Imagine hard braking with a 3500-lb. trailer rocking forward. Consider the interaction between the two chassis when your truck encounters dips. Picture the truck loaded with additional gear in the back, its front tires too light to steer and the rear springs slamming against the bump stops.

The equalizer attacks each of these problems, allowing the two chassis to move together. These torsion bars aren't just responsible for balancing the load, they also exert a counter-force as they flex. An equalizer works effectively to counter unwanted chassis movement. The truck and trailer frames move closely together on nearly the same plane.

A frame-mounted Class III hitch and equalizer help bring your trailer to a quicker, straighter stop. A stabilizer/equalizer unit can help stabilize your truck and trailer in crosswinds and on curvy and dipping roads. Most "whipping" comes under control. Here, a "sway control" friction brake can assist further. I always use an equalizing hitch and sway control in combination. These devices complement each other.

CAUTION —
Make certain that trailer brakes function properly. Use a sway control and equalizing hitch on larger trailers. Consult your Jeep dealer or a trailer/RV specialist if you have questions relating to trailer brake controls, sway controls or safe hitch types.

Fabricating Safe Trailer Hitches

Pre-fabricated trailer hitches are available for many Jeep truck models. Your Jeep dealer can supply a bolt-on Mopar/Jeep Accessories assembly. These hitches come as a "kit," with all hardware plus optional wiring harnesses for later model Jeep vehicles.

In some cases, however, a custom hitch will better suit your trailer or vehicle needs. A capable shop can build the right hitch for your Jeep. When choosing a custom trailer hitch, look carefully. You want a well-equipped shop, with all the necessary tools, welding apparatus and quality steel for building a hitch.

The highest grade steel, minimum 1/4" thick, should be used for braces and gussets. Quality 2-inch square, 0.188" wall thickness rectangular tubing works for most hitch assemblies. Required bends must be made on a press to prevent stress caused by heat-and-

Fig. 16-36. *A typical Class III-rated manufactured hitch can handle a 5000 lb. trailer. These hitches could also accommodate a Warn or Ramsey portable winch. Similar "platform/receiver" hitches are available from your local Jeep dealership.*

bend methods. Holes should be die-punched or drilled to size. All construction welds and actual frame attachment welds should follow rigid standards for reducing heat stress to frame members and other vital parts.

As off-pavement 4x4s tend to bury rear bumpers on occasion, a receiver-type hitch, tucked in close to the rear frame member, works well. You can remove the detachable ball mount assembly when the trailer is not in use. This will reduce rear (departure angle) hang ups and also discourage theft of expensive pieces.

NOTE —
A pin-and-clip disconnect eases removal of the ball mount. Some shops drill a hole through the side of the receiver and weld a nut on the outside. This provides for an "anti-rattle bolt" that helps eliminate the metallic noises associated with removable-type receiver ball mounts.

Rick's R.V. Center at El Cajon, California, specializes in trailer hitches. Rick Preston engineers and installs what I believe to be the safest frame-mount hitches available. When Rick constructs a Class III or higher rated hitch, his finished product includes strategic braces, side gussets and triangularly shaped support members that set his shop's work aside from others.

Fig. 16-37. *Pulling a 3500 lb. trailer is no light matter. This custom frame mount hitch/receiver easily pulled a 1600 lb. tent trailer. To resist fore-and-aft thrust of heavier trailer, hitch requires additional bracing between receiver and forward frame crossmember. Larger trailer will also benefit from an equalizing hitch and sway control.*

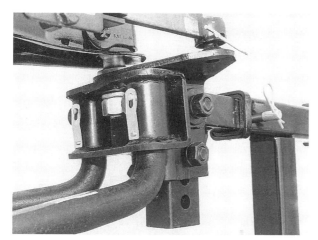

Fig. 16-38. *Hefty Drawtite receiver ball mount adjusts horizontally and also for tilt angle. Massive sockets for equalizer torsion bars can be seen here. The welded miniature ball bracket holds a sway control ball head. Sway control and equalizer assemblies make the whole package work. Without these devices, a truck and hefty trailer could wind up in serious trouble.*

Rick's final fit-ups include strategically placed MIG welds for the frame mounts, then installation of cross-bracing and supports. Rick adds nice touches like safety chain-holed plates at the receiver brace for channeling the trailer's safety chains through the hitch. An electrical connector bracket and glossy black engine enamel complete the job.

CAUTION —
Before towing any trailer with your Jeep, get an expert opinion about the required tow equipment. Your Jeep dealer's service and parts departments can supply information on proper equipment for later vehicles. Additionally, I rely upon the expertise of a professional like Rick Preston, whose clientele include owners of bus-size motorhomes, Airstream and other top-caliber travel trailers and valuable horse trailers.

Mopar/Jeep Accessories

When your later Jeep needs upgrades and accessories, consider Mopar. Your local Jeep dealership has access to a rapidly expanding range of factory-engineered accessory components. These pieces, engineered by the team that built your late model Jeep, meet rigid Chrysler Corporation standards—the same effort found in your Jeep truck.

Safety cannot be overlooked. Many aftermarket parts rely upon trial and error engineering, while the Mopar/Jeep Accessories pieces have been painstakingly designed to meet OEM frame, suspension, braking, lighting, engine cooling and safety requirements.

Mopar/Jeep Accessories wiring harnesses interface with your Jeep's chassis electrics. (Who knows better where the wires should go?) These harnesses have the same integrity as OEM wiring. When ABS and engine management electronics come into play, tapping into the wrong wiring could dangerously impair the function of your Jeep's brakes or engine. This is one more reason to depend upon Mopar/Jeep Accessories engineering. When I'm scores of miles from the nearest paved road, I find it reassuring that the accessories on my Jeep vehicle meet Jeep standards. "Mopar" parts and "Jeep Accessories" offer assurance that my Jeep will operate as designed.

Here is a sampling of the many Mopar/Jeep Accessories that you can access through your local Jeep dealer. See your dealer for catalogs on up-to-date product offerings.

Mopar AM/FM Stereo with Cassette is just one of many sound system upgrades for the Wrangler. Mopar sound system upgrades are available for XJ, ZJ, WJ and '87-up Wrangler models. Six- and 10-disc CD-changers, players, boom boxes and an overhead Sound Bar with speakers are other available items.

(continued)

"Add-A-Trunk" provides secure, lockable stowage space for TJ Wrangler. This could also serve as the location for items that should not be loose in the cab. A color-coordinated carpet cover is also available. Stowage box offers 3 cubic feet of secure cargo space.

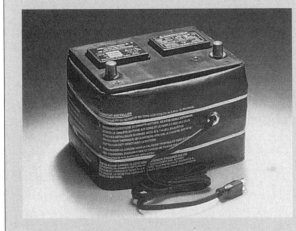

"Battery Blanket" and "Engine Block Heater" are just two of many utility items that Mopar and Jeep Accessories offer. Intended for extreme cold climates, these items fit properly and install quickly.

Tubular bumpers, side steps and brush/grille guards include this chrome item for Wrangler TJ. Available in

black aluminum, chrome, silver aluminum or colored finish (a precise match for specific OEM paint schemes), these steel products are popular. Mopar/Jeep Accessories' tubular steel components are mandrel bent for maximum strength, a superior look and quality fitup.

This front end cover for ZJ Grand Cherokee is black with silver Jeep logo—a distinctive and exclusive feature of Mopar/Jeep Accessories. Color-coordinated floor mats, cargo trays and interior enhancements appeal strongly to XJ and ZJ/WJ owners.

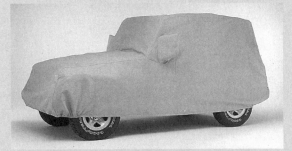

Vehicle covers with distinctive Jeep logo offer protection for your Wrangler (shown), XJ Cherokee, ZJ/WJ Grand Cherokees and 1985–86 CJ models.

Silver aluminum Grille/Brush Guard for '97–up XJ Cherokee reflects Jeep team engineering and fitup. This product meets Federal Motor Vehicle Safety Standards for lighting. The Grille/Brush Guard will not interfere with air flow to radiator or the functions of the vehicle's air bag system. Like Mopar/Jeep Accessories' line of wheels, proper fit and safety are primary design aims.

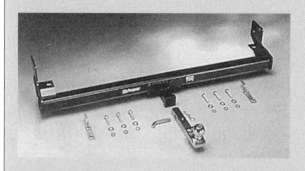

Trailer Hitch for TJ Wrangler comes complete with all mounting hardware and instructions. Optional wiring harness interfaces with OEM vehicle electrics. Hitch maximum load rating with 1.25" receiver/ball mount is 1000 pounds for TJ four-cylinder models and 2000 pounds for TJ six-cylinder models.

The earliest 4WD Jeep models offered exceptional utility. Mopar/Jeep snowplow for a TJ Wrangler continues this tradition. Tested and approved by the Mopar/Jeep Accessories engineering team, the modern snowplow comes with choice of steel or polyethylene blade. Jeep owners, take pride in this workhorse image!

I highly recommend one of Mopar/Jeep Accessories 'Oil Pan Skid Plate' protection. Designed to shield engine and transmission oil pans on TJ Wranglers with 4.0L six-cylinder (#82202538, top right) and 2.5L four-cylinder (#82202690, bottom right) engines, this is a "must item" for rough terrain driving.

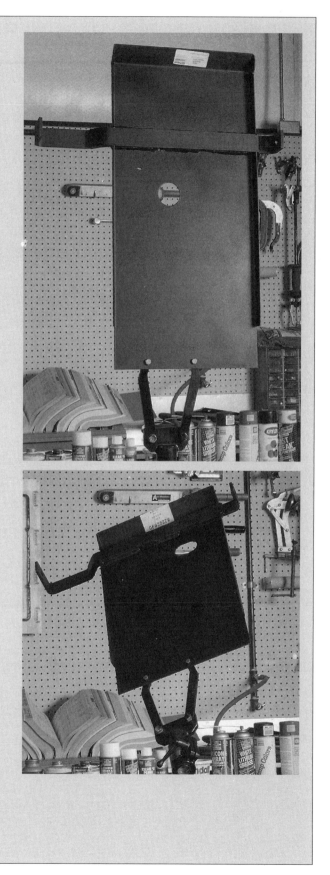

Chapter 17

Engine Performance Modifications

1. Performance and Smog Legal Modifications

The United States' Clean Air Act of 1990 was a watershed measure to curb environmental pollution. "This landmark bill will result in deep and lasting reductions in acid rain, of toxic industrial air pollutants and urban smog," President George Bush noted. "It also will limit U.S. greenhouse gas emissions and sharply reduce our potential contribution to climate change."

The President expressed this nation's commitment to protect the environment and added, "While national governments have an important role to play, progress in protecting our environment is also made community by community, street by street, person by person..."

Reflecting the Clean Air Act of 1990, the U.S. Environmental Protection Agency (EPA) targeted those motor vehicle engine modifications that defeat pollution controls. Since then, aftermarket performance manufacturers have been held to higher levels of accountability. In many instances, simple product disclaimers that read "for off-highway use only" are no longer enough.

Fig. 17-1. *Josh Solomon's modified CJ-8 features approved aftermarket modifications. Know what parts are legal before you begin modifying your engine or planning a conversion.*

The Message Is Clear

The U.S. EPA and California's Air Resources Board mean business. Many other states have adopted California-like standards. Cars and trucks manufactured and licensed for public road use must comply with clean air standards and emission control guidelines.

An EPA letter addressed to automotive parts manufacturers, distributors, retailers and installers clarifies the amended government policy: "The Clean Air Act now prohibits any person from manufacturing, selling, offering for sale, or installing any part or component intended for use with, or as part of, any motor vehicle, where a principal effect of the part or component is to bypass, defeat, or render inoperative any device or element of design, and where the person knows or should know the part or component is being put to such use."

As an example, the letter notes, "...EPA has determined that a catalytic converter replacement pipe, also known as a 'test pipe,' is a part or component intended for use with a motor vehicle for which a principal effect is to bypass, defeat, or render inoperative a vehicle's catalytic converter...EPA believes it is illegal for any person to manufacture, sell, offer for sale or install a catalytic converter replacement pipe...The penalty for violations is up to $2500 for each such device which is manufactured, sold, offered for sale or installed on a motor vehicle."

Ignorance is no excuse. Simply saying that the pipe "cannot be used on pollution controlled vehicles" won't satisfy the law. The manufacturer of such a device must now take full responsibility for the use of the product. The EPA warns, "We intend to focus our enforcement efforts not only on the manufacturers of these defeat devices, but also on auto parts houses and repair facilities who stock, sell or install such devices."

Taboos Under The New Law

How does this new policy affect your Jeep truck? Using the catalytic converter as an example, you cannot remove the converter for off-road driving. According to the EPA, "The federal tampering prohibition pertains to 'motor vehicles,' which are defined by section 216(2) of the Act as 'any self-propelled vehicle[s] designed for transporting persons or property on a street or highway.'"

The EPA emphasizes that in each model year, vehicle manufacturers certify engine-chassis configurations to meet certain tailpipe emission standards. Under the 1990 mandates, "...it is not legal for anyone to de-certify a motor vehicle for off-road use." This means that Jeep Corporation has certified your vehicle model. You cannot compromise any part of your Jeep's pollution control system.

This same law says that swapping an earlier non-catalyst engine into a later, catalytic-equipped chassis is illegal. The chassis still requires the use of a catalytic converter, and the engine must be either the same year or newer than your Jeep. Shops are now held accountable for knowing whether a vehicle originally required a catalytic converter.

Importantly, a muffler shop cannot install a non-certified (termed "non-exempt" in California) dual exhaust system in place of a single exhaust system—even if the shop installs dual catalytic mufflers. If your truck was originally a single exhaust model with a catalytic converter, certified by Jeep in that mode, the new EPA law restricts any kind of non-certified modification by a muffler shop.

> NOTE—
> These exhaust system rulings have spawned an aftermarket for single exhaust, "cat-back" upgrades. Such performance exhaust improvements do not interfere with the catalytic converter, oxygen sensor or any other device between the engine and back end of the cat.

So strong is this ruling that the only current exception is a vehicle that was converted to dual exhausts with dual catalytic converters prior to the 1990 Clean Air Act and these EPA rulings. Although the EPA encourages a shop to retrofit an OEM style single exhaust system in such cases, the agency currently allows shops to install replacement catalytic converters and pipes on a previously retrofit dual exhaust/dual cat system. The shop must be able to prove, however, that they did not replace the OEM single system with a dual exhaust setup after the date of the EPA rulings.

> NOTE—
> Check with your local muffler shop or the EPA for the latest rulings on this issue.

Catalytic converter rulings are just the beginning. EPA has adopted California's standards for exemption or certification of aftermarket engine parts. Components that the California Air Resources Board (CARB) finds acceptable also earn a federal stamp of approval. An Executive Order (EO number) from California indicates that an aftermarket part has undergone the testing necessary to meet OEM tailpipe emission compliance standards.

Legally "Exempted" Components

Before you limit the use of your Jeep 4x4, consider the legal issues. The EPA and CARB approve (exempt) many components that meet clean air requirements.

Certain other parts do not adversely impact tailpipe emissions. For that reason, a high output water pump, an improved cooling system, a high capacity charging circuit or chrome valve covers will not fail an emissions test.

Equally important, engine rebuilding can legally include many upgrade parts that will increase the reliability of your engine. Components like stronger pushrods, hardened exhaust valve seats, better bearings, improved piston rings, quality (stock compression ratio) pistons and a heavy duty timing chain have no effect on tailpipe emissions.

The issue here is tailpipe emissions. Changing the camshaft to a long duration grind for maximum mid-range and top end power is a sure way to raise measurable hydrocarbon and carbon monoxide output at lower engine speeds. (California-type biennial smog inspection tests take place at an idle and 2500 rpm.) Likewise, a non-approved high performance retrofit carburetor could raise tailpipe emissions.

> WARNING—
> A non-approved replacement carburetor will immediately fail the visual portion of a California-type smog inspection test.

Many aftermarket manufacturers have taken their components through the California emission certification process. Some performance items qualify as OEM replacement parts. Most of Edelbrock's Performer dual-plane manifolds, for example, provide a mount for the EGR valve. Although these manifolds improve flow and engine efficiency, they will not increase tailpipe pollution. Several exhaust header, ignition component and aftermarket camshaft manufacturers have passed the CARB tests and received executive order (EO) exemption numbers for their products.

For electronic fuel injected and turbocharged engines, a variety of aftermarket improvements in air flow and induction tuning parts have also met certification standards. If a part has an official California exemption number ("E.O.") for use on your specific engine, you can install the component without violating the law.

> NOTE—
> The Mopar Performance retrofit EFI/MPI induction system for 1981–90 4.2L/258 Jeep in-line six-cylinder engines has a California exemption number (Executive Order D265-7). This enhancement is "50-State Legal" and a smart alternative to the OEM 'BBD' carburetor. (For details, see later section in this chapter.)

Clean Air High Performance

Under the amended Clean Air Act, aftermarket manufacturers must certify any induction system component, ignition system piece, performance camshaft or exhaust device that differs from the OEM design or engineering. Additionally, each state has statutes or regulations which prohibit defeating or tampering with the pollution control equipment on a certified motor vehicle.

> CAUTION—
> The EPA emphasizes, "Vehicle owners who tamper with their own vehicles may be subject to substantial penalties under both federal and State law."

These laws, however, encourage lower tailpipe emissions. For this reason, California has no objection to the installation of a late model Jeep Cherokee High Output electronic fuel injected 4.0L engine, rated 190 horsepower, in place of a carbureted 258 six in a 1975 CJ-7. Despite the increase in horsepower, the tailpipe pollution from a late EFI engine is a fraction of that allowed for 1975 vehicles.

> NOTE—
> A late EFI conversion engine must include its OEM computer and all factory engine sensors. You must swap all parts that make up the engine/emission package.

Buy Legal Performance

A growing number of aftermarket parts have earned California EO exemptions. An exemption means the part will not defeat the design or intent of your engine's emission control system. When you find EO exempted parts, make sure that pieces have approval for use on your particular year and model engine. Some parts might fit your engine but still do not meet the emission requirements. EO exemptions apply to a specific engine type and/or model chassis.

There are a variety of devices that have EO numbers. Currently, the EPA accepts CARB tests and California's exemption criteria. Parts that have California exemption status also meet Federal/EPA standards. A complete list of California exempted components is available from the California Air Resources Board, or write: Haagen-Smit Laboratory, 9528 Telstar Avenue, El Monte, CA 91731-2990, phone 1-818-575-6800.

A Bright Future

Swapping late EFI engines into earlier Jeep chassis has become more common. Electronic fuel injection means an end to sidehill flooding and the negative effects of altitude. Also, without exception, later EFI engines have lower tailpipe emissions and far better fuel efficiency than earlier carbureted powerplants.

> NOTE —
> California provides a "referee" program for smog certification of vehicles with engine conversions. Referees determine whether you have made a complete conversion, including all necessary emission equipment. Tailpipe emissions from your new, upgraded engine must be equal to or less than your original Jeep engine in good operating condition. If you have questions, contact the California Consumer Affairs Department for a referral to the nearest Bureau of Automotive Repairs' referee station.

Imagine the performance of a late turbocharged Buick Grand National 231 V-6 engine in place of a 1971 225 Dauntless 225 V-6. How about a 360 Mopar EFI V-8 engine replacing a '77 AMC/Jeep 304 smog motor in a CJ-7? Your Jeep would gain torque and fuel efficiency, yet produce far less tailpipe pollution.

Reputable aftermarket manufacturers have responded to EPA requirements. Crane Cams tested and received the first California Air Resources Board EO numbers for several camshaft profiles. Crane camshafts with EO numbers have 50-State legal status when used in specific engines.

Gene Ezzell, President and CEO at Crane Cams, noted, "We are extremely proud to be the first performance camshaft company to receive exemption from ARB and to show the industry that it is possible to have products that meet emissions standards."

Ezzell credits the Specialty Equipment Market Association (SEMA) for encouraging the aftermarket to build California/EPA legal products. SEMA's effort helps assure the stability and future of the automotive performance aftermarket. Today, Competition Cams (CompCams) also offers several 50-State Legal 'High Energy' camshaft grind profiles that work remarkably well in Jeep off-pavement applications.

> NOTE —
> Look for an "E.O." number before buying a camshaft. A milder camshaft grind can enhance low speed torque output while easily meeting emission requirements.

As an active supporter of TREAD LIGHTLY! and clean air standards, I encourage Jeep owners to protect the environment. Please help by using aftermarket engine performance parts that bear a California EO number and "50-State Legal" status.

2. Engine Upgrades

When mud, rock and steep inclines grip all four of your Jeep's tires, engine speed can drop well below 2000 rpm. The engine begs to stall from the heavy load. In the raw realm of four-wheeling, your engine's character defines success.

Although an engine rebuild provides the opportunity for improving performance, many inexperienced mechanics turn to street performance formulas that offer the wrong ignition, carburetion and camshaft behaviors for off-pavement use.

> NOTE —
> Mopar Performance/Jeep Motorsport, the high performance Jeep factory source, offers the book, Mopar Jeep Engines: Speed Secrets & Racing Modifications for Jeep-Built 4, 6 & V-8 Engines (part #P4529529). This informative guide provides a condensed, engine-specific view of major overhaul and internal repairs for AMC/Jeep 2.5L and 2.46L fours, 4.0L and 4.2L sixes and the 5.9L (AMC design) V-8. Also covered are racing buildups for the AMC-design 2.5L, 4.0L and 5.9L engines. If your AMC- or Chrysler-Jeep engine goals include a factory "blueprint" rebuild or a racing buildup, see your Mopar or Jeep dealer for this valuable 350-page book.

Building a Jeep engine strictly for horsepower, a valid goal for desert racing, may actually inhibit low speed torque output and diminish trail running and rock crawling ability. Careful planning and selection of components can give your Jeep engine more usable torque, better breathing characteristics and greater stamina for tortuous off- pavement lugging and climbs.

> *CAUTION —*
> • *Many engine modifications are illegal for street or public highway use. If your Jeep must comply with vehicle registration and public highway requirements, make certain that aftermarket parts have California and federal EPA approval. It is illegal to remove, modify or degrade pollution control devices on vehicles licensed for use on public highways.*
>
> • *If you raise engine performance, the rest of the truck's powertrain must withstand the added torque. A light duty transmission, transfer case and drive axles often fail when subject to extreme increases in horsepower. Beware. You may need a host of powertrain modifications.*

Fig. 17-2. *The F-134 four has all exhaust valves fitted in the block and intake valves fitted within a removable cylinder head. This novel concept powered many Jeep trucks from the early 1950s until the '70s.*

Fig. 17-3. *Valve timing is a critical part of engine performance. When you install a new camshaft, sprockets and chain (or gears), set the valve timing accurately and according to the camshaft grinder's specifications. Use a degree wheel to verify and index valve timing.*

2.1 Begin with the Valvetrain

The typical Jeep engine's valvetrain consists of the camshaft, camshaft followers (lifters), pushrods, rocker arms, valve springs and valves. (Tornado overhead camshaft sixes operate without lifters and pushrods, as the rocker arms work directly from the camshaft lobes.) Jeep engine valves and springs fit either in a removable cylinder head (overhead valve configuration) or the block, like the early Jeep L-head engines and the exhaust valves of F-134 four-cylinder powerplants.

Camshaft followers or lifters ride on lobes of the camshaft. Pushrods connect the lifters to the rocker arms, which pivot and press against the valve stem ends. The intake and exhaust valves open and close ports that allow gases to enter and leave the engine's cylinders and combustion chambers.

The camshaft has an important job. Lobes, carefully ground to open and close the valves at precise times, rotate at one-half the speed of the crankshaft. Each two turns of the crankshaft, the camshaft will open and close each valve, doing so for the entire service life of the engine.

Spring tension at the camshaft and lifter contact points creates the highest pound-per-square-inch load within your Jeep's engine. The hardness of the camshaft and its compatibility with the lifter material affects the overall reliability of the engine. Lobe contours or profiles also dictate the degree of stress placed on pushrods, rocker arms and valve springs.

Camshaft Lobe Profiles and Valve Timing

Each Jeep engine type requires a camshaft of unique dimensions. Lobe profiles vary, and careful engineering determines the correct shape from low point (heel)

to peak lift. Lifter limitations also influence the lobe "ramp" shape. Radically high lobe contours increase stress and wear between the lobe and the lifter base. (Very high lift designs require roller lifters and special valve springs.)

Valve timing includes lift (the full range of lifter movement) and duration, the number of crankshaft degrees that the valve stays open. Valve timing controls the opening and closing time of the valves. The three concerns when choosing the right replacement camshaft are valve lift, opening duration, and valve timing. Your intended use of the engine dictates the correct profile.

Selecting Your Camshaft

Some general rules apply when meeting off-pavement and heavy duty pulling chores. For general four-wheeling, your engine will operate over a broad rpm range and need power from just off idle to at least 4000 rpm. The long duration street-performance camshaft is incorrect, as valve timing will overlap excessively. (Overlap is when the exhaust valve is still closing while the intake valve has already begun to open. Both valves are partially open at this point.)

Excess valve overlap creates two fundamental problems for an off-pavement 4x4 engine: 1) rough idle and poor low speed throttle response, and 2) low manifold vacuum at slower engine rpm.

Manifold vacuum is crucial to power, proper combustion and fuel economy. In effect, an automotive gasoline engine is a vacuum pump. Your Jeep engine's operating cycle begins with the vacuum characteristics of the intake stroke. If you plan serious rock crawling and trailer pulling, or want low speed economy and good throttle response, high manifold vacuum will be on top of your priority list. Especially at higher elevations, adequate engine breathing depends upon sufficient manifold vacuum.

Off-pavement Camshaft Profiles

The back country Jeep engine needs a camshaft that works well at highway cruising speeds (generally 2000–3000 engine rpm) and still can crawl smoothly through the Rubicon or your favorite rockpile. Not surprisingly, the Willys, Kaiser, General Motors, AMC and Chrysler engines found in Jeep trucks have mild camshaft profiles.

If light duty use, highway cruising, an occasional light trailer pull and reasonably good fuel economy are your goals, a camshaft close to the OEM specs would likely work fine. The formula for hard-core off-pavement success or ongoing trailer pulling, however, involves more low-rpm torque response and a smooth transition to the horsepower curve. This usually requires more valve lift than the OE camshaft provides.

Controllable power in an off-idle rock crawl relies on torque, not horsepower. Stronger valve lift with mild valve opening duration contributes to low-end torque. Lugging the engine prevents wheelspin. This requires strong low-end torque with very light use of the throttle. (See the chapter on operating your Jeep.)

Typical gasoline engines realize their full horsepower potential in the mid- to top-end rpm range, speeds upward of 3500 rpm. However, when your Jeep's tires need a solid grip, and rock shale threatens the sidewalls, running the engine at 3500 or more rpm is not only unsafe but also abusive to the truck and environment.

Low rpm control requires immediate off-idle torque, the product of healthy valve lift and higher manifold vacuum. Select a truck camshaft capable of at least 16 (preferably 18–20) in/hg of manifold vacuum at an idle. Such an "RV," "trailer towing" or "economy" camshaft will work well with milder carburetion. Four-wheeling benefits from readily available low speed torque.

> NOTE —
> For four-wheeling with a V-8 engine, Comp-Cams 252 High Energy grind is my favorite. Strong, useful torque by 2000 rpm and emission legal in many applications, this camshaft works well to 4500-plus rpm—plenty fast for a rock-crawler or trailer puller.

In general, seek a camshaft with slightly more lift than the OE Jeep profile. (OE specifications are available in factory level service guidebooks.) Keep both the valve opening duration and valve timing conservative.

Aftermarket Camshaft Options

For high torque within a reasonable rpm range, several camshaft profiles have worked well in Jeep engines. Surely the most popular OEM Jeep engine for a build-up has been the 232/258 AMC in-line six, which can be a real torque monster. Seven-main-bearing crankshaft support and a healthy stroke make the 258, in particular, a rugged, stump pulling engine.

The 258 and other in-line sixes can benefit from a hydraulic cam of approximately 0.444" gross lift and 264 degrees duration. Assuming that your Jeep 258 has a normal compression ratio (9.2:1 or less), the idle with this kind of camshaft is smooth, and your engine can develop usable low-end torque with respectable mid-range (2000–3500 rpm) horsepower. Like Comp-Cams' 252 High Energy grind for V-8s, expect the power curve for this type of six-cylinder camshaft to drop off above 4500 rpm.

For the Jeep AMC-type V-8 engines in the 304 to 401 cubic inch range, lift is again useful. For ultimate low-end torque and high manifold vacuum, I recommend Competition Cams' High Energy 252H grind. Lift is 0.433 inch intake and exhaust, duration is a mild 252 degrees at 0.006 inch valve lift. My tests show this camshaft delivers better fuel-efficiency and performs very well in the 800–4200 rpm range—great for rock-crawling or lugging a hefty load!

Another good overall camshaft profile has 195 degrees duration (figured at a 0.050" ramp measurement). Advertised or gross duration of 266 degrees coupled with a gross intake and exhaust valve lift around 0.425" works well. Lobe centerlines of 109 degrees intake and 112 degrees exhaust will take care of valve timing. Such a cam produces great torque plus good power from an idle through cruise. Expect the power drop to occur in the 4000–4500 rpm range.

Fig. 17-4. *Valve timing is critical to proper engine performance. This aftermarket roller chain sprocket has three keyways for varying camshaft timing. Here, the engine builder has the choice of normal (straight up) and an advance or retard of 4 degrees in either direction stock. Some kits use an offset bushing or key.*

Fig. 17-5. *Another function of most camshafts is to drive the distributor gear. Mesh of these gears is critical, as the oil pump may also run from the base of the distributor shaft. Make certain that your new camshaft's drive gear material is compatible with the distributor drive gear. Often, a bronze or specialty distributor gear is necessary. Follow the camshaft grinder's recommendation.*

NOTE —
These two camshaft profiles satisfy rock crawling, pulling a trailer and good gas mileage. With either camshaft, you can use OE carburetion or an improved carburetor with a near stock cubic-feet-per-minute (CFM) flow rate.

For higher horsepower aims, including competitive hill climbing, off-highway racing or sand drags, Mopar Performance offers a series of "factory engineered" performance camshafts for the AMC/Jeep V-8s and Chrysler's own 5.2L and 5.9L V-8s (found in the ZJ Grand Cherokee). See your Jeep or Mopar dealer or secure a copy of the latest Mopar Performance Catalog.

CAUTION —
Engines with EFI and computers will not tolerate racy camshaft profiles. AMC-design fours and in-line sixes or a Chrysler 5.2L or 5.9L V-8 with EFI/MPI are not candidates for a radical camshaft profile. There are some performance "computer cams" now available from prominent aftermarket camshaft suppliers. Look for an emission legal grind for best results.

Whenever you upgrade the camshaft, install new lifters and make certain that the valve springs are in top shape. The lifts I recommend here are relatively mild, and they only require that your OEM components, including valve springs, be in good condition. Install a high quality roller timing chain and sprocket set, and carefully follow the manufacturer's recommendations for setting camshaft timing degrees.

CAUTION —
For best results, always set valve timing to specifications. ("Degree" the camshaft.) Industry experts find that off-the-shelf timing sprocket and chain sets deviate as much as five degrees. To realize a camshaft's performance potential, valve timing must match cam design. If necessary and recommended by the camshaft manufacturer, use an offset bushing or key kit to degree valve timing.

For four-cylinder engines, in particular the Iron Duke Pontiac 151, manufacturers like Crane, Wolverine/Blue Racer and others offer camshaft upgrades. Mopar Performance provides an excellent "Factory Engineered" line of camshafts for the AMC-design (late '83–up CJs, the XJ Cherokee and Wrangler YJ/TJ) 2.5L fours.

CAUTION —
For the AMC/Jeep-design 2.5L EFI/MPI fours and 4.0L MPI sixes, or a Mopar 4.7L (OHC), 5.2L or 5.9L V-8 with EFI/MPI, be certain that any camshaft choice is "computer compatible." A milder grind would be advisable. "50-State Legal" for emissions is always your best bet.

The OE camshaft for the early Willys fours are industrial designs and provide remarkable smoothness at an idle. Ample low-end torque makes these L- and F-head 134 engines perform very well in the rough stuff. If rock crawling finesse, higher manifold vacuum at altitude and overall economy are your aims, stay with the stock 134 camshaft profile or consider a grind with a very slight increase in valve lift—Avoid the use of a camshaft with longer valve opening duration!

Before considering a camshaft change, assess your Jeep engine's condition. Check the carburetor, hunt down vacuum leaks, measure compression and analyze the ignition timing and spark. Confirm manifold vacuum. These are each areas where stable performance is won or lost.

Variable Duration Lifters
Most camshafts cannot satisfy every need. Some deliver bottom end power but weaker performance from 3500–4000 rpm upward. Others have little useful power at low speeds but great horsepower at higher rpm levels. For some Jeep engine applications, there's a solution.

Jack Rhoads pioneered a hydraulic lifter designed to bleed down at lower rpm, allowing lift to drop 0.020" to 0.030" and a milder valve opening duration in this phase. Precisely metered bleed-down makes several camshaft profiles out of one. Rhoads, Crane and others now offer variable duration lifters for many engine designs.

The reduction in lift and duration creates a tolerable idle and adequate low speed response, even with a hotter camshaft. The popular AMC/Jeep V-8 performance camshaft of 260–270 ("advertised") degrees duration becomes more acceptable. Valve lift, similarly, can be extended beyond 0.433" without an adverse effect on low speed performance. Low-end torque, reasonable manifold vacuum at low speeds and great mid-range and top-end power can be possible with the same camshaft grind.

CAUTION —
Be aware that bleed-down lifters may create more valvetrain noise than stock hydraulic lifters.

Lubrication and Oil Cooling

Internal combustion engines produce heat and energy. Hot, expanding gases move the pistons. Thermal loss is tremendous, as heat dissipates throughout the engine. On later Jeep engine designs, emission control and fuel economy standards lean the fuel mixes and advance the spark timing. As smaller engines do bigger jobs, upper cylinder temperatures increase further. The radiator, engine fan and coolant draw heat away from the engine, yet there's far more to cooling.

Oil, lubricating and battling friction, is another conductor for heat. Buildup of engine heat increases the oxidation rate and acid content in the oil. Oxygen combines with oil hydrocarbons, producing easily recognizable sludge. This sludge may include varnishes, waxes, corrosive acids and the water of hydration compounds. According to Hayden, a respected manufacturer of engine and transmission oil coolers, each 20 degrees of excess oil temperature doubles oil oxidation and bearing wear.

Launching a Second Front Against Heat

Traditionally, water/coolant circulation and dissipation of heat through a fan-assisted radiator have provided adequate Jeep cooling. Porsche and Volkswagen, however, have proven the effectiveness of direct oil-to-air cooling. The Porsche and VW air-cooled engines have survived in desert dune buggies and Baja racers, proving that enough air, moving through the right oil cooler, can offer substantial engine cooling.

Sceptics of air cooled engines need only look at their own water cooled Jeep engine. Outside the block's water jackets and cylinder head coolant ports, your entire engine is oil cooled. The valves and valvetrain, including the camshaft and timing chain or gear mechanisms, the connecting rods, pistons, rings, all bearings—even the crankshaft—rely on the oil's ability to continuously carry heat away.

For many years, truck and industrial users have recognized the usefulness of engine oil coolers. Many trucks have optional OE engine oil coolers, an obvious choice for the aware buyer. Mini-coolers appear on other automotive systems, too, including power steering.

Aftermarket automatic transmission coolers, offered since the 1960s, can dramatically extend transmission life. Despite OE radiator cooling, in-line automatic transmission fluid coolers and engine oil coolers are a must for trailer pulling and other heavy duty uses.

Subjected to loads, hills and towing, oil heat rises substantially. The best radiator and fan can only address coolant temperature, while oil temperature continues to increase. An add-on, external oil-to-air cooling system could prove vital to your Jeep engine. If hot climate driving, hard-core four-wheeling or trailer pulling fit your plans, an aftermarket engine or transmission oil cooler is practical protection.

Engine Oil Cooler Installation Tips

Like any other accessory, an engine oil cooler requires careful fitup. Mounted improperly, the cooler may actually inhibit air flow through the radiator. Most oil cooler kits provide detailed instructions. Necessary hardware should include quality hose and fittings, designed for exposure to high temperature oil. Usually, an oil filter spacer/adapter provides the cooler's source for both pressurized oil and the return flow.

Many aftermarket kits include quality coolers and adapters, but fall short with attaching hardware. For simple installation, manufacturers have resorted to through-the-radiator plastic ties to secure the cooler. For off-pavement use and situations where vehicles jar, vibrate and twist, plastic ties lead to trouble.

Radiator experts and I suggest fabricating a lightweight metal framework for the oil cooler. The cooler may still mount in front of the radiator, isolated from the expensive fins and tubes of the radiator core. Also route hoses carefully, and consider potential road hazard damage or any risk of chafing on body or chassis edges.

High GCW capacities require every ounce of engine energy available. Great expectations from smaller V-8, 4- and 6-cylinder engines, compounded by higher thermostat settings, endanger the engine oil and all lubricated parts. Heat is the number one cause of parts fatigue. Lowering oil temperatures can extend an engine's life.

NOTE —
Installed correctly, an oil cooler provides protection. I also use high-quality, 100% synthetic motor oil as a means for countering engine oil heat.

Axle Gearing for Your Camshaft

When making a camshaft choice, consider your axle gearing and tire diameter. These two factors determine the cruising rpm and low-speed responsiveness of your Jeep engine. Unless the tire diameter is oversize, very low axle ratios (4.27:1 to 5.38:1) will substantially raise your highway cruising rpm. Likewise, mid-'70s and later Jeep trucks often have taller axle ratios (3.08:1 to 3.73:1). Here, oversize tires may drop the cruising rpm range below 2000 rpm—especially with a fifth-gear overdrive transmission.

Tall gearing and oversize tires require a camshaft that provides plenty of low end torque. Forget 5000 rpm performance. The Jeep with 3.08:1 gearing, 33" diameter tires and a non-overdrive transmission spins the engine 1882 rpm in high gear at 60 mph. By contrast, an early model CJ or military Jeep with 5.38 gears and 30" diameter tires will spin the engine 3617 rpm at 60 mph. Usable power is your primary concern. With careful choices, your Jeep 4x4 can have realistic performance gains—both for off-pavement crawling and at highway cruise speeds.

2.2 Hot, Reliable Ignition

Hard-core four-wheeling requires consistent performance. The sport you've chosen requires the best an engine can muster. Fuel must flow precisely and spark cannot falter. A misfire at the wrong moment could prove catastrophic. Battling weather, high altitude, extreme climates, precarious road surfaces and marginal fuels, your Jeep engine needs a quality ignition system. For serious off-pavement users, a variety of aftermarket ignition enhancements are available.

Accel Performance Products offers a wide range of high performance ignition components. Racing Coils, the Super Coil, GM HEI intensifier kits, and an HEI Super Coil are designed to work in conjunction with various Jeep OE ignition systems. Super Stock Coils replace many OE Jeep coils. Electrical accessories, including ballast resistors and coil brackets, round out the OE replacement components.

Accel is also serious about racing, and a number of all-out performance distributors are available. A 37-Series Dual-Point provides performance to 9000 rpm. The 43-Series Magnetic NASCAR-developed distributor has an adjustable spark curve, making the unit useful for many racing and performance applications. Accel's 44-Series Direct Drive distributor, with rigid timing, could serve a radical sand drag or mud bog racing engine.

Four-wheelers find the Accel 41-Series electronic distributor attractive and available in optional me-

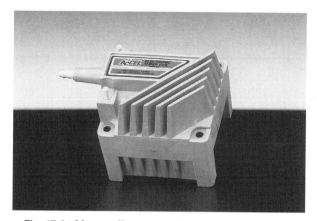

Fig. 17-6. *Mopar offers a complete line of distributors and high performance ignition components. Included is the Super Coil by Accel.*

chanical with vacuum advance form. In an off-road emergency, a GM HEI module and Chrysler distributor cap can bring your rig home.

Allison, now a division of CRANE Cams, has a long history of quality ignition products. Popular is the street-legal, California-approved XR-700 electronic ignition conversion for older breaker point ignitions. This system allows use of your stock distributor with all the benefits of an electronic high energy spark. For many Kaiser and AMC Jeep engines, the XR-700 kit can upgrade the OE breaker point ignition performance.

Crane/Allison claims performance and mileage gains, along with easier starting. The XR-700 kits are about as simple to install as breaker points. In addition to a lifetime warranty, the XR-700 conversion offers the ideal off-road backup system: the OE set of points and condenser. If the electronic parts fail in the field, simply re-install the OE ignition pieces.

Mallory pioneered high performance ignitions. Racing and high performance distributors, coils, electronic conversion kits, modules, rev limiters and much, much more make Mallory a strong choice for Jeep spark needs. Mallory offers OE replacement upgrades, computer chips and a traditional line of accessories. The popular Unilite breakerless distributors or a Unilite conversion kit can provide dependable spark. Racing dual-point and Unilite units are also popular.

Mopar Performance brings factory-level engineering to a full line of ignition and even EFI/spark management computer upgrades. Targeting both AMC/Jeep design and popular Chrysler-built engines, Mopar Performance is the first choice with enthusiasts and users who demand high quality and ready Mopar/Jeep dealership access to parts.

The Mopar Performance line includes complete Jeep replacement distributors, distributor caps and ro-

Fig. 17-7. *Mopar Performance offers a complete line of factory-approved ignition upgrades. Your local Jeep dealer and other Mopar outlets can supply complete electronic distributor units for the Jeep 2.5L, 4.0L, 304/360 AMC-design V-8 and other Chrysler engines.*

Fig. 17-8. *Mopar Performance computer provides more spark advance and improved fuel flow for off-road racing. This computer, designed for 4.0L in-line sixes, will enhance other performance modifications.*

tors, ignition control modules, wiring harness kits, the Super-Coil, ignition switches, spark timing devices and EFI/spark management computer units. See your local Jeep dealer's Mopar Performance Catalog.

MSD Ignition/Autotronic Controls Corporation is distinguished by a full line of ignition distributors, emission legal ignition enhancements and all-out racing hardware. MSD electronic devices interface with stock, aftermarket or complete MSD ignitions.

> NOTE—
> I have used and tested a variety of MSD Ignition components. In my experience, these exceptionally well-built products have met every claim. Early L- and F-head engines to later model Jeep four-, six- and V-8 ignitions can benefit from a range of MSD enhancements.

MSD's adjustable timing controls provide more complete combustion and a cure for high altitude and poor fuel grades. Want to compensate for thin air or Mexican gasoline? The MSD timing controls place spark timing at your fingertips.

Performance Distributors provides completely reworked OE-type units that wield a whopping spark. Performance Distributors claim nearly twice the spark of a magneto and fire to the 9,000 crankshaft rpm range. Custom spark curves meet your exact engine needs. Each unit undergoes thorough pre-testing before shipment.

Running 0.050"–0.055" recommended spark plug gaps, these distributor units yield tremendous gains from idle through high rpm. A bronze terminal cap and racing coil accompany each distributor. Most Kaiser and AMC Jeep engines have common GM or Ford type distributors. Performance Distributors can rework these units to meet high performance standards.

2.3 Supercharging

The first light four-wheel drive vehicle to use turbocharging was a mid-'Sixties four-cylinder Scout. Aftermarket retrofit superchargers now fit a wide range of popular engines. Perhaps in the near future, in step with demands for greater fuel economy and performance, domestic and import trucks will offer models with OE supercharging.

Acceleration, mid-range power, and volumetric efficiency improve drastically with supercharging, yet a sensibly staged blower or turbocharger usually has no impact on engine start-up, idle quality or off idle tip-in performance. As rpm rises, the blower boosts both manifold and cylinder pressures. The higher the speed, the greater the performance and efficiency.

Blower Basics

Mechanical superchargers or blowers receive power directly from the engine via a belt- or gear-drive mechanism. Altering the blower shaft speed can regulate air displacement. There are five popular mechanical blower designs: Roots-type, sliding-vane, spiral, centrifugal and rotary piston.

GM's Detroit diesels popularized the Roots-type blower. Plentiful and relatively inexpensive, the 6-71 and 4-71 blowers have served the racing community for over three decades. Fitted to a gasoline engine, a blower increases torque, mid-range and top-end power.

The Roots-type blower, like other positive-displacement superchargers, provides smooth volumetric flow rates and high pressures—even at relatively low blower speeds. Although some pressure loss occurs through "backflow," Roots-type superchargers can provide useful boost over a wide rpm range.

In the Roots-type blower, two rotors spin in a blower housing/cavity. (These twin rotors never touch each other or the housing.) The close tolerance fitup between the rotors and housing create high boost pressures.

> **NOTE —**
> Other mechanical superchargers share this common theme: Timed phases first draw air then squeeze, forcing air into the plenum. (Centrifugal superchargers compress air within the blower rather than in the intake plenum.) On OEM diesels, injectors spray pressurized fuel into each combustion or pre-combustion chamber as compression peaks.

When retrofitting Roots-type blowers to gasoline engines with carburetion or throttle body injection, fuel passes through the compressor chamber. Tuned port (TPI) or multi-point (MPI) injection requires a different approach, as injectors spray fuel directly into the intake ports. For TPI and MPI, the high speed, close tolerance centrifugal-type blower has become popular, as fuel does not pass through the compressor.

Exhaust Turbocharging

Turbochargers, usually of single-flow turbine design, deliver a slight excess of boost. Excess boost bypasses through a wastegate system. The wastegate prevents cylinder over-charging and minimizes the energy spent spinning the turbine/compressor.

The turbocharger operates at all engine speeds. Intake air flow assists the compressor rotation, while exhaust gases press the turbine into action. The result is an energy balance, as engine power increases with boost. Like a mechanical blower, turbocharger boost occurs when engine rpm (i.e., exhaust pressure/turbine speed) reaches a suitable level.

High manifold vacuum reduces exhaust pressure and also the demand for boost. Reciprocally, low manifold vacuum (heavy loads) increase exhaust pressure and create turbo boost. The adjustable wastegate sets a ceiling on boost pressure.

Intercoolers have provided a significant breakthrough for turbocharging. Compressed air generates heat. This heat expands the air/fuel mix and absorbs vital space. Cooling the air between the turbo unit and the intake plenum provides a denser, more energy-packed air/fuel mass for each cylinder.

Aftermarket Blowers

B&M has put years of product development into a complete line of blowers and an extensive blower accessory line. B&M focuses on both street and off-high-

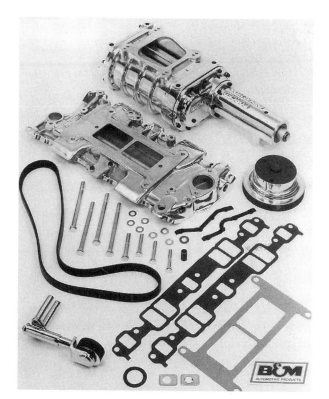

Fig. 17-9. *A typical B&M supercharger kit.*

Fig. 17-10. *K.F. Engineering pioneered the first emission legal blower system in the United States. Designed for the 2.8L GM 173 V-6, this system met 50-State emission requirements. Mild, precisely engineered boost enhanced performance without jeopardizing reliability. Kit for 1984–86 Cherokee applications came complete with all hardware and detailed instructions.*

way applications, ranging from streetable boost to the highly acclaimed and popular MegaBlower, a 6-71 size unit made completely from new materials. A Chevy 350 V-8 with 7.5:1 compression ratio and a MegaBlower claims 540 horsepower at 6500 rpm. A torque peak of 520 ft/lbs is achieved by 4500 rpm. Maximum boost for this dual 750 Holley carbureted engine is 12 psi at 6500 rpm.

For milder engines, B&M offers much tamer superchargers. Kits permit use of stock factory accessories, a real savings. B&M engineering also offers a low-profile blower for the 60- and 90-degree GM V-6 engines. This includes the 1984–86 2.8L GM/Jeep Cherokee V-6s. With a 390 CFM Holley carburetor, such a 2.8L engine can wield 220 horsepower on the dynamometer. Kits are available for most V-8s and the Buick V-6 231/252s.

Dyer Machine Service is one of the few aftermarket suppliers of blowers for AMC and Buick V-8s. The focus is V6-71 and R6-71 GMC blower systems. Upgraded for longevity, Dyer Machine Service blower kits feature all parts except the carburetors, which Dyer offers separately.

> NOTE —
> Before you buy any blower system, I recommend a review of the B&M Supercharger Technical Manual. This manual is a valuable resource tool. See your local B&M dealer for details.

> CAUTION —
> *A five-pound boost limit helps assure engine longevity for stock compression engine applications. Do not install a blower on an engine that has over 10% leakage at any cylinder. Always use lower compression ratio pistons when building an engine to run with a blower.*

Supercharging: Compression Ratios, Camshafts and Air Filtration

Supercharging works with compression ratios of 7:1 to 9:1 on engines with good cylinder sealing (10% maximum leakdown). Drive ratios determine boost levels. Forged aluminum pistons, quality stainless valves, and hard steel valve seats are minimal requirements for higher boost pressures.

Weiand's research reveals that peak performance camshaft blower grinds feature 112- to 114-degree lobe centers, 0.450" to 0.500" lift and 220–234 degree duration at 0.050" lift (272 to 288 degrees gross duration). Logically, the exhaust valve must remain closed while the intake valve is open to prevent pressurized air/fuel charges from racing out the exhaust port.

True blower camshaft grinds also have slightly longer duration on the exhaust side to totally clean out cylinders during the exhaust cycle. For mild supercharging, a stock or RV cam works fine. Weiand produces a full range of blowers and blower system products.

> NOTE —
> Weiand's camshaft recommendations pertain to racing and high performance use of blowers, not for street-driven vehicles or rock-crawling 4x4s. Near-stock camshafts work satisfactorily when blower boost is mild.

Air/fuel ratios are critical with blowers, so carburetor jetting and adequate air flow are essential. K & N and similar filtration systems provide the protection needed for expensive, close-tolerance blower systems. Carburetor CFM requirements rise somewhat above stock demands, although many OEM air cleaner assemblies provide enough reserve capacity when used with a K & N-type element.

HESCO Superchargers and 4.7L Stroker Kits

Lee Hurley lives and breathes Jeep engines. I first met Lee at Walker Evans' Race Shop in the late 1980s. Engrossed in the pioneering development of potent laptop-programmable Jeep electronic fuel and spark management, Lee stepped aside, momentarily, from the harried race prep scene. He grinned broadly, then spoke glowingly of the highly successful Jeep 4.0L racing engine program.

Hurley Engine Service Co. (HESCO) at Birmingham, Alabama, has evolved into a premier research and development center for Jeep performance. Today, many of HESCO's race-proven products, especially for 4.0L in-line six-cylinders, have gained prominence. HESCO performance gains and reliability are legend.

HESCO offers two items of special interest: the HESCO Supercharger Kits, designed for the 4.0L Cherokee/Grand Cherokee and Wrangler 4.0L applications, and the stroker crankshaft kits that turn 4.0L in-line sixes into 4.7L torque monsters.

Turning the 4.0L MPI Jeep in-line six into a HESCO supercharged, 4.7L stroker engine is nothing short of a performance coup. Dyno results for a supercharged 4.7L powerplant produced 303.5 peak horsepower at 4900 rpm. Torque of 387 ft-lbs at 3000 rpm was equally impressive. Such a powerplant in an XJ Cherokee, ZJ Grand Cherokee or a Wrangler would be more than enough performance for any enthusiast.

Used alone, the HESCO stroker kit puts stump pulling low-end torque into late 4.0L Jeep in-line sixes. While many rock crawling four-wheelers lamented the passing of the longer stroke 4.2L/258, Lee Hurley has eclipsed the stock 4.0L and 4.2L engine designs with the HESCO 4.7L stroker crankshaft. Whether you want more usable torque or the massive gains of a supercharger, HESCO engineering reflects years of professional Jeep racing experience.

2.4 Miscellaneous Tuning

Tuning with a Rich/Lean Indicator

A practical engine tuning device uses an exhaust-mounted oxygen sensor to read air/fuel mixture. Sending a signal to LED display lights, the instrument provides an instant account of carburetor air/fuel mixtures. With the A/F meter, deviations from 14.7:1 (stoichiometric) air/fuel ratio are easy to detect. For the tuner, adjusting retrofit fuel injection or jetting a carburetor becomes simple.

You can fine tune a carburetor by using an oxygen sensor and A/F meter. Understanding the circuits of a carburetor, a tuner can run the engine at cruise and other engine/throttle loads—virtually simulating a dynamometer test. Reading main jet air/fuel ratio becomes a matter of maintaining the engine's cruise throttle/load—without allowing the carburetor's power valve to open.

> NOTE—
> You will know when the power valve opens by a dramatic enriching of the A/F ratio. Meter readouts will help you determine which power valve setting is best for your carburetor. Holley and other carburetor designs have replaceable or adjustable power valves. An A/F meter takes the guesswork out of selecting the right valve or setting.

An air/fuel ratio meter provides instantaneous, ongoing readouts of the fuel mixtures at various throttle positions and engine loads. Once you determine which carburetor fuel circuit is operative, jetting changes and correct readouts can produce optimal performance and fuel efficiency.

Fig. 17-12. *Rich/Lean Indicator provides reading of air/fuel ratio and combustion patterns at your dash. If you understand carburetor circuits, an A/F meter serves as a "road dynamometer" for real world tuning and jetting.*

Holley Carburetor Footnotes

Holley carburetors are popular in performance circles. Many Holley carburetors use side-hung float bowls. Holley offers both center-hung bowls and off-road racing side-hung bowls that offset starvation and flooding tendencies. Racing bowls replace the standard side-hung assembly in minutes.

> NOTE—
> The center pivot or special side-hung racing float will better tolerate the jostling and angles of off-pavement rock crawling.

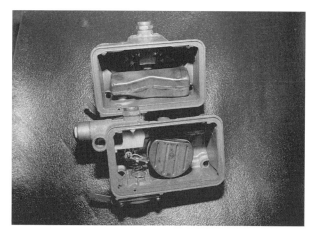

Fig. 17-13. *Center-hung floats fit a variety of two- and four-barrel Holley end float carburetors. Holley recommends a side hung racing bowl and high pressure needle/seats for desert racing and hard off-pavement pounding.*

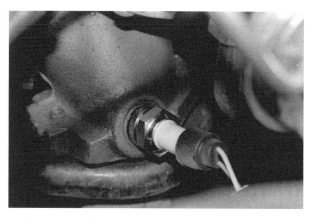

Fig. 17-11. *MSD's "Rich/Lean Indicator" receives voltage signals from an OEM-type oxygen sensor. Stock late CJ or Jeep Wrangler 4.2L manifold has this port, or exhaust tubing can be fitted with a threaded coupler to accept the sensor.*

A correctly jetted Holley carburetor is efficient and able to transit fuel circuits while maintaining stable air/fuel ratios. Such smooth transitions contribute to quick starts, good driveability and reasonable economy. Using the arsenal of Holley tuning parts, and an MSD Rich/Lean Indicator or similar A/F ratio meters from K&N and Edelbrock, you can tune a Holley carburetor for good results.

> CAUTION —
> *I have never found an off-the-shelf "universal" carburetor to be jetted correctly for my Jeep engines. Unless you intend to use an air/fuel ratio meter for staging such a carburetor, the new carburetor may perform worse than your OEM Jeep unit. If available, seek a designated OEM replacement.*

> NOTE —
> Installation of non-exempted aftermarket performance parts may violate pollution control laws. A generic or "universal" (non-OEM replacement) carburetor may fail a California-type smog inspection. (See beginning of this chapter.)

Conversion Engines

Very early in the Jeep's history, enthusiasts began swapping engines. The Willys four-cylinder and small L-head sixes were anemic by most standards, and the postwar hot rodding community knew a good deal about six-cylinder and V-8 conversions.

Some of the earliest Jeep conversion attempts were flathead Ford V-8s, Studebaker sixes and other mild performers. The real attraction to conversions, however, came with the Chevrolet small-block V-8. Unlike an in-line six, the 265 V-8 was light and short—compact enough for use in the WWII surplus MB and early CJ models.

Fig. 17-14. *This late CJ features a tuned port injected Chevrolet V-8 transplant. Using the entire engine with its emission hardware keeps the truck within legal bounds.*

Fig. 17-15. *Melody and Jerry Steele's early '80s CJ-7 enjoys the smooth off-pavement performance of a Ford 302 V-8 and Central Fuel Injection (CFI). Such engines are readily available from recycling sources and can attach to a T-18 Ford-type truck transmission with Ford OE components.*

Installing a higher output overhead valve (OHV) small-block Chevy or Ford V-8 could more than triple the horsepower in an early Jeep! The early '60s Oldsmobile 215 aluminum V-8 (with factory exhaust turbocharging available) also appealed to Jeep CJ owners.

Today, engine conversions are still popular, although emission constraints place restrictions on engine choices. Advance Adapters has an extensive line of conversion kits for transplanting V-6s and V-8s into various Jeep chassis. Novak Enterprises builds conversion kits for more popular Jeep changeovers. Kits accommodate both popular automatic transmissions and a long list of manual transmissions.

More common swaps are the small block Ford or Chevrolet V-8 engines into CJ and early truck chassis. (The Mopar 5.2L and 5.9L V-8s have gained some popularity since the Chrysler acquisition of AMC/Jeep.) Larger GM V-8 engines into earlier J-trucks and full-size Wagoneers have some following.

Consider the entire powertrain when increasing horsepower. The late model Jeep transmissions and lighter axle units have severe limitations. You may want to upgrade the entire geartrain. (See the chapter on geartrain upgrades.) On compact XJ Cherokee, Grand Cherokee and Comanche pickup models, the unibody design also limits modifications.

> CAUTION —
> *Do not compromise the structural integrity of your Jeep's frame or unibody. If necessary, consult a race truck fabricator or shop that specializes in safe engine swaps before attempting an engine conversion.*

NOTE —
• The current availability of AMC V-8 pieces is good, so don't overlook the obvious. Here, OE V-8 engine and transmission parts can serve CJs and other Jeep models.

• When considering a conversion, make certain that your Jeep will still meet emission standards and requirements. Often, the use of a complete late model engine, even EFI versions, will comply. Check first.

2.5 Maximizing 2.8L GM/XJ Cherokee V-6 Power

The 1984–86 Cherokee and Comanche 4x4s were very popular. Equipped with the AMC 2.5L four and GM 173/2.8L V-6, many of these trucks are in the used marketplace. If you like everything about these trucks except the modest horsepower, read further.

Automotive engine technology suffered severely in the 1970s. Pressure to reduce pollution, improve fuel economy and maintain some measure of performance vexed most manufacturers. Anticipating the '80s 4x4 market, GM's vast resources countered this challenge by designing a line of down-sized sport/utility trucks. In 1982, the all new S/T pickups emerged, followed a year later by the popular S-Blazer/Jimmy.

The new engine paradigm for the S-trucks included Chevrolet's metric 173 (2.8L) V-6. This engine also powers AMC/Jeep's first XJ Cherokee and Comanche trucks. Although these Jeep 4x4s are compact, demands for creature comforts and power accessories drove curb weights above 3000 pounds. Emission control constraints reached a peak with these models, which feature a closed loop carburetion system.

First Impressions

Extremely narrow across the intake manifold, with a light iron block casting and cylinder heads, the 173/2.8L V-6 engine was originally the answer to EPA/CAFE standards. Closed-loop carburetion and a host of emission control measures put a huge bite on performance, however, and the 2.8L V-6s begs for horsepower. Plagued with a nuisance oil leak at the crankshaft rear seal, the earlier 2.8L V-6s gained only modest support from GM S-truck and Jeep truck owners.

Two weaknesses of 1984 and some '85 2.8L V-6 engines are the rear main seal design and a smaller crankshaft main bearing journal size. During the 1985 model run, GM introduced a modified cylinder block with a larger main bearing crankshaft and a wide, single piece rear main seal. This is a desirable improvement. Any replacement engine for an 1984–86 Jeep 2.8 V-6 should have the later style cylinder block, improved (bigger main journal) crankshaft and wide, one-piece main seal.

Once past the rear main seal leak, the carbureted 2.8L engine meets most transportation needs. The compact XJ Cherokee's large cargo area and stable ride provide great value.

By 1986, the 2.8L reaches peak form, as TBI and more sophisticated electronic spark control provide performance and fuel economy gains. Unfortunately, the XJ Cherokee continued to use the carbureted version of the 2.8L V-6 until the release of the '87 AMC 4.0L in-line six with multipoint fuel injection.

The 2.8L engine is unique. Unlike the 229 and 262 (4.3L Vortec) V-6s, which share basic features with small-block V-8s, the 60-degree 2.8L V-6 was a fresh design. Meeting the multi-national aims of modern auto production, the V-6/60-degree design involves metric tooling and hardware. Cylinder bores measure 89mm, the stroke 76mm. The included 60-degree angle between the cylinder banks provides lighter weight yet adequate support. These compact engine blocks, with main caps in place, weigh only 106 lbs.

NOTE —
From a reliability standpoint, 173 V-6 engines have two crankshaft main bearing journal diameters. Early versions have a less desirable small journal crankshaft, while some '85 and all later blocks feature 67mm (2.6478") diameter journals. These big-journal engines are also distinguished by improved, one-piece rear main bearing seals.

Consider using the later block/crankshaft for any high performance buildup. The pounding in off-road racing has proven these rugged dynamos, with many

Fig. 17-16. *The 2.8L V-6, unlike a V-8, has each rod on its own journal. Note more radically offset 60-degree cylinder banks, with #1 cylinder at front of right bank. 60-degree V-6 engines are far easier to balance than 90-degree types.*

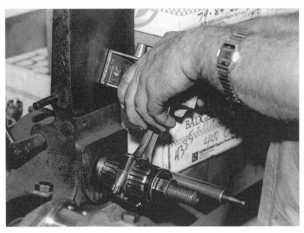

Fig. 17-17. *Stock 173 V-6 connecting rods are surprisingly stout. Good for 7000 rpm when blueprinted (shot-peened, magnafluxed, sized, and aligned), these rods work well with cast or forged pistons. Rod center-to-center bore measurements are same as early small-block V-8 at 5.700".*

Fig. 17-18. *Weak link in early, 2.8L small-journal crankshafts is rod journal/flange cheek area. Over-tightening of front drive belts and load of accessories have been known to break crankshafts at this point. Later large-journal 173 crankshaft is much preferred for serious buildups.*

engines approaching 300 horsepower and staying together. This far exceeds the 135 horsepower realm of factory 'high output' versions.

Bore centers of 4.40 inch allow adequate spacing for cooling ports and reasonable cylinder wall thicknesses. Although small, the iron powerplant offers top-notch oiling capability and durability, especially with the larger diameter main journal crankshaft. Stock, later nodular iron crankshafts have exhibited stamina, where earlier, smaller diameter cranks fail under severe service.

NOTE —
A qualified machine shop can line bore the main journal saddles/caps and machine new bearing tang slots on an early block, allowing retrofit of the bigger journal crankshaft.

2.8L V-6 Buildups

An outstanding resource book packed with insight into all popular Chevrolet V-8 and V-6 engines, including the 60-degree V-6, is the Chevrolet Power Book, Sixth Edition. (This is now a dated edition, and you may have difficulty securing a copy.) The book served as the most comprehensive and authoritative discussion of Chevrolet engine buildups available. Among other details, data for an all-out racing 2.8L V-6 engine included:

1) Spark Advance Limit: 36–40 crankshaft degrees

2) Max. Oil Temp: 300° F, measured in oil pan

3) Fuel Pressure (carbureted engine): 4–5 psi

4) Piston to Cylinder Wall Clearance (measured 90 degrees from the wrist pin centerline): Chevrolet forged pistons run 0.006"–0.007". Cast pistons require 0.002"–0.003" clearance.

5) Minimum Piston Ring End Gap: Top ring, 0.016"/2nd ring, 0.014"/Oil rails, 0.016".

6) Wrist Pin Clearance: 0.0006"–0.0008" in piston bore/0.0010"–0.0012" fit in the rod small end bore. A floating pin with a bushed rod requires 0.0005"–0.0008" fit and a recommended 00.005" end play.

7) Rod and Main Bearing Clearance (requires high oil pressure and volume): 0.0020"–0.0025"

8) Connecting Rod Side Clearance: 0.008"–0.012"

9) Crankshaft End Play: 0.002–0.007"

10) Piston-to-Cylinder Head Clearance: 0.035" minimum

11) Minimum Valve Head to Piston Clearance: 0.050" for engines run below valvetrain's maximum speed, otherwise 0.100" for tightly revved engines (for drag racing or hill climbs)

Additional components are available for high performance off-highway V-6/60-degree engine buildups. Although many aftermarket suppliers offer similar pieces, Chevrolet Special Products are available through any authorized GM dealership. For product integrity and a vast array of tested components, try this sampling of 2.8L V-6 heavy duty pieces from The Chevrolet Power Catalog:

1) S-10 Truck Fitted Partial Block: GM Part No. 14089006

2) X-11 and EFI Iron Cylinder Heads 14054884 (order two)

3) Late Camaro/X-11 and EFI Camshaft 14031378 (for milder, semi-street performance)

4) Piston sets are available from Chevrolet in 8.5/8.9/and 12:1 compression ratios. Ring sets to match

5) 1985–up 2.6478" Journal Nodular Iron 10048682 Crankshaft for iron cylinder head engines (with extensive block machining, may be retrofitted to earlier engine)

6) Conventional centrifugal/vacuum S-truck distributors: 1110581 ('82) 1103520 ('83/'84), which allow for re-curving the spark timing advance

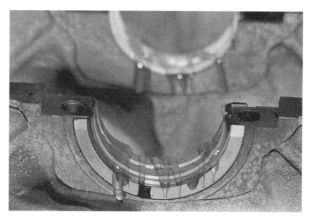

Fig. 17-21. *Main thrust bearing controls end play of crankshaft. Crank alignment is easy to control on these 2.8L V-6 engines.*

Fig. 17-22. *Rear main cap provides pedestal for oil pump. Chevrolet V-8 buffs should recognize the similarity with original small block V-8.*

Fig. 17-19. *Early 2.8L blocks were leak prone, with a rope-type replacement rear main bearing seal. Here, a contemporary neoprene seal replaces OE rope item. Other cures include machining rear lip from block and main cap, a means for installing an improved, full circumference seal.*

Fig. 17-20. *Chamfer and polish oil feed holes during machining.*

Fig. 17-23. *Stock rods and OE replacement cast pistons are one option for a mild performance hop-up. Serious racing requires forged pistons. Cast rings, fitted to cast pistons, again serve well in milder applications. Thin (minimum 0.175" thickness) iron cylinders tolerate only mild overbores. Sweetwood & Sons limits 2.8L rebores to a maximum of 0.030" oversize pistons.*

Fig. 17-24. *Checking ring gap is a standard blueprint procedure. This verifies cylinder bore relationship to ring diameter. Various piston designs call for different ring gaps. Read piston ring set instructions and gap accordingly.*

Fig. 17-25. *Assembly of 2.8L V-6 is straightforward. Camshaft bearings take more time to install than the six rod/piston and ring assemblies.*

Fig. 17-26. *Often overlooked during overhaul or rebuilding, the inexpensive pressure relief valve is critical to oiling and engine survival. Always renew this item.*

Fig. 17-27. *OE-type timing chain works with a unique spacing slipper. This curbs excess chain slap and helps maintain accurate valve timing on 2.8L V-6.*

Fig. 17-28. *Stock V-6 cast-iron heads are relatively light and durable. Screw-in rocker studs, steel pushrod guide-plates, dampened valve springs and other pluses follow years of small-block V-8 development that preceded the 1980 introduction of 2.8L metric V-6s. Valve sizes vary between standard applications and high output engines.*

Fig. 17-29. *Magnum Roller Rocker Arms from RHS/Competition Cams can be a quick route to torque for the 2.8L V-6. The 1.60 ratio arms, installed without a major engine teardown, offer a bolt-on increase in valve lift.*

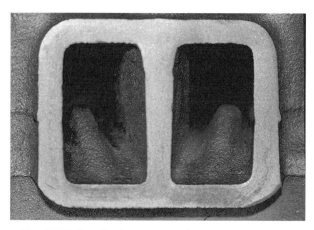

Fig. 17-30. *Iron intake port begs for custom porting work. Flow improvements on small displacement engines always raise horsepower and torque.*

Fig. 17-31. *Late model 2.8L engines with multi-port injection feature aluminum heads with large valves. Note port improvements and canted valve angles. Weight saving is substantial on an already lightweight engine. High performance off-road engine builders, however, stay with iron heads in most cases.*

Timely Alternative:
3.4L Replacement for GM 2.8L V-6

As the 1990s come to a close, so does the era of the 2.8L V-6 engine. GM's official "Chevrolet Race Shop" and GM Performance Parts now offer the 3.4L replacement engine for 1982–85 S-10 trucks and Blazers. These models use the same engines as 1984–86 XJ Cherokee Jeep trucks.

The 3.4L 60-degree V-6, GM part #12363230, is currently regarded as "49-State Emission Legal." As a precise replacement for the 2.8L V-6, it would not be unlikely that this engine will also meet California standards. (Check with your local Chevrolet dealer or California's Clean Air Resources Board before making this changeover for use in California.)

At 207 cubic inches, the stock profile 3.4L replacement engine provides an immediate 40 horse-

power gain over the original 2.8L powerplant. A better camshaft, 9:1 compression and improvements in the valvetrain and cylinder head design contribute to this impressive gain.

You original intake manifold, ignition system and water pump will fit. An oil pan swap and an electric in-line fuel pump may be necessary for some installations, although Chevrolet regards this as a "bolt-in for the tired 2.8 liter engine."

The rugged 3.4L engine features all of the later 2.8L improvements plus cast iron cylinder heads, a nice camshaft profile for street, highway and light trail use, a "regular (unleaded) gas" label, and an impressive 155 horsepower @ 4850 rpm, with 195 ft/lbs torque @ 2700 rpm. This is a complete, assembled engine, ready for bolting-on your peripherals and renewing that early XJ or Comanche.

Whether the 3.4L V-6 will revive interest in the 1984–86 XJ Cherokee models or not, GM's offering presents a very smart alternative to the more complicated 90-degree V-6 or V-8 swap. Even the in-line '87–up 4.0L engine is not an easy or inexpensive changeover for these mid-'80s XJ and Comanche models. The GM 3.4L V-6 option could very well provide the cost effective alternative that Jeep XJ owners seek.

2.6 Building the AMC/Jeep 232/258 Six

When AMC bought the Kaiser/Jeep Corporation in 1971, many Jeep enthusiasts awaited the fate of the CJ models. Buick 225 Dauntless V-6s had earned wide popularity, yet AMC had built Jeep's J-truck powerplants since the mid-'Sixties. The 232 and later 258 in-line sixes powered many full-size pickups and Wagoneers. For the pre-'72 CJ engine bays, however, the 232/258 block was too long.

Despite the need for chassis changes, the '72 CJs did offer the iron, seven-main-bearing in-line sixes, and also a 304 AMC V-8. Within months, the torque twisting ability of in-line sixes had won the hearts of four-wheelers. With the Warner T-18 truck four-speed option and an iron Spicer 20 transfer case, seventies Jeep buyers enjoyed terrific performance.

Despite emission constraints, the versatility of 258 (4.2L) sixes moved into the '80s. The proven design launched the YJ Wrangler and carried through 1990. Its replacement, the 4.0L powerplant, reveals many 258 design features.

What makes the 258 six so desirable? Torque, fuel economy and reliability. Despite the heaviest emission control constraints, the '79/'80 258 still managed a respectable 110 horsepower @ 3200 usable rpm. Torque is even more impressive: 210 ft/lbs at a roguish

1800 rpm—the stuff of true four-wheeling! (Counterpart '79 304 Jeep V-8s netted a mere 10 ft/lbs more torque at a higher, less desirable 2400 rpm.)

Clifford Research: Six = Eight

For building a 258 (4.2L) Jeep in-line six, Clifford Performance Products is a good place to start. Since the late '60s, Jack Clifford has turned 232 and newer 258 Jeep sixes into serious stump-pullers.

> NOTE—
> Although relatively light in weight, the 258 is very rugged. Light weight and durability make this engine a strong candidate for performance modifications.

Starting with a stock street engine, Clifford's Stage I kits can gain approximately 25% rear wheel horsepower. Bolt-on product consists of a single-outlet head-er set and a tuned intake manifold that accepts popular two- or four-barrel (Holley pattern) carburetors.

Clifford Stage I targets the 2000–4500 rpm range, a functional level for general off-highway use. Good performance and snappier overall response have made this manifold set popular.

The Clifford Performance Products Stage II kits promise even greater gains, aimed at the 2000–5000 rpm range. Here, rear wheel horsepower can jump 40%. This kit includes the intake/exhaust modifications of Stage I plus a high performance camshaft. A compression ratio of 9 or 10:1 is necessary, often accomplished by cylinder head milling or a change in piston design. Distributor re-curving or an aftermarket ignition with the right curve will round out the buildup.

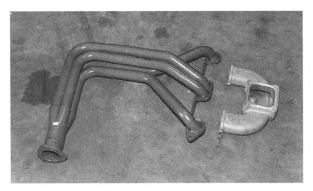

Fig. 17-32. *Highly modified 153 Chevy four-banger benefits from Clifford manifolds. Many of these engines have found their way into lightweight early MB and CJ Jeep chassis.*

Fig. 17-34. *Clifford intake manifold with an adapter provides a good foundation for retrofit TBI or MPI. AirSensors' multi-point injection claims a 28% increase in rear wheel horsepower and torque when introduced with a performance camshaft, header, and spark tuning.*

Fig. 17-33. *Jack Clifford explains strategy for 258 Jeep six performance. This single-outlet header and ram-tuned four-barrel intake combination has increased off-road torque and horsepower for over two decades.*

Fig. 17-35. *Clifford/AirSensors off-highway retrofit TBI uses four-barrel intake manifold and 2300 Holley two-barrel adapter. AirSensors TBI unit shows strong resemblance to Ford's CFI system.*

Racing victories are also within Clifford's scope. Full blueprinting and major modifications lead to Stage III claims of double the original rear wheel horsepower. Stage III engines operate in the 3000–7000 rpm range. This package adds dual outlet headers, competition head work, and a maximum overbore with 11 or 12:1 compression ratio forged aluminum pistons. Fuel demands dictate the use of a retrofit EFI system, dual four-barrel carburetors or exotic Webers.

Although Stage III transcends most recreational four-wheeling, such kits satisfy desert racers' needs. Clifford suggests that six-cylinder torque wins at any level of competition. Mud bogs, competitive hill

Fig. 17-36. *Spreadbore adapter enables use of GM Quadrajet or Carter Thermo-Quad as an alternative to Holley square flange carburetor. Quadrajet can be fitted to any Clifford in-line six manifold—including 232/258 AMC sixes. (Hudson manifold shown here.) In my experience, OEM Rochester Quadrajet has proven the best stock four-barrel carburetor for off-pavement and overall use. I look for a GM Q-jet from the same displacement engine as mine. Example: The 231 and 252 Buick V-6 non-feedback Quadrajets might work nicely on 232 and 258 Jeep in-line sixes (respectively).*

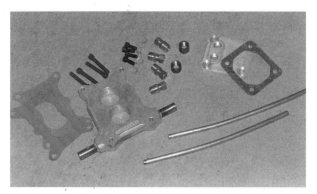

Fig. 17-37. *These Clifford heaters operate with hot engine coolant or exhaust heat. Here, a hot water baseplate for 2300 Holley two-barrel features a cast-in steel pipe. This serves well on Clifford's Jeep replacement manifolds. Heat at intake manifold is necessary for choke and carburetor to function properly.*

climbing or sand drags warrant Stage III performance. Combination trail four-wheelers and street users, however, do better with Stage I or II modifications.

> *CAUTION —*
> *If your Jeep must be registered for use in California, make certain that any engine modification parts bear a California "E.O." number. When you consider Clifford or other parts, always confirm whether these pieces are legal for public highway use on your Jeep vehicle.*

Summing Up Six-cylinder Performance

Although V-8s develop dazzling mid-range and top-end horsepower, the six cylinder has a reputation for endless low rpm work. This humble character has encouraged use of in-line four- and six-cylinder engines in Jeep 4x4s.

Torque is a prime goal for trailering and off-pavement use, and in-line sixes make torque, producing 30% more than same size V-8s. The main challenges in performance six-cylinder buildups are harmonics and balancing, which can be accomplished with a performance flywheel and fluid crankshaft damper.

Mopar's High Tech Retrofit EFI

Electronic fuel injection has proven its worth. Every truck manufacturer knows how well EFI meets fuel economy, tailpipe emission and performance needs. Instantaneous control of air/fuel ratios and immediate response to varied climes and engine loads makes EFI the ideal choice for off-pavement use.

Fig. 17-38. *Mopar Performance's 4.2L Jeep MPI Retrofit Kit includes all necessary components for an EFI and electronic spark management conversion. As shown, kits come ready to install. This 50-State Legal system resolves a variety of problems associated with Jeep carburetion. Expect substantial gains in horsepower, torque and fuel efficiency.*

Owners of 1981–90 Jeep 4x4s equipped with 258/4.2L in-line sixes can now benefit from Mopar Performance's MPI Fuel Injection Kit. Bolt-on pieces replace the original distributor, two-barrel manifold and carburetor. The "50-State Legal" kit (Part Nos. P5249610 for manual transmission and P5249686 for automatic transmission) raises horsepower to the 160 range with torque in excess of 230 ft/lbs from slightly above idle to 3500 rpm.

Gone is the troublesome Carter BBD carburetor; here is a sequential, multi-point fuel injection and electronic spark management system that will take a Jeep above 12,000 feet elevation without a whimper or puff of black tailpipe smoke. The kit utilizes many components from a '95 circa 4.0L MPI system, and Mopar Performance includes every piece of hardware for a neat and thorough installation.

Fig. 17-39. *Clifford/Air Sensors' retrofit EFI uses mass air flow as the primary signal. Control box interprets data and translates air flow rate into fuel discharge at the injectors. (Check with Clifford about emission legality.)*

Fig. 17-40. *Another EFI retrofit is a two- or four-barrel manifold coupled with Holley's Pro-Jection TBI. (Use with an adapter for the 2300 Holley two-barrel carb pattern.) Optional oxygen sensor feedback kit helps control air/fuel ratio and emissions.*

You will need a special vibration damper (Part #P5249687 for V-belt drive or #P5249688 for serpentine belt drive), also available from Mopar Performance. The package will transform your 4.2L six into a smooth, high torque rock crawler and mountaineer. Meets California's emissions requirements under Executive Order D265-7 of CARB.

The 4.0L EFI Cylinder Head Swap

Jack Clifford, Steve Dose and Lee Hurley (HESCO) now retrofit the 4.0L multi-point fuel injection cylinder head to earlier 258 (4.2L) engine blocks. With minor modifications to cooling ports, a change of pushrods and a few other details, the EFI cylinder head conversion can provide better breathing, larger valves, port injection fittings and quicker access to a factory-type MPI fuel injection system.

The 4.0L cylinder head retrofit can play a role in 258 engine upgrades. The most significant drawback with the original 232 or 258 heads is poor port design, small valve sizing and poor combustion chamber design. The advantages of EFI are multiple: better fuel economy, more torque, smooth engine operation at all altitudes (and vehicle attitudes!) and greater reliability.

258 Fuel System and Spark Magic

Mopar Performance, Dose Fuelmaster, Electromotive, HESCO, Howell and other electronic fuel and spark management systems provide the ultimate, high tech performance solutions. In the wake of Lee Hurley's pioneer work with Walker Evans' racing Jeep program,

Fig. 17-41. *Here, Walker Evans Racing relies on Lee Hurley's handiwork. Lee exploits the virtues of the 4.0L multi-point fuel injection engine, extracting massive horsepower through performance modifications and use of computer programmable Electromotive fuel and spark management components.*

the PC-computer programmable fuel and spark management systems have swept into off-road racing.

Many 258 engine tuners, however, have budgets that dictate the use of a carburetor and distributor. The Carter BBD carburetor found on later 258 engines leaves much room for improvement.

For carburetion, Holley has always been popular. The 258 Jeep six requires modest fuel flow, which suggests Holley's 2300-series two-barrel, a design with four decades of OEM use on Ford, AMC/Jeep, and I-H truck engines.

The Holley #0-7448 350 CFM model is a high performance version featuring a manual choke, center hung float bowl and a host of throttle linkage options. Holley's #17-3 adapter provides a bolt-on installation to the stock Jeep BBD manifold. Clifford offers a Ram Flow manifold with two- or four-barrel Holley base pattern options.

To prevent throttle valve binding with the larger throats of the 350 CFM Holley carburetor, a #108-52 heat insulator spacer and additional gaskets must be used on the carburetor side of the adapter. The adapter also requires careful carburetor positioning. If the carburetor is even slightly misaligned, the throttle valves may bind.

WARNING—
Always check for free throttle movement both before and after tightening your carburetor mounting hardware. Binding could cause the throttle to stick open, an extreme safety hazard. Make certain that hardware will not loosen in service and allow the carburetor to shift.

The Model 2300 is a simple carburetor to master. Holley's parts interchangeability allows a high degree of refinement. Armed with a Holley catalog of parts and technical books, fine tuning is possible.

NOTE—
Don't overlook the Holley OEM replacement carburetors. With Holley's adapter and spacer, I used an International-Harvester 266 V-8 OEM replacement carburetor (a Holley 2300 series manual choke version) on a 258 Jeep six (originally equipped with a BBD two-barrel). The carburetor was a near perfect match for A/F ratios. My only tuning change was a simple main jet drop, from 53s to 51s, as I tuned for use at 1400 feet elevation and higher. This was the most successful, least fussy Holley "performance" installation I've done to date.

Fig. 17-42. *Holley adapter permits installation of a 2300 series two barrel on the stock Jeep BBD carb manifold.*

Fig. 17-43. *Heat insulator spaces carburetor above adapter. This is necessary for throttle valves to clear the adapter.*

Fig. 17-44. *Jacobs custom fitted this stock Jeep Motorcraft distributor with Ford DuraSpark pieces. Both Jacobs and MSD offer replacement spark wires.*

Fig. 17-45. *Holley parts availability is ideal for serious tuning. Note center hung float and optional electric choke assembly.*

K&N air filtration can provide maximum air flow and engine protection with a reusable air cleaner element. In tight quarters, K&N's compact filter works well for the 2300 Holley fitup.

Spark enhancement can benefit from the wizardry of Jacobs Electronics or MSD components. You can build a suitable and reasonably priced Jacobs ignition upgrade using your 232 or 258's OEM Delco or Motorcraft distributor (maintaining stock centrifugal and vacuum advance).

On Jeep sixes with Motorcraft electronic ignition systems, the similarities between a Ford six and Jeep 258 ignition permit use of several Ford OEM replacement pieces, including a DuraSpark distributor cap, spacer and rotor.

David Freiburger, who worked with Jacobs Electronics years ago, notes several advantages to the Ford DuraSpark upgrades. "The larger diameter Ford cap prevents cross-fire and tracking under high voltage/heavy load conditions or if moisture gets into the distributor. The stock Jeep cap and rotor are not available with brass terminals and high dielectric plastic, but the Ford units offer this superior design. The Ford parts are A-moving items, and more likely to be available in one-horse towns." Now that's a Rubicon veteran's reasoning!

NOTE —
A popular OEM replacement Chrysler module will interface with the Jeep distributor and Jacobs' Energy Coil.

3. Engine Rebuilding

As your Jeep engine reaches the upper end of its service life, you have two options: an in-the-chassis "ring-and-valve job" (overhaul) or a complete, out-of-chassis engine rebuild.

An in-chassis overhaul is relatively easy with many Jeep engines. Following your factory-level service guide, you'll remove the cylinder head, oil pan and timing cover, ream the cylinder ridges before removing the pistons and rods, fit new rod and main bearings, along with new piston rings.

Most likely, you will sublet the cylinder head assembly to a machine shop for reconditioning. You'll carefully hone the cylinder bores (protecting the crankshaft bearing journals from any debris or abrasive materials) and restore cleanliness wherever possible. A new or reground camshaft, new lifters, a timing chain/sprocket set and a new oil pump round out the job.

Overhauls like this will work on mildly worn engines and those having hard, durable cylinder bores. An overhaul buys extra miles of driving yet falls short of a complete rebuild. Restricted by the chassis, many rebuilding steps are neglected during an overhaul. By contrast, a complete, professional rebuild involves replacement or precision machining of every moving part in the engine.

A 258 Engine Rebuild

NOTE —
Although I use the 258 as a rebuild example, this engine design is similar to the earlier 232 and even the later 4.0L in-line sixes. The 258 "family" includes the 2.5L AMC/Jeep design four-cylinder engine. Many 258 features and rebuilding steps apply to these other engines as well. When you perform engine work, use a factory-level Jeep service manual for your model and engine type.

The AMC-design 258 features seven main bearings and an undersquare bore and stroke configuration of 3.750" x 3.895". Capable of building huge torque with reliable rod length and angularity, the 258 Jeep engine commonly gives 120,000 or more miles of trouble-free service. This is an accomplishment for a high-temp emission engine operated under severe stress on lean-burning, low-octane fuel.

Emission control hardware and a maze of carburetor plumbing overwhelm most '79 and newer 258 Jeep engines. The basic long-block engine assembly, however, is much the same as earlier, less complicated versions of this engine. AMC/Jeep 232/258 and 4.0L engines remain simple to rebuild.

A quality rebuild will virtually remanufacture your engine. Caustic block and head cleaning, replacing hard-to-reach freeze plugs and installing camshaft bearings are just a few of the procedures. The typical 120,000 mile 232/258 six will have 0.008" or more cylinder taper. (A simple overhaul would serve little purpose, as rings cannot operate properly against a widely tapered cylinder wall.) Restoration of OE tolerances takes place during the remanufacture of your Jeep engine.

Step-by-step Rebuild

CAUTION —
Never fill hydraulic lifters with oil. Filling or "pumping up" lifters can cause valve-to-piston interference during initial cranking of the engine. After the engine is completely assembled and the valves are adjusted to specification, prime the engine's lubrication system for start-up.

NOTE —
The late Jeep Wrangler 4.2L's 9.2:1 compression ratio is too high for low octane fuel and rock crawling. A fix for this problem is replacement of the factory shim head gasket with a thicker (Detroit) composition type. Install the gasket according to the manufacturer's guidelines. Use Permatex's Teflon Thread Compound on head bolt threads.

Fig. 17-47. *Flywheel shows normal scoring for 120,000 miles of freeway driving and four-wheeling. Re-surfacing and balancing are in order here to restore smooth clutch action.*

Fig. 17-48. *Cylinder head's combustion chambers reveal early signs of oil seepage past piston rings and valve guides. This rugged engine had never been apart.*

Fig. 17-46. *At Sweetwood & Sons, this 258 long block engine leaves an '81 CJ-7's engine bay. The rebuild begins with dismantling all components and readying them for hot tank cleaning. Maze of carburetor/emission control hardware remains in the truck.*

Fig. 17-49. *Cylinders reveal scoring and taper. Cylinder re-boring, honing and fitting of new pistons is necessary.*

Fig. 17-50. *Engine reveals piston wear and signs of ring blowby. Oil consumption was a quart in 250 miles. Sludge and slight bearing wear are common at this mileage. A simple overhaul would neglect much of the engine's needs.*

Fig. 17-51. *Timing chain wear causes late valve timing and poor lower speed engine response. A 4x4 suffers drastically from late valve timing, as idle and low-speed manifold vacuum drop.*

Fig. 17-52. *Boring bar creates a new cylinder surface. On this OE engine, Sweetwood found that a 0.030" (diameter) rebore makes an ideal size. Power honing on a CK-10 Sunnen machine is best assurance of true, concentric and long-lasting bores. Machinists use a bore gauge regularly during finish honing. Exactitude here pays off in years of rugged, reliable four-wheeling service.*

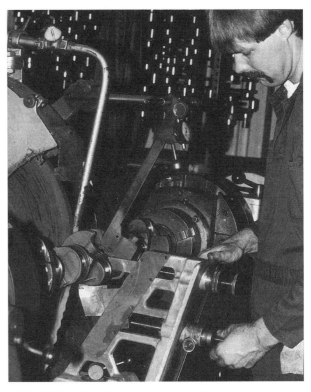

Fig. 17-53. *Gary Sweetwood mans the crankshaft lathe. Relatively light wear on 258 crank required minimum 0.010" undersize re-grind.*

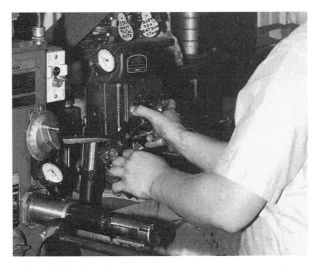

Fig. 17-54. *Resizing and truing each connecting rod restores new performance to seasoned rods. All critical parts undergo magnafluxing for cracks.*

Fig. 17-55. Hot tanked block now holds little resemblance to greasy engine that came from chassis. Note uniform, precise cross-hatch finish on each cylinder.

Fig. 17-56. Clean cylinder head receives new iron valve guide inserts. Manufacturer's tolerances, uniform compression and restored oil sealing result from fitting new valve guides and seals.

Fig. 17-57. Machinist carefully machines three-angle seats during cylinder head reconditioning. After cutting valve seats, cylinder head is re-surfaced. Head gasket seal and trueness of head are primary goals.

Fig. 17-58. Re-faced or new valves assure compression seal. Clifford's performance 264-degree camshaft comes with heavy duty valve springs and dampers.

Fig. 17-59. Machinist closely checks valve stem heights after grinding new valve seats. Since AMC engine has non- adjustable rocker arms, cutting of valve stem ends will restore proper lifter clearance. Adjustable pushrods are an alternative, available from Clifford.

Fig. 17-60. Heating machine takes load off pistons and pins during fitup. Heating small end of rod expands bore temporarily to accept the new piston pin.

Fig. 17-61. *Once pistons are installed, machinist checks rod/piston alignment. At a quality machine shop, every step is taken to assure close tolerances and true alignment of all parts.*

Fig. 17-62. *Camshaft bearings are installed first. Machinist wants a correct cam fitup before fitting any other parts. New bearings in 258 six fit precisely, with oil feed holes aligned carefully. Oil hole alignment is critical to proper engine oiling.*

Fig. 17-63. *Oil check valve is an often overlooked item. Wiser shops like Sweetwood always replace this valve, as age and hot tanking create questionable reliability.*

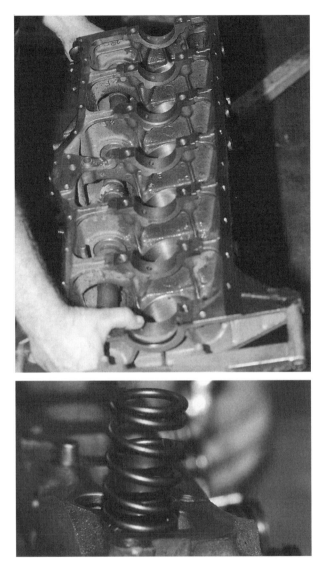

Fig. 17-64. *These heavy valve springs and 264-degree duration camshaft will enhance mid-range and top-end performance. Engine balancing and upgrade parts help assure smooth engine operation at higher rpm.*

Fig. 17-65. *Main bearing halves are fitted to spotless block saddles. Every piece is thoroughly lubricated with special assembly oil.*

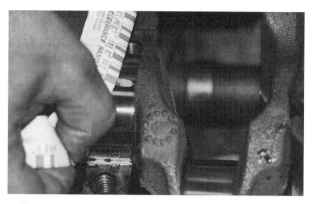

Fig. 17-66. *Plastigage of main bearings is final assurance of correct fitup. After confirming fit, main cap bolts receive final torque in sequence and to specification.*

Fig. 17-67. *New crankshaft sprocket is tapped into position.*

Fig. 17-68. *Timing sprockets align to specification. This step is crucial to performance and engine survival. Use of a degree wheel is advisable for performance tuning.*

Fig. 17-69. *New rings mate carefully to new pistons. Note "030" on crown of piston, a common oversize. With protective plastic caps on rod bolts, pistons are readied for installation. Sized ring compressor eliminates struggle during piston installation.*

Fig. 17-70. *Carefully, assembler slides each rod into proper position. Rod bearings lubed, matching rod caps fitted, torquing new OEM-type nuts is the final step. (Note rod bolt covers used to protect crankshaft journals during procedure.)*

Fig. 17-71. *New brass freeze plugs resist corrosion and premature failure. Shops like Sweetwood use OE or better pieces during a major rebuild.*

Fig. 17-72. *Bases of new lifters and lifter bores are lubed before installation of hydraulic lifters. (Warning: Never soak or pump new lifters full of oil before installation!)*

Fig. 17-73. *Head installation brings engine to complete form. A rebuilt long block assembly includes re-machining or replacement of all moving and critical parts.*

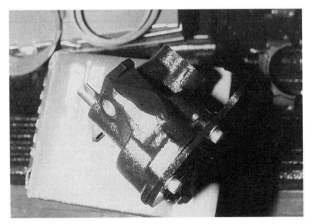

Fig. 17-74. *High-volume oil pump and new crankshaft bearings help keep the 258 alive on those rock crawls and hard pulls. Once completely assembled, with new oil in a spotless oil pan and a new oil filter in place, engine's oil pump and entire lubrication system must be primed before you install the distributor and attempt to start your new engine.*

Fig. 17-75. *Pushrods installed, new rocker arms and a new oil pump will complete the 258 assembly. Valve adjustment is not required on this engine design. Simply tighten rocker pivots to spec.*

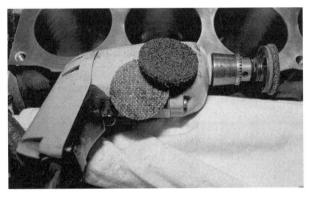

Fig. 17-76. *For an in-chassis overhaul, Eastwood's Velcro and Scotchbrite pads leave ideal finish on block deck and cylinder head. Always protect the crankshaft from abrasive contamination during an in-chassis overhaul.*

Final Notes on Rebuilding

During an engine overhaul or rebuild, you can upgrade performance with high-quality aftermarket parts. Speed-Pro Performance now recognizes the potent 258 AMC six, offering race-quality #R-10469 Plasma Moly file-fit gap piston rings. Another approach is Sealed Power's high grade Premium OEM replacement rings.

After refinishing and measuring each cylinder wall, wash your bores thoroughly and coat them with clean oil. Many shops recommend Speed-Pro/Sealed Power rings, fitted to the stock or OE type Jeep cast alloy pistons, to help provide greater durability. Likewise, a full set of Speed-Pro valves and a three-angle valve seat grind will assure consistent cylinder sealing and longevity.

Your newly rebuilt engine produces more horsepower and greater torque, and needs proper break-in and care. This requires adequate cooling, good water pump circulation and a working fan. Often, a marginal OE radiator, fan clutch or water pump becomes a glaring problem when new found horsepower demands far more from the cooling system.

> NOTE—
> Remember that horsepower equates to BTUs. More horsepower requires more radiator and cooling system efficiency.

A plugged, soldered or damaged radiator core, or a radiator filled with rust and scale, will prevent your new engine from cooling adequately. Engine break-in taxes the cooling system. Protect your newly rebuilt engine, with its hot tanked, scale-free block and cylinder head. Have the radiator hot tanked, rodded and pressure checked to assure adequate coolant flow.

In addition to installing a new water pump and reconditioning the radiator, pay attention to all hoses, clamps, the thermostat and drive belts. New parts here are cheap insurance. Test the fan clutch and replace if necessary. Any transmission or clutch parts that appear worn or marginal need replacement. Your new engine

Fig. 17-77. *Jeff and Karen Sugg, owner's of MIT at El Cajon, California, needed a testbed Wrangler YJ for research and development. Ford H.O. 302 makes a neat fit, provides high performance to California-legal standards. An NV4500 transmission and Dana 44 axles back up the engine. This is a contemporary, beautifully executed conversion that meets 50-State legal requirements and readily turns heads at Moab, Utah. Note ample radiator and OEM-style molded radiator hoses. (Avoid using flex-type "universal" hoses.)*

will work the geartrain heavily, especially in the off-pavement environment.

> NOTE—
> Now is the time to re-surface the flywheel. The renewed flywheel should receive balancing with other reciprocating crankshaft assembly parts.

Precision Engine Balancing

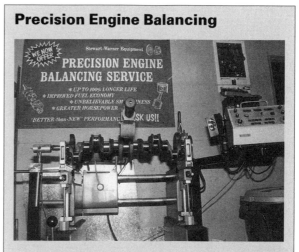

Your Jeep engine faces the perils of hard-core off-pavement driving, extremes of heat, stress, sustained rpm and abrupt runs up the rpm scale. Fortunately, AMC/Jeep 258 engines boast seven main bearings. Regardless of design, any engine benefits from balancing.

Careful matching of rod weights involves both ends of the connecting rod. All reciprocating pieces require close weighing.

Precision balancing and match-weighting of rod/piston are practical during your engine buildup. Balancing leads to maximum engine smoothness and reduced stress as the weights of pistons, rods, rings and bearings conform to blueprint tolerances. The machinist can spin and balance the crankshaft, pulley/damper, flywheel and clutch cover. Through the extra step of balancing, your Jeep engine will enjoy vibration-free, responsive performance over a long service life.

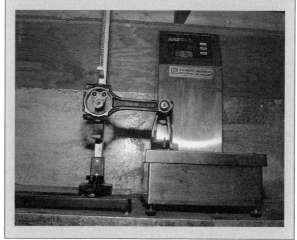

Chapter 18

Geartrain Modifications

The CJ Jeep was originally a truck. Long before the public thought of a "sport-utility 4x4" vehicle, civilian and military Jeep models were beasts of burden. Rated officially as 1/4-ton utility trucks, large numbers of early CJ-2A, CJ-3A, CJ-3B and CJ-5 Jeep vehicles toiled unceremoniously from their first tank of fuel forward.

In the mid-fifties, to handle the hard pounding that a work Jeep suffered, Kaiser introduced Borg-Warner's T-98A four-speed transmission option for the new CJ-5 and CJ-6s. This was a significant move. A 2600 lb. vehicle, powered by a small displacement four-cylinder F-head engine, could boast a two-ton truck gearbox. Beefy T-98 series Borg-Warner units were then popular in Ford, I-H, Studebaker, Diamond-T, Divco, Reo, and White trucks.

Equally impressive about CJ3-A to 1975 CJ Jeep models are their Spicer 44 rear axles. (All but the earliest CJ-2As offer a similar 41-2 axle.) This 1/2-ton truck unit was surely more than adequate for a light-

weight 80" and 81" wheelbase utility truck—Such stuff built the Jeep legend.

The T-98A Warner compound-low truck four speed (with its PTO outlet for a post-hole digger) was available in four-cylinder Jeep trucks through 1971. The AMC purchase of Kaiser's Jeep Corporation began an eight-year run (1972–79) of AMC-built CJs with optional Warner T-18 heavy duty four speed transmissions.

> **NOTE —**
> AMC CJs offered the T-18 almost exclusively with six-cylinder engines. Some 1979 and carryover 1980 models with the 304 V-8 have the T-18 four-speed.

The T-18 coupled to a Spicer 20 transfer case provides two-ton truck strength with a non-synchromesh compound-low gear. Through 1979, Jeep CJs continued to benefit from stout transmission options.

1. Transmission/Transfer Case

Beginning in 1980, the Jeep CJ model transmissions changed drastically. Lighter all-synchromesh four-speeds, of passenger car strength with close ratios, became the Jeep CJ's standard offering. Soon, a lightweight aluminum T-5 Warner five-speed overdrive transmission strayed further yet from the heavy-duty truck designs of earlier years.

> **NOTE —**
> The Dana 300 gear-drive transfer case, found in 1980–86 Jeep CJs, has great stamina. Coupled to a passenger car-grade transmission like the T-176, T-4, SR-4 or T-5, this transfer case has little opportunity to show its worth. In the same league as the earlier Model 20 through-drive transfer case, the iron cased Dana 300 makes an excellent foundation for a beefy powertrain. It enjoys the added benefit of a lower geared low range (2.61:1), quieter helically-cut gears and a compact, tough profile.

Fig. 18-1. *A row of transmissions illustrate design and size standards. Massive unit at left is 465 Muncie box, dwarfing the late T-5 overdrive. Jeep T-14 and T-90 (with Chevy V-8 adapter attached) three speeds set in middle, while huge T-18 truck box rests to right. In foreground is an early (pre-'68) Muncie SM420 truck four-speed unit.*

Fig. 18-2. *Transmission countergears show the relationship between truck four-speeds and Jeep's lighter OE offerings. Left to right, the Jeep T-18, T- 90, T-14, and T-5 gears stand next to GM's 465 Muncie truck quality gear. Five-speed NV4500 gears are even larger than most four-speed truck types.*

Fig. 18-3. *Three-speed T-14 countergear (here swallowed by Muncie SM420 assembly) was Jeep CJ's first offering of an all-synchromesh transmission.*

The Need To Change Gears

If your CJ Jeep has serious off-pavement rock crawling intentions, the use of a heavy-duty truck four-speed or the newer five-speed NV4500 overdrive unit makes sense. Aside from the virtually indestructible nature of truck gearboxes, most feature extremely low ratios in compound (granny) low.

Although individual applications vary, most compound-low truck gearboxes feature first-gear ratios of at least 6:1. GM's 465 Muncie is 6.54:1, while one version of the earlier SM420 yields a 7.05:1 ratio compound low gear. The New Process 435 four-speed is 6.69:1. An NV4500 five-speed is either 6.34:1 (early version) or the more common 5.61:1—either ratio very low.

Common Ford truck applications of Warner's T-18 rate a 6.4:1 first gear, common to many Ford/Jeep T-98 offerings. Coupled to a Dana 300 transfer case, an overall gear reduction (crawl ratio) of 68:1 is attainable with a 4.10 axle gearset. Taller, more economical axle gearing, say 3.73:1, still yields a compound low, low range crawl ratio of 62:1. This is true Rubicon or Moab gearing for your Jeep.

> NOTE —
> If you need even lower crawl ratios, see section on Advance Adapters' products and Atlas II transfer case.

While the Jeep Model 18 and 20 transfer cases yield slightly taller low range crawl ratios (moreso the Spicer 20 unit with its modest 2.03:1 ratio), a truck four-speed provides enough gear reduction and power for most reasonable situations. Such low gearing, coupled to the stamina of a real truck gearbox, also lends itself to high horsepower engine conversions. The gearbox strength found in a T-18 or T-98A four-speed (in good condition, of course) will easily handle 250–300 horsepower and torque to 400 ft/lbs.

Truck Four-speed Changeover

Once committed to a change, you'll find necessary components at Advance Adapters or Novak Enterprises. Each outlet builds conversion kits for installing several types of heavy-duty four-speed truck gearboxes into CJ and military Jeep models. The use of Jeep OE pieces should not be ruled out, although availability may make the aftermarket parts route easier.

> NOTE —
> The Jeep CJ version of the T-18 most often has a 4.02:1 first gear ratio. If you want a low crawl ratio, the conversion kits typically call for a common Ford two-wheel drive truck transmission, which has the desired 6.4:1 ratio compound first gear.

Choosing a truck four speed for your Jeep 4WD depends largely on engine and transfer case plans. The use of a stock four-cylinder engine, a V-6, in-line six or AMC V-8 affords one route. When converting to a Ford, Chevrolet or Mopar V-8 engine, you can also include a truck four-speed.

> NOTE —
> The NV4500 five-speed is a popular swap as well. If your budget can handle this later model, rugged transmission with overdrive, see this chapter's section on Advance Adapters' products.

'71 and earlier four-cylinder rigs can actually upgrade from the OE three-speed transmission (T-84, T-90 or T-14) to the factory T-98A. This method, however, is offset by the rare numbers of CJ-5 and CJ-6 Jeep trucks that featured such an optional four-speed. It is unlikely that you will find a recyclable CJ with a T-98A transmission and four-cylinder engine.

> NOTE —
> I am currently mating a T-18/T-98A hybrid to an F-134 CJ powerplant. The retrofit involves use of a special T-98-type Jeep input gear and adapter plate with the more common T-18 transmission. Discuss this approach with Novak Enterprises or Advance Adapters. There are also a number of I-H Scout pieces that can help complete this mate-up to a Model 18 transfer case. Transmission to transfer case adapter plates are similar for Model 18 and Spicer 20 units.

Even scarcer are Kaiser-era Buick 225 V-6 equipped CJs with the rare four-speed truck transmission option. These vehicles used a 4.02:1 ratio first gear (like later AMC/Jeep T-18s). This design, although strong, lacks the low gear advantage of four-cylinder CJ T-98A units and 6.4:1 ratio T-18 transmissions.

Adapters are available for mating a close-ratio passenger car type four speed to the Jeep transfer case. The advantage is the close gear ratios and lighter/compact size, though the durability of these transmissions is well below that of a truck-type four speed. (Also, the first gear ratio typically offers less than half the reduction of compound low gear in a truck four-speed.) Un-

less you are sand dragging your Jeep, the truck-type four speed would be a better choice than a close-ratio T-10 four-speed.

For V-6 Buick powered CJ and Jeepster models or the Jeep with a GM engine transplant, the truck four-speed conversion can use GM factory hardware and a transmission-to-transfer case adapter. Both the pre-'68 Chevrolet truck V-8 bellhousing or a Buick passenger car bellhousing (indexed for a 4.686" diameter retainer) readily accept the early Muncie SM420 truck box.

> NOTE —
> The 1966 and newer Ford T-18 transmission can be adapted to work with GM bellhousings. An advantage of the T-18 is its shorter overall length.

If your Jeep engine conversion plans include a Chevrolet V-6 or V-8, consider a '68 or newer Chevrolet truck bellhousing, distinguished by the 5.125" indexing bore, and the later 465 Muncie four speed.

> NOTE —
> For installing a 465 Muncie with a stock Buick bellhousing, you can re-machine the bellhousing to accept the 5.125" retainer. Fitup is critical, so machining requires concise location of the hole and adherence to factory tolerances for the retainer's fit.

GM engine conversions follow this pattern. Advance Adapters and Novak Enterprises provide transfer case adapters for the Muncie SM420 four-speed truck transmission to the Model 18 Spicer, Spicer 20 and later Dana 300 transfer cases. Advance Adapters and Novak also offer an adapter kit for the 465 Muncie to Model 18 or Spicer 20 unit (using the 4x4 version of the 465 transmission).

The 465 Muncie is newer by design and features massive components and a 6.54:1 first gear ratio. Earlier 420s are slightly shorter and take up less overall space. Most users find either gearbox very rugged, and for GM engine conversions, these are top choices.

If you plan a Ford or Dodge/Mopar V-8 swap for your Jeep, Ford and Dodge truck hardware can couple the engine to a T-18 or NP435 four-speed transmission. An Advance Adapters or Novak Enterprises transfer case adapter and motor mount kit will complete the swap. Consider this alternative closely, as the T-18 was AMC's choice for factory four-speeds in 1972–79 Jeep CJs. The NP435 has an even larger gear set and a 6.69:1 first gear ratio.

The T-18 conversion is smart. For Ford V-8 buffs, this is the simplest conversion link. Remember, however, that the transmission of choice is not the Jeep

Fig. 18-4. *Jeep CJ transfer cases include (clockwise) iron Dana 20 unit, aluminum late chain-drive assembly, a partially disassembled Dana 300 model, and a new replacement assembly for early Model 18 Spicer unit.*

version of the T-18 but rather the common two-wheel drive Ford truck unit.

Using an appropriate Ford truck bellhousing, clutch assembly and T-18 transmission, the conversion affords use of stock Ford components from the engine through the transmission. Two adapters are available. One mates the T-18 to Model 18 and Spicer 20 transfer cases, the other works with the Dana 300 unit and other late Jeep transfer cases.

If your CJ has an AMC engine, you can fit a 1972–79 Jeep CJ version of the T-18 by using the correct Jeep factory bellhousing and OE transmission-to-transfer case adapter for the Spicer 20 transfer case. You'll need an aftermarket adapter, however, to attach the T-18 transmission to a Dana 300 or later transfer case.

> NOTE —
> The T-18's shorter overall length permits use of a normal length rear driveshaft. This is especially important with short wheelbase CJ-5 models.

A conversion kit is also available for attaching a Ford version of the NP435 truck four-speed to a Wrangler transfer case. For the Mopar 'A' series V-8 enthusiast, Advance Adapters or Novak Enterprises can turn up a similar conversion approach.

Conversion Footnotes

The Model 18 transfer case is of side-drive design, used with an offset differential on the Spicer 25, 41-2 and 44 rear axles. A Model 18 tends to have more wear potential than a Spicer 20 unit. The Spicer 20 and Dana 300 transfer cases are quieter and more durable. As high range power flows straight through these units, friction is greatly reduced.

Fig. 18-5. *Base for Advance Adapters or Novak's T-18 conversion is Ford truck version of this heavy duty four speed. Popular, this gearbox is available from used '66 and newer Ford trucks, or as a new unit through OE and aftermarket outlets.*

Fig. 18-6. *Advance Adapters' T-18 to Dana 300 transfer case adapter boasts iron casting. Adapter replaces the short tailhousing extension, and kit includes a new mainshaft. Primary machined component of the conversion is a new output/mainshaft. The package replaces the stock T-18 mainshaft (seen at lower left).*

> CAUTION —
> *A Spicer 20, Dana 300 or chain drive transfer case creates a short, more steeply-angled rear driveshaft when installed in an 80" or 81" wheelbase pre-AMC/Jeep. Avoid U-joint binding and risk of driveshaft failure. A suspension lift kit and/or longer transmission will make this problem worse. (See earlier chapter for details on driveshaft angularity.)*

The Model 18 and Spicer 20 transfer cases often share transmission adapter pieces. Gear drive Dana 300 and later chain drive transfer cases share mounting flange patterns; these patterns differ from the earlier Jeep Model 18 and Spicer 20 pattern. Input splines and transmission mainshaft length requirements also vary between transfer case types.

If your CJ or military Jeep currently has a V-6 or V-8 conversion with a stock Jeep transmission, or even a stock engine and three-speed transmission, your choice of any four-speed truck box should also take its length into account. Engine and/or transfer case relocation may become necessary.

The combination of an SM420 Muncie and an aftermarket adapter is 15.3" long from the transmission face to the rear of the transfer case adapter. A 465 truck gearbox adds an additional 1.57" to this measurement. While the T-18 shares the same gearcase length as the earlier T-98A transmission (11.87"), both of these transmissions with their adapter plates are longer than the common T-90 transmission. Each of these four-speed installations requires driveshaft length changes.

> CAUTION —
> *CJs and the Wrangler have short rear drivelines. (The 80–84-inch wheelbase CJs and military models are the shortest.) When considering a transmission or engine/transmission swap, make every effort to maintain or increase (if you install a suspension lift kit) the original rear driveshaft length. Any less length creates severe loads on the U-joints. A suspension lift will increase and aggravate the driveshaft angles.*

You must also account for the transmission input shaft length. This will determine the distance from the engine block to the front face of the transmission (in effect, this is the depth of the bellhousing). Here, the Ford and GM truck four speeds streamline the engine-to-transmission distance. Their input shaft lengths are considerably shorter than many Jeep OEM applications.

> NOTE —
> • Novak Enterprises' Ford T-18 to Model 18 and Spicer 20 transfer case adapter is only one inch in thickness. (Overall length from bellhousing face to transfer case is 12.87".) Novak's T-18 to Dana 300 adapter matches overall length of factory SR-4 and T-5 units in '80-up CJ models. No driveline modifications are necessary with this conversion.
>
> • Bellhousing depth must be considered when determining engine/transmission/transfer case location.

By maintaining a stock transfer case location and not altering the chassis height, you can avoid driveshaft cutting and lengthening. A chassis lift will require rear driveline lengthening, so there are rare instances where a transmission conversion and simultaneous lift kit installation will result in no need for a rear driveline length change—the front shaft would still need lengthening. All other installations will require length changes to both the front and rear drivelines.

Fig. 18-7. *MIT often modifies the long nose on a Ford T-18 input gear (bottom shaft) for installation with a Jeep six or AMC V-8 engine. This method eliminates the search for a rare AMC/Jeep T-18 input gear. As an option, Novak Enterprises offers a custom pilot bushing that allows use of Ford input gear without modification.*

Fig. 18-8. *Close-up view of Advance Adapters' T-18 conversion mainshaft. You must disassemble the transmission to install this piece. Kit's installation instructions include a blueprint of parts layout.*

Fig. 18-9. *Muncie SM420, popular in 1948–67 Chevrolet and GMC trucks to two-ton capacity, mates to Model 18 and Spicer 20 transfer cases with this mainshaft and iron adapter from Advance Adapters.*

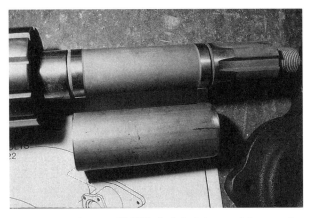

Fig. 18-10. *Longer SM420 shaft is Advance Adapters design. Jeff Sugg at MIT in El Cajon, California, adds a spacer sleeve to eliminate risk of dislodging snap rings.*

Aftermarket Overdrive

One advantage of the Model 18 transfer case is its power take-off (PTO), in-line with the transmission's output shaft. This access served as the installation point for the classic Warn Industries' overdrive unit. Advance Adapters acquired the tooling and rights to continue producing these units, which are available today. (See Advance Adapters section and 'Saturn Overdrive.')

The retrofit Warn-design Saturn 25% overdrive operates through all forward gears and reverse. When Warn first offered these units for the Model 18 transfer case, most Jeep trucks had 5.38 or 4.88:1 axle gearing. A 1941–71 Jeep with the Model 18 transfer case and this overdrive can gain fuel economy, longer engine life and the advantage of split shifting at each gear.

Fig. 18-11. *Advance Adapters acquired rights and tooling to continue production of Warn-type overdrive unit. Advance Adapters markets new units and assures the availability of service parts for older Warn assemblies.*

If your Jeep has a longer wheelbase, Advance Adapters offers a two-speed gearbox/overdrive unit, the Torque Splitter, that fits between the clutch bellhousing and a manual transmission. Installation requires some chassis and driveshaft fabrication. Such a unit could work with a 94-inch or longer wheelbase CJ or Wrangler.

The NV4500 five-speed overdrive transmission conversion has nearly eliminated the need for a Torque Splitter. Many current Torque Splitter users, especially trailer pullers, enjoy the split shifting feature. (Contact Advance Adapters for information and details on availability.)

Wrangler and XJ Rear Driveline Fix

The XJ Cherokee and Wrangler YJ introduced a slip-coupler rear driveshaft. This type of driveline poses two distinct disadvantages. First, if the driveline becomes damaged, you cannot remove the shaft for an emergency trip home in front-wheel drive. (Transfer case oil would pour out the tailhousing with the driveshaft's splined slip-coupler removed.) Second, due to the length of the splined coupler, the transfer case tailhousing extension requires a very short rear driveshaft on YJ and TJ Wranglers.

The MIT rear yoke conversion kit provides a cure for each of these problems. This kit eliminates the transfer case tailhousing and provides a conventional seal and Spicer U-joint yoke (double Cardan type shown below). The yoke accepts the common Jeep/Spicer joint. A new rear driveshaft, supplied with the kit (custom lengths available), includes a splined slip-yoke. The XJ, YJ, TJ or ZJ can benefit from features found in the rugged, earlier Jeep driveline designs.

MIT transfer case output yoke kit, shown here on Wrangler transfer case, eliminates extension housing and slip coupler driveshaft. Note longer driveshaft, which reduces angularity problems. Kit is popular for suspension lifted vehicles.

Advance Adapters: NV4500 Conversion

The current offerings from Advance Adapters for the latest Wrangler, XJ Cherokee and ZJ Grand Cherokee include retrofit kits for the New Venture 4500 five-speed overdrive truck transmission, four-speed truck transmission adapters, engine conversion bellhousings, the Saturn Overdrive and the Orbitor. An Orbitor kit (transfer case output drop box) serves the Jeep owner who chooses to install a moderate-to-severe chassis lift and wants to eliminate a radical driveshaft angle.

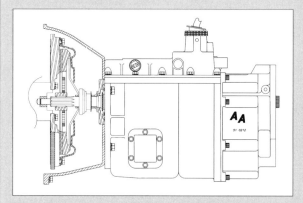

GM and Dodge versions of the rugged NV4500 transmission represent the most significant breakthrough in retrofit options for Jeeps. This massive transmission provides two sets of gear ratio choices: 1992–94 versions offer 6.34, 3.44, 1.71, 1:1 and 0.73 overdrive; 1995–up versions provide 5.61, 3.04, 1.67, 1:1, and 0.73; reverse ratio is the same as first gear in each of these series.

This is an iron-cased, extreme duty transmission. The "regular duty" version rates 14,500 pound maximum GVW, while the heavy duty Dodge version used with V-10 and Cummins diesel engines ranks even higher. For a vehicle of 3000 pounds, like the trail-equipped CJ or Wrangler, such excessive strength means a lifetime transmission.

Though somewhat costly, especially with a new transmission, this conversion has gained popularity with all segments of Jeep users, especially those who use their Jeep for hard-core trail running and serious rock crawling. The unique synchromesh compound low gear contributes to desirable crawl ratios, while some versions even offer synchromesh on reverse. The 27% overdrive on top means exceptional fuel economy, even with low (numerically high) axle gearing.

Advance Adapters makes kits available for installing the NV4500 transmission into CJ, YJ and TJ Wranglers, using stock engines as well as V-6 and V-8 conversions.

> **NOTE —**
> Before considering or selecting an NV4500, I recommend a thorough review of the Advance Adapters catalog and detailed installation instructions.

TJ Wrangler has all the ingredients for rugged back-country travel. MIT at El Cajon, California, installed an NV4500 and Advance Adapters' Atlas II transfer case with ultra-low range ratio into this TJ Wrangler, now the ultimate rock crawler. Owner of '97 model uses Jeep extensively on trails like the Rubicon and at Moab, Utah.

Another owner of a late XJ Cherokee with the NV4500 five-speed uses his vehicle for the Rubicon Trail and daily driving. Transmission adapter pieces from Advance Adapters made this swap possible. MIT performed the conversion. As new and pre-owned XJs continue to hit the trail, this swap will become more common.

(continued)

Advance Adapters' NV4500 conversion kits come complete with shift lever, linkages, machined adapters, mounts, detailed instructions and installation hardware. Despite number of variations, Advance Adapters keeps track of each application's needs. Different versions of the NV4500, however, require a close look at which transmission unit best suits your conversion.

Saturn Overdrive

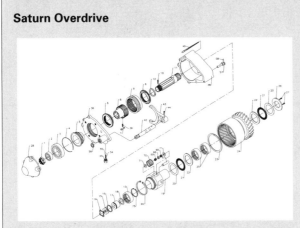

Many owners of 1941–71 Jeep trucks are perfectly satisfied with the Model 18 transfer case, yet an overdrive unit is always appealing. The Warn-design Saturn Overdrive from Advance Adapters provides the best of both worlds.

A 25% overdrive, rated 300 ft/lbs torque limit, the Saturn unit is right for the Jeep that has a stock engine, a lightly modified V-6 or a stock V-8 conversion. Especially with 5.38:1 axle gearing, the overdrive permits highway driving with the equivalent gearing of 4.04:1. Add a set of 30x9.5x15 or 31x10.5x15 tires on 8-inch wide rims, and that earlier Jeep can actually go down the road in overdrive without droning.

Saturn Overdrive from Advance Adapters has roots to original Warn Industries design. Ingeniously tapping into the PTO provision at rear of Model 18 transfer case, this 25% overdrive is easy to install and allows split shifting of all forward and reverse gears. With a truck four-speed, this means 16 speeds forward and four reverse. Synchronizer permits shifting just like a transmission: Depress the clutch, move the shift lever, and you're in overdrive.

Orbitor: Suspension Lift Solution

Short rear drivelines and chassis lift kits do not mix! Jeep CJs and Wranglers with short wheelbase lengths have real trouble with severe lifts. The Wrangler compounds this problem with a long tailhousing on the transfer case and an even shorter driveline than the CJ-7s.

Advance Adapters has solved each of these problems with the Orbitor drop box. Without removing the transfer case, you can install this output gear kit and housing. A conventional and shorter U-joint yoke replaces the OEM driveshaft coupler. The low output location improves rear driveline angle up to 50%. Kit coverage includes NP207, NP231 and NP241 chain drive units and Spicer 20, Dana 300 and Advance Adapters' own Atlas transfer case.

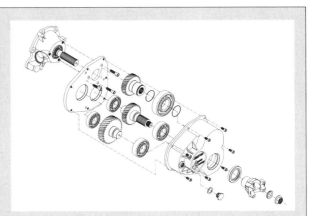

Kit installs without removal of transfer case and eliminates the rear driveshaft slip coupler nemesis on Wrangler and XJ/ZJ Cherokee/Grand Cherokee models. You must fabricate a new rear driveshaft with a conventional U-joint at the front end of the shaft.

Atlas Transfer Case: Tough, Ultra-low Gearing

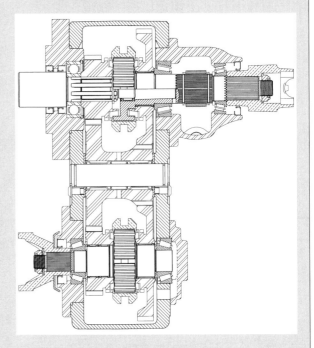

The push toward low crawl ratios has spawned a variety of modified and hybrid Jeep transfer cases. Advance Adapters pursued this demand and developed the heat-treated aluminum alloy, gear-drive Atlas II transfer case to replace all Wrangler and many AMC-era CJ applications.

Available in 3.8:1 and 4.3:1 low range ratios, the alloy case encloses helically cut gears, a Borg-Warner type synchronizer assembly and ample bearings. This unit meets or exceeds the torque ratings of all Jeep transfer cases, including the gear-drive Spicer 20 and Dana 300. This unit would make a terrific factory option for Jeep Wranglers, a suitable match for the OEM Dana 44 rear axle.

Overall Gains

The installation of a truck four-speed or NV4500 five-speed overdrive transmission could prove the best investment you'll ever make for your CJ, military or Wrangler Jeep. Compound low gear will give your Jeep a real crawling and pulling advantage. Such low gearing can save your chassis and powertrain. In hardcore rock-crawling, your Jeep will inch its way through the roughest terrain, with only light use of the brakes, less tire spin and less skidding.

Stalled on a precarious slope, you can engage the clutch with the transmission in compound first gear and the transfer case in low range four-wheel drive. The 12-volt starter motor can easily pull the truck up the steep incline while firing the engine. Little starter drag occurs, and the low gearing affords a smooth chug forward as the engine catches (providing you have your foot very lightly on the throttle). By keeping the truck in gear with the clutch engaged, you will not roll backward or battle wheelspin while trying to let out the clutch.

> *CAUTION —*
> *Know how your Jeep will respond to a start-up in gear. Practice this technique in a safe place before traveling dangerous terrain.*

> *NOTE —*
> This starting procedure will only work with a truck that does not require depressing the clutch pedal to engage the starter motor circuit. You cannot start your Jeep with the clutch engaged if the truck's wiring includes either a neutral or clutch pedal safety switch.(See the chapter on operating your Jeep for further details.)

Installing a four-speed or NV4500 five-speed truck box eliminates the chassis abuse so characteristic of three-speed CJs with 3.73 and taller axle gears. In rough terrain, tall geared CJs bend springs as they bash and skid their way through the rockpiles. By contrast, an F-head four cylinder CJ with the versatile T-98A transmission will perform far better, despite its "meager" 72–75 horsepower. Ultra-low gearing yields great dividends in chassis life, vehicle safety and control—and driver/passenger comfort. Also, high-powered engines have great difficulty breaking an iron truck gearbox in good condition.

A truck four-speed or NV4500's second gear has a lower ratio than the first gear of most three-speeds. Synchromesh down to second gear affords normal three-speed driving (or four speeds with the NV4500's overdrive) until you need heavy lugging power. With the ultra-light weight of CJs and military counterpart

models, the use of compound low gear is rare under most driving conditions.

Unless sand dunes, 4x4 sand drag racing or similar speed contests suggest the use of a close-ratio, fast-shifting passenger car four speed, you are always better off with a heavy duty truck transmission. Coupled to a two-speed transfer case, the heavy duty four- or five-speed truck gearbox helps reduce chassis wear and off-pavement fatigue. This is one option every backcountry 4WD Jeep could use.

2. The Clutch

Eventually, your clutch will fatigue and fail. When it does, the aftermarket clutch industry offers a variety of rebuilt and new clutch units to restore or improve your Jeep's performance. You can choose from a variety of clutch units that will handle your engine's torque and horsepower demands.

Traditionally, a high performance clutch was a non- diaphragm design. Two popular clutches were centrifugal arm/fulcrum type (Long) and a high spring rate type (Borg & Beck). A variation was the semi-centrifugal type.

Centrifugally weighted clutch fingers allow two distinct clutch behaviors. To ease take-off and reduce shock loads to the transmission and transfer case, the initial squeeze or clamp pressure is lower. As engine rpm increases in each gear, the centrifugal weights move outward. At speed, the fingers' fulcrum leverage applies increasingly more pressure to the clutch disc.

The complaint with older centrifugal clutch designs is high pedal pressure at higher rpm. In racing and high performance activities, a high revving clutch with hydraulic linkage can actually blow out the slave and clutch master cylinder seals. Similarly, mechanical linkage will place an overwhelming load on the driver's left foot.

> *CAUTION —*
> *In contrast, a relatively low apply pressure could allow unwanted and hazardous slippage of the clutch.*

Borg & Beck Type Clutch

One alternative, the non-centrifugal, three-finger clutch popularized by Borg & Beck, eliminates guesswork about apply pressure at any given rpm. Spring pressure type clutches apply the entire spring force of the pressure plate at one time. This means that the spring rate built into the clutch cover unit is exactly the rate sandwiching the clutch disc against the flywheel face.

Accurate clutch pressures can be set for vehicle weight, engine power output and the vehicle's usage.

In heavy duty 4x4 applications, such as a V-8 powered Jeep J-20 truck intended for brute work like trailer pulling, the range of recommended clutch pressure may reach 2000 pounds.

> NOTE —
> • Some OEM Jeep spring force clutches use centrifugal rollers to add clamping pressure at higher rpm. Jeep called this a "semi-centrifugal clutch cover," which resembles the three-finger Borg & Beck.
>
> • The OEM replacement clutch recommended by Jeep is generally adequate for most uses, although a large increase in horsepower or continual trailer hauling with a J-truck would call for a heavy duty replacement clutch. (Typical Jeep 10-1/2" replacement clutches range from 1600–1800 pound ratings. "High performance" might mean 2000 pounds. For still more performance, or if you increase tire diameter significantly, see section on Midway's Centerforce clutches.)

For a conversion V-8 engine with a large flywheel, an 11- or 12-inch clutch unit could range from 2000–2300 pounds rating. In a lighter vehicle, say a Jeep Wrangler with a 2.5L four-cylinder engine, peak load demands, even severe rock crawling and an increase in tire diameter, would seldom require more than a 1500–1600 pound rating clutch.

> NOTE —
> While high spring pressure aftermarket clutches decrease the chance of slippage, shock to vital gear parts increases on initial clutch engagement. By design, the Centerforce clutch does not shock the geartrain, yet this unique clutch type provides high clamping force.

Diaphragm Clutch

The third common clutch design is the multi-fingered diaphragm type. General Motors popularized the use of diaphragm clutches many years ago, and early high performance enthusiasts discarded them regularly in favor of Borg & Beck and Long type clutches. Diaphragm clutches were unable to handle high performance demands and offered few means for increasing apply pressures. Worse yet, overheat quickly damages the flat diaphragm clutch springs.

A diaphragm clutch has two advantages, however. First, the pedal pressure to disengage the clutch is minimal, as sixteen fingers apply leverage instead of three. The long spring fingers allow relatively high pressure plate force with minimal driver effort. Pedal take-up distance is relatively short with a diaphragm design, and clutch engagement occurs very smoothly.

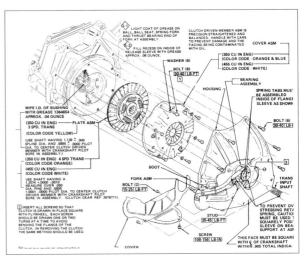

Fig. 18-12. *Factory installation guidelines prevent trouble. Note emphasis on critical measurements and proper tightening techniques to prevent warpage of a new clutch cover. Grease applied sparingly at these locations assures longevity of moving parts. Diaphragm clutch affords smooth engagement and immediate application of full spring pressure.*

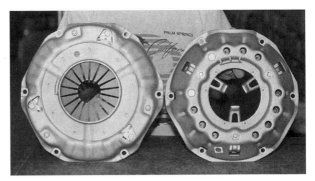

Fig. 18-13. *OEM-type Buick/Jeep diaphragm clutch (left) shows multiple spring/lever design. Spring tension alone squeezes the disc between the pressure plate and flywheel. At right is a common Borg & Beck OEM replacement clutch for AMC/Jeep engines.*

A High Performance Centerforce Clutch

Thanks largely to aftermarket innovation, several performance clutch designs are available for your Jeep. One of the more exciting options is Midway's Centerforce clutch. A diaphragm clutch with unique centrifugal weights, the Centerforce unit uses the best features of each popular clutch design.

Borrowing from the diaphragm unit, the Centerforce clutches have low release pressure, short pedal effort and smooth take-up. Drawing on centrifugal principles, the Centerforce clutch cover design incorporates an ingenious weighting of the diaphragm fin-

Fig. 18-14. *Midway's Centerforce clutch unit is a diaphragm design with the addition of centrifugal weights for higher clamp pressures as rpm increases.*

gers to allow higher apply pressure as clutch rpm rises. Centerforce claims increased disc and pressure plate life, and weights can be designed to accommodate a variety of user needs.

Many clutch manufacturers build high force aftermarket replacement clutches. Midway's Centerforce II and Dual Friction designs, however, have the widest reputation among four-wheelers. These clutch units are known for their rugged performance, reliability and light pedal apply pressure. I have thoroughly tested the Centerforce II and Dual-Friction type clutches. In my experience, there is no better clutch for backcountry use or heavy duty service. A claimed 60% (Centerforce II) to 90% (Dual-Friction) greater holding capacity than a stock clutch makes these Centerforce units popular with Jeep four-wheelers.

My tests have included extensive backcountry, towing and four-season chores, including rock crawling in V-8 transplant Jeep CJs along the Rubicon and pulling a tandem axle travel trailer with a 3/4-ton 4x4 pickup—the truck weighed nearly three tons when unloaded and had 300 horsepower and 410 ft/lbs of engine torque on tap. Despite such challenges, in over 120,000 miles of true testing, I have never seen appreciable wear or a defect in a properly installed Centerforce clutch.

> NOTE —
> Driving technique plays a large role in clutch life. Years ago, as a heavy equipment operator, I learned to use a clutch only for starting the vehicle moving and changing gears. Rather than downshifting without applying the brakes (using the clutch as a "friction brake"), I select the right gear for the terrain or load. This extends clutch life dramatically.

Clutch Linkage

Jeep trucks have a long history of clutch linkage problems. If you have plans to upgrade your powertrain, don't overlook the clutch linkage. Advance Adapters, Novak Enterprises and other aftermarket sources provide upgrade hardware for Jeep clutch linkage.

Some of the more reliable alternatives are hydraulic linkages. Either OE Jeep, aftermarket or a conversion from another make or model truck can improve your Jeep's reliability. Mechanical linkage fails more often than any other type and is difficult to improve. The twisting, flexing and jarring of the Jeep chassis places enormous demands on mechanical linkage.

The Jeep clutch linkage successes were models with hydraulic clutch master cylinders and the slave cylinder mounted at the bellhousing. This began as early as the first Kaiser/Jeep J-trucks and Wagoneers. Many early '80s and newer CJs feature hydraulic

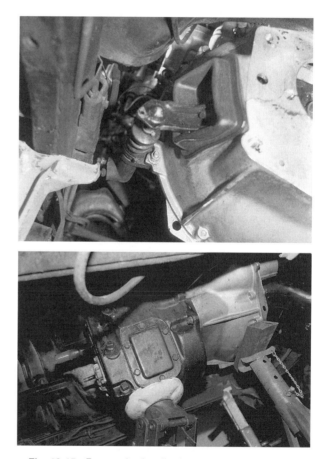

Fig. 18-15. *Factory hydraulic clutch linkage like this system on a 1981 CJ-5 works very well. Originally an Iron Duke four model, the truck now features a 258 six with a conversion Ford-type NP435 truck transmission that bolts directly to a Jeep factory part #8133951 bellhousing. The original clutch slave cylinder attaches to the OE Jeep bellhousing.*

Fig. 18-16. *#8133951 factory Jeep bellhousing mates a 258 (4.2L) six to Ford 2WD version of the NP435 truck transmission. Note mount for an OEM hydraulic clutch cylinder. Longer rod to the clutch release arm is the only modification necessary.*

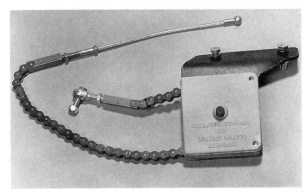

Fig. 18-17. *Available from Advance Adapters, roller chain clutch linkage is a retrofit kit for any CJ Jeep. Jeep models with either cable or mechanical linkage benefit from this conversion. Reduced friction and ability to flex are obvious advantages over factory mechanical linkage.*

clutch linkage. Several AMC/Jeep bellhousings provide flanges for mounting a slave cylinder.

> NOTE —
> • Hydraulic clutch linkage requires components capable of operating your Jeep's clutch. Some high performance clutches require a hydraulic linkage system upgrade.
>
> • Wranglers and other Jeep models use a hydraulic throwout bearing. The drawback with this design is that the simplest leak repair or seal replacement requires removal of two driveshafts, the transfer case, the transmission and other parts. Any time you perform work that accesses the hydraulic clutch release assembly, make certain that parts are in top shape. If in doubt, replace the release bearing assembly to avoid trouble later.

For the early, through the floorboard pedal Jeep, a durable alternative to the stock and failure prone cable release mechanism is a roller chain linkage kit marketed by Advance Adapters. This approach or a hydraulic clutch linkage conversion can work well on CJs and other Jeep 4x4s.

3. Jeep Axles and Traction

Jeep 4x4s prove their worth battling climate extremes, stretching over rocks, clawing at mud, navigating fast flowing streams and pulling through deep snow on barren winter paths. Many four-wheelers, seasoned by unruly trails, argue that there's no such thing as too much traction.

When your Jeep truck is in high- or low-range four-wheel drive, the power flow is constant through the transmission, transfer case and drivelines. Each driveshaft rotates an axle pinion shaft and gear. At the differential, power changes direction. The differential also determines the amount of power flow and traction for each wheel.

Spiral-beveled or hypoid ring and pinion gears turn the power flow 90 degrees. A case, commonly known as the differential carrier, holds the ring gear. Bearings, mounted on the differential carrier, support the differential either in the axle housing or within a removable center member housing.

The ring and pinion gear set has two functions: 1) changing the power flow 90 degrees, and 2) increasing torque by reducing rotational speed. A 4.10 gear ratio (41 teeth on the ring gear and 10 on the pinion) rotates the ring gear and axle shafts with approximately four and one-tenth times the torque available at the driveshaft. This ring gear turns at slightly less than one-fourth the driveshaft's speed.

Differential Action

The differential distributes torque to each axle shaft and also allows for axle shaft speed differences when your Jeep turns. During turns, the inside wheels at the front and rear axles rotate slower than the outside wheels. If all four wheels turned at equal speed in corners, sets of tires would skid, and the axle shafts at each axle would work against each other.

> NOTE —
> In the straight ahead mode on an even surface, the differential turns both axle shafts at equal speeds.

If the axle shafts connected directly to the ring gear's case, both wheels would spin continuously at the speed of the ring gear. This is a fully locked unit

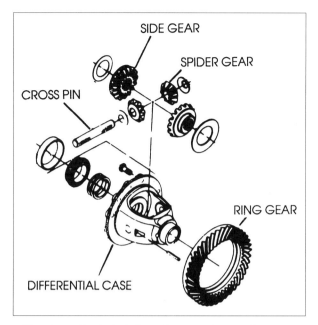

Fig. 18-18. *Exploded view of conventional differential shows gear locations.*

like a racing spool, which provides maximum traction. However, a spool or locked axle is incapable of negotiating left or right turns without tire spin and stress to the axle shafts.

Gears inside the differential allow for variations in axle shaft speeds and power flow. The differential consists of small pinions or spider gears and side gears. The axle shafts do not attach directly to the ring gear carrier, or they would turn at the same speed. Instead, the carrier is hollow at each end, and the axle shafts enter the differential through these openings. The inner ends of the axle shafts are splined to slip into the differential side gears.

The side gears have beveled teeth that mesh with the two spider gears. Spider gears ride on a shaft that fits rigidly into the differential carrier case. This shaft, pinned to the case, delivers power to the spider gears, which then transmit power to the side gears. These four differential gears rotate independently of the housing.

If resistance or road speed at both wheels stays equal, the spider and side gears remain static. (The spiders and side gears would move as a solid unit, traveling at the same rate of speed as the differential carrier.) When turning a corner, however, these four gears vary their speeds, applying more rpm to the axle at the outside wheel and proportionately less to the inside wheel.

Unfortunately, conventional differential action has a severe limitation: When the truck encounters loose traction, the differential directs power to the wheel with the least resistance. This inherent weakness in open differentials has a negative impact on four-wheel-drive traction. In loose terrain, it's easy to spot the 4x4 with a conventional or open differential because one wheel spins furiously while the opposite wheel, on a better traction surface, stands still.

Traction Differentials: Controlling Wheelspin

A factory positive-traction or limited-slip differential helps deliver traction yet still provides vital differential speed between the axle shafts. Factory traction axles have a variety of trade names. New vehicles can be ordered with Trac-Lok, Posi-Traction, or Power-Lok units. A number of aftermarket performance systems, well suited for severe off-pavement traction demands, are also available.

The typical Jeep posi-traction or limited slip unit features a clutch mechanism within the differential. Loss of traction at one wheel reads as "no resistance" in the differential unit. By design, the clutching device then continues to apply torque at the axle shaft that has more resistance, i.e., power flows to the wheel with traction.

Most original equipment limited slip units incorporate a multi-plate spring loaded clutch assembly and a standard spider and side gear arrangement. Under normal driving conditions, these differentials flow power through the spider and side gears in the conventional manner. When the clutches apply, power flows directly from the differential case to the side gears.

When one tire loses traction and spins, the clutches within the differential provide torque to the other

Fig. 18-19. *This 9-inch Ford axle spool is the ultimate traction device. Axle shafts fit directly into spool splines, eliminating the differential completely. Spools serve strictly for sand drags, pulls and competitive activities.*

wheel by directly driving that axle shaft's side gear. The spider gears, driving through beveled teeth, want to separate or spread the side gears. As the side gears move apart, they exert force on the clutch plates. When the load increases, so does the side gear pressure against the clutch plates. This directs more power to the wheel with traction.

While part of the load on the clutches comes from springs in the differential assembly, the majority of the force is from spreading the side gears. Torque load acting as the decisive factor, this explains why slight application of the brakes will cause a limited slip

Fig. 18-20. *The Dana 30 Power-Lok is a limited slip aftermarket differential engineered for Jeep, Scout, and early Bronco front ends. Dana 44 units are popular in most full size Jeep truck front ends and many rear axle applications. Users find OEM limited slip units deliver increased traction without severe shock loads.*

Fig. 18-21. *Multi-plate, OEM Jeep style limited-slip differential provides power/torque to the axle with traction. The spider gears press the side gears against the clutches to deliver more torque to the traction wheel.*

differential to direct more power to the wheel with good footing.

The clutch type limited slip unit, which retains the standard spider gears and side gears, still allows wheel speed to vary on corners. Varied wheel speed under normal load causes the clutches to slip, which allows the spider gears to perform their function. Applying heavy power in a turn, however, can load the clutches enough to lock the side gears against the differential case. This causes both wheels to turn at the same speed.

Although various clutch styles exist, the principle remains the same: provide a direct flow of power from the differential case to each of the side gears and wheels—rather than only to the wheel with the least traction. Although their method is entirely different, aftermarket lockers also accommodate this need.

Which Differential?

Your driving habits and four-wheeling tastes will dictate which traction differential to buy. Yes, there is such thing as too much traction, and driver caution is a must with any traction differential. Jeep trucks and other vehicles will go sideways when both wheels lose traction at the same time.

> *WARNING—*
> *On ice or slick off-camber pavement, torque application at both ends of an axle can create real trouble. If your Jeep has a traction differential(s) and you're traveling on ice, be very careful.*

As an expert on differentials, Tom Reider, president of Reider Racing Enterprises notes, "While differential choices vary enough to satisfy most everyone's needs, the differential that satisfies everyone's wants still hasn't been invented. For most highway situations, an open differential is all that most people need and is, therefore, found in 90% of all vehicles. Its ability to move the vehicle, however, is limited by the minimum traction available to any of the driving wheels. When operated in slippery conditions or with minimum weight on any of the drive wheels, it often causes the vehicle to become a land locked barge.

"The alternatives available to us are to install limited slip or locking type differentials which will then provide the type of power flow to the ground that we expect out of our vehicle. Benefits and drawbacks exist for both types of differentials."

The trade-offs are obvious. While manual and automatic lockers have the advantage of providing 100% traction to the opposite wheel when an axle shaft breaks, if you break a semi-floating rear axle shaft, or snap a front axle shaft anywhere near the steering knuckle, you cannot drive safely.

Full-floating rear axles, like those found on most 3/4-ton and larger 4x4s, will continue to work safely with a broken axle shaft. If possible, remove the broken axle section to protect other parts. Re-install the flange to keep debris out and prevent gear oil loss. You can make it home for repairs. Firewood haulers might find this reassuring.

Traction Device Buyers Guide

WARNING—
Jeep vehicles, especially short wheelbase models, handle and steer differently with automatic lockers and limited slips. Make certain that you understand these steering and control differences before installing an automatic locker or limited slip unit in the rear or front axle of your Jeep. Full automatic lockers are often excessively rough on front axle components and cause awkward steering. Before you install an automatic locker or combination automatic locker in the rear/limited slip unit up front, decide whether your Jeep will be a multi-purpose vehicle, with predictable handling for the highway, or primarily a rock-crawling, all-out traction recreational vehicle for off-pavement use.

NOTE—
If possible, before you install any limited slip, automatic locker or other traction device, drive a Jeep vehicle similar to yours that has the equipment you have considered. Drive the vehicle on the highway, curvy roads and off-pavement. Decide whether the handling and steering characteristics are acceptable.

A variety of aftermarket and OE-type traction differentials are available for your Jeep's axles. The need for these devices depends upon your driving environment and the importance of delivering torque to each wheel. Several manufacturers offer kits for increasing traction.

Detroit Locker/NoSPIN and TrueTrac: A highly respected differential unit that has stood the test of time is the Detroit Locker or NoSPIN unit, built by Tractech, Inc., a subsidiary of Dyneer Corporation.

Speed sensitive, the NoSPIN automatic locker allows your truck to maneuver corners and operate over irregular terrain. The unique design offers the equivalent of a completely locked differential (similar to a spool) during straight ahead driving conditions.

For differential action, the NoSPIN has a central spider assembly with dog teeth on both sides, two driven clutches (one for each axle shaft) with dog teeth to engage the spiders, and a pair of side gears. This spider assembly fits in the middle of the differential case. The

Fig. 18-22. *Detroit Locker/NoSPIN has a loyal following. The Detroit Locker features positive engagement to the wheel with greater traction. This display model shows high quality and the simple mechanism. Display model has survived years of customer abuse on parts counter.*

case drives the spider assembly, while the driven clutch assemblies ride on splines machined on the outside of the side gears. Coil springs keep the clutches engaged with the spider assembly. This directs power from the spider to the side gears.

As the truck corners and the outside wheel speeds up, cam ramps on the inside edges of the spider unit cause the clutch assembly for that wheel to disengage from the spider. The wheel now coasts freely. As with conventional or factory limited slip differentials, NoSPIN also prevents axle binding on turns. The method differs, however, as NoSPIN completely disconnects the power flow to the outer wheel as the vehicle makes a turn.

When wheel speeds are again equal, the freewheeling clutch re-engages with the spider. Power now flows evenly to both wheels. The unique factor with this differential is that power flow is either equal at both wheels or going to the wheel with the greater amount of traction.

If one wheel hangs in the air, the NoSPIN unit stays locked, providing as much torque to the wheel on the ground as traction will allow. If you spin the inside wheel on a turn, once the inner wheel's speed reaches that of the outside wheel, the unit will return to a locked mode.

The "TrueTrac" limited slip/locker device melds the tamer behaviors of a limited slip with those of the classic Detroit Locker/NoSPIN automatic locker. Some find that the combination of a Detroit Locker at the rear and the smoother gear mechanism of a TrueTrac locking differential up front serves well in hardcore off-pavement use. Among those who value traction above all else, a TrueTrac or limited slip front axle and a Detroit Locker/NoSPIN rear axle have been popular for years.

ARB Air Locker: After seven years of testing and use in Australia, the ARB Air Locker hit the U.S. market by storm a number of years ago. This differential locking system now has a loyal following among those who prefer manual control of their differentials. Winner of the coveted 1989 SEMA Best Product Award, the ARB Air Locker is a popular item with hard-core off-pavement users.

By design, the Air Locker provides conventional open differential operation for normal driving conditions. When your Jeep needs power to both wheels, Air Locker has a pneumatically operated shift mecha-

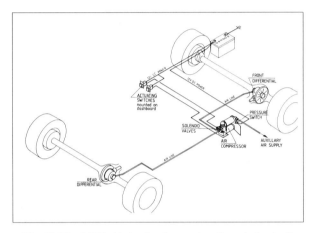

Fig. 18-23. *ARB's Air Locker leaves traction choice to the driver. With the push of a button, the differential locks up and both axle shafts rotate in unison, much like a spool. When disengaged, Air Locker provides the smooth operation of a conventional axle.*

nism for completely locking the spider gears and side gears within the differential.

Inside the differential case, the Air Locker has a slider mechanism, much like sliders found in manual transmissions or a transfer case. The outside of the slider has splines. They engage and slide inside the differential case. The slider also attaches to a hollow piston which surrounds the spider and side gears.

Actuated by pressurized air, the piston moves the slider. Teeth on the inside of the slider match a set of teeth on the outside of one side gear. When the piston moves the slider over the outer teeth of the side gear, the side gear, slider and differential case lock up. The locked side gears and spiders rotate both axle shafts at the same speed as the differential case.

> NOTE —
> The manual ARB Air Locker engages solid, fully locked up power flow to each wheel, much like a spool. The driver now bears full responsibility for unlocking and locking the unit.

Most units have four spider gears, compared to the two spiders found in most OEM conventional axle designs. An Air Locker requires electrical wiring and installation of an air compressor and air lines to the differentials. Although installation is more involved than other traction devices, kits include full instructions and all necessary parts.

Auburn Gear: For Jeep owners looking for a high-quality limited-slip differential, Auburn Gear provides heavy duty units to fit most popular axles.

Like OE limited-slip designs, Auburn Gear delivers power to both wheels through a clutching mecha-

Rating Differential Traction Devices*

Differential style	Smoothness of operation	Tractability	Adverse effect on tires/driveline	Cost	Used for
Conventional (open)	Excellent	Poor	None	Lowest	Highway
OEM Limited slip	Very good	Good	Very little	Modest	Modest off-road
Aftermarket limited-slip	Good	Very good	Modest	Moderate	Modest off-road
Automatic lockers (Lock-Right and Detroit)	Good to poor	Extremely good	Modest	Higher	Heavy off-road
Manual locker (ARB)	Good to excellent	Excellent (locked) Poor (unlocked)	Poor (locked) None (unlocked)	Highest	Heavy off-road
Spool/welded diff.	Poor	Excellent	Poor	Modest	Racing

*Source: Tom Reider, Reider Racing Enterprises

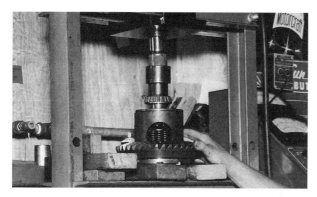

Fig. 18-24. *Auburn Gear's SureGrip is a rugged, heavy duty traction device.*

nism. However, instead of using clutch plates with high frictional loads, Auburn Gear uses a cone type clutch. (A cone attaches to the back side of a side gear and nests inside a matching machined surface in the differential case.) When loaded by either the differential springs or the spider gears, the side gear wedges itself within the differential case.

By design, much less force is necessary to lock the side gear to the differential case. Since there is direct steel-to-steel contact without clutch plates to wear out, peak performance can last much longer than with other units. Auburn enjoys an excellent reputation in the drag racing and high performance field. If you seek a heavy duty limited slip, consider Auburn.

Powertrax's LOCK-RIGHT and No-Slip: The LOCK-RIGHT differential functions much like the NoSPIN/Detroit Locker. Designed for military Dodge trucks and larger W300 civilian Power Wagons, the design has gone widely civilian since 1986. In addition to big Dodge trucks, LOCK-RIGHT automatic lockers fit Jeep/AMC Model 20 axles, Jeep's Spicer/Dana 30, 35 and 44 designs, and many other axle types.

The difference between a LOCK-RIGHT Locker and some traction devices, including NoSPIN, is its quiet operation during clutch lockup. Much like the popular NoSPIN, the LOCK-RIGHT Locker delivers 100% of the available torque to the traction wheel(s) at all times. This design offers very simple cam action and lockup, shifting easily enough for rear and front axle use (if applicable and advisable).

> WARNING—
> *At the rear, an automatic locker like the LOCK-RIGHT or the Detroit Locker/NoSPIN can create unique steering habits (even "torque steer"), especially in a short wheelbase vehicle. Understand how acceleration and deceleration affect cornering and steering with an automatic locker at the front or rear axle.*

> WARNING—
> *I advise against the use of any automatic locker or limited slip differential for the front of a Wrangler or other Jeep models that do not have a provision for free-wheeling hubs. Such a device will defeat the purpose of the OEM axle disconnect system; the front driveshaft will turn the transfer case's chain and other components whenever the vehicle is moving. Steering drag is also an issue. I highly recommend Warn Industries' full-floating front wheel hub conversion kit for any XJ, YJ, TJ or ZJ Jeep model—whether you install an aftermarket locker or not. This quality kit provides the benefits of free-wheeling hubs and an improved, safer front wheel hub and bearing arrangement.*

> CAUTION—
> *Like the Detroit Locker/NoSPIN, pay close attention to the LOCK-RIGHT's operating guidelines and any comments on vehicle handling or steering in two- or four-wheel drive. If you install an automatic locker in the front axle, you should shift to 2WD and unlock your front free-wheeling hubs before driving on hard pavement.*

The LOCK-RIGHT Locker installs in the existing differential case, which saves considerable cost. During installation, there's no need to remove differential bearings, so re-setting ring gear backlash is often unnecessary. The LOCK-RIGHT is a tough, military-proven design. If you seek the no-nonsense traction of a Detroit Locker/NoSPIN or ARB Air Locker, this quiet and rugged, fully automatic locker deserves a look.

"No-Slip Differential" is a Powertrax alternative to the harsher on-off engagement of a LOCK-RIGHT-type automatic locker unit. Without spring loaded dog teeth, frictional clutch plates or cones, these units lock up more like a limited slip yet provide more positive torque application to each wheel at the axle—whether or not the wheel(s) can get traction. Like the LOCK-

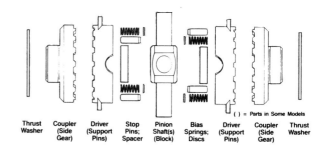

Fig. 18-25. *LOCK-RIGHT Locker diagram shows components of the differential. Cam teeth on each coupler allow overrun and disengagement when the axles rotate at uneven speeds.*

Fig. 18-26. *Ford 9-inch axle Traction-Loc unit shows stout ring gear flange. Currie Enterprises builds 9-inch Ford conversion axles for Jeep CJs. These rugged axles are excellent candidates for a traction differential.*

RIGHT, this device installs within the OEM carrier to reduce setup procedures, although Powertrax also offers a high-strength differential case for those who want to upgrade from the OEM case.

Spicer and Other OEM Limited Slips: Many Jeep trucks have factory-installed limited slip differentials. Spicer has supplied OE traction differentials since the 1950s, and satisfied users often restore their worn differentials with Spicer or Jeep/Mopar replacement parts.

Spicer traction units also work as retrofits for conventional Spicer/Dana axles. Since all Jeep 4x4s use Spicer/Dana axles in the front (many models use them at the rear, too), a Spicer Trac-Lok or Power-Lok unit is an option. Users who prefer a milder application of power and subtler traction at the front axle choose the Trac-Lok.

Traction Differential Footnotes

Installing a differential carrier assembly involves close tolerances. Ring gear backlash settings require a dial indicator and patience. Before buying a traction differential, read the installation instructions carefully. Decide whether to sublet the job to a capable shop or tackle the work yourself.

Give the broader traction issue some thought, too. Consider tires, traction bars and shock absorbers. Added traction to the wheels means a greater challenge keeping traction on the ground. Expect more wheel hop and spring wrap up, especially with large tires.

The ARB Air Locker

Having tested the ARB Air Locker in many 4x4 applications, I regard this device as the best traction differential concept in the current market. The driver's ability to manually set an axle in open or locked mode is both a safety and traction advantage.

I do not like limited slip axles and "automatic lock" traction devices on off-camber, icy highways and curvy, muddy backroads—especially for a shorter wheelbase Jeep. I much prefer the option of setting the differential in conventional/open mode to achieve better vehicle control and steering stability under these conditions.

On ice or slick mud, both tires spinning at an axle can be a safety liability, not an asset. For the steeply off-camber situation, the axle with both tires spinning will slip to the low side of the road or trail.

I once tested a non-Jeep compact 4x4 SUV with OEM limited slip axles at the front and rear. On a steeply off-camber and lightly snow covered dirt road, the vehicle slid to the low side. I drove over half a mile in this posture, objectively trying every imaginable trick and theory to steer the truck away from the gentle earth berm at the lower edge of the slippery trail. In my experience with open differentials and similar driving situations, I have never experienced this phenomenon.

> NOTE—
> The truck had stock, marginal "M&S" rated tires. Had the vehicle been equipped with more aggressive, cleated traction tires or sets of snow chains, I likely could have driven to the road center and painstakingly maintained that position. By themselves, however, the limited slip traction axles provided no measure of assistance, and instead, the truck could not gain traction without remaining snugly against the slight dirt berm at the lower road edge.

I like the ARB Air Locker for its ability to leave traction decisions to the driver. In Rubicon or Moab rock-crawling situations, there is nothing more impressive or environmentally sensitive than a fully locked axle. Every traction device has its place—and time. The ARB Air Locker offers the best of both worlds.

Conversion Axles

A variety of axle assemblies have met Jeep truck needs. Spicer/Dana has played a large role in the Jeep's development. All Willys, Kaiser, AMC and Chrysler built Jeep trucks feature Spicer or Dana front axles. Most rear axles are also Spicer/Dana designs with only a few exceptions. 1976–85 CJs have AMC Model 20 rear axles, although Spicer/Dana-type rear axles continued to dominate the larger trucks. To date, all Wranglers, XJs, ZJs and WJs have Dana axles both front and rear.

Although Spicer/Dana is one of the most respected names in the automotive industry, the use of a Dana/Spicer axle is no pat assurance that your Jeep axle is bulletproof. The size or model of the axle is the determining factor. CJs with Spicer 25 front or 23-2 rear axles and Spicer 27 front axle units—even the Dana 30 front axles and 35 rear axles—are often too light for severe duty four wheeling or high horsepower engine conversions. A number of aftermarket builders construct Dana 44 front and rear axle conversions for Jeep CJs, Wranglers—and even XJs and the front of ZJs.

The AMC Model 20 rear axle has a weak axle shaft/hub arrangement. Summers Brothers, Currie Enterprises and others offer heavy duty one-piece or full-floating replacement axle shaft assemblies that make the Model 20 a far more reliable rear end. The Model 20 has an 8-7/8" ring gear, which makes this unit as durable as the Dana 44. (Model 20s served well in full-size V-8 Grand Wagoneers/Cherokees and J-trucks.)

Another approach for the rear of lighter Jeep CJ and Wrangler models is use of either a custom Dana/Spicer 44 rear axle assembly or a Currie Enterprises' 9-inch Ford conversion. Currie also makes a unique 9-inch Ford front axle assembly with steering that links to the OE Jeep components.

As an extreme duty alternative, the rugged Dana/Spicer 60 model axle has become the ultimate retrofit. MIT at El Cajon, California, builds a variety of Dana 44 and 60 retrofit axle assemblies for severe duty Jeep use. In ongoing discussions with owners Jeff and Karen Sugg, it is clear that a properly built 44 is

Fig. 18-28. *Jeff and Karen Sugg's own Wrangler YJ test-bed sports a potent 302 Ford H.O. V-8 and does exceedingly well with Dana 44 axles front and rear. Although their shop, MIT at El Cajon, California, has built numerous Dana 60 axles for custom Jeep trucks, the Dana 44 and quality traction devices remain the practical option for most hard-core four-wheelers.*

Fig. 18-29. *Currie Enterprises specializes in 9-inch Ford axle assemblies. A custom built retrofit (front or rear axle) unit is available for CJ models.*

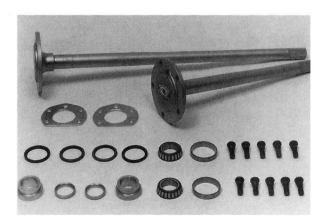

Fig. 18-27. *Summers Brothers manufactures one piece axle shaft kits (shown) and also a full-floating-kit for the '76-up CJ Model 20 AMC rear axle. Axles shown eliminate weaker press-on OEM wheel hub/axle shaft arrangement. Fitted with a pair of one-piece or full-floating axles, the Model 20 axle is far more reliable.*

sufficient for all but the wildest or highest horsepower CJ or Wrangler.

NOTE —
Unsprung weight for a Dana 60 axle assembly is high. The lighter weight Dana 44 axle can handle most challenges that any stock or reasonably modified Jeep CJ, Wrangler or XJ will encounter. Dana 60s suit the "monster Jeep" used for exhibition or mud bog racing with a 500 horsepower engine. The Dana 60 center section hangs lower than a 44 and demands very large diameter tires to create ample ground clearance.

Warn's Full-Floating Front and Rear Axle Hub Conversion and Disc Brake Upgrades

Warn Industries offers full-floating rear axle shaft conversion kits for Willys and Kaiser era CJs with a Spicer 44-type rear axle, the AMC/CJ Dana 44 axles, AMC/Jeep CJ Model 20 axles, '84-up XJ Cherokee axles, and all YJ/TJ Wrangler axles. Full-floating hubs and bearings support the rear wheels. The one-piece axle shafts consist of 4340 chrome nickel moly aircraft alloy, heat treated to 230,000 pounds-per-square-inch yield strength. Inner axle splines are available for Jeep 19, 29 and 30 tooth differential side gear types. The outer axle spline count is 30.

Rugged wheel hubs are also ample and accept Warn's tough internal spline manual locking hubs, the all-metal variety. Wheel hubs fit up with a more contemporary and higher quality spindle nut/lock nut system. Kit comes complete with all bearings, spindles, wheel hubs, manual locking hubs, axle shafts and quality installation hardware.

Additionally, Warn offers Front Wheel Hub Conversions which also accept Warn's high quality internal spline steel manual hubs. These wheel hubs and manual locking hubs seal out water and eliminate the time-honored nemesis of the six- or, worse yet, five-bolt (late '81-up) drive plate/OEM manual locking hub flanges. (No more loose or broken locking hub bolts.) Warn's upgrade hub bearing adjuster/lock nut system, included in each kit, is an additional improvement.

Even better, Warn's Front Wheel Hub Conversion is also available for the XJ Cherokee/Comanche and YJ/TJ Wrangler front axles. This is the simplest, smart-

Fig. 18-31. *Front Wheel Hub Conversion by Warn Industries allows use of superior internal spline manual locking hubs. Kit provides better sealing, high-grade parts and improved bearing adjustment method. This kit can also serve as the basis for installing disc front brakes on an earlier CJ—or military MB, M38 or M38A-1.*

est upgrade for these OEM semi-floaters. The conversion to safer full-floating front wheel hubs using high quality spindles, plus the added bonus of manual locking hubs, allows use of a locker or limited slip—Disengage the front locking hubs for highway use, just like the CJ folks.

If you're thinking of a disc brake conversion, these components can serve as a foundation for two- or four-wheel disc brakes. Warn offers high quality disc brake caliper brackets. When used with a Warn Front Axle Wheel Hub Conversion Kit, these brackets will fit 1941-up military Jeep models and all CJs. Brackets provide for rear disc brake conversions when you install a Warn Full-Floating Rear Axle Conversion Kit. By using OEM Jeep rotors with a common GM (metric fitting) caliper, you can install front and rear disc brakes—Warn engineers have done their homework on these setups.

> *WARNING—*
> *Aftermarket disc brake conversions require correct front/rear brake proportioning. One solution is an aftermarket manual proportioning valve. When you install such a valve on a Jeep, make certain you begin test settings with the rear braking set for very light brake apply pressure. Otherwise, you run the risk of locking up the rear brakes or spinning your Jeep—even rolling it over during tests. Always test brakes in a secluded area, free of traffic and hazards. Follow manufacturer's criteria when adjusting the manual proportioning valve.*

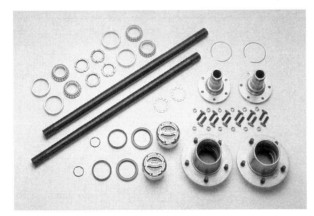

Fig. 18-30. *Warn Industries' full-floating rear axle kit is a quick upgrade for better axle shaft stamina, rear wheel hub safety and improved sealing. This is also the foundation for a four-wheel disc brake conversion. Kits available for all CJ semi-floating rear axles, YJ and TJ Wranglers, and even the XJ Cherokee/Comanche.*

Fig. 18-32. *Warn's full-floating front wheel hub conversion kits with high quality machined spindles are available for XJ, YJ and TJ models. You can turn your semi-floating Dana 30 front axle into a versatile, full-floating style with provision for manual locking hubs. Bring back the utility of the military and civilian Jeep CJ models that built the Legend. Very well conceived with highest quality materials, this is a Warn exclusive.*

Driveshaft Footnotes

The common 1310 size Spicer U-joint used on many Jeep applications is sufficient for most powertrains. These U-joints fit trucks through 1/2-ton capacity and handle reasonable power. Your driveshafts must be straight, within close tolerances and in balance. (The driveshaft built straight and true requires very little, if any, balancing.)

If your Jeep is a hard-core off-pavement runner, low driveshaft speeds and twisty, constantly changing driveshaft angles require stronger tubing sizes and a heftier rear coupler/splined shaft. A competent driveline shop can increase both tube diameter and wall thickness. For most CJs, Wranglers and XJs, the 1310 Spicer U-joint flange size is adequate. This applies to OE axle flanges and the transfer case flanges.

Driveshaft parts for handling more than 300 horsepower, however, should be one-ton truck variety (1350 Spicer size). A complete conversion includes heavier driveshafts and larger U-joint flanges. For most full-size 4x4 pickup owners, 1350-type Spicer joints can handle severe loads. Dana/Spicer 44 and 60 axle units can be fitted with 1350 replacement flanges.

> NOTE—
> For radical chassis lifts, double Cardan CV-joints will help reduce the vibration caused by steep driveshaft angles. Advance Adapters' Orbitor drop box is also a solution.

Steep driveshaft angles reduce the load capacity and safety of driveline assemblies. Shaft speed also de-

Hub-A-Lert: Protecting Your Drivetrain

Knowing whether your Jeep's free-wheeling hubs or transfer case have engaged or disengaged may require more than the '4-Wheel Drive' light on the console or dashboard. OEM warning lamp signals originate at the transfer case and simply indicate that the shifter/fork has moved to 4-High or 4-Low. While power flows to the front axle, without complete locking hub engagement, no torque moves to the wheels. Likewise, backing the truck up is no guarantee that the automatic hubs have disengaged. Dash lights cannot see inside the hub mechanisms.

There's a better method. Hub-A-Lert, an easy-to-install device built by 4x4 Specialty Products, is designed to read front driveshaft rotation. Simple and designed by a savvy "victim" of automatic hub and transfer case failures, the device sends a signal to a readable LED dash lamp, taking the guesswork out of hub disengagement.

During normal two-wheel drive operation, no shaft rotation (other than the minor lubricant drag/spin common to gear-drive transfer cases) will display at the LED light. If a defective hub drags, however, the front driveshaft will spin and flash an rpm-governed signal to the LED lamp.

termines safe driveline angles. Modified trucks often violate both of these considerations with steep driveshaft slopes and lower axle gear ratios (higher numerically). (See chapter on driveshafts for more information.)

> CAUTION —
> *Driveshaft length and angles are critical. A driveshaft is easy to remove and install, but there is nothing simple—or safe—about a driveline failure.*

Chapter 19

Suspension Upgrades

Most states now have mandates setting limits on vehicle chassis height and body modifications. Motor vehicle safety administrators, law enforcement agencies and a wary public have targeted unsafely modified 4x4 trucks and multipurpose trucks. Evidence of sensational accidents and senseless traffic deaths support their case.

> NOTE—
> More reputable aftermarket suspension manufacturers share many of the views of state legislators. Raising a truck's height has become an issue of safe engineering versus homespun efforts to achieve a particular "look."

Teams of factory engineers work endlessly at improving the ride, handling, safe steering and brakes of Jeep trucks. These mechanical engineers, versed in chassis dynamics and equipped with elaborate computer and laboratory equipment, build trucks to comply with known standards of safe handling and braking. Before you consider any modification to your Jeep's chassis or body height, prioritize safety.

> *WARNING—*
> *Suspension modifications can affect the handling characteristics of your Jeep truck. Incorrect modifications create poor braking, risk of a rollover, loss of vehicle/steering control, failure of driveline parts and marginal braking. Take extreme care when modifying your Jeep's suspension. Always adhere to the safety objectives set forth by Jeep OEM engineering.*

1. Chassis Modification

A challenge with any 4x4 multipurpose vehicle is chassis and suspension engineering. Highway driving, trail running and hard-core desert racing each require different chassis dynamics. Visualize your Jeep sweeping through corners, braking hard, bracing against a loose

traction surface or negotiating a precarious, off-camber sidehill. The interaction of the springs, shocks, stabilizers, brakes and tire/wheel mass is a blur! An automotive engineer or race truck fabricator must address each of these conditions.

On the test course or skidpad, a safe truck meets many criteria. Along with center of gravity, terms like Ackerman steering angles, lateral acceleration, roll axis, roll center, roll couple distribution, roll steer and toe change, roll stiffness, shock damping, spring/wheel rate, and vertical load transfer each apply to handling. The frame, suspension and axle design (Hotchkiss, IFS or multi-link and coil, just to name a few) also enter the equation.

At speed, aerodynamics and road load add to the burden. Braking is critically dependent upon load distribution and the anti-dive/anti-lift characteristics of the overall chassis design. Tire slip angle also becomes

Fig. 19-1. *Custom fabrication work on Walker Evans' race truck reveals high-caliber engineering and ultra-heavy duty components. A homespun look-alike cannot duplicate the stamina, materials and concern for safety displayed here. Your safety and that of others should be the ultimate consideration when approaching your Jeep's suspension needs.*

a factor. The safest Jeep truck balances each of these demands into a balanced overall chassis package.

Modifying Your Jeep Chassis

Changes in front end geometry, roll center, center of gravity, unsprung weight and tire design each have an effect on your Jeep's handling. Jeep engineers generally set up a chassis for good ride, safe steering control and manageable braking. Aftermarket components often meet the additional needs of special terrain, loads and driving conditions.

The better engineered aftermarket spring, link arm and shock absorber kits offer substantial improvements for the off-pavement Jeep truck. Additional clearance for specialty tires, improved spring rates, massive shock absorbers and stout steering damper shocks make our vehicles far better suited for back-country perils. In some instances, these parts enhance the handling and control of our trucks under an even wider range of driving conditions.

For Jeep owners, trends and fads also motivate chassis modifications. Achieving a certain status or "look" may override safety considerations. This leads to needless driving challenges on the highway and risk to vehicle occupants and other motorists.

The Culprits

Unfortunately, some Jeep owners go far beyond the OE and reputable aftermarket parts sources, seeking to establish a record for the highest, biggest, fastest and widest tread width Jeep. Without the benefit of engineering credentials or a sense for chassis dynamics,

Fig. 19-2. *No nonsense in the front suspension department on this Jeep Cherokee race truck. Again, although truck owners mimic the height profile of these trucks, they fail to match SCORE/HDRA's rugged, race tested standards.*

Fig. 19-3. *The ride height may look hot, but this front end geometry is unsafe. Note the radical slope angle on the draglink. As springs compress and the solid axle rises, "bump steer" will shift the wheels to the right.*

Fig. 19-4. *Here's an illegal setup in many states. Two sets of stacked spacer blocks make up this rear lift. Shifting of blocks and failure under load are possible. Never stack rear spacer blocks. Never install spacer blocks at a front axle.*

builders of homespun, radically lifted trucks have encouraged the wrath of motor vehicle and public safety administrators.

Improperly modified trucks sport crude and unsafe spacer block lifts, disfigured springs, bound up steering linkage, stretched brake hoses and pipes,

SEMA: Growth of a Truck Parts Aftermarket

The truck aftermarket has come of age, and the future is bright for quality, well-engineered and safe suspension and body lift products. SEMA and the suspension/body lift kit manufacturers strive hard to protect consumer interests, making every effort to rid the highways of unsafe equipment while lobbying to preserve truck owners' rights to reasonable tire, chassis and body modifications.

When selecting aftermarket components for your Jeep truck, you will find that SEMA supports the quality manufacturers within the industry. Look for the SEMA label on products and in advertising literature.

Massachusetts Has the Formula for Safe Suspension Modifications

Here's an example of one lift law that applies to sensibly modifying Jeep (and other) vehicles. Massachusetts has devised a formula for allowable mechanical (body and suspension) lift that accounts for both vehicle stability and safe handling: Wheel base multiplied by Wheel Track (the tire tread center-to-center measurement at the wider axle) divided by a factor of 2200. The wheel track width may be increased up to four inches—by way of wheel rim offset only—no wheel spacers allowed.

The formula is relatively easy. Suppose your Jeep CJ-7 or YJ/TJ Wrangler has a 94" wheelbase and wide rims that provide a 62" tread width. 94" x 62" = 5828 divided by 2200 = 2.65" lift. Under Massachusetts' Sections 6.04 and 6.05, tire diameter (based on the largest size available as an OEM option) may also be increased the same amount as the mechanical lift.

Simply put, the Jeep could have tires up to 2.65" larger diameter than stock plus a 2.65" mechanical lift by way of chassis and/or a body lift kit. (Accordingly, the body/door height could set a total of 3.975" over stock.)

All parts must be equal to or better than OEM standards, and the vehicle safety cannot be compromised. Here, Massachusetts has addressed OEM vehicle design, roll center, center-of-gravity and all other handling concerns with this statute. Other equipment on the truck must comply with general safety standards.

This is a sound approach, allowing reasonable lift for both off-pavement and highway usage. I am very pleased that Massachusetts took the initiative to advance such a formula. The guideline serves those who earnestly want a safe, versatile 4x4 truck.

overheight bumpers and ridiculous headlamp angles that glare menacingly into the eyes of oncoming drivers. These same trucks, with massively oversize tires that create an unsprung weight imbalance, have overtaxed brake systems that prevent safe stops. Radically sloped steering linkage and drag link angles, common to poorly constructed chassis lifts, create bump steer. The slightest blip in the road can cause the truck to veer uncontrollably.

Many law enforcement officers are also Jeep owners and recreationalists, yet most have a profound bias against radically lifted trucks. Each state's motor vehicle safety offices has files on highway mayhem caused by poorly crafted, radically lifted 4x4s. Horror stories of homespun junk run the gamut, including cases of these trucks rear ending other vehicles—with the lower edge of the truck's front bumper overrunning the entire trunk of the demolished car!

All agree that personal expression is a fundamental human right. Highway safety, however, is a collective responsibility.

State Lift Laws and Accountability

All states have laws directly regulating chassis lift and/or excessively oversize tires. Federal safety laws, interstate highway funding, and the issues of public liability make each state accountable to the same issues. The aftermarket suspension and body lift manufacturers have similar accountability. For a reputable company to survive, product liability insurance is essential. The cost of this insurance can be excessive. Here, a safely engineered kit effectively reduces product liability and, ultimately, reflects as lower insurance premium costs.

OEM standards remain the baseline for safety. Jeep Corporation and other new vehicle manufacturers must comply with U.S. Department of Transportation (D.O.T.)/National Highway and Traffic Safety Administration (NHTSA), Society of Automotive Engineers (SAE), and other professional engineering guidelines when building their vehicles.

Before investing time and money raising your Jeep's body, making suspension modifications or mounting a set of expensive oversize tires, review the laws for your state. If you've heard rumors of a changing law, consult your nearest state police or highway patrol office for the new rulings. These agencies will prove very helpful. Their primary concerns are public safety and compliance with motor vehicle regulations.

2. Off-Pavement Suspension Tuning

Suspension tuning enhances off-pavement performance. An upgraded spring and shock absorber package transforms a multipurpose 4x4 into a highly versatile trail machine. Correct handling, suspension travel and shock damping provide better vehicle control, stability and greater utility. Several factors determine the need for spring rate and chassis changes.

Conversion to a heavier engine, the addition of a hefty front winch or a protective front bumper/brush guard places additional load on the front springs. An oversize fuel tank, heavy duty truck-type manual or automatic transmission, a trailer towing package or heavy cargo can weight the rear springs. When your fatigued OE shocks and sagging springs need replacement, an upgrade spring and shock absorber package can improve your Jeep's performance.

Sagging springs allow the axle housings to rest close to the rubber bump stops. Suspension travel suffers, and your Jeep has difficulty negotiating twisty terrain. Poor off-pavement traction, excess body roll and steering control problems emerge. When a Jeep's springs and shock absorbers cause these troubles, or if reasonably oversize tires create tire-to-body interference, many owners consider an aftermarket suspension/chassis lift kit.

Aftermarket Suspension Improvements

Your goal should be a nicely tuned spring rate for solid traction and good wheel travel—without harsh rebound and overly stiff leaf stacks. Spring rebound damping and deflection control remain vital to maximum traction, and timid shocks can lose effectiveness in just a few miles of trail pounding. The best all around kits have "easy ride" spring rates and quality shock absorbers.

> *WARNING*—
> • *Limit your Jeep lift to just that amount necessary for safe tire installation and a full range of suspension travel. Select your tire size with care. Follow practical and safe tire and chassis guidelines, and make certain the wheel rim size is correct for your tires.*
>
> • *Use extreme caution when working under your Jeep vehicle. Use jackstands rated for the load. Do not rest the vehicle only on the jack, on cinder blocks or on pieces of wood.*

One example for later CJs is Rancho's well engineered 1" soft-ride suspension package. Once installed, this kit places the frame/front bumper height at just under 22" when running 31" dia. tires. This provides a 50-

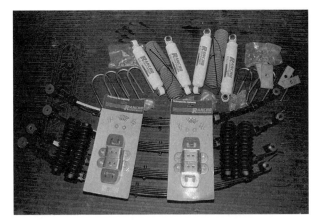

Fig. 19-5. *Rancho's Jeep CJ kit takes a full day to install. All hardware and instructions come with the kit. Here, springs are an easy ride rate and afford 1" lift over stock height. Tough urethane bushings provide long service life and durability while helping to eliminate side sway and other handling quirks.*

Fig. 19-6. *These stock '81 Jeep CJ springs are four-leaf and sag from age. Limited suspension travel, an in-line six in place of the original four-cylinder engine, and weak shock damping call for new suspension.*

Fig. 19-7. *CJ's 31-1/4" Goodyear Wrangler tire diameters produced limited clearance at rear wheel tubs. Rancho's 1"-plus spring lift and a set of mild drop bump stops eliminate the problem.*

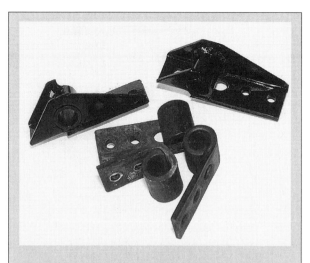

Jeep Frame Improvements

Under severe operating conditions, Jeep OE spring hangers and frame brackets are vulnerable to cracking. The use of hard urethane bushings and stiffer aftermarket springs can place additional stress on these chassis components. For this reason, many Jeep owners have found that softer OE rubber shackle bushings decrease the risk of parts failure.

For 1976-86 Jeep CJs, Full-Traction Suspension (see Appendix 1, Sources) manufactures heavy duty replacement frame brackets for front and rear springs. These machine-formed and reinforced shackle supports offer the option of using either stock OE or aftermarket bushings and shackles.

Full-Traction Suspension also offers shackle reversal kits for relocating the front spring anchors to the front end of each spring. With this changeover, the front axle pivots easily, arcing upward from the forward mounted spring anchor. As a bonus, these kits provide a mild lift and are available for 1976–86 CJs and the YJ Wranglers.

> NOTE—
> With the stock layout, trail obstructions cause the front axle and leaf springs to thrust rearward against the OEM spring anchors. Over time, rough trail pounding can lead to frame fatigue, and on many trucks (especially 1972–75 AMC/CJs), the frame cracks behind the anchors.

Off-pavement, a shackle reversal means reduced jarring, less frame stress and good steering control. On the highway in 2WD mode, the shackle reversal enables the front axle to trail from the frame instead of being constantly pushed forward. The frame and spring anchors pull the front springs and axle along. This reduces steering wander and darting while improving overall vehicle handling and control.

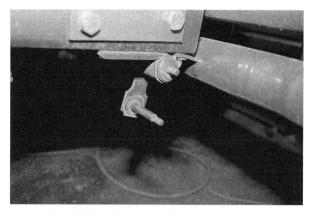

Fig. 19-8. *Sliding the springs from the shackles gains access to the rubber frame end bushings. If worn, replace the bushings.*

Fig. 19-9. *When installing U-bolts, tighten nuts evenly and in a cross pattern. At final torque, all exposed threads should be equal length. Re-check the torque periodically.*

Fig. 19-10. *Rancho front bump stops install easily, although rear stops require slight bending of the bracket to fit frame rail contours. These 1" dropped stops will prevent tire interference with fender wells.*

Fig. 19-11. *OEM front stabilizer will work with this mild lift. Actually, the "easy ride" spring rate and fifth leaf per spring account for just over an inch of extra ride height. OEM and Rancho hardware match perfectly.*

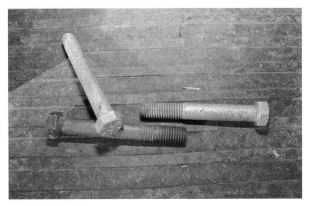

Fig. 19-12. *9/16" rear spring bolts, Grade 5 from the factory, wore and became unsafely distorted. This is a good time to replace hardware. Grade 8 bolts now secure spring anchor points.*

Fig. 19-13. *Rancho supplies 2.5-degree caster shims for the rear axle to restore pinion and driveshaft angle. These wedges are a tough aluminum alloy; hard steel wedges would serve even better.*

state legal Jeep with greater tire-to-body clearance, plus improved spring rate and better handling—on- and off-pavement. 31x10.50x15 tires on 8-inch wide rims offset the effects of such a height increase.

> *WARNING—*
> • *A lift or oversized wheels and tires will exaggerate any suspension problems. Inspect the steering linkage, make certain the frame is intact, and check all frame/suspension hardware torque settings. Follow lift kit instructions. On any lift installation, you must re-torque/tighten spring U-bolts, link- arm attachments and shackle hardware shortly after you put the vehicle in service.*
>
> • *Many chassis lifts create the need for long- er brake hoses at wheels or frame-to-axle. Most aftermarket lift kits address this issue, but you should check brake hose fitup close- ly to ensure that the hoses and pipes will not be stressed or damaged. Check each hose's movement over the full range of suspension travel. Turn the front wheels full left-to- right and make certain each hose does not interfere with the wheel, tire or chassis.*

> *CAUTION —*
> *Always be certain that a lift will accommo- date your tire and wheel plans. Discuss your Jeep model and proposed tire size with the suspension kit supplier, and follow recom- mendations. Do not buy new tires without making certain the size will fit your Jeep's chassis height while clearing the body and frame. Consider tire clearance at full range of suspension travel.*

2.1 Shock Absorbers

Jeep owners who use their vehicle in the backcountry or along washboard roads will find that some shock absorbers fail quickly. In Chapter 12, I describe the various shock absorber types and their uses. (Refer to that section for details on shock absorber design and the intended uses of various shock absorber types.)

For performance upgrades, I again emphasize that OEM shock absorber mounting and bracket systems vary in strength. Any shock absorber upgrade must take the vehicle's frame and shock brackets into ac- count. Upgrade each of these components to match the shock absorber damping pressures.

> *WARNING—*
> *The earliest Jeep shocks are held to the bracket posts with a washer and cotter pin. This kind of bracketry is not acceptable for severe service shock absorbers and certainly does not qualify for gas-pressurized shocks.*

Be very clear of your vehicle's intended use before selecting shock absorbers. A common misfortune is the

Axle Trusses

The pounding of off-pavement running can bend or break an axle housing. Often, Jeep owners concentrate on stiff spring rates and hefty shock absorbers without concern for the axles. If serious trail running or high performance driving is your Jeep's lot, consider axle trusses as part of your suspension buildup.

Bill Broyes at Autofab in Santee, California has built a show winning truck. Bill likes GO Rhino's combination rear axle truss/skid plate, which doubles as shock mount. Rhino clamps provide a simple installation. Although some tube support results from this design, the stronger point is skid plate protection.

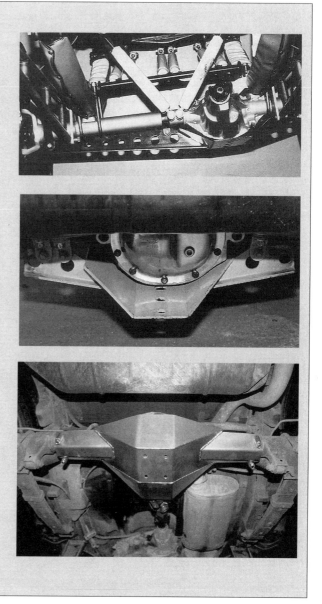

Dana 44 open-knuckle front axle (right, top) receives GO Rhino truss and skid plate combination. Open-knuckle support at axle housing end generally holds up without bracing. This truss design focuses on tube bracing.

Jeep Wrangler boasts a combination skid plate/truss on rear axle. Near stock, low running clearance benefits from protection (right, center).

Full-Traction Suspension's Axle Truss/Skid Plate (right, bottom) offers maximum protection for front or rear axles. Unique design wraps entire axle housing in a layer of 3/16" steel plate. Bolt-on, this highly protective design is a top candidate for serious trail running. Available for Model 20 AMC, Dana 30, 35 and 44 axles.

belief that if a certain degree of stiff damping worked well, even more damping will work better. I have RS9000 Rancho shock absorbers with the five-position Remote Cab Control (RC9700 kit), yet my settings range from "2-1/2" to "3" (front) and "3" to "3-1/2" (rear) on a three-ton 3/4-ton 4x4 truck. (Setting "3" equates to Rancho's RS5000.) This range works for highway and washboard roads.

So, in this case, the RS5000s would provide a fairly good approach. The RS9000s, however, provide the tuning edge that makes driving the truck a pleasure. On a near stock or lightly modified Jeep CJ, the RS9000's five setting range readily covers any reasonable use.

Single Versus Multiple Shocks

Show trucks, lifted trucks and even some OEM suspensions feature multiple shock absorbers per wheel. On factory dual-shock installations, the mounting angle and position of the additional shock is vital to the truck's handling. The shocks must counter jarring, chassis/spring oscillation and friction forces along the critical paths of frame travel.

Many homespun, multi-shock assemblies defy logic. Few hobbyists have the expertise to properly engineer shock absorber locations. Unless looks override every other consideration, do your homework.

If your Jeep 4x4 operates off-pavement, begin your suspension buildup around a healthy set of single

ARB's "Old Man Emu" (OME) Suspension: One Sensibly Equipped YJ Wrangler

Focused on safety and reliability, an Old Man Emu suspension kit transforms the stock YJ Wrangler into a multi-purpose, rough and ready back country machine. For optimal ground clearance, without compromising handling and stock driveline performance, the Old Man Emu Suspension package provides a two-inch chassis lift using OEM suspension mounting points.

The springs have a unique and highly efficient design. To assure matched rates, minimize stress and allow use of popular 31x10.5x15 to 32x11.5x15 tire sizes, the Old Man Emu springs feature flat sections through the spring plate attachment areas.

Additionally, the springs limit inter-leaf friction by employing a unique shape. Each spring is individually cambered on rotary dies and bears its weight at plastic sliders near the tips of the spring. This measure eliminates inter-leaf friction by a remarkable 75%. Although incurring more work in the spring manufacturing process, Old Man Emu springs operate more smoothly and claim longer life.

This ride height is practical, and 32x11.50R15 tires on 8-inch wide rims offer an excellent ride quality and

traction. For two-inches of chassis lift, the OME suspension kit includes transfer case lowering spacers.

NOTE—
Following a common industry practice, ARB/OME uses transmission/transfer case drop spacers for maintaining rear driveline angles. I do not use these spacers. I prefer to install M.I.T.'s transfer case output kit, which eliminates the YJ's OE transfer case tailhousing. The M.I.T. kit includes a longer, stouter rear driveshaft with a CV-joint (double Cardan). The rear axle/pinion shaft angle must fit properly with the transfer case output shaft angle. Consult with M.I.T. about proper operating angles for the M.I.T. driveshaft, CV-joint (transfer case end) and single U-joint (rear axle end).

The kit's urethane injection molded spring bushings match the movement and smooth action of the springs. Unlike many designs, these bushings permit expansion and the necessary torsional twist. An outer ring resists contamination by debris and road dust.

By limiting lift to two-inches, the stock chassis and steering components work fine, with minimal, if any, bump steer from the sloping draglink. (A two-inch dropped aftermarket pitman arm could eliminate nearly all bump steer. However, the stock arm and linkage work reasonably well and satisfy most users.)

Use of stock stabilizers and other steering control items helps assure a high level of engineering. This is another advantage of a mild lift with moderately oversized tires. Off-pavement, the package offers enough ground clearance for trails as severe as the Rubicon—Of course,

---

aftermarket replacement shocks. Should this not be enough, the main advantage of a dual shock conversion is that properly selected dual shocks can provide a sensible ride quality yet offer greater resistance to short and long travel bounce and fade.

NOTE—
Two moderate rate shocks per wheel can provide nearly twice the resistance to fade—without creating an unbearably harsh ride. As an example, two RS5000 shocks might produce a firmer, yet still acceptable ride. Under severe pounding, however, there is far less likelihood that both shocks will fade out.

2.2 Urethane Bushings

Polyurethane, a product of mid-1930s German pharmaceutical technology, meets a wide range of automotive challenges. Found in dashboards, arm rests, paints, door panels, foam seats and suspension components, urethane meets a host of challenges.

Urethane suspension and roll cage bushings provide the chassis tuning and durability that many desert racers demand. Recreational four-wheelers also benefit from urethane suspension pieces.

Why is urethane desirable? First, unlike rubber products, urethane resists road salt, ozone, gasoline and automotive oils. Precise hardness control provides a variety of stiffnesses for suspension uses. More importantly, urethane offers high resistance to abrasion,

OME Suspension (cont'd)

rocker sill protectors and added skid-plates are advisable for such use.

Matching Shock Absorber Design
The Old Man Emu shock absorbers focus on ride quality and wheel control. For testing, there's no place like Australia—Heat generated by extensive operation on "corrugated" Outback roads can melt the paint off shock housings and blue a hard chrome shaft.

These low-pressure gas charged shocks have a high rebound effect for maximum control and "in phase" contact with a washboard road surface. Use of an 18mm hard chrome shaft, a special heavy duty strut-type "check-valve" seal, and a "four-lip with garter" spring seal help keep the fluid within each shock.

'OME' shocks offer the thickest outside casing available on any twin-tube shock absorber. As a final consideration, these shocks use a steel bell sleeve instead of the typical rubber boot found on other aftermarket shocks. This prevents debris from accumulating within a boot. Debris can cause boot tearing and abrasive damage to a shock absorber.

The Safari Snorkel is an interesting accessory. Here in the U.S., we "live with" the dust levels of our occasional off-road ventures. In the Australian Outback, however, thick dust is a chronic nemesis. Dry paper air filter elements, with intakes beneath the hood or in the grille opening, can plug up in just a few miles.

The Safari Snorkel raises the intake to the roof height of a vehicle. Tests claim that drawing from this air zone can increase filter life by at least 50%. Another use is deep water fording, which requires additional precautions like relocating all gearcase vents and preventing water from entering wheel bearings, the brakes and the axle assemblies.

Although ARB Air Lockers front and rear provide the most traction available anywhere, a winch backup (Warn unit shown) is smart. So equipped, the YJ Wrangler can tackle challenging terrain. When the going gets easier, a flick of dash switches can "open" the differentials for smooth highway travel—the best of both worlds.

> NOTE—
> Using proper driving technique, ARB Air Lockers can serve as TREAD LIGHTLY devices, limiting impact to the environment by minimizing wheel spin.

The properly upgraded Wrangler is an excellent on- and off-pavement vehicle. U.S.A. VenturCraft's 'Trailblazer Camper' makes a nice adjunct to any Jeep. For backcountry travel, this Wrangler and trailer provide a light and maneuverable package. Trailer top lifts to provide large cargo space. Two- to three-person tent delivers a good night's sleep—anywhere!

---

yet engineers can factor elasticity into the product during the molding process. Manufacturers of urethane suspension bushings can control the characteristics of the finished product.

The Right Mix For Your Jeep Chassis
Don Bunker, founder of Energy Suspensions, comments on the differences in urethane materials...."Obviously," Don notes, "bump stops have to be somewhat soft to perform their duties, where high performance control arm bushings are generally of a firmer 'durometer' hardness for maximum control. Urethane can be as soft as the Slime toys that kids buy or as hard as a bowling ball."

Poor mixes create low quality finished products. Noting the disparity between good and poor product, Don Bunker states flatly, "All urethane is not created equal!"

Don cites the bitter experience of early urethane users who broke eyelets loose from their shock absorbers. Although owners often condemned the shocks, the real problem was the bushings. When excessively hard, the urethane acts as rigid as metal. Shock eyes, which actually travel in an arc, can bind up if the bushings are too hard. Eyelets break from the force.

Warn/Black Diamond: TJ Wrangler Backcountry Suspension Engineering

In showroom stock form, the '97-up TJ Wrangler has seven inches more suspension articulation than the former leaf-sprung YJ Wrangler. The TJ Wrangler is eminently qualified for backcountry use, and a suspension lift kit adds just the assurance that you can tackle the rougher, rockier trails.

Using a 3-D computer, Warn/Black Diamond engineering staff took a hard look at the TJ's Quadra-Coil link arm-and-coil spring suspension. The result was a three-inch suspension lift kit that increases both the axle articulation and wheel travel. By maintaining an OEM ride quality and limiting lift to three inches, Warn avoided rear driveline problems and premature chassis wear issues.

Warn knew that anyone planning for three inches of lift on a TJ would likely want a front-mounted winch. The Black Diamond engineers sized and rated the coil springs accordingly. Lab and extensive "real world" field tests, using a full complement of popular accessories and typical backcountry cargo, proved the stability of the springs.

Two grades (AT and XT) of shock absorbers were developed for the TJ lift kit. Anti-sway bar functions, crucial to safety on the highway, were maintained. (Anti-sway bars pivot at the stock locations.) The front sway bar benefits from the kit's quick-disconnect links, which you can easily disconnect and connect in the field—without tools. Dis-connects provide a means for unhooking the sway bar for maximum suspension travel when driving in rough, crawl-pace backcountry.

Warn's engineering staff of avid outdoor enthusiasts know the 4WD Jeep owner's needs. They provided room for 33x12.50x15 tires mounted on 8-inch rims (with 3-1/2-inch backspacing). Using the Warn/Black Diamond suspension system, tires to this size will not interfere with the fenders, flares or vehicle's frame.

Kits come complete and include a new dropped pitman arm for proper steering linkage alignment, extended bump stops to prevent over-extension of axle travel, hardware to re-position front and rear track arms for normal vehicle tracking, rear sway bar drop links, plus the front sway bar quick-disconnect components. Estimated time for installation is 7–8 hours for the home mechanic, 4.5 to 5.5 hours for the well-equipped shop.

Now, let's see....add one of Warn's winches, a full-floating front wheel hub conversion kit, a set of 32x11.50x15 tires on 8-inch wide wheels, front and rear ARB Air Lockers, an NV4500 five-speed transmission with Atlas II transfer case attached, and, by golly, I'd have one unbeatable backcountry Jeep TJ Wrangler!

NOTE—
Following a common industry practice, Warn/Black Diamond uses transmission/transfer case drop spacers for maintaining rear driveline angles. I do not use these spacers. I prefer to install M.I.T.'s transfer case output kit, which eliminates the TJ's OE transfer case tailhousing. The M.I.T. kit includes a longer, stouter rear driveshaft with a CV-joint (double Cardan). The rear axle/pinion shaft angle must fit properly with the transfer case output shaft angle. Consult with M.I.T. about proper operating angles for the M.I.T. driveshaft, CV-joint (transfer case end) and single U-joint (rear axle end).

NOTE—
If you upgrade your Jeep chassis with urethane suspension bushings, squeak is not uncommon, especially in twisting situations. Several manufacturers have addressed this problem. Some offer graphite-impregnated bushings to counter noise and friction.

Urethane Construction

There are two methods of urethane bushing production: injection molding and liquid cold pour casting. Injection molding provides the more precise results. Liquid cold pour castings serve in parts that require less critical tolerances.

Aftermarket urethane producers invest substantially in each bushing mold. Molds determine the fitup and ultimate reliability of the parts. Intricate machining is necessary to produce a quality mold. Correct mixture ratios complete the process, while colorful finishes are merely a "looks" consideration.

NOTE—
When selecting urethane sleeved bushings, seek seamless sleeves wherever possible.

Fig. 19-14. *Greg Williams' pre-runner, a support truck for Nelson & Nelson Racing, features rollbar brackets with versatile urethane bushings. Urethane comes in a variety of colors. The correct hardness of finished bushings, however, is far more important than color considerations. There are locations where OEM rubber bushings work best. Leaf spring bushings and suspension articulation often benefit from the flexibility of OEM-type rubber spring bushings.*

Fig. 19-15. *All '72-up AMC and Chrysler Jeep trucks use Saginaw steering gears. This '81 CJ-5 with an Iron Duke four has power steering. The OE Pontiac engine, built by GM, makes the GM power steering system an easy installation. Use an OEM Jeep system as a prototype for your power steering retrofit.*

Where Does Urethane Work Best?

Urethane control arm and strut rod bushings are popular. Front and rear stabilizers also benefit from urethane bushings, which allow greater application of force (unlike the loose action of factory rubber bushings). Urethane mounts offer a major gain over factory rubber cab and body mounts. Unlike aftermarket aluminum spacers, which deliver a rigid and harsh ride, urethane provides firm yet functional suspension while maintaining the alignment of body panels.

Aftermarket leaf spring bushings, mounting pin kits and most lift kits use urethane bushings. The trick is to select the right bushings for your particular driving style. Before grabbing the most colorful set off the shelf, consider options like graphite-impregnated bushings.

> NOTE —
> If your Jeep truck demands more stamina and a finely tuned suspension system, consider the urethane bushing option. The right bushings can drastically improve your Jeep's handling.

3. Steering Gear Conversions

Early Jeep models offer very crude steering gears. CJs and some trucks use the Ross cam-and-lever boxes, while other earlier Jeep trucks use worm-and-roller type gear units. Both designs are high in friction and offer shorter service than the later Jeep's Saginaw type steering gears.

By the end of the Kaiser/Jeep Corporation era, Saginaw manual and power steering gears were an industry standard. These recirculating ball-and-nut designs offer better service under rough duty, and far smoother operation, than any other gear available. 1972–up AMC Jeep trucks benefit from the GM Saginaw power and manual steering gearboxes.

If your early Jeep truck has worn out another OE steering gearbox, consider converting to a Saginaw gear. Advance Adapters makes a kit for this purpose, including steering linkage to eliminate the cumbersome bellcrank and twin tie-rod arrangement found on Jeep Universal/CJ and lighter military models.

Either a Saginaw integral power gear or a Saginaw manual steering unit will deliver superior service in your Jeep truck. If your Jeep has a GM V-6 or V-8 engine conversion, the power gear option is always practical. (A GM pump will fit up easily using GM mounting brackets.) 1972–up AMC/Jeep engines are also easy candidates for a changeover using Saginaw/AMC power steering pieces.

Setting Up the Right Gear

If you make the conversion with later OE Jeep parts, the steering gear ratio and other factors are already engineered. Should you choose the more universal route, select a common Saginaw power gear with four turns lock-to- lock.

Pitman arm length contributes to the final steering ratio. Select an arm that provides good road feel and correct travel of the steering arms/knuckles. When setting up the Saginaw steering gear and linkage, keep the steering drag link on a level plane with the tie-rod. This will prevent bump steer. (Check the linkage alignment with the Jeep parked on flat ground and loaded normally.) A dropped Pitman arm, common to many lift kits, can help align the linkage.

> CAUTION —
> *The quicker (three turn) gears are entirely too fast and give a CJ model the steering character of a sprint car. Avoid ultra-quick steering ratios. Many Jeep Wrangler and late CJ owners find that even the factory power steering ratios are too fast—especially with smaller steering wheels.*

> WARNING—
> *Many suspension lift kits require a dropped Pitman arm to maintain normal steering and handling. Failure to install a dropped arm can result in bump steer and other vehicle control problems.*

> CAUTION —
> *Power steering systems require careful engineering. The force of a Saginaw integral power unit is sufficient to rip a gear loose from the frame. When setting up a power gear and Pitman arm, care must be taken to prevent excess pressure build-up when the steering knuckles rest against their stops.*

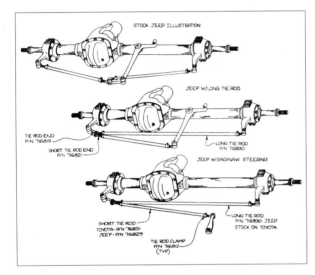

Fig. 19-16. *Advance Adapters offers a conversion kit for Saginaw manual or power steering gears to the pre-'72 Jeep CJ, Jeepster and Jeep truck chassis. Popularity and rugged service of Saginaw gears makes this a very practical swap. One-piece tie-rod assembly, included in kit, eliminates chronic wander associated with OEM draglink, bellcrank and two tie-rods.*

Fig. 19-17. *Often, an aftermarket or OE dropped Pitman arm can help realign the tie-rod and draglink. Aftermarket arm for CJ Jeep steering gear accommodates a 2"–3" suspension lift. Slightly shorter from stud center to center, this arm also slows steering ratio. Many owners prefer the slower feel, especially with power steering.*

Steering Linkage Fix for a Lifted Jeep

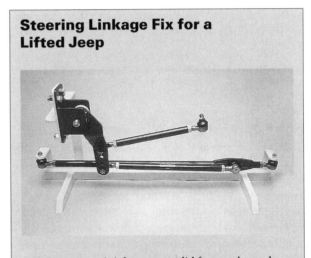

Bump steer is inherent to solid front axle trucks. Various OEM steering linkage designs help minimize bump-steer, but the challenge remains. When you install a mild chassis lift, a dropped Pitman arm can compensate for bump-steer by restoring the original steering linkage alignment. Some lifts, however, are beyond the reach of a safe dropped Pitman arm.

Full-Traction Suspension offers a linkage steering system that tackles bump-steer in a unique way. This system adds an idler/lever arm that pivots vertically at the passenger side frame rail. A draglink connects the Pitman arm to an upper locating point at the idler/lever arm. Below the idler/lever arm's pivot, there are several relay rod attachment points. This enables setting the relay rod parallel with the long tie-rod. (The long tie-rod runs between the steering knuckle arms.) The upper idler/lever arm section offers several draglink attachment positions to adjust steering ratio/leverage.

Full-Traction Suspension claims three improvements from this kit: 1) virtually eliminates bump-steer, 2) better steering ratio/leverage with quick adjustments of the steering ratio, and 3) reduction in driver fatigue by distancing the steering gear and steering wheel from rough trail kickback.

• Consult factory service manuals for pump and gear pressure specifications. Test your system for correct travel and pressure in all positions.

• Make certain that the steering gear does not reach its full range of movement before the steering knuckles reach their stops. Hyper-extending the steering gear can severely damage the ball races, nut or power rack. Always make sure that the steering gear is on its center with the front wheels and tires in the straight-ahead position. (See Chapter 12 for further details.)

• Always make sure that steering linkage moves freely and on a normal arc. Check for clearance over the full range of chassis/axle operating angles.

4. Tires

Preparing your Jeep for a special environment always includes tires. For rock crawling in the Rubicon or scaling a wagon road to an abandoned silver mine, you need the right rubber. Ground clearance, superior traction and resistance to rock abrasions each depend on your tire choices.

WARNING —
• Wider wheels and oversize tires will affect handling characteristics. Take extreme care when selecting your Jeep wheels. When in doubt, always follow Jeep and wheel manufacturers' recommendations.

• Wider wheels and oversize tires usually require other changes to your Jeep truck. Larger tires and wheels may place excessive stress on suspension and chassis components, including bearings, hubs, and brakes. Interference with brake drums, rotors and hoses is an additional concern.

There are mildly and wildly oversize wheels and tires. Oversize tires run anywhere from one or two sizes larger than your stock Jeep rubber to monstrous tires. Concerned with safety and liability issues, the majority of light truck tire manufacturers limit their maximum tire sizes to 35" diameter.

Why is 35" the usual limit? When it comes to mounting massive rubber on a light truck, the major tire manufacturers don't have time to conduct safety schools. Product abuse and consumer negligence occur regularly from the improper use of radically oversized tires.

Where Do "Monster" Tires Serve Best?

Lifted show trucks and boulevard cruisers have monster tires. Are these tires simply an artistic expression?

Fig. 19-18. *Wider wheels are necessary with most oversize tires. This 33"x12.50x15 tire mounts on Golden Wheel Corporation's Enkei 89-series one piece alloy rim. Rim bead width is ten inches.*

Not always. The 35" to 44" tire is also a workhorse. At highly specialized jobsites, such as logging and mining operations, heavy loads and deep mud packs make a rubber-tire loader cringe! Here, a heavy duty 3/4- or one-ton Jeep pickup truck, given the unceremonious task of lugging supplies and equipment over miles of primitive road, might benefit from jumbo tires.

Warren Guidry of Interco Tire Corporation comments on the merits of monster tires. "...for 4WD vehicles to obtain their full potential, bigger tires need to be used. Nothing will raise the axles except the tires, which in turn gives greater ground clearance, and this is very important to off-road use."

Obviously, there's a limit to monster tire use. These tires, which mount on specially built rims, fit a radically lifted truck. Huge tires require an elaborate spring and body lift for clearance, plus many other modifications to the engine, chassis, geartrain, steering and brakes.

Way Up Has a Downside

On some Jeep trucks, even a 32" diameter tire can threaten chassis and axle safety and create a precariously high center of gravity. Making any light truck

Fig. 19-19. In the Pacific Northwest logging country, oversize tires have utility value. Here, traction on muddy and rutted roads benefits from large tires, which actually reduce environmental impact when the driver keeps wheel spin under control.

Fig. 19-20. Handling big rubber means serious chassis and powertrain modifications. Full-floating 3/4-ton truck rear axles are common on show trucks. A very large tire size would demand the safety advantage of an eight-stud wheel and a full-floating axle.

safe with the mass and unsprung weight of 36"–44" tires involves radically altering the vehicle's track width, brakes, powertrain, steering and suspension. Neither Jeep nor any other light truck builder designs an OE brake system capable of safely handling the rolling mass of four 44" diameter, 130-pound tire and wheel assemblies.

Furthermore, manufacturers match gearing to their truck's OE tire diameter. If a Jeep Wrangler has 28" diameter OE tires and 3.31:1 axle gear ratios, a switch to 44" tires (if you could ever find a way to fit such a size) would require axle ratios near 5.20:1 to restore the engine's original operating rpm.

The radically lifted show trucks have extensive frame, suspension, geartrain and engine upgrades to handle the taller vehicle profile and huge rubber. If you're serious about duplicating this look, don't stop with wheels, tires and a spring lift. Pay attention to the rest of your Jeep's needs, those engineering measures that will maintain safe tractability, handling, steering, braking and control.

Safety First

"The truth is," Warren Guidry notes, "if a vehicle is professionally modified to accommodate larger tires, and if the larger tires are not just taller but also wider, the vehicle can be more stable than when it was stock...We would like to see "60 Minutes"* take Jeep CJs, install stronger shackles and remove the stock tires that they used in the tests, put on tires such as our 31x13.50s on a nine-inch wide wheel, and run through the same test at the same speeds..."

> NOTE—
> *In the early 1980s, the television program "60 Minutes" evaluated the CJ-5 Jeep. Investigative reporters alleged that the vehicle was unsafe and handled in such a manner that roll-over was likely. Warren Guidry's comments refer to that allegation.

Guidry concludes, "The wider tire and wheel combination increases the track of the vehicle and adds a tremendous amount of stability. The bigger, wider tires can carry more load with the same air pressure, and because of the greater volume of air are not under the load stresses that the smaller tires have to bear, and are thereby safer."

There's a clear relationship between track width and center of gravity. The savvy state laws, those that aim at restoring a stable center of gravity, suggest the use of a wider track width whenever height changes have been made to a vehicle.

As Warren Guidry suggests, the professional modification of a vehicle takes safety factors into account.

If you're unsure of the safety requirements for your Jeep truck, consult a 4x4 racing or competitive exhibition truck fabrication shop that has built its credential around maximizing safety.

In general, larger tires represent more unsprung weight, which immediately suggests stouter springs, hefty gangs of shock absorbers, added steering stabilization, traction bars or torsion arms and a whole arsenal of heavy duty wheel and brake parts. Oversize brake rotors, pads, rear brake shoes and drums—even heavier drive axles—may be necessary. Any truck that runs 39" and larger tires should have heavy duty, full-floating front and rear axles. The full-floater adds stamina and better wheel and axle bearing support.

Shock loads transfer back through the entire geartrain to the engine. U-joint upgrades, increased driveshaft wall thickness and/or diameter and other precautions help assure parts survival. Also, by changing axle gearing to restore the original engine speeds, you'll give the manual clutch or automatic transmission a chance to survive. Even so, consider upgrading the clutch or torque converter to handle the extra inertial loads of big tires.

Tried Trail Running Formulas

I've never installed tires larger than 33" diameter on any of my 4x4 trucks, including the 3/4-ton models. I firmly believe that driving skill and a decent tire will handle even the more challenging off-pavement environments. Beyond a mud-bog racer, logging rig or swampland runner, successful traction for your Jeep is as close as a good tread pattern on a set of moderately oversized tires.

Specifically, I feel that a 31" tire is plenty for a relatively stock Wrangler, CJ, Jeepster, Commando, Comanche or compact Jeep Cherokee and Grand Cherokee. (In cases where a lift is not desired, a 29"–30" diameter tire often serves as a reasonable limit.) I'm intrigued by Warren Guidry's 31x13.50x15 concept, although most light Jeep 4x4s require a mild lift to fit these tires.

> NOTE—
> The only drawback to a very wide tire on a lightweight CJ is the high flotation effect of the wide tire print. These tires would work great on sand, but a narrower tire would assure better traction on ice.

The 6.00x16 tires on early MBs and CJs teach a great lesson. These trucks, at a curb weight of 2215 lbs. (CJ-2A), get exceptional traction in rock and snow. The narrow tire tread places more weight on each tire print.

Fig. 19-21. *This '81 CJ has custom 7"x16" steel wheels from California Wheel in Gardena, California. Goodyear 235R85x16 Wrangler MT radial tires, 31-1/4" diameter and load range E rated, give the truck a lift without an exceptionally wide tire print.*

A prime traction factor, tread design, has nothing to do with tire size. You can choose from a host of tire tread patterns. Fifty years of off-pavement testing, complemented by three decades of desert racing, has produced specialized and multipurpose tread patterns for a wide range of Jeep uses. An extra set of tires, mounted and balanced on spare rims, make a good investment for your Jeep truck. Consider a specialized tread pattern that aims at your driving terrain and habits, tires that you can install when you're ready for the rough stuff.

Tire Inflation and Other Safety Concerns

Despite nail holes, rock punctures and other natural hazards of four-wheeling, the top two causes of tire blowout are under-inflation and worn tread. Low tire pressure places tremendous stress on sidewalls and generates unsafe heat levels.

> CAUTION —
> *For off-pavement use, tires showing over 50% tread wear are highly susceptible to rock breaks. Damage in the tread area increases substantially when tread is too worn to protect the tire carcass. Worn tread also creates more tire heat on pavement, which raises risk of belt separation and blowouts. Despite legal minimum tread depth allowances, tread wear beyond 50% is risky for travel in rugged backcountry.*

Goodyear: Jeep-Proven Tires

Goodyear Tire and Rubber Company has been an OE supplier to Jeep since the first Model MB. My earliest recollection of the Jeep-Goodyear relationship was my folks' shiny new '64 CJ-5 equipped with Goodyear's "Suburbanite" GX 7.00x15 Mud-and-Snow tires. Those original, tube-type 4-ply (bias) tires matched that Jeep's performance and willingness to tackle blizzards, icy and snow-covered highways, desert washes, remote mountain passes and, yes, even the rugged Rubicon Trail.

The Goodyear OE connection carries forth to the latest Jeep models. Today, however, Goodyear tires cover a much broader range of usage and offer new Jeep buyers the right original tire choice for their vehicles.

> NOTE—
> OE tire engineering takes a vehicle's precise chassis design and handling characteristics into account. For ride quality, minimal vibration and a factory-engineered handling/steering response, your surest tire choice is the original equipment type that Jeep Corporation recommends.

Jeep and Goodyear make a good match when new, and Goodyear can remain a top tire choice when replacing your Jeep's tires. When looking for a special-use tire, I select particular Goodyear tire types for four-wheeling, highway use and all-season, multipurpose driving. Here are my favorite Goodyear tire picks for Jeep 4x4 models.

Wrangler MT Radial: Want maximum traction? Willing to hear more from your tires, perhaps give up a bit of smoothness? The MT is a tough, aggressive tire that works well on the CJ or Wrangler headed for the back-country. I tested these tires on a CJ-5 in the Pacific Northwest: MTs get the bite many look for in muddy, loose traction terrain. Not your ideal highway tire, the MT is functional for that asphalt drive to where the pavement ends and your favorite 4WD trail begins. Available to 33x12.50x15 sizing. Wear is quicker if used extensively for highway driving.

Wrangler GS-A Radial: I tested these tires long before they appeared as OE equipment on the TJ Wrangler. This is a smooth riding, good cornering, all-season tire with a unique multi-tread pattern. In my experience, the correctly sized GS-A will serve in any kind of Jeep use. Larger sizes work well on the Rubicon. OE sizes can handle light mud, snow, ice and washboard. A quieter, stable tire, the GS-A is my "multipurpose" choice for the Jeep truck that spends a good deal of time on the highway but escapes to the outback every now and again.

Wrangler AT/S Radial: "Dual Traction Lug Channels" self-clean readily and purge mud, snow and water. Great traction, I use these tires on- and off-pavement. In larger sizes, tread opens up and becomes more "aggressive," making this a practical 32x11.50x15 size. (I keep tread depth to 50% minimum for rocky terrain use, where open channels expose more carcass.) One thing I really like about this tire is its lateral stability on slippery road surfaces. Ride is harsher than OEM tires as the AT/S has a very tough, two steel-belt design with stiff sidewalls. Good wear character.

Workhorse Extra Grip Radial: Not a "Wrangler"-series design, this one's the bulletproof commercial users' secret. Popular with fleet owners, the Workhorse Extra Grip is among the toughest, best wearing tires available. In 31x10.50x15 size, just right for a trail running rig that sees some highway driving, this tire offers aggressive traction, exceptional resistance to chipping, chunking and

tearing, very good self-cleaning ability, and long life, steel-belted stamina....I'm a heavy equipment operator at heart: The Workhorse Extra Grip won my respect.

Wrangler RF-A Radial: A new concept as of this writing, the "Axle-Specific" tire tread patterns are specially designed for front or rear axle handling traits. The RF-A provides maximum handling benefits on the highway and serves as a true "all-season" setup that does not require periodic tire rotation. If you need superior traction on wet and snowy highways, the RF-A may be your choice for the XJ, ZJ or WJ. Trail runners would be wise to stick with a matching tread at all four tire positions, which will allow the spare to easily rotate into a front or rear axle location.

One manufacturer notes, "Do not allow the air pressure to get below 20 PSI regardless of how light the vehicle may be. Pressures below 20 PSI may let the bead of the tire become unseated, especially from lateral forces. An exception would be while running in soft sand, where you may wish to reduce air pressure below 20 PSI. This should be an emergency procedure only. As soon as possible, pressure must be brought back up. Remember, overloading and/or under-inflation causes excessive heat build up which can cause separation of the tire body."

The manufacturer also recommends that you maintain correct air pressure, checking each tire cold at least once a month. (Cold means the truck has parked out of direct sunlight at least 3 hours.) Match pressure to the weight of your Jeep and load.

Tire wear depends on proper wheel alignment, inflation pressures, balancing and rotation. Rotation at 2,500 to 4000 miles is a good interval. The traditional pattern of rotation for radial tires has been front-to-rear and rear-to-front. Many manufacturers now recommend a modified cross-rotation method. Consult your tire manufacturer/dealer for proper tire rotation procedures.

Maximum load capacity is at the maximum pressure rating for the tire. If you lower the pressure to improve the ride, or for any other reason, load capacity also decreases. Big tires stand up easily, so give them more than a glance. Invest in a quality tire pressure gauge—Cheap gauges seldom read the same pressure twice.

Many oversize tires benefit from balancing on the truck. When you have your tires balanced with a floor balancer (wheels mounted on the truck), tire rotations involve one more step: Your tires will require re-balancing each time. Once rotated, or even re-positioned on the wheel hub, tire balance changes. Beware!

Installing Your Wheels

Your new tires, safely mounted to the correct rim, may be ready to install—but are the OE wheel bolts/studs and nuts ready? Grossly oversize wheel and tire packages have a lot of mass. Even if your new wheels fit the axle hub flange properly, there's still the matter of stamina. The inertial load may place excess stress on your Jeep's OE wheel studs and nuts.

Jeep trucks have used 7/16", 1/2", 9/16" and 5/8" wheel studs. 7/16" studs, designed for six-stud wheel applications, emerged in 1974. The most common Jeep stud size is 1/2", found on light GVWR rated trucks, CJ's, Wranglers and Cherokees. 3/4-ton and one-ton trucks use 9/16" and 5/8" wheel studs.

Before mounting a set of monster size alloy wheels and big tires, consider the OE wheel stud size. Consult your wheel and tire manufacturers guidelines for recommendations. For safety sake, your tires and wheels may demand an upgrade in stud diameter or length.

Be sure to tighten the wheel nuts securely. Use a torque wrench to prevent under- or over-tightening. Over-torquing is a common cause of wheel damage and stud breakage. Jeep and wheel manufacturers rec-

---

The Tire Glossary

Bias (Diagonal) Ply—Before radial tires, all trucks rode on bias ply tires. Bias plies run in a diagonal direction to the tire centerline. Plies cross in an "X" pattern, making a very strong but stiff tire. Today's Jeep owners demand the better ride and handling of radial ply designs.

Load Carrying Capacity—All highway-legal tires have load capacity ratings (A, B, C, etc.), reflecting tire size and design. Inflation pressure, however, affects a tire's load capacity. Lower pressures decrease load carrying capacity.

Maximum Inflation—This is a tire's air pressure limit, which influences load carrying capacity. A tire with a load range 'E' and a maximum inflation pressure of 80 PSI may have a 3000 pound rating. This means that the tire can safely support 3000 pounds only at 80 PSI inflation. As pressure drops, so does the tire's carrying capacity. Know your tires' load capacity at various tire pressures.

Ply Rating—Plies are supporting layers of synthetic cord and/or steel built into a tire casing. These layers or belts mold within the tire's rubber. Ply ratings for big radial tires can get confusing. Load range C tires qualify for a traditional 6-ply rating. A closer look, however, may reveal a four-ply tread and two-ply sidewall. Plies also vary in thickness and strength, so evaluate a tire by its load rating, the ply materials and overall construction.

Rear- or Back-spacing—To clear vital brake and steering parts, a wheel rim needs a certain amount of back-spacing. Measure back-spacing between the wheel mounting surface and the back edge of the rim (using a straight-edge across the wheel rim flange). Your Jeep requires a certain amount of wheel back-spacing. Total rim width and back-spacing determine the amount and type of wheel offset.

PSI—Pounds per Square Inch refers to the air pressure in your tires. Adding air increases PSI, while "airing down" reduces pressure. Always maintain your tires at recommended inflation levels. If you drop pressure too low, your tubeless tire bead may unseat from the rim. Excess air pressure can damage the plies or destroy a bead.

Radial Ply—Belts, whether steel or synthetic cord, circle the tire at a perpendicular angle to its tread centerline. Radial belts flex, allowing the sidewalls to cushion the ride. Tread conforms to the road, providing a better grip. Most new tires, including 36" to 44" monster tires, are radials.

Rim Offset—Wheel rim offset determines track width and affects tire clearance. Rarely is a wheel's mounting surface aligned with the centerline of the tire. When OEM rims place the wheel's mounting surface outboard of the tire centerline, this is called "positive offset." Aftermarket wide wheels typically place the wheel mounting face inboard of the tire centerline, and this is "negative offset." Too much negative offset impacts steering geometry and causes stress to wheel bearings, spindles, axle shafts and steering components.

Rim Width—Every tire has a rim width requirement. We measure rim width between the inside flanges where the tire beads seat. Rim width is crucial to safety. Sidewall and tread shape, the bead angle and even the vehicle's handling depend on rims that correctly match the tires.

Speed Rating—Although most trucks with big tires stay within posted speed limits, speed ratings also indicate a tire's margin of safety. Letter symbols represent maximum speed: 'S' to 112 mph; 'T' to 118 mph; 'H' to 130 mph; 'V' to 149 mph; and 'Z' over 149 mph. Take heed.

Compensating for the Unbalanced Hub, Rotor or Drum

If you know one wheel hub and brake drum or rotor is out of balance, you can balance all wheels/tires off the truck. Now, install a balanced wheel/tire at the unbalanced hub/drum/rotor, and balance the assembly on the truck. Make note of where and how much weight the wheel/tire takes during the on-the-truck balance job.

Mark/paint the hub/drum/rotor in the place where you added extra weight. Each time a wheel/tire rotates to this hub/drum/rotor location, extra weight (the same as the first time around) can be added at the same wheel position as you added weight to the first wheel/tire.

> NOTE—
>
> An alternative is to mark/paint a wheel stud tip near the first wheel's valve stem hole. You can then mount any wheel at this location with its valve stem in this position and place the extra weight at the same place on the wheel rim as you did with the original wheel/tire assembly.

When moving tires away from this unbalanced hub/drum/rotor, simply remove the extra weight before installing the wheel/tire at its next rotation position. In this way, you do not need to re-balance on the truck each time you rotate tires to the hub/rotor or drum with imbalance.

ommend specific torque settings. (Consult your Jeep workshop manual or owners handbook for specs.)

Factory wheel nut torque settings take load, braking, vehicle weight and stud diameter into account. For safety sake, use a torque wrench whenever possible to verify the torque setting. Always tighten Jeep wheel nuts gradually and in "cross pattern." This prevents distortion of the rim or damage to nut seats.

> WARNING—
>
> Even if your studs have the correct diameter, the use of aftermarket wheels with thicker mounting flanges may require longer wheel studs. Always make certain that wheel studs reach sufficiently through the wheel mounting flanges.

Choose a Safe Wheel

Big tires increase unsprung mass, raise load capacities and present special mounting concerns. Many OE and aftermarket wheels cannot match the big tire loads. Mickey Thompson/Alcoa and Clement Composite wheels address big tire requirements.

Fig. 19-22. *Many aftermarket wheels will "fit" your Jeep. Mopar's Jeep Accessories wheels, however, fit exactly to OEM standards. Note that the wheel center hole matches the axle flange. This rim rides on true center and does not depend solely upon the wheel studs for centering. Safety tests of Mopar wheels meet rigid Chrysler and federal safety standards.*

Other wheel suppliers, including Chrysler's Mopar/Jeep Accessories (OEM replacement sizes only), American Racing Equipment, Golden Wheel Corporation and Ultra Wheel, cover a cross-section of user needs. Before selecting your wheels, make sure that the load rating and warranty will satisfy your usage and demands.

Sources for BIG Specialty Tires

For most Jeep four-wheelers, tires built by major tire companies like Goodyear, B.F. Goodrich, General Tire, Michelin, Yokohama or Bridgestone provide excellent selection and designs for four-wheeling. When your plans lean toward the extraordinary, however, several specialty manufacturers produce 36"–44" monster tires.

> CAUTION—
>
> When shopping for your Jeep's tires, look closely at construction, ply ratings and the load capacity—not just diameter and price. Consider each of the safety hazards associated with grossly oversized wheels and tires before making such a choice.

> WARNING—
>
> Many chassis lifts create the need for longer brake hoses at wheels or frame-to-axle. Most aftermarket lift kits address this issue, but you should check brake hose fitup closely to ensure that the hoses and pipes will not be stressed or damaged. Check each hose's movement over the full range of suspension travel. Turn the front wheels full left-to-right and make certain each hose does not interfere with the wheel, tire or chassis.

Interco's "Swamper" Tires: The original 78-series Swamper tire has been around for over two decades. Originally a 6- or 8-ply bias ply tire, Swamper offers a popular tread pattern. Interco also builds grossly oversize tires, including the Super Swamper TSL 36"x12.50-15LT through 18.5/44-15 sizes and a 18.5/44-16.5 tire. These heavy duty bias ply tires with massive lugs and self-cleaning ability meet on- and off-pavement demands for a Jeep with a very stout, heavily modified chassis and an appetite for massive unsprung wheel/tire weight and huge rubber.

Super Swamper Radial/TSL tires come in LT315/85R15, 38x15.50R15 and 38x15.50R16.5LT sizes. These are smoother riding, low noise level big-

Fig. 19-23. *The B.F. Goodrich Baja T/A tire (right), developed through desert racing tests, is an excellent off-pavement performer. Hard compound makes a harsher ride, but sidewall stamina is unexcelled in rocky terrain. Note: I do not recommend this tire for highway use.*

Fig. 19-24. *Interco's Swamper series tires make a big impression! The tire has a strong following among 4x4 competitors, recreationalists and show truck users. Traction gains are obvious.*

gies with a six-ply rating. If noise, handling and ride are top priorities, consider these tires. For the Rubicon and other rocky terrain, Super Swamper TSL/SX features 36x12.50-15 and 16.5 sizes, rated six ply with a nylon bias body and steel belt reinforcement under the tread. Sidewall lugs protect and add extra traction in ruts and rocks.

Gateway Buckshot and Gumbo Mudders: Campfire talk has the Buckshot Radial Mudder pegged as the hot setup for tall, narrow traction. The QR78-15LT and QR78-16 varieties fit the 36" big tire category, yet they still fit a 7JJx15 or 6.5Hx16 rim. These are tubeless, 6-ply rated tires with a polyester and steel belt cord. Stiff bead areas and provision for ice studs make the Buckshot a versatile choice, without the need for exotic wheels.

Also available from Gateway are the Buckshot Wide Mudder, Buckshot Metric Radial Mudder and the famed Gumbo Monster Mudders. Gumbo Monster series tires fit the big tire category with easy. These tires begin at 36-inch diameter and grow to 43.6" giants for 15" or 16.5" rims. Tread widths for the 6-ply rated tires range from 10.4" to 14.1", which requires wide rims. For the radial user, the Gumbo Monster Radial Mudder is available in 36"–38" sizes with a width of 10.4" to 10.7" (cross-sections 14.2" to 15.2"). These radials require 10x15 or 9.75x16.5 rims.

Mickey Thompson Tires/Alcoa Wheels: Mickey Thompson and off-road desert racing go back to the beginning. Mickey Thompson's Baja-Belted polyester and fiberglass belt tires offer an aggressive tread pattern with a soft ride, long wear and Sidebiters for extra traction. The Tall Baja-Belted tire line offers several big tire sizes, including 15/39 and 18/39 for 15" and 16.5" rims.

Mickey Thompson has joined with Alcoa Aluminum to produce the M/T Alcoa Aluminum Wheel. Most wheel manufacturers void their warranties when you mount really big tires. Alcoa has engineered these wheels of one-piece forged aircraft aluminum, with a non-porous and leak proof surface. Polished and machined for a 0.020" maximum runout, these wheels have a 2600 or 3000 pound load rating per wheel—depending upon application. Available in 15" x 10", 12" or 14" width (3000 lbs. rated) and 8" width (2600 lbs. rated), these wheels are available in popular 5- and 6-stud truck patterns.

Dick Cepek Tires: Dick Cepek is a household name among Jeep recreationalists. A full line of vehicle and outdoor equipment makes Cepek a one-stop shopping center for Jeep four-wheelers. When buyers want tires, Dick Cepek has a full line to match every imaginable need.

Fig. 19-25. *M/T Alcoa aluminum wheels carry a rating for big tires. Load capacity to 3000 lbs. and 8", 10", 12" and 14" widths meet a range of requirements and fitups.*

Fig. 19-26. *The Dick Cepek Radial F-C offers the ride and handling benefits of a radial tire. Radial tires satisfy users who do most of their driving on the highway but still need superior traction off-pavement.*

Radial F-C/Fun Country tires aim at mileage. As a steel belted flotation tire, these tires run quietly, yet the tread design offers self-cleaning. These are legitimate mud and snow tires, much like the popular Fun Country

nylon bias-ply design. Dick Cepek's Mud Country I tires can be used for snow plowing or logging trails, while Mud Country II boasts better flotation characteristics.

Cepek has recently introduced a Super Wide Radial F-C tire available to 38" diameter. These tires concentrate on width, providing all around performance in mud, snow, sand, rock and on the highway. Quietness, an aggressive tread design, steel belts for a 50,000 mile limited warranty and tread at least 4" wider than competitor's tires distinguish the Super Wide Radial F-C.

Denman Tire's Ground Hawg: Denman's line of big tires has a huge following with the show truck crowd. The roguish "Ground Hawg" is a beefy tire hell-bent on maximum traction. For a flexible tread and superior traction, Denman delivers radial benefits with a deep, self-cleaning tread design. The biggest Ground Hawg is 18.5/44x16.5 inches.

Goodyear—One Big Wrangler RT: Goodyear Tire and Rubber Company is the only major tire producer to offer tires in the really big category. The Wrangler RT-GC0530 provides a rugged, multipurpose tread design and is available in 36-12.50-16.5 size only. Hummer drivers will recognize this design, as Goodyear developed the tire for HUMVEE military use.

> NOTE —
> A Wrangler MT 37x12.50R16.5LT load range D tire is also available through Goodyear retailers. Also little known, the highly versatile Wrangler GS-A has a listing in the 37x12.50R16.5LT, load range D category.

Although Goodyear offers a complete line of Wrangler light truck radial tires (see sidebar), the RT was the first entry in the 36" or larger light truck market. If you're looking for big tires, these load range "C" biggies (Goodyear's product code No. 309-552-321) and the even stouter 37" diameter Wrangler MT and GS-A tires may meet your needs. Goodyear builds quality tires and offers a widespread, service-oriented authorized dealership network.

5. Brake System Upgrades

Years ago, one cure for the weak 9" Jeep brakes was to retrofit an in-line Bendix Hydrovac booster (common to older medium duty trucks with hydraulic brakes). This fix applies more pressure to the hydraulic cylinders and brake shoes, raising the likelihood of brake fade or rupturing a fluid seal. If your early Jeep has 9" brakes and an add-on vacuum booster, find a safer alternative.

One popular method for increasing brake performance on an early CJ Jeep 4x4 is a conversion to 11"x2" drum brakes. Aftermarket kits, patterned after the '72-up AMC/CJ factory design, provide larger wheel cylinders, brake drums, backing plates, brake shoes and all necessary installation hardware. Factory (OEM) 11" brakes on '72 to early-'77 CJs worked very well, a significant improvement over Willys/Kaiser-era CJs.

Of course, there is now the disc brake option. Warn Industries' offers Jeep full-floating rear axle conversion kits and matching front axle hub conversion for upgrading the manual locking hub design to internal spline type. Here is also a platform for a disc brake conversion. Disc brake caliper brackets can accompany these Warn parts. Consider the four-wheel disc brake alternative or disc front brakes with large drum rear brakes.

WARNING—
• Changing to disc brakes on an early Jeep model requires upgrading the hydraulic master cylinder and installing a proportioning valve to balance the front-to-rear braking. A dual master cylinder and manual proportioning valve are the customary approaches. Always make certain that the master cylinder provides sufficient fluid displacement to safely activate disc brake calipers or larger drum brake wheel cylinders.

• Modifying the braking system may require larger (inside diameter) brake hoses and pipes. Be certain that the master cylinder, brake piping and hoses match the fluid demands of the new disc calipers or drum brake wheel cylinders. Check hydraulic system fitup closely to assure that the hoses and pipes will not be stressed or damaged. Check each brake hoses's movement over the full range of suspension travel. Turn the front wheels full left-to-right and make certain each hose does not interfere with the wheel, tire, or chassis. Always use approved fittings, brake hoses and double-flared brake pipe specified for brake useage.

• Use extreme caution when testing and adjusting a brake proportioning valve. Start by backing the rear brake apply pressure off to avoid rear brake lockup and risk of spinning your Jeep around (or rolling the vehicle over) while testing the proportioning valve settings. Always follow the manufacturer's guidelines when installing and testing an aftermarket manual proportioning valve.

Hydraulic Brake System Improvements

Before 1967, most brake system manufacturers recommended annual flushing and rebuilding of all hydraulic brake cylinders. Some vehicles tolerate years of neglect without a brake system flush or rubber cup/seal replacement. Off-pavement vehicles, however, are far more susceptible to fluid contamination than other vehicles. This is especially true of early Jeep models with master cylinders mounted beneath the floorboard.

Most post-'66 Jeep tandem master cylinders have air bellows in the cap gasket. The gasket completely seals the system and eliminates the need for a master cylinder vent to atmosphere. Problems from moisture, debris, dust and corrosives occur far less often with 1967 and newer Jeep brake systems.

One cure for the early military/CJ brake problems is to custom fit a 1967 or newer tandem master cylinder system, including pedal linkage and hydraulic hardware. Such a retrofit could also include a hydraulic clutch master cylinder (both cylinders mounted on the firewall), a hydraulic clutch slave cylinder with linkage and a set of suspended brake and clutch pedals. A vacuum brake booster with 11" drum brake, disc/drum or a four-wheel disc brake conversion could complete the package.

WARNING—
On any brake conversion, make certain that the master cylinder bore and brake pipe sizes can move enough fluid to safely operate the brakes. Always maintain proper front-to-rear brake proportioning and balance. Find a safe place for hard braking tests to determine whether the front-to-rear brake balance ("proportioning") is correct.

CAUTION —
When installing a brake system upgrade kit, your Jeep may require additional hydraulic system components to meet the demands of larger wheel cylinders/brake shoes or disc brake calipers/rotors. Adequate master cylinder fluid displacement and proper hydraulic proportioning between the front and rear braking systems are crucial to your safety.

NOTE—
When converting to 11-inch drum brakes on 1967–71 CJ Jeeps with dual braking systems, front-to-rear brake imbalance can often be remedied by installing a proportioning valve for an AMC-era CJ with factory 11" drum front brakes. (Adjustable proportioning valves are also available through aftermarket high performance sources.) Test brakes in a safe and prudent manner.

Chapter 20

Epilogue

Dawn was still several hours away. The F-head four started confidently, idling steadily with the hand choke pulled out halfway. In minutes, the temperature gauge crept slowly past the cold line, and the engine whined as I backed out the driveway. Chilling fall air swept in gusts from the Sierras. Opening day of deer season, a tapestry of stars filled the sky above Carson Valley. We'd hunt Genoa Peak, hiking our way down toward the valley.

The Jeep's engine droned as the heater streamed warm air toward our Red Wing boots. Instinctively, Nathan and I hunched forward, away from the stiff vinyl seats. As the canvas-covered cab began to thaw, our conversation picked up. In minutes, the straight, narrow lane toward the Sierras gave way to Foothill Road. Two quick turns and Kingsbury Grade, known locally as the Pony Express Trail, came into view.

Steady light from the Jeep's tall headlamps skirted the stark pine trees. The steep, thinly paved switchbacks now narrowed to less than two car widths, and I worked the T98A four-speed, shifting between third and second gear. Far below, on the moonlit valley floor, miles of frosted alfalfa stubble glistened.

Just over the pine-crested summit, near 8,000 feet, a sharp right turn put us on the backside of Genoa Peak, heading up a narrow dirt road that in daylight would have furnished a view of Lake Tahoe. Ponderosa pine and sagebrush reflected the Jeep's round 12-volt headlights, their ghostly white light piercing the waning night.

As the road became rocky, I stopped and locked the front hubs. Minutes later, my right hand gripped the 4WD lever, and I backed off the throttle, nudging the stick. The front axle came to life, and the steering took a firm set. Ahead, granite rock and gravel became the roadbed, and the trail squeezed narrowly through thick pine trees. Abruptly, a loose, rocky stretch angled steeply up the mountain's face.

I stopped the Jeep and carefully moved the transfer case lever to Low Range. As the gearshift slid into compound first gear, I lifted the clutch pedal slowly. The CJ inched forward.

Second gear barely increased the truck's speed, as the Jeep's 67:1 crawl ratio worked its magic. My heart pounded, and I glanced quickly at my pal, Nathan. His eyes were wide, staring straight ahead. Shadows of tree branches and a starry black sky filled the windshield.

Fuel in the tank beneath the seat sloshed, then washed against the rear of the metal cell. The F-head engine's whine reached a higher, yet reassuringly steady pitch, cutting the silence. The Jeep climbed willingly up the mountain, its 7.00x15 Goodyear Suburbanite tires pawing patiently at decomposed granite and loose shale.

After running on straight adrenaline for what must have been several minutes, I steered the Jeep onto a flat bench. Our stomachs settled as the truck came to a halt atop a wide granite bluff.

Black sky filled the rear view mirror. Eastward, through the base of the windshield glass, townsfolk at Gardnerville and Minden slept peacefully. Twenty miles away, above the juniper covered peaks of the Pine Nut Range, the sky streaked rose and purple as the temperature dipped below freezing. A dawn wind's chill factor caused the exhaust system to crackle, and day broke....

Nathan and I were just sixteen years old that dawn. Since 1965, I have driven perhaps a hundred thousand miles on dirt roads and trails. Despite travels through British Columbia, the Yukon, Alaska, Ontario and each of the eleven Western States, the image of that near-new Spruce Green '64 CJ-5, framed against the pine forest of the Sierra Nevada Mountains southeast of Lake Tahoe, remains vivid today....Surely, your Jeep truck will provide such moments, places beyond time, where a starlit night plays host to the fresh dawn.

In The Rubicon

Spanning just over twenty miles, the Rubicon Trail has drawn thousands of Jeep enthusiasts. Scenic Lake Tahoe lies to the east, and the route runs adjacent to the Desolation Wilderness Area. Southwest of the region, Placerville and Georgetown serve as traditional staging areas. Popularized by the Jeepers Jamboree,

Rubicon Jeep Jamboree and a slew of organized four-wheel drive odysseys, the Rubicon remains ever rugged and a haunting challenge.

Pine, granite and pristine lakes best describe the area. For horse packers and hikers, the Pacific Crest Trail cuts off the easternmost corner of the Wilderness, while numerous trails of the Eldorado National Forest lace the lakes and valleys of this high country. Peaks rise to over 9,000 feet. Icy streams and springs feed the pocket lakes. Meadow grass and flowers grow deep in late spring and early summer, retreating in early fall beneath a mantle of snow. Summer is short for mosquitoes and humans alike. Even the lower reaches lie above 6,000 feet, quickly yielding to the seasons and chilling winds of October.

In July of 1988, I returned to the Rubicon. My first trip, twenty-one years earlier, was still sharp in my memory. July is a month of life and activity in the dense forests of the Rubicon. The Jamboree and its lively procession of Jeep 4x4s was still weeks ahead. Deer, chipmunks and early visitors could still relax in the quietude of Rubicon Springs. Although a lax winter left the reservoirs menacingly low, late patches of snow dotted north-facing slopes of the higher peaks.

Fig. 20-1. *On trail, just past Wentworth Springs, everyone's rolling fine. It's 4:15 in the afternoon.*

More Fun In Numbers

This was a good time to travel the Rubicon Trail. I accepted an invitation from Rollie Scarselli, an old friend and member of the Washoe County Search and Rescue Team. The plan called for our group to rendezvous at Ice House, northeast of Placerville and past Riverton, then head up the steep Ice House Road. The Reno, Nevada-based faction would come through Carson City, then drive west past Lake Tahoe and down U.S. Highway 50 to Riverton.

We arrived within twenty minutes of each other. The Search and Rescue rigs, all Jeep models in various

forms, parked tightly in line with camping gear stacked neatly in open cargo bays. Our intent was a five day trip, with one day assigned for accessing the trailhead, two days on trail, plus two "R & R" days at Rubicon Springs. Overall, the rigs looked hardy and well-stocked, although suspicions about a bad alternator had one member concerned.

Topping fuel tanks at the Ice House Shell pumps, we headed up the last few miles of steep paved road. At the Gerle Creek/Wentworth Springs fork, the smooth asphalt ended. Dipping through the shallow creek, the momentary tire quenching gave way to a dusty stretch of silt in the pine forest. Civilization in our rearview mirrors, the trail began to deteriorate. Its surface soon fell to patches of rock, well trafficked ruts and crawl-pace bumps.

Loon Lake Road was an alternate route. Too easy, we concluded. After all, a Rubicon Run demands commitment. Rather than drive the paved road to Loon Lake, followed by a vague path below the spillway to a trail junction just past Wentworth Springs, we chose the direct assault of a rockier trail. Passing through Wentworth Springs at 4:30 in the afternoon, Buck Island Lake became our campsite goal.

Travail On The Trail

An itinerary makes good sense—everywhere except a Rubicon run. The Little Sluice Box and five miles separated us from Buck Island Lake. We felt there was enough daylight to attempt the run despite stretches where one mile per hour would be the average speed. If the first night's camp were at the lake, Friday would easily see us into the Rubicon Springs.

A bit past Wentworth Springs, the roadbed turned into a rock pile, the kind so common to the Rubicon. The spillway of Loon Lake, approximately 800 yards away, was within sight. Motorhomes could easily cruise to the dam on a graded road.

We stopped and locked hubs, shifted to low range and drew on our off-pavement savvy. The trail's camber shifted, granite boulders replaced soil, and just ahead, an ominous crevice cleaved through a stretch of huge rocks. That was our "road!"

We stopped and carefully plotted the approach. 18" rocks made steps up the left side of the trail. A bold granite wall tilted 45 degrees to the right, narrowing our access as we approached a precarious, angular face. Two Jeep models, a CJ-5 and CJ-2A, went through. I followed their line. Traction was awkward but my pass was uneventful.

Rollie came next, driving his 350 Chevy V-8 powered '70 Jeepster. The truck has a wonderful early Muncie SM420 truck transmission with a "granny low." Rollie, a top notch four-wheeler, built his Jeep-ster with enough horsepower to easily tackle the verti-cal walls along the Rubicon Trail. At a 101" wheelbase, however, the Jeepster is longer than all CJ models ex-cept the CJ-6 and Scrambler (CJ-8). Without rear posi-traction, the truck railed stubbornly against this steep, loose rock face.

Rollie postured his Jeepster for the assault. Easily climbing the rocks, the truck began clawing against the right-sloping granite boulder. Inhibited by the wheel-base length, the chassis resisted the tight swing to the right. With the right front wheel precariously clutch-ing the rock's surface, the opposite tire left the ground.

Hanging three feet in the air, the left front wheel received torque. A dangerous lurching began as the rear axle grappled in the rocks. The excessive angle complicated the maneuver. Several jolts took place be-fore the inevitable. A sickening "snap," metallic and profound, echoed through the forest.

"Oh," one of the onlookers exclaimed, "Rollie's wheel has come loose." We should have been so lucky. The Jeepster's fate was far worse.

A somewhat common early Jeep trait reared itself. The right spindle's six bolts had ripped cleanly from the threaded holes in the steering knuckle. Brake fluid puked down the side of the huge granite rock, and grease oozed from the naked steering joint.

One For All

Traveling as a group, several rigs waited behind the broken Jeepster. Rumor had it that a Jeep club from Sacramento was due soon, even at this late hour. A temporary repair was necessary. The goal: Move the truck out of the rock chasm and onto higher, flat ground beside the trail.

Here, just a few hours off-pavement, was the Ru-bicon, a place where mechanical risk runs high and ob-stacles go on forever. Parts outlets seem light years away, and the best mechanical skills go only so far without shop tools and a parts inventory. Time flies, and thin air weighs heavily on a flatlander's lungs.

Guessing which spare parts to carry, even for a search and rescue organization, isn't easy. Our trailers, full of hardware, certainly didn't hold a right-side steering knuckle for a Spicer 27 front axle—and an-other knuckle was the only cure!

Seven hours later, by sheer effort, the front end had a very temporary fix, and Rollie started his engine. Tied together with under-capacity hardware, the front end stood shakily on the rock. Realizing the risk, Rol-lie wisely shut off the engine. A recovery strap and winch cable replaced the 350 V-8's power. Gradually, the truck inched forward. The spindle held, staying to-

Fig. 20-2. *Here's the place for a Hi-Lift jack and a bunch of friends. Once lifted safely, the Jeepster's plight be-came apparent.*

gether as the truck leveled onto the nearby flat.

A closer look with several flashlights revealed the brevity of the fix. Already, the temporary bolts showed strain, and the spindle had begun to spread once more from the steering knuckle. A decision followed. We'd camp here for the night, just out of the trail. Early in the morning, we'd organize a parts run back to Placerville.

Dinner plans long lost, the group shared cold cuts and aged Kentucky Fried Chicken. Coolers and camp-boxes full of food lay buried in the rigs. Exhaustion en-croached, and even the tents stayed packed. We pitted our ribs and hips against the granite floor of the Rubi-con, dropping hastily to sleep beneath the Milky Way and towering Jarrett and Guide Peaks.

The quarter moon rose just before dawn, a pho-tographer's dream. I shot two-thirds of a roll as my son, Jacob, and the rest of the group stayed fast asleep. The pine trees and tiers of granite, spreading into the distance, picked up rose-colored dawn light as Rollie, Ken, and my son woke. In the light breeze and high-thirties air temperature, we prepared for a run into Placerville. The rest of our weary travelers hid deep in their bedrolls.

After taking a two-hour "shortcut" to the Loon Lake spillway, we reached the pavement. By ten forty-five, we arrived at Earl Warden Auto Repair. In the town of Placerville, four-wheeling and the Warden family are synonyms. Earl had by then retired from ga-rage work, concentrating his energy on used Jeep and Land Cruiser parts sales, but his son, Danny, ran the shop, and he immediately came to our aid.

"Yeah, typical Model 27 spindle and steering knuckle," Danny noted. "The 3/8" bolts pull from the threads....I think we've got a used knuckle. Can you wait till one o'clock?"

Two of our rigs had come to town. Five of us looked at each other and then at Danny. His shop swarmed with people, but he sensed our frustration.

"I'll go check now," he said, smiling as he grabbed the defective piece. An hour later, Danny had secured a right side steering knuckle from a mid-'Sixties Gladiator, a set of new knuckle seals and enough grease to service the knuckle and wheel bearings. We ran around town, finding the proper length 3/8" Grade-8 SAE threaded bolts and some cleaning solvent.

At four o'clock, we hit camp. The rough road that had beaten the Scarselli's Jeepster into submission was behind us, and a thorough repair lay ahead. By 6:30, as a low sun cast long shadows across the granite mountain faces, we'd fixed the Jeepster—properly. Now, the Rubicon Trail beckoned, and our tight line of 4x4s aimed for Buck Island Lake.

Two Sluice Boxes and Unquarried Rock

It was Friday night, 24 hours later than our original schedule. Talk in Placerville confirmed that the Dirty Dozen 4x4 gang had planned their midnight run through the Rubicon for this evening. Pressed to set up at Buck Island Lake before that lively group arrived, we stepped up our pace.

With a few utility trailers in tow (more like dragging an anchor through the rocky stretches!), the go-

Fig. 20-3. *At 6 p.m. Friday, we pulled back onto the trail. Buck Island Lake was the goal.*

ing went slowly in the rough stuff. The Mud Lake region told us we were close to the Little Sluice Box, as a setting sun now blackened the backside of rocks and denser reaches of the forest. Undaunted and determined to make camp at Buck Island Lake, we pitted our 4x4s against the first sluice box.

Here, the rocks look like grotesque steps. Driving becomes an abstraction. No longer does any confusion exist, like which route to choose or how to straddle a boulder. The approach gets very simple: Conserve the truck. One route lies ahead, and it's first gear, low range only. Steep, treacherously loose, and constantly shifting, the road transforms itself between vehicles.

Light throttle succeeds, tire spin fails. Torque control, careful aim and preservation of steering components takes precedence. Knowing the strength of our brawny Saginaw power steering units, we instinctively lightened our grips. Constant feel for each rock's counterforce could prevent a perilous breakdown.

As the sun dipped, turning the sky dark purple, our jarred trucks went through their last contortions. Having mastered the twisting rock climbs, we now faced the challenge of night driving. A broad hillside ahead harbored no road markings at all, but the team's knowledge from years of wheeling this trail led us on. Solid granite blackened, and our headlights skittered across rocks, trees and brush.

Moments later, the camp below the spillway came into view. Here, with room for tents and small campfires, we landed. A nine-o'clock dinner, the quick pitching of our sleeping gear, and everyone went to bed.

Some Normalcy Along the Trail

When the sound sleepers finally rose at 7:30, breakfast sizzled at each campsite. Once past the domestic chores, we gathered all trash and packed the trucks. Murmurs about the Big Sluice Box began as the staccato of four-, six- and eight-cylinder engines harmonized in the cool morning air. Buck Island Lake, a pristine body of trout-inhabited water, made a sweet sight. One at a time, the 4x4s crawled carefully over the sill of the spillway and back onto the trail.

As the trip to the Rubicon Springs involved several nasty rock runs and tight, twisty spring stretchers, we began to catch up with some Dirty Dozen members who had passed us during the night. Bashing through rock at night had taken its toll. Some rigs stood with their hoods open. Others perched on logs and high rocks. Fortunately, the camaraderie and resourcefulness of that group resolved even the more dire situations.

We crept down the Big Sluice Box, through the saw-toothed rocks, and over the gnarled trail that led, finally, to the Springs. With lack of sleep, hours of white ing both our triumph over the trail and a tolerance for the chilling, emerald green water.

The worst was behind us. Cadillac Hill, with its notorious "V", held no great threat for the moment. Days later, a few hours of careful climbing, straining gears and piling rocks in strategic places would bring us to the plateau.

There, Miller Meadows and Miller Lake lie just down the road. The last glimpse of panoramic peaks, towering over the grandeur of the Desolation Wilderness Area, soon vanishes from view. The deep blue waters of Lake Tahoe appear an hour later.

Indelible Memories

Where Highway 89 traffic intersects the Miller Lake or Barrett Pass junctions, civilization returns. Some say this is the trail's end. Others suggest that the Rubicon lives on, deep within the psyche.

"Once through," they say, "you'll never forget the Rubicon!" I'd surely agree that the majesty of the Desolation Wilderness makes a lasting imprint. For hikers, horseback riders and four-wheelers, the far reaches of the Rubicon stir our primordial senses. At the edge of this vast, timbered lake country, carved against rugged granite slopes, winds a trail of long memories.

Fig. 20-4. *Here, the edge of Buck Island Lake became the road. The Buck Island Lake to Rubicon Springs leg is pure hell. Rock lurks everywhere and drivers meet their greatest challenge. The Big Sluice box and saw-toothed rocks signal the approach to the Rubicon River.*

knuckled driving and the 7,000-foot elevation affecting each of us, the trail's end came none too soon.

At the Rubicon Springs, we each took time to assess our rigs. Once we felt confident that the squeaking springs would cool down and survive, tents and camping gear emptied from the trailers. Champagne for Saturday evening's annual dinner went into a gunny sack, sealed and dropped into the cold stream. Bathing suit clad bodies followed, with whoops and hollers declar-

Fig. 20-5. *Crossing the Rubicon! Here is the the reward, a feeling of accomplishment that each trail savvy four-wheeler can appreciate. Suddenly, it's worth the effort.*

Sources

Axle, Transfer Case and Transmission Service

M.I.T.
1112 Pioneer Way
El Cajon, California 92020
619-579-7727
(Geartrain, axle, transmission rebuilding; custom gearbox and axle retrofits; shortened transfer case output kits)

Holbrook Specialties/4 Wheel Drive Center
115 E. Arlington
Gladstone, Oregon 97027
503-655-4747
(Geartrain, axle and transmission rebuilding)

Manual Clutch and Automatic Transmission

Art Carr Performance Products
14305 Mt. McClellan Street
Reno, Nevada 89506
702-677-6610
(Performance and retrofit automatic transmissions; transmission electronic computer controls)

B&M Automotive
9142 Independence Ave.
Chatsworth, CA 91311
818-882-6422
(High performance automatic transmission kits)

Midway/Centerforce Clutches
2266 Crosswind Drive
Prescott, AZ 86301
520-771-8422
(Performance replacement and retrofit manual clutch assemblies; billet steel flywheels)

Engine/Transmission Conversion Kits

Advance Adapters
P.O. Box 247
Paso Robles, CA 93447
805-238-7000
(Transmission/transfer case adapters; Atlas II transfer case, Saturn overdrive and Orbitor drop box; source for NV4500 and other transmissions)

Novak Enterprises
13321-A Alondra Blvd.
Santa Fe Springs, CA 90670
562-921-3202
(Noted for engine/transmission and transfer case adapters)

Electrical

Wrangler NW Power Products
4444 S.E. 27th Avenue
Portland, OR 97202
503-235-1038
(High output alternators and battery management systems; quality electrical components)

Premier Power Welder/Pull-Pal
P.O. Box 639
Carbondale, CO 81623
970-963-8875
(High output alternators and on-board welder/electrical power sources)

Centech Wiring
7 Colonial Drive
Perkiomenville, PA 18074
610-287-5730
(Replacement wiring kits; rebuilt steering columns and power steering gears)

Painless Wiring
9505 Santa Paula
Ft. Worth, TX 76116
817-244-6898
(Chassis wiring harnesses patterned after OEM design; multiplex chassis wiring harnesses)

Harnesses Unlimited
Box 435
Wayne, PA 19087
610-688-3998
(Reproduction wiring harnesses for authentic restoration of early Jeep trucks)

Engine

Clifford Performance Products
2330 Pomona-Rincon Road
Corona, CA 91720
909-734-3310
(Specializes in high performance components for in-line sixes and four-cylinder engines)

Dyers Machine Service, Inc.
7665 W. 63rd Street
Summit, IL 60501
312-496-8100
(Racing superchargers)

Edelbrock
2700 California St.
Torrance, CA 90509
310-781-2222
(Performance manifolds, camshafts, carburetors; A/F meters; exhaust systems and shock absorbers)

Flex-A-Lite Fans
P.O. Box 9037
Tacoma, WA 98409
206-475-5772
(Engine cooling products)

Jacobs Electronics
500 N. Baird St.
Midland, TX 79701
915-685-3345
(Ignition specialty items)

K&N Engineering
P.O. Box 1329
Riverside, CA 92502
909-684-9762
(Performance air and oil filtration products; A/F meters)

Mopar Performance/Jeep Accessories
See your Jeep dealer or Mopar Performance supplier.
("Factory engineered" performance components for AMC- and Mopar-design Jeep engines; a full line of high quality utility items, sound systems and appearance enhancements for later model Jeep vehicles)

MSD/Autotronic Controls Corp.
1490 Henry Brennan Drive
El Paso, TX 79936
915-857-5200
(Ignition performance products; emission legal ignition systems; A/F meters)

Competition Cams
3406 Democrat Road
Memphis, TN 38118
901-795-2400
('High Energy' grind camshafts for rock-crawling off-pavement use)

Speed-Pro Performance/Sealed Power
A Division of Federal Mogul: See your local dealer.
(OEM and high performance engine components)
Exterior Trim, Tops, Light Bars, Roll Cages and Seat Harnesses

Exterior Trim, Tops, Light Bars, Roll Cages and Seat Harnesses

Beachwood Canvas Works
P.O. Box 137H
Island Heights, NJ 08732
732-929-3168
(Restoration canvas, trim items, upholstery and drive-train pieces for the vintage models)

Bell Auto Racing
Route 136 East
Rantoul, IL 61866
217-893-9300
(Harnesses/safety equipment and helmets)

BesTop
2100 W. Midway Blvd.
Broomfield, CO 80020
303-465-1755
(Jeep tops and accessories)

Bushwhacker
9200 N. Decatur
Portland, OR 97203
503-283-4335
(Jeep body and custom trim parts)

Crown Automotive Sales Co.
Fax: 617-826-4097 or contact nearest dealer.
(1941-up replacement parts)

Filler Products
9017 San Fernando Rd.
Sun Valley, CA 91352
818-768-7770
(Racing safety equipment)

Grizzly/Mercury Tube
1802 Santo Domingo Ave.
Duarte, CA 91010
818-301-0226
(Steel tubing products)

Hobrecht Enterprises
15632 Commerce Lane
Huntington Beach, CA 92649
714-893-8561
(Roll cages/steel tubing products)

Kentrol
550 W. Pine Lake Road
North Lima, OH 44452
216-549-2235
(Stainless steel trim/body panels)

Schroth (See your local performance parts outlet)
(Safety harnesses/rally belts)

Smittybilt
2090 California Ave.
Corona, CA 91719
909-272-3176
(Roll cages/steel tubing products)

TRW (See your local performance parts outlet)
(Safety harnesses/equipment)

Free-Wheeling Front Hubs, Electric Winches

Warn Industries
12900 S.E. Capps Road
Clackamas, OR 97015-8903
503-722-3019
(Winches/supplier to Mopar/Jeep Accessories; Black Diamond suspension kits, full-floating axle conversion kits and wheel hubs; free-wheeling hubs; fender flares and accessories)

Ramsey Winch Company
1600 N. Garnett Road
Tulsa, OK 74116
918-438-2760
(Winches and winch accessories; supplier to Mopar/Jeep Accessories)

Superwinch
Winch Drive
Putnam, CT 06260
203-928-7787
(Winches and winch accessories; free-wheeling hubs)

HUB-A-LERT
4x4 Specialty Products
P.O. Box 813
Highland, CA 92346
(LED monitor for detecting front axle engagement)

Manuals and Books

The Willys and Jeep Corporation factory workshop manuals provide official information. Highly detailed, with all specifications, the factory workshop manual is your assurance of a professional-level repair.

Currently, official AMC/Jeep and Chrysler/Jeep Service Manuals are available for later CJ and newer Jeep trucks. Your local Jeep/Eagle dealer can provide manuals for CJs, J-trucks, full-size (Grand) Wagoneers and Cherokees, the compact XJ Cherokee/Comanche/Wagoneer, ZJ or WJ Grand Cherokee and Wrangler YJ or TJ models. Here you will find *first-generation*, detailed mechanical specifications for your vehicle.

> NOTE —
> Later Jeep models may require an engine, chassis, electrical, emissions, geartrain and/or body book. Read the catalog carefully. Make sure you get the manual(s) that cover your year and model Jeep truck.

For the early (194171) Jeep owner, Original Reproductions, P.O. Box 5161, Newport Beach, California 92662 reproduces Willys and Kaiser/Jeep Corporation factory manuals. These guides serve as an excellent reference for the early Jeep CJ, Station Wagon, Utility Pickup, Jeepster, Wagoneer or J-truck models. Equipped with such a manual, you could completely rebuild your early Jeep truck.

The Willys Club (719 Lehigh Street, Bowmanstown, PA 18030) publication, *Willys World*, caters to owners of Willys trademark vehicles, Jeep models through 1963 included.

For all Jeep model owners, the Jeep Registry, "An International Club Dedicated to Jeeps," publishes *Tracks*. The informative newsletter brings many Jeep enthusiasts and historical facts together. Jeep Registry, Inc., is a non-profit club and states clearly that "We receive *no* support from and are *not* affiliated with Chrysler [Jeep] Corporation." For information, contact The Jeep Registry, Inc., 172 Long Hill Road, Oakland, New Jersey, U.S.A. 07436-3113, phone 1-201-405-0480 or explore the website: http://members.aol.com/jeepreg1/ for details.

Additionally, four-wheel drive enthusiast magazines provide performance tips and review aftermarket Jeep accessories. A healthy aftermarket exists for Jeep performance parts and accessories.

Catalogs from Mopar/Jeep Accessories (available through your Jeep dealer) provide a standard for well-engineered accessories and upgrades. Advance Adapters and Novak Enterprises (engine and transmission conversion parts for Jeep trucks) can provide useful reference guides for Jeep geartrain components and modifications. Similarly, catalogs from 4WD Hardware, Dick Cepek, 4-Wheel Parts Wholesalers, Leon Rosser Jeep and other outlets serve as valuable information sources.

Book Sources:

Brian's 4WD Parts & Literature
260 Tyler Street
East Haven, CT 06512
203-469-4940
(Willys, Kaiser, AMC and Chrysler era books)

Classic Motorbooks
Osceola, WI 54020-0001
Fax: 294-4448/www.motorbooks.com
(Jeep-related books and workshop manuals)

Military Vehicles
12-H4 Indian Head
Morristown, NJ 07960
(Bi-monthly magazine covering military MB/GPW, MC/M38, MD/M38A1 and derivative models, M151 and civilian CJs)

Walter Miller
6710 Brooklawn Parkway
Syracuse, NY 13211
315-432-8282/www.autolit.com
(This large auto literature source likely covers each Jeep model ever built)

Maps And Travel Guides

A variety of map sources and atlas guides serve Jeep travelers. U.S. Forest Service and B.L.M. topographical maps remain my primary choices.

Specialty map sources include a series by Sidekick, which produces a range of maps on popular Western U.S. and Baja California four-wheel drive trails. A Sidekick Map details each region, including highlights of local sites, the area's history, minesites, ghost towns, directions from major highways, access costs, camping facilities and public agency offices in the area. Sidekick map/pamphlets are printed on high quality paper stock and include color pictures.

Sidekick
12188 Central Avenue, Suite 352
Chino, CA 91710
909-628-7227

Parts: General

Your Jeep is a popular vehicle, and parts availability seldom presents a problem. Currently, Jeep/Eagle dealers can provide many pieces for later AMC/Jeep models and even the last (Chrysler-built) full-size Grand Wagoneers. Dealers stock faster-moving replacement parts and routine service items for all Chrysler built Jeep trucks. Your dealer can order other items for Wranglers, the XJ, ZJ and WJ. Owners of 1941-86 Jeep models will find a variety of parts sources throughout North America.

Retail auto parts outlets can supply tune-up, powertrain and most chassis parts. NAPA provides excellent parts coverage for Jeep trucks. Quality filters and oil products are available from NAPA and other outlets.

For Jeep geartrain parts sources, Border Parts at Spring Valley, California, and M.I.T. at El Cajon, California, remain my top choices. 4WD Hardware, Inc., 4-Wheel Parts Wholesalers, Dick Cepek, and Reider Racing Enterprises also provide geartrain and axle pieces. Each of these outlets can provide OEM-style replacement parts or aftermarket performance components. Warn Industries offers full-floating rear axle conversion kits and upgrade (full-floating type) front wheel hub conversions for the CJ, YJ, TJ, XJ and ZJ models.

Jeep engine parts are readily available. From the earliest L-134 engine to the latest Chrysler/Jeep SMPI powerplant, Jeep replacement engine parts abound. Popular aftermarket suppliers, including TRW, Federal Mogul/Sealed Power, Dana Corporation, Perfect Circle, Hastings, Wolverine, Badger and Silv-O-Lite, offer Jeep engine parts. Mopar Performance continues to develop and offer "factory engineered" performance upgrades for AMC- and Mopar-design Jeep engines.

Parts: Rare, OEM and Restoration

4WD Hardware, Inc.
P.O. Box 57
44488 State Rte. 14
Columbiana OH 44408
330-482-4924
(Serves Jeep owners with popular accessories, performance parts and quality replacement parts; rugged fiberglass replacement bodies, trim, utility items and enhancements; knows what satisfies a loyal following of Jeep owners)

Asssi-Willys Jeep Parts
P.O. Box 4189
Yuma, AZ 85366
Fax: 520-343-1200
(Focus is Willys era: parts source for CJs plus military MB, M38 and M38A1 Jeep models; literature/shop manuals)

Archer Brothers
19745 Meekland Ave.
Hayward, CA 94541
415-537-9587
(A Bay Area institution for many decades, the supplier of surplus and replacement Jeep parts)

Capitol Jeepers Supply
3130 Fulton Ave.
Sacramento, CA 95821
916-481-2326
(Complete parts line for '41-up Jeep vehicles)

AJ's Four-Wheel Drive Center
RD-3, Box 284A
Jersey Shore, PA 17740
717-398-7520
(Specializes in body pieces and other Jeep items)

Border Parts
3875 Bancroft Drive
Spring Valley, CA 92077
619-461-0171
(Need a right side hand wiper for a Burma MB Jeep? Jon Compton likely has a box full of them. Stores of military surplus and civilian geartrain, axle and engine pieces)

J.C. Whitney
P.O. Box 3000
La Salle, IL 61301
312-431-6102
(Valued mail-order source for body panels, fuel tanks, axle, engine, chassis, cooling system and tune-up parts)

MEPCO
7250 So. 620 West
Midvale, UT 84047
801-561-3299
(Parts source for Jeep components, replacement parts and accessories)

Brian Chuchua Jeep
777 W. Orangethorpe Ave.
Placentia, CA 92670
714-879-5337
(A longstanding Jeep dealer and enthusiast/rally competitor, Brian has promoted Jeep since the Kaiser era)

Dick Cepek, Inc.
17000 Kingsview Ave.
Carson, CA 90746
310-217-1805
(Dick Cepek, an avid Jeep 4WD enthusiast and family recreationalist, served as mentor for many of us....Tom Cepek has expanded the Cepek tradition with a huge inventory of Jeep accessories, geartrain parts, tops and specialty tires)

Don-A-Vee Jeep/Eagle/Motorsports
17308 So. Bellflower Blvd.
Bellflower, CA 90706
213-867-7256
(A Jeep dealership totally committed to the Jeep lifestyle. Supplier of genuine Mopar/Jeep Accessories and Mopar Performance components)

Walck's Four Wheel Drive
700 Cedar Street
Bowmanstown, PA 18030
610-852-3110
(Full line of Jeep new and used parts for all years of Jeep trucks. Manuals, literature and military pieces, including tires)

The Jeepster Man
238 Ramtown-Greenville Road
Howell, NJ 07731
732-458-3966
(Source for Jeepster as well as Willys/Kaiser era CJ, truck and wagon body panels, trim and hard parts. Restorers will find repair and restoration body pieces, books, manuals and parts guides)

Red River Parts and Equipment
I-30 West, Exit 206 N.
P.O. Box 817
New Boston, TX, 75570
903-547-2226
(A vast store of military surplus parts including Jeep geartrain, axle and body components)

REWECO Truck Parts Co.
711 E. Rosecrans Ave.
Los Angeles, CA 90059
310-217-1800
(Geartrain, military Jeep parts, steel bodies and more)

Leon Rosser Jeep/Eagle
1724 1st Avenue North
Bessemer, AL 35020
205-424-1640
(Leon Rosser staunchly serves the Jeep community. A catalog full of Mopar/Jeep Accessories, Mopar Performance products and aftermarket specialty items distinguishes the Leon Rosser Jeep dealership. A huge OEM parts inventory meets Jeep owner needs. Leon Rosser also supports four-wheel drive activities and recreation.)

Sarafan Auto Supply, Inc.
23 N. Madison Ave.
Spring Valley, NY 10977
914-356-1080
(Vintage Jeep parts, military models included; canvas products)

Shell Valley Fiberglass
Route 1, Box 69
Platte Center, NE 68653
402-246-2355
(Durable replacement panels and full bodies for those salt-eaten and beaten Jeep CJs and Wranglers!)

Specialty Parts Four Wheelin'
1617 Old Country Road, #8
Belmont, CA 94002-3931
415-592-2130
(Source for military surplus and civilian Jeep replacement parts)

Surplus City Parts
11796 Sheldon Street
Sun Valley, CA 91352
818-767-3666
(Source for military and civilian Jeep vehicle parts)

Restoration and Specialty Tools

Eastwood Company Tools
Box 296
Malvern, PA 19355
1-800-345-1178
(Niche tools for the restorer or home mechanic; unique products for those wanting original appearance or show quality results)

Easco/K.D. Tools
(Contact Eastwood Company or your local tool supplier)

Mark Williams Enterprises
765 South Pierce Avenue
Louisville, CO 80027
303-665-6901
(Precision ring-and-pinion gear setup tools; the 'Bench Mule' fixture)

Suspension/Chassis

Rancho Suspension (USA)
P.O. Box 5429
Long Beach, CA 90805
562-630-0700
(Complete suspension packages for Jeep trucks; steering stabilizer shocks, RS5000 and RS9000 shock absorbers and springs kits)

Warn/Black Diamond Suspension
12900 S.E. Capps Road
Clackamas, OR 97015-8903
503-722-3019
(Full suspension lift kit packages, shock absorbers and axle enhancements for CJs, YJs, TJs, XJs and Grand Cherokees; full-floating front hub conversions for YJ/TJ/XJ/ZJ; rear axle full-floater conversion kits)

Full-Traction Suspension
6600-B McDivitt Drive
Bakersfield, CA 93313
805-398-9585
(Chassis/frame spring bracket upgrades and shackle reversal kits; steering linkage systems; axle trusses; suspension lift kits)

Old Man Emu/OME
1425 Elliott Avenue W
Seattle, WA 98119
206-284-5906
(Australia tested, rugged spring lift packages; heavy duty gas-charged shock absorbers)

Skyjacker
212 Stevenson Street
West Monroe, LA 71294
318-388-0816
(Suspension/lift kits, shock absorbers, springs; dropped Pitman arms)

Superlift
211 Horn Lane
West Monroe, LA 71292
318-322-3458
(Complete suspension/lift kits, traction bars; dropped Pitman arms)

Dick Cepek, Inc.
17000 Kingsview Ave.
Carson, CA 90746
310-217-1805
(Full suspension kits, shocks and more)

Trail Master
420 Jay Street
Coldwater, MN 49036
517-278-4011
(Complete suspension kits, springs, shock absorbers; dropped Pitman arms)

National Spring
1402 N. Magnolia Ave.
El Cajon, CA 92020
619-441-1901
(Bonafide spring manufacturer; need springs made or duplicated, National Spring can do it; suspension kits)

Explorer/Pro Comp
2758 Via Orange Way
Spring Valley, CA 91978
619-670-5222
(Suspension systems, lift kits and shock absorbers; chassis enhancements)

Tera Manufacturing/Teraflex
7055 S. 700 West
Midvale, UT 84047
801-256-9897
(Suspension lift kit packages; Tera Low gear reduction kits for transfer cases)

Heckethorn Off Road/Rough Country
P.O. Box 526
Dyersburg, TN 38024
901-285-9000
(Shocks/steering stabilizers; Rough Country Suspension Systems)

Tuff Country (TCI)
1806 W. 3500 South Street
Salt Lake City, UT 84119
1-800-288-2190 (orders only)
(Suspension kits; spring packages)

AutoFab
10996 N. Woodside Ave.
Santee, CA 92071
619-562-1740
(Suspension products and custom steel fabrication)

Tomken Machine
36580 U.S. Highway 24 North
Buena Vista, CO 81211
719-395-2526
(Lift kits and chassis enhancements for Jeep CJs, Wranglers, XJs and ZJs)

Advance Adapters
P.O. Box 247
Paso Robles, CA 93447
805-238-7000
(Steering linkage kits and Saginaw gear mounting brackets for upgrades)

Flaming River Industries
17851 Englewood Drive
Cleveland, OH 44130-3489
440-826-4488
(Custom Saginaw manual steering gears; steering columns for retrofit manual and power steering)

Edelbrock
2700 California St.
Torrance, CA 90509
310-781-2222
(Unique, quality shock absorbers)

Air Lift Company
P.O. Box 80167
Lansing, MI 48908-0167
517-322-2144
(Air suspension kits)

Energy Suspension Systems
1131 Via Callejon
San Clemente, CA 92673
714-361-3935
(Urethane bushings)

Tires

Bridgestone Tire
See your local dealer

Dunlap & Kyle Co.
P.O. Box 720
Batesville, MS 38606

Dick Cepek, Inc.
17000 Kings View Avenue
Carson, CA 90746

Denman Tire Corporation
216-898-5256

The Goodyear Tire & Rubber Company
See your local Goodyear dealer

B.F. Goodrich T/A
See your local dealer

Interco Tire Corporation
P.O. Box 486
Rayne, LA 70578

Mickey Thompson Performance Tires
P.O. Box 227
Cuyahoga Falls, OH 44222

Trailside Toolbox and Spare Parts Kit

Properly maintained, your Jeep may never break in the back country. Yet for long and remote trips, like the spur roads from the Alaska Highway or the remote reaches of Baja California, a full set of tools and spare parts provide the likelihood that you can keep going and remain safe.

Store your tools and spare parts securely. Take into account the worst case scenario, the possibility that your Jeep could break in desolate country. There, you would need ready access to your winching accessories kit or tools!

> *WARNING—*
> *Be certain that your tools have been neatly boxed and strapped down firmly to avoid severe physical injury or even death in the event of a vehicle roll-over. Loose tools, jacks or cargo become lethal objects during an accident or roll-over situation.*

On-board Tools for Remote Trailside Fixes

1. A complete socket set
2. A full set of common hand tools
3. Oil filter wrench
4. Compact volt-ohmmeter
5. Induction ammeter and starter current meter
6. Flare nut wrench set
7. Plumber's small chain wrench
8. Snap ring plier set
9. Front wheel bearing spindle nut wrench
10. Sizable pry bar
11. Vacuum gauge
12. Compact timing light
13. Wire repair kit and crimping pliers
14. Tubing flare tool and repair fittings
15. Grease gun with chassis lube
16. Enough tools to break down and repair a tubeless tire
17. Air compressor
18. High output alternator and on-board welder; welder's face shield, protective welding gloves and assorted, dry welding rod (stored in a waterproof container)
19. Jacks for tire repairs and transmission/axle work
20. Minimum 8000-pound capacity (single line pull) winch in top working condition with a complete winch accessories kit; dual battery system with isolator/manager
21. "Pull-Pal" winch cable anchor
22. "Hi-Lift" jack with cast iron foot
23. Multi-purpose Max Tool Kit
24. Assortment of *properly graded* hardware
25. Factory-level workshop manual(s) that thoroughly covers troubleshooting and unit overhaul procedures for your Jeep truck model
26. An installed CB radio plus a spare CB radio backup
27. A quality first aid kit: I recommend taking American Red Cross or equivalent 'First Aid' and 'CPR' classes.
28. Fire extinguisher(s), approved and within expiration period (*Caution: Securely mount fire extinguishers to prevent unplanned dislodging or discharge!*)
29. GPS and cellular telephone—and knowledge of areas where phone reception will be available.*

*In serving at search-and-rescue, I found a cellular phone to be much more effective for emergencies than a CB radio. A cell phone can serve as your link to prompt medical and law enforcement services. A CB radio has limited range and function in mountainous country.

> *WARNING—*
> *When choosing hardware for field backup use, select fasteners of the appropriate grade and type. Do not use lower-grade, "general purpose" hardware on safety items! Match hardware to OEM grading. Follow tightening/torque guidelines in your factory workshop manual(s). Use proper tightening procedures. Note torque and whether threads should be dry or lubricated. Use liquid thread-locking compound where recommended.*

Spare Parts for the Long Trail

1. Fuses, light bulbs and at least one headlamp, wrapped securely to prevent damage

2. 25-foot rolls of 10-, 12-, 14- and 16-gauge automotive wire; for high amp charge system, carry extra 4-gauge wire

3. Two rolls (minimum) of electrical tape

4. Solderless crimp connectors and terminals

5. Roll of duct tape

6. Package of radiator and gas tank repair putty

7. Proper fuel hose and spare clamps for carbureted engines; high pressure (steel braid or OEM replacement) fuel hose with attached, pressure-rated fittings for EFI/MPI systems

8. Spare drive belt(s)

9. Upper and lower radiator hoses and spare clamps

10. Thermostat and housing gasket

11. Tubes of silicon gasket sealant

12. Tube of metal mender (Permatex's LocWeld or equivalent)

13. Exhaust system patch kit

14. Liquid thread locking compound

15. Teflon tape

16. Clean, sealed brake fluid

17. A fuel pump with pump mounting gasket or fuel tank gasket

18. Roll of mechanic's wire

19. Spare tire valve stems

20. Patch kit for repairing tubeless (radial or bias ply) tires

21. Spare axle and driveline universal joints

22. Front wheel grease seals (full-floating axles)

23. At least one oil filter and enough oil for a crankcase refill (plastic bottles wrapped and stored properly)

24. An oversized, self-tapping oil pan drain plug with gasket

25. Two squeeze bottle quarts (minimum) of gear lubricant

26. Clean tub of wheel bearing grease

27. Clean shop rags or towels

28. Fuel filter(s)

29. Air cleaner element

30. Spare fuel and potable water (minimum 5 gallons of each), secured safely with a vehicle roll-over in mind!

31. Ignition distributor cap, rotor, points or module

32. Ignition spark plug wire set

33. Carburetor float and air horn gasket

33. Water pump and mounting gasket

34. Bucket/pan for draining and saving fluids

35. Roll of mechanic's or "baling" wire!

NOTE —
Always carry a quality first aid kit, safety flares and dry matches. Stow a waterproof ground cloth, shelter materials and rope for setting up an emergency habitat or weather-proof "garage." Freeze dried or canned rations and a portable stove will provide a means for survival in the event that your Jeep becomes stranded.

New or Rebuilt Engine Break-in Procedure

There is little information available on the proper break-in of a new or freshly rebuilt engine. Your Jeep engine's performance and longevity depend upon correct break-in. The following procedures are those recommended by Sealed Power Corporation, a major supplier of parts to the engine remanufacturing industry.

> *CAUTION —*
> *These run-in schedules are "good basic procedures" to follow for engine break-in. They are recommended as a practical guide for engine rebuilders who are not advised of specific factory run-in schedules. If a factory manual is available, carefully follow the break-in procedure outlined.*

Engine Run-in Procedure (engine in vehicle)

A) Before starting engine, make preliminary adjustments to the carburetor (diesel injection system—where applicable) tappets and ignition timing

B) Install new oil and air filters

C) Priming of the engine lubrication system before starting is definitely recommended

> NOTE —
> A common cause of scuffing and seizure, when an engine is started for the first time, is effected by a "dry start." This can happen in a short length of time before the oil, under pressure, is delivered to bearings and other vital parts. Priming the oil system can be accomplished with a pressure tank or pre-lubricator attached to the system or mechanically driving the pump to supply the necessary oil throughout all oil passages.

(D) Clean crankcase ventilation components—breathers road draft tubes or positive crankcase ventilation system

E) Check Installation of coolant and crankcase oil levels

Initial Starting (before run-in schedule)

(A) Start engine and establish throttle setting at a fast idle (1000 to 1500 RPM) and watch oil pressure gauge. If oil pressure is not observed immediately, shut engine down and check back on assembly of oil pump and lubricating system

When engine running is resumed, continue at the fast idle until coolant reaches normal operating temperature.

(B) Stop engine and recheck oil and water levels

(C) Make necessary adjustments to carburetor (or injectors), ignition timing, tappets, fan belt tightness, etc.

(D) Retorque cylinder heads following engine manufacturer's recommendations

(E) Check for oil and coolant leaks, making corrections where necessary

Run-in Schedule
For Passenger Cars

Begin the break-in schedule by making a test run. Accelerate to 30 miles per hour and then immediately to 50 miles per hour and decelerate to 30 miles per hour. Repeat this cycle for approximately 30 to 50 miles avoiding any periods of slow idling except for minor adjustments.

For Buses, Light, Medium and Heavy Duty Trucks

Set engine at a fast idle. Put vehicle under a moderate load and accelerate to 50 miles per hour with alternate deceleration. Continue this intermittent cycling under this load for at least 50 miles. Additional time is desirable.

> NOTE —
> Many Jeep engines have passenger car origins. Early Jeep engines were bonafide light truck designs.

Note: Harmful Practices

(A) Avoid lugging under any load condition. Lugging exists when the vehicle does not "readily respond" as the accelerator is depressed. The engine speed being too low, does not allow the engine to develop sufficient horsepower to pull the load. (Keep rpm up)

(B) Avoid long periods of idling. Excessive idling will drop engine temperature and can result in incomplete burning of fuel. Unburned fuel washes lubricating oil off cylinder walls and results in diluted crankcase oil and restricted (poor) lubrication to all moving parts. The relatively dry cylinder walls depend upon oil throw-off to lubricate them and a speed above a slow idle is necessary for this. Long idling periods produce glazing of cylinder walls, detrimental to ring and cylinder wall seating.

(C) Avoid stopping engine too quickly. When an engine has completed the test run-in schedule or at any time it becomes heavily worked, it is a good policy to disengage the load from the engine and decelerate gradually. Allow it to idle a few minutes before turning the ignition to the "off" position.

The few minutes of idling will allow the engine to cool gradually and promote a desirable dissipation of heat from any localized area of concentrated temperature. Such good practice avoids the rapid cooling that can cause valve and seat warpage, block distortion, etc.

Engine Run-in procedure (engine on dynamometer)

NOTE—
Follow necessary "preliminary" procedures outlined for engine in vehicle.

Gasoline Engines: Light Truck and Passenger Car*

Stage of test	Complete test cycle of dynamometer break-in						
	1st	2nd	3rd	4th	5th	6th	7th
RPM	800—1200	1500	2000	2500	3000	3000	800
Manifold vacuum in inches of mercury	No load	15 in.	10 in.	10 in.	6 in.	Full load	No load
Time limit	Warm-up 10 min.	10 min.	15 min.	15 min.	15 min.	5 min.	3 min.

*Dynamometer break-in is a loaded condition (manifold vacuum readings indicate degree of load). To simulate these loads, drive your Jeep on various grades. Match manifold vacuum noted for each rpm range.

About the Author

An avid fly fisherman, hunter, canoeist and four-wheeler, Moses Ludel took his first driver's license exam in the family CJ-5 Jeep. Two years later, at age eighteen, he drove the Rubicon Trail by the back route, entering from the Miller Lake access and tracking an unmarked trail across the Sierra Mountains to Placerville, California.

Moses worked as a master truck mechanic and heavy equipment operator before earning a Bachelor of Science (Pre-Law/Sociology) degree with honors from the University of Oregon. He has taught Adult Education level courses in Automotive and Diesel Mechanics and now has a fifteen year track record as an automotive journalist and photographer with emphasis on four-wheel drive vehicles. Moses' body of published work now exceeds 1900 technical features, stories and columns plus five *Owner's Bible* series books for Robert Bentley, Inc.

His magazine credits include *Off-Road, Four-Wheeler, 4WD SUV, 4x4 Magazine Japan, Trailer Life, Motorhome, Popular Hot Rodding, Chevy Truck, Jp Magazine* and many others. Moses served as Tech editor and columnist for *Jp Magazine*.

A past board member for the national TREAD LIGHTLY! program, Moses continues to serve on that organization's Environmental Relations Committee. He has consulted to 4WD truck/SUV manufacturers including General Motors, Jeep Corporation/Mopar and Mercedes-Benz.

Acknowledgements

Motivation for this book began in 1964, when my parents, Leonard and Ruth Ludel, bought a new Jeep CJ-5. Their appreciation for rural Nevada's history, artifacts and abandoned mining towns, aided by the Jeep's willingness to travel primitive backroads, left an indelible impression.

My commitment to detail stems from work with "old school" truck mechanics, heavy equipment operators, parts personnel and four-wheel drive community notables like Jon Compton, Tom Reider, Warren Guidry and Lloyd Novak. Several professional contacts have grown into much valued friendships: Jeff Sugg (MIT), Scott Salmon and Tom Telford (Warn Industries), Keith Buckley (Goodyear Tire and Rubber), Bill Vicencio (Yerington Tire Service), John Partridge (Advance Adapters), Gene Humrich (Midway/Centerforce), Stuart Hall (U.S.A. VenturCraft) and the enthusiastic staff at Mopar/Jeep Accessories and Mopar Performance.

I owe much to my former students at the San Diego Job Corps' mechanics program. They taught me how to convey information in a useful manner—despite my university degree.

In assembling historical facts and photographs, I relied upon the archival resources of Warn Industries, Ramsey Winch Company, Chrysler's Jeep Corporation and Mopar/Jeep Accessories. Personnel within these organizations and others lent valued support.

I thank Michael Bentley, President of Robert Bentley, Inc., for confidently backing my enthusiasm for Jeep 4WD products. Senior Editor John Kittredge continues to offer his exceptional professionalism and willingness to handle the monumental amount of material, photographs and text that I feel essential for this book. John provides the integrity and bearing of a true editor/friend. We now have a five-book track record and rapport.

As a foremost consideration, I thank my wife, Donna, and son, Jacob, for their patience and understanding. My commitment to each edition of this book has been intensive and time consuming, yet our home remains whole and happy. Thanks, family, for your support, presence and mutual interest in four-wheeling! Of course, Jacob has become a third generation Jeep enthusiast, equally at home behind the wheel of our vintage '55 CJ-5 or a new TJ Wrangler!

Special thanks to Randy Martin and family of Springfield, Oregon, for access to the remarkable '48 CJ-2A depicted on the back cover.

Automotive Books From Robert Bentley

HARLEY-DAVIDSON

Harley-Davidson Evolution V-Twin Owner's Bible™ *Moses Ludel*
ISBN 0-8376-0146-0

PONTIAC AND CHEVROLET

Glory Days: When Horsepower and Passion Ruled Detroit *Jim Wangers*
ISBN 0-8376-0208-4

Chevrolet & GMC Light Truck Owner's Bible™ *Moses Ludel* ISBN 0-8376-0157-6

Chevrolet by the Numbers™**: 1955–59** *Alan Colvin* ISBN 0-8376-0875-9

Chevrolet by the Numbers™**: 1960–64** *Alan Colvin* ISBN 0-8376-0936-4

Chevrolet by the Numbers™**: 1965–69** *Alan Colvin* ISBN 0-8376-0956-9

Chevrolet by the Numbers™**: 1970–75** *Alan Colvin* ISBN 0-8376-0927-5

FORD

Ford F-Series Pickup Owner's Bible™
Moses Ludel ISBN 0-8376-0152-5

Ford Fuel Injection and Electronic Engine Control: 1988–1993 *Charles O. Probst, SAE*
ISBN 0-8376-0301-3

Ford Fuel Injection and Electronic Engine Control: 1980–1987 *Charles O. Probst, SAE*
ISBN 0-8376-0302-1

ENGINEERING

Maximum Boost: Designing, Testing, and Installing Turbocharger Systems *Corky Bell*
ISBN 0-8376-0160-6

Race Car Aerodynamics *Joseph Katz*
ISBN 0-8376-0142-8

The Scientific Design of Exhaust and Intake Systems *Philip H. Smith and John C. Morrison* ISBN 0-8376-0309-9

The Design and Tuning of Competition Engines *Philip H. Smith, 6th edition revised by David N.Wenner* ISBN 0-8376-0140-1

Bosch Fuel Injection and Engine Management *Charles O. Probst, SAE*
ISBN 0-8376-0300-5

DRIVING TECHNIQUE

Going Faster: Mastering the Art of Race Driving The Skip Barber Racing School *Carl Lopez, with foreword by Danny Sullivan*
ISBN 0-8376-0227-0

Think To Win: The New Approach to Fast Driving *Don Alexander, with foreword by Mark Martin* ISBN 0-8376-0070-7

Sports Car and Competition Driving *Paul Frère, with foreword by Phil Hill*
ISBN 0-8376-0202-5

The Racing Driver *Denis Jenkinson, with foreword by Stirling Moss* ISBN 0-8376-0201-7

The Technique of Motor Racing *Piero Taruffi, with foreword by Juan Manuel Fangio*
ISBN 0-8376-0228-9

BMW ENTHUSIAST AND SERVICE MANUALS

Unbeatable BMW: Eighty Years of Engineering and Motorsport Success
Jeremy Walton ISBN 0-8376-0206-8

The BMW Enthusiast's Companion *BMW Car Club of America* ISBN 0-8376-0321-8

BMW Z3 Roadster Service Manual: 1996–1998, 4-cylinder and 6-cylinder engines
Bentley Publishers ISBN 0-8376-0325-0

BMW 5-Series Service Manual: 1989–1995 525i, 530i, 535i, 540i, including Touring
Bentley Publishers ISBN 0-8376-0319-6

BMW 5-Series Service Manual: 1982–1988 528e, 533i, 535i, 535is *Robert Bentley*
ISBN 0-8376-0318-8

BMW 3-Series Service Manual: 1984–1990 318i, 325, 325e(es), 325i(is), and 325i Convertible *Robert Bentley*
ISBN 0-8376-0325-0

ALFA ROMEO

Alfa Romeo Owner's Bible™ *Pat Braden with foreword by Don Black*
ISBN 0-8376-0707-9

VOLKSWAGEN ENTHUSIAST AND OFFICIAL SERVICE MANUALS

Volkswagen Beetle: Portrait of a Legend *Edwin Baaske* ISBN 0-8376-0162-2

Small Wonder: The Amazing Story of the Volkswagen Beetle *Walter Henry Nelson*
ISBN 0-8376-0147-9

Volkswagen Sport Tuning for Street and Competition *Per Schroeder*
ISBN 0-8376-0161-4

Passat Official Factory Repair Manual: 1995–1997 *Volkswagen of America*
ISBN 0-8376-0380-3

Jetta, Golf, GTI, Cabrio Service Manual: 1993–1997, including Jetta_III_ **and Golf**_III_
Robert Bentley ISBN 0-8376-0365-X

GTI, Golf, and Jetta Service Manual: 1985–1992 Gasoline, Diesel, and Turbo Diesel, including 16V *Robert Bentley*
ISBN 0-8376-0342-0

Corrado Official Factory Repair Manual: 1990–1994 *Volkswagen United States*
ISBN 0-8376-0387-0

Passat Official Factory Repair Manual: 1990–1993, including Wagon *Volkswagen United States* ISBN 0-8376-0378-1

Super Beetle, Beetle and Karmann Ghia Official Service Manual Type 1: 1970–1979 *Volkswagen United States* ISBN 0-8376-0096-0

Beetle and Karmann Ghia Official Service Manual Type 1: 1966–1969 *Volkswagen United States* ISBN 0-8376-0416-8

Rabbit, Scirocco, Jetta Service Manual: 1980–1984 Gasoline Models, including Pickup Truck, Convertible, and GTI *Robert Bentley* ISBN 0-8376-0183-5

Station Wagon/Bus Official Service Manual Type 2: 1968–1979 *Volkswagen United States* ISBN 0-8376-0094-4

Fastback and Squareback Official Service Manual Type 3: 1968–1973 *Volkswagen United States* ISBN 0-8376-0057-X

Volkswagen Fox Service Manual: 1987–1993, including GL, GL Sport and Wagon *Robert Bentley* ISBN 0-8376-0340-4

Eurovan Official Factory Repair Manual: 1992–1999 *Volkswagen of America*
ISBN 0-8376-0335-8

Vanagon Official Factory Repair Manual: 1980–1991 including Diesel Engine, Syncro, and Camper *Volkswagen United States* ISBN 0-8376-0336-6

SAAB OFFICIAL SERVICE MANUALS

Saab 900 16 Valve Official Service Manual: 1985–1993 *Robert Bentley* ISBN 0-8376-0312-9

Saab 900 8 Valve Official Service Manual: 1981–1988 *Robert Bentley* ISBN 0-8376-0310-2

AUDI OFFICIAL SERVICE MANUALS

Audi 100, A6 Official Factory Repair Manual: 1992–1997, including S4, S6, quattro and Wagon models.
Audi of America. ISBN 0-8376-0374-9

Audi 80, 90, Coupe Quattro Official Factory Repair Manual: 1988–1992 including 80 Quattro, 90 Quattro and 20-valve models *Audi of America*
ISBN 0-8376-0367-6

Audi 100, 200 Official Factory Repair Manual: 1988–1991 *Audi of America*
ISBN 0-8376-0372-2

Audi 5000S, 5000CS Official Factory Repair Manual: 1984–1988 Gasoline, Turbo, and Turbo Diesel, including Wagon and Quattro *Audi of America*
ISBN 0-8376-0370-6

Audi 5000, 5000S Official Factory Repair Manual: 1977–1983 Gasoline and Turbo Gasoline, Diesel and Turbo Diesel *Audi of America* ISBN 0-8376-0352-8

Audi 4000S, 4000CS, and Coupe GT Official Factory Repair Manual: 1984–1987 including Quattro and Quattro Turbo *Audi of America* ISBN 0-8376-0373-0

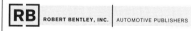

Robert Bentley has published service manuals and automobile books since 1950. Please write Robert Bentley, Inc., Publishers, at 1734 Massachusetts Avenue, Cambridge, MA 02138, visit our web site at http://www.rb.com, or call 1-800-423-4595 for a free copy of our complete catalog.